Fodor's Road Guide USA

Maine
New Hampshire
Vermont

First Edition

Fodor's Travel Publications
New York Toronto London Sydney Auckland
www.fodors.com

Fodor's Road Guide USA: Maine, New Hampshire, Vermont

Fodor's Travel Publications
President: Bonnie Ammer
Publisher: Kris Kliemann
Executive Managing Editor: Denise DeGennaro
Editorial Director: Karen Cure
Director of Marketing Development: Jeanne Kramer
Associate Managing Editor: Linda Schmidt
Senior Editor: Constance Jones
Creative Director: Fabrizio La Rocca
Director of Production and Manufacturing: Chuck Bloodgood

Contributors
Editor: Arabella Meyer
Additional Editing: Stephanie Adams, Ensley Eikenburg, Elizabeth Kugler, Karen Licurse
Writing: Tom Atwell (Maine lodgings and attractions), Robin Bloksberg (New Hampshire restaurants), Elisa Fitzgerald (Vermont restaurants), Paula Flanders (New Hampshire), Elizabeth Peavey (Maine), and Bill and Kay Scheller (Vermont), with William Fox, Eric Reymond, Frances Schamberg, and Daniel Taras
Black-and-White Maps: Rebecca Baer, Robert Blake, David Lindroth, Todd Pasini
Production/Manufacturing: Bob Shields
Cover: Mae Scanlan (background photo), Bart Nagel (photo, illustration)
Interior Photos: Artville (Maine), Photodisc (New Hampshire and Vermont)

First Edition
ISBN 0-679-00514-5
ISSN 1528-1523

PRINTED IN THE UNITED STATES OF AMERICA
10 9 8 7 6 5 4 3 2 1

CONTENTS

Great Road Trips

Of all the things that went wrong with Clark Griswold's vacation, one stands out: The theme park he had driven across the country to visit was closed when he got there. Clark, the suburban bumbler played by Chevy Chase in 1983's hilarious *National Lampoon's Vacation,* is fictional, of course. But his story is poignantly true. Although most Americans get only two precious weeks of vacation a year, many set off on their journeys with surprisingly little guidance. Many travelers find out about their destination from friends and family or wait to get travel information until they arrive in their hotel, where racks of brochures dispense the "facts," along with free city magazines. But it's hard to distinguish the truth from hype in these sources. And it makes no sense to spend priceless vacation time in a hotel room reading about a place when you could be out seeing it up close and personal.

Congratulate yourself on picking up this guide. Studying it—before you leave home—is the best possible first step toward making sure your vacation fulfills your every dream.

Inside you'll find all the tools you need to plan a perfect road trip. In the hundreds of towns we describe, you'll find thousands of places to explore. So you'll always know what's around the next bend. And with the practical information we provide, you can easily call to confirm the details that matter and study up on what you'll want to see and do, before you leave home.

By all means, when you plan your trip, allow yourself time to make a few detours. Because as wonderful as it is to visit sights you've read about, it's the serendipitous experiences that often prove the most memorable: the hole-in-the-wall diner that serves a transcendent tomato soup, the historical society gallery stuffed with dusty local curiosities of days gone by. As you whiz down the highway, use the book to find out more about the towns announced by roadside signs. Consider turning off at the next exit. And always remember: In this great country of ours, there's an adventure around every corner.

HOW TO USE THIS BOOK

Alphabetical organization should make it a snap to navigate through this book. Still, in putting it together, we've made certain decisions and used certain terms you need to know about.

LOCATIONS AND CATEGORIZATIONS

Color map coordinates are given for every town in the guide.

Attractions, restaurants, and lodging places are listed under the nearest town covered in the guide.

Parks and forests are sometimes listed under the main access point.

Exact street addresses are provided whenever possible; when they were not available or applicable, directions and/or cross-streets are indicated.

CITIES

For state capitals and larger cities, attractions are alphabetized by category. Shopping sections focus on good shopping areas where you'll find a concentration of interesting shops. We include malls only if they're unusual in some way and individual stores only when they're community institutions. Restaurants and hotels are grouped by price category then arranged alphabetically.

RESTAURANTS

All are air-conditioned unless otherwise noted, and all permit smoking unless they're identified as "no-smoking."

Dress: Assume that no jackets or ties are required for men unless otherwise noted.

Family-style service: Restaurants characterized this way serve food communally, out of serving dishes as you might at home.

Meals and hours: Assume that restaurants are open for lunch and dinner unless otherwise noted. We always specify days closed and meals not available.

Prices: The price ranges listed are for dinner entrées (or lunch entrées if no dinner is served).

Reservations: They are always a good idea. We don't mention them unless they're essential or are not accepted.

Fodor's Choice: Stars denote restaurants that are Fodor's Choices—our editors' picks of the state's very best in a given price category.

LODGINGS

All are air-conditioned unless otherwise noted, and all permit smoking unless they're identified as "no-smoking."

AP: This designation means that a hostelry operates on the American Plan (AP)—that is, rates include all meals. AP may be an option or it may be the only meal plan available; be sure to find out.

Baths: You'll find private bathrooms with bathtubs unless noted otherwise.

Business services: If we tell you they're there, you can expect a variety on the premises.

Exercising: We note if there's "exercise equipment" even when there's no designated area; if you want a dedicated facility, look for "gym."

Facilities: We list what's available but don't note charges to use them. When pricing accommodations, always ask what's included.

Hot tub: This term denotes hot tubs, Jacuzzis, and whirlpools.

MAP: Rates at these properties include two meals.

No smoking: Properties with this designation prohibit smoking.

Opening and closing: Assume that hostelries are open year-round unless otherwise noted.

Pets: We note whether or not they're welcome and whether there's a charge.

Pools: Assume they're outdoors with fresh water; indoor pools are noted.

Prices: The price ranges listed are for a high-season double room for two, excluding tax and service charge.

Telephone and TV: Assume that you'll find them unless otherwise noted.

Fodor's Choice: Stars denote hostelries that are Fodor's Choices—our editors' picks of the state's very best in a given price category.

NATIONAL PARKS

National parks protect and preserve the treasures of America's heritage, and they're always worth visiting whenever you're in the area. Many are worth a long detour. If you will travel to many national parks, consider purchasing the National Parks Pass ($50), which gets you and your companions free admission to all parks for one year. (Camping and parking are extra.) A percentage of the proceeds from sales of the pass helps to fund important projects in the parks. Both the Golden Age Passport ($10), for those 62 and older, and the Golden Access Passport (free), for travelers with disabilities, entitle holders to free entry to all national parks, plus 50% off fees for the use of many park facilities and services. You must show proof of age and of U.S. citizenship or permanent residency (such as a U.S. passport, driver's license, or birth certificate) and, if requesting Golden Access, proof of your disability. You must get your Golden Access or Golden Age passport in person; the former is available at all federal recreation areas, the latter at federal recreation areas that charge fees. You may purchase the National Parks Pass by mail or through the Internet. For information, contact the National Park Service (Department of the Interior, 1849 C St. NW, Washington, DC 20240-0001, 202/208—4747, *www.nps.gov*). To buy the National Parks Pass, write to 27540 Ave. Mentry, Valencia, CA 91355, call 888/GO—PARKS, or visit www.national-parks.org.

IMPORTANT TIP

Although all prices, opening times, and other details in this book are based on information supplied to us at press time, changes occur all the time in the travel world, and Fodor's cannot accept responsibility for facts that become outdated or for inadvertent errors or omissions. So always confirm information when it matters, especially if you're making a detour to visit a specific place.

Let Us Hear from You

Keeping a travel guide fresh and up-to-date is a big job, and we welcome any and all comments. We'd love to have your thoughts on places we've listed, and we're interested in hearing about your own special finds, even the ones in your own back yard. Our guides are thoroughly updated for each new edition, and we're always adding new information, so your feedback is vital. Contact us via e-mail in care of roadnotes@fodors.com (specifying the name of the book on the subject line) or via snail mail in care of Road Guides at Fodor's, 280 Park Avenue, New York, NY 10017. We look forward to hearing from you. And in the meantime, have a wonderful road trip.

THE EDITORS

Important Numbers and On-Line Info

LODGINGS

Adam's Mark	800/444—2326	www.adamsmark.com
Baymont Inns	800/428—3438	www.baymontinns.com
Best Western	800/528—1234	www.bestwestern.com
	TDD 800/528—2222	
Budget Host	800/283—4678	www.budgethost.com
Clarion	800/252—7466	www.clarioninn.com
Comfort	800/228—5150	www.comfortinn.com
Courtyard by Marriott	800/321—2211	www.courtyard.com
Days Inn	800/325—2525	www.daysinn.com
Doubletree	800/222—8733	www.doubletreehotels.com
Drury Inns	800/325—8300	www.druryinn.com
Econo Lodge	800/555—2666	www.hotelchoice.com
Embassy Suites	800/362—2779	www.embassysuites.com
Exel Inns of America	800/356—8013	www.exelinns.com
Fairfield Inn by Marriott	800/228—2800	www.fairfieldinn.com
Fairmont Hotels	800/527—4727	www.fairmont.com
Forte	800/225—5843	www.forte-hotels.com
Four Seasons	800/332—3442	www.fourseasons.com
Friendship Inns	800/453—4511	www.hotelchoice.com
Hampton Inn	800/426—7866	www.hampton-inn.com
Hilton	800/445—8667	www.hilton.com
	TDD 800/368—1133	
Holiday Inn	800/465—4329	www.holiday-inn.com
	TDD 800/238—5544	
Howard Johnson	800/446—4656	www.hojo.com
	TDD 800/654—8442	
Hyatt & Resorts	800/233—1234	www.hyatt.com
Inns of America	800/826—0778	www.innsofamerica.com
Inter-Continental	800/327—0200	www.interconti.com
La Quinta	800/531—5900	www.laquinta.com
	TDD 800/426—3101	
Loews	800/235—6397	www.loewshotels.com
Marriott	800/228—9290	www.marriott.com
Master Hosts Inns	800/251—1962	www.reservahost.com
Le Meridien	800/225—5843	www.lemeridien.com
Motel 6	800/466—8356	www.motel6.com
Omni	800/843—6664	www.omnihotels.com
Quality Inn	800/228—5151	www.qualityinn.com
Radisson	800/333—3333	www.radisson.com
Ramada	800/228—2828	www.ramada.com
	TDD 800/533—6634	
Red Carpet/Scottish Inns	800/251—1962	www.reservahost.com
Red Lion	800/547—8010	www.redlion.com
Red Roof Inn	800/843—7663	www.redroof.com
Renaissance	800/468—3571	www.renaissancehotels.com
Residence Inn by Marriott	800/331—3131	www.residenceinn.com
Ritz-Carlton	800/241—3333	www.ritzcarlton.com
Rodeway	800/228—2000	www.rodeway.com

Sheraton	800/325—3535	www.sheraton.com
Shilo Inn	800/222—2244	www.shiloinns.com
Signature Inns	800/822—5252	www.signature-inns.com
Sleep Inn	800/221—2222	www.sleepinn.com
Super 8	800/848—8888	www.super8.com
Susse Chalet	800/258—1980	www.sussechalet.com
Travelodge/Viscount	800/255—3050	www.travelodge.com
Vagabond	800/522—1555	www.vagabondinns.com
Westin Hotels & Resorts	800/937—8461	www.westin.com
Wyndham Hotels & Resorts	800/996—3426	www.wyndham.com

AIRLINES

Air Canada	888/247—2262	www.aircanada.ca
Alaska	800/426—0333	www.alaska-air.com
American	800/433—7300	www.aa.com
America West	800/235—9292	www.americawest.com
British Airways	800/247—9297	www.british-airways.com
Canadian	800/426—7000	www.cdnair.ca
Continental Airlines	800/525—0280	www.continental.com
Delta	800/221—1212	www.delta.com
Midway Airlines	800/446—4392	www.midwayair.com
Northwest	800/225—2525	www.nwa.com
SkyWest	800/453—9417	www.delta.com
Southwest	800/435—9792	www.southwest.com
TWA	800/221—2000	www.twa.com
United	800/241—6522	www.ual.com
USAir	800/428—4322	www.usair.com

BUSES AND TRAINS

Amtrak	800/872—7245	www.amtrak.com
Greyhound	800/231—2222	www.greyhound.com
Trailways	800/343—9999	www.trailways.com

CAR RENTALS

Advantage	800/777—5500	www.arac.com
Alamo	800/327—9633	www.goalamo.com
Allstate	800/634—6186	www.bnm.com/as.htm
Avis	800/331—1212	www.avis.com
Budget	800/527—0700	www.budget.com
Dollar	800/800—4000	www.dollar.com
Enterprise	800/325—8007	www.pickenterprise.com
Hertz	800/654—3131	www.hertz.com
National	800/328—4567	www.nationalcar.com
Payless	800/237—2804	www.paylesscarrental.com
Rent-A-Wreck	800/535—1391	www.rent-a-wreck.com
Thrifty	800/367—2277	www.thrifty.com

Note: Area codes are changing all over the United States as this book goes to press. For the latest updates, check www.areacode-info.com.

Fodor's Road Guide USA

Maine
New Hampshire
Vermont

Maine

Tucked in the northeasternmost corner of the United States, bordered by Canada, New Hampshire, and the Atlantic Ocean, the state of Maine conjures romantic images of a distant outpost, a frontier untouched by the hand of civilization. Some view the population as folksy with hardworking farmers, fishermen, and loggers; others, who may have visited the state around the end of cabin-fever season in March, might feel (or fear) that its residents have stepped straight out of a Stephen King novel. (The winters can grow a tad long.) Its 5,000-mi, rock-bound coast and deep woodlands inspire thoughts of lobsters crawling right out of the Atlantic into stew pots, or moose lounging by the side of the road waiting for someone to show up and take their picture.

And to a certain extent these perceptions hold true. Kind of.

With tourism a major industry in the state, years of waterfront development, and a population increasingly made up of "people from away," it gets harder and harder to find the authentic Maine. The state is the largest in New England; in fact, you could fit all other New England states within its borders—and in the high summer months, it sometimes feels like this has happened. Since the 19th century, crowds have poured into the Pine Tree State each summer for its cool ocean breezes, craggy coast, pristine lakes and mountains, and miles of rivers and streams. This influx means some of the Maine you've come to see has been built up or crowded out. Many of the onetime remote backwoods towns and quaint fishing villages now border on the Disney-esque, but the authentic Maine still exists. It just takes a little digging and backroading to find it.

Aside from tourism, the state's major industries are logging, fishing, farming, and, more recently, aquaculture. A number of the mainstays of the economy have been around for some time. Maine's blueberry crop—the bulk of which is harvested in Washington County—is the largest in the nation. The state ranks third nationally in potato production, and Aroostook County is Potato Central, although broccoli is becoming another

CAPITAL: AUGUSTA	POPULATION: APPROXIMATELY 1.2 MILLION	AREA: 33,215 SQUARE MI
BORDERS: NH; CANADA; ATLANTIC OCEAN	TIME ZONE: EASTERN	POSTAL ABBREVIATION: ME
WEB SITES: WWW.MAINETOURISM.COM, WWW.STATE.ME.US, AND WWW.VISITMAINE.COM		

important crop there. And just to show some stereotypes are true, Maine is responsible for 90% of all U.S. lobster production—although they do not crawl out of the sea for the taking. Industry also plays a role in the economy. Major employers are shipbuilder Bath Iron Works, the credit card giant MBNA, and outdoor outfitter extraordinaire L. L. Bean. Economic development continues to be a hotbed topic at the statehouse, as politicos try to use Yankee ingenuity to stimulate the state's often sluggish economy.

If there's anyone who can figure a way, it's a Mainer. Yankee ingenuity and the Yankee work ethic are more than aphorisms, they are, indeed, a way of life. Mainers, as a rule, are a hardworking lot. Even transplants to the state tend to feel a twinge of guilt if they quit work too early. (Fortunately, this quality rarely rubs off on visitors.)

In its history, Maine has produced or been home to its share of notable residents, ranging from the Civil War hero Joshua Chamberlain to the aforementioned local-boy-gone-creepy Stephen King. Chester Greenwood, the inventor of the earmuff, Helen and Scott Nearing, who practically invented the back-to-the-land movement with their book *Living the Good Life,* and sexual energy researcher Wilhelm Reich are just a few of the forward (or sideways) thinkers who have called Maine home. Maine has also been the subject for numerous pens and paintbrushes. The state claims such arts and letters luminaries as Winslow Homer, Henry Wadsworth Longfellow, Louise Nevelson, Rockwell Kent, Harriet Beecher Stowe, Andrew Wyeth, and E. B. White as natives or adoptees. But Maine might be best known for its presence in national politics. Margaret Chase Smith, Edmund Muskie, and, more recently, George Mitchell and William Cohen have all distinguished themselves with their straightforward, no-nonsense Yankee thinking and problem solving.

No, Maine is more complex than the stereotypes imply. The idyllic postcard version of the state might be a bit skewed, but as you cross the border into Maine, see if the air doesn't seem a bit clearer, the sky wider, the pace slower (except at the backed-up traffic at the York tollbooth). Being back on Maine turf makes anyone who calls Maine home—even for a week—know they have arrived at a place unlike any other on earth.

History

It all started with a great sheet of ice that ripped and gouged its way across Maine some 25,000 years ago. By the time it had fully receded 14,000 years later, the sheet left in its wake a fingery coastline, massive boulders, eskers, drumlins, beaches, 3,000 islands, and even a fjord.

Maine's first known inhabitants, the Red Paint People, were so named because they lined the graves of their dead with red clay. Early native tribes that followed included the warlike Micmacs and the peaceful Abenakis (or Wabanakis). If you have trouble pronouncing the names of some of Maine's streams and rivers, chalk it up to the many tribes who inhabited the state and christened its natural features. Today, only two tribes remain: the Passamaquoddies and the Penobscots.

Throughout the 15th and 16th centuries, European explorers reportedly visited the area, but it was not until 1607 that the first British colony was settled at Popham—

ME Timeline

25,000 years ago	11,500 years ago	AD 1000	1524
A great ice sheet spreads over Maine.	Paleo Indians settle in Maine.	Leif Eriksson and crew arrive in Newfoundland and Nova Scotia. Some now say his visit included Maine.	Giovanni da Verrazano is the first confirmed European to explore the coast of Maine.

INTRODUCTION
HISTORY
REGIONS
WHEN TO VISIT
STATE'S GREATS
RULES OF THE ROAD
DRIVING TOURS

the same year as the Jamestown settlement. Winter proved too much for the Popham settlers, however, and the colony didn't last.

The advent of the French and Indian wars slowed settlement, but things picked up again in the mid-1700s, when 100-acre parcels of land were granted to anyone who would settle in the northern wilderness. The Revolutionary War saw active participation from the colonists, with the first naval battle of the Revolution taking place off the coast of Machias. During this war, Colonel Benedict Arnold—prior to turning traitor and join-ing the cause of the redcoats—marched his men though Maine's North Woods in a failed attempt to capture Québec. (Today, this path is still known as the Arnold Trail.)

Growing resentment toward Massachusetts's rule led to Maine's statehood in 1820. The capital was sited in Portland, then moved two years later to the more central town of Augusta. Rapid growth followed statehood. Lumbering, shipbuilding, ship-ping, and fishing were important industries. Textile and leather manufacturing surged. Mills began springing up on the banks of Maine's rivers. After the Civil War, the boom slowed, and a new industry came to the fore—tourism. Resort hotels were constructed, and visitors arrived by rail and steamship. Wealthy rusticators found the climate and shoreline enough to their liking that they, too, commenced construction. Their grand summer "cottages" still dot the coastal communities. Soon vacationing in Maine was no longer restricted to the upper crust, and visitors of all socioeconomic levels flocked to the state.

Today Maine is something of a work in progress—trying to strike a difficult balance between strengthening the economy and preserving the environment. Forest manage-ment, infrastructure improvement, and waterfront development are just a few of the issues that currently stir lively debate at town meetings and in the state legislature.

Regions

1. SOUTH COAST

Stretching from Kittery to Old Orchard Beach, the south coast of Maine is so popular among tourists that many people never realize there's much more to the state. This section, which also rolls west through pastoral countryside to the New Hampshire border, is rich in history. The first European settlers laid stake to this part of Maine not long after the *Mayflower* arrived at Plymouth Rock. Many examples of the architecture of this era survive, particularly in York Village. But what really distinguishes the South Coast is the abundance of broad sand beaches and its elbow-to-elbow resort towns, packed with shops, inns, and restaurants, which heat up—both liter-ally and figuratively—in summer.

Summer is the time to visit the south coast if you don't mind crowds; all attractions and businesses are open then. For more breathing room,

1604		1607	1614	1622
French nobleman Pierre du Gua, sieur de Monts, and car-tographer Samuel de Champlain establish the first recorded European colony in Maine at the mouth of the St. Croix River. While	exploring, Cham-plain names Mt. Desert Island (*L'Ile des Monts Déserts*).	The British establish the Fort Popham Colony, which does not last the brutal winter.	Capt. John Smith explores and maps the coast from the Penobscot River to Cape Cod. He is the first to use the term "New England."	Sir Ferdinando Gorges and John Mason are granted rights to lands that make up what is now Maine and New Hampshire. Gorges became the first per-son to title the terri-tory "Maine."

move farther down the coast or don't come until off-season. The area is highly developed, more like a playland than authentic Maine. Chances are that that charming "local" shopowner or innkeeper is from New Jersey.

Towns listed: Biddeford-Saco, Kennebunk, Kennebunkport, Kittery, Ogunquit, Old Orchard Beach, Wells, The Yorks

2. GREATER PORTLAND AND CASCO BAY

Metropolitan Portland is an ideal four-seasons vacation destination if you want to enjoy Maine's splendid coast with a Seattle-style cup of coffee in hand and easy access to the arts, shopping malls, and latest movies. Within a matter of minutes from downtown Portland, you can find yourself poised atop a cliff head, strolling on a wooded hiking trail, lolling on a sandy beach, or riding a ferryboat to one of the many islands in Casco Bay—and still be back in time to catch a first-rate dinner and a show.

The islands of Casco Bay, known as the Calendar Islands, are accessible by ferry, and while most of them are not designed for heavy tourist traffic, they make excellent hiking or biking day trips.

Towns listed: Cape Elizabeth, Chebeague Islands, Freeport, Portland, Scarborough, Yarmouth

3. MIDCOAST

Although there is some disagreement over borders, Midcoast Maine can be said to extend from the town of Brunswick east to the Penobscot River. One thing about this region, however, defies dispute: it is one of the most highly touristed areas in the state—and for good reason. As you move east from Portland, the coastline begins to change. Sandy beaches give way to more rugged coast, taking the shape of glacier-carved peninsulas and sheltered harbors. Picturesque fishing villages, quaint tourist towns, and first-rate resorts all jockey for their piece of the shoreline. Midcoast U.S. 1 clogs in summer, as do many of the narrow state roads that reach down each peninsula. The best advice is to roll down the windows, take a deep breath, and enjoy the ride.

Towns listed: Bailey Island/Orr's Island, Bath, Belfast, Boothbay Harbor, Brunswick, Bucksport, Camden, Damariscotta, Georgetown, Harpswell, Lincolnville, Monhegan Island, Newcastle, Pemaquid Peninsula, Phippsburg, Rockland, Rockport, Searsport, Wiscasset

4. ACADIA AND DOWN EAST

The Acadia and Down East region comprises three discrete parts:

East Penobscot Bay: The rolling hills, islands, and peninsulas ambling out between Penobscot and Blue Hill bays offer a more serene (some might even say more dignified) version of the Midcoast. You can find excellent meals and accommodations, but the activity is subdued—designed more for the locals than a large influx of visitors.

1632	1652	1675	1675–1760	1762
York is incorporated as America's first chartered city.	Maine is annexed as a frontier territory by Massachusetts.	King Philip's War spurs conflicts between the English, French, and Indians for control of the North American territories.	The Indian Wars continue.	Peace is at last formally made at Fort Pownell.

INTRODUCTION
HISTORY
REGIONS
WHEN TO VISIT
STATE'S GREATS
RULES OF THE ROAD
DRIVING TOURS

Mt. Desert Island: Home to Acadia National Park and Bar Harbor, Mt. Desert is, in a word, a tourist Mecca. The combination of natural scenic splendor, amusements, and amenities jammed on this small island means crowds. But places don't get crowded for no reason. It is *the* vacation spot in the state.

Washington County: A trip to this region of the state, which is also known as the Sunrise County, is a step back in time. The terrain is covered with blueberry barrens (low bushes) that blaze a fiery red in autumn. (Sixty-five million pounds of blueberries are harvested here annually.) It is also home to some of the state's most dramatic tides, pristine woodlands, historic villages, and two Native American reservations.

Towns listed: Acadia National Park, Bar Harbor, Blue Hill, Calais, Castine, Cranberry Isles, Deer Isle/Stonington, Eastport, Ellsworth, Hancock/Hancock Point, Lubec, Machias, Northeast Harbor, Southwest Harbor

5. THE COUNTY

Capping the state is Aroostook County, Maine's largest (6,500 square mi) and northernmost. "The County" as it is affectionately termed, often gets short shrift from Maine visitors, owing to its distant locale. (The town of Fort Kent is as far from Portland as is New York City.) But those willing to go the extra mile(s) will find a land of endless, rolling fields of potato blossoms (farmlands produce over a million and a half tons of potatoes each year), and unspoiled wilderness. Bordered all around by Canada, The County has a deep Acadian heritage, 2,000 lakes, rivers, and streams, and a way of life all its own. Excellent snowmobile trails attract thousands of "sledders" each winter.

Towns listed: Allagash Wilderness Waterway, Caribou, Fort Kent, Houlton, Presque Isle

6. KATAHDIN AND MOOSEHEAD

This region, which includes the heart of the North Woods, stretches from the remote Allagash Wilderness south to the urban Bangor area and encompasses some of the wildest and most hyperbolic terrain in the state—the largest state park, Maine's highest mountain, the state's biggest lake, and one of the most difficult stretches of white water in the country. Undeveloped townships in this region are owned, operated, and harvested (yes, that means clear-cut) by international paper companies. Once the heart of log drives, forever popular with hunters and sport fisherfolk, and more recently with eco-tourists, the area is not exactly the undeveloped wilderness you might expect, but there are still plenty of wild places to explore.

Towns listed: Allagash Wilderness Waterway, Bangor, Greenville, Lincoln, Millinocket, Moosehead Lake, Orono, Rockwood

7. KENNEBEC AND MOOSE RIVER VALLEYS

Sliced in two by the mighty Kennebec River, this region begins at the state capital of Augusta and ambles northwest to the Canadian border. Rolling hills, farmlands, and

1775	1775	1794	1815	1820
The first naval battle of the Revolutionary War takes place off the coast of Machias.	Benedict Arnold marches a band of revolutionaries through Maine in a failed attempt to capture British strongholds in Québec City and Montréal.	Bowdoin College becomes Maine's first post-secondary institution.	The world's first Total Abstinence Society is founded in Portland. The temperance movement would dominate the state for the next century.	Under the Missouri Compromise, Maine gains statehood and becomes the 23rd state in the Union, with Portland its capital.

lakeside summer communities distinguish the lower half of the region. Things get a bit wilder as you move north. Wooded hills and mountains, world-class white water, deep gorges, and miles of scenic back roads (U.S. 201 is especially popular during fall foliage) take you to a more rustic Maine. The appeal of this rustic quality, however, has meant a growing population of outdoor adventurers. The Forks is to white-water rafting what Times Square is to traffic.

Towns listed: Augusta, Belgrade Lakes, Bingham, Hallowell, Skowhegan, Waterville

8. WESTERN MAINE MOUNTAINS

As you move west from the urban center of Lewiston/Auburn, hills and mountains dominate this part of the state that hugs the New Hampshire and Canadian border and stretches into southern Maine. The area's popular ski resorts keep a steady stream of traffic moving along its country roads all winter. When the last of the snow melts, things quiet down some. You can find lakefront summer communities, farmlands, and orchards in the southern corner; to the north and west, dramatic mountain vistas and chains of lakes.

Towns listed: Bethel, Bridgton, Carrabassett Valley, Center Lovell, Farmington, Fryeburg, Kingfield, Lewiston/Auburn, Norway, Poland Spring, Rangeley, Rumford, Sebago Lake

When to Visit

"There are two seasons in Maine: winter and August."

The weather in Maine is so frequently the butt of jokes that it's hard to get a straight read on the climate. Like most clichés, these jokes hold a kernel of truth. The weather in Maine is, indeed, volatile and unpredictable, but Maine also enjoys a unique, healthful, and moderate climate. (Some people claim they can actually "taste" the pine or salt air.) The best way to deal with the Maine climate is to pack an extra sweater and a raincoat, and to remain flexible.

The state is broken into three climatic regions: Coastal, Southern Interior, and Northern Interior. The Coastal region, extending 20 mi inland, is tempered by the Atlantic, yielding lower summer temperatures and higher winter ones. Annual rainfall here averages around 46 inches, with 50 to 70 inches of snowfall. The Southern Interior, which covers about 30% of Maine, is the warmest area of the state in summer, and gets around 42 inches of annual rainfall and 60 to 90 inches of snow. The Northern Interior, taking up nearly 60% of the state, has a Continental climate and receives about 40 inches of annual rainfall, and 90 to 110 inches of snowfall.

Statewide summer temperatures average around 70 degrees, although temperatures can sometimes creep into the 90s for a few days. You can also get a "scotcha" (Maine talk for "scorcher") in both early May and late September. Winters are, well, cold, but not without respite. The Northern Interior can have as many as 60 days of

1822	1839	1842	1851	1860
The capital is moved from Portland to Augusta.	Governor Fairfield declares war on England over a boundary dispute between New Brunswick and northern Maine.	The Webster-Ashburton Treaty of 1842 settles the Maine/New Brunswick border dispute.	Harriet Beecher Stowe begins writing her antislavery novel, *Uncle Tom's Cabin*, in Brunswick.	Hannibal Hamlin is named Abraham Lincoln's vice president.

INTRODUCTION
HISTORY
REGIONS
WHEN TO VISIT
STATE'S GREATS
RULES OF THE ROAD
DRIVING TOURS

sub-zero temperatures, while the Coast usually sees only 10 to 20. Fog, nor'easters, and thunderstorms spice up the mix, as has global warming, which some say has resulted in milder winters and hotter summers recently.

Traditionally, the most popular time to come to Maine has been summer. Long, languid days unspool into cool evenings. Seasonal attractions are open, business hours are extended, and an endless selection of events and festivals takes place. And summer is the only time you can brave a dip in the Atlantic, where ocean temperatures generally hover in the 50° to 60° range. The summer season is in full tilt July 4 through Labor Day, so if you are visiting popular tourist spots and want the warm weather as well, prepare to buck up and share your part of the Maine experience with many like-minded visitors.

Autumn means an influx of "leaf-peepers"; tour buses and motorists career and crawl over back roads as people ogle the fall foliage spectacle. The shoulder season between Labor Day and Peeper Season is one of the best times to visit the state. Indian summer weather conditions are not uncommon, and the crowds thin significantly.

Maine's crystalline winters bring their own crowds. Skiing and snowmobiling are wildly popular in winter months. "Mud season" (thinly disguised as spring) is the unloved spinster of Maine seasons, but clad in Wellies and a warm jacket, you can have much of the state to yourself.

And one further word of warning: early summer means black fly and mosquito season. Inland and marshy areas are especially attractive to these pests, who view your skin as an all-you-can-eat buffet. The worst of it is usually over by July, but to be safe, pack your bug repellent, mosquito netting, and a baseball bat. (Just kidding about the bat. These insects don't get that big, although some locals will claim they do take a swing or two at them.)

CLIMATE CHART

Average High/Low Temperatures (°F) and Monthly Precipitation (in inches)

	JAN.	FEB.	MAR.	APR.	MAY	JUNE
PORTLAND	30/11	33/14	41/25	52/34	63/43	73/52
	3.5	3.3	3.7	4.0	3.2	3.4
	JULY	AUG.	SEPT.	OCT.	NOV.	DEC.
	78/58	77/57	69/49	59/38	47/37	35/28
	3.1	2.9	3.1	3.9	5.2	4.6
	JAN.	FEB.	MAR.	APR.	MAY	JUNE
PRESQUE ISLE	19/-2	23/1	34/15	46/29	62/40	72/49
	2.4	1.9	2.4	2.5	3.1	2.9
	JULY	AUG.	SEPT.	OCT.	NOV.	DEC.
	77/55	74/52	64/43	52/34	38/30	24/18
	4.0	4.1	3.5	3.1	3.6	3.2

1863
Brunswick native Joshua Chamberlain successfully defends Little Round Top against Confederate troops at the Battle of Gettysburg in the Civil War. Chamberlain's actions are said to

be the turning point of that battle.

1868
A great fire levels much of downtown Portland.

1931
Governor Percival Baxter begins buying land in northern Maine, which would eventually become Baxter State Park.

1948
Margaret Chase Smith is elected to the U.S. Senate. She is the first woman to ever be voted into this office and also the first women to serve in both houses of Congress.

ON THE STATE CALENDAR
WINTER

Dec.   **Christmas Prelude.** Street shows, tours, shopping, and special events, including Santa's arrival in a lobster boat, highlight this holiday celebration in the pretty coastal villages of Kennebunk and Kennebunkport. | 207/967–0857.

New Year's Portland. This citywide celebration attracts thousands of revelers, as the streets and halls of Portland are filled with dance, song, and family fun in Portland's downtown. Things kick off with an afternoon parade and don't slow down until the old year is ushered out with fireworks. One ticket buys admission to all events and performances. | Dec. 31 | 207/772–9012.

Feb.   **U.S. National Toboggan Championship.** A 400-ft toboggan chute sets the stage for this unique Maine event. More than 250 teams arrive in Camden from across the country to test their skill on the slippery slope. There's also a Chili and Chowder challenge, plus other amusements and activities. | 207/236–3438.

SPRING

Mar.   **Maine Maple Sunday.** A statewide event celebrating the tapping of sap. From York to Aroostook counties, over 60 syrup-producing sugarhouses open their doors to demonstrate the maple-syruping process. Events range from site to site, but you can count on finding pancake feeds, syrup sales, tours, and pony rides. | 207/289–3871.

May–June   **MooseMainea.** In and around Moosehead Lake is a month-long tribute to the ungainly, antlered beast in one of its favorite hangouts. Activities include a fly-casting tournament, canoe race, biking events and races, moose calling, moose spotting, moose safaris, moose photo contest, moose facts, tales, and lore, moose slide shows, and, believe it or not, moose d'oeuvres. | 207/695–2702.

SUMMER

July   Slightly subdued to full-scale **Fourth of July celebrations** take place in towns and cities across the state. Check local papers and area visitor centers for the lowdown on the celebration nearest you.

1968	**1974**	**1980**	**1988**	**1994**
The University of Maine system is established.	James Longley's election to governor marks the first popularly elected independent governor in the history of the United States.	Senator Edmund Muskie replaces Cyrus Vance as President Carter's secretary of state.	Senator George Mitchell is named the U.S. Senate Majority Leader.	Angus King becomes the second-ever popularly elected independent governor in United States history.

INTRODUCTION
HISTORY
REGIONS
WHEN TO VISIT
STATE'S GREATS
RULES OF THE ROAD
DRIVING TOURS

Yarmouth Clam Festival. This clamorama celebrates our bivalved friend in all its glory. Started over 30 years ago as a town clambake, the festival has evolved into one of the area's most popular and peopled events, with crafts fair; parade; carnival; games; bike, road, canoe, and duck races; fireworks; live music and entertainment; and seafood treats galore. | 207/846-3984.

Aug. **The Maine Festival.** takes place at Thomas Point Beach, Brunswick. Maine's top artists, crafters, musicians, and dancers converge at this coveside park for day and evening demonstrations and performances. You will find craft and food booths, plenty of activities to keep the kiddies busy, and a veritable smorgasbord of cultural and artistic offerings. | 207/772-9012.

Maine Lobster Festival. A Maine tradition for over 50 years, the Lobster Festival in Rockland's Harbor Park has gained the attention of lobster devotees from all over the world. There's a parade, crafters, a wide variety of live entertainment and demonstrations, boat and train rides, lobster crate races, an appearance by King Neptune, and the crowning of the Maine Sea Goddess. And, of course, the festival is simply crawling with crustaceans. | 207/596-0376.

Wild Blueberry Festival. Washington County is the blueberry capital of the world, and this festival in Machias celebrates the fact with all things berryish: pies, cakes, muffins, pancakes, or straight off the bush. There's also a fish fry, crafts fair, a parade, games, live entertainment, various other amusements, and lots of blue-stained tongues and fingers. | 207/255-4402.

AUTUMN

Sept. **Common Ground Fair.** Think of a classic county fair, and then think vegetarian chili and tabbouleh salad instead of fried dough and corn dogs; recycling demonstrations instead of Tilt-a-Whirls; and thousands of Birkenstock tracks on the midway. Sound as exciting as a bowl of mullet? Far from it. The Common Ground Fair in Unity (near Waterville) is perhaps the finest fair in the state, with countless earth-friendly demonstrations and products, live entertainment and animals, and lots of good, wholesome fun. | 207/622-3118.

1997
Senator William Cohen is sworn in as President Clinton's secretary of defense.

1999
George Mitchell is awarded the Presidential Medal of Freedom for brokering the Good Friday Peace Accord in Northern Ireland.

Oct.   **Fryeburg Fair.** Maine's largest agricultural fair was founded in
         1850 and has been a popular event since the first local farmers
         got together to show off their produce to the local commu-
         nity. Maine's last country fair of the season, the Fryeburg Fair
         has it all: wall-to wall exhibition halls, a farm museum, craft
         demonstrations, and midway; poultry, llama, flower, and sheep
         shows; ox, horse, and tractor pulls; harness racing, parade, live
         music—and many, many Fry-o-lators. | 207/935–3638.

State's Greats

With a nickname like "Vacationland," tourism a major industry, and with 8 million visitors annually, Maine nearly throws down the gauntlet, challenging you to just try and
not have a good time.

Maine's appeal is as varied as its geography. With its rugged 5,200-mi coastline,
pristine lakes and streams, deep woods, and majestic mountains, there is no end to
the outdoor adventures you can experience. But Maine is not just all rugged, natural
beauty. Cultural and historical attractions, tony resorts, outlet hot spots, and picturesque
villages round out the mix that makes the state such a popular tourist destination.

Whether your idea of vacation means snoozing in an Adirondack chair on a piney
point, hanging from a sheer cliff face, browsing through blocks of shops and boutiques,
or delving into early American history, Maine has a bit of something for everyone.

The only question is: How to fit it all in?

Beaches, Forests, and Parks

No matter your shorefront preference—long sand beaches or dramatic craggy cliffs—
the Maine coast has it. The best sand beaches are concentrated in the south coast: **York
Beach, Long Sands Beach, Ogunquit Beach, Kennebunk-area beaches,** and **Old Orchard
Beach** are just a sampling of places you can spread out your blanket and slather on the
sunscreen. The metropolitan area of Portland also has some excellent sand beaches nearby:
Crescent Beach, Ferry Beach, and **Scarborough Beach.** And don't overlook **Popham
Beach** and **Reid State Park,** near Bath. **Sand Beach** in Acadia National Park is one of the
few sand beaches Down East. These popular and peopled beaches get crowded in high
summer, and swimming can be a chilly proposition. (You'll be lucky to find the water
temperatures getting out of the 50s in some areas.) Those looking for warmer waters
might try an inland lake beach, such as **Damariscotta, Moosehead,** or **Sebago Lake.**

If there's one thing the Pine Tree State is not short on, it's forests. Seventeen million
acres of woodlands cover 89% of the state. Maine's North Woods is a sea of trees—
but don't expect a pristine wilderness. Much of this land is owned and harvested by
timber companies, and clear-cutting scars are not uncommon. The **White Mountain
National Forest** outside Bethel has great hiking and stunning fall foliage drives.

Thirty-three state parks have been carved out all over the state. These, along with
nature preserves and land trusts, provide ample public land for hiking, fishing, swimming, picnicking, and camping, despite the fact that Maine has one of the lowest percent-
ages of publicly owned land in the country. **Acadia National Park,** the second-most-visited
national park in the United States, offers both wild spaces and first-rate resorts (yes,
you *can* have it all); **Baxter State Park** remains the wilderness paradise Governor Percival Baxter intended it to be. Both parks get, as they say, "wicked" busy in summer months,
so it's best to plan ahead.

Culture, History, and the Arts

On rainy days you can soak up art or steep yourself in history. From maritime history to Moxie memorabilia to music boxes, there are collections statewide to dazzle the eye and spark the imagination. Among the notable museums in the state are the **Portland Museum of Art**; the hands-on **Children's Museum of Maine**, also in Portland; the **Maine Maritime Museum** in Bath; the **Penobscot Marine Museum** in Searsport; Rockland's **Farnsworth Museum**, with its Wyeth wing; the **Maine State Museum** in Augusta; **Franklin D. Roosevelt's cottage** on Campobello Island, near Lubec; and collections at both Bowdoin and Colby colleges.

The term "historic Maine" is something of a redundancy. From austere meetinghouses to stately churches to solitary lighthouses to grand and gothic mansions, historical sights and districts spring up at almost every bend in the road. The **Old York Historical Society** takes you back to colonial days with its historic buildings and museums; the Pemaquid Peninsula has a number of historical attractions, from the **Thomson Ice House,** where ice is still harvested, to the ancient shell heaps, or middens, on the banks of the Damariscotta River. If forts are your forte, you may want to check out **Fort Knox** or **Fort Popham.**

Maine is home to a number of excellent performance spaces, opera houses, and concert halls, including the **Merrill Auditorium** in Portland. You can hear first-rate jazz and classical concerts in a historic opera house with the **Bay Chamber Concerts** in Rockport. The **Kneisel Hall Chamber Music Festival** is a venerable institution in Blue Hill; concerts by both students and faculty are presented over the summer. The splendidly piney **Deertrees Theater** in Harrison hosts the **Long Lakes Chamber Music Festival,** in addition to other musical and theatrical offerings. You'll find myriad classical and contemporary concerts from which to choose throughout the year in Portland, Maine's cultural hub. The best bet—particularly in summer—is to check local listings for in- and outdoor concerts and performances.

Maine also lays claim to a number of professional and amateur theater groups, which present everything from offbeat performance art to classical drama to light comedy and musicals to full-blown opera. The state's arts organizations and universities also bring many national touring companies and world-class performers to Maine stages. Summer brings an additional wave of footlights action. The **Ogunquit Playhouse** is a favorite with southern Maine visitors, owing to its well-executed light fare and brand-name stars. The **Maine State Music Theater** in Brunswick has presented perennial musical favorites since the 1950s. **Lakewood Theater,** Maine's oldest summer theater located just outside Skowhegan, rolls out a variety of offerings in a decidedly bucolic setting. The **Theater at Monmouth** has long highlighted works of the Bard, even before Hollywood made them fashionable. The productions are consistently solid, but a visit to the theater's 1900 Romanesque Victorian Cumston Hall makes a trip here worthwhile all on its own.

Sports

Maine's expansive coastline, deep forests, and soaring mountains mean more than a pretty backdrop to your vacation. Whether you wish to tame white water or have a quiet wander in the woods, you can carve out any number of ways to frolic in the state.

Man once battled and tried to tame waterways for food, power, or transport. Today that battle takes the form of adventure. The coast and inland lakes and rivers are ideal for sailing, canoeing, kayaking, white-water rafting, and fishing. Landlubbers have ample bicycling, birding, camping, hiking, and golfing available. Those interested in more offbeat adventuring can try ballooning, llama trekking, dog sledding, or moose-watching expeditions. Fall sees a very active hunting season, and sporting camps are available to facilitate the process. Things don't slow down when the snow flies. There's skiing and snowboarding at the state's 20 ski areas, ranging from dinky lumps to such top-rated ski resorts as **Sugarloaf/USA** and **Sunday River Ski Resort.** With a 10,000-mi trail network crisscrossing the state, snowmobiling is becoming an increasing tourist draw. But there's still plenty of pastoral calm in the form of cross-country skiing, snowshoeing, and ice skating in secluded woodland spots.

If you prefer more passive sports, you can jump aboard a whale- and/or bird-watching cruise from almost any port on the coast. Or if even that's too much effort, grab a hot dog and take a bleacher seat for some Double-A baseball at a **Portland Sea Dogs** game.

Other Points of Interest

Sport, to some, means bagging a bargain, and two towns in Maine—Kittery and Freeport—have become synonymous with **outlet shopping.** Kittery serves up its shopping smorgasbord, strip-mall style, with over 120 stores clustered in mini-malls along U.S. 1. Freeport's 170 outlet shops and stores are in attractive houses and storefronts that cluster like pawns around the Freeport retail king **L. L. Bean.** Both of these places are perennially peopled, so bring your credit cards—and your patience.

Rules of the Road

License Requirements: Any person with a valid driver's license may drive in Maine.

Speed Limits: The speed limit on Interstate 95 (Maine Turnpike) is 65 mi per hour, although it occasionally drops to 50 or 55 in more congested areas. Speed limits on U.S. 1 and state roads top out at 55 mph but can quickly change as you approach settled areas. The best bet is to keep alert. If not posted, the speed limit on back roads is 45 mph.

Right Turn on Red: Right turns on red are permitted throughout the state, unless otherwise posted.

Seat Belt and Helmet Laws: Seat belts are mandatory. While you cannot be stopped for not wearing one, you can be cited if stopped for another reason. Motorcycle helmets are required for drivers under 18 years of age and for those holding a license for under one year.

Headlights: A 1997 law requires motorists to have their headlights on any time their windshield wipers are in use or other weather conditions dictate. Headlights must also be on one half hour after sunrise and before sunset.

Snow Tires: Some Maine municipalities require cars to have snow tires in season. (All-season tires do not qualify.)

Drinking and Driving: Maine has a tough drunk-driving policy.

For More Information: Contact the State Department of Highway Safety at 800/452-4664.

The Down East Coast Driving Tour

ALONG U.S. 1, FROM ELLSWORTH TO CAMPOBELLO ISLAND

Distance: approximately 100 mi, detours excluded   Time: 2 days

Breaks: A stay around the Jonesport area is necessary, if you choose to take the puffin watch. Otherwise, try camping at Cobscook State Park or a stay in Lubec or at Campobello Island.

This tour will take you into a Maine of another era. The historic towns and villages that dot this stretch of coast smack of authenticity. Natural sites are less crowded, roads less congested. Time seems to move a bit more slowly. Fall is an especially good time for this tour, as the hundreds of acres of blueberry barrens that parallel the road blaze red. Build in time for plenty of detours down the peninsulas to get a full glimpse of a rapidly vanishing Maine. This is not an appropriate tour if you're looking for luxury resorts, shopping malls, or scintillating nightlife. If, however, you want space, quiet, and an open stretch of road, this tour will dish it up.

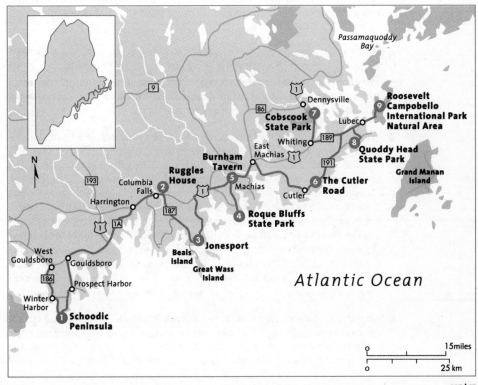

❶ Starting in **West Gouldsboro** (located just off U.S. 1), you will make your way to the **Schoodic Peninsula** (take Route 186 south from the town of West Gouldsboro, through Winter Harbor, until you see the park entrance sign). Part of the **Acadia National Park** system, these 2,000 acres are traversed by a 6-mi, one-way loop road that winds through dense woods, picnic spots, and scenic lookouts, with dramatic views and pounding surf (tides willing) at **Schoodic Point.**

❷ From the loop road, return to Route 186; follow it through the town of Prospect Harbor to Gouldsboro and proceed north on U.S. 1. Take U.S. 1A out of Milbridge (it rejoins U.S. 1 in Harrington) to **Columbia Falls.** Here you'll find the historic **Ruggles House** (Main St., ¼ mi east of U.S. 1, 207/483–4637), a wee manse and an impressive example of Federal-style design, complete with flying staircase, carvings, and period pieces.

❸ In **Jonesport** (Route 187 out of Columbia Falls), take a **puffin-watching cruise.** Since 1940, Captain Barna B. Norton has been guiding naturalists to Machias Seal Island for an up-close-and-personal glimpse of these comical and ultra-adorable birds. (Cruises leave at 7 AM; reservations required: 207/497–5933.) If you choose to extend your detour, **Great Wass Island** (take the bridge to Beals Island to the Great Wass causeway, then go 3 mi on Duck Cove Road to the parking area on the left) offers excellent hiking, sublime ocean views, abundant wildlife, and spruce- and fir-studded paths. This 1,579-acre preserve is owned and maintained by the Nature Conservancy (207/729–5181). From Jonesport, return to U.S. 1 via Route 187 and continue north to Machias.

❹ In **Machias,** depart U.S. 1 and head south for another quick detour: **Roque Bluffs State Park** (6 mi south of U.S. 1, Roque Bluffs Rd., 207/255–3475) is a great family park for sunning, picnicking, and an icy dip in the Atlantic. (There is also a freshwater pond for the more faint of heart.) Or just take in the island views from the sandy (albeit windy) mile-long beach. From Roque Bluffs State Park, take Roque Bluffs Road and reconnect with U.S. 1 north. You will soon arrive in Machias.

❺ Back in **Machias,** Revolutionary War history comes alive at **Burnham Tavern** (Main St., 207/255–4432). Built in 1770, it is the oldest building east of the Penobscot. Job and Mary Burnham raised their 11 children here, but it also served as an infirmary and a gathering place for local patriots, who hatched schemes against the British. Period furnishings, documents, clothing, and weapons are on display.

❻ In **East Machias,** just north of Machias on U.S. 1, head south on Route 191, better known as the **Cutler Road.** If you have chosen this tour to get away from it all, the Cutler Road is it. This beautiful coastal drive will take you past fishing shanties, island vistas, and through rolling wooded hills into the picturesque and teeny town of Cutler. (Don't be alarmed by the giant spires towering over the landscape—it's North Cutler's Naval Computer and Telecommunications Station.) There's good hiking along the way: **Western Head** (Destiny Bay Rd., Cutler) has an easy 3- to 4-mi loop trail that emerges through dense woods onto an ocean panorama. The 5-mi loop of the **Bold Coast Trail** (4½ mi northeast of Cutler to your right on Rte. 191) requires a bit more effort, but the rugged cliffs and ocean views are worth it. Approximately 3 mi south of where Route 191 rejoins U.S. 1, visit **Bailey's Mistake,** where one Captain Bailey purportedly wrecked his schooner and decided to stay. Was it laziness or the black-sand beach? You decide.

❼ From this point, take a slight detour to **Cobscook State Park** (located just off U.S. 1 in Dennysville, 207/726–4412). For your viewing pleasure, nature has carved out inlets and coves in the seclusion of dense stands of trees, where the 24-ft tides surge and drop. Be sure to check out the adjacent **Reversing Falls Park** (Mahar Point, Pembroke).

INTRODUCTION
HISTORY
REGIONS
WHEN TO VISIT
STATE'S GREATS
RULES OF THE ROAD
DRIVING TOURS

(To get here from U.S. 1, go to the Leighton Road; turn right at the SHORE ACCESS, 5.5 MILES sign, go 3¾ mi and turn right again at the not highly visible REVERSING FALLS sign and then left onto a gravel road.) Persevere through these twists and turns. If you catch these falls a couple hours before high tide, it will be worth your trouble.

❽ Retrace your path on U.S. 1 to Whiting, then head northeast on Route 189 to **Lubec.** You'll know you've arrived at the easternmost point in the country at **Quoddy Head State Park** (W. Quoddy Head Rd., 207/733–0911) by the sight of the famed 1858 red-and-white stripe lighthouse that seems to lurch up out of the horizon at you. This 480-acre park has breathtaking hiking trails, great ocean views, and a picnic area.

❾ After a visit to the town of Lubec, cross over the international bridge at Lubec to New Brunswick, Canada, and the **Roosevelt Campobello International Park Natural Area.** These 2,800 acres of land are under joint U.S. and Canadian jurisdiction. Stop first at the visitors center (just on your right, immediately after customs, 506/752–2922), where you can obtain maps and other information. Perhaps best known as the summer retreat of Franklin D. Roosevelt, this island offers as much natural beauty as it does history. The **Roosevelt Cottage** features F.D.R.'s shingle-style "cottage" and manicured grounds and gardens. Guides are posted in the 18-room house to offer insights into family artifacts. The cottage is a must-see, but also make time to explore the island's beaches and rocky cliffs.

The Western Maine Mountains Driving Tour

ALONG ROUTE 113, U.S. 2, AND ROUTE 17, AND ROUTES 16/4

Distance: approximately 100 mi, detours excluded   Time: 2 days
Breaks: Plan a stay in Bethel, which is approximately midway through the tour.

This tour takes you from Fryeburg to Rangeley, through breathtaking mountains and rural Maine. Naturally, foliage season is the best time, but you'll have to share these often winding roads with fellow leaf-peepers. Best to avoid this tour in winter and early spring: Route 113 closes in winter; in spring, you'll encounter a number of frost heaves, making the going even slower. This is an especially good tour for people who want to get out of their car and do some hiking and exploring.

❶ Start your tour with a detour. Just outside of Fryeburg is the **Hemlock Covered Bridge** (off U.S. 302, 3 mi northwest of East Fryeburg), a 116-ft-long bridge constructed in 1857.

❷ Return to Fryeburg and take Route 113 North. (You will weave in and out of New Hampshire, but you are still mostly in Maine.) The winding road leads you over steep twists and turns in the **White Mountain National Forest** (207/824–2134) and through **Evans Notch.** The route also travels alongside **Evans Brook,** a good swimming spot in summer. Lounge on the large boulders that dot the brook.

❸ At the terminus of Route 113, head east on U.S. 2 to the town of **Bethel.** The **Moses Mason House Museum** (Broad St., 207/824–2908) is a restored Federal-era home of one of Bethel's most prominent 19th-century citizens. Period furnishings and interesting murals can be seen within.

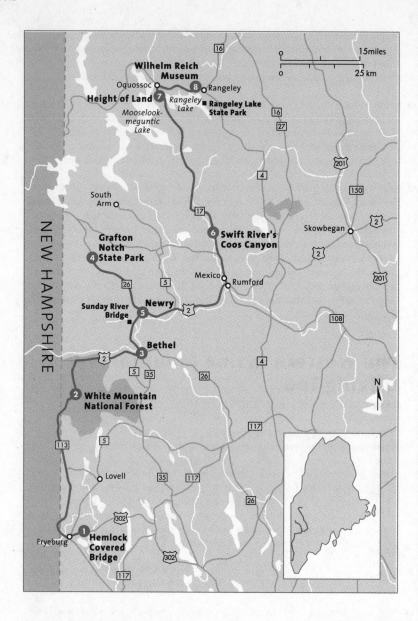

④ **Grafton Notch State Park** (Rte. 26, 14 mi north of Bethel, 207/824–2912) is a unique geological area, where the ice age made a big impression. Take short jaunts to **Screw Auger Falls, Moose Cave, Mother Walker Falls,** and the **Natural Falls**—all within the park. There are also trailheads for the Appalachian Trail and other major mountain hikes, including Old Speck, Table Rock, the Eyebrow Loop, and Baldpate. Return on Route 26 South to Newry.

⑤ In Newry, located just outside **Bethel** on U.S. 2 and Routes 5/26, the **Sunday River Ski Resort** (Sunday River Rd., Newry, 207/824–3000 or 800/543–2754) offers chairlift rides to take in the full panorama of fall foliage. Take in another covered bridge, the **Sunday River Bridge,** better known as the Artist's Bridge (on U.S. 2/Rte. 26, 4 mi northwest of North Bethel).

⑥ Return to U.S. 2 and travel east until you come to Rumford and Mexico. In Mexico, pick up Route 17 North. Near the towns of Roxbury and Byron, at the **Swift River's Coos Canyon,** there's a scenic gorge, where you can also pan for gold if you're feeling lucky.

⑦ From Coos Canyon, continue north on Route 17 to **Height of Land** (on Route 17, just outside the town of Oquossoc). An aptly named scenic overlook, it is rimmed by mountains that stretch to the horizon. Mooselookmeguntic Lake sprawls in a deep dish below.

⑧ From Height of Land, Route 17 will take you into the town of Oquossoc. There, a sharp right will put you on Routes 4/16 and lead you to Rangeley. **Rangeley Lake State Park** (South Shore Dr., 207/864–3858) covers over a mile of lakefront and offers an array of swimming, picnicking, fishing, and camping. Also plan to visit the **Wilhelm Reich Museum** (Dodge Pond Rd., 207/864–3443), the onetime home of the controversial Viennese psychoanalyst, who believed he could trap airborne sexual energy and use it to treat disease. See his "orgone" boxes, orgone gun, or just enjoy the views from his hilltop estate and impressive fieldstone mansion.

ACADIA NATIONAL PARK

MAP 3, F9

ACADIA
NATIONAL PARK

INTRO
ATTRACTIONS
DINING
LODGING

(Nearby towns also listed: Bar Harbor, Cranberry Isles, Northeast Harbor, Southwest Harbor)

With its dramatic coastline, stately forests, well-maintained trails, and 57 mi of carriage roads, it's not surprising that Acadia National Park is the second-most-visited national park in the United States. The park dominates the second-largest island in New England, Mt. Desert Island, which was named L'Isle des Monts-déserts (island of barren mountains) by Samuel de Champlain in 1604. But Acadia is anything but barren. Surrounded by bustling tourist towns, its 40,000 acres include four lakes, 120 mi of hiking trails, and 17 mountains—including Cadillac Mountain, the highest point on the eastern seaboard.

Information: National Park Service, Acadia National Park | Box 177, Bar Harbor, 04609 | 207/288–3338 | www.nps.gov/acad. **Hulls Cove Visitor Center** | Rte. 3, Hulls Cove, 04644 | 207/288–5262.

Attractions

★ **Acadia National Park.** There is lots of hiking, camping, and sightseeing in this second-most-visited national park in the United States. While you can see sheer cliffs, thick woods, and rolling meadows from your car, the best way to see the park is to hoof or cycle it. | Mt. Desert Island | 207/288–3338 | www.nps.gov/acad | $10 per vehicle for 7-day pass; $5 for pedestrians and cyclists for 7-day pass | Daily (some roads closed in winter).

Blackwoods Campground. This popular national park camping area in Acadia National Park has 300 primitive sites. There are no facilities or hookups, though each site has a fire pit and picnic table. Walk-in and drive-in sites. Make reservations well in advance for high season camping. | Rte. 3, Otter Creek | 207/288–3274, 800/365–2267 reservations | www.nps.org | $13–$19 | Daily.

Cadillac Mountain. At 1,530 ft, this is the highest mountain on the eastern seaboard. Expect to find stunning views of Frenchman and Blue Hill bays at the summit, so long as the fog stays away. | Acadia National Park, via South Ridge Trail, about 3½ mi each way | 207/288–3338 | www.nps.gov/acad.

Park Loop Road. This 27-mi, two-lane road provide access to many of the park's featured natural attractions and stunning shoreline views. You can do the loop in under an hour, but then this isn't a relay race, is it?

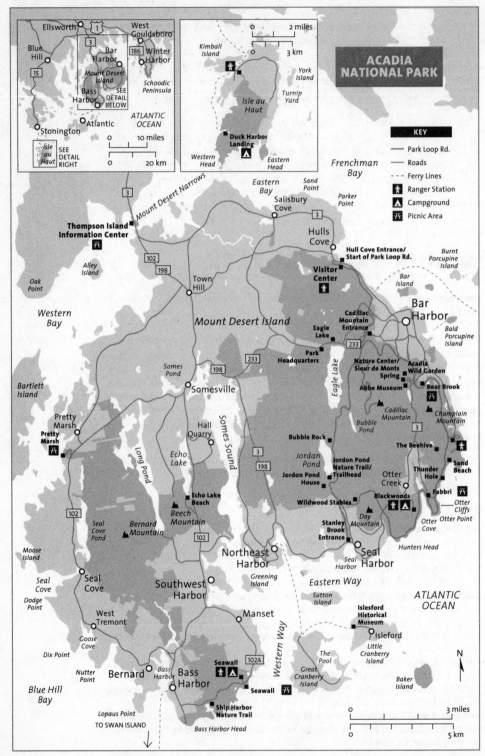

ACADIA
NATIONAL PARK

KEY

— Park Loop Rd.
— Roads
--- Ferry Lines
Ranger Station
Campground
Picnic Area

Schoodic Peninsula. Part of the Acadia National Park system, the Schoodic Peninsula comprises 2,000 acres, with panoramic views of the rocky coast and Mark Island lighthouse. | 207/288–3338 | Free.

Seawall Campground. This popular national park camping area in Acadia National Park has first-come, first-served service, beginning at 7 AM. There are no facilities on site. | Rte. 102A, Southwest Harbor | 207/244–3600 | www.nps.gov | $13–$19 | Late May–late Sept.

Thunder Hole. This celebrity attraction can either wow you or be a big dud. The trick is in the timing. As tides rush into this narrow granite channel, air becomes trapped and ba-booms. At low tide, you'll get little more than a slurp. | Midway between Great Head and Otter Cliffs.

Wild Gardens of Acadia. This is a planting of native wildflowers, divided into 12 sections reflecting the different habitats of Mt. Desert Island: mixed woods, roadside, meadow, mountain, heath, brookside or damp thicket, bird thicket, coniferous woods, bog, marsh, and pond. | Just south of Bar Harbor on Rte. 3, the Loop Rd., at Sieur de Monts spring.

Wildwood Stables. The 51 mi of carriage roads created by John D. Rockefeller, Jr. are perfect for a romantic horse-and-buggy ride. One- and two-hour trips take in the coast, the island's bridges, or the sunset trip to the top of Day Mountain for a 50-mi view to the mainland. Longer charters are available. | Park Loop Rd. | 207/276–3622 | www.acadia.net/wildwood | Mid-June–Columbus Day.

Dining

Jordan Pond House. Continental. Known for its fresh-baked goods like the famous popovers and strawberry jam and its prime view of Jordan Pond, this rustic inn is a great place to take afternoon tea on the lawn, a local tradition since the late 1800s. Fresh Maine seafood is the focus of the dinner menu, including regional favorites like lobster stew and crab cakes and meat dishes like Black Angus steak. | Park Loop Rd. | 207/276–3316 | www.jordan-pond.com | Reservations essential | Closed late Oct.–mid-May | $9–$18 | AE, D, MC, V.

ALLAGASH WILDERNESS WATERWAY

MAP 3, E3

(Nearby towns also listed: Fort Kent, Millinocket)

"Wilderness" is the operative term with this 92-mi-long chain of lakes, rivers, falls, and streams wending through the Maine's commercial forests. Largely undeveloped and uninhabited, this state-protected waterway stretches from just west of Baxter State Park and runs north to the tip-top of the state, ending at the town of Allagash. The canoe trip is said to be the best long-distance one in the state. (Parties should be made up of experienced paddlers or accompanied by a guide.) Camping and picnic sites are available along the waterway.

Information: Bureau of Parks and Lands | 106 Hogan Rd., Bangor, 04401 | 207/941–4014 | fax 207/941–4222 | www.state.me.us/boc/parks.

Attractions

Allagash Canoe Trips. Maine's oldest canoe guiding service offers weeklong trips from Chamberlain Lake to the St. John River. Nearly all equipment is provided. All trips are suitable for beginners. | Box 713, Greenville | 207/695–2492 | fax 207/695–2492 | www.allagashout-fitters.com.

Allagash Wilderness Waterway. This 92-mi-long, state-protected waterway travels through a chain of lakes, rivers, falls, and streams from just west of Baxter State Park and runs north-

ward to the town of Allagash. It's deep in the wilderness of the North Maine woods. | 207/941–4014.

Abandoned Railroad. These two giant steam locomotives that are only accessible by water are leftovers from the 1925–26 Eagle Lake and Umbazooksus Railroad. They come upon you rather suddenly and are something of a wilderness oddity. | Near the shore of Eagle Lake | 207/941–4014.

Allagash Falls. These 40-ft falls are considered by many to be the highlight of canoeing the Allagash. | 13 mi from where the Allagash joins the St. John River, near the Maine/New Brunswick border | 207/941–4014.

MOUNT DESERT ISLAND

You want it all: putt-putt golf and windswept cliffs, nature hikes and gourmet meals, blocks of boutiques and acres of barren islands. You want your own slice of the picturesque Maine coast, but you want to be where the action is. You want plenty of diversions for the kids, but you want activities for you, too. You want both hubbub and calm. Whether you know it or not, you want a trip to Mount Desert Island.

There is perhaps no place in the state that offers it all like the Bar Harbor/Acadia National Park region, located Down East on Mount Desert Island. That Acadia National Park is sited in such a remote locale and is the second-most-visited national park in the United States is telling. You'll find miles of shorefront and hiking trails, and numerous mountains and lakes. The Park Loop Road offers easy access to all of Acadia's amenities. A trip up Cadillac Mountain, the highest point on the eastern seaboard, gives you a sweeping overview of it all.

And when you feel you have exhausted your possibilities in the park (a mighty feat), there is the rollicking tourist town of Bar Harbor to explore, with its array of shops and restaurants clustered in a compact downtown. An endless list of ocean excursions and adventures is offered at its harbor. You can learn to lobster or a paddle a kayak, or just grab a table at an outdoor café and watch the day wind away. Or you can hop in the car and explore the rest of the island. The August summer community at Northeast Harbor or the working waterfront at Southwest Harbor provide good alternatives to the frenzy of Bar Harbor. Or, if you really want to get away from it all, plan a day trip to the Cranberry Isles. A visit to the nearby Blue Hill peninsula or to the wilder and less built-up peninsulas to the east of Mount Desert make great day trips.

Yes, you can have it all at Mount Desert Island, but you should know that this island is no secret Eden. Even with its ample open spaces, things get jammed here in summer months, and you will pay top dollar. Most Mainers snort in derision at the thought of even venturing on the island during the high season. If crowds give you the willies, you might think of scheduling an off-season trip. Although you might find many businesses and attractions closed, all the natural sights are still there for the viewing. (The park stays open year-round.) You might even catch a glimpse of the real Maine you came to see when the crowds thin.

© Artville

AUGUSTA

(Nearby towns also listed: Belgrade Lakes, Hallowell, Waterville)

Augusta, the state capital, is bisected by the Kennebec River. The city is built in a series of terraces on either side, with most of the state buildings on one, the downtown area on the other.

The Native Americans called Augusta "Cushnoc." Only 45 mi from open sea, it was valued by Plymouth Colony as a trading port. After the Kennebec Patent of 1628–29, trade was established, and a post was set up near the site of Fort Western, commanded, in part, by John Alden (made famous by Longfellow's "The Courtship of Miles Standish"). It is said the Kennebec fur trade was so profitable that Pilgrims were able to pay their *Mayflower* excursion debts from the profits. After 32 years of trading, peace was disrupted by the Indian Wars for nearly 75 years.

In 1754 the British erected Fort Western on the east bank of the river to attract settlers. Captain James Howard, the first and only commander of the fort, was Augusta's first permanent settler. After the peace of 1759, the Kennebec was once again safe for settlers, and the fort was dismantled, except for the garrison.

In 1762 Fort Western joined forces with Hallowell, a town to its south, and together they became known as the Fort and the Hook. The construction of a bridge in 1796 caused a rift between the two settlements, and they split. The Fort was named Harrington, but is said to have changed its name to Augusta two years later because it sounded too much like "Herring Town."

Augusta experienced a new era of development in the early 19th century. Fleets of schooners sailed weekly between Augusta and Boston by 1840. In 1832, Augusta was named the state's capital, and the impressive capitol building with its Charles Bulfinch facade was erected. When the river trade dimmed, the city became a textile and manufacturing center.

Today Augusta is home to a branch of the University of Maine and numerous state buildings. There are many notable historical sites and homes and a fine museum, but the city, after some rocky years following the decline of industry there, is still in the process of turning things around.

Information: **Kennebec Valley Chamber of Commerce** | 21 University Dr., Augusta, 04332–0192 | 207/623–4559 | kvcc@mint.net | www.augustamaine.com.

TRANSPORTATION INFORMATION

Airports: Augusta State Airport | 75 Airport Rd., | 207/626–2306. **Colgan Air** | 800/272–5488.

Bus Lines: Vermont Transit: Depot News Company | 312 Water St. | 207/622–1601 or 800/894–3355.

Driving Around Town–Augusta. Driving in Augusta can be a bit of an effort. Straddling the Kennebec River, Augusta has two bridges that can be particularly contentious, especially during rush hour with thousands of municipal workers commuting to downtown. Evening rush hour (4:30 PM–6 PM) can be pretty thorny throughout the area, but the traffic rotaries (circles) on either side of Memorial and Father Curran bridges can be bumper to bumper. Better to avoid it altogether or add 15–20 minutes to your travel time. Most of the tourist attractions are on the river's west side, locally famous for its lack of public parking. Most lots are designated for government workers, and there are no lots for the general public. You can try on-street parking around town or check out Commercial Street which has diagonal stalls on the road side good for half-hour or one-hour stints. Exceeding that will likely get you a modest fine. Traffic aside, downtown is fairly easy to negotiate in a passenger car. Roads are clearly marked, though

cars parked on either side of the street can make the going a bit tight, especially for RVs. You're best off leaving the RV on Commercial Street to avoid any problems. The main roads into Augusta are Route 202 from Bangor; Route 3 from Belfast and the coast; and Interstate 95 which runs from Portland 57 mi to the south and to Bangor 75 mi to the north.

Attractions

ART AND ARCHITECTURE

Blaine House. The current residence of Maine's governor's was built in 1833 in the Federal style and remodeled in 1872 and 1919, when it became the official residence of Maine governors. The public rooms, which you can visit on the guided tour, are filled with furniture from the early 1900s. | 192 State St. (U.S. 201), at Capitol St. | 207/287–2121 or 207/287–2301 | Tues.–Thurs. 2–4, unless there's an official event.

Maine State House. Built in 1829 from local granite, the original building was designed by noted Boston architect Charles Bulfinch. A 1910 redesign doubled the State House's size. A statue of Minerva, the goddess of wisdom, is perched atop the 185-ft dome. | State and Capitol Sts. (U.S. 201) | 207/287–2301 | Free | Weekdays 9–5, Sat. 10–4, Sun. 1–4.

BEACHES, PARKS, AND NATURAL SIGHTS

Capitol Park. This 10-acre park near the Kennebec River contains the 1985 Maine Vietnam Veterans Memorial. | Off State St., between the State House and the Kennebec River | Free | Daily.

Pine Tree State Arboretum. Directly across the Kennebec River from the state capitol, this 224-acre collection features trees and shrubs, a rock garden, rhododendron and lilac plantings, and one of the largest collections of hosta in New England. Three and a half miles of trails are available for hiking, jogging, mountain biking, horseback riding, snowshoeing, and cross-country skiing. | 153 Hospital St. | 207/621–0031 | www.communityforest.org | Free | Daily dawn–dusk.

CULTURE, EDUCATION, AND HISTORY

Old Fort Western. The 1754 original structure within this complex is a National Historic Landmark and the oldest surviving wooden fort in New England. There is more than military history on display here: you can also see the original barracks and store; reproduction blockhouses, watchboxes, and palisade; and demonstrations by the staff, dressed in reproduction costumes, of family and residential life of the period. | 16 Cony St., next to City Hall | 207/626–2385 | fax 207/626–2304 | www.oldfortwestern.org | $4.75.

Samantha Smith Memorial. This monument to peace was inspired by Samantha Smith, who in 1982 wrote a letter to Yuri Andropov to express her concerns about rising tensions between the United States and the Soviet Union. Andropov responded with an invitation to visit Moscow. Smith died in a plane crash in 1985 at age 13. | State St. and Capitol St., adjacent to the Maine State Museum | Free | Daily.

Theater at Monmouth. The historic and imposing Cumston Hall is home to one of Maine's finest repertory companies, but a look at the remarkable turn-of-the-20th-century Romanesque Victorian structure is worth a trip all its own. You can get a dose of Shakespeare here, or more contemporary works during Maine's summer-theater season. | 795 Main St. (Rte. 132) | 207/933–9999 | fax 207/933–2952 | $14–$24 | July–Aug.

MUSEUMS

Children's Discovery Museum. A hands-on center filled with a pretend diner, post office, and supermarket, a performing arts stage with costumes, and arts-and-crafts tables, and a toddler literature room. | 265 Water St. | 207/622–2209 | $3.50 | Weekdays 9–2, Sat. 10–4, Sun. 1–4. Call for extended summer hrs.

KODAK'S TIPS FOR TAKING GREAT PICTURES

Get Closer
- Fill the frame tightly for maximum impact
- Move closer physically or use a long lens
- Continually check the viewfinder for wasted space

Choosing a Format
- Add variety by mixing horizontal and vertical shots
- Choose the format that gives the subject greatest drama

The Rule of Thirds
- Mentally divide the frame into vertical and horizontal thirds
- Place important subjects at thirds' intersections
- Use thirds' divisions to place the horizon

Lines
- Take time to notice lines
- Let lines lead the eye to a main subject
- Use the shape of lines to establish mood

Taking Pictures Through Frames
- Use foreground frames to draw attention to a subject
- Look for frames that complement the subject
- Expose for the subject, and let the frame go dark

Patterns
- Find patterns in repeated shapes, colors, and lines
- Try close-ups or overviews
- Isolate patterns for maximum impact (use a telephoto lens)

Textures that Touch the Eyes
- Exploit the tangible qualities of subjects
- Use oblique lighting to heighten surface textures
- Compare a variety of textures within a shot

Dramatic Angles
- Try dramatic angles to make ordinary subjects exciting
- Use high angles to help organize chaos and uncover patterns, and low angles to exaggerate height

Silhouettes
- Silhouette bold shapes against bright backgrounds
- Meter and expose for the background illumination
- Don't let conflicting shapes converge

Abstract Composition
- Don't restrict yourself to realistic renderings
- Look for ideas in reflections, shapes, and colors
- Keep designs simple

Establishing Size
- Include objects of known size
- Use people for scale, where possible
- Experiment with false or misleading scale

Color
- Accentuate mood through color
- Highlight subjects or create designs through color contrasts
- Study the effects of weather and lighting

Maine State Museum. The varied exhibits at this museum cover both Maine's landscape and history. You will find everything from fossils and gems to 19th-century manufacturing technologies to space exploration. | State St. and Capitol St. (U.S. 201) | 207/287–2301 | Free | Weekdays 9–5, Sat. 10–4, Sun. 1–5.

SPORTS AND RECREATION

Beaver Brook Campground. This is a fully equipped 150-acre camping area on Androscoggin Lake, 15 mi southeast of Augusta. There's a pool, beach, fishing, boating, minigolf, rec hall, laundry facilities, convenience store, and activities for kids. | Wilson Pond Rd., N. Monmouth | 207/933–2108 | www.beaver-brook.com.

Kennebec River. Fish on the Kennebec River below the head of tide at Edwards Dam for Atlantic salmon, striped bass, trout, shortnose sturgeon, and other sea-run fish with this outfit that has a national reputation. The fishing is expected to improve now that Edwards Dam has been removed. No license needed until Augusta. | Access to the river at Washington St. on west side of river and at Maple St. on east side | 207/623–4559 | Daily.

ON THE CALENDAR

JUNE–JULY: *Great Kennebec River Whatever Family Festival Week.* This weeklong family festival celebrates the cleanup of the Kennebec River with entertainment, food, river-related events, and an anything-goes river race. | Throughout Augusta | 207/623–4559.

AUG.: *Annual Blistered Fingers Bluegrass Festival.* Bands from across Maine and Canada are pickin' and grinnin' till the cows come home at the Silver Spur Writing Club. You will also find amusements for the kiddies and camping at this event, 7 mi north of Augusta. | Rte. 104, West River Rd., Sidney | 207/873–6539.

AUG.–SEPT.: *Windsor Fair.* This is a classic family fair with all the fixings—parade, carnival, and agricultural exhibits—at the Windsor Fairgrounds, 10 mi east of Augusta. | Rte. 32, Windsor | 207/549–7121.

SEPT.: *Litchfield Fair.* This old-time agricultural fair has been around for over 140 years, with rides, pig scramble, exhibition hall, games, crafters, and food. | Litchfield | 207/683–2487.

WALKING TOURS

Historic Augusta
(approximately 1 hour without stops)
Start at the corner of State and Capitol streets at the **Blaine House,** the official residence of Maine governors since 1919. The mansion was first built in the Federal style in 1833, changed to Victorian and Italianate style in 1872, and given a Colonial Revival remodeling in 1919 by architect John Calvin Stevens. The mansion has limited hours for tours, so call ahead. Cross the street to the **Maine State House,** the center of state government. (Note the 185-ft dome crowned by a statue of Minerva, the Roman goddess of wisdom.) The original 1829 building was designed by Boston architect Charles Bulfinch and redesigned in 1910, doubling its size. A major restoration and renovation project took place in 1999. Feel free to wander the halls; self-guided tours are also available.

Continue south across the statehouse grounds to the **Maine State Museum,** where you will find an excellent assortment of exhibits documenting the natural and cultural history of the state. Adjacent to the museum is the **Samantha Smith Memorial.** This monument to peace was inspired by the child who wrote a letter to Yuri Andropov in 1982, expressing her concerns about the tense relations between the United States and the then–Soviet Union. Andropov responded with an invitation for the girl to visit Moscow. Samantha died in a plane crash in 1985 at the age of 13. End your tour by swinging back north on State Street to 1 Hichborn Street; grab a deli sandwich at **Burnsie's Sandwich Shop** and take it over to the 10-acre **Capitol Park,** located between the statehouse and the Kennebec River, for a picnic. There you can also view the 1985 **Maine Vietnam Veterans Memorial,** a "statue in reverse," which can be walked around and through. Return to State Street to conclude your tour.

Dining

Burnsie's Sandwich Shop. Delicatessen. At this popular local deli you can rub elbows with the state's politicos. It's known for thick sandwiches named in honor of the luminous and not-so-luminous politicians who have peopled the statehouse. Cafeteria service (no tables; you can picnic nearby). No liquor. No smoking. | 1 Hichborn St.; off State St., between the rotary and the capitol | 207/622–6425 | Closed Sat., Sun. No dinner | $6–$10 | No credit cards.

Hilltop Restaurant. American. A good place to tide you over if you're in or near the airport. This eatery serves sandwiches, pastas, steaks, fried seafood, and a host of appetizers like chicken nuggets and mozzarella sticks. Kids' menu. | 75 Airport Rd., Augusta State Airport | 207/623–2044 or 877/623–2044 | Breakfast also available Apr.–Oct. | $4–$17 | AE, D, MC, V.

North Park Grill. American. With five 10-ft TVs with table-side remote controls throughout the restaurant, carnival-style games, motion simulators, a dinner theater, billiards room, full-service pub, and café, there's something for everyone here. A large menu covers all the bases as well, including pizzas, burgers, fried seafood platters, pastas, and sandwiches. Kids' menu. | 330 Civic Center Dr. | 207/621–9776 | $6–$15 | D, MC, V.

Lodging

INEXPENSIVE
Motel 6. This two-story chain offering, next to several state government offices, is one of the newest hotels in the area. Cable TV. Laundry facilities. Some pets allowed. | 18 Edison Dr. | 207/622–0000 | fax 207/622–1048 | 70 rooms | $52 | AE, D, DC, MC, V.

MODERATE
Edwards House Inn. This 1872 Victorian home overlooking the Kennebec River is a pure slice of Americana with a shady front porch and restored period antiques. Rooms have wall-to-wall carpeting. Dining room, complimentary Continental breakfast. No room phones, cable TV. Pets allowed. | 53 Water St. | 207/622–2691, 207/622–3617 evenings and weekends | fax 207/622–2824 | river@ctell.net | www.ctell.net/~ninnian | 16 rooms (16 rooms share 4 baths) | $55–$85 | D, MC, V.

Susse Chalet Inn. This is a budget chain hotel near the turnpike and government offices. Complimentary Continental breakfast. Some kitchenettes. Pool. Laundry facilities. Business services. | 65 Whitten Rd. | 207/622–3776 | fax 207/622–3778 | ingleinns@aol.com | www.sussechalet.com | 59 rooms | $65–$70 | AE, D, DC, MC, V.

EXPENSIVE
Best Western Senator Inn. This standard hotel is just off the turnpike and near the state capitol and government offices. Restaurant, bar, picnic area, complimentary breakfast, room service. In-room data ports, some refrigerators, cable TV, VCR (and movies) available. 2 pools. Massage. Indoor putting green. Gym. Laundry facilities. Some pets allowed (deposit). | 284 Western Ave. | 207/622–5804 | fax 207/622–8803 | www.senatorinn.com | 103 rooms | $89–$139 | AE, D, DC, MC, V.

Maple Hill Farm Bed and Breakfast. A 130-acre working farm with an 1890s Victorian farmhouse, 5 mi south of Augusta. The large rooms are furnished with country antiques; some have private decks and fireplaces. Dining room, picnic area, complimentary breakfast. In-room data ports, some in-room hot tubs. Hiking. Cross-country skiing. No pets. No kids under 8. No smoking. | Outlet Rd., Kallowell | 207/622–2708 or 800/622–2708 | fax 207/622–0655 | stay@maplebb.com | www.maplebb.com | 8 rooms | $90–$160 | AE, D, MC, V.

Travel Lodge. This standard hotel is near the state capitol, government offices, and turnpike. Restaurant, bar, complimentary Continental breakfast. Some microwaves, cable TV. Pool, wading pool. Laundry facilities. Business services. Pets allowed. | 390 Western Ave. | 207/622–6371 | fax 207/621–0349 | www.travellodge.com | 98 rooms | $80 | AE, D, DC, MC, V.

BAILEY ISLAND/ORR'S ISLAND
MAP 3, C10

(Nearby towns also listed: Brunswick, Harpswell)

The eastern halves of Harpswell, Bailey, and Orr's islands are narrow spits of land connected to the mainland by a series of bridges. There are scenic ocean vistas at almost every bend in the road, where you can see deep-water harbors, fir-fringed shorefront, and lobster pots galore. Bailey Island is also home to the mortarless Cribstone Bridge.

Information: Chamber of Commerce of Bath-Brunswick Region | 59 Pleasant St., Brunswick, 04011 | 207/725–8797 or 207/443–9751 | ccbbr@horton.col.k12.us | www.mid-coastmaine.com.

Attractions
Bailey Island Cribstone Bridge. Built in 1928 with no mortar, this bridge is the only one of its kind in the world. The great granite blocks are actually laid in crib fashion, cross- and then lengthwise to allow the swift tides to flow freely through. | On Rte. 24 S, over Will Straits | Free | Daily.

Giant Staircase. This natural stone "staircase" makes a great backdrop for the sweeping ocean vistas near the end of Bailey Island. | Washington St., Bailey Island; near the corner of Ocean St. | Free | Daily.

ON THE CALENDAR
JULY: *Annual Bailey Island Tuna Tournament.* For more than 60 years, fisherfolk have reeled in the big ones for prizes and prestige at Cook's Lobster Pound in Garrison Cove. | 207/833–2818.

Dining
Cook's Lobster House. Seafood. Cook's is a pine-paneled, family-style eatery overlooking Harpswell Sound that is known for its stuffed-lobster shore dinners. There is open-air dining on the deck and a raw bar. Live music every other Sunday afternoon. Kids' menu. No smoking. | Garrison Cove Rd., just off Rte. 24 | 207/833–2818 | Closed Jan. | $10–$30 | D, DC, MC, V.

Lodging
Bailey Island Motel. This small motel, 13 mi south of Cook's Corner on Route 24, is on the ocean and offers daily nature cruises and fishing trips. Picnic area, complimentary Continental breakfast. No air-conditioning, some kitchenettes, cable TV, no room phones. | Rte. 24 | 207/833–2886 | fax 207/833–7721 | www.baileyislandmotel.com | 11 rooms | $105 | Closed late Oct.–May | MC, V.

Cook's Island View Motel. This is a well-located small coastal motel 13 mi from Brunswick, about ½ mi past Cribstone Bridge. No air-conditioning, some kitchenettes, cable TV, no room phones. Pool. No pets. | Rte. 24 | 207/833–7780 | 20 rooms | $95 | Closed through late Oct.–Memorial Day | AE, MC, V.

Driftwood Inn and Cottages. This classic 1910 getaway has stood the test of time, and hasn't changed much throughout the years. Secluded and private, the rooms have bare original wood and furnishings and overlook the coastline. The saltwater pool and patio are nice places to relax in the sun. Dining room. No air-conditioning, no room phones, TV in common area. Pool. Pets allowed (no fee). No smoking. | 81 Washington Ave., Bailey Island | 207/833–5461 | www.midcoastmaine.com | 24 rooms (10 with half bath, 14 share 6 baths), 6 cottages | $80–$90 | Closed mid-Oct.–late May | No credit cards.

BANGOR

(Nearby towns also listed: Bucksport, Orono)

Seat of Penobscot County and the urban hub of the northern three-quarters of the state, Bangor has a long and colorful logging history. Located on the Penobscot River, it was the Lumber Capital of the world in the 1800s.

First visited by Samuel de Champlain in 1604, the city was settled in 1769 and known as the Kenduskeag ("eel-catching place") Plantation and, later, Sunbury. In 1779, a Revolutionary expedition gone awry saw Americans, including settlers, destroy their fleet of nine ships and retreat to Kenduskeag. Those who remained found themselves under British control. Twelve years later, they petitioned for incorporation and took on the name Bangor. In the early 19th century, the lumber trade picked up, with certain wartime lapses. After the Civil War, Bangor became one of the leading lumber ports in the world.

This prosperity brought its own version of trouble in river city. If Maine had one rootin' tootin' Wild West town, Bangor of the 1900s was surely it. A section of town was known as the "Devil's Half Acre," where taverns and brothels sprang up to cash in on this

BANGOR

INTRO
ATTRACTIONS
DINING
LODGING

LITERARY MAINE

The state of Maine has sparked the imagination and inspired the pens of notable writers throughout its history. From Henry David Thoreau's meditations on the Maine North Woods and Portland's Henry Wadsworth Longfellow's numerous maritime themes, through the elegant, Shaker-style prose of E. B. White to the modern-day ghoulish gore of Stephen King, Maine has served prominently in the world of letters.

If you're wishing to make literary pilgrimages in the state, however, you might be disappointed if you go looking for the following places, which exist in imagination only: Stephen King's Castle Rock, Salem's Lot, Derry, and Ludlow; Crabapple Cove, the hometown of *M*A*S*H*'s Hawkeye Pierce; Cabot Cove from the TV show *Murder She Wrote* (OK, this isn't exactly a literary reference, but people believe it exists); Egypt, from Carolyn Chute's *The Beans of Egypt, Maine*; the Hardy Boys' Bayport; or the early-20th-century poet Edwin Arlington Robinson's Tilbury Town.

If you are interested in making more fulfilling literary treks, try Portland for Longfellow, the North Woods for Thoreau, Gardiner for Robinson, Bangor for King, Brooklin for White, Brunswick for Harriet Beecher Stowe, Camden and Rockland for Edna St. Vincent Millay, and South Berwick for Sarah Orne Jewett.

For the full lowdown on Maine letters, the Maine Writers and Publishers Alliance (12 Pleasant St., Brunswick, 207/729–6333) can help you out.

© Artville

boom time. After months in the North Woods, log drivers would arrive in Bangor with a pocketful of wages and a mighty thirst. Floors of taverns were scarred from these men's caulk (or spiked) boots, and brawls were frequent. These trips to Bangor by loggers continued well into the 20th century, until the last of the drives ended in 1971.

Shipbuilding and merchant trade followed, and many fine homes and churches were built, which helped define the Bangor landscape. Today, the city serves as the area's commercial center, with a sprawling mall, active downtown, and proximity to the flagship campus of the University of Maine, in nearby Orono. After a slump, the city is enjoying a resurgence, with a lively arts scene and bustling downtown. But Bangor's current claim to fame may very well be as the home of ghoulmeister Stephen King. Glimpses of the exterior of his gothic home on West Broadway are a big tourist draw.

Information: **Bangor Region Chamber of Commerce** | 519 Main St., Bangor, 04402 | 207/947–0307 | chamber@bangorregion.com | www.bangorregion.com. **State of Maine Visitor Information Center, Hampden North** | I–95 N, Mile 169, Box 319, Hampden, 04444 | 207/862–6628 | www.mainetourism.com.

TRANSPORTATION INFORMATION

Airports: Bangor International Airport | 207/947–0384 | 287 Godfrey Blvd.
Bus Lines: Concord Trailways | 1039 Union St. | 207/945–4000 or 800/639–3317 | www.concordtrailways.com. **Vermont Transit Company** | 158 Main St. | 207/945–3000 or 800/894–3355.
Driving Around Town–Bangor. All roads lead to Bangor. With seven main thoroughfares into town and three bridges linking it to its sister city of Brewer, Bangor is well suited to handle even the heaviest summer traffic. Though locals may gripe about the influx of cars and moderate back ups, most out-of-staters won't even bat an eye. The streets of Bangor run perpendicular or parallel to the Kennebec River. Downtown is full of one-way streets, but the roads are well signed and wide enough for RVs. Free on-street parking is available throughout downtown in half-hour and one-hour increments. Metered parking is available at public lots throughout town. There is a large lot at Pickering Square. Take note that public lots in Bangor use electronic, token-only meters. Pick up the tokens at the Pickering lot or the Chamber of Commerce and Visitors Bureau at 519 Main Street. Fifty cents gets you an hour. Enforcement is very strict, so don't take a chance. If you do get a ticket, it will cost you $7.50. The main roads into town are Route 202, which runs more or less parallel to Interstate 95, to Augusta (75 mi); Route 15 from the northwest to south and Bucksport (20 mi); Route 1 linking Ellsworth and the coast including Bar Harbor (46 mi); Route 9 which takes you generally east–west towards Calais (98 mi) and Nova Scotia; Route 2 which runs due west to Skowhegan (28 mi); and Route 222 which winds its way west to Sebasticook Lake (29 mi). Note that all state routes take on local street names when in downtown, but revert to numbers once out of the city.

Attractions

ART AND ARCHITECTURE

Paul Bunyan Statue and Park. Lumberjack legend Paul Bunyan is memorialized in this 31-ft-tall statue, towering over a pleasant park on Main Street. This behemoth was erected in 1959 for the city's 125th anniversary. | Next to the chamber of commerce office at 519 Main St. | Free | Daily.

Peirce Memorial. This sculpture remembers Maine's colorful river drivers in a bronze statue by Charles Tefft. A group of three drivers is depicted prying the key log out of a jam. They are shown with axe, cant dog, and peavey, engaged in the hazardous tasks of freeing the logs for the journey downstream. | Harlow St.; adjacent to the Bangor Public Library | Free | Daily.

CULTURE, EDUCATION, AND HISTORY

Bangor Public Library. The library was built in 1912, and has an excellent reading room, a domed roof inscribed with the names of 12 famous 19th-century New England authors, and a fine collection of paintings. Artists' works on view include those of the local Hardys and Waldo Pierce. Local resident, writer Stephen King, helped raise the money for the 1997 renovation. | 145 Harlow St. | 207/947–8336 | Free | June–Labor Day, Mon.–Thurs. 9–7, Fri. 9–5; Labor Day–May, Mon.–Thurs. 9–9, Fri.–Sat. 9–5.

Broadway District. This historic district, on the National Register, features many stately homes built during the lumber boom. A number of famous timber merchants and bankers lived here. The best way to visit the area is to take the Best of Bangor bus tours. These are run by the Bangor Historical Society out of the Thomas Hill House museum (*see below*), every Thursday and Saturday morning starting at 10:30 AM, from June to mid-September. | Bus leaves from the parking lot at the chamber of commerce, by the Paul Bunyan statue | 159 Union St. | 207/942–5766 | www.bairnet.org/organizations/bangorhist | Historic district free, bus tour $5 | Daily.

Remember the Maine Memorial. Created in 1922, the memorial contains the original shield and scroll of the battleship *Maine*, which was blown up in Havana Harbor in 1898. | Davenport Park; corner of Main and Cedar Sts. | Free | Daily.

MUSEUMS

Bangor Historical Society Museum. In the historic Thomas Hill House, this collection will give you everything you need to know about Bangor's colorful history. The first floor of this 1836 brick Greek Revival house is appointed with Victorian decorations and furnishings; galleries are located upstairs. | 159 Union St., at High St. | 207/942–5766 | $5 | Apr.–May and Oct.–Dec., Tues.–Sat. noon–4; June–Sept., Tues.–Sun. noon–4.

Cole Land Transportation Museum. The massive collection includes over 200 19th- and 20th-century Maine land transportation vehicles, ranging from prams to trams. It's also the site of a World War II memorial, and an engaging attraction for kids. | 405 Perry Rd.; near I–95 and I–395 | 207/990–3600 | fax 207/990–2653 | $3 | May–early Nov., daily 9–5.

PARKS

Cascade Park. A small, relaxing picnic area, with a waterfall, fountain, and gazebo, the park overlooks the waterfront on the Penobscot River. | State St. | Free. | Daily.

RELIGION AND SPIRITUALITY

Bangor Theological Seminary. This complex of buildings is listed on the National Register of Historic Places. | 300 Union St. | 207/942–6781 | Free | Daily.

St. John's Catholic Church. The 1856 Gothic Revival structure is on the National Register of Historic Places and was once led by John Bapst, S.J., who would later became the first rector of Boston College. | 207 York St., at Boyd St. | 207/942–6941 | Free | Daily 8–4.

SPORTS AND RECREATION

Blackbeard's USA Family Fun Park. This locally owned theme park includes miniature golf, go-carts, batting cages, and a climbing wall. | 339 Odlin Rd.; across from Howard Johnson's | 207/945–0233 | Free, miniature golf $5.50, go-carts $5, batting cages $1 | Wed.–Thurs. 3–8, Fri. 3–9, Sat. 10–9, Sun. 10–8.

ON THE CALENDAR

MAR.–APR.: *Downeast Boat and Marine Expo.* All things nautical are exhibited to get you rigged and ready for boating season. | Bangor Auditorium and Civic Center, 100 Dutton St. | 207/947–5555.

APR.: *Annual Kenduskeag Stream Canoe Race.* Sponsored by the Bangor Parks and Recreation Department, this race attracts hundreds of canoes and thousands of spectators for this spring runoff race. It finishes in downtown Bangor. | From Kenduskeag Village to downtown Bangor | 207/947–1018.

APR.: *Bangor Garden Show.* Local businesspeople get a jump on spring with displays of flowers and plants. | Bangor Auditorium and Civic Center, 100 Dutton St. | 207/990–1201.

JUNE: *World's Largest Garage Sale.* Sponsored by WLBZ radio, this enormous fundraising event takes over the local four-story parking garage, selling just about anything imaginable. | Pickering Sq | 207/942–4821 | 9–4.

JUNE–AUG.: *Band Concerts.* Band concerts are presented on Tuesday evenings in the shadow of logging legend Paul Bunyan. | Paul Bunyan Park | 207/947–1018.

JULY–AUG.: *Bangor State Fair.* This granddaddy of agricultural fairs has been around for 150 years. Ten days of critters, carnival rides, food, and live entertainment, featuring nationally known performers, attract thousands. | Bass Park | 207/947–5555.

JULY–AUG.: *Maine Shakespeare Festival.* A variety of live, outdoor Shakespeare productions at the Penobscot Theater. | On the Bangor Waterfront | 207/942–3333.

WALKING TOURS

Bangor East Side Tour
(approximately 2 hours without stops)
Begin at the **Bangor Public Library** at 145 Harlow Street, which was constructed after Bangor's 1911 fire and has a fine reading room and a collection of paintings. Adjacent to the library on Harlow Street is the **Peirce Memorial,** a bronze statue commemorating area river drivers. From the memorial, continue along Harlow Street to Center Street and Bangor's **City Hall** (visitors welcome), which was built in 1912–15 and modeled after a federal post office building in Danville, Illinois. Proceed up the Center Street hill, take Somerset Street to the historic **Broadway District,** which is on the National Register. Many of these stately homes were built during the lumber boom, and you will find myriad architectural styles, including Greek Revival, Italianate, colonial, Victorian, and Gothic Revival. At Garland Street, backtrack down Broadway to State Street, turn left and continue to Brown Street. At Brown and York Streets is **St. John's Catholic Church.** If you want to extend your walk, head farther out State Street to Cascade Park, where you can explore the grounds, which include a waterfall, fountain, and gazebo, and stop for a picnic. From either stopping point, take State Street back to Harlow Street to conclude your tour.

Dining

INEXPENSIVE

Bagel Central. Café. Maine's only kosher restaurant has a great selection of cold cuts, bagel sandwiches, and baked goods. Its specialties are spanakopita, pizza potpie, and split-pea soup with matzoh balls. | 33 Central St. | 207/947–1654 | Closed Sat. No lunch Fri. | $1–$7 | No credit cards.

MODERATE

Captain Nick's Seafood House. Seafood. These casual dining rooms on two levels feature a dining car fashioned out of an authentic railway sleeper. It's known for its wide variety of lobster dishes and seafood. Live music on weekends. Kids' menu, early-bird suppers. No smoking. | 1165 Union St. | 207/942–6444 | $12–$25 | AE, D, MC, V.

Miller's Restaurant. Seafood. Upscale dining is served in two distinct areas. It's famous for its 200-item, hot-and-cold buffet/salad bar. Kids' menu, early-bird suppers. Sunday brunch. No smoking. | 427 Main St. | 207/945–5663 | $12–$20 | AE, D, MC, V.

Pilots Grill. Seafood. This eatery, established in 1940, has tall windows, white linens, and deep banquettes. Try the baked stuffed lobster, baked stuffed shrimp, or prime rib. Homemade desserts. Kids' menu, early-bird suppers. No smoking. | 1528 Hammond St. | 207/942–6325 | Closed Sun. Jan.–Mar. | $6–$21 | AE, D, DC, MC, V.

Sea Dog Brewing Company. American. This microbrewery on the Penobscot River serves up typical bar fare such as burgers, grilled chicken, and fresh Maine seafood. Its specialty is homemade beer. Ask about the lobster bake boat trips on *River Dog*. | 26 Front St. | 207/947–8004 | www.seadogbrewing.com | $8–$17 | AE, D, MC, V.

Thistle's Restaurant. Contemporary. This downtown restaurant displays local artwork on the walls. Try the roast duck or cashew chicken. There's open-air dining on the patio and a salad bar. Live music nightly by a pianist or guitar player. Sunday brunch. No smoking. | 175 Exchange St. | 207/945–5480 | Closed Sun. | $13–$19 | D, MC, V.

Lodging

INEXPENSIVE

Best Western White House Inn. This standard, chain hotel is near the civic center. Bar, picnic area, complimentary Continental breakfast. In-room data ports, refrigerators, cable TV, in-room VCRs (and movies). Pool. Sauna. Laundry facilities. Business services. Pets allowed. | 155 Littlefield Ave., Hampden | 207/862–3737 | fax 207/862–6465 | 64 rooms | $45–$89 | AE, D, DC, MC, V.

Main Street Inn. This older, typical inn across from the Civic Center is well priced, near a variety of restaurants, and provides basic amenities. Complimentary Continental breakfast. Cable TV. Business services. Pets allowed. | 480 Main St. | 207/942–5281 or 800/928–9877 | fax 207/947–8733 | 64 rooms | $49–$59 | AE, D, DC, MC, V.

Ranger Inns. This family-owned, clean, efficient, and modern inn is near the airport and shopping. Bar. No air-conditioning, some kitchenettes. Laundry facilities. Pets allowed (fee). | 1476 Hammond St. | 207/945–2934 | fax 207/945–3456 | www.rangerinn.com | 90 rooms | $49–$59 | AE, D, MC, V.

Rodeway Inn. This standard chain inn is near the airport and shopping. Restaurant, picnic area. Cable TV. Business services, airport shuttle. Pets allowed (fee). | 482 Odlin Rd. | 207/942–6301 | fax 207/941–0949 | 98 rooms | $42–$70 | AE, D, DC, MC, V.

Tether's End Bed and Breakfast. This 1890s country home surrounded by gardens is 7 mi east of town. Rooms have antiques, quilts, and sitting areas. Complimentary breakfast. No air-conditioning, no room phones, no TV. No pets. No smoking. | 50 Church Rd., Holden | 207/989–7886 | tethers@agate.net | www.agate.net/~tethers | 3 rooms | $50–$60 | Closed mid-Dec.–May | MC, V.

MODERATE

Comfort Inn. This standard hotel is near the interstate, airport, and shopping malls. Restaurant, complimentary Continental breakfast. Pool. Video games. Business services, airport shuttle. Pets allowed (fee). | 750 Hogan Rd. | 207/942–7899 | fax 207/942–6463 | 96 rooms | $55–$90 | AE, D, DC, MC, V.

Days Inn. This is a typical chain motel. Complimentary Continental breakfast. Cable TV. Pool. Hot tub. Video games. Business services, airport shuttle. Pets allowed (fee). | 250 Odlin Rd. | 207/942–8272 | fax 207/942–1382 | www.daysinn.com | 101 rooms | $50–$80 | AE, D, DC, MC, V.

Econo Lodge. This standard chain is near the interstate and shopping malls. In-room data ports, cable TV. Laundry facilities. Business services. Pets allowed. | 327 Odlin Rd. | 207/945–0111 or 800/393–0111 | fax 207/942–8856 | 128 rooms | $50–$85 | AE, D, DC, MC, V.

Fairfield Inn by Marriott. This chain hotel is near shopping and the airport. Complimentary Continental breakfast. In-room data ports, cable TV. Pool. Hot tub, sauna. Gym. Laundry facilities. Business services. | 300 Odlin Rd. | 207/990–0001 | fax 207/990–0917 | 153 rooms | $59–$79 | AE, D, DC, MC, V.

Holiday Inn. This standard chain offering is near the airport and 3 mi west of Bangor on Interstate 395. Restaurant, bar with entertainment, room service. In-room data ports, microwaves,

some refrigerators, cable TV, some in-room VCRs. 2 pools. Hot tub. Video games. Laundry facilities. Business services, airport shuttle, free parking. Pets allowed. | 404 Odlin Rd. | 207/947–0101 | fax 207/947–7619 | bgror@aol.com | 207 rooms | $72–$92 | AE, D, DC, MC, V.

Holiday Inn–Civic Center. This standard chain, near the Civic Center, is across the street from the Paul Bunyan statue. Restaurant, bar with entertainment, room service. In-room data ports, cable TV. Pool. Laundry facilities. Business services, airport shuttle, free parking. Pets allowed. | 500 Main St. | 207/947–8651 | fax 207/942–2848 | www.holidayinn.com | 122 rooms | $69–$89 | AE, D, DC, MC, V.

Mann Hill Morgans Bed and Breakfast. A charming New England Colonial Saltbox inn with stables, this inn is 7 mi east of Bangor. Original oak floors and staircase, cathedral ceilings, and antiques greet you in the main room. Guest rooms have country antiques and fireplaces. Complimentary breakfast. No air-conditioning, no room phones, cable TV, TV in common area. No pets. No smoking. | 660 Mann Hill Rd., Holden | 207/843–5657 | mannhill@gateway.net | www.maineguide.com/bangor/mannhill | 2 rooms | $65 | D, MC, V.

EXPENSIVE

Four Points Sheraton. This standard chain at the airport is near shopping. An enclosed walkway connects the hotel to the airport. Restaurant, bar. In-room data ports, cable TV. Pool. Exercise equipment. Business services. Pets allowed. | 308 Godfrey Blvd. | 207/947–6721 | fax 207/941–9761 | www.fourpoints.com/bangor | 103 rooms | $125 | AE, D, DC, MC, V.

Lucerne Inn. It's an easy downhill stroll to Phillips Lake from this antiques-filled farmhouse, 10 mi northeast of Bangor. It has been an inn for nearly two centuries. Deer often pass across the lawns from the nearby woods. Dining room, complimentary Continental breakfast, room service. Pool. Business services. | U.S. 1A, East Holden | 207/843–5123 or 800/325–5123 | fax 207/843–6138 | info@lucerneinn.com | www.lucerneinn.com | 30 rooms | $99–$199 | AE, MC, V.

Best Inn. This downtown inn near the Civic Center has been well maintained. The restaurant features homemade baked goods and pastries. Restaurant, bar. Cable TV. Business services. Pets allowed. | 570 Main St. | 207/947–0566 | fax 207/945–3309 | 50 rooms, 1 suite | $75–$120 | AE, D, DC, MC, V.

Phenix Inn at West Market Square. This inn occupies a late-19th-century building that's on the National Register of Historic Places. Complimentary Continental breakfast. Some microwaves, some refrigerators, cable TV, some in-room VCRs. Gym. Laundry service. Business services. Pets allowed. | 20 Broad St. | 207/947–0411 | fax 207/947–0255 | www.maineguide.com/bangor/phenixinn | 32 rooms | $85–$169 | AE, D, DC, MC, V.

BAR HARBOR

MAP 3, F9

(Nearby towns also listed: Acadia National Park, Cranberry Isles, Ellsworth, Northeast Harbor, Southwest Harbor)

Ever since rusticators have been rusticating, this heavily trafficked tourist town has been a hot spot. Works by painters from the Hudson River School are credited with first attracting visitors in the mid-19th century. As the area's popularity grew, hotels and resorts began to pop up, and soon the nation's elite were building summer "cottages" here. Among those was John D. Rockefeller, Jr., who was responsible for the 57-mi of carriage roads constructed in Acadia National Park in the early 1900s. In 1947 a great fire devastated much of the island, but the region quickly bounced back, as evidenced by the numerous shops, inns, restaurants, excursions, amusements—and guests—in today's Bar Harbor. The area offers so many attractions and activities, you could stay here all summer and never run out of things to do. Fall is a lovely, less-peopled season for a visit.

Information: Bar Harbor Chamber of Commerce | 93 Cottage St., Bar Harbor, 04609 | 207/288–5103 or 800/288–5103 | www.barharborinfo.com.

Attractions

Abbe Museum. Housed in a National Historic Register building, this museum brings the ancient past to life with prehistoric and historic artifacts from its 50,000-item collection. Its emphasis is on Native American culture. In summer you'll find a number of events here. | 1 Park Loop Rd. | 207/288–3519 | www.abbemuseum.org | $2 | Mid-May–June and Sept.–mid-Oct., daily 10–4; July–Aug., daily 9–5.

Acadia Zoo. More than 40 species of wild animals such as reindeer, monkeys, moose, big cats, and reptiles are kept within this 15-acre property, designed to reflect the natural habitats of the animals. Be sure to check out the old barn–turned–rain forest filled with tropical plants and animals. It's 15 mi north of Bar Harbor. | Rte. 3, Trenton | 207/667–3244 | $6 | May–Dec., daily 9:30–dusk.

Atlantis Whale Watch. Set sail on a 116-ft, diesel-powered ship designed especially for watching whales. The *Atlantis* sails 20 mi off shore to an area where herring live and lure the whales. | 1 West St. | 207/288–3322 or 800/508–1499. | www.whalesrus.com | $32 for whales only, $35 for whales and puffins | May–Oct., daily 8:30 AM for whales and puffins, 12:30 and 4:30 for whales only.

Bar Harbor Historical Society Museum. Formerly St. Edwards Convent, this 1918 museum is on the National Register of Historic Places. Exhibits include a large collection of early photographs on local history, containing original *Life* magazine photographs and personal

KODAK'S TIPS FOR PHOTOGRAPHING PEOPLE

Friends' Faces
- Pose subjects informally to keep the mood relaxed
- Try to work in shady areas to avoid squints
- Let kids pick their own poses

Strangers' Faces
- In crowds, work from a distance with a telephoto lens
- Try posing cooperative subjects
- Stick with gentle lighting—it's most flattering to faces

Group Portraits
- Keep the mood informal
- Use soft, diffuse lighting
- Try using a panoramic camera

People at Work
- Capture destination-specific occupations
- Use tools for props
- Avoid flash if possible

Sports
- Fill the frame with action
- Include identifying background
- Use fast shutter speeds to stop action

Silly Pictures
- Look for or create light-hearted situations
- Don't be inhibited
- Try a funny prop

Parades and Ceremonies
- Stake out a shooting spot early
- Show distinctive costumes
- Isolate crowd reactions
- Be flexible: content first, technique second

From Kodak Guide to Shooting Great Travel Pictures © 2000 by Fodor's Travel Publications

accounts of the 1947 fire. | 33 Ledgelawn Ave., off Mt. Desert St. | 207/288–0000 | Donations accepted | Mid-June–mid-Oct., Mon.–Sat. 1–4.

Bar Harbor Whale Watch Co. Set sail on a steady catamaran and try your luck at spotting the huge sea mammals, as well as the unusual Maine bird, the puffin. | Rte. 3 at the Bar Harbor Regency Holiday Inn | 207/288–2386 or 800/WHALES–4 | www.whalesrus.com | $39 | May–Oct., daily 8:30 (whale and puffin trips), 1 (whales only), 4:45 (whales only, no 4:45 trip on Sun.).

College of the Atlantic. Set on beautiful Mt. Desert Island, this small college (300 undergraduates) offers a curriculum in human ecology. | 105 Eden St. | 800/528–0025 | www.coa.edu | Daily.

Natural History Museum. This museum features natural aspects of maritime Maine, including mounted birds and mammals and a whale skeleton model. | 105 Eden St. | 207/288–5015 | $3.50 | June–Labor Day, daily 10–5; mid-Sept.–mid-June, Thurs.–Fri. and Sun 1–4, Sat. 10–4.

Ferry service to Yarmouth, Nova Scotia. Car and passenger service on a high-speed catamaran. The ferry stops briefly in Yarmouth, then returns. | 888/249–7245 | $55 round-trip | June–mid-Oct., daily 7:30–3:30.

ON THE CALENDAR

JULY: *Fourth of July Festivities.* Public suppers and breakfasts, seafood festival, parade, and fireworks round out this popular event. | Downtown Bar Harbor | 207/288–5103.

JULY–AUG.: *Arcady Music Festival.* A Thursday-evening summer concert series in Gates Hall at the College of the Atlantic featuring a wide variety of musical offerings. | Eden St. | 207/288–2141.

JULY–AUG.: *Bar Harbor Music Festival.* Since 1967, classical, jazz, and pops concerts have been offered at various locations around town. | 212/222–1026 or 207/288–5744.

Dining

Anthony's Cucina Italiana. Italian. Friendly hosts, old-world family recipes, and local Maine seafood make for a charming, semiformal place for dinner. Try the lobster *Asiago al forno* (in a creamy cheese sauce with shallots, garlic, roasted red peppers, and mushrooms), and the *alla pescatore fra diavolo* (shellfish sautéed with onions, peppers, and mushrooms in a spicy tomato sauce, over linguine). | 191 Main St. | 207/288–3377 | No lunch Sun.–Thurs. | $12–$18 | D, MC, V.

Atlantic Brewing Company. American. The main draw here is the handcrafted beer made in small batches. But if you've got the urge for grilled chicken sausages, burgers, and typical pub fare, this is the place. Be sure to try the floats make from homemade root beer. Brewery tours are offered at 1, 2, 3, and 4 PM daily. Gift shop and beer tastings from 12 to 6. Inquire about the brewer's Saturday barbecues. | Knox Rd. | 207/288–2337 | Closed mid-Sept.–June | $4–$7 | D, MC, V.

The Burning Tree. Seafood. Boasting a menu of fresh organic produce and seafood, this friendly restaurant, with two dining rooms and a screened-in patio, uses locally grown ingredients. Try Ida's crab cakes, the pan-seared yellowfin tuna with sesame spinach in a ginger tamari sauce, or choose from one of several vegetarian items like the feta-stuffed eggplant roll with linguine, tossed in arugula, olive oil, and Parmesan. | Rte. 3, Otter Creek | 207/288–9331 | Closed Tues. and mid-Oct.–mid-June. No lunch | $17–$24 | MC, V.

Café This Way. Eclectic. The groovy, mismatched interior fixtures, eat-in counter, and packed bookshelves set the tone for a quirky, inspired menu with everything from crab cakes in tequila lime sauce and tuna sausage with wasabi, soy, and ginger to butternut squash ravioli with roasted red peppers in a rosemary maple cream sauce and filet mignon grilled with a horseradish, green peppercorn crust. Vegetarian substitutions and dishes are available. | 14½ Desert St. | 207/288–4483 | Breakfast also available; no lunch in summer, no dinner in winter | $12–$19 | MC, V.

Fisherman's Landing. Seafood. At this rustic, wharf-side setting, you can pick your own lobsters from the tank. There's open-air dining on the deck or right on the wharf. Cafeteria-style service. Kids' menu. Dock space. No smoking. | 35 West St. | 207/288–4632 | Closed Nov.–May | $5–$15 | MC, V.

Galyn's. Seafood. This two-story, former boardinghouse is the place where locals come for prime rib. The upstairs of the 1890s building has a bar and lounge with an antique mahogany bar. Seafood dishes like the mixed grill with lobster, scallops, and fresh fish are complemented by an extensive wine list and homemade desserts. Be sure to try the blueberry apple crisp made with locally grown fruit, and the chocolate truffle mousse cake with raspberry topping. | 17 Main St. | 207/288–9706 | No lunch | $12–$21 | AE, D, MC, V.

George's. Continental. This old summer cottage is an oasis off Main Street. It is known for fish, lobster, and lamb. Open-air dining overlooking the garden. Live music Wednesday–Saturday. Kids' menu. No smoking. | 7 Stephens La., off Main St. | 207/288–4505 | Closed Nov.–Memorial Day. No lunch | $25–$35 | AE, D, DC, MC, V.

Havana. South American. Fresh Maine seafood and locally grown ingredients prepared with a Latin flair are the trademarks of this bustling café. Try the salads such as the Peruvian quinoa with fresh fruit over spinach and greens and jicama and mango salad with a citrus vinaigrette or the sautéed jalapeño shrimp in a lime ginger coconut sauce. | 318 Main St. | 207/288–2822 | Reservations essential | No lunch | $14–$27 | AE, D, MC, V.

Island Chowder House. Seafood. A model train travels around the dining room in this cozy place. Known for lobster, chowder, and the homemade desserts. Kids' menu, early-bird suppers. | 38 Cottage St. | 207/288–4905 | Closed Nov.–Apr. | $8–$15 | AE, D, MC, V.

Lompoc Café and Pub. Eclectic. A quirky, fun local hangout that has a bocce court. Try the mango salmon with basil and ginger or the Indonesian peanut chicken with stir-fried vegetables and coconut milk. There's also a large selection of microbrewed beers on tap and a host of fine scotches. Patio dining and bocce, and live blues, bluegrass, and jazz weekend nights in summer. Kids' menu. | 36 Rodick St. | 207/288–9392 or 207/288–3251 | Closed mid-Oct.–Apr. | $10–$15 | MC, V.

Maggie's Classic Scales. Seafood. A converted Victorian house where you'll find fresh local seafood with organic vegetables. The lobster crêpes are highly recommended. Homemade desserts. No smoking. | 6 Summer St.; Rte. 3, left on Cottage St. to Bridge St. junction | 207/288–9007 | Closed late Oct.–Memorial Day. No lunch | $20–$30 | D, MC, V.

Miguel's. Mexican. This laid-back restaurant has Mexican artifacts, tiled floors, and a separate lounge. Try the blue-corn crab cakes. There's open-air dining on the patio. Kids' menu. No smoking. | 51 Rodick St. | 207/288–5117 | No lunch | $7–$24 | MC, V.

Michelle's Fine Dining. French. From the flatware and white linens to the complex menu and ornately framed artwork, an erudite perfection fills this small, romantic dining room in the Ivy Manor Inn. The French country influence fills every nook, including the menu layered with dishes like the pan-seared maple-sugared salmon, roast duckling *à la Provençal*, and the baked lobster and truffle *à la Maison*. Try the "Bag of Chocolate" for dessert—a white chocolate mousse with strawberries layered into a dark chocolate bag. | 194 Main St. | 207/288–2138 or 888/670–1997 | Closed Nov.–mid-May | $22–$60 | AE, D, MC, V.

124 Cottage Street. Continental. This warren of intimate dining rooms has a large airy garden for open-air dining. Known for fresh fish and desserts. Salad bar. Kids' menu, early-bird suppers. | 124 Cottage St. | 207/664–0454 | Closed Nov.–May | $20–$30 | AE, MC, V.

Poor Boy's Gourmet. Continental. Check out the all-you-can-eat early-bird pasta dinner with 12 types of noodles, from *farfalle* with garlic butter and Parmesan to linguine *al pesto*. The mushroom and bean stroganoff and vegetable scampi are suitable for vegetarians. The poor boy's porterhouse is a 16-ounce grilled steak with roasted garlic and parsley butter. | 300 Main St. | 207/288–4148 | Closed Oct.–May | $10–$20 | AE, D, MC, V.

Reading Room Restaurant. Continental. Once a gentleman's club, this restaurant in the Bar Harbor Inn offers panoramic views of the harbor and docks from the semicircular dining room. Known for fresh local seafood as well as creative chicken and beef dishes. Open-air dining on the terrace. Pianist or harpist nightly. Sunday brunch. Dock space. No smoking. | Newport Dr. | 207/288–3351 | Closed Nov.–Apr. | $25–$35 | AE, D, DC, MC, V.

Rinehart Dining Pavilion. Continental. Named after mystery writer Mary Roberts Rinehart, this restaurant with excellent views of Bar Harbor and Frenchman's Bay is set on a quiet hilltop on her former estate on the property of the Wonder View Inn. Dishes range from pasta and steaks to fresh local seafood. | 50 Eden St. | 207/288–5663 | $13–$21 | D, MC, V.

Rupununi. American. This busy spot in downtown Bar Harbor serves up a variety of dishes, like Louisiana gumbo, grilled swordfish, and pasta *barbarino*, spinach fettuccine tossed with bacon, chicken, peppers, onions, and mushrooms in a light cream sauce. There's outdoor dining in season and live Sunday jazz on the patio. Kids' menu. Visit the cigar bar and billiards room and check out the large selection of single-malt scotch. | 119 Main St. | 207/288–2886 | Closed Nov.–Mar. | $10–$19 | AE, D, DC, MC, V.

Terrace Grill. American. The casual, outdoor restaurant is part of the Bar Harbor Inn. Unlike its more elegant sibling, the Reading Room (*see above*), the Terrace Grill is home to lighter fare such as sandwiches, salads, and grilled fish. | Newport Dr. | 207/288–3351 or 800/248–3351 | $7–$21 | AE, D, DC, MC, V.

Lodging

Acacia House Bed and Breakfast. This late 1800s town house has a newly restored veranda, original 19th-century kitchen, and gardens. It's on a quiet side street with on-site parking. Two rooms have private decks. Complimentary breakfast. Free parking. No smoking. | 6 High St. | 207/288–8122 or 800/551–5399 | acaciahouse@acadia.net | www.acaciabarharbor.com | 9 rooms | $85–$150 | AE, D, DC, MC, V.

Acadia Inn. Opened in 1996, this inn offers deluxe accommodations 300 yards from the Nova Scotia ferry terminal—1½ mi from Acadia National Park. Picnic area, complimentary Continental breakfast. In-room data ports, some refrigerators, cable TV. Pool. Hot tub. Laundry facilities. Business services. | 98 Eden St. (Rte. 3) | 207/288–3500 or 800/638–3636 | fax 207/288–8424 | acadiainn@acadia.com | www.acadiainn.com | 95 rooms | $109–$155 | Closed Dec.–Mar. | AE, D, DC, MC, V.

Atlantic Eyrie Lodge. This lodge stands atop a bluff overlooking Frenchman's Bay. In this quiet, remote location, you'll have views of the ocean from your room and balcony. Picnic area, complimentary Continental breakfast. Some refrigerators, cable TV. Pool. Laundry facilities. Business services. | 6 Norman Rd. | 207/288–9786 or 800/422–2883 | fax 207/288–8500 | atlanticeyrie@acadia.net | www.barharbor.com/eyrie | 58 rooms | $110–$193 | Closed mid-Oct.–mid-May | AE, MC, V.

Atlantic Oakes Motel. This onetime estate has wonderful ocean views and is next to the Nova Scotia ferry terminal. Some kitchenettes, some refrigerators, cable TV. 2 pools. Tennis. Dock. Laundry facilities. Business services. | 119 Eden St. (Rte. 3) | 207/288–5801 or 800/336–2463 | fax 207/288–8402 | reservations@bhrhorisor.com | www.barharbor.com/oakes | 153 rooms | $135–$169 | AE, MC, V.

Balance Rock Inn. This luxury downtown bed-and-breakfast was built in 1903 for Scottish railroad tycoon Alexander Maitland and his family. It's on the historic Shore Path and has ocean views and gardens. Complimentary breakfast. Some in-room hot tubs. Pool. Gym. | 21 Albert Meadows | 207/288–2610 or 800/753–0494 | fax 207/288–5534 | rock@acadia.net | www.barharborvacations.com | 23 rooms | $255–$525 | Closed late Oct.–Apr. | AE, D, MC, V.

Bar Harbor Motel. This motel occupies a 14-acre, parklike site 1 mi from downtown Bar Harbor. Among its many amenities is direct trail access to Acadia National Park. Picnic area. Refrigerators, cable TV. Pool. Playground. Business services. | 100 Eden St. (Rte. 3) | 207/288–

3453 or 800/388–3453 | fax 207/288–3598 | bhmotel@acadia.net | www.barharbormotel.com | 78 rooms, 24 suites in 18 buildings | $48–$137 | Closed Nov.–Apr. | D, MC, V.

Bar Harbor Hotel–Bluenose Inn. This inn is on a hilltop and has stellar views of Frenchman Bay as well as many amenities and services. Restaurant, bar, room service. Refrigerators, cable TV, in-room VCR available. 2 pools. Hot tub. Exercise equipment. Laundry facilities. Business services. No smoking. | 90 Eden St. | 207/288–3348, 800/445–4077 outside ME, or 800/531–5523 in ME | fax 207/288–2183 | www.bluenoseinn.com | 97 rooms, 48 suites | $169–$349 | Closed Nov.–Apr. | AE, D, MC, V.

Bar Harbor Inn. At the head of picturesque Frenchman Bay, this inn is a full-service beach-front resort. Restaurant, bar with entertainment, complimentary Continental breakfast, room service. Minibars, some refrigerators, cable TV, some in-room VCRs. Pool. Beach, dock. | Newport Dr. | 207/288–3351 or 800/248–3351 | fax 207/288–5296 | bhinn@acadia.net | www.barharborinn.com | 153 rooms | $139–$279 | Closed Dec.–Mar. | AE, D, DC, MC, V.

Bar Harbor Regency Holiday Inn–Sunspree Resort. This resort on the waterfront with a nearby pebble beach is ideal for families. 3 restaurants, bar, room service. Refrigerators, cable TV. Pool. Putting green. Exercise equipment, dock. Children's programs (seasonal, all ages). Business services. | 123 Eden St. (Rte. 3) | 207/288–9723 or 800/HOLIDAY | fax 207/288–3089 | www.barharborholidayinn.com | 221 rooms, 2 suites | $245–$265 | Closed May–Oct. | AE, D, DC, MC, V.

Bass Cottage in the Field. Open to the public since 1928, this former summer estate just above the town pier is one of the area's best bargain destinations. Family-owned and operated since opening day, the lodge makes up in charm and sense of history what it lacks in modernity. No air-conditioning, no room phones. No pets. No smoking. | 14 the Field | 207/288–3705 | 10 rooms (4 with shared bath) | $75–$100 | Closed mid-Oct.–late May | No credit cards.

Bayview Hotel and Inn. This Georgian home on Frenchman Bay is filled with antiques and equipped with fireplaces. Bar, complimentary Continental breakfast. Some in-room hot tubs, cable TV. Pool. Massage. Exercise equipment. Library. Business services, airport shuttle. | 111 Eden St. (Rte. 3) | 207/288–5861 or 800/356–3585 | fax 207/288–3173 | www.barharbor.com/bayview | 38 rooms in 2 buildings, 6 apartments | $117–$440 | Closed late Oct.–late May | AE, DC, MC, V.

Best Western Inn. This typical chain hotel is 4 mi west of Bar Harbor and near the entrance to the mainland. Restaurant. Some refrigerators, cable TV. Pool. Laundry facilities. | Rte. 3 | 207/288–5823 | fax 207/288–9827 | bestwest@acadia.net | acadia.net/bestwestern | 70 rooms | $105 | Closed Nov.–Apr. | AE, D, DC, MC, V.

Black Friar. Surrounded by a perennial flower garden, this charming Victorian inn has book-cases, windows, and finely crafted woodwork salvaged from turn-of-the-20th-century "cottages" on Mt. Desert Island. The romantic guest rooms are furnished with period antiques and fine linens. Complimentary breakfast. No room phones, TV in common area. No kids under 11. No smoking. | 10 Summer St. | 207/288–5091 | fax 207/288–4197 | blackfriar@blackfriar.com | www.blackfriar.com | 7 rooms | $90–$145 | Closed Nov.–Apr. | D, MC, V.

Cadillac Motor Inn. This motel on the quiet end of Main Street is a half mile from the village and 1 mi from the park entrance. The nearby Shore Path offers a walk by the sea past some older mansions and ends at the town pier. Families are especially welcome. Picnic area. No air-conditioning in some rooms, some kitchenettes, cable TV. Laundry facilities. | 336 Main St. | 207/288–3831 | fax 207/288–9370 | cadillacmotorinn@acadia.net | www.cadillacmotorinn.com | 47 rooms, 4 apartments | $64–$165 | Closed Oct.–mid-May | AE, D, MC, V.

Castlemaine Inn. This sprawling, Victorian inn is furnished with antiques and fireplaces. It's 1½ blocks from the ocean. Complimentary Continental breakfast. Some refrigerators, some in-room hot tubs, cable TV, no room phones. No smoking. | 39 Holland Ave. | 207/288–4563 or 800/338–4563 | fax 207/288–4525 | www.castlemaininn.com | 17 rooms, 5 suites | $55–$185 | Closed late Oct.–mid-May | MC, V.

Cleftstone Manor. The rooms in this 1894 Victorian cottage have antiques and fireplaces. The manor is in the midst of Victorian gardens. Complimentary breakfast. No room phones. No smoking. | 92 Eden St. (Rte. 3) | 207/288–4951 or 888/218–4951 | fax 207/288–2089 | cleftstone@acadia.net | www.cleftstone.com | 16 rooms | $100–$195 | Closed Nov.–Apr. | MC, V.

Cromwell Harbor. This small, friendly, family-oriented hotel is a half mile from downtown. Picnic area. No air-conditioning in some rooms, some microwaves, some refrigerators, cable TV. Pool. | 359 Main St. | 207/288–3201 or 800/544–3201 | www.cromwellharbor.com | 25 rooms | $78–$115 | MC, V.

Edgewater Motel and Cottages. This motel is on a quiet cove on Frenchman Bay, 5 mi west of Bar Harbor. All rooms have views of the bay, spacious sitting areas, and outdoor decks. Picnic area. Some kitchenettes, refrigerators, cable TV. Beach. Laundry facilities. | Old Bar Harbor Rd., Salisbury Cove | 207/288–3491 or 888/310–9920 | fax 207/288–3491 | www.edgewaterbarharbor.com | 8 rooms, 4 apartments, 11 cottages | $102–$125 | Closed Dec.–Mar. | MC, V.

Emery's Cottages on the Shore. These 21 old-style family cottages on Frenchman Bay, 5 mi northwest of Bar Harbor, have a private pebble beach. There's a community kitchen for groups and some cottages have separate kitchens. They're 2 mi from the park entrance. Bicycle storage area, kayak rental available. Shuttle bus stop for access to park. Picnic area. No air-conditioning, some kitchenettes, refrigerators, cable TV. No room phones. Laundry facilities. | Sand Point Rd. | 207/288–3432 or 888/220–3432 | emerycottages@acadia.net | www.emeryscottages.com | 21 cottages | $75–$118 | Closed late Oct.–early May | AE, D, MC, V.

Golden Anchor Inn. This inn is on the waterfront in downtown Bar Harbor and within walking distance of shops and sights. The rooms are spacious and some have ocean views and views of Frenchman's Island. Sloop cruises in season. Restaurant, bar, complimentary Continental breakfast. Cable TV. Pool. Hot tub. Dock. Business services. | 55 West St. | 207/288–5033 or 800/328–5033 | fax 207/288–4577 | www.goldenanchorinn.com | 88 rooms | $120–$165 | Closed Nov.–Mar. | D, DC, MC, V.

Graycote Inn. This 19th-century inn near the ocean has fireplaces and antiques. Complimentary breakfast. No air-conditioning in some rooms, no room phones, no TV in some rooms. No kids under 9. No smoking. | 40 Holland Ave. | 207/288–3044 | fax 207/288–2719 | graycote@acadia.net | www.graycoteinn.com | 12 rooms, 2 suites | $95–$159 | AE, D, MC, V.

Hatfield Bed and Breakfast. Furnished with antiques, this B&B is on a quiet, residential side street. The decor is a mix of classic Victorian and casual. There's a front porch and third-floor sundeck, and there's cross-country skiing 2 mi away. Complimentary breakfast. No air-conditioning, no room phones. No kids under 10. No smoking. | 20 Roberts Ave. | 207/288–9655 | fax 207/288–0360 | rooms@hatfieldinn.com | www.hatfieldinn.com | 6 rooms (2 with shared bath, 3 with shower only) | $80–$115 | D, MC, V.

Hearthside Bed & Breakfast. This B&B's exterior is in a shingle, Arts and Crafts style. The rooms are decorated in a traditional style with antiques. Two rooms have porches. Dining room, complimentary breakfast. Some in-room hot tubs. No kids under 10. No smoking. | 7 High St. | 207/288–4533 | fax 207/288–9818 | hearth@acadia.net | www.hearthsideinn.com | 9 rooms | $65–$140 | D, MC, V.

High Seas Motel. This family hotel is 4 mi north of Bar Harbor and near the park entrance. It's surrounded by natural woodland. Restaurant. Some refrigerators, cable TV. Pool. Playground. | Rte. 3 | 207/288–5836 or 800/959–5836 | www.highseasmotel.com | 35 rooms | $80–$104 | Closed mid-Oct.–mid-May | D, MC, V.

Holbrook House. This cheery 1876 Victorian inn is furnished with four-poster beds, lots of lace, floral prints, and antiques. Two cottages have small patios, two bedrooms, and a living room and are suitable for families. Complimentary breakfast. No air-conditioning in some rooms, no room phones, TV in common area. Library. No pets. No kids under 12. No smoking. | 74 Mount Desert St. | 207/288–4970 or 800/860–7430 | info@holbrookhouse.com

| www.holbrookhouse.com | 10 rooms, 2 cottages | $125–$150 rooms, $155–$235 cottages | Closed Nov.–Apr. | MC, V.

Inn at Bay Ledge. With a view of Frenchman Bay, this 1907 inn has antiques and a country decor. An 80-step staircase takes visitors to the beach and caves at the base of the cliff. Complimentary breakfast. No air-conditioning, some in-room hot tubs, no room phones, cable TV in common area. Pool. Sauna, steam room. No kids under 15. No smoking. | 1385 Sand Point Rd. | 207/288–4204 | fax 207/288–5573 | bayledge@downeast.net | www.innat-bayledge.com | 8 rooms, 3 cottages | $140–$325 | Closed Nov.–Apr. | MC, V.

Inn at Canoe Point. This Tudor home built in 1889 stands on Frenchman's Bay and is cherished for its privacy and location abutting Acadia National Park. The master suite, with a gas fireplace and canopy bed, has antique doors opening onto a shared deck. The living room, with its open views and granite fireplace, is the perfect place to sit and watch the sea. Dining room, complimentary breakfast. No room phones, no TV. Fishing. No pets. No kids under 16. No smoking. | Eden St., Rte. 3 | 207/288–9511 | fax 207/288–2870 | info@innat-canoepoint.com | www.innatcanoepoint.com | 3 rooms, 2 suites | $170–$285 | D, MC, V.

Ivy Manor Inn. This 1940s English Tudor, all-suites inn has imported tiles, hardwood floors, stained glass, and mahogany wainscotting. The rooms are elegant, filled with original 19th-century antiques, embossed wallpaper, and Victorian fixtures like velvet sofas and armoires. Some bathrooms have claw-foot tubs and marble vanities. Restaurant, bar, complimentary breakfast. In-room data ports, cable TV. Library. Business services. No pets. No smoking. | 194 Main St. | 207/288–2138 or 888/670–1997 | fax 207/288–0038 | ivymanorinn@acadia.net | www.ivymanor.com | 8 rooms | $165–$325 | Closed Nov.–mid-Apr. | AE, D, MC, V.

Ledgelawn Inn. This beautiful three-story, 1904 summer cottage–style mansion has a historic air. Rooms are elegantly furnished, and many have fireplaces, porches, and canopy beds. Complimentary Continental breakfast. No air-conditioning in some rooms, some in-room hot tubs, cable TV. Pool. Pets allowed (fee). No smoking. | 66 Mount Desert St. | 207/288–4596 or 800/274–5334 | fax 207/288–9968 | www.barharborvacations.com | 33 rooms | $125–$275. | Closed mid-Oct.–Apr. | AE, D, MC, V.

Manor House. This restored Victorian (1887) house in the historical district is near both downtown and the ocean. It is filled with antiques and has fireplaces. Picnic area, complimentary breakfast. No air-conditioning in some rooms, no room phones, cable TV in common area and in cottages. Library. No kids under 10. No smoking. | 106 West St. | 207/288–3759 or 800/437–0088 | fax 207/288–2974 | manor@acadia.net | www.acadia.net/manor-house | 17 rooms, 5 suites, 2 cottages | $95–$195 | Closed Dec.–Mar. | AE, D, MC, V.

Maples Inn. This turn-of-the-20th-century Victorian inn is on a quiet side street in the center of Bar Harbor. You can relax on the front porch. Complimentary breakfast. No air-conditioning in some rooms, no room phones. Library. No kids under 12. No smoking. | 16 Roberts Ave. | 207/288–3443 | fax 207/288–0356 | maplesinn@acadia.net | www.maplesinn.com | 6 rooms, 1 suite | $90–$150 | D, MC, V.

Mira Monte Inn. An immense veranda fronts this Civil War–era inn, which is full of the appropriate antiques. Complimentary breakfast. No air-conditioning in some rooms, cable TV. Business services. No smoking. | 69 Mt. Desert St. | 207/288–4263 or 800/553–5109 | fax 207/288–3115 | mburns@acadia.net | www.miramonte.com | 16 rooms in 2 buildings, 2 suites | $145–$225 | Closed mid-Nov.–Apr. | AE, D, MC, V.

Nannau Seaside Bed and Breakfast. This stoic, peaceful 1904 seaside estate on Compass Harbor is listed in the National Register of Historic Places. Rooms are cozy and have antique furnishings including claw-foot tubs. Many have ocean views and fireplaces. Complimentary breakfast. No air-conditioning, no room phones, TV in common area. Beach. Library. No smoking. No pets. | 396 Main St. | 207/288–5575 | fax 207/288–5421 | nannau@acadia.net | www.nannau.com | 6 rooms | $65–$135 | Closed mid-Oct.–mid-June | MC, V.

Park Entrance Oceanfront Motel. This motel, on 10 acres of land, is near the beach 2½ mi north of downtown. All the rooms have water views and an open-air balcony or patio. Picnic area. No air-conditioning in some rooms, some kitchenettes, some refrigerators, cable TV. Pool. Hot tub. Dock. Business services. | Hamor Ave. | 207/288–9703 or 800/288–9703 | parkentrance@acadia.net | www.acadia.net/parkentrance | 58 rooms | $179 | Closed Nov.–Apr. | MC, V.

Quality Inn. This standard chain hotel is near both downtown and Acadia Park. It's four blocks from the ocean. Picnic area. Some kitchenettes, some refrigerators, cable TV. Pool. Laundry facilities. Business services. | 40 Kebo St. | 207/288–5403 or 800/282–5403 | fax 207/288–5473 | quality@acadia.net | www.acadia.net/quality_inn/ | 77 rooms | $149–$169 | Closed late Oct.–late Apr. | AE, D, DC, MC, V.

Ridgeway Inn. This elegant but relaxed inn was built in 1884 and has many antiques as well as a garden and a front porch. It is 1 mi from the park entrance and two blocks from the ocean. Complimentary breakfast. No air-conditioning, no room phones. No kids under 12. No smoking. | 11 High St. | 207/288–9682 or 800/360–5226 | www.maineguide.com/barharbor/ridgeway | 5 rooms | $90–$150 | Closed Nov.–mid-May | MC, V.

Stratford House. This English Tudor house was built in 1900 by the publisher of Louisa May Alcott's *Little Women*. Complimentary Continental breakfast. No smoking. | 45 Mt. Desert St. | 207/288–5189 | fax 207/288–5181 | inkeeper@midmaine.com | www.stratfordinn.com | 10 rooms (2 with shared bath) | $75–$175 | Closed Oct.–May | AE, MC, V.

Thornhedge Inn. This Queen Anne home was built in 1900. Complimentary Continental breakfast. No air-conditioning in some rooms, cable TV. No smoking. | 47 Mt. Desert St. | 207/288–5398 | www.maineguide.com/barharbor/thornhedge | 13 rooms | $80–$140 | Closed mid-Oct.–Apr. | MC, V.

The Tides. This 1887 Greek Revival home, right in Bar Harbor, is on the National Register of Historic Places with 1½ acres of manicured gardens, a half acre of ocean frontage, and magnificently appointed rooms filled with oversize beds, antiques, private sitting areas, and fireplaces. Complimentary breakfast. No pets. No kids under 12. No smoking. | 119 West St. | 207/288–4968 | fax 207/288–2997 | info@barharbortides.com | www.barharbortides.com | 4 rooms | $175–$325 | AE, D, MC, V.

Ullikana and the Yellow House Bed and Breakfast. The Ullikana is a charming and secluded 1885 Tudor home, surrounded by gardens and ocean views. Rooms are elegantly furnished with antiques, four-poster beds, and country finishes. Some have fireplaces and terraces. Its sister property, the Yellow House, is linked by a small path. It is simpler, with large rooms and a wraparound porch. Complimentary breakfast. No air-conditioning in some rooms, no room phones, no TV. Library. No pets. No kids under 8. No smoking. | 16 The Field | 207/288–9552 | fax 207/288–3682 | www.ullikana.com | 15 rooms, 1 suite | $135–$235 | Closed Nov.–Apr. | MC, V.

Villager Motel. This in-town family motel is minutes from the waterfront, restaurants, and shops. Everything is within walking distance and it is also on the island shuttle bus route. Cable TV. Pool. | 207 Main St. | 207/288–3211 | fax 207/288–2270 | villager@acadia.net | www.acadia.net/villager | 52 rooms | $98–$115 | Closed late Oct.–mid-May | AE, MC, V.

Wonder View Inn. This inn is on a 14-acre hilltop and there are ocean views from most rooms. Restaurant, bar, picnic area. Some refrigerators, cable TV. Pool. Business services. | 50 Eden St. | 207/288–3358 or 888/439–8439 | fax 207/288–2005 | wonderview@acadia.net | www.wonderviewinn.com | 79 rooms (10 with shower only) | $100–$145 | Closed mid-Oct.–mid-May | AE, D, MC, V.

BATH

(Nearby towns also listed: Brunswick, Georgetown, Phippsburg, Wiscasset)

For centuries, shipbuilding has been the driving force in this small, attractive city located on the Kennebec River. The inviting downtown features a waterfront park and many specialty shops, and the city's streets are lined with stately ship captains' homes. The Bath Iron Works, Maine's largest industry, is located here, and you can see large, gunmetal-gray ships harbored along the river and a massive red-and-white crane hovering over the town like a giant praying mantis. The opening of the four-lane Sagadahoc Bridge has made traveling much smoother. Bath also serves as a gateway to Georgetown and Phippsburg.

Information: Bath-Brunswick Region Chamber of Commerce | 59 Pleasant St., Brunswick, 04011 | 207/725–8797 or 207/443–9751 | ccbbr@horton.col.k12.us | www.midcoast-maine.com. **Visitors Center** | U.S. 1 N, West Bath, 04530 | 207/725–8797 or 207/443–9751 | www.midcoastmaine.com.

Attractions

Chocolate Church Arts Center. Bath's renowned cultural center hosts theater productions, live jazz, folk and classical concerts, and children's performances. | 804 Washington St. | 207/442–8455 | Tues.–Sat. 12–4.

★ **Maine Maritime Museum and Shipyard.** Devoted to Maine's maritime history, this extensive museum has a maritime history building; a historic 19th-century shipyard; demonstrations of seafaring, boatbuilding, and lobstering; a Kennebec River cruise that includes views of Bath Iron Works; and regularly changing exhibits. | 243 Washington St. | 207/443–1316 | www.bathmaine.com | $8.75 | Daily 9:30–5.

Sagadahoc Preservation Guided Walking Tours of Bath. Guided walking tours of the homes and buildings of Bath. | 880 Washington St. | 207/443–2174 | July–Aug., Tues. and Thurs. at 2.

ON THE CALENDAR

★ **JULY:** *Heritage Days.* There's a triathlon, carnival, parade, children's events, entertainment, vendors, fireworks, and craft and art shows all centering around the Fourth of July. | Waterfront and Library Park | 207/443–9751.
DEC.: *Old-Fashioned Christmas.* You'll find store displays, a festival of trees, and special events to help you celebrate the holidays. | Downtown Bath | 207/443–9751.

Dining

Beale Street Barbecue and Grill. American. Brimming with flavors of the South, this is a great place to get some down-home cooking. Try the jambalaya, blackened fish-and-chips, and the hickory barbecue sampler of ribs, sausage, chicken, pork chicken, or brisket on corn bread with beans and coleslaw. | 215 Water St. | 207/442–9514 | $7–$16 | MC, V.

Kristina's. Seafood. Bright and airy multilevel dining is offered in two connected restored Victorian houses. Try the Maine crab cakes, haddock Kristina, or the sticky buns. This eatery is renowned for its baked goods. There's open-air dining on the deck. Kids' menu. Saturday and Sunday brunch. No smoking. | 160 Centre St.; just off the High St. (Rte. 209) exit of U.S. 1 | 207/442–8577 | Closed Jan. | $15–$25 | D, MC, V.

Taste of Maine. Seafood. This capacious dining room, 1 mi north of town, overlooks the fork of Pleasant Cove and attracts the bus-tour crowd. There's dining outside on the deck, antiques, and a player piano. It's known for lobster, seafood, and steak. Kids' menu. | U.S. 1, Woolwich | 207/443–4554 | $10–$15 | AE, D, MC, V.

Lodging

The Donnell House. This is an 1850s Italianate home with a cupola and views of the Kennebec River. The dining room has high ceilings, rose-color walls, and a sense of history. All rooms have large private baths with tubs and showers and four-poster beds; some have oriental rugs. The suite has a mahogany sleigh bed. Complimentary breakfast. Some in-room hot tubs, no room phones, cable TV. Library. No pets. No kids under 12. No smoking. | 251 High St. | 207/443–5324 or 888/595–1664 | donlhseinn@clinic.net | www.mainelodging.com | 3 rooms, 1 suite | $85–$160 | D, MC, V.

Fairhaven. This 18th-century inn is loaded with antiques and is 1½ mi north of town. It has views of meadows, river, and woods. Picnic area, complimentary breakfast. No air-conditioning, no room phones. Cross-country skiing. Library. | 118 N. Bath Rd. | 207/443–4391 or 888/443–4391 | fax 207/443–6412 | fairhvn@gwi.net | www.mainecoast.com/fairhaveninn | 8 rooms (2 with shared bath) | $80–$130 | D, MC, V.

Galen C. Moses House. This stylish but quaint Victorian building (1874) is on the National Register of Historic Places. A full theater occupies the third floor and was once used to entertain officers from the local air-force base. Several ghosts are said to haunt the building, but they are "assuredly friendly"! Complimentary breakfast. No air-conditioning. Library. No smoking. | 1009 Washington St. | 207/442–8771 or 888/442–8771 | fax 207/443–6412 | galenmoses@clinic.net | www.galenmoses.com | 4 rooms | $68–$119 | MC, V.

Holiday Inn. This standard chain hotel is near U.S. 1 and downtown. Restaurant, bar with entertainment. In-room data ports, some refrigerators, cable TV. Pool. Hot tub. Exercise equipment. Business services, free parking. Pets allowed. | 139 Richardson St. | 207/443–9741 | fax 207/442–8281 | hibath@aol.com | www.holidayinn.com/bathme | 141 rooms | $79–$129 | AE, D, DC, MC, V.

The Inn at Bath. This beautiful 1810 Greek Revival home is in Bath's Historic District. It's filled with antiques yet polished off with modern amenities. Rooms are elegant but comfortable; some have wood-burning fireplaces and private terraces. Four rooms can be converted into two suites for families. Complimentary breakfast. In-room data ports. Some in-room hot tubs, cable TV, in-room VCRs. Laundry facilities. Business services. Pets allowed. No smoking. | 969 Washington St. | 207/443–4294 | fax 207/443–4295 | innkeeper@innatbath.co | www.innatbath.com | 8 rooms, 1 suite | $85–$145 rooms, $185–$370 suites | AE, D, MC, V.

Kennebec Inn. This Italianate mansion (circa 1860) is in downtown Bath, two blocks from the ocean. Complimentary breakfast. Some in-room hot tubs, cable TV. No smoking. | 11 High St. | 207/443–5202 or 800/822–9393 | www.bedandbreakfast.com | 7 rooms | $100–$165 | AE, D, DC, MC, V.

Linekin Bay Resort. With its waterfront location and host of activities, this is an ideal choice for families. Choose from the waterfront lodge or wooded cottage accommodations. The all-inclusive price includes meals as well as use of the resort's sailboats, instruction, and facilities. No air-conditioning, no room phones, TV in common area. No pets. | 92 Wall Point Rd. | 207/633–2494 | www.linekinbayresort.com | 35 rooms, 37 cabins | $140–$200 | MAP | MC, V.

Sebasco Harbor Resort. This old-style, 600-acre resort is on the ocean. It offers sailing lessons, cruises, and lobster boat rides. Families and golfers are especially welcome. There are sailboats and motorboats for rent for the nautically minded. Restaurants. Pool, lake. Golf course. Gym, hiking, boating. Children's activities (all ages). Laundry service. | Rte. 217, Sebasco Estates | 207/389–1161 or 800/225–3819 | fax 207/389–2004 | info@sebasco.com | www.sebasco.com | 115 rooms | $149–$269 | Closed late Oct.–early May | MAP | MC, V.

BELFAST

(Nearby towns also listed: Bucksport, Searsport)

Belfast was once home to more sea captains than any other port in the world, as evidenced by its abundance of Victorian, Federal, and Greek Revival manses. This pretty, small harborside city, perched on the Passagassawakeag River, has attracted artists and artisans for a number of years, many of whom came for a visit and never left. Its shop-lined, bricky downtown and strollable, shady streets have also made it a popular off-the-beaten-track destination. The Belfast and Moosehead Lake Railroad, which carried freight and passengers for 130 years, is now an excursion train. Recently, the telecommunications credit card giant MBNA moved its headquarters here.

Information: Belfast Area Chamber of Commerce | Box 58, 17 Maine St., Belfast, 04915 | 207/338–5900 | fax 207/338–3511 | chamber@belfastmaine.org | www.belfastmaine.org.

Attractions

Belfast and Moosehead Lake Railroad. A ride on the Belfast and Moosehead Lake Railroad is especially enjoyable during fall foliage season. It runs from the town of Unity, 20 mi west of Belfast, to Burnham Junction. It's a two-hour round-trip with the 1913 Swedish steam locomotive. | 1 Depot Sq., Unity | 207/948–5500 or 800/392–5500 | $16 | Mid-June–Dec., trains leave at noon.

Lake St. George State Park. This park, 19 mi west of Belfast, has a swimming area with life-guards on a crystal-clear lake and hiking trails. The fishing is good and a snowmobile trail is maintained from the park to Frye Mountain. There are 38 camping sites, and showers. | Rte. 3, Liberty | 207/589–4255 | $2 | Mid-May–Oct. daily 9–sunset.

ON THE CALENDAR

JULY: *Belfast Bay Festival.* This city festival includes food, crafts, live entertainment, a duck race, parade, and fireworks. | City Park, Northport Ave. | 207/338–5719 or 207/338–1722.
AUG.: *Sankofa Festival and Street Dance.* An annual multicultural event featuring ethnic music, poetry, and dance that takes place on the third weekend of the month. | Church St. | 207/338–5380.
DEC.: *New Year's by the Bay.* A family festival with events scheduled throughout the day, including ice sculpting, musical entertainment, food, and fireworks. | Downtown Belfast | 207/338–4501.

Dining

Darby's. Contemporary. This refurbished 1865 pub has tin ceilings and an original 1920 mahogany Brunswick bar with stained-glass fixtures. It is known for its wide-ranging menu, from macrobiotic dishes to steaks and seafood. Try the pad Thai. Kids' menu. Sunday brunch. No smoking. | 155 High St. | 207/338–2339 | $14–$25 | AE, D, DC, MC, V.

90 Main. Seafood. There's a bakery and deli beneath the restaurant here. It is known for fresh seafood, lobster, and vegetarian/vegan/macrobiotic dishes. Open-air dining on a deck out the back. Live entertainment Thursday and Friday. Kids' menu. Sunday brunch. | 92 Main St. | 207/338–1106 | $10–$20 | AE, D, MC, V.

Young's Lobster Pound. Seafood. Young's has ultracasual dining at picnic tables, with water views. Here you'll find basic seafood at fair prices: lobster rolls, chowders, and shore dinners. While it's open year-round, the dining room is unheated. Open-air dining on the deck. Cafeteria service. BYOB. Dock space. No smoking. | 4A Mitchell St., East Belfast | 207/338–1160 | fax 207/338–5652 | $7–$24.95 | MC, V.

Lodging

The Alden House. This meticulously restored 1840s Greek Revival home is in historic downtown Belfast. Cherry stairways, marble fireplaces, and parlors fill the common areas. Guest rooms are filled with antiques and hardwood furnishings, including the 7½-ft-tall carved burled walnut bed in the Elizabeth Waller room. Dining room, complimentary breakfast. No air-conditioning, no room phones, no TV. Library. No pets. No kids under 12. No smoking. | 63 Church St. | 207/338–2151 | innkeeper@thealdenhouse.com | www.thealdenhouse.com | 7 rooms (2 with shared bath) | $86–$120 | MC, V.

Belfast Bay Meadows. This turn-of-the-20th-century country inn on 10 acres has a view of Penobscot Bay. It's richly decorated with antiques, but retains a relaxed atmosphere. There's outdoor dining on the deck and views of bay. You'll find many activities nearby, including whale-watching boat trips, steam-train excursions, tennis, golf, hiking, biking, and winter sports. Complimentary breakfast. Some refrigerators, no TV in some rooms, cable TV in common area. Business services. Pets allowed. No smoking. | 192 Northport Ave. | 207/338–5320 or 800/335–2370 | fax 207/338–5715 | bbmi@baymeadowinn.com | www.baymeadowsinn.com | 20 rooms | $85–$165 | AE, D, MC, V.

Belfast Harbor Inn. This family-style inn and motel sits on 6 acres overlooking Penobscot Bay. You'll find excellent views of the bay and the historic port of Belfast from here. Picnic area, complimentary Continental breakfast. Cable TV. Pool. Business services. Pets allowed (fee). | U.S. 1 | 207/338–2740 or 800/545–8576 | fax 207/338–5205 | stay@belfastharborinn.com | www.belfastharborinn.com | 61 rooms | $84–$119 | AE, D, MC, V.

Belhaven Bed and Breakfast. This 1851 Victorian inn is in the heart of town. Rooms are filled with lace and country antiques and furnishings. The efficiency suite has a fully equipped kitchen, sundeck, and private entrance and is suitable for families. Dining room, complimentary breakfast. No air-conditioning, no room phones, TV in common area. Library. Pets allowed (fee). No smoking. | 14 John St. | 207/338–5435 | stay@belhaveninn.com. | www.belhaveninn.com | 4 rooms (3 with shared bath), 1 suite | $65–$105 | MC, V.

Gull Motel. This small family motel with a bay view is 3 mi north of Belfast. Cable TV. Pets allowed (fee). | U.S. 1 | 207/338–4030 | 14 rooms | $65–$79 | MC, V.

Jeweled Turret Inn. This storybook 1898 Victorian inn on the National Register of Historic Places is packed with charming turrets, columns, gables, local hardwoods, and period antiques. The inn's namesake is the stained-glass window, in the stairway turret, that glimmers like a jewel. Rooms are warm, with lace curtains, ornate wood trim, and antique and wicker beds. Complimentary breakfast. No air-conditioning, no room phones, TV in common area. Library. No pets. No kids under 12. No smoking. | 40 Pearl St. | 207/338–2304 or 800/696–2304 | jturret@gwi.net | www.maineguide.com/belfast/jeweledturret/ or www.jeweledturret.com | 7 rooms | $85–$135 | AE, MC, V.

The White House. This 1842 Greek Revival home, topped with an octagonal cupola, is fixed with ornate trim, Italianate fireplaces, and an elliptical flying staircase. Asian rugs, chandeliers, and antiques fill the elegant guest rooms. The inn is surrounded by gardens and Maine's largest copper beech tree. Dining room, complimentary breakfast. No air-conditioning, some in-room hot tubs, some in-rooms VCRs. Library. Business services. No pets. No kids under 14. No smoking. | 1 Church St. | 207/338–1901 or 888/290–1901 | fax 207/338–5161 | whitehouse@mainebb.com | www.mainebb.com | 4 rooms, 2 suites | $90–$150 | D, MC, V.

Wonderview Cottages. On the property's own Penobscot Bay beach, 3 mi northeast of Belfast, these cottages have screened-in porches and fireplaces. Picnic area. No air-conditioning, kitchenettes, cable TV. Playground. Pets allowed. | Searsport Ave. | 207/338–1455 | wondercottages@acadia.net | www.maineguide.com/belfast/wonderview | 20 1–3 bedroom cottages | $485–$860 (7–day minimum stay) | Closed mid-Oct.–mid-May | D, MC, V.

BELGRADE LAKES

(Nearby towns also listed: Augusta, Hallowell, Waterville)

The Belgrade Lakes are a chain of seven lakes and ponds surrounded by deep woods and open farmland in mid-Maine. Summer cottages and children's camps dot the shorelines, and all varieties of water sports are available. If, standing on the shore, you hear a loon and think of Katharine Hepburn, you probably won't be the first. Belgrade Lakes' Great Pond served as the inspiration for the novel *On Golden Pond*—even though the movie was filmed in New Hampshire.

Information: Belgrade Lakes Region, Inc. | Rte. 27, Box 72B, Belgrade Lakes, 04917 | 207/495–2744 or 888/895–2744 | www.mint.net/~belgrade.

ON THE CALENDAR

JULY: *July Fourth Celebration.* This annual parade, fireworks show, fire department chicken barbecue, and loon-calling contest is always a big draw. Other events change from year to year, but have included church concerts and kayaking demonstrations. | Belgrade Lakes | 207/495–2744 or 888/895–2744.

Dining

The Village Inn. Contemporary. At this restaurant between Great and Long ponds, you can eat in the dining room or on decks by the water. It's famous for its roast duck and also known for steaks, seafood, and vegetarian dishes. Kids' menu, early-bird suppers. Sunday brunch. Dock space. No smoking. | Main St. (Rte. 27) | 207/495–3553 | www.villageinndecks.com | Limited hrs Dec.–Feb. No lunch Sept.–June | $10–$20 | AE, MC, V.

Lodging

Pressey House Bed and Breakfast. This white, all-suites, octagonal 1850s Greek Revival inn on the shores of Messalonskee Lake is on the National Register of Historic Places and is 10 mi south of town. Rooms are fully furnished with country antiques and have full kitchens; some are large and are suitable for families. Some have fireplaces and/or private decks overlooking the water. Dining room, complimentary breakfast. No air-conditioning in some rooms, cable TV, no room phones. Lake. Dock, boating, fishing. Ice-skating. No pets. No smoking. | 32 Belgrade Rd., Oakland | 207/465–3500 | presshse@mint.net | www.pressey-house.com. | 5 rooms | $75–$110. | No credit cards.

Wings Hill Inn. This farmhouse was built in 1800. Complimentary breakfast. No air-conditioning, no room phones, no TV, cable TV in common area. No smoking. | Rte. 27 | 207/495–2400 or 800/509–4647 | fax 207/495–3920 | winghill@aol.com | www.virtualcities.com | 9 rooms (5 with shower only) | $95–$110 | D, MC, V.

BETHEL

(Nearby town also listed: Rumford)

Incorporated in 1796, Bethel is a quaint village that epitomizes small-town New England living. White clapboard historic homes, a village green, the brick buildings of Gould Academy—a prep school founded in 1836—and a sprawling country resort define the town's landscape. Best known as the gateway to the Sunday River Ski Resort, Bethel also provides easy access to Maine's White Mountain National Forest and Grafton Notch State Park.

Information: Bethel Area Chamber of Commerce | 30 Cross St., Bethel, 04217-1247 | 207/824–2282, 800/442–5826 hotel reservations | www.bethelmaine.com. **Maine Tourism Association** | 18 Mayville Rd., Bethel, 04217 | 207/824–4582 | www.mainetourism.com.

Attractions

Artist's Bridge. Also known as the Sunday River Bridge, this is the most painted and photographed of Maine's eight covered bridges and is 4 mi northwest of Bethel. | Sunday River Rd. off Rte. 26 | Free | Daily.

Carter's X-C Ski Center. This site has 1,000 acres of cross-country skiing terrain, including beginner trails and a slope from the top of Farwell Mountain. Two lodges, including one on the Androscoggin River with outstanding views of Mt. Will, the Mt. Washington Range, and Sunday River. Ski shop and lounge are on site. | Intervale Rd. | 207/539–4848 | $10 | Mid-Dec.–early Apr., Fri.–Sun. and holidays (depending on snowfall).

Dr. Moses Mason House Museum. In the National Historic District, this Federal-era house was built in 1813 and highlights the life of Dr. Moses Mason and his wife, Agnes Staw Mason, as well as local history. | 14 Broad St. | 207/824–2908 | http://orion.bdc.bethel.me.us/~history | $2 | July–Labor Day, Tues.–Sun. 1–4; Labor Day–June, Tues.–Fri. 1–4, or by appointment.

Gould Academy. This local prep school has been open since 1836 and specializes in visual arts and snow-related sports and courses. Prospective students can enjoy its Georgian architecture and classic New England campus feel on one of the guided walking tours. | Church St. | 207/824–7777 | www.gouldacademy.org.

Grafton Notch State Park. The high point of this wonderfully scenic area, 9 mi northwest of Bethel, at the end of the Mahoosuc mountains is Screw Auger Falls. But there also is Mother Walker Falls, Spruce Meadow, Old Speck Mountain, and Moose Cave. The Appalachian Trail traverses the park, but there are many other hiking options as well. A main artery snowmobile trail, maintained by a local club, also passes through the park. | Rte. 26, Newry | 207/824–2912 | Free | Mid-May–mid-Oct., daily 9–dusk.

Mt. Abram Ski Resort. This good-size mountain, 8 mi south of Bethel, has excellent trail grooming, challenging runs, and a friendly family environment all at bargain prices. | Off Rte. 26, Locke Mills | 207/875–5003 | www.mtabram.com | $17–$32 | Nov.–Mar., daily 9–4.

Sunday River Ski Resort. One of Maine's premier ski resorts is 6 mi northeast of Bethel and has high-speed lifts serving 126 trails on eight different peaks. There's plenty of nightlife after the ski lifts close. In summer, the slopes are turned over to mountain bikers. Canoeing, fishing, golf, tennis, and other sports are also available. | Sunday River Access Rd., off U.S. Rte. 2 | 207/824–3000 or 800/543–2SKI | www.sundayriver.com | Daily.

White Mountain National Forest. Although the White Mountains and most of this national forest are in New Hampshire, a portion of it juts into Maine, 10 mi west of Bethel. There are dozens of hiking trails and the views on the Evans Notch Road (Route 113 beginning in Gilead) are among the best in the state. The fishing in the Wild River isn't what it once was. The Patte Brook demonstration area can be an educational course in ecology. Hastings campground is well maintained and peaceful. | U.S. Rte. 2 | 207/824–2134 or 603/528–8721 | Free | Daily dawn–dusk.

ON THE CALENDAR

JAN.: *Carter's Last Stand Cross-Country Ski Race.* An annual 3-mi race in the scenic western Maine mountains at Carter's Cross-Country Ski Center. | Middle Intervale Rd. | 207/824–3880 or 207/539–4848.

JULY: *Bethel Historical Society Fourth of July Celebration.* You'll find fireworks, fun, games, and food at this annual event. | Broad St. | 207/824–2908.

JULY: *Mollyockett Day.* A celebration in homage to the Indian healer of the same name, with entertainment, crafts fair, food, and a parade. | The Common | 207/824–3575.

Dining

Bethel Inn and Country Club. Continental. The menu of this renowned inn leans to the formal, serving dishes like hazelnut crusted duck, pastry-wrapped shrimp, lobster, and roasted rack of lamb. The in-house tavern has lighter fare like sandwiches and burgers and is open for lunch. Kids' menu. | Village Common | 207/824–2175 or 800/654–0125 | Closed mid-Oct.– Dec. and Mar.–May. No lunch | $16–$21 | AE, D, DC, MC, V.

Mother's Restaurant. American. This turn-of-the-20th-century gingerbread house with a filligreed exterior has four small dining rooms with antique wood tables, fresh flowers, decorative woodstoves, a den, and bookshelves filled with old law texts. The crowd includes skiers and locals who come for a meal of scallops *au gratin,* Mother's meat loaf, and the stuffed mushroom appetizer. There is a patio and screened-in porch for seasonal outdoor dining. Kids' menu. | 43 Main St. | 207/824–2589 | No dinner Sun. Oct.–May | $8–$17 | D, MC, V.

Sudbury Inn. Continental. Three distinct semiformal dining areas give you the option of sitting next to a fireplace, overlooking Main Street, or enjoying the formal country room with a tin ceiling. Fine New England fare is the house specialty. Be sure to start off with the grilled seafood bisque, and continue with the wild mushroom and potato lasagna or the grilled seafood trio *cassoulet,* a melange of salmon, shrimp, and scallops with white beans and spinach. | 151 Lower Main St. | 207/824–2174 | No lunch | $14–$20 | AE, D, MC, V.

Suds Pub. American. Come mingle with a rough-and-tumble bunch of outdoorsy Mainers, particularly in winter, when the place is packed with ski guides. The menu is typical of a college bar, with burgers and sandwiches. The pizza is a real specialty and you can choose from 25 microbrewed beers, many of them products of Maine. Kids' menu. | 151 Lower Main St. | 207/824–2174 | No lunch | $5–$14 | AE, D, MC, V.

Sunday River Brewing Company. American/Casual. A modern, family-friendly brewpub, with an open dining room, wide windows, and fireside dining. Try the ribs or vegetarian items. Open-air dining on the deck. Live music throughout the week. Kids' menu. No smoking. | 1 Sunday River Rd., at U.S. Rte. 2 | 207/824–4ALE. | $10–$20 | AE, D, DC, MC, V.

Victoria Inn. Contemporary. Victorian-style fixtures like chandeliers and stained glass fill this restored mansion. The menu has been created by a transplanted San Francisco chef, bringing a more sophisticated touch to food in the area. Local organic produce is used in dishes like a house-cured tequila-lime salmon, sesame grilled shrimp, petite hen with Gorgonzola polenta, and a tomato *confit* and Moroccan duck over quinoa with preserved orange. A long, reasonably priced wine list is filled with unique titles from around the world. | 32 Main St. | 207/824–8060 or 899/774–1235 | $16–$21 | MC, V.

Lodging

Bethel Inn and Country Club. An elegant country inn (circa 1913) on the town square, the Bethel has its own golf course and is tucked in the Mahoosuc. Dining room, bars with entertainment. No air-conditioning in some rooms, cable TV, some in-room VCRs. Pool. Hot tub. Driving range, 18-hole golf course, putting green, tennis. Exercise equipment, boating. Cross-country skiing. Kids' programs (June–Labor Day, ages 4–12). Business services. Pets allowed. | 1 Broad St. | 207/824–2175 or 800/654–0125 | fax 207/824–2233 | connorsa@nxi.com | www.bethelinn.com | 60 rooms in 5 buildings, 40 condominiums | $109–$199, $119–$189 condominiums | MAP | AE, D, DC, MC, V.

Briar Lea Inn and Restaurant. This 1850s farmhouse filled with antiques is 1 mi north of town. Restaurant, complimentary breakfast. Hiking, cross-country skiing. Some pets allowed. | 150 Mayville Rd. | 207/824–4717 or 888/479–5735 | fax 207/824–7121 | briarlea@megalink.net | www.briarleainnrestaurant.com | 6 rooms (3 with shower only) | $73–$103 | AE, D, MC, V.

Chapman Inn. This 1865 colonial inn, named for the 19th-century composer William Chapman, is right on Bethel's town square. Guest rooms are simply furnished with antiques and local art. Dormitory bunk accommodations are available in the barn and are perfect

for those on a modest budget, or for the kids. Dining room, complimentary breakfast. In-room data ports. Hot tub. Sauna. Exercise equipment, bicycles. Ice-skating. Laundry facilities. Business services. Pets allowed (fee). No smoking. | Bethel Town Common | 207/824–2657 or 877/359–1498 | fax 207/824–7152 | info@chapmaninn.com | www.chapmaninn.com | 7 rooms (2 with shared bath), 1 suite, 24 dorm beds | $45–$119 rooms, $119 suites, $25–$30 dorm | AE, D, MC, V.

Evans Notch Motel and Cottages. This relaxed family motel is on 2 acres, just outside the White Mountain National Forest and 10 mi west of Bethel. It is near both fishing and the Appalachian Trail. Complimentary Continental breakfast. Some kitchenettes. | U.S. Rte. 2 and Rte. 113, Gilead | 207/836–2300 | fax 207/824–0640 | www.evansnotchmotel.com | 5 rooms, 6 cottages | $69–$85, $55–$85 cottages | AE, D, MC, V.

Holidae House. A beautiful 1851 Victorian inn, the Holidae is a short walk to the NTL (National Training Laboratories). Rooms are clean and quiet and feature period antiques. Efficiency units are available. Dining room, complimentary Continental breakfast. No air-conditioning in some rooms, in-room data ports, some kitchenettes, some in-room hot tubs, cable TV. No pets. No smoking. | 85 Main St. | 207/824–3400 or 800/882–3306 | fax 207/824–0276 | denniss@nxi.com | www.travelbase.com/destinations/bethel/holidae/ | 7 rooms, 2 suites | $75–$180 | AE, D, MC, V.

Inn at the Rostay. This friendly country inn is near both skiing and outdoor activities. Some microwaves, some refrigerators, cable TV, in-room VCRs. Cross-country skiing. | 186 Mayville Rd. (U.S. Rte. 2) | 207/824–3111 | athrall@bdc.bethel.me.us | www.rostay.com | 18 rooms (10 with shower only) | $55–$110 | AE, D, MC, V.

Jordan Grand Resort Hotel. About 12 miles east of Bethel, these fully furnished, condominium accommodations are a hit with local ski aficionados, and have access to the Jordan Bowls trails. Many units have fireplaces and full kitchens. 3 restaurants. Some microwaves, some refrigerators, cable TV, in-room VCRs. Pool. Massage, sauna, steam room. Health club, hiking. Cross-country skiing. Shops, video games. Baby-sitting, kids' programs (6–12). Laundry facilities. Business services. No pets. No smoking. | 1 Grand Circle, Newry | 207/824–5000 or 800/543–2754 | fax 207/824–5399 | www.sundayriver.com | 185 units | $160–$260 | AE, D, MC, V.

L'Auberge Country Inn. The Auberge is a charming, white 1880s converted carriage house on 5 wooded acres, just off the town common. Rooms are large and sunlit, and have king-size beds and antiques. Dining room, complimentary breakfast. No air-conditioning, no room phones, TV in common area. Library. Laundry facilities. Business services. Pets allowed (no fee). No smoking. | 32 Mill Hill Rd. | 207/824–2774 or 800/760–2774 | fax 207/824–0806 | reservations@laubergecountryinn.com | www.laubergecountryinn.com | 7 rooms | $79–$129. | MAP available | AE, D, MC, V.

Norseman Inn and Motel. This is a convenient roadside inn and motel with easy access to Sunday River. Picnic area, complimentary Continental breakfast. No air-conditioning in some rooms, cable TV. Cross-country skiing. Video games. Laundry facilities. No kids under 16 (inn). | 134 Mayville Rd. (U.S. Rte. 2) | 207/824–2002 | fax 207/824–0640 | norsemaninn.com | 32 rooms in 2 buildings | $98–$138 motel, $108–$148 inn | D, MC, V.

River View. This family-style hotel above the Androscoggin River 2 mi northeast of Bethel has a wide variety of activities. Picnic area. Kitchenettes, cable TV. Pool. Hot tub, sauna. Tennis. Video games. Playground. | 357 Mayville Rd. | 207/824–2808 | fax 207/824–6808 | rview@nxi.com | www.newmarket.com/maine.htm | 32 2-bedroom suites | $99–$129 | AE, D, MC, V.

Sudbury Inn. This 1873 white clapboard country inn in the heart of Bethel is known as a great place for families. The warm hosts and casual eclectic furnishings make this a local favorite and the two-room suites are good for families. 2 restaurants, complimentary breakfast. Air-conditioning in some rooms, no rooms phones, cable TV. No pets. No smoking. | 151 Lower Main St. | 207/824–2174 or 800/395–7837 | fax 207/824–2329 | sudbury2@thesudburyinn.com | www.thesudburyinn.com | 10 rooms, 7 suites | $65–$95 | Closed parts of Nov. and Apr. | AE, D, MC, V.

Summit Hotel and Conference Center. The Summit is a mountainside ski resort hotel 4 mi north of Bethel and near the White Mountain National Forest. A mountain-bike park, moose tours, and kayak trips are among the many activities available in summer. Restaurant, bar. Some kitchenettes, some microwaves, cable TV, some in-room VCRs. Pool. Hot tub. Exercise equipment, hiking. Cross-country skiing, downhill skiing. Children's programs (mid-Dec.–Apr., ages 6 weeks–12 years). Laundry facilities. Business services. Free parking. | Sunday River Access Rd. | 207/824–3500 or 800/543–2754 | fax 207/824–3993 | reservations@sundayriver.com | www.sundayriver.com | 230 rooms | $99–$129 | AE, D, MC, V.

Sunday River Inn. This casual, family-style winter-only inn, 6 mi north of Bethel and ½ mi from Sunday River Ski Resort, is popular with families and skiers. Private rooms are available, and dorm-style accommodations are suitable for students and skiers. Buffet meals are hearty and filling (breakfast and dinner are included in the price). It will accommodate groups in summer. Dining room, complimentary breakfast. No air-conditioning, no room phones, TV in common area. Outdoor hot tub, sauna. Ice-skating, cross-country skiing, tobogganing. Library. No pets. No smoking. | 23 Skiway Rd., Newry | 207/824–2410 | fax 207/824–3181 | www.sundayriverinn.com | 19 rooms (16 share bath), 5 dorms with 30 beds (sharing 2 baths) | $140–$172, $45 per person in dorms | Closed Apr.–late Nov. | MAP | AE, D, MC, V.

Telemark Inn. A unique place geared toward the outdoor lover, this rustic, turn-of-the-20th-century, handcrafted Adirondack-style lodge is on 360 acres in the White Mountain National Forest. With llama treks, canoeing, skajoring (a combination of cross-country skiing and dog sledding—the dogs pull you along as you ski), and trips focusing on natural history, ecology and education, the prevailing theme is understanding and living with nature. It can be reserved for group retreats. Three-, 5-, and 7-day packages are available, as are bed-and-breakfast rates in off-season. Dining room, complimentary breakfast. No room phones, no TV. Sauna. Hiking, horseback riding. Ice-skating, cross-country skiing, sleigh rides. No pets. No smoking. | Kings Hwy. | 207/836–2703 | telemark@nxi.com | www.telemarkinn.com | 5 rooms (all share 2 baths) | $95 per person | MAP | AE, MC, V.

BIDDEFORD-SACO

MAP 3, B11

(Nearby towns also listed: Kennebunk, Old Orchard Beach, Scarborough)

The twin cities of Biddeford and Saco are divided by the Saco River, the former being the more industrial side, the latter the more residential. Franco-American heritage runs deep in Biddeford, once a thriving a mill town and now in the process of revitalization, which includes plans for a new riverfront park. U.S. 1 cuts through the center of Saco, which has an inviting downtown and a number of architecturally impressive homes and churches. The outlying areas of Biddeford Pool and Camp Ellis are snug summer communities.

Information: **Chamber of Commerce** | 110 Main St., Saco, 04072 | 207/282–1567 | chamber@int-usa.net | www.biddefordsacomaine.com.

Attractions

Aquaboggan Water Park. This water park, 4 mi north of Saco, has just about everything wet a person could want, from a swimming pool to three water slides, wave pools, bumper boats, water wars, and more. For those who prefer to play out of the water, there is also miniature golf, shuffleboard, and race cars. | U.S. 1 | 207/282–3112 | www.aquabogganwaterpark.com | $18 | May–Sept., daily 10–6.

Dyer Library and York Institute Museum. Dyer Library has an extensive Maine history collection, local genealogy, and City of Saco records. The York Institute Museum has exhibits on regional and natural history, art, culture, and industry. | 371 Main St., Saco | 207/283–3861 or 207/282–3031 | $4 | Tues.–Fri. 12–4, Thurs. 12–8.

Ferry Beach State Park. While the beach is the big draw at this park 3½ mi north of Saco, the tupelo or black gum trees, rare at this altitude, and nature trails also lure visitors to this 100-acre area. The beach has a changing area, and there are picnic areas. | Rte. 9; 3½ mi north of Saco via Rte. 9 | 207/283-0067 | $1.

Funtown/Splashtown USA. This longtime theme park, 2 mi north of Saco, has a roller coaster and other carnival-type rides, as well as water slides, bumper boats, and other wet activities. There are also arcades, miniature golf, and batting cages. | 774 Portland Rd. (U.S. 1) | 207/284-5139 or 800/878-2900 | funtown@ime.net | www.funtownsplashtown.com | $14-$20 | Mid-June-Labor Day: Funtown 10-10; Splashtown 10-6. Weekends in May and September, Funtown only 10-5.

Seashore Trolley Museum. Founded in 1939, this unique collection of electric railway units is the largest in the world. Visit the three car barns or the restoration shop or take the 1¾-mi ride on one of six working cars. It's 4 mi south of Biddeford. | 195 Log Cabin Rd. | 207/967-2800.

ON THE CALENDAR
JUNE: *La Kermesse.* A four-day block party, with parade, entertainment, traditional dancing, ethnic dishes, and fireworks celebrating Biddeford's Franco-American heritage. | Downtown Biddeford | 207/282-2894.
JUNE: *Saco Sidewalk Art Festival.* A combination of visual and performing arts in the middle of Saco. | Main St. | 207/282-6169.

Dining
Governor's Restaurant and Bakery. American. If the Lionel train set cruising the perimeter of the restaurant doesn't get your attention, the diversity of the menu will. It runs the gamut from shepherd's pie and spaghetti and meatballs to fried seafood and roast pork. All breads, rolls, and desserts are made on the premises. Don't miss the chocolate and strawberry creme pies. | 431 Elm St. | 207/282-2992 | Breakfast also available | $5-$16 | AE, D, DC, MC, V.

Wormwood's. Seafood. People have been enjoying family-style dining here for over 50 years. The restaurant is near a scenic breakwater and has river and ocean views from its four dining rooms. Try the baked stuffed haddock or fried clams. Kids' menu. No smoking. | 16 Bay Ave., Camp Ellis, Saco | 207/282-9679 | $10-$20 | D, MC, V.

Lodging
Classic Motel. The Classic is convenient to Old Orchard Beach and other beaches. Picnic area. In-room data ports, some kitchenettes, refrigerators, cable TV. Pool. Some pets allowed. | 21 Ocean Park Rd. (Rte. 5), Saco | 207/282-5569 or 800/290-3909 | www.classicmotel.com | 17 rooms | $55-$85 | AE, D, MC, V.

Crown 'n Anchor Inn Steeped in local lore, this grand Federal inn listed on the National Register of Historic Places consists of two distinct homes built in 1760 and 1827. The guest rooms are filled with antiques and contain memorabilia from the local historical figures and events for which they were named. On three acres. Dining room, complimentary breakfast. No air-conditioning, in-room hot tubs, cable TV, TV in common area. Library. Pets allowed (no fee). No smoking. | 121 North St. | 207/282-3829 or 800/561-8865 | 6 rooms | $75-$120 | AE, MC, V.

Eastview Motel. This motel 3 mi north of Saco has spacious rooms with business services. Refrigerators, cable TV. Pool. No pets. | 924 Portland Rd. (U.S. 1) | 207/282-2362 | fax 207/282-2362 | 22 rooms | $70-$80 | Closed Nov.-Apr. | AE, D, MC, V.

Hobson House Celtic Inn Bed and Breakfast. This is an 1820s Federal mansion in the heart of town. Rooms have antiques, custom furnishings, and four-poster beds. Some also have fireplaces. Picnic area, dining room, complimentary breakfast. No air-conditioning, some room phones, TV in common area. Pool. Library. Business services. No pets. No smoking. |

398 Main St. | 207/284–4113 | info@hobsonhouse.com | www.hobsonhouse.com | 4 rooms | $85–$145 | MC, V.

BINGHAM

(Nearby town also listed: Skowhegan)

Settled in 1785, Bingham is just south of the 155-ft-high Wyman Dam. For generations, Bingham was an outfitting village for sportsmen, who came to the wilds of Maine to hunt and fish. Today it is the jumping-off point for popular white-water rafting centers, such as The Forks, where the backed-up raft traffic on the Kennebec makes coastal U.S. 1 look like a cakewalk.

Information: Upper Kennebec Valley Chamber of Commerce | Main St., Box 491, 04920 | 207/672–4100. **Visitor Center** | Old Scott Paper building, off Main St., Bingham, 04920.

Attractions

Maine Whitewater. Full-service rafting guides for trips on the Kennebec and Dead rivers. All levels are welcome. | Gadabout Gaddis Airport, U.S. 201 | 207/672–4814 | www.mainewhitewater.com | Memorial Day–Labor Day.

Wilderness Expeditions. This offshoot of the Birches wilderness resort offers white-water rafting expeditions on the Kennebec, Dead, and Penobscot rivers. | 1 Birches Rd., Rockwood | 207/534–7305, 800/825–9453 for reservations | www.birches.com | May–Oct., daily.

ON THE CALENDAR

SEPT.: *Annual Bingham Fly-In.* If it flies, it's at the Gadabout Gaddis Airport. Ultralights, helicopters, vintage and modern craft, and parachuters gather among vendors, musicians, and craftspeople for their annual preening. | Rte. 201 | 207/672–4100.

Lodging

Bingham Motor Inn and Sports Complex. This family motel 1 mi north of town caters to hunters and fishermen and has downhill skiing 5 mi away. Picnic area. Some kitchenettes, some refrigerators, cable TV. Pool. Hot tub. Basketball, hiking, volleyball. Cross-country skiing, snowmobiling. Pets allowed (no fee). | Rte. 201 | 207/672–4135 | fax 207/672–4138 | www.ctel.net/~bmisc | 20 rooms | $61 | AE, MC, V.

Inn on the River. This inn is on a bluff over the Kennebec River, 20 mi north of Bingham, and in the heart of the Maine white-water rafting region. You can pick up the Appalachian Trail eight minutes away, or see the impressive Moxie Falls. Bar with entertainment. Cable TV in common area, no TV. Hiking, boating, fishing. Snowmobiling. | U.S. 201, West Forks | 207/663–2181 | fax 207/882–9294 | www.innbytheriver.com | 10 rooms | $90–$120 | MC, V.

Mrs. G's Bed and Breakfast. The warm welcome, reasonable rates, and home cooking make this a popular stop for white-water rafters. The 1920s Victorian home is very simple; rocking chairs on the front porch help while away the time. The third-floor loft has nine beds, a private bath and entrance, and is perfect for groups. Ask about moosing trips. Complimentary breakfast. No air-conditioning, no room phones, TV in common area. No pets. No smoking. | Meadow St. | 207/672–4034 or 888/267–4833 ext. 2460 | 4 rooms, 1 loft with 9 beds | $30 per person | Closed Dec.–Apr. | No credit cards.

MAINE | BLUE HILL

BLUE HILL

(Nearby towns also listed: Castine, Deer Isle-Stonington, Ellsworth)

Tucked between Blue Hill mountain and bay, the small community of Blue Hill is a refined summer colony that was settled in 1762. Shipbuilding and the granite industry were the mainstays of this coastal town for years. This prosperity attracted warm-weather visitors, generations of whom continue to summer here. Home to the Kneisel Hall Chamber Music School, as well as a number of artists, craftsmen, and musicians, Blue Hill is a seaside town without a lot of fanfare—and residents seem content to keep it that way.

Information: **Ellsworth Chamber of Commerce** | Box 267, Ellsworth, 04605 | 207/667–5584 | woisard@bluehillme.com | www.ellsworthchamber.org.

Attractions
Blue Hill Mountain Hiking Trail. This easy ³⁄₄-mi hike to the top of Blue Hill gives great views from the peak. | Rte. 172/Rte. 115 | 207/667–5584.

Holt House. There have been no structural changes to this handsome two-story house built in 1825, which still boasts its original four chimneys and eight fireplaces. Operated by the Blue Hill Historical Society, the house has artifacts and other items related to town history. | Water St. | 207/374–2339 | July–Aug., Tues. and Fri. 1–4.

Parson Fisher House. This 1814 house was built by Jonathan Fisher, the town's first settled minister. He not only designed and built the house, but some of the tools needed to build it and the furniture inside. | Rte. 15 at Rte. 176 | 207/374–2459 | $3 | July–mid-Sept., Mon.–Sat. 2–5.

Rackliffe Pottery. Operated by the Rackliffe family, the shop, 1 mi from town, welcomes people to watch potters at work. | Ellsworth Rd. | 207/374–2297 | Free | Sept.–June, Mon.–Sat. 8–4; July–Aug., daily 8–5.

Rowantrees Pottery. This is another shop with a tradition of great glazes. It welcomes visitors. | Union St. | 207/374–5535 | Free | June–Sept., Mon.–Sat. 8–5; Oct.–May, weekdays 8–5.

ON THE CALENDAR
JUNE–AUG.: *Kneisel Hall Chamber Music Festival.* Summerlong series featuring faculty and student talent from the Kneisel Hall Chamber Music School. | 207/374–2811.
SEPT.: *Blue Hill Fair.* This popular agricultural fair at Mountain Park on Labor Day weekend has displays and demonstrations, whole and junk food, a carnival, and live entertainment. | Rte. 172 | 207/374–3701.

Dining
Blue Hill Inn. French. Intimate, candlelight dining is offered in this 1830 colonial inn with garden views and a five-course, prix fixe menu. It's known for imaginative preparations with local seafood and organic produce such as the wolffish in parsley sauce or the organic roast rack of lamb. Frequent performances are given by students from the nearby Kneisel Hall Chamber Music School. No smoking. | Union St., Rte. 177 E | 207/374–2844 | www.bluehillinn.com | Reservations essential | Closed Dec.–mid-May. No lunch | $75 prix fixe | D, MC, V.

Jonathan's. Seafood. A nautical theme reigns throughout this two-floor restaurant, filled with polished wood, seafaring knickknacks, and captain's chairs. The menu reflects the interior and is filled with fresh seafood dishes like lobster and salmon as well as free-range chicken and Black Angus steaks. | Main St. | 207/374–5226 | $16–$20 | MC, V.

Tavern at Firepond. Contemporary. Dine casually in this refurbished late-18th-century blacksmith shop overlooking a stream. It has exposed beams and three separate dining areas. It's known for fresh fish, onion rings, and specialty burgers. Outdoor dining on a deck and patio. Live music—jazz, rock, and classical. No smoking. | Main St. at Mill Stream | 207/374–9970 | Reservations not accepted | $15–$25 | D, MC, V.

Lodging

Auberge Tenney Hill Bed and Breakfast. This charming 1870s Victorian home is filled with antiques and artwork. Common areas are elegantly furnished with country touches; the common room opens up to a sundeck. Complimentary breakfast. No air-conditioning, cable TV in common area. Library. No pets. No smoking. | 1 Mines Rd. | 207/374–5710 | raguay@hypernet.com | www.inn-guide.com/tenneyhill | 5 rooms | $65–$95 | MC, V.

Blue Hill Inn. This Federal-style inn was built in 1830. It has antiques, fireplaces, and a 1-acre perennial garden, which is on the National Register of Historic Places. Elm trees surround the property. The suite is in a modern building called the Cape House next door. Dining room, complimentary breakfast. No air-conditioning in some rooms. No smoking. | Union St., Rte. 177 E | 207/374–2844 or 800/826–7415 | fax 207/374–2829 | bluehillinn@hotmail.com | www.bluehillinn.com | 11 rooms, 1 suite | $138–$175, $190–$245 suite | Closed Dec.–mid-May | MC, V.

Eggemoggin Reach Bed and Breakfast. This modern post-and-beam home on 5½ waterfront acres and 10 mi north of Blue Hill is built in the the Maine farmhouse style. Individual units are plush, charming wood cottages and studio rooms with excellent views of Penobscot Bay, Eggemoggin Reach, and Pumpkin Island and have private, screened-in porches. All accommodations are fully furnished and have woodstoves and full kitchens. Units can be rented for three- or four-day periods only, beginning on Sunday or Thursday. No air-conditioning, no TV. Hiking, dock, boating, fishing. No pets. No kids under 16. No smoking. | 92 Winneganek Way, Brooksville | 207/359–5073 or 888/625–8866 | fax 207/359–5074 | www.eggreachbb.com | 9 units | $150–$175 | Closed mid-Oct.–mid-May | MC, V.

Heritage Motor Inn. This modern motor inn is on a hill overlooking Blue Hill inner harbor and bay and is ½ mi east of Blue Hill. Cable TV. | Ellsworth Rd. | 207/374–5646 | hmi@acadia.net | www.bhheritagemotorinn.com | 22 rooms, 1 suite | $89–$95 rooms, $130 suite | MC, V.

BOOTHBAY HARBOR

MAP 3, D10

(Nearby towns also listed: Damariscotta, Monhegan Island, Newcastle, Wiscasset)

Once a simple port and shipbuilding center, Boothbay Harbor has evolved into one of Maine's top tourist destinations. Motels, cottages, restaurants, and gift shops crowd and cluster around the scenic, mast-studded harbor. It's all here: serene ocean cruises, lobster-pot key chains, spectacular shorefront vistas, fried clams, and a 1,000-ft-long footbridge spanning the harbor. The kitsch factor can run a little high at times, but views from the craggy shoreline are pure Maine.

Information: Boothbay Harbor Region Chamber of Commerce | 192 Townsend Ave., Rte. 27, Boothbay Harbor, 04538 | 207/633–2353 or 800/266–8422 | fax 207/633–7448 | seamaine@boothbayharbor.com | www.boothbayharbor.com.

Attractions

Boating Expeditions. Boothbay has many opportunities for seafaring adventures.
Balmy Days. This boat offers daily trips to Monhegan Island, as well as two-hour supper cruises on Tuesday and Thursday in July and August. | Pier 8, Commercial St. | 207/633–2284 | $30 round-trip to Monhegan | June–Sept., daily.
Bay Lady. This sailboat provides 1½-hour sails near the islands and lighthouses around the harbor. This 31-ft Friendship Sloop was once the workboat of Maine lobstermen. | Pier 8, Commercial St. | 207/633–2284 | June–Sept., call for schedule.

Novelty. Daily cruises of the shores, coves, lighthouses, and islands around Boothbay Harbor. | Pier 8, Commercial St. | 207/633–2284 | $9; special rates for children | Mar.–mid-Oct., 8–8; some summer cruises at 9:30.

Basket Barn of Maine. An unusual store, 1 mi north of Boothbay center, featuring woven Native American, domestic, and imported baskets. | Rte. 27 at River Rd. | 207/633–5532 | Free | Daily 9–5.

Boothbay Railway Village. An entertaining and educational compound, 1 mi north of Boothbay center, where you can take a 1½-mi ride on a narrow-gauge steam locomotive, visit a restored railroad station from 1911, and see more than 60 antique vehicles. There are also beautiful gardens and a village green surrounded by an 1847 town hall and the 1923 Spruce Point Chapel. Special events through the season. | Rte. 27 | 207/633–4727 | www.railwayvillage.org | $7 | Memorial Day–mid-June, weekends 9:30–5; mid-June–Oct., daily 10–5:30.

Cap'n Fish's Boat Trips. This outfitter offers a wide variety of boat trips and fishing excursions, including a seal-watching cruise, a harbor cruise, and a cruise up the Kennebec River. | Pier 1 | 207/633–3244 or 207/633–2626 | Memorial Day–Oct., daily; call for schedule.

Coastal Maine Botanical Garden. This garden on Sheepscot Bay, 1 mi north of town, has hiking trails and many attractive native plants. Nonprofit groups have saved the more than 100 acres from becoming a housing subdivision and are preserving and highlighting native plants, while slowly adding interesting new plant materials. | Barter's Island Rd., off Rte. 27 | 207/633–4333 | Free | Apr.–Nov., daily dawn–dusk.

Department of Marine Resources Aquarium. Focusing on species endemic to Maine's coastal tide pools and shores, this one-room aquarium houses a touch tank and a center tank where you can pet a live shark. The lobster presentation is a very popular event, where you will learn everything you wanted to know about Maine's most famous crustacean. | McKown Point Rd. | 207/633–9559 | $3 | Mid-May–Sept., daily, 10–5.

ON THE CALENDAR

APR.–MAY: *Fisherman's Festival.* Seafood, fishing demonstrations, the Blessing of the Fleet, races, pageants, and boat parade kicks off the summer season. | Throughout town | 207/633–2353.

JUNE: *Annual Lobster Boat Races.* Watch from any of the waterfront promenades as local lobstermen race their boats across the harbor for fun. | Boothbay Harbor | 207/633–4900.

JUNE: *Windjammer Days.* Windjammers arrive full rigged into the harbor, and the town goes all out to celebrate with concerts, a Best of the Harbor Food Competition, fireworks, and live entertainment. | Throughout town | 207/633–2353.

JULY: *Antique Automobile Show.* This two-day celebration of antique cars showcases over 200 restored and running vehicles. | At Boothbay Harbor YMCA | 207/633–4727.

JULY: *Harbor Jazz Weekend.* A variety of jazz players from Maine and elsewhere are featured in a number of concerts. | Throughout town | 207/563–3328.

OCT.: *Fall Foliage Festival.* Crafts, culinary booths, entertainment, and steam train rides all add to this autumn spectacle at Boothbay Railway Village. | Rte. 27 | 207/633–2353.

DEC.: *Harbor Lights Festival.* A crafts fair, carols and stories, wagon rides, and a lighted boat parade combine to celebrate this event. | In Boothbay Harbor | 207/633–2353.

Dining

Andrews' Harborside. Seafood. This comfortable dining room in a former early-19th-century shooting gallery has columns, hand stenciling, and marina views. The cinnamon buns are great. There's open-air dining on the screened-in deck. Kids' menu. No smoking. | 12 Bridge St. | 207/633–4074 | Closed Nov.–Apr. | $12–$25 | D, DC, MC, V.

Brown's Wharf. Seafood. If you're a fan of nautical artifacts, then this waterside dining room packed with model ships will make you feel right at home. Serving up traditional

Maine sea specialties for nearly five decades, it's got a lock on lobster. The downeast dinner comes with chowder, steamed clams, baked potato or fries, and choice of vegetable. The cedar-plank salmon in teriyaki sauce or nut-crusted chicken with an almond, hazelnut crust served in a Frangelico cream sauce are of equal renown. Kids' menu. | 105 Atlantic Ave. | 207/633–5440 or 800/334–8110 | Breakfast also available. Closed Oct.–mid-June. No lunch | $12–$25 | D, MC, V.

Carousel Music Theatre. American. This is prix fixe with a twist. Listen, watch, and dine as old-time vaudeville and Broadway acts are performed in a turn-of-the-20th-century theater. Choose from entrées like Atlantic salmon, lobster, steak, or chicken. | Townsend Ave. | 207/633–5297 or 800/757–5297 | www.boothbaydinnertheatre.com | $25 prix fixe | MC, V.

China by the Sea. Chinese. Dine in a relaxed setting with a subdued interior and 25 tables. | 96 Townsend Ave. | 207/633–4449 | $8–$20 | AE, D, MC, V.

Christopher's Boathouse. Eclectic. The open kitchen and great views of the harbor draw plenty of couples here for a romantic meal. You can watch as the chefs prepare high-end dishes like lobster and mango bisque and grilled scallops *fra diavolo* with artichokes, kalamata olives, roasted garlic, and pine nuts, tossed with linguine in a light tomato sauce, and topped with Parmesan and anchovies. | 25 Union St. | 207/633–6565 | Closed mid-Oct.–mid-May | $15–$21. | MC, V.

Ebb Tide. Seafood. This popular, family-style local eatery has the feel of a knotty-pine diner. It is known for fresh seafood and homemade desserts and serves breakfast all day. Kids' menu. No smoking. | 43 Commercial St. | 207/633–5692 | Breakfast also available | $9–$14 | No credit cards.

HOW TO EAT A BOILED LOBSTER

The first thing you need to know is how *not* to eat a lobster: do not eat a lobster while wearing your favorite silk blouse, by using a knife and fork, or with a copy of *Emily Post* anywhere in sight. Tackling the mighty crustacean is a participatory sport. Decorum's out the window. Dig in.

Next, the equipment: lobster crackers (mallets, rocks, or hammers have been known to substitute), a cocktail fork, and a plastic bib. In a number of eateries, these bibs are often tied around your neck for you by your server. You will only feel foolish until you see the same thing happening to the guy sitting next to you.

Grab the lobster by the body and gently twist off the claws. There is usually water inside them, so don't do this over your lap. Crack open the claws, remove the meat (fingers are fine, use your small fork if you must), dip in butter, and eat. Next, twist the tail from the rest of the body, as though you were gently wringing out a dish towel. Remain calm at the sight of the green fluffy substance inside the body cavity. This is the lobster's liver, called tomalley (it's quite edible, although palatable only to a select few). Set the body and tomalley aside. Remove the small tablike flippers at the sealed end of the tail. Straighten out the tail and grasp it with one hand. With your index finger, force the tail meat from the flipper end out through the shell. Don't use too much force, or you might send this prize piece flying across the picnic table, and that would be very sad. There is also meat inside the body and the feelers, which is worth extracting, especially on larger, hard-shell lobsters. Finish up with a Wet Nap bath (the Maine version of a finger bowl).

Note: If this procedure seems too daunting, opt, instead, for a lobster roll or bowl of stew.

© Artville

Fisherman's Wharf Inn. Seafood. You'll find panoramic views from floor-to-ceiling windows at this inn built on pilings over the harbor. You can add a lobster to any entrée for $8. Try the cedar-plank salmon. Open-air dining on the deck. Kids' menu. Dock space, by reservation. No smoking. | 22 Commercial St. | 207/633–5090 | fax 207/633–5092 | Closed mid-Oct.–mid-May | $20–$40 | AE, D, DC, MC, V.

Gray's Wharf. Seafood. This dockside eatery is popular with locals and tourists alike. There's live music, pool tables, pinball, video games, and plenty of outdoor seating. Enjoy regional treats like lobster stew, chowders, and the famous lobster roll. Seafood pie, sirloin steaks, and the clam and lobster bakes are not to be missed. In winter the menu simplifies to burgers, pizza, and seafood. Kids' menu. | Pier One | 207/633–5629 | $7–$29 | AE, D, MC, V.

J.H. Hawk. Seafood. This laid-back and festive seaside restaurant has a nautical theme. The menu is definitely Maine, with plenty of clams, lobster, steamers, and fried fish. Lunch has a variety of sandwiches like the seafood cheddar melt and the Maine shrimp roll. Kids' menu. | Pier One | 207/633–5589 | www.jhhawk.com | Closed Oct.–mid-May | $9–$23 | AE, D, MC, V.

Kaler's Crab and Lobster House. Seafood. This affordable, casual dockside restaurant is filled with ocean-faring memorabilia. The menu is full of Maine specialties like lobster, fried clams, swordfish, and lobster stew. Burgers and lighter fare are also available. Kids' menu. | 48 Commercial St. | 207/633–5839 | Closed Oct.–mid-May | $6–$21 | MC, V.

Lobsterman's Coop. Seafood. This working lobster farm doubles as a local favorite for simple, down-home shellfish, burgers, and hot dogs. Kids will be happy with fried cheese sticks, clams, veggies, chicken nuggets, and watching the lobstermen from the outdoor dining area. Daily lobster specials. | Atlantic Ave. | 207/633–4900 | Closed mid-Oct.–mid-May | $11–$19 | D, MC, V.

Mac Nabs Tea Room. Café. Take a break and relax with a cup of tea and a light baked treat in this old Cape-style home. Learn all about tea, from how to make it to what ails it cures. Choose from more than 50 brews, from vanilla almond and Japanese genmaicha to Moroccan mint and good old English breakfast. One mile before Boothbay Harbor. | Back River Rd. | 207/633–7222 | Closed Sun., Mon. | $2–$4 | MC, V.

Rocktide Inn. Seafood. Choose from a casual or more formal setting for your dinner of classic Maine seafood. Either way, you'll be on the water's edge, enjoying lobster, steaks, and poultry. | 35 Atlantic Ave. | 207/633–4455 or 800/762–8433 | Breakfast also available; closed Oct.–mid-June. No lunch | $9–$20 | D, MC, V.

Spruce Point Inn. Contemporary. Enjoy the incredible view of Boothbay Harbor and the Atlantic while feasting on lobster cakes with tomatillo salsa or the Australian rack of lamb with an herb crust. There's a poolside barbecue for lighter fare. | Atlantic Ave. | 207/633–4152 or 800/553–0289 | Breakfast also available; closed mid-Oct.–mid-May. No lunch | $20–$29 | AE, D, DC, MC, V.

Tugboat Inn. American. Built right on the superstructure of the tugboat *Maine,* this restaurant and pub in the Tugboat Inn is perched right over the water for excellent views. Choose from a standard selection of lobster, steaks, chops, and seafood. Try the seafood fettuccine. Outdoor seating and live music in season. Kids' menu. | 80 Commercial St. | 207/633–4434 or 800/248–2628 | www.tugboatinn.com | Closed late Nov.–early Apr. | $16–$26 | AE, D, MC, V.

Lodging

1879 Seafarer Inn. This stately 1879 former sea captain's Victorian home is on the water and just a two-minute walk from the harbor. Guest rooms are modestly furnished with period antiques, and there are great views of the harbor from the wraparound deck and most guest rooms. Dining room, picnic area, complimentary breakfast. No air-conditioning, no room phones, no TV. No pets. No smoking. | 58 Union St. | 207/633–2116 or 800/531–0065 | seafarer@clinic.net | www.seafarerinn.com | 5 rooms (3 with shared bath) | $110–$130 | MC, V.

Admiral's Quarters Inn. Built in 1830, this elegant but laid-back inn overlooks the harbor and is furnished with antiques and a wood-burning stove. It has a wooded location. Picnic area, complimentary breakfast. Cable TV. Laundry service. No kids under 12. No smoking. | 71 Commercial St. | 207/633–2474 | fax 207/633–5904 | loon@admiralsquartersinn.com | www.admiralsquartersinn.com | 6 rooms (2 with shower only), 4 suites | $135–$155, $145–$155 suites | Closed mid-Dec.–mid-Feb. | D, MC, V.

Anchor Watch Bed & Breakfast. This relaxing inn has a lawn that slopes down to the shore of Boothbay Harbor. You'll find ocean views here, as well as great places to go for walks. Complimentary breakfast. No air-conditioning in some rooms, some in-room hot tubs, no room phones, cable TV in common area. No kids under 9. No smoking. | 9 Eames Rd. | 207/633–7565 | fax 207/633–5317 | diane@lincoln.midcoast.com | www.anchorwatch.com | 5 rooms (3 with shower only) | $115–$145 | MC, V.

Atlantic Ark Inn. A peaceful retreat across the street from the harbor, this 1850s classic Maine home has rooms furnished with antiques, mahogany four-poster beds, and fresh flowers. The third-floor suite has a cupola, 17 windows, oak floors and staircase, cathedral ceilings, and two sets of double French doors —one leading to a private balcony, the other to a two-person hot tub. The cottage is fully furnished, has a cathedral ceiling and oriental rugs, and backs up to a 1-acre pond. Complimentary breakfast. No air-conditioning, some in-room hot tubs, no room phones, no TV. Pond. Library. No pets. No kids under 12. No smoking. | 62 Atlantic Ave. | 207/633–5690 or 800/579–0112 | fax 207/633–7912 | donna@atlanticarkinn.com | www.atlanticarkinn.com | 5 rooms, 1 cottage | $99–$175 | Closed Nov.–Memorial Day | AE, MC, V.

Brass Bed Bed and Breakfast. This large, white colonial home is in a quiet residential neighborhood. The rooms' namesake brass beds are covered with fine bedding. Two of the rooms have dressing areas and claw-foot tubs. Dining room, complimentary breakfast. No air-conditioning, TV in common room. No pets. No smoking. | 10 Fullerton Rd. | 207/633–4313 | info@brassbedb-b.com | www.brassbedb-b.com | 4 rooms | $75–$80 | MC, V.

Brown Bros. Wharf Inn. This modern, family-run, waterfront motel and marina 1 mi southeast of Boothbay Harbor is serviced by two trolley buses and convenient to everything. All rooms have balconies and harbor views. Restaurant, bar. Cable TV. Dock. Business services. | 121 Atlantic Ave. | 207/633–5440 or 800/334–8110 | fax 207/633–5440 | brownswharf@clinic.net | www.brownswharfinn.com | 67 rooms, 3 apartments, 1 cottage | $129–149, $199 apartments, $1,500 cottage (7–day minimum stay) | Closed Nov.–Apr. | AE, MC, V.

Cap'n Fish's. This modern motel is just a walk over a footbridge from downtown Boothbay Harbor. From here you can take cruises and whale-watching trips. Restaurant, picnic area. Some kitchenettes, cable TV. Dock. Business services. | 65 Atlantic Ave. | 207/633–6605 or 800/633–0860 | fax 207/633–6239 | www.capnfish.com | 54 rooms | $79–$120 | Closed mid-Oct.–mid-May | AE, MC, V.

Captain Sawyer's Place. This former sea captain's home was built in 1877 and has a cupola from which there are fine views of the harbor. There are also porches and a English front garden. Complimentary breakfast. No air-conditioning, no room phones, cable TV. No smoking. | 55 Commercial St. | 207/633–2290 or 800/434–9657 | www.captainsawyer.com | 10 rooms | $70–$95 | MC, V.

Fisherman's Wharf Inn. The rooms of Fisherman's Wharf Inn offer commanding views of the harbor like nowhere else in Boothbay Harbor. All rooms have balconies. Restaurant, bar, complimentary Continental breakfast. Cable TV. Business services. | Pier 6, 22 Commercial St. | 207/633–5090 or 800/628–6872 | fax 207/633–5092 | fishermanswharf@clinic.net | www.fishermanswharfinn.com | 54 rooms | $95–$175 | Closed mid-Oct.–May | AE, D, DC, MC, V.

Five Gables Inn. Built in 1890, this Victorian inn has a large wraparound veranda and gardens and is 2½ mi east of town. All rooms overlook the bay, and some have fireplaces. Complimentary breakfast. No air-conditioning. No kids under 12. No smoking. | Murray

Hill Rd., East Boothbay | 207/633–4551 or 800/451–5048 | info@fivegablesinn.com | www.fivegablesinn.com | 15 rooms (10 with shower only) | $100–$170 | Closed mid-Oct.– mid-May | MC, V.

Flagship Motor Inn. This standard motel on the main route into Boothbay Harbor is convenient to all regional locations. Restaurant, bar. Cable TV. Pool. | 200 Townsend Ave. (Rte. 27) | 207/633–5094, 800/660–5094 in ME | fax 207/633–7055 | infor@boothbaylodging.com | www.boothbaylodging.com | 83 rooms | $39–$70 | AE, D, MC, V.

Greenleaf Inn. This restored New England Cape-style home overlooks the harbor. All rooms have ocean or bay views and porches with wicker furniture. The inn is 5 mi from rugged Ocean Point. Complimentary breakfast. No air-conditioning. Cable TV. | 66 Commercial St. | 207/633–7346 or 888/950–7724 | fax 207/633–2642 | info@greenleafinn.com | www.green-leafinn.com | 5 rooms | $105–$135 | Closed Nov.–Apr. | AE, MC, V.

Harborage Inn. Boothbay Harbor's oldest original guest house is a three-generation effort. Perched at the water's edge, the inn boasts a grassy waterside terrace and two floors of rooms. All rooms have a private entrance from one of the wraparound verandas and Laura Ashley stencils and touches. Suites are larger, with sofas or love seats, and a sitting area. Vouchers are given for breakfast from the bakery next door. No air-conditioning, some kitchenettes, cable TV. No pets. No kids under 6. No smoking. | 75 Townsend Ave. | 207/633–4640 or 800/565–3742 | info@harborageinn.com | www.harborageinn.com | 9 rooms | $70–$160 | MC, V.

Harbour Towne Inn on the Waterfront. This restored 1870s Victorian town house on the waterfront is within walking distance of all downtown sights. Complimentary breakfast. No air-conditioning, some kitchenettes, cable TV. No pets. No smoking. | 71 Townsend Ave. (Rte. 27) | 207/633–4300 or 800/722–4240 | gtme@gwi.net | www.acadia.net/harbour-towneinn | 12 rooms | $129–$159 | Closed late Nov.–Feb. | AE, D, MC, V.

Hillside Acres Cabins and Motel. This old-style motel with cabins on a hill is just outside Boothbay. Picnic area. No air-conditioning, some kitchenettes, cable TV, no room phones. Pool. Pets allowed in cottages. | Adams Pond Rd. | 207/633–3411 | fax 207/633–2295 | hillside@clinic.net | www.gwi.net/~hillside | 14 rooms (2 with shared bath), 7 cabins | $54–$75 | MC, V.

Howard House Lodge. This unique chalet is surrounded by trees and is 1 mi north of Boothbay Harbor. It has ponds, flowers, and a garden. No air-conditioning, cable TV, no room phones. | 347 Townsend Ave. (Rte. 27) | 207/633–3933 | fax 207/633–6244 | howardhs@gwi.net | www.howardhouselodge.com | 14 rooms | $71–$87 | No credit cards.

Kenniston Hill. This restored 18th-century house was built by David Kenniston, a prominent shipbuilder and landowner. It is filled with antiques and has acres of wildflowers, gardens, and shady maples. Complimentary breakfast. No air-conditioning, no room phones. No smoking. | Rte. 27 | 207/633–2159 or 800/992–2915 | fax 207/633–2159 | innkeeper@maine.com | www.maine.com/innkeeper | 10 rooms (7 with shower only) | $79–$120 | MC, V.

Lawnmeer Inn. This historic inn 2 mi south of Boothbay Harbor is on a quiet inlet, but near shopping, galleries, and boat rides. Restaurant, bar. No air-conditioning in some rooms, cable TV. Dock. Pets allowed (fee). | Southport Island, West Boothbay Harbor | 207/633–2544 or 800/633–7645 | fax 207/633–7198 | cooncat@lawnmeerinn.com | www.lawnmeerinn.com | 35 rooms | $95–$150 | Closed mid-Oct.–mid-May | MC, V.

Lion D'Or. This cozy, intimate Victorian home (1857) is a five-minute walk from the center of town. It has a front porch and is close to the water. Complimentary breakfast. Cable TV. No smoking. | 106 Townsend Ave. (Rte. 27) | 207/633–7367 or 800/887–7367 | liondor@gwi.net | www.gwi.net/liondor | 5 rooms | $70–$95 | MC, V.

Newagen Seaside Inn. This informal seaside resort-inn built in 1816 is on 85 acres of Southport Island and is 6 mi south of Boothbay Harbor. There's a mile-long seaside trail, heated freshwater pool, gazebo, and rowboats available. Restaurant, bar, complimentary breakfast. No air-conditioning, no smoking, no room phones. Pool. Tennis. Library. | Rte. 27, South

Port Island, Cape Newagen | 207/633–5242 or 800/654–5242 | fax 207/633–5340 | seaside@wiscasset.net | www.newagenseasideinn.com | 23 rooms, 3 suites | $120–$175, $175–$200 suites | MC, V.

Ocean Gate Motor Inn. This waterfront inn is 2½ mi southwest of Boothbay Harbor, on extensive wooded grounds with views of harbor. Most rooms have a porch. Complimentary breakfast. No air-conditioning in some rooms, some refrigerators, cable TV. Pool. Hot tub. Tennis. Exercise equipment, dock, boating. Playground. Laundry facilities. | Rte. 27, Southport Island | 207/633–3321 or 800/221–5924 | fax 207/633–9968 | ogate@oceangateinn.com | www.oceangateinn.com | 66 rooms, 5 suites, 2 cottages | $120–$170, $150–$200 suites, $300–$320 cottages | Closed mid-Oct.–late May | D, MC, V.

Ocean Point Inn. At this inn 6½ mi southeast of Boothbay Harbor, you can relax as you're surrounded by nature. Go swimming in the area's largest heated outdoor pool or in the invigorating bay, play golf and tennis nearby, or try fishing from the community pier. The decor of rooms varies from traditional to modern. Dining room, bar. No air-conditioning in some rooms, some kitchenettes, refrigerators, cable TV. Pool. Hot tub. | Shore Rd., East Boothbay | 207/633–4200 or 800/552–5554 | opi@oceanpointinn.com | www.oceanpointinn.com | 50 rooms in 5 buildings, 6 cottages | $105–$175, $108–$175 suites, $102–$108 cottages | Closed mid-Oct.–late May | AE, D, MC, V.

The Pines. This hotel's spacious rooms offer views of the harbor. It's 1¼ mi southeast of Boothbay Harbor and welcomes families. Refrigerators, cable TV. Pool. Tennis. Playground. Pets allowed. | Sunset Rd. | 207/633–4555 | 29 rooms | $80 | Closed late Oct.–early May | D, MC, V.

Rocktide Inn. This old Boothbay standby, a five-minute walk to the harbor, has simple rooms with motel-style furniture, armchairs, and water views. The outdoor patio decks for lounging reach right out over the water. The trolley shuttle runs from the hotel to town and back. Restaurant, complimentary breakfast. Pool. No pets. No smoking. | 35 Atlantic Ave. | 207/633–4455 or 800/762–8433 | popover@rocktideinn.com | www.rocktideinn.com | 97 rooms | $89–$154 | Closed mid-Oct.–mid-June | D, MC, V.

Seagate Motel. This standard motel is near the scenic waterfront and harbor. Picnic area, complimentary breakfast. Some kitchenettes, refrigerators, cable TV. Pool. | 124 Townsend Ave. (Rte. 27) | 207/633–3900 or 800/633–1707 | fax 207/633–3998 | walshan@lincoln.midcoast.com | www.seagatemotel.com | 25 rooms | $90–$100 | Closed mid-Oct.–Mar. | AE, D, MC, V.

Smugglers Cove Inn. This inn, 4¼ mi east of Boothbay Harbor, has a wooded location and is on the ocean. You'll even find a swimming beach nearby. Restaurant, bar, complimentary Continental breakfast. No air-conditioning, some kitchenettes, cable TV. Pool. Business services. Some pets allowed. | Rte. 96, East Boothbay | 207/633–2800 or 800/633–3008 | fax 207/633–5926 | www.smugglerscovemotel.com | 60 units | $99–$149 | Closed mid-Oct.–late May | AE, D, MC, V.

Spruce Point Inn. This traditional Maine coastal inn is over a century old and is on extensive wooded grounds. You can walk along the rocky shore or relax in one of the pools. Dining room, bar. No air-conditioning in some rooms, some in-room hot tubs, cable TV, some in-room VCRs. 2 pools. Putting greens, tennis. Dock. Library. Playground. Business services. | 1 Spruce Point | 207/633–4252 or 800/553–0289 | fax 207/633–7138 | thepoint@sprucepointinn.com | www.sprucepointinn.com | 9 rooms in inn, 54 rooms in cottages, 37 suites | $150–$230 inn, $270–$290 suites, $275–$465 cottages | Closed mid-Oct.–late May | AE, D, MC, V.

Tugboat Inn. This inn has waterfront views and is within walking distance of the shops and boat cruises. Restaurant, bar with entertainment. Some kitchenettes, some refrigerators, cable TV. Laundry facilities. Business services. | 80 Commercial St. | 207/633–4434 or 800/248–2628 | www.gwi.net/~tugboatinn | 64 rooms | $125–$165 | Closed late Nov.–early Apr. | AE, D, MC, V.

Welch House Inn. This 1873 home is on peaceful McKown Hill with a great view of Boothbay Harbor. Rooms are filled with an eclectic array of antiques like four-poster beds and

oriental rugs; most have water views. Breakfast is served on a glassed-in patio overlooking the harbor. Dining room, complimentary breakfast. No room phones, cable TV. Library. Pets allowed (fee). No kids under 8. No smoking. | 56 McKown St. | 207/633–3431 or 800/ 279–7313 | fax 207/633–3752 | welchhouse@wiscasset.net | www.welchhouse.com | 16 rooms | $80–$145 | Closed Dec.–Mar. | MC, V.

BRIDGTON

MAP 3, B9

(Nearby towns also listed: Center Lovell, Fryeburg, Sebago Lake)

U.S. 302 starts to quiet down in Bridgton, which has something of the feel of a frontier town. Traffic is not quite as congested, and open fields and woodlands replace businesses and strip malls. Incorporated in 1794, the town has many fine homes and historic sites and is part of the Sebago and Long Lakes Region. Nearby Shawnee Peak, just 45 minutes from Portland, is a popular ski area and offers good hiking in summer.

Information: **Bridgton Lakes Region Chamber of Commerce** | Portland Rd., U.S. 302, Box 236, Bridgton, 04009 | 207/647–3472 | director@mainelakeschamber.com | www.mainelakeschamber.com.

Attractions

Bridgton Museum and Archives. Operated by the Bridgton Historical Society and housed in a 1901, wooden fire station, this museum has local and historic items from the founding of the town in 1768 to the present day. | Gibbs Ave.; 2 blocks west of U.S. 302 and Main St. | 207/647–3699 | $1 | Sept.–June, weekends 1–4; July–Aug., Fri.–Sun. 11–3.

Deertrees Theater. This theater in the wood, 7 mi north of Bridgton, dates back to the late 1930s and was revived in the 1970s after slipping into disrepair. You'll find an eclectic mix of theater, music, and cultural events on offer throughout the summer. Past performers have included Ethel Barrymore, Tallula Bankhead, Rudy Vallee, Arthur Treacher, and Joe E. Brown. It now hosts the Sebago Long Lake Chamber Music Series, other concerts, humorists and storytellers, and theater. | Deertrees Rd., Harrison | 207/583–6747 | Late June–Labor Day.

Narramissic, Peabody-Fitch Farm. Operated by the Bridgton Historical Society, this house built in 1797 is largely decorated with original furnishings. It includes a working blacksmith shop. | Ingalls Rd. | 207/647–3699 | $3 | June–July, Wed.–Sun. 11–3, or by appointment.

Shawnee Peak at Pleasant Mountain Ski Area. A medium-size family-oriented ski area overall, but New England's largest night skiing area, it has enough challenging terrain to keep all skiers happy. | Mountain Rd.; 6 mi west of Bridgton, off U.S. 302 | 207/647–8444 | Weekdays 9–9, Sat. 8:30–10.

ON THE CALENDAR

FEB.: *Mushers Bowl.* A weekend-long festival with races, family activities, and public suppers. | Highland Lake | 207/647–3472.

JULY: *Pondicherry Days.* An art show, parade, live music, food, and fireworks highlight this family festival. | Downtown Bridgton | 207/647–3472.

JULY: *Quilt Show.* Chickadee Quilters show off their handiwork with this exhibit and sale of quilts and wall hangings at the Bridgton Town Hall. | N. High St. | 207/655–3991.

JULY–AUG.: *Long Lakes Chamber Music Festival.* A popular Tuesday-night chamber music concert series that takes place at the historic Deertrees Theater. | Deertrees Rd., Harrison | 207/583–6747.

AUG.: *Western Maine Heritage Festival.* This event at the Peabody-Fitch House celebrates life on the farm with period clothing, demonstrations, food, and music. | Off Rte. 107 and Ingalls Rd., South Bridgton | 207/647–2765.

Dining

Black Horse Tavern. Seafood. This restored 200-plus-year-old home in the heart of Bridgton has equestrian artifacts everywhere. It's known for the lobster pie, steak, seafood, and gumbo. Open-air dining on the screened-in porch. Kids' menu. Sunday brunch. No smoking. | 8 Portland Rd., on U.S. 302 | 207/647–5300 | $12–$25 | D, MC, V.

Olde Mill Tavern. American. You'll find casual, family-style dining in this converted early-19th-century gristmill. Antique tools and curios are displayed on the walls. Try the meat loaf and roast chicken. Kids' menu. Sunday brunch. No smoking. | Main St., Harrison | 207/583–4992 | $8–$22 | AE, D, DC, MC, V.

Tom's Homestead. Eclectic. At this eatery in an old Maine home, a mix of locals and tourists come for such choices as baked stuffed haddock, rack of lamb, veal Parmesan, veal piccata, or poultry dishes. | U.S. 302 | 207/647–5726 | $11–$20 | AE, D, MC, V.

Lodging

Bridgton House. This turn-of-the-20th-century white clapboard cottage-style inn was built from the remains of an old Civil War hotel on the same site. Rooms are bright and airy, and furnished with simple antiques and brass and four-poster beds. It's a short walk to shops and restaurants and to Highland Lake park and beach. Dining room, complimentary breakfast. No air-conditioning, no room phones, cable TV. No pets. No smoking. | 2 Main St. | 207/647–0979 | www.mainelakeschamber.com | 6 rooms (3 with shared bath) | $95 | Closed Nov.–Apr. | No credit cards.

Grady's West Shore. This sports-oriented, one-story, off-road motel is on Highland Lake, 3/4 mi north of Bridgton. Kitchenettes. Beach, boating. Ice-skating. | 2 Main St. | 207/647–2284 | gradywst@megalink.net | www.megalink.net/~gradywst | 4 rooms | $65–$99 | AE, D, MC, V.

Inn at Long Lake. This small, turn-of-the-20th-century lodging is a stone's throw from Long Lake and 8 mi south Bridgton. All rooms are individually decorated in Laura Ashley style. Picnic area, complimentary breakfast. No smoking. | Lakehouse Rd., Naples | 207/693–6226 or 800/437–0328 | innatll@megalink.net | www.innatlonglake.com | 14 rooms, 2 suites | $120–$128, $160 suites | Closed Jan.–Mar. | D, MC, V.

Noble House Bed and Breakfast. This large, yellow, Victorian manor is on 3 acres overlooking Highland Lake. Rooms are bright and filled with country furnishings. Dining room, picnic area, complimentary breakfast. No air-conditioning, no room phones, TV in common area. Some in-room hot tubs. Beach, dock, boating, fishing. No pets. No smoking. | 37 Highland Rd. | 207/647–3733 | fax 207/647–3733 | noblehousebb@hotmail.com | www.noblehousebb.com | 9 rooms (3 with shared bath) | $90–$149 | MC, V.

BRUNSWICK

MAP 3, C10

(Nearby towns also listed: Bailey Island/Orr's Island, Bath, Freeport, Harpswell)

Settled in 1628 around the falls of the Androscoggin River, Brunswick enjoys a varied history. Native Americans called the falls Ahmelahcogneturcook, "place of much fish, fowl, and beasts" (and syllables). Later, the power of these falls was harnessed to run sawmills and textile mills. It was in Brunswick that Harriet Beecher Stowe penned *Uncle Tom's Cabin*. Nathaniel Hawthorne graduated from Bowdoin College, founded in 1794 and considered to be one of the finest small colleges in the country. And Civil War hero Joshua Chamberlain put down roots here. The broad main street (198 ft wide) is lined with shops and restaurants and has an expansive village green. The Brunswick Naval Air Station and the college give the town a lively mix of people. Brunswick also serves as a gateway to Harpswell Peninsula.

Information: **Chamber of Commerce of Bath-Brunswick Region** | 59 Pleasant St., Brunswick, 04011 | 207/725–8797 or 207/443–9751 | fax 207/725–9787 | www.mid-coastmaine.com | ccbbr@horton.col.k12.us.

Attractions

Bowdoin College. This small liberal arts college is the alma mater of Nathaniel Hawthorne, Henry Wadsworth Longfellow, and Franklin Pierce. | Maine St. | 207/725–3000 | www.bow-doin.edu | Daily.

Maine State Music Theater. This professional music theater has operated for more than 40 years at Bowdoin College's Pickard Theater, and presents five musicals per season as well as two children's shows. | 14 Maine St. | 207/725–8769 | $17–$35 | June.–Aug., Tues.–Sat. Call for details.

Museum of Art. A wide-ranging college museum that houses 19th- and 20th-century art, the Warren collection of classic antiquities, portraits, and old masters' drawings. | Walker Art building | 207/725–3275 | Donation suggested | Tues.–Sat. 10–5, Sun. 2–5.

Peary-MacMillan Arctic Museum. Named for Arctic explorers and Bowdoin graduates Robert E. Peary and Donald B. MacMillan, the museum is a center for the study of human cultures and natural environments in the Arctic regions. It includes gear used by the two Arctic explorers. | Hubbard Hall | 207/725–3416 | Donations accepted | Tues.–Sun. 10–5:30.

General Joshua L. Chamberlain Museum. Memorabilia from the life and times of Maine's most celebrated Civil War hero are on display here. Chamberlain also served as state governor and as president of Bowdoin College. | 226 Main St. | 207/729–6606 | www.curtisli-brary.com/pejobscot.htm | $3 | Tues.–Sat. 10–4.

Pejepscot Historical Society. These rotating exhibits and research collections reflect the history and accomplishments of the towns of Brunswick, Topsham, and Harpswell. | 159 Park Row | 207/729–6606 | www.curtislibrary.com/pejepscot.htm | $4 | Tues.–Wed. and Fri. 9–5; Thurs. 9–8, Sat. 9–4.

Skolfield–Whittier House. This house-cum-museum reflects the three generations of sea captains and physicians who lived within its walls. Virtually unchanged since the 1880s, the home can be seen on one of four guided tours offered daily in season. | 161 Park Row | 207/729–6606 | www.curtislibrary.com/pejepscot.htm | $4 | June–mid-Oct., Tues.–Sat. at 10, 11:30, 1, 3.

Thomas Point Beach. This 80-acre compound comprises a sandy beach overlooking tidal water on Thomas Bay. Facilities include areas for softball, volleyball, a large free playground, an ice-cream parlor, an arcade, bathhouses, and 500 picnic tables. It hosts the Maine Festival of the Arts in early August, the Maine Highland Games in late August, and the Bluegrass Festival Labor Day weekend. | 29 Meadow Rd. | 207/725–6009 | www.thomas-pointbeach.com | $3 | June–Sept., daily.

ON THE CALENDAR

JULY–AUG.: *Bowdoin Summer Music Festival and School.* These Friday-evening concerts at Brunswick High School's Crooker Theater feature chamber music played by festival faculty. | 207/725–3322.

AUG.: *Highland Games.* Take the high or the low road to this festival at Thomas Point Beach featuring bagpipes, kilts, dancing, arts, and crafts. Sponsored by St. Andrews Society of Maine. | 29 Meadow Rd. | 207/549–7451.

AUG.: *The Maine Festival.* Top Maine artists, crafters, and performers converge at Thomas Point Beach for day and evening demonstrations and performances. | 29 Meadow Rd. | 207/772–9012.

AUG.: *Topsham Fair.* A classic agricultural fair with exhibits, carnival, and harness racing at the Topsham Fairgrounds. | Elm St., Topsham | 207/725–2735.

SEPT.: *Bluegrass Festival.* Bring the tent and make a weekend of this top-rated Labor Day festival at Thomas Point Beach, with world-class entertainers, 24-hour food, and security. | 29 Meadow Rd. | 207/725–6009.

Dining

Fat Boy Drive-In. American/Casual. An authentic 1950s drive-in, with curb service and carhops. There's limited seating available inside. Known for burgers, onion rings, fried seafood, and shakes. Kids' menu. No liquor. No smoking inside. | 111 Bath Rd. | 207/729-9431 | Closed mid-Oct.–late Mar. | $5–$10 | No credit cards.

Great Impasta. Italian. This snug and casual booth-lined dining room has an open kitchen and is extremely popular with locals. Try the seafood lasagna. Kids' menu. No smoking. | 42 Maine St. | 207/729-5858 | Closed Sun. | $9–$15 | AE, D, DC, MC, V.

MacMillan and Company. American. This two-level establishment is a good place to sample regional Maine cuisine. On the ground level is the Explorer's Pub, with pool tables, darts, and music. Upstairs is a bit more formal, with high ceilings, cloth napkins, and some booths for more private dining. Try the house special French onion soup, or main dishes like the chicken *cordon bleu*; the MacMillan sirloin topped with roasted onions, peppers, mushrooms, and garlic and topped with white cheddar; or the baked, stuffed lobster. Kids' menu. | 94 Maine St. | 207/721-9662 | $5–$23 | AE, D, MC, V.

Lodging

Atrium Inn and Convention Center. This business and traveler's hotel is convenient to the Naval Air Station and Bowdoin College. Restaurant, bar, room service. Refrigerators, cable TV, some in-room VCRs (and movies). Pool, wading pool. Hot tub. Exercise equipment. Video games. Laundry facilities. Business services. Pets allowed. | 21 Gurnet Rd. (Rte. 24) | 207/729-5555 | fax 207/729-5149 | 186 rooms | $74–$125 | AE, D, DC, MC, V.

Brunswick Bed and Breakfast. This stately 1849 Greek Revival home has a common area with a blend of contemporary and antique furnishings, fireplace, and hardwood floors. Guest rooms have a mix of antique and modest country furnishings. The cottage is fully furnished and has a kitchen and is suitable for families. Complimentary breakfast. No TV in some rooms. Business services. No pets. No kids under 5. No smoking. | 165 Park Row | 207/729-4914 or 800/299-4914 | info@brunswickbnb.com | www.brunswickbnb.com | 5 rooms 3 suites, 1 cottage | $90–$130 | Closed Jan. | MC, V.

Captain Daniel Stone Inn. The antiques-laden home of the eponymous mariner is in a quiet area of town and has an enclosed veranda. It faces the Androscoggin River. Dining room, bar, complimentary Continental breakfast. Cable TV. Business services. | 10 Water St. | 207/725-9898 | fax 207/725-9898 | cdsi@netquarters.net | www.netquarters.net/cdsi | 30 rooms, 4 suites | $139–$215, $195–$215 suites | AE, DC, MC, V.

Captain's Watch Bed and Breakfast and Sailing Charters. This 1862 inn on the National Register of Historic Places was originally known as the Union Hotel and is the oldest accommodation on the Maine coast. The original cupola remains and the ocean views are stunning. Guest rooms are comfortable and modest and have either views of the harbor or the woods. Day or overnight sailing trips aboard the 37-ft sloop *Symbion* are run by the inn's host. Dining room, complimentary breakfast. No air-conditioning, no room phones, TV in common area. Dock, boating, fishing. Library. Business services. No pets. No kids under 10. No smoking. | 926 Cundy's Harbor Rd. | 207/725-0979 | cwatch@gwi.net | www.gwi.net/~cwatch | 4 rooms, 1 suite | $115–$175 | MC, V.

Comfort Inn. This typical chain hotel is near shopping, the interstate, and Bowdoin College. Complimentary Continental breakfast. Cable TV, some in-room VCRs. Business services. | 199 Pleasant St. (U.S. 1) | 207/729-1129 | fax 207/725-8310 | 80 rooms | $109–$119 | AE, D, DC, MC, V.

Econo Lodge. This chain hotel, 2 mi south of Brunswick, is near Interstate 95, Bowdoin College, and downtown. Cable TV. Pool. Laundry facilities. | 215 Pleasant St. | 207/729-9991 | fax 207/721-0413 | 29 rooms | $77–$84 | AE, D, DC, MC, V.

Pelletier Bed and Breakfast. This former convent was built in the 1930s, and still retains a small chapel for quiet meditation. Rooms are large and include furnishings like antiques,

king-size beds, fine linens, and writing desks. The upstairs room covers the entire floor, sleeps four adults, and has a private bath. Complimentary breakfast. No air-conditioning, cable TV, no room phones. No pets. No kids under 8. No smoking. | 40 Pleasant St. | 207/725–6538 | jean22@blazenetme.net | www.pelletierbedbreadfast.com | 4 rooms (3 with shared bath) | $80–$120 | MC, V.

Super 8 Motel. This chain hotel is convenient to Brunswick Naval Air Station. Picnic area. Cable TV, some in-room VCRs (and movies). | 224 Bath Rd. | 207/725–8883 or 800/800–8000 | fax 207/729–8766 | 70 rooms | $70 | AE, D, DC, MC, V.

BUCKSPORT

MAP 3, E8

(Nearby towns also listed: Bangor, Belfast, Castine, Ellsworth, Searsport)

Travelers anxious to motor farther Down East very often bypass this second-largest town in Hancock County. At the mouth of the Penobscot River, Bucksport was settled in 1764 as a shipping port by Jonathan Buck. (His gravestone in the local cemetery is said to be cursed by the mysterious outline of a woman's leg.) The town's most distinguishing feature is the bright-green, 2,040-ft-long suspension bridge, which was built in 1931—the first long-span bridge in Maine.

Information: **Bucksport Bay Area Chamber of Commerce** | 236 Main St., Bucksport, 04416-1880 | 207/469–6818.

Attractions

Craig Brook National Fish Hatchery and Atlantic Salmon Museum. The nation's oldest salmon hatchery has been helping restock the region's rivers since 1871. There's a 1-mi interpretive hike and salmon viewing areas. | 306 Hatchery Rd. | 207/469–2803 | Free | Hatchery daily, museum Memorial Day–Labor Day. Call for hrs.

Fort Knox. Built between 1844 and 1869, the fort features stunning military architecture and master granite craftsmanship. It was used during the Civil and Spanish American wars but never saw combat. | Off U.S. 1, across Waldo Hancock Bridge | 207/469–7719 | $2 | May-Oct., daily 9–dusk.

Fort Point State Park. This park on a Penobscot Bay peninsula, 8 mi south of Bucksport, incorporates historic Fort Pownall (circa 1759) and Fort Point Light (1836). It has a 200-ft pier for those arriving by boat. | U.S. 1, Stockton Springs | 207/469–6818 or 757/422–8945 | $1 | Late May–Labor Day, daily.

Northeast Historic Film Museum. This museum at the Alamo Theater, one of the oldest in New England, dating from 1916, preserves, archives, and shows films and other art from the past 100 years that relates to northern New England. | 379 Main St. | 207/469–0924 | fax 207/469–7875 | www.oldfilm.org | Museum free, fee for screenings | Weekdays 8–4.

ON THE CALENDAR

JULY: *Fort Knox Bay Festival.* The event includes water races, entertainment, home and garden show, fireworks, and fort tours. | On Main St. and the waterfront in Bucksport and at Fort Knox | 207/468–6818.

SEPT.: *Penobscot River Festival.* Maine businesses, government agencies, and members of the Penobscot Nation present programs, projects, and wildlife. | Bucksport Waterfront | 207/469–7300.

Dining

MacLeod's. Contemporary. This restaurant in a Victorian brick building in Bucksport's historic Bradley Block is 100 yards from dock space at the town landing. Try the ribs, tomato

Cognac soup, or scallop strudel. Kids' menu. No smoking. | Main St. | 207/469–3963 | $10–$20 | AE, D, MC, V.

Stewart's Pizza and Take Out. Pizza. Hearty subs and hand-tossed pizza make up the majority of the menu at this busy local joint. Try the loaded pie with ham, sausage, mushrooms, black olives, and hamburger meat. | Main St. | 207/469–2750 | $4–$12 | MC, V.

Lodging

Alamoosook Lodge. The call of loons and morning mist on the lake are Maine trademarks and a common sight at this rustic lodge right at the water's edge and 4 mi east of Bucksport. All rooms open up to the grassy lawn overlooking Alamoosook Lake. Dining rooms, picnic area, complimentary breakfast. Beach, water sports, boating, fishing. Ice-skating, cross-country skiing. No pets. No smoking. | Soper Rd., Orland | 207/469–6393 | fax 207/469–2528 | info@alamoosooklodge.com | www.alamoosooklodge.com | 6 rooms | $98 | AE, MC, V.

Best Western Jed Prouty Motor Inn. This hotel is convenient to coastal areas on the Penobscot River. In-room data ports, cable TV. Business services. Some pets allowed. | 53 Main St. | 207/469–3113 | fax 207/469–3113 | 40 rooms | $89–$99 | AE, D, DC, MC, V.

Bucksport Motor Inn. This standard roadside motel is convenient to coastal areas. Cable TV. Pets allowed. | 151 Main St. | 207/469–3111 or 800/626–9734 | 24 rooms | $72 | AE, D, MC, V.

River Inn Bed and Breakfast. This 1793 colonial home was built by the founder of Bucksport and overlooks the Penobscot River and Fort Knox. Some rooms have fireplaces. Many have views of the fort. Complimentary breakfast. Cable TV, no room phones. Library. Business services. Pets allowed (fee). No smoking. | 210 Main St. | 207/469–3575 | fax 207/469–0008 | stngry22@aol.com | 7 rooms (3 with shared bath) | $50–$75 | AE, D, MC, V.

Sign of the Amiable Pig Bed and Breakfast. With as wry a history as its name, this inn 2½ mi east of town was a stop on the Underground Railroad, a stable, and an antiques shop. Named after the weather vane atop the roof, the inn has maintained much of its original flavor, including pegged wood floors and the large cooking fireplace with built-in bake oven. Rooms are large and filled with antiques. The guest house, in the restored barn, has cathedral ceilings, is fully furnished with a kitchen, and accommodates up to four adults. Dining room, complimentary breakfast. No air-conditioning, some room phones, no TV in some rooms. Laundry service. No pets. No smoking. | 74 Castine Rd. (Rte. 175), Orland | 207/469–2561 | fax 207/469–9009 | wpipher@hotmail.com | www.bedandbreakfast.com/usa/maine/orland | 2 rooms, 1 suite, 1 cottage | $60–$75 rooms, $550/wk guest house | No credit cards.

CALAIS

MAP 3, H7

(Nearby towns also listed: Eastport, Lubec)

Calais (pronounced Cal-us, not Callay) in the St. Croix Valley lays claim to being the sixth-busiest port of entry into the United States on the Canadian border. The town's roots go back to precolonial days, when French settlers established a short-lived colony, but it was not until 1851 that it was incorporated as a city. During the tall-ship era, lumber, shipbuilding, and shipping were vital industries. Things are a little sleepier here now. Along with its across-the-border neighbor—St. Stephen, New Brunswick—Calais hosts an annual International Festival, which promotes goodwill between the two countries.

Information: Calais Regional Chamber of Commerce | 16 Swan St., Calais, 04619 | 207/454–2308 | calcham@nemaine.com | www.visitcalais.com.

Attractions

Calais Memorial Park. A public park with a playground and veteran's memorial that is one block from the banks of the St. Croix River. Take the walkway to the St. Croix River walk, a 2-mi trail following the old railroad tracks along the water. | Main St. | 207/454–2308.

Moosehorn National Wildlife Refuge. This migratory bird refuge comprises 24,390 acres on two sites and is maintained primarily for woodcocks and waterfowls. Four miles north of Calais you'll find nature and hiking trails. | Charlotte Rd. | 207/454–7161 | Free | Daily.

St. Croix Island International Historic Site. This site, 8 mi south of Calais, marks an early attempt (1603) by Frenchman Pierre de Gua, Sieur de Monts, to establish a colony in America. It is accessible only by boat. | Opposite Red Beach on the St. Croix River | 207/288–3338 | Free | Daily.

ON THE CALENDAR

AUG.: *International Festival Week.* A celebration of goodwill between the border towns of Calais and St. Stephen, New Brunswick, Canada. Street dances, outdoor concerts, craft fairs, and a large parade. | 207/454–2308 or 800/377–9748.

Dining

Calais Motor Inn. American. You'll find hearty food in this family restaurant. Try the seafood marinara, sirloin tips with mushroom gravy, or the chicken *cordon bleu.* Kids' menu. | 293 Main St. | 207/454–7111 | $8–$15 | AE, D, DC, MC, V.

Heslin's Motel & Dining Room. American. This casual, family-friendly restaurant has plenty of Maine specialties like lobster and haddock chowders, and meats like New York sirloins and Friday-night prime-rib dinners. All breads are made on the premises. Kids' portions available. | U.S. 1 | 207/454–3762 | Closed Nov.–Apr. No lunch | $11–$21. | D, MC, V.

Wickachee. American. In this friendly, casual dining room you'll find such favorites as orange honey-glazed chicken and homemade breads and desserts. Kids' menu. Beer and wine only. No smoking. | 282 Main St. | 207/454–3400 | $5–$24 | MC, V.

Lodging

Downeaster Motel. This simple, red, single-story stopover spot with large rooms overlooks the water. Rooms are furnished with standard motel fixtures. No air-conditioning, no room phones, cable TV. Pets allowed (fee). No smoking. | U.S. 1 | 207/454–3376 or 800/899–3376 | cwing@calais-maine.com | www.calais-maine.com/downeast | 7 rooms | $45. | Closed Nov.–Apr. | D, MC, V.

Heslin's Motel & Dining Room. In this rustic setting 5 mi south of Calais, you have views of the Canadian countryside. Restaurant, bar. Cable TV, no phones in cottages. Pool. | U.S. 1 | 207/454–3762 | fax 207/454–0148 | 15 rooms, 10 cottages | $55–$100 | Closed Dec.–Apr. | D, MC, V.

International Motel. This central roadside motel is near the Canadian border. Cable TV. Business services. | 276 Main St. | 207/454–7515 or 800/336–7515 | fax 207/454–3396 | 61 rooms | $65–$100 | AE, D, DC, MC, V.

Redclyffe Shore Motor Inn. This mid-19th-century Gothic inn is high above the St. Croix River and Passamaquoddy Bay and 12 mi south of town. Restaurant. | U.S. 1, Robbinston | 207/454–3270 | fax 207/454–8723 | redclyffeinn@aol.com | www.redclyffeinn.com | 17 rooms | $62–$73 | Closed Nov.–Apr. | AE, D, MC, V.

CAMDEN

(Nearby towns also listed: Lincolnville, Rockland, Rockport)

Boats, boats, and more boats are what you (and the others who throng here each summer) will find in Camden's famed harbor. But popular tourist spots don't happen by accident. Crowds aside, this is the Maine you came to see. The deep, secluded harbor surrounded by rolling hills has made Camden a popular destination since the days steamships brought wealthy urbanites to vacation here. Once a shipbuilding hub, Camden's shady streets are lined with graceful, well-maintained homes from that era, many of which have been turned into B&Bs.

Information: Camden-Rockport-Lincolnville Chamber of Commerce | Commercial St., Public Landing, Camden, 04843 | 207/236–4404 or 800/223–5459 | fax 207/236–4315 | chamber@camdenme.org | www.visitcamden.com.

Attractions

Camden Hills State Park. This park, 2 mi northeast of Camden, includes outstanding views from Mt. Battie—depicted spectacularly in the movie *Peyton Place*—which is accessible by car as well as hiking. The park has 30 mi of hiking trails and a 112-site camping area. During winter a local club maintains several snowmobile trails. | U.S. 1 | 207/236–3109 | $2 | Daily.

Camden Snow Bowl. This is an attractive ski area with great views of Penobscot Bay and the Atlantic, but it's often closed because of lack of snow along the coast. It also has a 400-ft toboggan chute and a 500-ft snow-tubing hill. | 3 mi west of Camden; drive south of Camden via U.S. 1 to John St. and then to Hosmer Pond Rd. | 207/236–3438 or 207/236–4418 | www.camdensnowbowl.com | Weekdays 10–9, weekends 9–4.

Merryspring Horticultural Nature Park and Learning Center. This 66-acre park features numerous gardens and has trails through its fields and woods. It has a large gazebo surrounded by rose, herb, and perennial gardens. There is also a 10-acre arboretum of native species and a woodland garden with pool. | Conway Rd. | 207/236–2239 | Free | Daily dawn–dusk.

Mount Battie Trail. You can pick up the trail to the peak of Mount Battie (800 ft) at the north end of Megunticook Street, just a short walk from the town common. The 45-minute, ½-mi hike to the peak gets you excellent views of Camden and the harbor. Some rocky and steep patches may not be suitable for all hikers. | Megunticook St. | 207/236–4404 | Free | Daily.

Old Historical Conway House Complex. This is an 18th-century restored farmhouse and barn, furnished with authentic period materials. It has a working blacksmith shop, an 1820 maple sugar house, a Victorian privy, and the Camden Rockport Historical Society collection. | U.S. 1, near Rockport border | 207/236–2257 | $2 | June–Aug., Tues.–Fri. 10–4.

Riverdance Outfitters. Run by the hosts of the Belmont Inn, these hiking, canoeing, and kayaking excursions on the Maine mid-coast are led by experienced, licensed guides. All levels are welcome, and equipment is provided. | 6 Belmont St. | 207/230–0033 | Year-round.

Sailing trips. The area from Camden through Rockland is the center for the Maine Windjammer sailing industry. These trips last up to a week, and most overnight stays include all meals. Passengers can either help sail the ship or just relax and let the crew do the work. | May–Oct.

Angelique. The 130-ft, 31-passenger topsail ketch makes three-, four-, and six-day cruises that vary with the wind. | Library Park, off Atlantic Ave. | 800/282–9989 | fax 207/785–6036 | www.sailangelique.com | $550–$975 | May–Oct.

Appledore. The 82-ft schooner makes four two-hour sails a day out of Camden Harbor. | At the end of Bayview Landing | 207/236–8353 | $20–$25 | Mid-June–end Oct.

Maine Windjammer Cruises. Three sailing boats (the *Grace Bailey* and *Mercantile* carrying 29 passengers and the *Mistress* carrying 6) go for three- to five-day cruises. | Public Landing | 207/236–2938 or 800/807–9463 | www.mainewindjammercruises.com | $295–$800 | May–Oct.

Olad and Northwind. *Olad* does five two-hour sails on a 55-ft schooner off the Public Landing. It can carry 21 passengers. *Northwind*, a 75-ft schooner that runs out of Middle Pier in Rockland, is used for day-sailing trips. All trips feature maritime history and lighthouses. Saturday-night's sail and lobster dinner is by reservation only. | Public Landing | 207/236–2323 | www.sailingsojourns.com | $20 for 2-hr tour | May–Oct.

Schooner *Lewis R. French*. Three-, four-, and six-day cruises on a 64-ft schooner carrying 22 passengers leave from Harbor Park in Camden. | Harbor Park, at Atlantic Ave. | 800/469–4635 | fax 207/236–2463 | $425–$775 | May –Oct.

Schooner *Mary Day*. This 90-ft windjammer, built specifically for the modern windjamming industry, carries 29 passengers on four- and six-day cruises that leave from Camden Library Park. | Camden Library Park, Camden Harbor | 207/236–2750 or 800/992–2218 | www.midcoast.com/~maryday | May–Oct.

ON THE CALENDAR

FEB.: *U.S. National Toboggan Championship*. More than 250 teams from across the nation compete in the giant toboggan race at the Camden Snow Bowl. There's also food and activities. | Camden Snow Bowl | 207/236–3438.

JULY: *Open House and Garden Day*. For over 50 years, the public has been given license to snoop into some of Camden's finest homes and gardens. The Camden Garden Club sponsors this annual event on the third Thursday of the month. You can buy your tickets at a number of places around town. | Camden | 207/236–9630.

SEPT.: *Annual Windjammer Weekend*. The largest single gathering of these stately sailing ships takes place on Labor Day weekend. There's also live music, nautical activities, boat parade, fireworks, and more. | 207/236–4404.

OCT.: *Fall Festival Arts and Crafts Show*. Nearly 100 artists and craftsmen show and sell their work in Camden's open spaces. You'll also find live entertainment, food, and kids' stuff. | Harbor Park | 207/236–4404.

DEC.: *Christmas by the Sea*. Shopping, open houses, Santa sightings, live entertainment, and tree-lighting at this annual celebration. | 207/236–4404.

Dining

Atlantica Gallery and Grille. Seafood. This is not your typical "lobster in a pot" restaurant. You might find glazed ginger scallops, crab-encrusted halibut, or homemade coconut sorbet on the revolving menu. The chef is flexible and all meals can be cooked to order. Locally crafted microbrews are also offered. | One Bay View Landing | 207/236–6011 or 207/236–6019 | Closed Mon. | $16–$30 | AE, MC, V.

Cappy's Chowder House. Seafood. Serving up heaps of its namesake chowder, this local favorite packs in the tourists and old-timers to sample its down-east grub, including lobster, mussel beach pasta in a Mediterranean tomato sauce over linguine, and the margarita half chicken in a tequila-lime sauce. | 1 Main St. | 207/236–2254 | $10–$17 | MC, V.

Peter Ott's. Steak. This casual eatery has a rustic brick interior with prints and paintings on the walls. It's known for seafood and Black Angus beef. Salad bar. Kids' menu. No smoking. | 16 Bayview St. | 207/236–4032 | Closed Mon.–Tues. No lunch | $15–$23 | MC, V.

Sea Dog Brewing Company. American. This local brewhouse in an old wooden mill serves up typical pub fare like burgers, turkey clubs, and a fried seafood platter. Beer is the specialty, with more than 13 home brews on tap. Kids' menu. | 43 Mechanic St. | 207/236–6863 | $7–$12 | AE, D, MC, V.

Waterfront. Seafood. With a post-and-beam interior and brick fireplace, this eatery, as its name suggests, also has water views. Try the fresh seafood (especially the lobster). You'll

VACATION COUNTDOWN Your checklist for a perfect journey

Way Ahead

- ❏ Devise a trip budget.
- ❏ Write down the five things you want most from this trip. Keep this list handy before and during your trip.
- ❏ Book lodging and transportation.
- ❏ Arrange for pet care.
- ❏ Photocopy any important documentation (passport, driver's license, vehicle registration, and so on) you'll carry with you on your trip. Store the copies in a safe place at home.
- ❏ Review health and home-owners insurance policies to find out what they cover when you're away from home.

A Month Before

- ❏ Make restaurant reservations and buy theater and concert tickets. Visit fodors.com for links to local events and news.
- ❏ Familiarize yourself with the local language or lingo.
- ❏ Schedule a tune-up for your car.

Two Weeks Before

- ❏ Create your itinerary.
- ❏ Enjoy a book or movie set in your destination to get you in the mood.
- ❏ Prepare a packing list.
- ❏ Shop for missing essentials.
- ❏ Repair, launder, or dry-clean the clothes you will take with you.
- ❏ Replenish your supply of prescription drugs and contact lenses if necessary.

A Week Before

- ❏ Stop newspaper and mail deliveries.
- ❏ Pay bills.
- ❏ Stock up on film and batteries.
- ❏ Label your luggage.
- ❏ Finalize your packing list—always take less than you think you need.
- ❏ Pack a toiletries kit filled with travel-size essentials.
- ❏ Check tire treads.
- ❏ Write down your insurance agent's number and any other emergency numbers and take them with you.
- ❏ Get lots of sleep. You want to be well-rested and healthy for your impending trip.

A Day Before

- ❏ Collect passport, driver's license, insurance card, vehicle registration, and other documents.
- ❏ Check travel documents.
- ❏ Give a copy of your itinerary to a family member or friend.
- ❏ Check your car's fluids, lights, tire inflation, and wiper blades.
- ❏ Get packing!

During Your Trip

- ❏ Keep a journal/scrapbook as a personal souvenir.
- ❏ Spend time with locals.
- ❏ Take time to explore. Don't plan too much. Let yourself get lost and use your Fodor's guide to get back on track.

also find steaks and vegetarian items. Open-air dining on the deck overlooking the harbor. Kids' menu. No smoking. | Bayview St. | 207/236–3747 | $12–$25 | AE, MC, V.

Whitehall Dining Room. Contemporary. This classic turn-of-the-20th-century summer hotel, ¼ mi north of town, has an upscale dining room overlooking its gardens. Try the baked breaded haddock or the chicken St. Millay. It has a great wine list. Kids' menu. No smoking. | 52 High St. | 207/236–3391 | www.whitehall-inn.com | Closed mid-Oct.–mid-June. No lunch | $16–$20 | AE, MC, V.

Youngstown Inn. French. This Federal inn's French-inspired kitchen presents its ethnic fare with a flair. Be sure to try the lobster ravioli, pheasant, duck, or rack of lamb. | Rte. 52 at Youngstown Rd. | 207/763–4290 or 800/291–8438 | No lunch | $17–$23 | MC, V.

Zaddik's Pizza. Pizza. Serving up some of the best pie around, this easygoing spot also offers a menu of Mexican and pasta dishes. Specialty pies include the Mexican pizza with jack cheese, barbecued beans, chilies, chips, sour cream and salsa, and the white Mediterranean pizza with feta cheese, kalamata olives, sun-dried tomatoes, and oregano. Kids' menu. | 20 Washington St. | 207/236–6540 | $6–$18 | MC, V.

Lodging

Belmont Inn. This elegant, 19th-century Edwardian inn is only a three-minute walk from downtown. Rooms are individually decorated with a variety of country furnishings, including a king-size sleigh bed. The innkeeper hosts guided hiking, kayaking, and canoeing trips on the mid-coast and is a licensed Maine guide. Restaurant, dining room, complimentary breakfast. Air-conditioning in some rooms, no TV. Library. No pets. No kids under 10. No smoking. | 6 Belmont Ave. | 207/236–8053 or 800/238–8053 | fax 207/236–9872 | belmont@mid-coast.com | www.thebelmontinn.com | 6 rooms | $115–$175 | AE, MC, V.

Best Western Camden River House Hotel. Typical of the chain, this option is in downtown Camden. Complimentary Continental breakfast. In-room data ports, microwaves, refrigerators, cable TV. Pool. Hot tub. Exercise equipment. Business services. | 11 Tannery La. | 207/236–0500 | fax 207/236–4711 | riverhouse@camdenmaine.net | www.camdenmaine.com | 35 rooms | $159–$199 | AE, D, DC, MC, V.

Black Horse Inn. This inn's colonial building has a view of the bay and mountains at the back. One and a half miles from Camden Hills State Park, it is 4 mi north of Camden. Refrigerators, some in-room hot tubs, no cable TV in some rooms. Business services. No smoking. | U.S. 1, Lincolnville Beach | 207/236–6800 or 800/374–9085 | fax 207/236–6509 | www.midcoast.com/~blkhorse | 21 rooms | $88–$135 | AE, D, MC, V.

Blue Harbor House. An antiques-filled 1810 house. Complimentary breakfast. No air-conditioning in some rooms, some kitchenettes, no TV in some rooms. No kids under 12. No smoking. | 67 Elm St. | 207/236–3196 or 800/248–3196 | fax 207/236–6523 | balidog@midcoast.com | www.blueharborhouse.com | 8 rooms, 2 suite | $95–$165, $165 suites | AE, D, MC, V.

Camden Maine Stay. This 1802 Greek Revival clapboard inn is listed on the National Register of Historic Places. It has manicured gardens, a country kitchen open to guests, hiking trails at the edge of the property, comfortable common areas and guest rooms, and trademark hospitality that makes you feel relaxed and at home. Complimentary breakfast. Cable TV in common area. No pets. No kids under 10. No smoking. | 22 High St. | 207/236–9636 | fax 207/236–0621 | innkeeper@mainestay.com | www.mainestay.com | 5 rooms, 3 suites | $100–$150 | AE, MC, V.

Camden Windward House. Mt. Battie hiking trails run past this mid-19th-century house, which is two blocks from the sea. Some of the rooms have fireplaces. Picnic area, complimentary breakfast. Some in-room hot tubs, some in-room VCRs. No kids under 12. No smoking. | 6 High St. | 207/236–9656 | fax 207/230–0433 | www.windwardhouse.com | 8 rooms (5 with shower only) | $125–$195 | AE, MC, V.

Cedar Crest Motel. This family-oriented hotel is ¾ mi from the ocean, on the edge of historic Camden. Some rooms overlook Mt. Battie. Restaurant. Refrigerators, cable TV. Pool.

Playground. Laundry facilities. | 115 Elm St. | 207/236–4839 or 800/422–4964 | fax 207/236–6719 | www.mainesunshine.com/ccrest/ | 37 rooms | $106–$129 | Closed Nov.–Apr. | AE, D, DC, MC, V.

Cedarholm Garden Bay. Sixteen acres of manicured perennial gardens and waterfront woods are home to four two-bedroom, luxury, cedar cottages perched over the coast. They have cobblestone fireplaces, two-person hot tubs, and modern kitchens and are very private. Other clapboard cottages are set back, but still have views of the shore. A common deck by the shore is open for all guests. Complimentary breakfast. No air-conditioning in some rooms, some kitchenettes, some in-room hot tubs, some room phones. No pets. No smoking. | U.S. 1, Lincolnville Beach | 207/236–3886 | www.cedarholm.com | 8 units | $80–$300 | Closed Jan.–Mar. | MC, V.

Dark Harbor House. This imposing turn-of-the-20th-century home furnished with antiques is 6 mi north of Camden. Dining room, complimentary breakfast, room service. No air-conditioning in some rooms, no room phones. Bicycles. Library. No kids under 12. No smoking. | 117 Jetty Rd., Islesboro | 207/734–6669 | fax 207/734–6938 | www.darkharborhouse.com | 11 rooms, 3 suites | $115–$185, $275 suites | Closed Oct.–Mar. | MC, V.

The Elms Bed & Breakfast. This 1806 colonial home is filled with lighthouse and seafaring books and lore. Rooms are on the smaller size, but make up for it in charm and warm country furnishings. Inquire about lighthouse tours. Picnic area, dining room, complimentary breakfast. No air-conditioning in some rooms, in-room data ports, no TV. Library. No pets. No kids under 5. No smoking. | 84 Elm St. | 207/236–6250 or 800/755–3567 | fax 207/236–7330 | theelms@midcoast.com | www.elmsinn.net | 6 rooms | $85–$115 | D, MC, V.

Glenmoor by the Sea. This property with 14 acres on the ocean is in the quiet community of Lincolnville, 4 mi north of Camden. Complimentary breakfast is delivered to every room. No smoking, some kitchenettes, some refrigerators, cable TV. 2 pools. Tennis. | U.S. 1, Lincolnville | 207/236–3466 or 800/439–3541 | fax 207/236–7043 | www.glenmoorbythesea.com | 22 rooms, 4 suites, 21 cottages | $109–$255, $159–$325 cottages | Closed Nov.–late May | AE, MC, V.

Hawthorn Inn. Stained glass embellishes this turreted turn-of-the-20th-century Victorian home. There are views of the harbor through the trees, and spacious guest rooms. Complimentary breakfast. No air-conditioning, some in-room hot tubs, cable TV, in-room VCRs. No kids under 12. No smoking. | 9 High St. (U.S. 1) | 207/236–8842 | fax 207/236–6181 | hawthorn@midcoast.com | www.camdeninn.com | 10 rooms in 2 buildings | $100–$205 | Closed Jan. | AE, MC, V.

Inn at Ocean's Edge. So named for its location overlooking Penobscot Bay, this modern inn has all the creature comforts, with each room having ocean views, a fireplace, king-size bed, and whirlpool for two. It's 3 mi north of Camden Hills State Park. Watch for signs on the right onto a private road. Complimentary breakfast. In-room data ports, in-room hot tubs, cable TV. Exercise equipment. Business services. No pets. No kids under 14. No smoking. | U.S. 1 | 207/236–0945 | fax 207/236–0609 | ray@innatoceansedge.com | www.innatoceansedge.com | 14 rooms, 1 suite | $220–$250 | MC, V.

Inn at Sunrise Point. This inn is on 4 acres on Penobscot Bay and 4 mi north of Camden. The cottages have porches. Complimentary breakfast. No air-conditioning, in-room hot tubs, cable TV, some in-room VCRs. No kids under 17. No smoking. | Sunrise Point Rd. (U.S. 1), Lincolnville | 207/236–7716 or 800/43–LOBSTER | fax 207/236–0820 | www.sunrisepoint.com | 3 rooms, 4 cottages | $175–$375 | Closed end Oct.–mid-May | AE, MC, V.

Lodge at Camden Hills. Rooms and cottages are scattered over 5 peaceful, forested acres 1 mi north of Camden. There's an abundance of wildflowers, rocks, birds, and trees, and Mt. Battie is in the background. Each guest room has a private deck or porch from which to enjoy sea and wooded vistas. In-room data ports, microwaves, refrigerators, some in-room hot tubs, cable TV, some in-room VCRs. Business services. No smoking. | U.S. 1 | 207/236–8478 or 800/832–7058 | fax 207/236–7163 | burgess@thelodgeatcamdenhills.com | www.acadia.net/lodge | 12 rooms, 4 suites, 4 cottages | $129–$225 | AE, D, MC, V.

Mt. Battie Motel. Near Camden Hills State Park, this B&B combines rural seclusion with convenience. Complimentary Continental breakfast. Refrigerators, cable TV. Business services. No smoking. | U.S. 1, Lincolnville Beach | 207/236–3870 or 800/224–3870 | fax 207/230–0068 | mountbattie@acadia.net | www.acadia.net/~mountbattie | 23 rooms | $75–$165 | Closed Nov.–Apr. | AE, D, MC, V.

Norumbega Inn. This Victorian castle-by-the-sea, with lavish oak woodwork and romantic fireplaces, holds murder mystery weekends. Complimentary breakfast. No air-conditioning in some rooms, no TV in some rooms. No kids under 7. No smoking. | 63 High St. (U.S. 1) | 207/236–4646 | fax 207/236–0824 | norumbeg@acadia.net | www.norumbegainn.com | 11 rooms, 2 suites | $160–$340, $365–$475 suites | AE, D, MC, V.

Snow Hill Lodge. This wooded property, 4½ mi north of Camden, has views of the bay and caters to families. There's a public beach 1 mi away. Restaurant, picnic area, complimentary Continental breakfast. No air-conditioning, cable TV. | U.S. 1, Lincolnville Beach | 207/236–3452 or 800/476–4775 | fax 207/236–8052 | theview@midcoast.com | www.midcoast.com/~theview | 30 rooms | $45–$79 | Closed end Nov.–end Feb. | AE, D, MC, V.

Swan House B&B. This beautiful 1870 Victorian home is close to the Mount Battie trailhead. Rooms are comfortable in the country style; some are filled with rich wood and rustic furnishings, others are more provincial, with lace and quilts. Complimentary breakfast. No air-conditioning, TV in common area. No pets. No kids under 12. No smoking. | 49 Mountain St. | 207/236–8275 or 800/207–8275 | fax 207/236–0906 | hikeinn@swanhouse.com | www.swanhouse.com | 6 rooms | $90–$145 | MC, V.

Victorian by the Sea. This Victorian summer cottage, 5 mi north of Camden, was built in 1881 and is furnished with antiques. The rooms have fireplaces and remarkable views of the ocean and nature. Complimentary breakfast. No air-conditioning in some rooms. No kids under 12. No smoking. | Sea View Dr., Lincolnville | 207/236–3785 or 800/382–9817 | fax 207/236–0017 | victbb@midcoast.com | www.victorianbythesea.com | 7 rooms (2 with shower only) | $135–$205 | AE, D, MC, V.

Whitehall Inn. This inn emphasizes chessboards, jigsaws, and books, rather than television. There's also a garden with patio. Restaurant, bar, complimentary breakfast. No air-conditioning, cable TV in common area. Tennis. Business services. | 52 High St. (U.S. 1) | 207/236–3391 or 800/789–6565 | fax 207/236–4427 | www.whitehall-inn.com | 50 rooms (4 with shared bath) in 3 buildings | $150 | Closed mid-Oct.–late May | AE, MC, V.

CAPE ELIZABETH

MAP 3, C11

(Nearby towns also listed: Portland, Scarborough)

This tony bedroom community of Portland got an early start as a summer retreat for urban Portlanders seeking ocean breezes. Shingle-style "cottages" (a number of which were designed by noted architect John Calvin Stevens) and other manses cluster along Shore Road. The area also has excellent parks and sand beaches. Cape Elizabeth's greatest claim, however, is the 1791 Portland Head Light, long reputed to be the most photographed lighthouse in the world.

Information: Convention and Visitors Bureau of Greater Portland | 305 Commercial St., Portland, 04101 | 207/772–5800 | fax 207/874–9043 | www.visitportland.com.

Attractions

Crescent Beach State Park. The area's largest sand beach (and often the most crowded) is 1 mi long and has picnic tables, a bathhouse, charcoal grills, and a concession stand.

There's a lifeguard on duty from the 3rd week of June through the third week of October. | Rte. 77 | 207/799–5871 year–round | $2.50 | Memorial Day–Columbus Day 9–8.

Portland Head Light. Built in 1791 and commissioned by George Washington, Portland Head is Maine's oldest lighthouse. It has great views of crashing surf, particularly after a storm. | 1000 Shore Rd., in Fort Williams Park | 207/799–2661 | Free | Daily dawn–dusk.

   Museum at Portland Head Light. The keeper's house of Portland Head Light contains lighthouse memorabilia and local marine history. | 1000 Shore Rd., in Fort Williams Park | 207/799–2661 | $2 | June–Oct., daily 10–4; Nov.–Dec. and Apr.–May, weekends 10–4.

Two Lights State Park. A craggy coastal walk, World War II bunkers, picnic areas, and benches are featured in this park, as well as two lighthouses—the "two lights" of the title. | Two Lights Rd., off Rte. 77 | 207/799–5871 | $2 | Daily 9–dusk.

ON THE CALENDAR
JULY: _Portland Symphony Orchestra Independence Pops Concert._ These popular outdoor concerts feature patriotic favorites and fireworks. Concerts are held at Fort Williams Park and Southern Maine Technical College. Bring a picnic. | Southern Main Technical College, South Portland | 207/773–6128.

Dining
Audubon Room. American. This dining room overlooking the Atlantic has picture windows and tables set with crystal, Lenox china, linen tablecloths. House specials include the grilled tuna crusted with ginger and horseradish and served with sake soy sauce, and rack of lamb with rosemary mustard sauce. Kids' menu. Patio dining in season. | 40 Bowery Beach Rd. | 207/799–3134 | Breakfast also available | $18–$26 | AE, D, MC, V.

★ **Lobster Shack.** Seafood. This quintessential 1920s lobster shack has unparalleled views of the crashing surf. The rustic interior has a decidedly nautical motif. Known for boiled lobster and fried clams. Open-air dining at oceanfront picnic tables. Cafeteria-style service. Kids' menu. BYOB. No smoking. | 225 Two Lights Rd. | 207/799–1677 | Closed Nov.–Mar. | $5–$20 | MC, V.

Lodging
Inn by the Sea. This all-suites inn has excellent views of Crescent Beach and Kettle Cove. All units have a private porch or deck with ocean view, full kitchen, and living room. Rooms are fully furnished with many amenities; some have fireplaces. Suitable for families. Restaurant, dining room, room service. No air-conditioning, in-room data ports, cable TV, in-room VCRs. Pool. Tennis court. Beach, boating, bicycles. Pets allowed (no fee). No smoking. | 40 Bowery Beach Rd. | 207/799–3134 or 800/888–4287 | fax 207/799–4779 | innmaine@aol.com | www.innbythesea.com | 25 suites, 18 cottage units | $269–$549. | AE, D, MC, V.

CARIBOU

MAP 3, G3

(Nearby town also listed: Presque Isle)

Caribou, the easternmost city in the United States (and one of the chilliest), is less than 15 mi from the Canadian border. First incorporated in 1859 as Lyndon, the town was rechristened Caribou in 1877. Here, in the heart of potato country, the spud is king. Farmers in The County are said to plant some 80,000 acres of potatoes, and during picking season, life revolves around the harvest. In winter, Caribou is snowmobiling country, its central location serving as home base to the area's more than 1,600 mi of groomed trails.

Information: **Caribou Chamber of Commerce** | 24 Sweden St., Suite 101, Caribou, 04736 | 207/498–6156 or 800/722–7648 | www.cariboumaine.net.

Attractions

Caribou Historical Center. This museum, 3 mi south of Caribou, is in a T-shape log building and features artifacts, furniture, and documents from the community. | U.S. 1 | 207/498–2556 | Donations accepted | June–Aug., Tues.–Sat. 11–5, or by appointment.

Nylander Museum. This collection of Swedish-born naturalist Olaf Olsson Nylander includes American Indian artifacts as well as rocks, minerals, fossils, and marine specimens. It's ¼ mi south of Caribou. | 657 Main St. | 207/493–4209 | Free | Memorial Day–Labor Day, Wed.–Sun. 1–5.

***Rosie O'Grady's Balloon of Peace* Monument.** Local residents commemorated the spot, 2 mi south of Caribou, where Joe Kittinger took off for the first successful solo balloon flight across the Atlantic in 1984. The spot is marked by this small replica of the craft. | S. Main St. | 207/498–6156 | Free | Daily.

ON THE CALENDAR
FEB.: *Winter Carnival*. Canoe races, Great Outhouse Revival, Monte Carlo night, and snowmobile ride-in highlight this 10-day celebration of snow season. | 207/498–6156.
JUNE: *Midsommar Festival*. County Swedes celebrate the summer solstice with Swedish dancing, a public supper, maypole decorating, and a smorgasbord of other activities. | Museum grounds, New Sweden; 12 mi from Caribou | 207/896–5843.

Dining

Frederick's Southside. American. You'll find comfort food and plenty of it in this casual spot. It's a great place for the whole family and is known for baked beans, pot roast, and pizza. Kids' menu. Beer and wine only. No smoking. | 507 S. Main St. | 207/498–3464 | $5–$12 | AE, D, MC, V.

Jade Palace. Chinese. Caribou's only Chinese restaurant is adjacent to a tiki lounge. Known for seafood Worbar, sweet-and-sour chicken, and egg rolls. Kids' menu. No smoking. | Skyway Plaza | 207/498–3648 | $2–$13 | AE, D, MC, V.

Reno's. Italian. There's straightforward family fare here, including pizza and sandwiches. The dining room is outfitted with booths and tables. Salad bar. No liquor. No smoking. | 117 Sweden St. | 207/496–5331 | $5–$10 | MC, V.

Lodging

Caribou Inn. This full-service hotel and convention center is 2 mi south of town. Restaurant, bar with entertainment, room service. Minibars, refrigerators, cable TV, some in-room VCRs. Pool. Hot tub, sauna. Gym. Laundry facilities, laundry service. Business services, airport shuttle. | 19 Main St. | 207/498–3733 or 800/235–0466 | fax 207/498–3149 | www.mainerec.com/cnvntion.html | 73 rooms | $68–$74 | AE, D, DC, MC, V.

Crown Park Inn. This is a centrally located motel. Bar, complimentary Continental breakfast. In-room data ports, refrigerators, cable TV. Exercise equipment. Laundry facilities. Business services. | 30 Access Hwy. | 207/493–3311 | fax 207/498–3990 | 66 rooms | $64 | AE, D, DC, MC, V.

Old Iron Inn Bed and Breakfast. This red, two-story, early 1900s home is filled with antiques and memorabilia, including a large collection of its namesake old irons. High-back black oak beds, colonial vanities, and period knickknacks fill the rooms. Complimentary breakfast. No air-conditioning, no room phones, no TV. Library. No pets. No smoking. | 155 High St. | 207/492–4766 | oldiron@mfx.net | www.oldironinn.com | 4 rooms (2 with shared bath) | $45–$59 | AE, D, MC, V.

CARRABASSETT VALLEY

(Nearby town also listed: Kingfield)

With Sugarloaf/USA dominating this area, the valley itself is often overlooked as a drive-through. The Carrabassett River parallels Routes 27 and 16 and makes for a scenic drive, in any season, to the mountain. The Bigelow Range adds to the rugged terrain and provides great hiking. The megaplex on the mountain is everything you'd expect from a top ski resort: 119 trails, 15 lifts, a touring center, condos, lodging, dining, entertainment, conference centers, and loads of Spandex. Sugarloaf's 90 km of groomed cross-country trails, mountain-bike trails, and a top golf course make it an all-season resort. (*See* Kingfield for more Sugarloaf listings.)

Information: Sugarloaf Area Chamber of Commerce | Valley Crossing, Box 2151, Carrabassett Valley, 04947 | 207/235–2100 or 800/THE–AREA.

CARRABASSETT
VALLEY

INTRO
ATTRACTIONS
DINING
LODGING

Attractions

Sugarloaf Outdoor Center. More than 60 mi of cross-country ski trails, from beginner to expert, are connected to Sugarloaf's downhill ski area. The center has its own restaurant. In summer you can go fly-fishing and hiking. | Rte. 27 | 207/237–6830.

Sugarloaf/USA Ski Area. This is Maine's highest and one of its oldest ski mountains, with the only above–the–tree line skiing in the state. The views are phenomenal from the Snowfield, and the upper Narrow Gauge has one of the most challenging headwalls in the East. Fifteen miles west of Carrabassett Valley, Sugarloaf also has a world-class 18-hole golf course. | Sugarloaf Access Rd. off Rte. 16/Rte. 27 | 207/237–2000 or 800/THE–LOAF | Nov.–late May, weekdays 8–4; late May–Oct., daily 7–5.

ON THE CALENDAR

JAN.: *Sugarloaf/USA White, White World Week.* Parades, a chili cook-off, Celebrity Cup Races, and fireworks are just some of the features of this celebration of life at the Loaf. | Sugarloaf Access Rd. off Rte. 16/Rte. 27 | 207/237–2000 or 800/THE–LOAF.
APR.: *Reggae Ski Bash.* Live music, entertainment, dancing, and some of the last runs of the season at Sugarloaf/USA. | Sugarloaf Access Rd., off Rte. 16/Rte. 27 | 207/237–2000 or 800/THE–LOAF.

Dining

Hug's. Italian. This cozy dining room is just minutes from Sugarloaf/USA. It's known for veal and pasta dishes, and family-style dinners, where you can sample a number of dishes at once. Kids' menu. Beer and wine only. No smoking. | Rte. 27 | 207/237–2392 | Closed May–Sept.; No lunch; Wed.–Sun.,5-10 | $15–$25 | D, MC, V.

Sugarloaf Brewing Company and Theo's Restaurant. American. This cozy après ski restaurant and bar is right near the base of Sugarloaf ski resort and serves up seven different types of brews made on the premises. Choose from a menu of soups, sandwiches, grills, and pub appetizers. Kids' menu. | Sugarloaf Access Rd. | 207/237–2211 | www.sugarloaf-brewing.com | $8–$15 | MC, V.

Lodging

Grand Summit Hotel and Conference Center. This is an on-the-mountain, full-service hotel and conference center, 16 mi north of Kingfield, 2 mi southwest of Route 27 on Sugarloaf Mountain. Restaurant, bar. Refrigerators, cable TV, in-room VCRs available. Hot tub, massage. 18-hole golf course, tennis. Gym. Cross-country skiing, downhill skiing. Laundry facilities. Business services. Free parking. | Sugarloaf Access Rd. | 207/237–2222 or 800/527–9879 | fax 207/237–2874 | smhotel@somtel.com | www.sugarloafhotel.com | 119 rooms | $100–$210 | AE, D, DC, MC, V.

Sugarloaf Inn. This mountain-style inn is at the base of Sugarloaf Mountain ski resort. The rooms are either standard hotel rooms or studios with loft sleeping. Restaurant, bar, dining room. Air-conditioning in some rooms, cable TV, VCRs. 2 pools. Hot tub, massage. Golf course, tennis. Gym, hiking. Fishing. Cross-country skiing, downhill skiing. | Sugarloaf Access Rd. | 207/237–2000 or 800/843–5623 | fax 207/237–3773 | info@sugarloaf.com | www.sugarloaf.com | 42 rooms | $91.36–$154.47, prices include tax | AE, D, MC, V.

CASTINE

MAP 3, E9

(Nearby town also listed: Blue Hill)

For nearly 200 years, Castine was the center of conflicts among the French, Dutch, British, and colonists for control of the Acadian peninsula. Things are quieter today. Castine is the type of community that makes you wish you were from Old Money (in case you didn't feel that way already). It's not so much snobby as solid. Residents' histories with the town go back generations. The homes are well maintained—many are listed on the National Register—and there's a close-knit, year-round community feel. But just to even things out, Castine is also home to Maine Maritime Academy, where young men and women are rigorously trained for life at sea. It sounds like a culture clash, but the mix works.

Information: Castine Town Office | Court St., Castine, 04421 | 207/326–4502.

Attractions

Soldiers and Sailors Monument. A statue dedicated to the memory of Castine town residents who served in the Civil War. | Castine Town Common | 207/326–4502 | Free | Daily.

ON THE CALENDAR
JULY: *Kayak Symposium.* An event featuring all things related to kayaks and kayaking, including demonstrations, exhibits, and sales. | 207/326–4502.

Dining

Castine Inn. Contemporary. Owner-chef Tom Gutow combines an urban flair garnered in New York with a focus on locally grown vegetables, meats, and seafood, resulting in a menu that is a sophisticated respite from typical Maine fare. Try the warm oil-poached salmon with a red cabbage and snowpea slaw in a hot-and-sour broth or the sweet-and-sour mackerel and scallops in a mirin lime broth. A six-course tasting menu with wine is an excellent way to sample the broad menu. | Main St. | 207/326–4365 | www.castineinn.com | Reservations essential | Closed Dec.–May | $21–$30 | MC, V.

Dennett's Wharf. Seafood. This popular waterfront restaurant is in a converted town wharf and has a rustic interior with nearly 9,000 $1 bills attached to the ceiling. It is known for steaks, seafood, and lobster. Open-air dining on the deck. Raw bar. Occasional live dance music on Fridays. Kids' menu. Sunday brunch, spring and fall only. Dock space. No smoking. | Sea St. | 207/326–9045 | www.dennettswharf.com | Closed mid-Oct.–Apr. | $8–$20 | AE, D, MC, V.

Lodging

Castine Harbor Lodge. This stately 1893 mansion inn is right on the Harbor. Though it can be grand, it's still a good choice for families. Rooms are comfortable and filled with an eclectic mix of antiques and modern pieces. The efficiency cottage is a fully furnished studio right on the water's edge. Nine of the rooms have water views. Complimentary Continental breakfast. No air-conditioning, no room phones, TV in common area. Pets allowed (fee). No smoking. | 147 Perkins St. | 207/326–4335 | fax 207/326–0900 | chl@acadia.net | www.castinemaine.com | 15 rooms (6 with shared bath), 1 cottage | $75–$175 | D, DC, MC, V.

Castine Inn. This stately, three-story, 1898 Georgian-Federal inn with views of Penobscot Bay is surrounded by elaborate, manicured gardens. Rooms are furnished in the New England summer-resort style; some on the third floor have harbor views. Restaurant, bar. Complimentary breakfast. No air-conditioning, no room phones, no TV. Sauna. No pets. No kids under 8. No smoking. | Main St. | 207/326–4365 | fax 207/326–4570 | relax@castineinn.com | www.castineinn.com | 16 rooms, 3 suites | $85–$210 | Closed Oct.–Apr. | MC, V.

Pentagöet Inn. This relaxed, elegant 1894 Victorian home with a wraparound porch overlooks Main Street. The rooms in the separate 200-year-old colonial building are furnished with antiques. Complimentary breakfast. | Main St. | 207/326–8616 or 800/845–1701 | fax 207/326–9382 | pentagoet@hypernet.com | www.pentagoet.com | 16 units | $99–$129 | Closed mid-Oct.–early May | MC, V.

CENTER LOVELL

MAP 3, B9

(Nearby towns also listed: Bridgton, Fryeburg)

A blip on the map, albeit a lovely one, Center Lovell is one of three tiny burgs making up "The Lovells." It is exquisitely nowhere on a high, mountain-rimmed terrace overlooking Kezar Lake, just south of Maine's White Mountains National Forest. Center Lovell might be best known as the home of the premier "write an essay, win an inn" contest.

Information: **Bridgton Lakes Region Chamber of Commerce** | Portland Rd., Rte. 302, 04009 | 207/647–3472 | director@mainelakeschamber.com | www.mainelakeschamber.com.

Attractions

Sabattus Mountains Trail. This easy, 45-minute hike takes you to the 1,200-ft peak of Sabattus Mountain. You get views of the White Mountains and of Pleasant Mountain in Brunswick. Take Route 5 to Sabattus Road and follow signs. | Sabattus Rd. | 207/647–3472.

White Mountain National Forest. While most of the White Mountain National Forest lies in New Hampshire, the Maine section has magnificent rugged terrain and excellent hiking—in total, 770,000 acres of natural forest and 60 peaks over 4,000 ft. | North of Center Lovell on Rte. 5 | 207/824–2134. | www.fed.fs.us | Free | Daily dawn–dusk. **Evans Notch.** A visitors center with information on camping, climbing, and hiking in the White Mountain Forest. The Evans "notch," or pass, through the mountains is nearby. | I–91/93, then take Rte. 2, follow signs | Free | Daily.

ON THE CALENDAR

AUG.: *Annual Arts and Artisans Fair.* Over 60 juried works from local and regional craftspeople are on exhibition (and sale) to raise money for the Charlotte Hobbs Library. At the Newsuncook School. | Rte. 5 | 207/647–3472.

Dining

Center Lovell Inn. American. A rich country feeling fills the dining room of this stately 1805 inn. The menu offers smoked pheasant ravioli, herb-crusted rack of lamb, and seasonal variations as well as seafood in a mix of New England and continental cuisines. | Rte. 5 | 207/925–1575 or 800/777–2698 | No lunch | $20–$27 | D, MC, V.

Ebenezer Kezar's Restaurant and Pub. American. Roast half duckling, mussels marinara, and locally raised Black Angus beef are among the delicious fare at this restaurant 10 mi north of Fryeburg. Singer/songwriters and folk musicians entertain Tuesdays and weekends. | Rte. 5 North, Lovell | 207/925–3200 | www.ebenezerspub.com | Closed Columbus Day–Memorial Day | $5–$19 | MC, V.

Lodging

Center Lovell Inn. While the owners of this beautiful lodge won it from an essay contest, that doesn't mean it's not a well-run establishment. The impressive 1805 Victorian home, with a Manford roof and cupola, is surrounded by acres of fields and mountains. The adjacent Harmon House has five rooms. Restaurant, dining room. No air-conditioning, no room phones, no TV. No pets. No smoking. | Rte. 5 | 207/925–1575 or 800/777–2698 | info@centerlovellinn.com | www.centerlovellinn.com | 8 rooms, 1 suite | $73–$183, $175–$350 suite | Closed Nov. and Apr. | MAP available | D, MC, V.

Pleasant Point Inn. At this secluded 1911 inn on Kezar Lake both the cottages and condos are fully furnished. Rooms are simple and modest; some have king-size beds and water views. Complimentary Continental breakfast. No room phones, no TV. Lake. 2 tennis courts. Hiking, beach, dock, boating, fishing. | Pleasant Point Rd. | 207/925–3008 | fax 207/925–3828 | pleasantpt@landmark.net | www.pleasantpoint.com | 8 rooms, 4 cottages, 2 condos | $95–$260 | Closed May–Oct. | MC, V.

Quisisana Resort. This small lake resort is on the edge of the White Mountains. Inside you'll find wood-paneled walls and white wicker furniture. Some rooms have stone fireplaces, and all cottages have a private porch. Dining room. No air-conditioning, refrigerators, no TV. Lake. Tennis. Beach, water sports, boating, fishing. | Pleasant Point Rd. | 207/925–3500 | fax 207/925–1004 | quisisanar@aol.com | www.quisisanaresort.com | 16 rooms in 2 buildings, 38 cottages | $130–$135, $150–$175 cottages | Closed Sept.–mid-June | AP | No credit cards.

CHEBEAGUE ISLANDS

MAP 3, C10

(Nearby towns also listed: Portland, Yarmouth)

The islands of Casco Bay bear the nickname the "Calendar Islands" because an early explorer (mistakenly) believed there was an island for every day in the year. Of these islands, Great Chebeague (referred to simply as Chebeague) is the largest, at 4½ mi long and 1½ mi wide. Chebeague was first settled by Europeans in the mid-1700s but had long been inhabited by Native Americans prior to that time. Ferries from both Portland and Yarmouth service the island. Adjacent Little Chebeague (an uninhabited state park) has a great sand beach and can be accessed either by private boat or by foot at low tide from Chebeague. If you do walk, be sure to watch the time and the tide.

Information: Convention and Visitors Bureau of Greater Portland | 305 Commercial St., Portland, 04101 | 207/772–5800 | fax 207/874–9043 | www.visitportland.com.

Attractions

Casco Bay Lines. Trips out into Portland Harbor or to the Chebeague Islands leave several times a day from the Casco Bay Ferry Terminal in Portland. | Commercial and Franklin Sts. | 207/774–7871 | fax 207/774–7875 | www.cascobaylines.com | $8.10 to the islands, $9.75 around the harbor | Daily.

Chebeague Island Golf Club. A 9-hole golf course with lots of beautiful scenery. One of the water holes is over a small bay. Equipment rentals are available for $10. The cost of admission entitles you to unlimited rounds. | Stonewharf Rd., Chebeague Island | 207/846–9478 | $25 | Apr.–mid-Oct.

Chebeague Transportation. Regular ferry service from Cousins Island, Yarmouth, to Chebeague. | Stone Pier | 207/846–3700 | www.chebeaguetrans.com | $5 per adult per trip | Daily.

JULY: *Fourth of July Celebration.* A small, family-oriented barbecue and picnic with the residents of Chebeague Island. | Chebeague Island | 207/772–2811.

Dining

Chebeague Island Inn. Seafood. The dark wood dining room in this 1920s-era inn overlooks a golf course and the water. Known for seafood, lobster, and rack of lamb. Open-air dining on the wraparound, screened-in porch. Kids' menu. No smoking. | South Rd., near the Cousins Island ferry dock | 207/846–5155 or 800/597–3599 | www.chebeagueinn.com | Closed Oct.–mid-May | $14–$25 | D, MC, V.

Lodging

Chebeague Orchard Bed and Breakfast Inn. This beautiful Greek Revival home is on 2 acres with ocean views. The 3-acre property across the road has an apple orchard and organic vegetable and flower garden. Rooms are simply done with period antiques, hardwood dressers, and beautiful quilts. Complimentary breakfast. No air-conditioning, no room phones, no TV. Bicycles. Library. Pets allowed (winter only, no fee). No smoking. | 453 North Rd. | 207/846–9488 | orchard@nlis.net | www.chebeague-orchard.com | 5 rooms (2 with shared bath) | $75–$125 | MC, V.

CRANBERRY ISLES

MAP 3, F9

(Nearby towns also listed: Acadia National Park, Bar Harbor, Northeast Harbor, Southwest Harbor)

The Cranberry Isles—made up of Great Cranberry, Little Cranberry (or Islesford), Sutton, Baker, and Bear islands—are located off the tip of Mt. Desert Island. They were named for the great (erstwhile) cranberry bogs discovered by early settlers on Great Cranberry. While high on natural beauty, these islands (two of which include Acadia National Park property) are low on tourist amenities. A well-planned day trip is your best option. Great Cranberry and Islesford are served by the Beal & Bunker passenger ferry (207/244-3575) from Northeast Harbor and by Cranberry Cove Boating Company (207/244-5882) from Southwest Harbor. Baker Island is reached by the summer cruise boats of the **Islesford Ferry Company** (207/276-3717) from Northeast Harbor; Sutton and Bear islands are privately owned.

Information: Thompson Island Information Center | Rte. 3, Mt. Desert Island, 04660 | 207/288–3411. **Mt. Desert Chamber of Commerce** | Sea St., Box 675, Northeast Harbor, 04662 | 207/276–5040.

Attractions

Baker Island. This densely forested 123-acre island is home to seals, osprey, deer, and mink. Boat excursions are the best way to get to see the island up close. Check with the Acadia National Park Visitors Center for more information. | McFarland Hill, Eagle Lake Rd., Bar Harbor | 207/288–3338.

Islesford Historical Museum. Celebrating the heritage of the Cranberry Isles, this museum has artifacts used by past communities: navigational aids, boats, household, fishing, and farming equipment. | Islesford, on Little Cranberry Island | 207/244–9224 | Donations accepted | Mid-June–late Sept., daily 10–noon and 12:30–4:30.

Lodging

Braided Rugs Inn. This white clapboard home was built in 1892 and has been occupied by the same family ever since. It's popular with bird enthusiasts who come to see the island's migratory species. Rooms are simple, filled with period antiques. As there are few places to eat on the island, ask about receiving home-cooked meals. Complimentary breakfast. No air-conditioning. No room phones, TV in common area. Pets allowed. No smoking. | 1892 Main St., Islesford | 207/244–5943 | 3 rooms (all with shared bath) | $75 | MC, V.

DAMARISCOTTA

MAP 3, D10

(Nearby towns also listed: Boothbay Harbor, Newcastle, Pemaquid Peninsula, Wiscasset)

This pretty village just off U.S. 1 is the gateway to the Pemaquid Peninsula and is on the banks of the Damariscotta River. The town's name, meaning "meeting place of the alewives," came from the rich harvests of herring found at the river. With the right timing, you can still see the magnificent spring runs of these fish. Although tourist trade is brisk, Damariscotta preserves small-town life with its tidy white clapboard houses and snug downtown. There are still even swivel stools at the drugstore's soda fountain.

Information: Damariscotta Region Chamber of Commerce | Main St., Damariscotta, 04543 | 207/563–8340 | drcc@tidewater.net | www.drcc.org.

Attractions

Chapman-Hall House. Completed in 1754, this house has period furnishings and exhibits about shipbuilding. The kitchen reveals the original building methods and materials. | Main St., at Church St. | 207/442–7863 | $1 | July–early Sept., Mon.–Sat.

Colonial Pemaquid. The museum, 14 mi south of Darmariscotta, displays materials found on the site from prehistoric artifacts to musket balls, coins, hardware, and other items from the colonial period. Archaeological excavations have found 14 foundations of 17th- and 18th-century buildings, including Fort William Henry and Fort Frederick. | Rte. 130 in New Harbor | 207/677–2423 | $1 | Memorial Day–Labor Day, daily 9–5.

Pemaquid Point Lighthouse Park. A 6-acre park surrounds the Pemaquid Point lighthouse, 15 mi south of Damariscotta, which is closed to the public. Picnic areas. | Pemaquid Point at the end of Rte. 130 | 207/677–2494 or 207/677–2726 | $1.

Round Top Center for the Arts. A local community center for visual and performing arts, with a gallery and studio space for several local artists. | U.S. 1 | 207/563–1507 | Donations accepted.

ON THE CALENDAR

AUG.: *Annual Summer Fair and Art Show.* Held at the Congregational Church 7 mi southeast of Damariscotta, this family fair hosts a silent auction, an art show featuring local artists, a white elephant table, children's games, food, and live music. | Rte. 130 | 207/563–8340.

Dining

Backstreet Landing. Seafood. This family-style restaurant is in an airy building with wide windows overlooking the Damariscotta River. Try the crab cakes or mussels. Kids' menu. No smoking. | Elm St. Plaza off Main St. | 207/563–5666 | Closed Feb. and Wed. Nov.–Apr. | $14–$29 | D, MC, V.

Moody's Diner. American. This authentic 1920s-style diner has original wooden booths and counters. Known for tripe and rib-eye steak. No liquor. No smoking. | 1400 Atlantic Hwy. (U.S. 1), Waldoboro, 10 mi from Damariscotta | 207/832–7785 | $9–$15 | No credit cards.

Romeo's Pizza. Italian. This family-style, no-frills pizza joint has some creative pies like the Casablanca, with alfredo sauce, garlic, onion, and chicken or the spanakopita with ricotta cheese, sausage, spinach, and mushrooms. Pasta, subs, and beer are also available. | U.S. 1 | 207/563–1563 | $8–$15 | MC, V.

Lodging

Anniversary Farm Bed and Breakfast. Forty-three acres of woods and gardens surround this 18th-century farmhouse, 10 mi northwest of Damariscotta. Vegetables grown in the certified organic garden make their way onto your plate. Rooms have simple country antiques; one has a fireplace. Two rooms can be combined to make a large suite. A four-course prix-fixe dinner is available with prior arrangement. Dining room, complimentary breakfast. No air-conditioning, no room phones, no TV. Hot tub. Library. No pets. No smoking. | 2282 Alna Rd. | 207/586–5590 or 877/781–0455 | fax 207/586–5108 | stay@anniversaryfarm.com | www.anniversaryfarm.com | 2 rooms, 1 cottage | $85–$95 | MC, V.

Barnswallow Bed and Breakfast. This 1837 Cape home is on 1 wooded acre in a quiet residential neighborhood. The downstairs parlors and dining rooms have five fireplaces; the guest rooms have antiques and oriental pieces. One room has a sitting area. Dining room, complimentary Continental breakfast. No air-conditioning, no room phones, TV in common area. Library. No pets. No kids under 12. No smoking. | 362 Bristol Rd. | 207/563–8568 | 3 rooms | $80 | MC, V.

Bradley Inn. From this inn you can swim at Pemaquid Beach near Pemaquid Lighthouse and go on boat trips to Monhegan Island with its puffins and seals. The spacious guest rooms in this 1880 structure have private tiled baths. Restaurant, complimentary breakfast. No air-conditioning, cable TV in common area. Hiking, boating, fishing, bicycles. | 3063 Bristol Rd., New Harbor | 207/677–2105 or 800/942–5560 | fax 207/677–3367 | bradley@lincolnmidcoast.com | www.bradleyinn.com | 9 rooms (4 with shower only), 6 suites, 1 cottage | $135–$195, $195–$225 suites, $195 cottage | AE, MC, V.

Brannon-Bunker Inn. This antiques-filled charmer, 4½ mi south of Damariscotta, occupies a couple of early 19th-century structures on the river. Complimentary Continental breakfast. No air-conditioning, some kitchenettes, no room phones, TV in common area. No smoking. | 349 State Rte. 129, Walpole | 207/563–5941 or 800/563–9225 | brnbnkinn@lincoln.midcoast.com | 8 rooms (2 with shared bath) | $60–$75 | Closed Dec. 1–Apr. 1 | AE, MC, V.

Broad Bay. Built in 1830 and loaded with antiques, this inn is 8 mi northeast of town and has an art gallery in the barn, where the owner offers summer watercolor classes. You can relax in the lovely garden. Complimentary breakfast. No room phones, cable TV in common area. Library. No kids under 10. | 1014 Main St. (Rte. 220), Waldoboro, 11 mi north of Damariscotta | 207/832–6668 or 800/736–6769 | brdbayinn@midcoast.com | www.midcoast.com | 5 rooms (all with shared bath) | $60–$80 | MC, V.

Down Easter. This Greek Revival home is filled with antiques. Complimentary Continental breakfast. No air-conditioning, no room phones. | 222 Bristol Rd. | 207/563–5332 | fax 207/563–5332 | 22 rooms | $64–$85 | Closed mid-Oct.–late May | MC, V.

Mill Pond Inn. This 1780s colonial, 2½ mi north of Damariscotta, has antiques-filled rooms and lakeside views. Loons, otters, and bald eagles reside on the lake, and you can arrange a trip with the owner, a Registered Maine Guide, on the inn's 17-ft antique lapstrake boat. The rooms are warm and inviting and there's a pub for guests, though you may find it hard to tear yourself away from the hammocks-for-two overlooking the pond. Complimentary breakfast. No air-conditioning. No room phones, TV in common area. Boating, fishing, bicycles. Ice-skating. No pets. No kids under 10. No smoking. | 50 Main St., Nobleboro | 207/563–8014 | www.millpondinn.com | 5 rooms, 1 suite | $95 | No credit cards.

Newcastle Inn. In this mid-19th-century inn on the Damariscotta River, some rooms have four-poster or canopy beds, and all are individually decorated and furnished with antiques. Dining room, complimentary breakfast. No room phones. No kids under 12. No smoking. | River Rd., Newcastle | 207/563–5685 or 800/832–8669 | fax 207/563–6877 | www.newcastleinn.com | 14 rooms | $145–$245 | AE, MC, V.

Oyster Shell Motel. Overlooking the Great Salt Bay 1½ mi north of Damariscotta, this motel is a convenient choice for families or guests who come to fish the nearby Damariscotta River. Kitchenettes. Pool. No smoking. | R.R. 1, Box 267, Damariscotta | 207/563–3747, 800/874–3747 outside ME | fax 207/563–3747 | oyster@lincoln.midcoast.com | www.lincoln.midcoast.com/~oystrshl | 19 suites | $105–$139 | AE, MC, V.

DEER ISLE–STONINGTON

MAP 3, F9

(Nearby town also listed: Blue Hill)

Deer Isle is both the name of the island and the town contained therein. It is joined to the mainland by an impressively high and narrow suspension bridge. This area is part of the true Maine that seems to be getting squeezed from the state's coastline. Fishing is still the mainstay of the economy here, particularly in the town of Stonington, at the island's tip, where houses and businesses crowd along the water's edge. There, you can glimpse the pink granite cliffs of Isle au Haut—or better yet, board a ferry for memorable day trip.

Information: Deer Isle-Stonington Chamber of Commerce | Rte. 15, Box 459, Stonington, 04681-0459 | 207/348–6124 | deerisle@acadia.net | www.acadia.net/deerisle.

Attractions

Haystack Mountain School of Crafts. Overlooking Jericho Bay, this renowned institute attracts skilled craftspeople from the world over to its summer classes. Most of the campus is closed to the public, but you are permitted on the flag deck and the nearby nature walks. A guided tour is offered on Wednesdays at 1 PM. | Sunshine Rd. | 207/348–2306 | Free | June–Aug.

West Quoddy Head. This easy family hike skirts the unspoiled and spectacular southern shoreline of Isle au Haut. Narrow passages through dark spruce forest connect high, dramatic headlands and isolated stony beaches. Enjoy a wealth of panoramic ocean vistas featuring seabirds, lobster boats, and crashing waves. Hikers must travel to the island by a mail boat from Stonington. There is no auto ferry, and there is no service to or from Isle au Haut on postal holidays. | Destiny Bay Rd. | Ferry, 207/367–5193 | Free | Daily.

ON THE CALENDAR

JULY: *Fisherman's Day.* Come celebrate the old salty dog life with Coast Guard demonstrations, rowboat races, and a codfish relay race. At the Stonington fish pier. | Main St. | 207/348–6124.

Dining

Café Atlantic. Seafood. This casual harborside restaurant is run by the owners of the Inn on the Harbor (*see below*), and maintains the inn's relaxed but romantic flair. The indoor dining rooms have water views, linen tablecloths, and wide pine floors. The upstairs is more elegant and suitable for private parties. The outdoor deck is right over the water and is great for families. There is an enormous lobster cauldron where they steam up your choice of local seafood which you can pick from the holding tank. Lunch has your choice of burgers, sandwiches, or lobster rolls; dinner the classic Maine seafood and steaks. | Main St., Stonington | 207/367–6373 | Closed Dec.–Apr. | $13–$21 | AE, D, MC, V.

Eaton's Lobster Pool. Seafood. This comfortable dining area has water views and a fireplace. It's known for fresh seafood: lobster, stews, and salads. Open-air dining on deck and terrace. BYOB. Dock space. No smoking. | Blastows Cove Rd., Little Deer Isle | 207/348–2383 | Closed mid-Oct.–mid-May. No lunch | $12–$30 | No credit cards.

Fisherman's Friend. Seafood. This is a bustling local hangout serving fresh local fish and lobster. Be sure to try the house-special lobster stew, lobster rolls, and the fried or broiled mixed-seafood plate. Kids' menu. | School St., Stonington | 207/367–2442 | Closed Oct.–May | $5–$20 | D, MC, V.

Goose Cove Lodge. Eclectic. The family-style seating and views of the islands make this a destination in itself. The kitchen puts out a great mix of exotic seafood like Arctic char and seared wolffish in season, sautéed lobster with sun-dried tomatoes and capers in a black bean sauce, and a vegetarian tofu with bok choy over Portobello mushrooms. Don't miss the Friday-night lobster feast down on the beach. | Goose Cove Rd., Sunset, about 3 mi from Stonington | 207/348–2508 | Reservations essential | $18–$28 | AE, D, MC, V.

Pilgrim's Inn. American. Rustic farm tools fill this barn–turned–dining room where you will dine on a gourmet four-course prix fixe including an hors d'oeuvres hour, appetizers like mahogany clams in thyme cream sauce, salads, and main courses like salmon crusted with mustard and horseradish. | Rte. 15A, Deer Isle | 207/348–6615 | Reservations essential | Closed mid-Oct.–mid-May | $33 | MC, V.

Lodging

Burnt Cove Bed and Breakfast. This is a shorefront B&B operated by a lobstering family. There is a large deck for sunbathing and dining that overlooks Penobscot Bay. No air-conditioning, no room phones. | Whitman Rd., Stonington | 207/367–2392 | fax 207/348–2624 | goosecove@hypernet.com | www.goosecovelodge.com | 3 rooms (2 with shared bath) | $55–$90 | MC, V.

Goose Cove Lodge. Informal and rustic, the lodge and cabins anchor 21 acres with water views. You can play golf and tennis at the nearby Island Country Club. The property has a large private beach, nature trails, and amateur astronomy nights. Dinner is included in the price of rooms. Complimentary breakfast. No air-conditioning, some kitchenettes, refrigerators. Hiking, beach, bicycles, lake. Library. Children's programs (ages 1–12), playground. Business services. | End of Goose Cove Rd., Sunset | 207/348–2508 | fax 207/348–2624 | goosecove@goosecovelodge.com | www.goosecovelodge.com | 2 suites in lodge, 21 rooms in cabins | $180–$210 suites, $360–$450 cabins | Closed mid-Oct.–mid-May | MAP | AE, D, MC, V.

Inn on the Harbor. This unassuming set of four attached Victorian buildings masks the excellent location and views. Rooms are simple and modest, but comfortable, and 10 have ocean views. Many have fireplaces and water views. Rooms in the rear are quieter. There is a large deck overlooking the harbor. Dining room, picnic area, complimentary Continental breakfast. No air-conditioning, cable TV. No pets. No kids under 12. No smoking. | Main St., Stonington | 207/367–2420 or 800/942–2420 | fax 207/367–5165 | webmaster@innontheharbor.com | www.innontheharbor.com | 13 rooms, 1 suite | $100–$130 | AE, D, MC, V.

The Keeper's House. This tranquil getaway is geared toward naturalists in need of a retreat. Built in 1907 as the lighthouse keeper's home and now on the National Register of Historic Places, it's perched on the rocks adjacent to the Isle au Haut Lighthouse, and surrounded by woods. All rooms have water views and are furnished with simple antique furnishings. Be forewarned: there is no electricity or phones on the property. Isle au Haut is accessible only by passenger mail boat (207/367–5193 or 207/367–6516). Complimentary breakfast. No air-conditioning, no room phones, no TV. Hiking, fishing, bicycles. No pets. No smoking. | Isle au Haut | 207/367–2261 | www.keepershouse.com | 5 rooms (4 with shared bath) | $280–$319 | Closed Nov.–mid-May | No credit cards.

Pilgrim's Inn. This is an attractive 18th-century inn on the water, with pine floors and many antiques. Dining room, complimentary Continental breakfast. No air-conditioning. | Rte. 15A, Deer Isle | 207/348–6615 | fax 207/348–7769 | www.pilgrimsinn.com | 13 rooms (3 with shared bath) | $160–$215 | Closed mid-Oct.–mid-May | MC, V.

DEER ISLE–
STONINGTON

INTRO
ATTRACTIONS
DINING
LODGING

EASTPORT

MAP 3, H7

(Nearby town also listed: Lubec)

Once one of America's busiest ports (with a smuggling business in the early 1800s) and later a hub of the sardine-canning industry, Eastport is in the process of redefining itself. Large commercial vessels, along with working and pleasure craft, now dominate the waterfront, and aquaculture has replaced the once-abundant canning factories. Yet, there is something singularly appealing about this very small Down East town. On Moose Island and connected to the mainland by a scenic causeway, Eastport makes you feel like you've slipped into another time. Water Street's historic, bricky downtown district hugs the harbor. Fine Federal, Greek Revival, and Victorian homes stack up along the hillside reaching above the waterfront. And the dramatic tides—some 28 ft at their peak—punctuate the craggy coastline.

Information: **Eastport Area Chamber of Commerce** | 23A Water St., Eastport, 04631 | 207/853–4644 | fax 207/853–4747 | eastportcc@nemaine.com.

Attractions

Barracks Museum. Operated by the Border Historical Society, this museum includes part of the barracks and officers quarters of the original Fort Sullivan, built in 1809. | 74 Washington St. | 207/853–6630 | Donations accepted | Memorial Day–Labor Day, Tues.–Sat. 1–4.

Cobscook State Park. A calm and scenic park 20 mi northeast of Eastport that has many camping sites on the waterfront. The park contains a reversing falls, which changes direction with each reversal of the 24-ft tides. Groomed cross-country ski trails are available in winter. | On Edmonds Township off U.S. 1 | 207/726–4412 | $2 | Daily 24 hrs.

Ferry to Deer Island, New Brunswick. Ferries run between Deer Island and Campobello (*see* Lubec), which was the summer vacation spot for Franklin Delano Roosevelt. Visitors traveling to New Brunswick can save nearly 100 mi by taking the ferry. | Water St. | 506/747–2159 | www.deerinet.nb.ca/eastcoast | $15 for car and passengers | Late June–mid-Sept., daily 9:15–6:15 from Deer Island.

Old Sow Whirlpool. Said to be the second-largest whirlpool in the world, it can be seen two hours before high tide. | Between Dog and Deer islands | 207/853–4644 | Free | Daily.

Passamaquoddy Indian Reservation. The Passamaquoddies have lived on this reservation, 5 mi north of Eastport, for decades. The Waponahki Museum displays artifacts and art of the Passamaquoddies, and a library is designed to preserve the tribe's culture. | Pleasant Point Perry, Rte. 190 | 207/853–2600 | Free | Weekdays 8–4:30.

Raye's Mustard Mill. Established in 1903, this mill still makes mustard according to its original recipe, and sells it all around the country. There are historical exhibits, and the most interesting tours are before 4 PM Monday through Friday, when mustard is being made. | 83 Washington St. | 207/853–4451 or 800/853–1903 | www.rayesmustard.com | Free | Mon.–Wed. 8–5, Thurs.–Fri. 8–6, weekends 9–5.

Reversing Falls Park. The best time to see these reversing falls is a couple of hours before high tide. | Mahar Point, Pembroke, about 12 mi from Eastport | 207/853–4644.

Shakford Head. For excellent views of Passamaquoddy Bay, take this short hike up to the top Shakford Head, a large rocky outcropping. When the tide is out, take the trail down to the beach. | Deep Cove Rd. | 207/853–4644 | Free | Daily.

ON THE CALENDAR

JULY: *Fourth of July Week Celebration.* This weeklong party centers on the town homecoming and parade; the two-hour procession is the largest in the state. Events take place throughout the week, including cod fish races and blueberry-pie-eating contests for kids. The week is capped with a big fireworks display. | Downtown Eastport | 207/853–4644.

AUG.: *Indian Ceremonial Days.* Native American dances, crafts, and food are featured at the Pleasant Point Reservation. | Rte. 190, 5 mi north of Eastport | 207/853–2600.

SEPT.: *Salmon Festival.* Farm-raised Atlantic salmon dinner, aquaculture tours, smoked-salmon sales, and live music are featured at this tribute to the flavorful fish. | Water St. | 207/853–4644.

DEC.: *Festival of Lights.* A Christmas theme is the big draw for this annual event, with a tree-lighting ceremony, caroling, and all the town's fishing boats decorated with lights. There are contests for the best-decorated house, business, and boat. | Downtown Eastport | 207/853–4644.

Dining

Eastport Lobster and Fish House. Seafood. The Eastport offers informal dining in an open, airy, wood-paneled dining room with water views. Try the lobster dinners. Open-air dining at picnic tables on the wharf. Kids' menu. Dock space. No smoking. | 167 Water St. | 207/853–6006 or 888/327–8767 | $18–$25 | AE, D, MC, V.

Happy Landing. American. This family-oriented dinette has a walk-up counter. Burgers, franks, and sandwiches make up a good portion of the menu; the fish-and-chips are the big draw for locals. Try the lemon squares or homemade pies for dessert. | 35 Water St. | 207/853–2565 | Breakfast also available | $2–$10 | MC, V.

La Sardina Loca. Mexican. Try the good, cheap south-of-the-border fare in a festive setting at the easternmost Mexican restaurant in the United States. Full Mexican regalia and Christmas lights cover the walls. Boiled lobster with rice and beans is an interesting change of pace. | 28 Water St. | 207/853–2739 | Closed Mon. No lunch | $6.50–$12.95 | MC, V.

Lodging

Brewer House Bed and Breakfast. This 1830s Greek Revival home on the National Register of Historic Places, 17 mi north of Eastport, was built by Captain John Brewer and is on 5 wooded acres across from the public picnic area and boat launch. The prize is in the details with a circular staircase, cathedral ceilings, marble fireplaces, and an array of Victorian fixtures. Rooms are warm and plush and furnished with antiques. The housekeeping cottage is fully furnished and has a kitchen. Dining room, complimentary breakfast. No room phones, no TV. No pets. No kids under 12. No smoking. | U.S. 1, Robbinston | 207/454–2385 or 800/821–2028 | fax 207/454–8770 | landing@aol.com | www.brewerhouse.com | 4 rooms (2 with shared bath), 1 apartment | $60–$85 | D, MC, V.

Kilby House Inn. This 1887 Queen Anne Victorian is filled with family heirlooms and antiques. Rooms are light and many have ocean views. There is a guest parlor with a fireplace and grand piano. Breakfast is offered only during July and August. Dining room. Complimentary breakfast. No air-conditioning, no room phones, no TV. No pets. No kids under 16. No smoking. | 122 Water St. | 207/853–0989 or 800/435–4529 | info@kilbyhouse.com | www.www.kilbyhouseinn.com | 5 rooms | $80 | MC, V.

Milliken House. This ornate, well-preserved 1846 Victorian inn is two blocks from the Eastport waterfront. Marble-topped furnishings, books, and antiques are remnants from Benjamin Milliken, a shipbuilder and the home's founder. Rooms are filled with Victorian and Eastlake furniture, and with fresh flowers in season. Complimentary breakfast. No air-conditioning, no room phones, TV in common area. Library. Pets allowed (no fee). No smoking. | 29 Washington St. | 207/853–2955 | millikenhouse@eastport-inn.com | www.eastport-inn.com | 5 rooms (2 with shared bath) | $50–$65 | AE, D, MC, V.

Motel East. This waterfront motel has spacious rooms with ocean views. Picnic area. No air-conditioning, some microwaves, some refrigerators, cable TV. Business services. | 23A Water St. | 207/853–4747 | fax 207/853–4747 | moteleastonocean@acadia.net | 14 rooms, 1 cottage | $90–$95 | AE, D, DC, MC, V.

Seaview. This bayfront property has cookouts in summer. Restaurant, picnic area. No air-conditioning, some kitchenettes, cable TV, no room phones. Hiking. Playground. Laundry facilities. | 16 Norwood Rd. (Rte. 190) | 207/853–4471 | www.EastportMaine.com | 13 rooms (12 with shower only), 9 cottages | $45–$60 | Closed mid-Oct.–mid-May | D, MC, V.

Todd House. This vintage New England charmer, a few hundred feet from the ocean, is filled with antiques and has fine views of the bay. Picnic area, complimentary Continental breakfast. No air-conditioning, some kitchenettes, no room phones, cable TV in some rooms. Pets allowed. | 1 Capen Ave. | 207/853–2328 | fax 207/853–2328 | 8 rooms (6 with shared bath) | $55–$80 | MC, V.

Weston House Inn. This 19th-century inn 1½ blocks from the waterfront has a spacious lawn that leads down from its a large front porch. Picnic area, complimentary breakfast. No air-conditioning. No pets. | 26 Boynton St. | 207/853–2907 or 800/853–2907 | www.virtualcities.com/me/westonhouse.htm | 5 rooms (2 with shared bath) | $50–$75 | No credit cards.

ELLSWORTH

MAP 3, F8

(Nearby towns also listed: Bar Harbor, Blue Hill, Bucksport, Hancock-Hancock Point)

Ellsworth, Hancock County's shire town, was first settled in 1763 on the Union River, which flows through the city. Once a thriving lumber town, Ellsworth is now primarily known as the clogged gateway to the Bar Harbor Region. Route 3 is lined with strip malls, but Ellsworth's downtown maintains a small-town look (in 1855 a fire ripped through the town, which was largely rebuilt in the Victorian style), and there are many fine homes, historic buildings, and churches located away from the fray.

Information: Ellsworth Area Chamber of Commerce | 163 High St., Ellsworth, 04605 | 207/667–5584 | fax 207/667–2617 | eacc@downeast.net | www.ellsworthchamber.org.

Attractions

John Black Mansion. This splendid example of Georgian architecture has been preserved with its original furnishings and tapestries. The circular staircase is outstanding, and it has some wonderfully restored gardens. | W. Main St. | 207/667–8671 | $5 | June–mid-Oct., Mon.–Sat. 10–4.

Lamoine State Park. This state park is 8 mi southeast of town on Frenchman's Bay near Acadia National Park. It has a 61-site campground, fishing pier, boat-launching ramp, picnic area, and playground. | Rte. 184, Lamoine | 207/667–4778 | $2 | Daily 8–dusk.

Patten Pond Camping Resort. This is a full-service location, 5 mi from downtown Ellsworth, with camping, cottage, and RV accommodations, and private lake access. A modem center, laundromat, store, playground, and a host of boats are available. Basketball, horseshoes, volleyball, and fishing will keep the kids occupied. There are full hookups and a dumping station for RVs. | 1470-M Bucksport Rd., junction U.S. 1 and Rte. 3, | 207/667–7600 or 877/667–7376 | www.pattenpond.com | May–Oct.

Stanwood Sanctuary (Birdsacre) and Homestead Museum. This country home of Cordelia J. Stanwood, an ornithologist, photographer, and author, is on 130 acres of a bird sanctuary. The museum, built in 1850, has original furnishings and mounted birds and eggs. The sanctuary has nature trails and rehabilitation facilities for birds. | Bar Harbor Rd. (Rte. 3) | 207/667–8460 | Donation suggested | Daily, open 24 hrs.

ON THE CALENDAR

SEPT.: *Autumn Gold Days.* A busy, three-day event with music, classic car shows, sidewalk sales, chowder fests, and theater performances. Events take place throughout town, so stop by the chamber of commerce or check the local paper for locations and times. | 163 High St. | 207/667–5584.

Dining

Hilltop House. Contemporary. This eatery, 1 mi south of Ellsworth, has a cheerful interior with booths, tables, and plants. It's a great place to bring the kids and is known for steak, seafood, and pizza. Kids' menu. No smoking. | Bar Harbor Rd. | 207/667–9368 | fax 207/667–4834 | $9–$15 | AE, D, MC, V.

Riverside Cafe. Café. This busy and friendly local favorite with big, open windows serves home-style breakfasts, soups, sandwiches, and vegetarian specials like tofu scramble and vegan French toast. Smoothies and fresh-squeezed juices are made to order. Breakfast is served all day. | 151 Main St. | 207/667–7220 | Breakfast also available; no dinner | $5–$8 | AE, MC, V.

Union River Lobster Pot. Seafood. Ellsworth's only waterside dining is a casual affair. The focus is on Maine-style seafood like chowders, fried haddocks and, of course, lobster. Steaks, chicken, ribs, and nightly fresh seafood specials are also available. Kids' menu. | 8 South St. | 207/667–5077 | Closed Nov.–May | $13–$20. | MC, V.

Lodging

Berry Cove House. This seaside, 1857 fisherman's home has great views of Frenchman's Bay and Cadillac Mountain. Much of the original structure remains, including wood-plank floors and the double gables. Rooms all have views and are furnished with antiques. Complimentary breakfast. No air-conditioning, no room phones, TV in common area. Library. Business services. No pets. No smoking. | 47 Berry Cove Rd., Lamoine, about 7 mi from Ellsworth | 207/667–7989 | bcove@ctl.com | www.berrycovehouse.com | 3 rooms (2 with shared bath) | $55–$80 | No credit cards.

Colonial Travel Lodge. This efficient, modern motel is on the way to Bar Harbor. Restaurant, picnic area, complimentary Continental breakfast (May–Oct.). Some kitchenettes, some refrigerator, cable TV. Pool. Hot tub. Business services. Pets allowed. | 321 High St. | 207/667–5548 | fax 207/667–5549 | colonial@acadia.net | www.acadia.net/colonial | 69 rooms, 3 suites | $88–$108, $139 suites | AE, D, MC, V.

Ellsworth Motel. This small downtown hotel is just 20 minutes from Bar Harbor. Cable TV. Pool. | 24 High St. | 207/667–4424 | fax 207/667–6942 | 16 rooms | $49–$60 | Closed Nov.–Mar. | MC, V.

Holiday Inn. This sparkling hotel is 18 mi from Bar Harbor. Restaurant, bar, room service. In-room data ports, cable TV. Pool. Hot tub. Tennis. Exercise equipment. Laundry facilities. Business services. | 215 High St. | 207/667–9341 or 800/HOLIDAY | fax 207/667–7294 | hielwme@acadia.net | 103 rooms | $105–$139 | AE, D, DC, MC, V.

Mrs. Bancroft's Bed and Breakfast. This simple 1876 Victorian home is a 10-minute walk to town and just seconds from a quiet country road, perfect for a morning jog. Rooms are finished with a country feel. There's no common room or sitting area, but the price more than makes up for any lack of facilities. Complimentary breakfast. No air-conditioning, no room phones, no TV. No pets. No smoking. | 6 Wood St. | 207/667–4696 | mrsbancroft@webtv.net | www.w5.downeast.net/mrsbancroft | 2 rooms | $40 | AE, MC, V.

Twilite. This old-style roadside motel is 1 mi west of town and convenient to downtown, Acadia, and the ferry to Yarmouth, Nova Scotia. All rooms have individual decks. Picnic area, complimentary Continental breakfast. No air-conditioning in some rooms, some refrigerators, cable TV. Pets allowed (fee). | U.S. 1 (Rte. 3) | 207/667–8165 or 800/395–5097 | fax 207/667–0289 | twilite@downeast.net | www.twilitemotel.com | 23 rooms | $40–$78 | AE, D, MC, V.

FARMINGTON

(Nearby town also listed: Rumford)

One of the more populous towns of the western Maine mountains and home to a branch of the University of Maine, Farmington is anything but a rowdy college town. As the shire town of Franklin County, it serves as the gateway to the area's mountains and lakes. Although SUVs en route to ski resorts and logging trucks rumble through town, its sprawling, brick-lined main street has the quiet feel of the friendly frontier village it was when incorporated in 1794.

Information: **Greater Farmington Chamber of Commerce** | R.R. 4, Box 5091, Farmington, 04938 | 207/778–4215 | fax 207/778–2438 | www.farmingtonchamber.org.

Attractions

Nordica Homestead. Birthplace of the opera star Madam Lillian Nordica (née Norton), this museum 2½ mi northeast of town displays some of her costumes, jewelry, and mementos as well as original 19th-century furnishings. | 121 Nautica La. | 207/778–2042. | $2 | June–Labor Day, Tues.–Sat. 10–noon and 1–5; Sun. 1–5; or by appointment.

Norlands Living History Center. The 19th-century home of Israel and Martha Washburn is 25 mi north of Lewiston. The center includes a Victorian country mansion with well and barn, a granite library, a church, a one-room schoolhouse, and much of the original family farmland. Tours present rural life during the post–Civil War period from the perspective of people who lived there. | ½ hr southwest of Farmington at 290 Norlands Rd., Livermore | 207/897–4366 | www.norlands.org | July 4–Labor Day, daily 10–4; Labor Day–Columbus Day, weekends 10–4.

ON THE CALENDAR

MAR.: *Maple Days.* One of the featured venues in Maine's Maple Sunday, this event at the Norlands Living History Center (½ hr southwest of town) has a sap house, syrup making, building tours, and hayrides. | 290 Norlands Rd., Livermore | 207/897–4366.
JUNE: *Strawberry Festival.* A tribute to all things agrarian: farm tours, crafts, music, draft horses, 4-H events, live music, strawberry shortcake, and hayrides at the Norlands Living History Center (½ hr southwest of Farmington). | 290 Norlands Rd., Livermore | 207/897–4366.
AUG.: *Wilton Blueberry Festival.* Road race, fireman's muster, live entertainment, parade, crafts, pancake breakfast, blueberry bazaar, pie-eating contest, pie bake-off, and lots of berries at this event, 9 mi south of Farmington. | Main St., Wilton | 207/778–4726.
SEPT.: *Franklin County Fair.* An agricultural fair, with livestock shows, harness racing, midway, and nightly entertainment at the Farmington Fairgrounds. | Farmington Fairgrounds | 207/778–4215.
OCT.: *Autumn Celebration.* A traditional harvest fest, with cider, live animals, demonstrations, and country meals at the Norlands Living History Center (½ hr southwest of town). | 290 Norlands Rd., Livermore | 207/897–4366.
DEC.: *Chester Greenwood Day.* A daylong celebration of the famed earmuff inventor and Farmington's favorite son, featuring a parade where ear coverings are a decided motif; there's also a Polar Bear Club dip. | Main St. | 207/778–4215.

Dining

Greenfield's. American. This comfortable, unpretentious restaurant is always a sure bet for a satisfying meal. Favorites include fresh seafood and prime rib. | Rtes. 2 and 27, | 207–778–5000 | Breakfast also available | $4–$17 | AE, D, MC, V.

Homestead Bakery Restaurant. American. This sunny bakery/restaurant is in a converted storefront, with tall arched windows and take-out service. Known for baked goods, seafood, and vegetarian items. Kids' menu. Saturday and Sunday brunch. No smoking. | 20 Broadway . | 207/778–6162. | No dinner Sun. | $16–$28 | AE, D, MC, V.

Lodging

Colonial Valley Motel. Although 30 years old, this stately motel prides itself on its modern interiors, which are frequently updated. Cable TV. | Rtes. 2 and 4 | 207/778–3391 or 800/684–2800 | fax 207/778–5475 | www.mainewest.com/colonial-valley | 28 rooms, 2 efficiencies | $55–$75 | AE, D, MC, V.

FORT KENT

MAP 3, F2

(Nearby town also listed: Allagash Wilderness Waterway)

On the Canadian border at the tip-top of the state and northernmost terminus of U.S. 1, Fort Kent is steeped in Acadian culture. It's not uncommon to hear locals ping-pong back and forth between French and English. Incorporated in 1869, it took its name from the historic, rough log blockhouse at the town's center. Despite its far-flung locale, it is a bustling place with a lively downtown, a branch of the University of Maine, and friendly, community-oriented people. Adjacent to the Allagash Wilderness Waterway and surrounded by rolling hills, lakes, and forest, Fort Kent and the St. John Valley retain some of the wildness of Maine.

Information: Greater Fort Kent Area Chamber of Commerce | 76 W. Main St., Fort Kent, 04743 | 207/834–5354 or 800/733–3563 | fax 207/834–6868 | www.fortkentchamber.com.

Attractions

Fort Kent. This blockhouse was built in 1839 to secure Maine's claim to the northern forest after the Aroostook War. It's at the confluence of the Fish and St. John rivers and has a picnic area maintained by the local Boy Scout troop. | Off U.S. 1 at the north edge of town | 207/941–4014 | Free | Memorial Day–Labor Day, daily dawn–dusk.

Fort Kent Block House. Established in 1839 to protect American timber interests during border disputes with Canada, this historic building will transport you to a time when Fort Kent was still on the edges of the frontier. Inside you will find artifacts such as rifles, tools, small boats, and a cannonball. | Block House Rd. | Free | Memorial Day–Labor Day during daylight hrs.

ON THE CALENDAR

★ **FEB.–MAR.:** *Can Am Crown Sled Dog Races.* Maine's answer to the Iditarod includes races, finish-line party, and mushers and huskies galore. | Downtown Fort Kent | 800/733–3563.
SEPT.: *Scarecrow Festival.* Merchants and citizens build scarecrows and participate in this costume contest. There is also a parade, a pumpkin hunt, bingo, and vendors. | 207/834–5354.

Dining

Pierrette's Kitchen. American. This modest restaurant is known for its pesto pizza and Tex-Mex chili. The wooden booths and red tables are reminiscent of a big-city family restaurant. | 57 E. Main St. | 207/834–6888 | $4–$6 | No credit cards.

Sirois' Restaurant. American. You can dine in one of two dining rooms or in the lounge or banquet room. It's known for pasta and prime rib. Salad bar. Kids' menu. No smoking. | 84 W. Main St. | 207/834–6548 | Closed Mon. | $9–$22 | AE, MC, V.

Lodging

Northern Door Inn. This pleasant inn derives its name from the fact that you can literally see Canada from your room. It is mere feet from the International Bridge into Canada. It was renovated in 1999 and has a brand new addition. Complimentary Continental breakfast. Cable TV. | 91 W. Main St. | 207/834–3133 | northerndoorinn@fkglobal.com | 43 rooms | $54–$58 | AE, D, MC, V.

FREEPORT

MAP 3, C10

(Nearby towns also listed: Brunswick, Yarmouth)

Internationally known, outdoors-outfitter L. L. Bean put Freeport on the map some time ago, and the store has become a top destination for visitors to the state. Other retailers have since followed suit, and Freeport is now one of the state's top outlet towns. Pre-Bean, in the 18th century, ships' masts were brought from surrounding forests to Mast Landing to be shipped to England and the town square was created to give ample room for them to swing as they were turned en route. Freeport also purportedly saw the signing of the papers that established Maine as an independent state in 1820. Despite the fact that almost every inch of Freeport's downtown is crammed with retail and outlet space (over 170 shops and stores), it has somehow managed to maintain the architectural look of a small village.

THE BOOT THAT BUILT AN EMPIRE

In 1912 an avid sportsman by the name of Leon Leonwood Bean returned from a hunting trip with sore and soggy feet and vowed to have this happen no more. He set to work designing a new outdoor boot that would be both lightweight and durable, stitching leather uppers to gum (or rubber) soles. The result was the now world-famous Maine Hunting Shoe—or more simply, the Bean Boot.

Armed with a list of nonresidents who held hunting licenses, Bean advertised his $3.50 boot and received 100 orders. However, his marketing skills proved better than his design skills, as many of the initial boots came unstitched. He refunded the money, redesigned the boot, and recanvassed his target audience. With that a multi-million-dollar business was born.

Today, the name L. L. Bean is synonymous with outdoor gear. (Locals refer to the store as Bean's.) The Freeport flagship store, which stays open 24 hours per day, 365 days per year, has become a tourist destination for many visitors (3½ million per year, at last count). It is not uncommon for visiting celebrities to make shopping excursions there in the wee hours. Once a warehouse of a building with foot-worn staircases and rickety metal shelving, the L. L. Bean of today is a modern, multilevel, multi-department mall of a store, replete with a trout pond—think of a piney Neiman Marcus.

© Artville

Information: Freeport Merchants Association | 23 Depot St., Freeport, 04032 | 207/865–1212 or 800/865–1994 | fax 207/865–0881 | freeportcc@maine.com | www.freeportusa.com.

Attractions

Atlantic Seal **Cruises.** The *Atlantic Seal* goes to Eagle Island State Park, former home of Arctic explorer Robert E. Peary. | Depart from Town Wharf, foot of Main St. in South Freeport | 207/865–6112 | $20 | May–mid-Oct, daily.

Desert of Maine. A tribute to bad agricultural practices, this area (3 mi southwest of town) has a motorized tour of the shifting sand dunes that remain, and a museum. | 95 Desert Rd. | 207/865–6962 | $7 | Daily 9–5; last tour at 4:30.

L. L. Bean. Founded in 1912 as a mail-order business selling products to hunters and fishermen, L. L. Bean today attracts more that 3½ million visitors yearly to its flagship store in Freeport. | 95 Main St. (U.S. 1) | 800/341–4341 | www.llbean.com | Open daily 24 hrs.

Mast Landing Sanctuary. This spot on a tideway of the Harraseeket River was once a delivery point for famed Maine timbers used as masts on British ships. The 140-acre site, 1½ mi east of Freeport, now has fields, marshes, and forests that house a wide variety of wildlife. Picnic grounds and an old mill are also on site. | Upper Mast Landing Rd. | 207/781–2330 | www.maineaudubon.org | Free | Daily.

Thos. Moser Cabinetmakers. A 26-year-old company making traditionally styled furniture, the shop has demonstrations of furniture making on several Saturdays from May 29 to October 9. | 149 Main St. (U.S. 1) | 207/865–4519 | www.thosmoser.com | Free | Mon.–Sat. 10–6, Sun. 11–5.

Winslow Memorial Park. This town-operated park, 5 mi south of town, has picnic areas and swimming. | End of Staples Point Rd. | 207/865–4198 | $1.50 | Daily 8:30–dusk.

Wolfe's Neck Woods State Park. Hiking, picnicking, and wildlife-watching are the main attractions on more than 200 acres of shoreland and forest, 4½ mi south of downtown. | 426 Wolfe's Neck Rd. | 207/865–4465 | www.state.me.us/doc/dochome.htm | $2 | Memorial Day–Labor Day, daily 9–dusk; Apr.–Memorial Day and Labor Day–Oct., daily 9–6.

ON THE CALENDAR

AUG.: *South Freeport Festival.* You'll find lobster and chicken dinners, live music, games—and no outlet stores at this family festival. | S. Freeport Rd., South Freeport | 207/865–4012.

Dining

Chowder Express and Sandwich Shop. Seafood. You can sit at the 14-seat counter while enjoying chowder, or take out a lobster or crab sandwich. The restaurant is tiny and no frills; think of it as fast-food seafood. | 2 Mechanic St. | 207/865–3404 | Closed Dec., Jan. | $4–$9 | No credit cards.

The Corsican. Italian. There's reasonably priced, home-style cooking on the menu in this restored 19th-century carriage-repair shop. Try the lazy lobster stew. There's also open-air, garden dining (takeout only). Kids' menu. Beer and wine only. No smoking. | 9 Mechanic St. | 207/865–9421 | $12–$20 | DC, MC, V.

Gritty McDuff's. Pub. You'll find pub-style dining in an open and airy brewpub at this spot ¼ mi from Freeport Village. Try the fish-and-chips or the shepherd's pie. Open-air dining on two decks. Kids' menu. No smoking. | 187 Lower Main St. (U.S. 1) | 207/865–4321 | $9–$15 | AE, D, MC, V.

Harraseeket Lunch and Lobster. Seafood. There's ultracasual dining at this classic, ocean-front Maine lobster shack, 2¼ mi south of town. It's a great spot for the whole family and is known for boiled lobster and fried seafood baskets. Open-air dining at picnic tables, half of which are awning covered. Cafeteria service. Kids' menu. BYOB. No smoking. | Main St., Town Landing, South Freeport | 207/865–4888 | Closed mid-Oct.–Apr. | $7–$17 | No credit cards.

Jameson Tavern. Seafood. Legend has it that the document separating Maine from Massachusetts was signed and sealed here, when this tavern was nearly ½ century old. Today it's a restaurant that has such dishes as *fruits de mer* (seafood over pasta). Open-air dining on the patio. Kids' menu. No smoking. | 115 Main St. (U.S. 1) | 207/865–4196 | fax 207/865–6769 | $20–$30 | AE, D, DC, MC, V.

Lobster Cooker. Seafood. This renovated early-19th-century barn has exposed beams and brick foyers. It's known for its soups and lobster rolls and there's open-air dining on the patio. Cafeteria service. Kids' menu. Beer and wine only. No smoking. | 39 Main St. (U.S. 1) | 207/865–4349 | www.lobstercooker.com | $5–$20 | No credit cards.

Maine Dining Room. American. The dining room at the Harraseeket Inn has fireplaces and views of gardens. Try the tableside rack of lamb for two. Open-air dining on the patio. Kids' menu. Sunday brunch. No smoking. | 162 Main St. | 207/865–1085 | www.harraseeketinn.com | $20–$35 | AE, D, DC, MC, V.

Lodging

Atlantic Seal Bed & Breakfast. This mid-19th-century B&B, 2 mi south of Freeport, is filled with sea-related motifs and many antiques. There are wood-burning fireplaces. Complimentary breakfast. Cable TV, some room phones. Dock, boating, bicycles. No smoking. | 25 Main St., South Freeport | 207/865–6112 | www.burnicechesler/atlanticsealbnb.com | 4 rooms | $105–$175 | MC, V.

Bagley House Inn. Rugged beams, wide-board wood floors, and many antiques decorate this 18th-century inn, 6 mi north of Freeport. Picnic area, complimentary breakfast. No air-conditioning. Cross-country skiing. Library. No smoking. | 1290 Royalsborough Rd., Durham | 207/865–6566 or 800/765–1772 | fax 207/353–5878 | bglyhse@aol.com | www.bagley-house.com | 8 rooms | $95–$150 | AE, D, MC, V.

Brewster House Bed & Breakfast. This beautiful Queen Anne house has antique furnishings and tasteful traditional decorating that complements the 19th-century fixtures such as tin ceilings and carved moldings. Complimentary breakfast. No room phones, cable TV in common area. No kids under 7. No smoking. | 180 Main St. | 207/865–4121 or 800/865–0822 | fax 207/865–4221 | www.brewsterhouse.com | 7 rooms (1 with shower only) | $100–$150 | AE, D, MC, V.

Captain Briggs House Bed & Breakfast. Though an easy jaunt from downtown Freeport, this historic home is set on a street so quiet you will imagine you are in the country. Rooms are bright and immaculate, and there is a gorgeous flower garden. Complimentary breakfast. Some room phones, TV in common area. No smoking. | 8 Maple Ave. | 207/865–1868 or 800/217–2477 | www.bbonline.com/me/johnbriggs | 6 rooms | $90–$120 | MC, V.

Casco Bay Inn. This hotel is on U.S. 1 and near Interstate 95, convenient to outlets and L. L. Bean. Complimentary Continental breakfast. Cable TV. | 107 U.S. 1 S | 207/865–4925 or 800/570–4970 | www.gardinns.com | 30 rooms | $79–$95 | AE, D, MC, V.

Coastline Inn. This standard chain motel is convenient to L. L. Bean and outlets. Picnic area, complimentary Continental breakfast. Cable TV. Laundry facilities. | 537 U.S. 1 S | 207/865–3777 or 800/470–9494 | fax 207/865–4678 | www.coastlineinnmaine.com | 108 rooms in 3 buildings | $70–$100 | AE, D, MC, V.

Freeport Inn and Cafe. This inn is on 25 acres and has canoeing nearby. Restaurant, picnic area. Some refrigerators, cable TV. Pool. Business services, free parking. Some pets allowed. | 31 U.S. 1 S | 207/865–3106 or 800/998–2583 | fax 207/865–6364 | www.freeportinn.com | 80 rooms | $110 | AE, D, DC, MC, V.

Harraseeket Inn. Rooms in this hotel on several acres occupy an 18th-century Federal house, a vintage Victorian, and a contemporary structure. Dining room, complimentary breakfast, room service. In-room data ports, some in-room hot tubs, cable TV. Pool. Business services. | 162 Main St. (U.S. 1) | 207/865–9377 or 800/342–6423 | fax 207/865–1684 | harraseeket@aol.com | www.harraseeketinn.com | 84 rooms | $160–$245 | AE, D, DC, MC, V.

Kendall Tavern. Antiques fill this mid-19th-century farmhouse. Complimentary breakfast. No air-conditioning, no room phones, cable TV in common area. No smoking. | 213 Main St. (U.S. 1) | 207/865–1338 or 800/341–9572 | fax 207/865–3544 | 7 rooms | $100–$115 | AE, D, MC, V.

Maine Idyll Motor Court. These old-style cabins in a wooded grove on a 20-acre plot have been operating since 1932. It's 2½ mi north of Freeport. No air-conditioning in some rooms, some kitchenettes, refrigerators. | 1411 U.S. 1 N | 207/865–4201 | www.freeportusa.com/maineidyll | 20 cabins | $46–$90 | Closed Nov.–Apr. | No credit cards.

Maple Hill Bed & Breakfast. The owners of this B&B emphasize a warm family-friendly environment; the cheery golden retriever will even welcome you into the home. Formerly a farmhouse, Maple Hill's barn and garden preserve the traditions of its rural heritage. Complimentary breakfast. Cable TV. Pets allowed. No smoking. | 18 Maple Ave. | 207/865–3730 or 800/867–0478 | www.web-knowledge.com/maplehill | 3 rooms | $110–$150 | AE, D, MC, V.

181 Main Street. This mid-19th-century inn filled with antiques is in a quiet area of Freeport, only a five-minute walk from its center. Complimentary breakfast. No air-conditioning in some rooms, no room phones, cable TV in common area. Pool. Library. Free parking. No kids under 14. No smoking. | 181 Main St. (U.S. 1) | 207/865–1226 | bb181main@aol.com | 7 rooms | $85–$110 | MC, V.

Shepard Seaside Cottage. This secluded cottage sits amid woods and affords splendid view of the ocean. It's only 5 mi from downtown Freeport. The cottage will accommodate four adults and a child, or two adults and four children. Kitchenette, microwave, refrigerator, cable TV, in-room VCR. Beach, boating, bicycles. Laundry facilities. | 17 Merganser Way | 215/236–3658 | www.members.aol.com/~hhshepard | 3 bedrooms in single cottage | $1,500 (7-day minimum stay) | No credit cards.

The Village Inn. The inn, built in 1855, has retained its historic feel—the dining room has an original wood interior and fireplaces. The rooms, however, have all the modern touches of a contemporary motel. Complimentary breakfast. Cable TV. | 186 Main St. | 207/865–3236 or 800/998–3649 | fax 207/865–4243 | www.freeportvillageinn.com | 9 rooms | $80 | MC, V.

White Cedar Inn. This inn is on landscaped grounds and its tidy rooms have antique white iron beds. Picnic area, complimentary breakfast. No room phones, cable TV in common area. No kids under 11. No smoking. | 178 Main St. | 207/865–9099 or 800/853–1269 | capandphil@aol.com | www.whitecedarinn.com | 7 rooms (6 with shower only) | $95–$130 | AE, D, MC, V.

FRYEBURG

MAP 3, A10

(Nearby towns also listed: Bridgton, Center Lovell)

Home to the state's largest agricultural fair, Fryeburg is a quiet town with trim houses, in the Saco River valley, close to the New Hampshire border. Settled in 1763, Fryeburg was once home to the famed orator Daniel Webster, who taught at Fryeburg Academy (founded in 1791). Fryeburg also serves as a gateway to abundant outdoor recreation at area mountains, lakes, and the Saco River, which is popular with canoeists.

Information: Bridgton Lakes Region Chamber of Commerce | Portland St. (Rte. 302), Box 236, Bridgton, 04009 | 207/647–3472 | director@mainelakeschamber.com | www.mainelakeschamber.com. **Maine Tourism Association** | Rte. 302, Fryeburg, 04037 | 207/935–3639.

Attractions

Fryeburg Flea Market. Over 50 tables, both indoor and outdoor, feature a mix of arts, crafts, and antiques. Located at the Fryeburg Fairgrounds. | 203 Main St. | 603/447–6857 | Memorial Day–Labor Day, Sun.

Hemlock Covered Bridge. This 116-ft-long covered bridge, 3 mi northwest of Fryeburg, was constructed in 1857. | Off U.S. 302.

Saco River Canoe and Kayak. The Saco River, although often crowded, is one of the most beautiful and friendly places to canoe in Maine. Sand bars from Swan's Falls to Brownfield make for plentiful stops for swimming and picnicking. Use of the river is free if you have your own canoe and a way to transport it. If you don't, go to Saco River Outfitters who will rent you a canoe and do the shuttling for you. | Rte. 5, North Fryeburg | 207/935–2369 | www.sacorivercanoe.com | $25.

ON THE CALENDAR

OCT.: *Fryeburg Fair.* Maine's largest agricultural fair has been the last country fair of the season since 1851. It's a Sunday-to-Sunday event with wall-to-wall exhibition halls, farm museums, craft demonstrations, midway, and lots of livestock at the Fryeburg Fairgrounds. | 203 Main St. | $5 | 207/935–3268.

Dining

Oxford House Inn. Contemporary. This Edwardian inn has a fireplace and mountain panoramas. Try the veal Oxford or the champagne-poached salmon. Open-air dining on screened porch. No smoking. | 105 Main St. | 207/935–3442 or 800/261–7206 | www.oxfordhouseinn.com | Reservations essential | Closed Mon.–Wed. Nov.–June. No lunch | $8–$25 | AE, D, DC, MC, V.

Lodging

Admiral Peary House. Arctic explorer Robert E. Peary once called this Civil War–era (1865) structure home. It's beautifully situated on 10 acres of lawns, gardens, and woods. Complimentary breakfast. No room phones, cable TV in common area. Outdoor hot tub. Tennis. Bicycles. Cross-country skiing. Library. Airport shuttle. No smoking. | 9 Elm St. | 207/935–3365 or 800/237–8080 | fax 207/935–3365 | admpeary@nxi.com. | www.admiralpeary-house.com | 6 rooms | $80–$138 | AE, MC, V.

Jockey Cap Motel. This affordable motel is within reach of rock climbing, skiing, golf, and other activities. There is also a well-stocked country store on the premises. Restaurant, complimentary Continental breakfast. Some microwaves, some refrigerators, cable TV. Hiking. Snowmobiling. Shops. Pets allowed. | 16 Bridgton Rd. | 207/935–2306 | fax 207/935–2351 | www.jockey-capmotel.com | 7 rooms | $42–$56 ($87–$97 during Fryeburg Fair) | AE, D, MC, V.

Oxford House Inn. This antiques-filled turn-of-the-20th-century home has a characteristic porch and fine mountain views. Restaurant, complimentary breakfast. Cable TV. Cross-country skiing. No smoking. | 105 Main St. | 207/935–3442 or 800/261–7206 | fax 207/935–7046 | innkeeper@oxford.com | www.oxfordhouseinn.com | 4 rooms | $95–$125 | AE, D, DC, MC, V.

GEORGETOWN

MAP 3, D10

(Nearby town also listed: Bath)

Connected to the mainland by a series of bridges, the island of Georgetown lays claim to Reid State Park, a nature preserve, twisting woodland roads that give way to ocean vistas, and sheltered fishing communities. Work your way over to Five Islands for a classic view of pure Maine coast.

Information: Chamber of Commerce of Bath-Brunswick Region | 59 Pleasant St., Brunswick, 04011 | 207/725–8797 or 207/443–9751 | ccbbr@horton.col.k12.us | www.mid-coastmaine.com.

Attractions

Reid State Park. This park, 15 mi north of Georgetown, has more than a mile of sand beaches, dunes, marshes, ledges and oceans, and a warm saltwater pond for swimming. Hiking trails run through much of the property. | Seguin Rd. | 207/371–2303 | $2.50 | Daily 9–dusk.

ON THE CALENDAR
JULY: *Fire Department Auction.* You will find everything from locally made fudge to paintings and sculptures at this auction, which takes place at the Five Islands Fire Station on the first Saturday after the 4th. An unfinished 35-ft cape dory boat was included in the 2000 event. | Old Schoolhouse Rd. | 207/371–2375.
AUG.: *Georgetown Working League Fair.* A huge white elephant sale on the second Tuesday of the month at the Georgetown Central School with books, weaving, and other crafts. There is a luncheon and kids' games as well. | Baypoint Rd. | 207/371–2221.

Dining

The Love Nest, the Lobster Pound, and Annabelle's Ice Cream. Seafood. All part of one complex, you'll find everything from "the best lobster roll in the world," to crab cakes, to homemade ice cream. The restaurants are on a working dock, and seating is outdoors on picnic tables. | Rt. 127 to Five Islands | 207/371–2990 | Closed Oct.–Apr. | $4–$15 | MC, V.

Robinhood Free Meetinghouse. Contemporary. This lovingly restored 1855 Greek Revival meetinghouse has wood floors, tall windows, and loft seating. Try the Szechuan swordfish or crab-stuffed fillet. No smoking. | Robinhood Rd. | 207/371–2188 | www.robinhood-meetinghouse.com | No lunch | $17–$25 | AE, D, MC, V.

Lodging

Grey Havens Inn. You'll find this elegant, shingle-style inn tranquil and inviting. A wrap-around porch, great ocean views from most rooms, and savory blueberry muffins add up to a perfect getaway vacation. Bar, complimentary breakfast. No TV. Dock, boating. | Seguinland Rd. | 207/371–2616 or 800/431–2316 | fax 207/371–2274 | www.greyhavens.com | 13 rooms | $100–$210 | MC, V.

GREENVILLE

MAP 3, D6

(Nearby towns also listed: Moosehead Lake, Rockwood)

Greenville is at the southern tip of Moosehead Lake and is the official gateway to the Great North Woods. Incorporated in 1836, the town has long been an outpost for rugged outdoor enthusiasts. Its amenities and services, ranging from moose-watching expeditions to comfortable resorts, mean visitors no longer come here to get away from it all—because it's all here. Greenville also serves as a back-door gateway to Baxter State Park, which is due northeast from town and can be reached via dirt road.

Information: Moosehead Lake Region Chamber of Commerce | Main St. (Rte. 15), Box 581, Greenville, 04441 | 207/695–2702 or 207/695–2026 | moose@mooseheadarea.com | www.mooseheadarea.com.

Attractions

Big Squaw Mountain Resort. This old-style ski resort, 2 mi northwest of Greenville, is remote but a lot of fun. It has low prices and a low-key, friendly base lodge as well as great views of Moosehead Lake and Mt. Katahdin. A slope-side hotel has rooms for $40. | Rte. 15 | 207/695–1000 | Thanksgiving–Apr., daily.

Folsom's Air Service. This floatplane service flies people into remote areas for fishing and hunting, and also does sightseeing flights. | Lincoln St. | 207/695–2821 | www.folsoms.com | $30 per person for 30-min sightseeing flight | Year-round.

Katahdin Cruises. This 1914 lake steamboat, operated by the Moosehead Marine Museum, makes regular sightseeing and Mt. Kineo cruises. | N. Main St. | 207/695–2716 | fax 207/695–2367 | www.katahdincruises.com | $18–$25 | July–Columbus Day, Tues.–Thurs. and weekends; closed Mon. and Fri for cruises.

Lily Bay State Park. This park on the shore of Moosehead Lake is 8 mi north of Greenville and has 91 well-spaced camping sites in two areas, many on the shore, two boat-launch sites, a swim area, a playground, and a shoreline hiking area. | Lily Bay Rd., 10 mi from Greenville | 207/695–2700 | www.state.me.us/doc/prkslnds | $2.50 | Memorial Day–mid-Oct., daily dawn–dusk.

Moosehead Marine Museum. The museum contains memorabilia, including items pertaining to the history of shipping on the lake. | N. Main St. | 207/695–2716 | fax 207/695–2367 | www.katahdincruises.com | $3 | July–Columbus Day, daily 10–2.

★ **MooseMainea.** Once virtually near extinction, moose are back—so much so that they are a hazard on the roads. Moosehead Lake is the area of highest concentration, and there are dozens of ways to get to see them. MooseMainea, run by the chamber of commerce in the peak viewing season of mid-May to mid-June, offers sighting possibilities by plane, boat, ground vehicles, bicycles, and hiking. Call for information on other moose-sighting tours

MOOSE WATCH

Sighting a moose has become an integral part of the Maine mystique. Seeing one of these massive creatures feeding in a secluded pond or lumbering along the roadside can be both a memorable and startling experience.

Maine has more moose per square mile than any other state in North America. Some of your best chances for spotting moose are in the western mountains or in the North Woods, but moose don't read guidebooks, so you never know where one will show up. (Moose, on occasion, have even wandered into Portland's city limits.) Between mid-May and late July, black flies drive moose from the deep woods, making this the best season to spot them. They tend to hang around swamps and lakes, where they are likely to be found feeding. The best time of day to see them is early morning and dusk. If you need help in your search, there are a number of moose safaris and moose-spotting tours available, particularly in the, you guessed it, Moosehead area.

A word of caution: Moose are not exactly the Einsteins of the animal kingdom. Plus, they're big. A full-grown moose stands 6–7 ft at the shoulder and can weigh near half a ton. Big and not-too-bright is not a good combination for safety. Always give moose a wide berth—particularly cows with calves in tow and during rutting (mating) season in fall. Moose are responsible for numerous highway accidents. Neither their fur nor their eyes reflect light, so use extreme caution when traversing Maine's back roads.

offered in the area. | Moosehead Lake Region Chamber of Commerce, Rte. 15, Greenville | 207/695–2702 | www.mooseheadarea.com | Mid-May–mid-June, daily.

ON THE CALENDAR

JAN.: *Down East Sled Dog Race.* The two-day race also has activities and events to keep you busy while the mushers are mushing. | 207/695–2702.

MAY–JUNE: *MooseMainea.* This family festival includes a fly-casting tournament, moose calling, moose spotting, moose photo contest, moose facts and lore, slide shows, and moose d'oeuvres. | 207/695–2702.

AUG.: *Forest Heritage Days.* The North Woods come alive with forest tours, logging competitions, crafts fair, and steamboat rides. | 207/695–2702.

SEPT.: *Sea Plane Fly-In.* Planes fly in from all over New England for air shows, games, slide shows, crafts fair, and public breakfasts. | Greenville and Greenville Junction | 207/695–4571.

Dining

The Boom Chain. American. This restaurant has an unpretentious interior and serves dishes such as no-frills burgers and homemade soups. The walls are decorated with photographs of Old Greenville. | Main St. | 207/695–2602 | Breakfast also available; no dinner | Under $8 | MC, V.

Fiddlehead Grill. Eclectic. At this restaurant, part of the Blair Hill Inn, all meals are cooked on an indoor mesquite or cherry-wood grill and fuse Southwestern and Asian cuisines. | Lily Bay Rd. | 207/695–0224 | fax 207/695–4324 | Closed Sun.–Thurs. No lunch | $50 prix fixe | AE, D, MC, V.

Flatlanders. American. Old wood accents abound in this 45-seat, homey restaurant. Roasted chicken and specials such as lobster casserole are the favorites. | Pritham Ave. | 207/695–3373 | Closed Mon. and Apr. | $3–$12 | MC, V.

Greenville Inn Restaurant. American. Try the New York strip, roasted half duckling, and filet mignon in this restaurant that is less than ¼ mi from downtown. | Norris St. | 207/695–2206 | Closed Nov.–May. No lunch | $19–$28 | D, MC, V.

Trailside Family Restaurant. American. Steaks, seafood, and sandwiches abound in this country-style spot. It also has a sports-theme bar and is ¾ mi from downtown. | Lily Bay Rd. | 207/695–3737 | $7–$11 | D, MC, V.

Lodging

Blair Hill Inn. A luxurious inn in the wilds of Maine with bright, tasteful rooms that include fresh flowers, aromatherapy soaps, and wood-burning fireplaces. It has 15 acres of meticulous gardens. Restaurant, complimentary breakfast. TV in common area. Lake. Outdoor hot tub. No pets. No smoking. | Lily Bay Rd. | 207/695–0224 | fax 207/695–4324 | www.blairhill.com | 8 rooms | $195–$265 | AE, D, MC, V.

Captain Sawyer House. Moosehead Lake and a cruise ship, the steamship *Katahdin,* are within view of this colonial farmhouse, built in 1849. The house has comfortable rooms and a large porch. TV in common area. No pets. | Lakeview St. | 207/695–2369 | fax 207/695–2480 | www.moosehead.net/sawyer | 4 rooms | $85–$95 | Closed Mar.–Apr. | MC, V.

Chalet Moosehead Motel. Most rooms here have lake views, and some have private balconies and Jacuzzis. Beds are either double or queen, and paddleboats and canoes are available at no charge. Squaw Mountain is 5 mi to the north. Picnic area. No air-conditioning, in-room data ports, some kitchenettes, some refrigerators, some in-room hot tubs, cable TV. Lake. Dock, boating. Shops. Some pets allowed (fee). | Rte. 15, Greenville Junction | 207/695–2950 | www.mooseheadlodge.com | 27 rooms | $68–$105 | AE, D, MC, V.

Evergreen Lodge Bed and Breakfast. This cedar post-and-beam home, built in 1974, looks like a typical Adirondack structure. The property spans 30 acres, and the home is surrounded by lovely gardens. Complimentary breakfast. TV in common area. Outdoor hot tub. Cross-

country skiing. No pets. No kids under 12. No smoking. | Rte. 15 | 207/695–3241 or 888/624–3993 | fax 207/695–3084 | www.mainlodge.com | 6 rooms | $110–$135 | AE, MC, V.

Greenville Inn. Return to another era in this restored Victorian mansion, the former residence of a lumber baron, built in 1895. Elegant and relaxing, with cherry-wood and mahogany antiques, porches with view of mountains, and flower gardens. Dining room, bar, complimentary Continental breakfast. Some refrigerators, no room phones, no TV in some rooms. Lake. | Norris St. | 207/695–2206 or 888/695–6000 | fax 207/695–0335 | gvlinn@moosehead.net | www.greenvilleinn.com | 5 rooms, 1 suite, 6 cottages | $135–$175, $225 suite, $165 cottages | D, MC, V.

Greenwood Motel. This is a family-owned and well-maintained motel near Moosehead Lake, 3 mi northwest of town. Picnic area, complimentary Continental breakfast. Refrigerators, cable TV. Pool. Hiking. Business services. Pets allowed (fee). | Rte. 6 and 15, Rockwood Little Squaw | 207/695–3321 or 800/477–4386 | fax 207/695–2122 | grenqoos@moosehead.net | www.mooseheadlake.net | 16 rooms | $65–$75 | AE, D, DC, MC, V.

Kineo View Motor Lodge. This modern motel with spectacular views of Moosehead Lake and mountains is on 55 acres of unspoiled landscape 2 mi south of Greenville. Picnic area. Hot tub. Cross-country skiing. Pets allowed (fee). | Rte. 15 | 207/695–4470 or 800/659–8439 | fax 207/695–4656 | www.kineoview.com | 12 rooms, 1 suite | $55–$65 | AE, MC, V.

Lakeview House. The view of Moosehead Lake is as stunning here as it is at more expensive lodges. This quiet bed-and-breakfast is only 3 mi from Greenville. Complimentary breakfast. In-room VCRs, no room phones. Some pets allowed. No smoking. | Lily Bay Rd. | 207/695–2229 | fax 207/695–8951 | www.lakeview.com | 2 rooms, 1 suite | $110–$150 | MC, V.

Lodge at Moosehead Lake. Rooms in this fine 1918 inn, 2½ mi north of town, are at once elegant and rustic: each is unique. Beds in three are suspended from the ceilings with logging chains. There are great views of Moosehead Lake and Squaw Mountain from the dining room and public spaces. Complimentary breakfast. In-room hot tubs, no room phones, cable TV, in-room VCRs. Cross-country skiing. Business services. No kids under 14. No smoking. | Lily Bay Rd. | 207/695–4400 | fax 207/695–2281 | innkeeper@lodge.mooseheadlake.com | www.lodgeatmooseheadlake.com | 5 rooms, 3 suites | $185–$395 | D, MC, V.

Spencer Pond Camps. Looking for an escape from the modern world? These secluded and rustic camps, 34 mi north of Greenville, are in a remote wilderness location (your nearest neighbor is 14 mi away). You'll find no plumbing (outhouses are out back), and proprietors maintain two vegetable gardens for use by guests. Other features include woodstoves, quilts, and rocking chairs. Hiking, boating, fishing, bicycles. Library. | Star Rte. 76 | 207/695–2821 radio contact service | fax 207/695–2281 | innkeeper@lodge.mooseheadlake.com | www.lodge@mooseheadlake.com | 6 cabins | $175–$395 | Closed Dec.–Apr. | No credit cards.

HALLOWELL

MAP 3, D9

(Nearby towns also listed: Augusta, Belgrade Lakes, Waterville)

This historic city (one of the smallest in Maine) astride the Kennebec River vied with Augusta as the prominent commercial center of the area into the 19th century. Settled in 1762, it was formerly known as Hook, named for its Bombahook Stream. Hallowell was once an active port with a booming lumber trade, but things are quieter now. Its brick-lined downtown is a National Historic District, and its eclectic assortment of restaurants, antiques stores, and bookshops are meant for meandering.

Information: Kennebec Valley Chamber of Commerce | 21 University Dr., Augusta, 04332–0192 | 207/623–4559 | fax 207/626–9342 | kvcc@mint.net | www.augusta-maine.com.

JULY: *Old Hallowell Day.* Loads of children's activities, crafts fair, church breakfasts and suppers, parade, live entertainment, and fireworks—all in homage to the good old days. | Main St. | 207/623–4021.

Dining

A 1 Diner. Contemporary. This 1945, stainless-steel Worcester diner with an art deco-style interior and an original marble counter is 4 mi north of Hallowell. The menu is creative and eclectic. Try the Vietnamese bouillabaisse or pork bayou dirty rice. Sunday brunch. Beer and wine only. No smoking. | 3 Bridge St. (U.S. 201), Gardiner | 207/582–4804 | www.a1diner.com | No dinner Sun. | $10–$20 | MC, V.

River Cafe. Lebanese. This eatery, in a historic building built in the early 1800s, has tapestries and photographs from Lebanon that mingle with original brickwork. | 119 Water St. | 207/622–2190 | Closed Sun. No lunch | $11–$14 | AE, D, MC, V.

Slates. Contemporary. This 200-year-old building, 4 mi south of Hallowell, has tin ceilings, a dark-wood bar, and a rotating display of art. The menu is wide ranging and eclectic. Try one of the Asian or Mexican dishes, or the chicken potpie at lunch. There's live acoustic music on weekends, rock and folk concert series Monday nights. No smoking. | 167 Water St., Gardiner | 207/622–9575 | No dinner Sun. | $11–$19 | D, MC, V.

Lodging

Maple Hill Farm Bed and Breakfast Inn. This large, restored Victorian inn has great charm and its 130 wooded acres are gorgeous year-round. Bar, complimentary breakfast. Some in-room hot tubs, in-room VCRs. Hiking. Cross-country skiing. No pets. No smoking. | Outlet Rd. | 207/622–2708 or 800/622–2708 | fax 207/622–0655 | www.maplebb.com | 8 rooms | $90–$160 | AE, D, DC, MC, V.

HANCOCK–HANCOCK POINT

MAP 3, F8

(Nearby town also listed: Ellsworth)

Hancock and Hancock Point are often used as spillover from their more popular and populous next-door neighbors, Bar Harbor and Acadia National Park, but the two towns are destinations in themselves. Incorporated in 1828, Hancock Point was once a retreat for the religious and, later, for the well-heeled, as evidenced by the sprawling "cottages" that cluster around the water's edge at its point. By the end of the 1920s, there were numerous lodging and dining establishments, owing to ferry service that connected the point to Mt. Desert Island (MDI). The stock market crash and the construction of a bridge to MDI caused the Point to revert to the sleepy village it is today. You'll find splendid views of Frenchman Bay and Cadillac Mountain, a couple of fine inns and restaurants, an octagonal library, and one of the teeniest post offices in the world.

Information: Ellsworth Area Chamber of Commerce | 163 High St., Ellsworth, 04605 | 207/667–5584 | eacc@downeast.net | www.ellsworthchamber.com.

Attractions

Sullivan Harbor Farm Smokehouse. Hot and cold smoked salmon, duck, chicken, scallops, and mussels are all available here. Featured in Dean and Deluca. | U.S. 1, Sullivan Harbor, 12 mi east of Ellsworth | 207/422–3735 or 800/422–4014 | fax 207/422–8229.

JUNE–JULY: *Pierre Monteux School for Conductors Summer Concert Series.* This school was founded by a world-renowned conductor to prepare advanced students for careers in orchestral conducting. Students give six Sunday concerts in the main hall, featuring works from Strauss to Bartok. | Just off U.S. 1 | 207/422–3931.

Dining

Crocker House Inn. Contemporary. Two dining rooms in a restored 19th-century inn make up this restaurant with bay windows, skylights, and views of woods and gardens. Try the Crocker House scallops, peppered quail, or rack of lamb. There's a pianist on weekends. Sunday brunch. No air-conditioning. No smoking. | Hancock Point Rd. | 207/422–6806 | www.maineguide.com/downeast/crocker | Closed Jan.–Apr. No lunch | $17–$24 | AE, D, MC, V.

Le Domaine. French. This country inn is full of Provençal fabrics and antiques, like copper kettles in a wall-size fireplace. Try the pâté or the rabbit. Open-air dining in the screened-in garden room. All-French wine cellar, with over 5,000 labels. No air-conditioning. No smoking. | U.S. 1 | 207/422–3916 | www.ledomaine.com | Closed Sun., Mon. and Dec.–May | $22–$28 | AE, D, MC, V.

Ristorante Armando's. Italian. The woodwork interior of this eatery has an impressive two-sided stone fireplace and views of both the river and mountain. Try the filet mignon in Dijon brandy sauce. Kids' menu. No smoking. | U.S. 1 | 207/422–3151 | No lunch | $9–$18 | MC, V.

Ruth and Wimpy's. American. The menu is wide ranging, but seafood fettuccine is a favorite. The unpretentious interior and deck seats 50. | U.S. 1 | 207/422–3723 | Closed Thanksgiving–Christmas | $4–$12 | D, MC, V.

Lodging

Crocker House Inn. The Crocker House offers simple country elegance only 350 yards from the ocean. Fine dining is also available. Restaurant, complimentary breakfast. Hot tub. | Hancock Point Rd. | 207/422–6806 | fax 207/422–3105 | www.arcadia.net/crocker | 11 rooms | $110–$135 | AE, D, MC, V.

Le Domaine. The French-country-style rooms, sprawling 95 wooded acres, and top-shelf dining will transport you to Provence, the region of France on which this bed-and-breakfast is modeled. Luxurious rooms, a superb wine collection, and extensive gardens are some of the other treats you will encounter. Restaurant, complimentary breakfast. Pond. Hiking, fishing. Pets allowed (fee). | U.S. 1 | 207/422–3395 or 800/554–8498 | fax 207/422–2316 | www.ledomaine.com | 3 rooms, 2 suites | $110–$135 | AE, D, MC, V.

Sullivan Harbor Farm. This handsome colonial home built in 1820 overlooks Sullivan Harbor. A pleasant stream, carefully tended gardens, and a salmon smoker give unique touches to the grounds. Complimentary breakfast. Some kitchenettes, some room phones, no TV in some rooms. | U.S. 1 | 207/422–3735 or 800/422–4014 | fax 207/422–8229 | 3 rooms, 2 cottages | $95 rooms, $675–$900/wk cottages | Closed Oct.–May | D, MC, V.

HARPSWELL

MAP 3, C10

(Nearby towns also listed: Bailey Island/Orr's Island, Brunswick)

Harpswell refers to both the name of a town and an area. Ancient glaciers carved out the ragged peninsulas and islands that make up Harpswell. Long, narrow Harpswell Neck dangles out into Casco Bay, astride Bailey, Orr's, and Great islands, which make up the other sectors of the Harpswell peninsula. With 150 mi of shoreline, Harpswell boasts the longest coastline of any town in the nation. On the Neck, hills and farmlands give over to stunning vistas of fir- and island-studded inlets and bays. Tidy white clapboard houses, austere churches, rolling meadows, and dense woods typify the north end of the peninsula. By the time you reach the southern tip, summer homes and cottages jostle and piggyback for their slice of the shorefront.

Information: **Bath-Brunswick Region Chamber of Commerce** | 59 Pleasant St., Brunswick, 04011 | 207/725–8797 or 207/443–9751 | ccbbr@horton.col.k12.us | www.midcoast-maine.com.

Attractions

Summer Home of Admiral Robert E. Peary. Accessible by boat from the marinas in Harpswell or Freeport, you can tour the arctic explorer's home and enjoy a picnic or nature walk. The home is part of the Eagle Island State Park, 3 mi from Harpswell. | Eagle Island | 207/624–6075 | $2 | June 15–Labor Day, daily 10–6.

ON THE CALENDAR
JULY–AUG.: *Beanhole Bean Supper.* For nearly 50 years, this public supper has been a Harpswell institution. | Rte. 123, Harpswell Neck | 207/647–3472.

Dining

Dolphin Restaurant. Seafood. Water surrounds this peninsular restaurant on three sides. It's small and intimate. Try the fish chowder and the blueberry muffins. | Basin Point | 207/833–6000 | $12–$25 | MC, V.

J. Hathaway's Restaurant and Tavern. American. Fish-and-chips and pork spareribs are the most popular dishes at this open restaurant with 45 seats. Call ahead if you're visiting Harpswell in spring, as it does not open at a fixed date each year. | 923 Harpswell Neck Rd. | 207/833–5305 | Closed Nov.–Mar. or Apr. | $9–$16 | D, MC, V.

Lodging

Bethel Point Bed and Breakfast. This is a stately 1830s home just steps from the ocean. Rooms are clean and simply furnished with hardwood furniture and floors. The suite has a fully equipped kitchen, private entrance, washer and dryer, and sleeps four adults. Dining room, complimentary breakfast. No air-conditioning, no room phones, TV in common area. No pets. No smoking. | 331 Bethel Point Rd. | 207/725–1115 or 888/238–8262 | bethelpt@gwi.net | www.bethelpoint.com | 2 rooms, 1 suite | $90–$140 | MC, V.

Harpswell Inn. This stately house overlooks Middle Bay. The 3½ acres grounds include gardens, a pond, and a stream. Complimentary breakfast. Some kitchenettes, some in-room hot tubs, some room phones, no TV in some rooms. Pond. Dock. No pets. No kids under 10. No smoking. | 108 Lookout Point Rd. | 207/833–5509 or 800/843–5509 | www.gwi.net/~harpswel | 9 rooms, 3 suites | $78–$135, $155–$185 suites | D, MC, V.

HOULTON

MAP 3, G4

(Nearby town also listed: Presque Isle)

A spud's throw from New Brunswick, Canada, Houlton is the shire town and commercial hub of southern Aroostook County, plus the terminus of Interstate 95. Houlton started as a lumber town, but forests soon gave way to potato fields, the farming of which remains the area's mainstay. In 1839, Houlton was put on the map as the center of a border dispute, which was peaceably settled. The town's square includes a number of historic turn-of-the-20th-century buildings that are listed on the National Register.

Information: **Greater Houlton Chamber of Commerce** | 109 Main St., Houlton, 04730 | 207/532–4216 | chamber@houlton.com | www.mainerec.com/houlton.html.

Attractions

A. E. Howell Wildlife Conservation Center and Spruce Acres Refuge. Nature trails, a trout pond for kids, and raptor education programs are found on over 50 acres at this site 14 mi south of Houlton. Critters from bobcats to bears are rehabilitated for release into the wild at Spruce Acres. | Lycette Rd. off U.S. 1, North Amity | 207/532–6880 or 207/532–0676 | fax 207/532–0910 | www.members.xoom.com/spruceacres/index.html | $5 suggested donation | May–Nov., weekdays 10–4, Sat. 10–3.

Aroostook Historical and Art Museum. Housed in a 1902 Colonial Revival building containing Aroostook County artifacts, this museum also contains tools, vintage clothing, and other items. | 109 Main St. | 207/532–4216 | Donation suggested | By appointment only.

Hancock Barracks. The barracks site for the American troops in the bloodless 1839 "war" between the United States and Canada is 1 mi east of town. Maine and New Brunswick quarreled over the border of Aroostook County and local logging rights. At one point 50,000 U.S. troops were to be sent to the area, but the dispute was settled without fighting. Only the site of Hancock Barracks remains today, but a scale model may be seen in the Aroostook Museum (*see above*). | Garrison Hill | 207/532–4216 | Free | Daily dawn–dusk.

Market Square Historic District. An area of outstanding turn-of-the-20th-century architecture, listed on the National Register. | Main St. between Kendall and Broadway | 207/532–4216 | www.greaterhoulton.com | Free | Daily.

Museum of Vintage Fashions. This eclectic museum, 25 mi southwest of town, displays old clothing from the Edwardian era to the 1950s, in themed rooms including a millinery shop and haberdashery. | Sherman St., Island Falls | 207/463–2404 or 207/862–3797 | $3 | June–early Oct., Mon.–Thurs. 10–4, Fri.–Sun. by appointment only.

ON THE CALENDAR
FEB.: *MooseStompers Weekend.* Three days of winter fun with snowmobiling, cross-country skiing, and a wild game buffet. | 207/532–4216.
APR.: *Meduxnekeag River Canoe Race.* Intrepid contestants take on the spring runoff. | 207/532–4216.
JULY: *Houlton Fair.* Agricultural exhibits, rides, pig scramble, food, contests, pageants, carnival, and fireworks in Community Park. | Park Ave. | 207/532–4216.
AUG.: *Houlton Potato Feast Days.* A festival concerning all things spudly: potato contests and games, Potato Feast supper, arts, and crafts. | 207/532–4216.

Dining
Elmtree Diner. American. The Elmtree serves home-cooked meals in a down-home spot. You can enjoy clams and grilled ham or steak and then purchase one of the crafts that decorate the diner. | 146 Bangor St. | 207/532–3181 | Breakfast also available | $6–$13 | AE, D, MC, V.

Lodging
Ivey's Motor Lodge. This central hotel is good for businesspeople and travelers. It has convenient, quiet accommodations. Bar. Refrigerators, cable TV. Business services. | North Rd. | 207/532–4206 or 800/244–4206 | fax 207/532–4206 | www.houlton.com/iveys | 24 rooms | $52–$68 | AE, D, DC, MC, V.

Scottish Inns. This chain option 1 mi south of Houlton is near businesses, U.S. 1, and the interstate. Some refrigerators, cable TV. Business services. Pets allowed (fee). | 239 Bangor St. | 207/532–2236 | fax 207/532–9893 | 43 rooms | $40–$80 | AE, D, MC, V.

Shiretown Inn. This downtown hotel is convenient to businesses and the interstate. Restaurant, bar. Refrigerators, cable TV. Pool. Tennis. Exercise equipment. Laundry facilities. Business services. | 282 North Rd. (U.S. 1) | 207/532–9421 or 800/441–9421 | fax 207/532–3390 | 51 rooms | $58–$72 | AE, D, DC, MC, V.

Stardust Motel. Extensively renovated in 2000, this small motel will appeal to you if you prefer a no-frills, inexpensive room. Pets allowed (fee). | 672 North St. | 207/532–6538 or 800/437–8406 | fax 207/532–4143 | 11 rooms | $50 | AE, D, MC, V.

KENNEBUNK

(Nearby towns also listed: Biddeford-Saco, Kennebunkport, Wells)

Sometimes bypassed in order to get to its more touristed sister town, Kennebunkport (the two are popularly referred to as the "Kennebunks"), Kennebunk has its own appeal. Situated inland on the Mousam River, the town was settled in the mid-1600s and was established as an important shipbuilding center by the mid-1700s. Kennebunk is a classic small New England town, with an inviting shopping district, steepled churches, and fine examples of 18th- and 19th-century brick and clapboard homes. There are also plenty of natural spaces for walking, swimming, birding, and biking.

Information: Kennebunk-Kennebunkport Chamber of Commerce | 17 Western Ave., Kennebunk, 04043 | 207/967–0857 | fax 207/967–2867 | kkcc@maine.org | www.kkcc.maine.org.

Attractions

Brick Store Museum. This museum in a former brick store (1825) has three additional buildings with historic artifacts, fine and decorative arts, and imaginative displays. Architectural tours of the town begin at the museum on Thursday in summer. | 117 Main St. | 207/985–4802 | fax 207/985–6887 | $5 | Tues. and Thurs.–Sat. 10–4:30, Wed. 10–8.

Taylor-Barry House. An early 19th-century sea captain's house, also owned by the Brick Store Museum, that provides a glimpse into life in the era of tall ships. | 24 Summer St. | 207/985–4802. | Free with admission to Brick Store Museum | June–Sept., Tues.–Fri. 10–4.

Kennebunk Beach. Adjoined by Beach Road, the beach includes Gooch's Beach, Mother's Beach, and Kennebunk Beach. It has a playground, wading pools, and swimming lessons. Mother's Beach is favored by families with young children. | Beach Rd. | Parking $5 a day, $15 a wk, and $30 for season | Daily 9–5.

Wedding Cake House. Although not open to the public, you will find this architectural oddity to be worth a peek. There are a gallery and an art studio on the grounds, which are open sporadically. | 104 Summer St., at Rte. 35 .

ON THE CALENDAR

FEB.: *Annual Winter Carnival Weekend.* Take the chill off with this family festival that features a variety show, chili and chowder contest, games, and sleigh rides. | Parson's Field (off Park St.) | 207/985–6890.

MAR.: *Annual Home, Food & Craft Show.* Business displays, food, crafts, and entertainment at the Kennebunk High School. | Rte. 35 | 207/967–0857.

AUG.: *Teddy Bear Show and Sale.* All things cute and cuddly can be found at the Kennebunk High School. There are over 40 exhibitors, old and new bears, clothes, furniture, and bear repairs. | Rte. 35 | 207/967–0857.

Dining

Atlantic Pizza. Pizza. Greek pizza is one of the popular choices, among the more typical pies and sandwiches. This tiny restaurant has windows all around, affording a great view of the Kennebunk River. | 8 Western Ave. | 207/967–0033 | $6–$12 | No credit cards.

Grissini. Italian. The main dining room has a stone fireplace and patio and many dishes are cooked in a wood-burning oven. Try the fish, pasta, or rack of lamb. | 27 Western Ave., Lower Village | 207/967–2211 | $11–$19 | AE, MC, V.

Kennebunk Inn. Contemporary. Though this inn dates back to 1799, the restaurant's menu is modern. You'll relish dishes such as tempura soft-shell crab and marinated lamb loins. | 45 Main St. | 207/985–3351 | $13–$21 | AE, D, MC, V.

Windows on the Water. Contemporary. A wall of windows overlooks the river and a marina in this comfortable modern restaurant with white linen, candlelight, and an open kitchen. Try the rack of lamb or lobster ravioli. Open-air dining on the deck. No smoking. | 12 Chase Hill Rd. | 207/967–3313 | www.windowsonthewater.com | $15–$36 | AE, D, DC, MC, V.

Lodging

Arundel Meadows. Antiques and original art add style to this lovely early-19th-century farmhouse-turned-inn with beautiful sloping lawns that is next to the Kennebunk River and 2 mi north of town. Picnic area, complimentary breakfast. Cable TV in some rooms, no room phones. Pool. Hot tub. No kids under 11. No smoking. | 1024 Portland Rd., Arundel | 207/985–3770 | bach@cybertours.com | www.gwi.net/arundel_meadows_inn | 5 rooms, 2 suites | $75–$135, $110–$135 suites | MC, V.

Beach House Inn. This turn-of-the-20th-century inn is on the quiet end of Kennebunk's beach, 1½ mi from Kennebunkport. It is furnished with wicker and country Victorian antiques and ringed with gardens. There's whale-watching, deep-sea fishing, and hiking at the nearby Rachel Carson Wildlife Refuge. Cable TV. Beach. No smoking. | 211 Beach Ave. | 207/967–3850 | fax 207/967–4719 | sundial@lamere.net | www.beachhseinn.com | 33 rooms, 2 suites | $210 | AE, D, DC, MC, V.

Econo Lodge. A chain hotel near beaches, shopping, and the interstate. Complimentary Continental breakfast. Microwaves in some rooms, refrigerators in some rooms, cable TV. Pool. | 55 York St. | 207/985–6100 | fax 207/985–4031 | www.econolodge.com | 46 rooms | $59–$149 | AE, D, DC, MC, V.

English Meadows. This attractive 1860s Victorian farmhouse and attached carriage house are furnished with antiques. You can wander over the lawns and flower gardens. Complimentary breakfast. No air-conditioning in some rooms, some kitchenettes, no room phones, no TV in some rooms. Library. No smoking. | 141 Port Rd. | 207/967–5766 or 800/272–0698 | fax 207/967–3868 | emi@cybertours.com | www.englishmeadowsinn.com | 13 rooms (2 with shared bath), 2 suites | $90–$155, $175 suites | AE, D, MC, V.

Kennebunk Inn. A late-18th-century in-town inn with many gables. Bar, dining room, complimentary Continental breakfast. Some room phones, no TV in some rooms, cable TV in some rooms. Library. Business services. | 45 Main St. | 207/985–3351 | fax 207/985–8865 | jmartin@cybertours.com | www.thekennebunkinn.com | 28 rooms, 4 suites | $95–$105, $155 suites | AE, D, MC, V.

St. Anthony's Franciscan Monastery Guest House. The rooms are simple yet modern and the landscaped grounds span 30 acres. Much of the property is wooded and adjoins a river. Cable TV, no room phones. Pool. Playground. No pets. No smoking. | 28 Beach Ave. | 207/967–2011 | 60 rooms | $64–$69 | Closed Oct.–May | No credit cards.

Turnpike Motel. A small, roadside motel right off the Maine Turnpike (Interstate 95). Picnic area. Refrigerators, cable TV. | 77 Old Alewive Rd. | 207/985–4404 | 24 rooms | $70 | AE, D, MC, V.

William Lord Mansion. This 1801 federal building, restored in 1994, is right in the middle of Kennebunk's historic district. Rooms are bright, sunny, and lovingly detailed. Complimentary breakfast. In-room data ports, refrigerators, cable TV. | 20 Summer St. | 207/985–6213 | www.cybertours.com/~thewmlordmansion | 2 rooms | $150–$200 | No credit cards.

KENNEBUNKPORT

MAP 3, B11

(Nearby towns also listed: Kennebunk, Wells)

A perennially popular seaside resort, Kennebunkport was made famous during the George Bush presidency, and tourists still crowd along Ocean Avenue to get a distant glimpse of his Walkers Point estate. Much more interesting are the stately summer homes that jostle for space along this byway, the stretch of sand beaches, or the well-preserved colonial buildings in town. The Lower Village and Dock Square serve as the shopping-dining-lodging hotbeds.

Information: **Kennebunk–Kennebunkport Chamber of Commerce** | 17 Western Ave., Kennebunk, 04043 | 207/967–0857 | fax 207/967–2867 | kkcc@maine.org | www.kkcc.maine.org.

Attractions

Goat Island Lighthouse. This 25-ft white, cast-iron cylindrical light is at the entrance to Cape Porpoise. Although there is no formal public access to the lighthouse, those owning boats can visit Goat Island. | 207/967–4243.

The Nott House. Also known as White Columns, this Greek Revival mansion has Doric columns that rise to the height of the house, and period furnishings. | 8 Maine St. | 207/967–2751 | www.kporthistory.org | $5 | Mid-June–mid-Oct., Tues.–Fri. 1–4 and Sat. 10–1.

Pasco Exhibits Center. Run by the Kennebunkport Historical Society, the Pasco center has ongoing revolving exhibits about Kennebunkport's history. | 125 North St. | 207/967–2751 | www.kporthistory.org | $3 | Nov.–Mar., Tues.–Fri. 10–4; Apr.–Oct. Tues.–Fri. 10–4, Sat. 10–1.

Seashore Trolley Museum. This museum, 3½ mi north of Kennebunkport, features a 4-mi circuit through woods and fields, a replica old depot, and a collection of more than 200 trolleys from around the world. Also includes a restoration shop. | 195 Log Cabin Rd. | 207/967–2800 or 207/967–2712 | www.trolleymuseum.org | $7 | June–mid-Oct., daily 10–5; May and late Oct., weekends 10–5.

ON THE CALENDAR

JUNE: *Annual Bed-and-Breakfast, Inn, and Garden Tour.* A chance to tour some of the most outstanding homes and gardens in the Kennebunks. | 207/967–0857.
JUNE: *Blessing of the Fleet.* Help set the season into full sail with a cocktail cruise, trivia contest, fleet-blessing ceremony, regatta and other races, and a band concert. | At the mouth of the Kennebunkport River at Dock Square | 207/967–0857.
DEC.: *Christmas Prelude.* Shopping and special events, including tree lighting, concerts, and Santa's arrival in a lobster boat. | Throughout town | 207/967–0857.

Dining

Alisson's. Seafood. The first floor in this converted storefront is casual and publike; the second floor is a bit more formal with a view of Dock Square. Try the seafood fettuccine or seafood medley. Kids' menu. No smoking. | 5 Dock Sq | 207/967–4841 | $13–$24 | AE, D, MC, V.

Arundel Wharf. Seafood. Deep-sea fishing boats tie up at the nearby wharf and are best viewed from this restaurant's deck overlooking Kennebunkport River and marina. Try the clambake dish with lobster on top or one of the eight individual lobster recipes. | 43 Ocean Ave. | 207/967–3444 | www.arundelwharf.com | Closed Nov.–Mar. | $11–$30 | AE, D, DC, MC, V.

Bartley's Dockside. Seafood. A casual spot with water views and lighthouse decorations. Try the lobster pie or haddock à la Dockside. Open-air dining on the deck. Kids' menu. No smoking. | Western Ave. (Rte. 9) | 207/967–5050 | www.bartleysdockside.com | $13–$29 | AE, D, DC, MC, V.

The Belvidere Room at the Tides Inn. Contemporary. In the dining room of this historic, ocean-view inn (6 mi northeast of town), cobalt-blue water glasses and pink lanterns are complemented by striped sea-green table linen. Theodore Roosevelt and Sir Arthur Conan Doyle both signed the guest book, and the inn is said to be haunted by the ghost of its first owner, Emma Foss. Try the lobster burrito or the game-and-fowl trio specialty. Homemade bread, pastries, desserts, and ice cream. Kids' menu. No smoking. | 252 Kings Hwy., Goose Rocks Beach | 207/967–3757 | www.tidesinnbythesea.com. | Breakfast also available; closed mid-Oct.–mid-May. No dinner Tues. | $18–$30 | AE, MC, V.

Breakwater Inn. American. Comfortable dining in a Victorian guest house furnished with country antiques and with water views. There's also a cozy pub. Known for lobster, seafood, steak, and chicken. Kids' portions. No smoking. | 133 Ocean Ave. | 207/967–3118 | www.break-waterinn.com. | Closed late Oct.–May | $18–$24 | AE, MC, V.

Cape Arundel Inn. Continental. You can enjoy stuffed lobster or chicken Wellington in a comfortable, rather than ornate, Victorian interior. All tables have a view of the ocean. | 208 Ocean Ave. | 207/967–2125 | fax 207/967–1199 | Reservations essential | Closed Jan.–Mar. | $19–$29 | AE, D, MC, V.

Cape Pier Chowder House. Seafood. In addition to the steamed lobster, you'll relish the lobster roll, which was voted best in Maine by *Down East Magazine.* Most of the seating is on a outdoor deck with a view of Goat Island Lighthouse. | Pier Rd. | 207/967–0123 | Breakfast also available weekends; closed Dec.–Apr. | $14–$24 | MC, V.

Clam Shack. American. If you want a quick, uncomplicated meal, you can't go wrong with the fried clams, shrimp, or a burger. In Dock Square just below the Kennebunkport Bridge, the Clam Shack only has takeout. | Western Ave. | 207/967–2560 | Closed Columbus Day–Mother's Day | $2–$27 | No credit cards.

Federal Jack's. Eclectic. Typical bar fare mingles with lemon-roasted halibut and potato-encrusted haddock. The interior is open and light and has wood beams and great views of the Kennebunk River. A deck with an awning is open in summer. It produces the nationally distributed Shipyard Ale, and you can savor such treats as their pumpkin and raspberry ales, which are produced on the premises. | 8 Western Ave. | 207/967–4322 | $10–$27 | AE, D, MC, V.

Green Heron Inn. American. Homemade breakfast is served every morning at this bed-and-breakfast to guests and nonguests alike. Eggs Florentine and Benedict, Mexican eggs, and corned beef are favorites dishes. | 126 Ocean Ave. | 207/967–3315 | fax 207/967–4973 | Closed Jan. No lunch or dinner | $3–$8 | No credit cards.

Mabel's Lobster Claw. Seafood. A cozy, 50-seat dining room with knotty-pine walls and water views that is one of the area's longest-running restaurants. Try the baked stuffed lobster or lobster roll. Open-air dining on front porch. No smoking. | 124 Ocean Ave. | 207/967–2562 | Closed Nov.–Mar. | $15–$30 | AE, MC, V.

Ooh-La-La French Creperie. French. An adorable and bright space with hot pink accents and a "kiddie corner" playroom for kids. Favorite crêpes are creamy lobster and french chocolate, and soups and quiches are also available. The crêperie is on the second floor above Julia's Gifts. | 16 Dock Sq. | 207/967–5115 | Breakfast also available; closed Jan.–Mar. No dinner | $4–$9 | No credit cards.

Seascapes. Contemporary. Built on pilings over the water, this bright and airy dining room, 2 mi northeast of Kennebunkport, has pastel colors and wide windows that overlook a working harbor. Try the roasted lobster or marinated salmon. Open-air dining on the patio (lunch only). Pianist nightly. No smoking. | 77 Pier Rd., Cape Porpoise | 207/967–8500 | Closed Jan.–mid-Apr. | $28–$36 | AE, D, DC, MC, V.

★ **White Barn Inn.** Contemporary. Ultra-elegant dining in a converted 18th-century barn filled with art and antiques. The floor-to-ceiling picture windows overlook sculpted gardens. The four-course, prix fixe menu changes weekly. Try the steamed lobster on fettuccine or the lobster spring rolls. There's a pianist nightly. No smoking. Free parking. | 37 Beach St. | 207/967–2321 | www.whitebarninn.com | Reservations essential | Jacket required | No lunch | $67 prix fixe | AE, MC, V.

Lodging

Austin's Inn Town Hotel. In a secluded location on an old wharf in the historic district. Some kitchenettes, cable TV, no room phones. | 28 Dock Sq | 207/967–4241 or 888/228–0548 | www.austinsinntown.com | 14 rooms, 2 suites | $54–$169, $198–$218 suites | Closed Nov.–Apr. | D, MC, V.

Breakwater Inn. A late 19th-century inn at the mouth of Kennebunkport Harbor, 1 mi south of Kennebunkport. Restaurant, complimentary Continental breakfast. Some refrigerators, cable TV, no room phones. | 133 Ocean Ave. | 207/967–3118 | www.breakwaterinn.com | 20 rooms (2 with shower only) in 2 houses | $90–$165 | Closed late Oct.–May | AE, MC, V.

Bufflehead Cove Inn. Six acres of flower gardens, lawns, and pines surround this late-19th-century cottage-turned-inn on the edge of the Kennebunk River; the porch is archetypal with its row of white Adirondack chairs. Boats are available. Picnic area, complimentary breakfast. No room phones. Hot tubs. No kids under 12. No smoking. | Bufflehead Cove Rd. | 207/967–3879 | fax 207/967–3879 | www.buffleheadcove.com | 5 rooms (3 with shower only) | $145–$295 | D, MC, V.

Cabot Cove Cottages. Separate spacious cottages on landscaped grounds adjacent to a tidal cove of the Kennebunk River. Each has white wicker furniture and pine floors. Picnic area. Kitchenettes, cable TV. Boating. Laundry facilities. No smoking. | 7 S. Main St. | 207/967–5424 or 800/962–5424 | www.cabotcovecottages.com | 15 cottages | $125–$160 | Closed Columbus Day.–mid-May | D, MC, V.

Cape Arundel Inn. A Victorian inn 2 mi north of Kennebunkport that has an adjacent small motel called "Rockbound." You'll find views of the Atlantic sea coast from its cliff-top perch. Restaurant. No air-conditioning, no TV in some rooms. | 208 Ocean Ave. | 207/967–2125 | fax 207/967–1199 | www.capearundelinn.com | 14 rooms in 2 buildings | $200–$250 | Closed Jan.–Feb. | AE, MC, V.

Cape Porpoise Motel. This motel, 2 mi northeast of Kennebunkport, is ideal if you are simply looking for an inexpensive place to sleep—it's small and has no frills. Cable TV. No pets. No smoking. | Rte. 9, Cape Porpoise | 207/967–3370 | 10 rooms | $73 | Closed Oct.–May | D, MC, V.

Captain Fairfield Inn. The Fairfield is named for the sea captain who once made his home in this 1813 structure. It is within walking distance of the ocean, restaurants, shops, and galleries. Complimentary breakfast. No room phones, cable TV in common area. Business services. No smoking. | At the corner of Pleasant and Green Sts. | 207/967–4454 or 800/322–1928 | fax 207/967–8537 | jrw@captainfairfield.com | www.captainfairfield.com | 9 rooms | $165–$250 | AE, D, DC, MC, V.

Captain Jefferds Inn. Kennebunkport has many Federal-style sea captains' homes-turned-inns and this is a good one with its solarium and antique furnishings. Rooms have fresh flowers, down-filled comforters, working fireplaces, private porches, oversize showers, and CD players. Complimentary breakfast. In-room hot tubs, no room phones, TV in common area. Pets allowed (fee). No smoking. | 5 Pearl St. | 207/967–2311 or 800/839–6844 | fax 207/967–0721 | captjeff@captainjefferdsinn.com | www.captainjefferdsinn.com | 15 rooms | $135–$285 | AE, MC, V.

Captain Lord Mansion. Antiques embellish the elegant spaces in this fine Federal-style (1812) mansion topped with a cupola. Complimentary breakfast. Refrigerators in some rooms. Business services. No kids under 12. No smoking. | 6 Pleasant St. | 207/967–3141 | fax 207/967–3172 | captain@biddeford.com | www.captainlord.com | 16 rooms | $175–$399 | D, MC, V.

Captain's Hideaway. A luxurious and romantic bed-and-breakfast. You can see the Kennebunk River and a distant view of the Atlantic from the upstairs, and Dock Square is five blocks away. Complimentary breakfast. Refrigerators, in-room hot tubs, cable TV, in-room VCRs. No pets. No kids. No smoking. | 12 Pleasant St. | 207/967–5711 | fax 207/967–3843 | www.captainshideaway.com. | 2 suites | $179–279. | V, MC.

Chetwynd House Inn. The best feature of this 1840 colonial home is the location: Dock Square is mere steps away and parking is provided. The river inlet is right across the street. Complimentary breakfast. Cable TV, no room phones. Free parking. | 4 Chestnut St. | 207/967–2235 | fax 207/967–5406 | www.chetwyndhouse.com | 4 rooms | $149–$169 | Sometimes closes in winter | MC, V.

Colony Hotel. A family-operated resort on a peninsula, with a surf beach and organic gardens. Bar, dining room, complimentary breakfast, room service. No air-conditioning, no TV in some rooms. Pool. Putting green. Beach, bicycles. Business services. Pets allowed (fee). No smoking. | 140 Ocean Ave. | 207/967–3331 or 800/552–2363 | fax 207/967–8738 | info-me@thecolonyhotel.com | www.thecolonyhotel.com/maine | 123 rooms in 3 buildings | $175–$425 | Closed mid-Oct.–mid-May | AE, MC, V.

Cove House. Period antiques and a meticulous restoration help preserve the original flavor of this 1793 colonial home. It has a fine view of Chick's Cove, and Dock Square is less than a mile away. A separate cottage is also available. Complimentary breakfast. No room phones, TV in common area. | 11 S. Main St. | 207/967–3704 | www.covehouse.com | 3 rooms, 1 cottage | $92, $125 cottage | MC, V.

English Meadows Inn. This Victorian home, built in 1860, is ¼ mi from Kennebunkport Harbor and 1 mi from a public beach. The inn's lawns, gardens, and woods cover 3 acres. Parking, which can be a problem in Kennebunkport, is ample. Complimentary breakfast. Some kitchenettes, no room phones, TV in common area. No pets. No smoking. | 141 Port Rd. | 207/967–5766 or 800/272–0698 | fax 207/967–3868 | www.englishmeadowsinn.com | 10 rooms, 1 efficiency, 1 carriage house | $95–$160 | AE, MC, V.

Fontenay Terrace Motel. Don't let the term "motel" deceive you: you'll find the rooms and grounds as charming as those at most bed-and-breakfasts. It's 600 ft from the ocean and has a view of President Bush's summer home. Refrigerators, cable TV. No pets. No smoking. | 128 Ocean Ave. | 207/967–3556 | fax 207/967–4973 | www.fontenaymotel.com | 8 rooms | $96–$116 | Closed Jan. | D, MC, V.

Green Heron Inn. This bed-and-breakfast abuts a small tidal inlet, and is 1 mi from Dock Square. The inn was built in 1900 and fully renovated in 1988. Complimentary breakfast. Some kitchenettes, cable TV. | 126 Ocean Ave. | 207/967–3315 | fax 207/967–4973 | www.green-heroninn.com | 10 rooms, 1 cottage | $105–$125 | Closed Jan. | No credit cards.

Harbor Inn. This 1902 home retains all of its authentic Victorian touches inside and out. It's ¼ mi from the ocean, and mere feet from the Kennebunk River. Complimentary breakfast. No air-conditioning, some kitchenettes, no room phones, TV in common area. | 90 Ocean Ave. | 207/967–2074 | www.harbor-inn.com | 5 rooms, 2 suites, 1 cottage | $95–$150 | MC, V.

Inn at Harbor Head. Lovely murals distinguish this vintage farmhouse inn with breezy sea views. Complimentary breakfast. Some room phones. Beach. No kids under 12. No smoking. | 41 Pier Rd. | 207/967–5564 | fax 207/967–1294 | www.harborhead.com | 5 rooms, 2 suites | $190–$330 | Closed last 2 wks in Dec. | MC, V.

Kennebunkport Inn. This Victorian mansion has been an inn since the Roaring '20s. Many rooms have antiques and four-poster beds, one has a gas fireplace, and all have private baths. Bar with entertainment, dining room. Cable TV. Pool. Business services. | 1 Dock Sq | 207/967–2621 or 800/248–2621 | fax 207/967–3705 | www.kennebunkportinn.com | 34 rooms | $152–$299 | AE, MC, V.

Kilburn House. In the center of Kennebunkport village, this turn-of-the-20th-century house is furnished with antiques. It's close to restaurants, shops, galleries. Picnic area, complimentary breakfast. No room phones, cable TV in common area. Kids in suite only. No smoking. | 6 Chestnut St. | 207/967–4762 | fax 207/967–1065 | www.kilburnhouse.com | 5 rooms (2 with shower only, 2 with shared bath), 1 suite | $115–$135, $125 suite | AE, MC, V.

Lake Brook Bed and Breakfast. The gardens and tidal brook are as enjoyable as the interior of this restored farmhouse: both are extravagant. Local artists are featured inside, and the porch affords a stunning view of the grounds. Complimentary breakfast. Some kitchenettes, no room phones, no TV. No pets. No smoking. | 57 Western Ave., | 207/967–4069 | www.lakebrookbb.com | 3 rooms, 1 suite | $90–$130 | MC, V.

Maine Stay Inn and Cottages. This property is in the historic district, not far from the harbor and the beach. It has a suspended spiral staircase, sunburst crystal glass windows, chandeliers, fireplaces, cupola, wraparound porch with views of village, and many antiques. Picnic area, complimentary breakfast. Some kitchenettes, some refrigerators, cable TV, no room phones. Business services. No smoking. | 34 Maine St. | 207/967–2117 or 800/950–2117 | fax 207/967–8757 | innkeeper@mainestayinn.com | www.mainestayinn.com | 4 rooms, 2 suites, 11 cottages | $160–$185, $225 suites, $180–$225 cottages | AE, MC, V.

Ocean View. This modernized Victorian home has bright and cheery spaces, but the best feature is that it's right on the ocean. All rooms have a view of the water. Complimentary breakfast. Refrigerators, no TV in some rooms. No pets. No kids under 13. No smoking. | 171 Beach Ave. | 207/967–2750 | fax 207/967–5418 | www.theoceanview.com | 9 rooms | $210–$295 | Closed mid-Dec.–Apr. or May | AE, D, MC, V.

Old Fort Inn. An elegant, tranquil retreat (1800), nestled amid aged trees and bountiful gardens, one block from the Atlantic Ocean. Complimentary breakfast. Microwaves, refrigerators, cable TV. Pool. Tennis. Laundry facilities. Business services. No smoking. | 8 Old Fort Ave. | 207/967–5353 or 800/828–3678 | fax 207/967–4547 | ofi@ispchannel.com | www.oldfortinn.com | 16 rooms | $155–$350 | Closed mid-Dec.–mid-Apr. | AE, D, MC, V.

Rhumb Line Motor Lodge. On a 4-acre wooded property 3 mi southeast of Kennebunkport, this hotel is less than a mile from former President Bush's Summer White House. It's also near a coastal, pebble beach and a short drive to beautiful sandy beaches. It's on a trolley route. Bar, picnic area, complimentary Continental breakfast. Refrigerators, cable TV. 2 pools. Hot tub. Exercise equipment. Business services. | Ocean Ave. | 207/967–5457 or 800/337–4862 | fax 207/967–4418 | rhumblinemaine.com | 59 rooms | $129–$149 | Closed Jan. | AE, D, MC, V.

Schooners Inn. This inn is on the harbor, where the river meets the sea. All rooms overlook the Kennebunk River and Atlantic Ocean and are furnished with Thos. Moser furniture. Restaurant, complimentary Continental breakfast. Refrigerators, cable TV. Business services. | 127 Ocean Ave. | 207/967–5333 | fax 207/967–2040 | www.schoonersinn.com | 17 rooms | $155–$275 | AE, MC, V.

Seaside Inn. This beachside hotel and cottages complex designed for family vacations is ³/₄ mi south of Kennebunkport. No air-conditioning, some kitchenettes, refrigerators, cable TV. Beach. Playground. Laundry facilities. Some pets allowed (fee). | Gooch's Beach | 207/967–4461 | fax 207/967–1135 | www.kennebunkbeach.com | 22 rooms, 10 cottages | $179–$199, $975–$1,295/wk cottages | Cottages closed Nov.–Apr. | AE, MC, V.

Shawmut Ocean Resort. A vintage oceanfront inn on extensive grounds that is 3 mi east of Kennebunkport. Town transportation by trolley. Restaurant, bar, picnic area, complimentary breakfast. Some kitchenettes, cable TV. Pool. Business services. | Turbats Creek Rd. | 207/967–3931 or 800/876–3931 | fax 207/967–4158 | shawmutreservations@juno.com | 74 rooms, 20 suites | $129–$159, $179–$199 suites | Closed mid-Dec.–mid-Apr. | AE, D, DC, MC, V.

Tides Inn by-the-Sea. This shingle-style Grand Yellow Lady of Goose Rocks Beach has welcomed generations of Maine summerfolk since she was built in 1899. The food is exceptional (see The Belvidere Room at the Tides Inn, above), and the inn is said to be haunted. Dining room. No air-conditioning, some kitchenettes, no room phones, no TV in some rooms, TV in common area. Beach. | 252 Kings Hwy. | 207/967–3757 | fax 207/967–5183 | www.tidesinnbythesea.com | 25 rooms (3 with shared bath, 3 with shower only) | $185–$265 | Closed mid-Oct.–mid-May | AE, MC, V.

Village Cove Inn. A family-oriented inn ½ mi southeast of Kennebunkport. Restaurant, bar with entertainment. Cable TV. 2 pools. Business services. | 29 S. Main St. | 207/967–3993, 800/879–5778 outside ME | fax 207/967–3164 | info@villagecoveinn.com | www.villagecoveinn.com | 34 rooms | $169–$189 | AE, D, MC, V.

★ **White Barn Inn.** Rooms in this 1820s farmhouse-turned-inn come with fresh flowers and fruit, a CD system, voice mail, toiletries, and lovely gardens. It has morning-through-evening valet service, same-day laundry service, and room service at breakfast. Restaurant (see Dining, above), complimentary Continental breakfast, room service. Some in-room hot tubs, no TV in some rooms. Pool. Boating, bicycles. No kids under 12. | 37 Beach Ave. | 207/

967–2321 | fax 207/967–1100 | innkeeper@whitebarninn.com | www.whitebarninn.com | 16 rooms, 9 suites | $230–$255, $395–$425 suites | AE, MC, V.

Yachtsman Lodge. This is a quiet retreat on the river's edge, just a short walk from Dock Square in the heart of Kennebunkport. The rooms resemble the interior of a handsomely appointed yacht. French doors open onto patios overlooking the private marina. Picnic area, complimentary Continental breakfast. No air-conditioning in some rooms, refrigerators, cable TV. Business services. | Ocean Ave. | 207/967–2511 or 800/992–2487 | fax 207/967–5056 | yachtsman@kport.com | www.yachtsmanlodge.com | 30 rooms | $195–$235 | Closed Jan.–Feb. | AE, MC, V.

KINGFIELD

MAP 3, C7

(Nearby town also listed: Carrabassett Valley)

Kingfield is the official gateway to Sugarloaf/USA. Surrounded by mountains, woodlands, and waterways, there's plenty to do here (mud season aside) year-round. Named for the state's first governor, William King, it has a bit of a Wild West feel—rustic storefronts line the broad main street, and a large hotel dominates the town's center. Kingfield is also the birthplace of the Stanley twins, of Stanley Steamer fame.

Information: **Sugarloaf Area Chamber of Commerce** | Valley Crossing, Box 2151, Carrabassett Valley, 04947 | 207/235–2100 or 800/THE-AREA.

Attractions

Nowetah's American Indian Museum and Gift Store. Privately owned and operated, this museum and store, 6 mi southwest of Kingfield in New Portland, has a display of Native American art from all over the United States and Canada, with a special emphasis on Maine. Items include old stone artifacts, moccasins, carved necklaces, and baskets and bark containers. | 2 Coldgrove Rd., Rte. 27, New Portland | 207/628–4981 | Donation suggested | Daily 10–5.

Stanley Museum. Dedicated to Kingfield native twin brothers F. E. and F. O. Stanley, inventors of the Stanley Steamer automobile more than a century ago, this Georgian structure has a few of the steam-powered cars and such items as violins the twins built, an airbrush F. E. invented, and more. The brothers were partners in the Stanley Dry Plate Co., which they sold to Eastman Kodak. | School St. | 207/265–2729 | www.stanleymuseum.com | $2 | May–Oct., Tues.–Sun. 1–4; Nov.–Apr., weekdays 1–5.

Wire Bridge. Built in 1866, this bridge over the Carrabassett River in New Portland uses a unique suspension system of imported English free cables. It's 4 mi south on Route 27, then east toward West New Portland village. | 207/628–4981 | Free | Daily.

ON THE CALENDAR
AUG.: *Kingfield Festival Days.* This family celebration has a parade, public suppers, dances, games, and craft exhibits. | Throughout town | 207/235–2100.

Dining
Herbert Inn. Contemporary. A classic 1917 inn, with comfortable lobby, hardwood floors, and lace tablecloths. It has a wide-ranging menu that changes seasonally and that includes prime rib, seafood, and vegetarian items. | Main St. (Rte. 27) | 207/265–2000 or 800/843–4372 | fax 207/265–4594 | www.mainemountaininn.com | Closed mid-Apr.–June, mid-Oct.–mid-Nov., and Tues.–Wed. No lunch | $11–$20 | AE, D, DC, MC, V.

Inn on Winter's Hill. Continental. The menu continually changes, but you can expect dishes like trout almondine, filet mignon, and lamb chops. The restaurant is in the Georgian

Revival portion of the inn, and has intimate, fireside dining. | Winter's Hill Rd. | 207/265–5421 | fax 207/265–5424 | Reservations essential | Closed May–Jan. | $17–$23 | AE, D, MC, V.

Longfellow's. Contemporary. Wholesome dining in one of Kingfield's oldest buildings (1860s). It has a rustic interior with barn board and exposed beams. Try the chicken pot-pie at lunch. Open-air dining on the deck overlooking river. Kids' menu, early-bird suppers. No smoking. | Main St. (Rte. 27) | 207/265–4394 | $10–$15 | MC, V.

Nostalgia Tavern. Continental. You'll certainly find something to enjoy on this expansive menu; steak tips and scallops and salmon are among the favorites. Two-for-one entrées are offered Tuesday nights. The tavern is rustic and whimsical, with a post-and-beam interior and an array of antiques, including a collection of snowmen figurines. | Rte. 27, N. Kingfield | 207/265–2559 | Closed Mon. | $8–$15 | D, MC, V.

Lodging

Herbert Inn. Built by the Carrabassett River in 1917, this inn has antiques, ornate woodwork, and marble terrazzo floors. Dining room, complimentary Continental breakfast. No air-conditioning in some rooms, in-room hot tubs, no room phones, no TV in some rooms, TV in common area. Massage. Pets allowed. | Main St. (Rte. 27) | 207/265–2000 or 800/843–4372 | fax 207/265–4594 | herbert@somtel.com | www.mainemountaininn.com | 27 rooms, 4 suites | $99–$119, $119–$149 suites | AE, D, DC, MC, V.

Inn on Winter's Hill. The inn is divided into the original Georgian Revival section with a restaurant and king-size luxury rooms, and a more contemporary 1989 addition. It's 15 mi from Sugarloaf. Cable TV. Indoor and outdoor pools. Hot tub. No pets. | Winter's Hill Rd. | 207/265–5421 | fax 207/265–5424 | www.wintershill.com | 20 rooms | $85–$150 | AE, D, MC, V.

KITTERY

INTRO
ATTRACTIONS
DINING
LODGING

KITTERY

MAP 3, B12

(Nearby towns also listed: The Yorks; Portsmouth, NH)

In recent years, Kittery—the gateway to Maine—has come to be known as one thing: Outlet Heaven (or Hell, depending on your orientation). Flanked on either side of U.S. 1 are over 120 stores, which attract hordes of shoppers year-round. Prior to Liz Claiborne and Dansk, however, Kittery had long been known as the home of the Portsmouth Naval Shipyard. Yet Kittery (Maine's oldest town) and Kittery Point have an abundance of historic sights and buildings, oceanfront, and off-the-beaten path wild spaces.

Information: **Chamber of Commerce** | U.S. 1, Kittery, 03904 | 207/439–7545 or 800/639–9645 | info@gatewaytomaine.org | www.gatewaytomaine.org. **State of Maine Visitor Information Center** | I–95 and U.S. 1, Box 396, Kittery, 03904 | 207/439–1319.

Attractions

Factory Outlet Stores. Over 120 name-brand outlet stores—including Eddie Bauer, J. Crew, DKNY, Esprit, and Ralph Lauren—line U.S. 1. Grab your credit cards and join the shop-till-you-drop crowds that swarm this chain of strip malls year-round. | U.S. 1 | Free | Daily, hrs vary from store to store.

Fort Foster Park. This 1872 fort was part of a military installation that was active until 1949. Now, white-sand beach, picnic and play areas, and exploring make up the activity. The park is open year-round to pedestrians; hours listed below apply to parking. | Pocahontas Rd., Kittery Point | 207/439–3800 | $10 per car, $5 per person to walk in | June–Aug., daily 10–7; May and Sept., weekends 10–7.

Fort McClary. Built in 1690 to protect the mouth of the Piscataqua River, the fort's prominent historical feature is its 1812 blockhouse. It's in a scenic harbor and has ocean views. | Rte. 103, Kittery Point | 207/439–2845 | $1 | Memorial Day–end Sept., daily 9–8.

Hamilton House. This Georgian Colonial house-museum with formal gardens, 5 mi from Kittery Point, overlooks the Salmon Falls River and was featured in Sarah Orne Jewett's novel *The Tory Lover.* "Sundays in the Garden," a summer concert series, presents musical offerings ranging from classical to folk. | Vaughan's La., South Berwick | 207/384–2454 | $4 | June–mid-Oct., Wed.–Sun. 11–5.

Kittery Foreside. This small commercial neighborhood at Wallingford Square contains a concentration of some of Kittery's nicer galleries, cafes, and antiques stores. | Wallingford Sq.

Kittery Historical and Naval Museum. Kittery's rich naval history is represented with this interesting collection of all things nautical. | U.S. 1 at Rogers Rd. | 207/439–3080 | $3 | June–Oct., Tues.–Sat 10–4, or by appointment; Nov.–May, by appointment.

Lady Pepperell's Mansion. Built in 1760, this private residence is a splendid example of the lavish Palladian style of architecture. The home is not open for tours, and can only be enjoyed from the outside. | Rte. 103, Kittery Point.

Sarah Orne Jewett House. The house dates from 1774, and the Jewett family lived here when author Sarah Orne Jewett was born in 1849. Now a museum, the house contains period furnishings. Jewett's bedroom remains as she left it. | 5 Portland St., South Berwick | 207/384–2454 | www.spnea.org | $4 | June–mid-Oct., Wed.–Sun. 11–5.

ON THE CALENDAR
JUNE: *Strawberry Festival.* Amid all the berries, there's a juried crafts show and live entertainment scheduled throughout the day. | South Berwick | 207/384–2263 | www.southberwickme.com.
JUNE–AUG.: *Sundays in the Garden.* This concert series presents musical offerings ranging from classical to folk in the formal gardens of Hamilton House. | 207/384–2454.
SEPT.: *Septemberfest.* This annual events focuses on life in the great outdoors—there are wilderness training and first-aid demonstrations, crafts, and events for the kids. | Kittery Trading Post, U.S. 1 | 207/439–2700.

Dining
Cap'n Simeon's Galley. Seafood. The dining room has a nautical theme with a heavy-beamed ceiling and a panorama embracing the pier, lighthouses, islands, and historic forts. It's great for kids. Try the fresh broiled haddock. Live music (acoustic to folk) in the lounge on weekends. Kids' menu. Sunday brunch. No smoking. | 90 Pepperell Rd. (Rte. 103), Kittery Point | 207/439–3655 | Closed Tues. Columbus Day–Memorial Day | $10–$25 | AE, D, MC, V.

Sunrise Grill. American. This restaurant provides a daytime alternative to the many seafood restaurants in Kittery. Pancakes, waffles, taco salad, and burgers are the favorites. The Grill is simply appointed with booths and a breakfast bar, but abundant fresh flowers add a touch of freshness. | 182 State Rd. | 207/439–5748 | Breakfast also available; no dinner | $6–$8 | No credit cards.

Warren's Lobster House. Seafood. This casual eatery was built right over the wharf and has water views. Try the lobster Thermidor. Open-air dining on the deck. Salad bar. Kids' menu. Dock space. No smoking. | 11 Water St. | 207/439–1630 | www.lobsterhouse.com | $10–$30 | AE, MC, V.

Lodging
Coachman Inn. Convenient to the Maine Turnpike and outlet shopping. Complimentary Continental breakfast. Cable TV. Pool. Business services. | 380 U.S. 1 | 207/439–4434 or 800/824–6183 | fax 207/439–6757 | 43 rooms | $105–$129 | AE, D, MC, V.

Days Inn Kittery/Portsmouth. Typical of the chain, near the New Hampshire border, convenient to outlet shopping. Bar, complimentary Continental breakfast. Microwaves, refrigerators, cable TV. Pool. Sauna. Gym. Laundry facilities. Business services. Free parking. | 2

Gorges Rd. | 207/439–5555 | fax 207/439–5555 | dayinn5078@aol.com | www.daysinn.com | 108 rooms | $89–$115 | AE, D, DC, MC, V.

Inn at Portsmouth Harbor. This brick Victorian home, with many antiques, is fully modernized. The inn offers a view of the Piscataqua River and Portsmouth Harbor, and is an ideal getaway for couples. Complimentary breakfast. In-room data ports, cable TV. No pets. No kids under 16. No smoking. | 6 Water St. | 207/439–4040 | fax 207/438–9286 | www.innatportsmouth.com | 5 rooms | $135–$175 | MC, V.

LEWISTON-AUBURN

MAP 3, C9

(Nearby town also listed: Poland Spring)

The Androscoggin River divides the twin cities of Lewiston and Auburn (L/A), yet their names are often uttered in the same breath. The river's powerful falls first attracted Native Americans for their rich stocks of salmon. Later, industrialists harnessed the falls' energy, creating a textile boom in the 19th century that attracted masses of Québecois and Acadian French, whose culture remains a large part of the cities' makeup. Large mills sprang up along the banks of the river, turning out such products as cotton and shoes. The roar of these mills has recently quieted, and L/A are currently in the throes of a renaissance, working to shake off their mill-town images. Lewiston, the second-largest city in the state, is home to Bates College, which offers numerous cultural programs. The cities share impressive churches and stately homes, as well as a lively arts scene, and they serve as gateways to many of the area's lakes and mountains.

LEWISTON-AUBURN

INTRO
ATTRACTIONS
DINING
LODGING

Information: Androscoggin County Chamber of Commerce | 179 Lisbon St., Lewiston, 04240 | 207/783–2249 | infor@androscoggincounty.com | www.androscoggincounty.com.

Attractions

Androscoggin Historical Society Library and Museum. A museum with an extensive collection of census and cemetery records and genealogical resources. | County Building, 2 Turner St., Auburn | 207/784–0586 | Donation suggested | Wed.–Fri. 9–noon and 1–5.

Atrium Gallery. This gallery on the campus of Lewiston-Auburn College has year-round exhibits. Local artists' works are shown in winter, and there is an art auction in spring. Franco-American exhibits are frequently highlighted as well. | 51 Westminster St. | 207/753–6554 or 207/753–6500 | www.usm.maine.edu/lac/art/art.html | Free | Daily.

Bates College. Bates is a prestigious liberal arts college established in 1864. | Campus Ave., Lewiston | 207/786–6255 or 207/786–6330 | www.bates.edu | Daily.
Mt. David. A 350-ft hill on the Bates College campus provides views of the Androscoggin Valley and Mt. Washington in New Hampshire. | 207/786–6255 | Free | Daily.
Olin Arts Center. This college museum provides space for traveling exhibits and displays from its permanent collection, including works from the 18th to 20th centuries and works by Marsden Hartley, a Lewiston native. | 75 Russell St., Lewiston | 207/786–6158 museum, 207/785–6135 center | Free | Tues.–Sat. 10–5, Sun. 1–5.

Lost Valley Ski Area. A family ski area with excellent snowmaking, night skiing, ski schools, and, for those pressed for time, hourly rates. | Lost Valley Rd., Auburn | 207/784–1561 | www.lostvalleyski.com | Call for details | Dec.–mid-Mar., daily.

Mount Apatite Park. This 325-acre park provides diverse activities, from mineral sleuthing to hiking to snowshoeing. There is no vehicle access on the park property, but parking is available at the park's entrance. From the Maine Turnpike, take exit 12, travel 3 mi and take a left on Minot Avenue; travel 2 mi and take a right on Garfield Road; continue another 2 mi and look for the park's entrance behind a baseball diamond and a National Guard building. | 207/784–0191 | Free | Daily dawn–dusk.

ON THE CALENDAR

MAY: *Maine State Parade.* Maine's largest parade, drawing over 30,000 spectators and participants from all over the state to see the floats. | Throughout Lewiston | 207/783–2249.

JULY: *Moxie Festival.* A homage to the Depression-era soft drink that was spawned by one Dr. Augustin Thompson's 1885 Moxie Nerve Food. Booths, expansive parade, food booths, recipe contest, and collectibles exhibits and sales. | Lisbon Rd. (Rte. 196), downtown Lisbon Falls | 207/783–2249.

JULY: *Lewiston-Auburn Garden Tour.* Ten gardens on display to benefit the Maine Music Society. | Throughout towns of Lewiston-Auburn | 207/782–1403 | $10–$12.

JULY–AUG.: *Bates Dance Festival.* Classes, workshop, lectures, and performances are included in this four-week festival on the Bates College Campus. | Campus Ave., Lewiston | 207/786–6381.

JULY–AUG.: *Festival de Joie.* A multicultural heritage celebration, featuring ethnic food, dances, music, and children's activities. | Central Maine Civic Center, Lewiston | 207/782–9265.

AUG.: *Great Falls Balloon Festival.* Hot-air balloon launches and rides (by reservation), food, games, road races, and live entertainment. | DowntownLewiston–Auburn | 207/783–2249.

Dining

Graziano's Casa Mia. Italian. This rambling, multiroom restaurant, 10 mi southwest of Auburn, is packed floor-to-ceiling with boxing memorabilia. Try the eggplant Parmesan or lasagna. Live jazz on Friday. Kids' menu. No smoking. | Lisbon Rd. (Rte. 196), Lisbon | 207/353–4335 | Closed Mon. | $8–$16 | D, MC, V.

Marco's. Italian. You can enjoy chicken Parmesan or seafood marinara in a classic room with exposed brick walls, oak accents, and burgundy linens. | 177 Lisbon St. | 207/783–0336 | Closed Sun. in summer | $8–$16 | AE, D, DC, MC, V.

Marois Restaurant. Eclectic. A Lewiston landmark since 1919, these two dining rooms have chandeliers, gilded mirrors, and art prints. It is known for Greek, French, Italian, American, and Cajun cooking. Kids' menu, early-bird suppers Monday–Thursday. No smoking. | 249 Lisbon St., Lewiston | 207/782–9055 | $10–$20 | AE, DC, MC, V.

Lodging

Auburn Inn. Near the turnpike and industrial parks, the Auburn Inn is en route to the lakes and mountains. Restaurant. Some refrigerators, cable TV. Pool. | 1777 Washington St., Auburn | 207/777–1777 | fax phone/fax: 207/777–1777 | 114 rooms | $70–$80 | AE, D, DC, MC, V.

Chalet Motel. A standard motel with services that is near Maine Turnpike's exit 13 and convenient to downtown businesses. Restaurant, bar, picnic area. Some kitchenettes, some refrigerators, cable TV. Pool. Hot tub, sauna. Laundry facilities. Business services. | 1243 Lisbon St., Lewiston | 207/784–0600 or 800/733–7787 | fax 207/786–4214 | 67 rooms, 8 suites | $45–$50, $60–$85 suites | AE, D, DC, MC, V.

Coastline Inn. This thoroughly modern facility is most notable for its location in the heart of Auburn. Complimentary Continental breakfast. In-room data ports, some microwaves, some refrigerators, cable TV. Laundry facilities. Pets allowed. | 170 Center St. | 207/784–1331 or 800/470–9494 | fax 207/786–2286 | www.coastlineinnmaine.com | 69 rooms, 3 suites | $72–$85 | AE, D, MC, V.

Ramada Inn. This chain option is convenient to downtown businesses, the turnpike, and Bates College. Restaurant, bar with entertainment, complimentary Continental breakfast. In-room data ports, cable TV. Pool. Hot tub, sauna. Exercise equipment. Laundry facilities. Business services. | 490 Pleasant St., Lewiston | 207/784–2331 | fax 207/784–2332 | www.ramadamaine.com | 117 rooms | $80–$100 | AE, D, DC, MC, V.

Super 8. A chain hotel that is convenient to the turnpike and downtown businesses. Complimentary Continental breakfast. Cable TV. | 1440 Lisbon St., Lewiston | 207/784–8882 | fax 207/784–1778 | www.super8.com | 49 rooms | $62 | AE, D, DC, MC, V.

Travel Motel. Although this motel is in Lewiston proper, it is surrounded by wooded lots that give a sense of quiet and calm. Extensive remodeling was undertaken in 1999, and the rooms are crisp and modern. Complimentary Continental breakfast. Some kitchenettes, microwaves, refrigerators, cable TV. Pool. Basketball. No pets. | 1968 Lisbon Rd., Lewiston | 207/784–5476 | 28 rooms | $40–$85 | AE, D, MC, V.

LINCOLN

MAP 3, F6

(Nearby town also listed: Millinocket)

A haven for outdoors enthusiasts, the greater Lincoln area encompasses more than 13 lakes and ponds. There's skiing at nearby Mt. Jefferson, water sports on the Penobscot River, and miles of snowmobile trails connected to Lincoln. The town itself, situated between the Penobscot River and Mattanawcook Lake, is small and friendly, easily accessed from Interstate 95.

Information: Greater Lincoln Area Chamber of Commerce | 75 Main St., Lincoln, 04457 | 207/794–8065 | www.mainrec.com/linchome.html.

Attractions

Lee Historical Society Museum. Formerly Lee's Town Hall, every floor of this three-story 1919 building, 12 mi east of Lincoln, is filled with artifacts dating back to Victorian times. Items from furniture to toys to musical instruments, are represented. | Rte. 6, Lee | 207/738–5014 | $2 (suggested) | Memorial Day–Veteran's Day, Wed. and weekends 1–4.

Mt. Jefferson Ski Area. A ski area 12 mi east of Lincoln, on Route 6 in Lee, that caters to families, most of whom live in the area. | 207/738–2377 | $15. | Jan.–Mar., Tues.–Thurs. and weekends.

ON THE CALENDAR
APR.: *Piscataquis River Canoe Race.* Paddlers take on the 8-mi course from Guilford to Dover-Foxcroft. A shorter race, geared for families, also takes place. It starts in Guilford. | 207/564–7533.

Dining
Wing Wah Restaurant. Chinese. You'll find traditional fare and decorative touches, right in the center of Lincoln. Popular dishes include the "Wing Wah Special," seafood and vegetables over lo mein noodles, and "Four Happiness," a shrimp, chicken, beef, and pork combination. | 76 Main St. | 207/794–3001 | $10–$25 | AE, D, MC, V.

Lodging
Briarwood Motor Inn. A standard motel by Interstate 95 and 1 mi south of Lincoln that is convenient to stores and services. Refrigerators available, cable TV. Pets allowed. | U.S. 2 and Rte. 6, on Outer W. Broadway | 207/794–6731 | 24 rooms | $65 | AE, D, MC, V.

Dunloggin' Bed and Breakfast. All the rooms in this 1980 home 12 mi east of Lincoln have a view of Mattakeunk Lake, and you can borrow the Dunloggin's boat to paddle across the water. In addition to breakfast, the inn offers High Teas every Wednesday from mid-June to mid-October. Complimentary breakfast. Some room phones. Dock. Pets allowed. No smoking. | Just off Rte. 6 at Silver Lake | 207/738–5014 | www.dunlogbnb.com | 3 rooms | $60 | D, MC, V.

LINCOLNVILLE

MAP 3, E9

(Nearby town also listed: Camden)

Just east of Camden on U.S. 1, Lincolnville is a quick strip of beachfront speckled with restaurants, inns, and antiques shops. Farther inland, Lincolnville Center is a rural outpost with a number of lakes and ponds, plus good back roads for biking. Both provide easy access to nearby Camden Hills State Park; the ferry for Islesboro departs from the Lincolnville waterfront.

Information: Camden-Rockport-Lincolnville Chamber of Commerce | Public Landing, Camden, 04843 | 207/236–4404 or 800/223–5459 | chamber@camdenme.org | www.visitcamden.com.

Attractions

Islesboro. Three miles offshore from Lincolnville, Islesboro is small island town whose population doubles and triples in summer. The island is separated into two parts by the Narrows: the north shore is the more rustic, working waterfront of the island; the southern shore is home to the exclusive summer community of Dark Harbor. A jaunt to this 12-mi-long island makes a great day trip, particularly for cyclists, but the narrow, winding roads tend to get congested in the high season.

Sailor's Memorial Museum. Dedicated to the memory and experiences of the mariners of Islesboro, this small museum contains nautical artifacts, paintings, and models. | 615 Ferry Rd. | 207/734–2253 | Donation suggested | July–Labor Day, Tues.–Sun. 10–4:30.

Kelmscott Farms. A rare-breeds farm established in 1995, the nonprofit conservation learning center has more than 200 animals and 10 species of rare livestock. The most common animals at the farm are Cotswold sheep, and many of the farm programs involve them. Special events are held throughout the year. | Rte. 52, 4 mi from Lincolnville | 207/763–4088 | fax 207/763–4298 | www.kelmscott.org | $5 | May–Oct., Tues.–Sun. 10–5; Nov.–Apr., Tues.–Sun. 10–3.

Maine State Ferry Service. The ferryboat *Margaret Chase Smith* makes the 3-mi, 20-minute crossing between Lincolnville and Islesboro several times daily, depending on the season. | U.S. 1, Lincolnville Beach | 207/789–5611 or 207/624–7777 | $4.50, $8 bicycles, $14 cars | Daily 7:30–5.

Schoolhouse Museum. This site still retains the original charming features from its days as a school. You will find prehistoric artifacts, implements used by Lincolnville's original settlers, and a vast array of genealogical research materials. | Rte. 173, 1/8 mi from U.S. 1 | 207/789–5445 | www.booknotes.com/lhs | Free | End June–Sept., Mon., Wed., and Fri. 1–4. Call about weekends.

ON THE CALENDAR

JUNE: *Rare Breeds Weekend.* If you've never seen a Kerry Cow or an Old Spots Pig, this is your chance. And don't worry if you miss the event, Kelmscott Farm is open weekends all summer long. | Kelmscott Farm (Off Rte. 52) | 207/763–4088.

Dining

Lobster Pound. Seafood. You can eat on the enclosed patio while looking at the lobster tanks or water views at this restaurant 6 mi north of Lincolnville. It's known for fish, turkey, steak, pasta, and the homemade desserts. Open-air dining on the patio. Kids' menu. | U.S. 1, Lincolnville Beach | 207/789–5550 | Reservations essential | Closed end Oct.–May | $25–$35 | AE, D, DC, MC, V.

Youngtown Inn. French. Rack of lamb, lobster ravioli, and soufflés are some of the favorite dishes presented by renowned chef Manuel Mercier. The inn has an extensive wine menu and includes a fine pub. | Rte. 52 and Youngtown Rd. | 207/763–4290 or 800/291–8438 | Closed Mon.–Tues. Oct.–June | $16–$25 | AE, MC, V.

Lodging
Youngtown Inn. This 1810 bed-and-breakfast has been glowingly reviewed in national journals such as *Better Homes and Gardens*. The rooms are bright and tasteful. And you won't need to travel far to locate a good meal or a drink, as the inn has an outstanding French restaurant and a pub. Complimentary breakfast. No room phones, no TV in some rooms. No smoking. | Rte. 52 and Youngtown Rd. | 207/763–4290 or 800/291–8438 | www.youngtowninn.com | 5 rooms, 1 suite | $110–$150 | Closed 2 wks in Apr. | AE, MC, V.

LUBEC

MAP 3, H7

(Nearby town also listed: Eastport)

The nation's easternmost town, Lubec often gets bypassed by travelers en route to Campobello Island. But with its dramatic tides, scenic Quoddy Head State Park, and open coastline, Lubec is worth more than just a passing glance. The town, settled in 1780, was once part of Eastport, which is just across the bay. Lubec was formerly home to numerous sardine-canning plants, but now they've closed and it's just a sleepy fishing village. Buildings and homes crowd along the water's edge in town, where you are highly likely to spot numerous seals and the occasional bald eagle.

Information: Lubec Chamber of Commerce | Box 123, Lubec, 04652-0123 | 207/733–4522.

Attractions
Quoddy Head State Park. This 480-acre park is the easternmost point in the nation and has dramatic views from 90-ft cliffs overlooking the Bay of Fundy, as well as the famed red-and-white striped lighthouse (1858). | South Lubec Rd. | 207/733–0911 | $1 | Mid-May–mid-Oct., daily 9–dusk.

Roosevelt Campobello International Park. Connected to Lubec by the Franklin Roosevelt Memorial Bridge, this 2,800-acre preserve, 1½ mi east of town, is where FDR spent his summers until 1921. It is the only international park in the world, administered jointly by Canada and the United States. As it is located within the province of New Brunswick, the park is within the Atlantic Time Zone, and is one hour ahead of Eastern Standard Time. | Off Rte. 189, Campobello Island, New Brunswick, Canada | 506/752–2922 | www.fdr.net | Free | Late May–Columbus Day, daily 10–6.

Roosevelt Cottage. Within the 2,800-acre Roosevelt Campobello International Park are the cottage and the grounds where Franklin Roosevelt vacationed. | Welshpool St. (Rte. 774), Campobello Island, New Brunswick, Canada | 506/752–2922 | Free | Mid-May–mid-Oct., weekdays 8–5.

ON THE CALENDAR
JULY: *Annual County Fair.* An old-time fair with food, live entertainment, activities for the kids, and other events. | 207/733–4522.

Dining
Home Port Inn. Seafood. A cozy, nine-table dining room in a Victorian country inn with garden views. Known for local fish dishes. Beer and wine only. No smoking. | 45 Main St. | 207/733–2077 | Closed mid-Oct.–mid-June. No lunch | $12–$25 | D, MC, V.

Phinney's Seaview. Seafood. This bright, casual dining room and lounge is perched on a hill above Johnsons Bay. It's known for lobster and you can see the lobster cookers outside.

Open-air dining on the deck. Live music on weekends. Kids' menu. No smoking. | Rte. 189 | 207/733–0941 | Closed Nov.–Mar. | $7–$20 | MC, V.

Uncle Kippy's. American. Shrimp supreme in Alfredo sauce, and baked stuffed haddock are offered in this large, open room. The restaurant is decorated in classic burgundy tones. | Rte. 189, County Rd. | Closed Mon. | $7–$17 | MC, V.

Lodging

Bayviews. This turn-of-the-20th-century farmhouse abuts Johnson Bay. The property includes a meadow, perennial gardens, and evergreens. Complimentary breakfast. No room phones, TV in common area. No pets. No smoking. | 6 Monument St. | 207/733–2181 | 3 rooms, 1 suite | $50–$80 | Closed for winter and early spring | No credit cards.

Eastland Motel. A small, family-oriented motel in the country, set back from the highway. It's minutes from Quoddy Head State Park, the home of the famous candy-stripe lighthouse that has guided Down East mariners for generations. Complimentary Continental breakfast. Cable TV. Some pets allowed. | Rte. 189 | 207/733–5501 | fax 207/733–2932 | eastland@nemaine.com | www.nemaine.com/eastland | 20 rooms | $54–$64 | AE, D, MC, V.

Home Port Inn. A late-19th-century inn with period furnishings. Restaurant, picnic area, complimentary Continental breakfast. No room phones, no in-room TVs, TV in common area. Library. No smoking. | 45 Main St. | 207/733–2077 or 800/457–2077 | carmant@nemaine.com | www.quoddyloop.com/hp1 | 7 rooms | $65–$85 | Closed mid-Oct.–late May | D, MC, V.

Owen House. On the water overlooking Passamaquoddy Bay. Complimentary breakfast. No room phones, TV in common area. No smoking. | 11 Welshpool St., Campobello Island, New Brunswick, Canada E0G 3H0 | 506/752–2977 | owen@campnet.nb.ca | www.campnet.nb.ca/~owen/ | 9 rooms (5 with private bath) | $62–$95 | Closed mid-Oct.–late May | V.

Peacock House. This 1860 Victorian home mixes modern and antique accents. Several rooms have good views of Fundy Bay, which surrounds this house on three sides. Complimentary breakfast. No room phones, some in-room cable TV and VCRs. No pets. No kids under 7. No smoking. | 27 Summer St. | 207/733–2403 | www.peacockhouse.com | 2 rooms, 3 suites | $70–$80 | Closed Oct. 15–May 15 | MC, V.

MACHIAS

MAP 3, H8

(Nearby towns also listed: Eastport, Lubec)

The Machias River flows through historic Machias, the county seat of Washington County. Machias is Micmac Indian for "bad little falls," and those very falls boil in the town's center. The first Revolutionary War naval battle took place here in 1775, when feisty local patriots took the British man-of-war *Margaretta*. The town grew prosperous with the lumbering and shipbuilding boom, but the blueberry is now top dog. (There's a large-scale blueberry festival held here each summer.) The downtown is a hilly ramble of stores, and the town claims a branch of the University of Maine. Machias also serves as a good base for exploring the area's scenic coastline.

Information: Machias Bay Area Chamber of Commerce | 112 Dublin St., Machias, 04654 | 207/255–4402 | mbacc@nemaine.com | www.nemaine.com/mbacc.

Attractions

Bad Little Falls Park. These falls, for which Machias is named, are a must-see. Right in the center of town, there is a also small park with picnic benches, and a bridge spanning the gorge of this lovely stretch of the river. | U.S. 1 | Free | Daily dawn–dusk.

Bold Coast Trail. Cutler Coast on Washington County's "Bold Coast" contains almost 5 mi of dramatic cliff-bound ocean shore. A network of hiking trails follows most of the shore, providing access to remote hike-in campsites, then returns to the trailhead through the stunted spruce, heaths, and grasslands of the interior. | Rte. 191, Cutler | 207/827–5936 | Free | Daily.

Burnham Tavern Museum. The oldest building in eastern Maine and the only one with a Revolutionary War history, this tavern served as a meeting place for planning the first naval battle of the Revolution. The gambrel-roof tavern was built in 1770 by Mary and Joe Burnham. It contains authentic furnishings from the period, many of them donated by Burnham descendants. | Main St. | 207/255–4432 | $2.50 | June–Sept., weekdays 9–5; or by appointment.

Cobscook Bay State Park. *See* Eastport | In Edmonds Township, off U.S. 1 | 207/726–4412 | $2 | Daily, 24 hrs.

Fort O'Brien. Built in 1775 and destroyed by the British that same year, the four-gun Fort O'Brien was rebuilt, then destroyed by the British again in 1814. The first naval battle of the Revolutionary War was fought off this site, 5 mi east of town, five days before Bunker Hill. | Rte. 92 | 207/941–4014 | Free | Daily.

Great Wass Island. This 1,579-acre nature preserve at the tip of Beal Island offers excellent hiking and bird-watching. Trails lead through the woods and open onto the rocky coast and magnificent ocean views. From Jonesport, cross the bridge over Moosabec Reach to Beals Island, continue to Great Wass Island, and follow the road to Black Duck Cove (about 3 mi). | 207/729–5181 | Free | Daily dawn–dusk.

Jasper Beach. A wild, undeveloped ½-mi stretch of beach that is known for its smooth, reddish rocks. The beach, 4 mi south of Machias, is a seabird and wildlife habitat. There are no bathrooms, and no swimming, due to the powerful undertow. | Rte. 92 | Free | Daily dawn–dusk.

Puffin Watch. For an up-close look at these adorable birds, join Captain Barna Norton for a puffin-watching cruise to Machias Seal Island. The boat leaves from Jonesport Marina. Look for the boat called *Chief*. Call ahead, as reservations are required. | 207/497–5933 | $50 for 5-hr cruise | Cruises leave Memorial Day–Labor Day, daily at 7 AM.

THE TERM "DOWN EAST"

To avoid getting hopelessly turned around in Maine, you must understand the term "Down East." For most people, the term "down" refers to south, as in "down south." Things are sort of turned around in Maine.

Say you are in the Midcoast town of Camden, and you need directions. You will be told (depending on who you ask) you need to go up to Portland and down to Bar Harbor. According to your map, Bar Harbor is decidedly up and Portland clearly down. But before you knock the bejesus out of your compass, you should know how this oddball orientation came about.

During the 18th and 19th centuries, Maine was a leading shipping center. Schooners carrying cargo from Boston to Maine caught the prevailing winds that blow from the southwest, pushing vessels downwind to the east. So, although ships were sailing up the Maine coast, they were actually traveling down with the wind. Hence, the term "Down East."

Too confusing? You can solve the problem by simply saying that you're planning to travel "up Down East."

© Artville

Roque Bluffs State Park. With a pebble beach on the ocean and a freshwater pond, this unique day-use park, 7 mi south of town, has both saltwater and freshwater swimming. There are picnic areas, changing areas with toilets, and playgrounds. | U.S. 1 | 207/255–3475 | $1 | Memorial Day–late Sept.

Ruggles House. A Federal-style house with intricately carved interiors and a magnificent flying staircase that is 20 mi south of town. It has been restored and furnished with period pieces. | Main St., Columbia Falls | 207/483–4637 or 207/546–7903 | $3 suggested donation | June–mid-Oct., Mon.–Sat. 9–4:30, Sun. 11–4:30.

ON THE CALENDAR
JULY: *Jonesport Lobster Boat Races.* Part of Jonesport's Fourth of July celebration, these races let fisherfolk put the traps aside and cut loose. There are also a number of activities and events going on in town, including public suppers, games, and fireworks. | Main St., Jonesport | 207/255–4402.

★ **AUG.: *Wild Blueberry Festival.*** This big berry blowout has been taking place for a quarter century and has a fish fry, crafts fair, parade, entertainment, and blueberry dessert buffet and pancake breakfast. | Centered around Center St. Congregational Church | 207/255–4402.

Dining
Bluebird Ranch. American. Seafood Alfredo vies with fried clams and shrimp as this restaurant's most popular dishes. You'll relish their homemade pies, especially their blueberry pies in August, when the berries are freshest. One room has nautical themes, while another pays homage to the region's wild blueberries. | 3 E. Main St. | 207/355–3351 | Breakfast also available | $7–$19 | AE, D, MC, V.

Riverside Inn. Contemporary. The small and large dining rooms in this carefully restored 1805 inn, 3½ mi north of town, have Victorian furnishings and river views. It's known for its all-inclusive menu that changes nightly and features fresh seafood, pasta, veal, and pork. BYOB. No smoking. | U.S. 1, East Machias | 207/255–4134 | www.riversideinn-maine.com | Reservations essential | Closed Sun.–Wed. No lunch | $14–$19 | AE, MC, V.

Lodging
Bluebird Motel. A rural motel 1 mi west of Machias that is near both downtown and the ocean. Cable TV. Pets allowed. | U.S. 1 | 207/255–3332 | 40 rooms | $60 | AE, MC, V.

Maineland Motel. This basic roadside motel is 1 mi east of town and near ocean and downtown. Picnic area. No air-conditioning in some rooms, some refrigerators, microwaves available, cable TV. Some pets allowed. | U.S. 1, East Machias | 207/255–3334 | maineland@memaine.com | www.freeyellow.com/members8/visitmaine | 30 rooms | $48–$53 | AE, D, DC, MC, V.

Riverside Inn. This 1805 inn is right on the East Machias tidal river, allowing you frequent sightings of eagles, seals, and other wildlife. The grounds have splendid vegetable and flower gardens, as well as a pond and waterfall. The inn also runs a fine restaurant. Restaurant, complimentary breakfast. Some kitchenettes, cable TV, no room phones. No pets. No kids under 12. No smoking. | U.S. 1 | 207/255–4134 | fax 207/255–3580 | www.riversideinn-maine.com | 2 rooms, 2 suites | $85–$95 | AE, MC, V.

MILLINOCKET

MAP 3, E6

(Nearby town also listed: Allagash Wilderness Waterway)

The timber industry virtually created the town of Millinocket, when the need for labor to man a pulp paper mill turned it into a turn-of-the-20th-century boomtown. In an area where logging looms large, Millinocket itself is basically still a mill town, but it also serves as a gateway to Baxter State Park. Sprawling over 204,733 acres, Baxter is Maine's largest state park, home to the state's highest peak—Mt. Katahdin; it's a naturalist's paradise. Millinocket is the last urban outpost before heading into the park, and in the parking lot of the town's local grocery, you'll often see people stocking coolers and scrutinizing maps.

Information: Katahdin Area Chamber of Commerce | 1029 Central St., Millinocket, 04462 | 207/723–4443 | kacc@kai.net | www.millinocket.com.

Attractions

Baxter State Park. Mt. Katahdin, almost a mile high and at the northern end of the Appalachian Trail, is the dominant feature of this beautiful wilderness preserve that is 18 mi northwest of Millinocket and was donated to the state by Governor Percival Baxter. There are more than 75 mi of hiking trails, including those up Katahdin, but parking at trailheads fills up quickly in peak season. Camping requires reservations. Fly-fishing in the park can be outstanding. | 24 mi northwest of Millinocket, Baxter State Park Rd. | 207/723–5140 | Free for Maine vehicles, $8 for out-of-state vehicles.

Patten Lumberman's Museum. This museum 25 mi north of town is a tribute to the lumber industry in Maine as it was in the 1800s through 1930. Housed in nine buildings, it includes the tools of the trade and the various horse-drawn logging sleds and tote sleds. An 1820 logging camp shows how the people lived. | Rte. 11, Patten | 207/528–2650 | $2.50 | Fri.–Sun. 10–4.

GOLDEN ROAD

In the Moosehead/Katahdin region, logging has long been king. While there remains a great deal of controversy about logging practices (such as clear-cutting and forest management), the forest industry continues to allow outdoor enthusiasts right-of-way on their lands.

And one way you can explore the North Woods is via the Golden Road, a mostly unpaved, 96-mi-long road that cuts across the state from Millinocket to the Canadian border and passes Chesuncook and Seboomook lakes, the West Branch of the Penobscot, and the Ripogenus Dam.

In 1970, Great Northern Paper Company began construction of a road for logging vehicles. The road is 30 ft wide, allowing enough room to prevent passing 18-wheelers from running each other off the road. It was completed in 1975 at a cost of $3.2 million. The Golden Road is said to have earned its name from paper-company accountants: after the costs of construction were tallied, they noted the price tag was $45,000 per mile, as opposed to the $3,500 per mile that simple, earlier tote roads cost.

To use the Golden Road, you must register at paper-company checkpoints (enter at Rockwood, Millinocket, or Greenville), where you will pay fees for both access and camping, and will be given regulations to follow. You must always give right-of-way to logging trucks, and bicycles and motorcycles are not permitted. You should also keep your eyes peeled for moose—in terms of both safety and spectacle. Additionally, there are no amenities along the Golden Road, so stock your cooler and fill up your gas tank before embarking into the wilds.

© Artville

ON THE CALENDAR

AUG.: *Patten Beanhole Dinner.* This annual bean feed takes place at the Patten Lumberman's Museum, 25 mi north of town, where you can also see the tools and the lore of the loggers' lives. | Rte. 11, Patten | 207/528–2650.

SEPT.: *End of the Trail Festival.* This celebration of the Appalachian Trail's terminus at Baxter State Park has live banjo music, outdoor games and challenges, and arts-and-crafts displays. | Millinocket | 207/723–4443.

Dining

Big Moose Inn. Seafood. Blackened swordfish and seafood casserole are a few of the popular dishes you can enjoy while dining in this solarium with a view of the woods. | Baxter State Park Rd. | 207/723–8391 | Closed Columbus Day–May | $11–$19 | MC, V.

Scootic Inn and Penobscot Room. Seafood. In addition to baked, broiled, or blackened haddock and a seafood combo, the menu offers prime rib and a variety of Italian dishes. You can dine in the carpeted dining room with linens, or in the less-formal room with booths and tables. | 70 Penobscot Ave. | 207/723–4566 or 207/723–4567 | Reservations essential weekends | $10–$17 | D, MC, V.

Lodging

Best Western Heritage Motor Inn. This chain motel is convenient to Baxter State Park and local industry, as well as snowmobiling and rafting. Restaurant, bar, complimentary Continental breakfast. Cable TV. Hot tubs. Exercise equipment. Business services. Some pets allowed. | 935 Central St. | 207/723–9777 | fax 207/723–9777 | 49 rooms | $89 | AE, D, DC, MC, V.

Big Moose Inn. Sandwiched between Lakes Millinocket and Ambajejus, and 8 mi south of Baxter State Park and 8 mi north of Millinocket, the attraction here is the natural setting, rather than the conveniences. You should be prepared to share bathrooms, bring your own towels, and use a pay phone. Restaurant. Some kitchenettes, no room phones, TV in common area. Lake. Boating. No pets. | Baxter State Park Rd. | 207/723–8391 | fax 207/723–8199 | www.bigmoosecabins.com | 11 rooms (3 with shared baths), 11 cottages | $36–$40 rooms, $34–$38 cottages | Closed Columbus Day–May | MC, V.

Katahdin Inn. A business and tourist hotel that is near both Baxter State Park and Millinocket's paper mills. Bar, complimentary Continental breakfast. Some microwaves, some refrigerators, cable TV, some in-room VCRs. Pool, wading pool. Hot tub. Exercise equipment. Playground. Laundry facilities. Pets allowed. | 740 Central St. | 207/723–4555 | fax 207/723–6480 | 72 rooms, 10 suites | $65–$70, $90 suites | AE, D, DC, MC, V.

MONHEGAN ISLAND

MAP 3, D10

(Nearby towns also listed: Boothbay Harbor, Rockland)

This craggy 700-acre island, roughly (in every sense of the word) located 10 mi offshore, has long attracted the brush-and-canvas crowd, including such luminaries as Robert Henri, Rockwell Kent, and Edward Hopper. The island's history includes visits by Captain George Waymouth in 1605, and Captain John Smith in 1614. But the real draw of this island is its quiet calm and its inspiring coastline, which continues to attract painters. It's also a great spot for hikers and birders. The island's 17 mi of scenic hiking trails range from a stroll through Cathedral Woods to hand-to-toe climbing along spectacular cliff heads. There's not much in the way of nightlife (woe be to those who drag teens here); there are only a handful of rustic inns, hotels, art galleries, and eateries, a teeny town center, and not much else in terms of amenities. Visitors are also asked to observe a number of rules while on the island, but all these things are just part of the Monhegan mystique.

Information: Rockland-Thomaston Area Chamber of Commerce | Box 508, Rockland, 04841 | 207/596–0376 or 800/562–2529 | www.midcoast.com/~rtacc.

Attractions

***Balmy Days II* ferry trip from Boothbay Harbor.** This boat offers daily trips to Monhegan Island, leaving from Boothbay Harbor. | Pier 8, Commercial St., Boothbay Harbor | 207/633–2284 | www.anchorwatch.com/balmy | $30 round-trip, $9 1-hr excursion | June–Oct., daily.

Ferry from Port Clyde. Ferry rides to Port Clyde, a quaint fishing village with a lighthouse and museum. Pick up the ferry at the foot of Route 131. | Monhegan Thomaston Boat Line, Box 238, Port Clyde | 207/372–8848 | fax 207/372–8547 | www.monheganboat.com | $25 round-trip | Year-round, call for schedule.

Monhegan Historical and Cultural Museum. Attached to the 1856 Monhegan Lighthouse, the museum offers displays on the island's history, information on shipwrecks, and ecology exhibits. | 1 Lighthouse Hill | 207/596–7003 | $2 (suggested) | July–Sept., daily 11:30–3:30.
Monhegan Lighthouse. This 47-ft gray-granite conical tower is easily seen by the approaching ferries. The grounds are open to the public. | Free | Daily.

Dining

The Periwinkle. Seafood. Walnut-and-crabmeat-stuffed sole and broiled halibut are a few of the dishes served along with the island's only salad bar. The dining room has a nautical theme and works of art by local artists. | 100 Main St. | 207/594–5432 | Closed Columbus Day–Memorial Day | $13–$30 | MC, V.

Lodging

Island Inn. This scenic inn has a museum about the indigenous people of the island. Restaurant, complimentary breakfast. No air-conditioning, no room phones. | 1 Ocean Ave., Monhegan Island | 207/596–0371 | fax 207/594–5517 | islandinn@midcoast.com | www.islandinnmonhegan.com | 34 rooms (19 with shared bath), 4 suites | $120–$185, $185–$210 suites | Closed mid-Oct.–late May | AE, D, MC, V.

Monhegan House. This 1870s island inn in the center of Monhegan Island's village has long been a haven for artists, bird-watchers, and nature lovers. It has views of both the ocean and the lighthouse. Restaurant. No air-conditioning, no room phones. No smoking. | Monhegan House, Monhegan Is. | 207/594–7983 or 800/599–7983 | fax 207/596–6472 | 33 rooms (with shared bath) | $60–$145 | Closed mid-Oct.–late May | MC, V.

Trailing Yew. This inn reflects the island's undeveloped condition; only one building has electricity, kerosene lamps provide the lighting, and only one room has its own bath. Restaurant, complimentary breakfast and dinner. No room phones, no TV. Pets allowed. No smoking. | 8 Lobster Cove Rd., Monhegan Island | 207/596–0440 or 800/592–2520 | 37 (36 with shared bath) | $60 per person | Closed mid-Oct.–mid-May | No credit cards.

MOOSEHEAD LAKE

MAP 3, C6

(Nearby towns also listed: Greenville, Rockwood)

At 40 mi long and covering 117 mi, Moosehead Lake sprawls across the heart of the North Woods. Its most imposing feature is the 763-ft Mt. Kineo, which seems to surge up and shrug over the lake. Native Americans came to the base of the mountain, which is made of flint, to gather shards to make tools. For years, sportsmen and outdoor enthusiasts have made the inland trek (early on by railroad) to Maine's largest lake, and the trend continues. From moose-watching to fly-fishing to white-water rafting—and everything in between—there are enough recreational activities to keep you at a steady clip.

Information: **Moosehead Lake Region Chamber of Commerce** | Box 581, Main St. (Rte. 15), Greenville, 04441 | 207/695–2702 or 207/695–2026 | moose@moosehead.net | www.mooseheadarea.com and www.mooseheadlake.org.

Dining
Kelly's Landing. American. One mile from the center of town, this eatery, with open-air dining overlooking Moosehead Lake, will fill you up. Try hash browns, homemade muffins, and pastries for breakfast, and typical fare like veal Parmesan or pasta dishes for dinner. Kids' menu and full bar. | Rte. 15 | 520/394–2366 | Breakfast also available | $8–$17 | MC, V.

NEWCASTLE

MAP 3, D10

(Nearby towns also listed: Boothbay Harbor, Damariscotta, Pemaquid Peninsula, Wiscasset)

Newcastle is often mistakenly lumped together with the town of Damariscotta, which lies due east across the Damariscotta River. There's not a great deal to distinguish it from its neighbor—there's no downtown to speak of, save a historic church, tidy clapboard and brick houses, and Newcastle Square, with its imposing brick structure and 4½-way stop. This former shipbuilding town is now a pleasant, shady spot with an excellent nature preserve.

Information: **Damariscotta Region Chamber of Commerce** | Main St., Damariscotta, 04543 | 207/563–8340 | drcc@tidewater.net | www.drcc.org.

Attractions
Dodge Point Preserve. These 506 acres of waterfront on Damariscotta River, 3½ mi south of Newcastle, are used for swimming, hiking, fishing, cross-country skiing, and skating. | Fire La. | 207/563–1393 or 207–778–8231 | Free | Daily dawn–dusk.

YOUR FIRST-AID TRAVEL KIT

- ❏ Allergy medication
- ❏ Antacid tablets
- ❏ Antibacterial soap
- ❏ Antiseptic cream
- ❏ Aspirin or acetaminophen
- ❏ Assorted adhesive bandages
- ❏ Athletic or elastic bandages for sprains
- ❏ Bug repellent
- ❏ Face cloth
- ❏ First-aid book
- ❏ Gauze pads and tape
- ❏ Needle and tweezers for splinters or removing ticks
- ❏ Petroleum jelly
- ❏ Prescription drugs
- ❏ Suntan lotion with an SPF rating of at least 15
- ❏ Thermometer

Excerpted from Fodor's: How to Pack: Experts Share Their Secrets
© 1997, by Fodor's Travel Publications

St. Patrick's Church. This church, 2 mi north of town, was built in 1808 and is said to be the oldest surviving Catholic Church in New England. The cemetery dates to 1760. | Rte. 215 | 207/563–3240 | Donation suggested | Daily 8–dusk.

ON THE CALENDAR
JULY: *Saint Andrew's Lawn Party and Auction.* This festive event takes place at St. Andrew's Church on the second Saturday of the month. It raises money for local non-profit organizations by auctioning off everything from artwork to silver to boat rides and extravagant dinners. Live music and catered food add extra incentive to attend this philanthropic evening. | Glidden St. | 207/563–3533.

Dining
Newcastle Inn. French. This comfortable country inn has a fireplace, French doors, three separate dining areas (one with river and garden views), and a cocktail deck. There's a four-course, prix fixe menu. Try the lobster and seafood bouillabaisse or the steak au poivre. | 60 River Rd. | 207/563–5685 or 800/832–8669 | www.newcastleinn.com | $40 prix fixe | AE, D, MC, V.

Lodging
Newcastle Inn. Overlooking the tidal Damariscotta River, this three-story, colonial inn is within walking distance of downtown. It has elegant rooms and suites that are especially appropriate for honeymoons or anniversaries. Beds are queen or king and the dining room is excellent. Complimentary breakfast. | 60 River Rd. | 800/832–8669 or 207/563–5685 | fax 207/563–6877 | www.newcastleinn.com | 11 rooms, 3 suites | $145–$240 | AE, MC, V.

NORTHEAST HARBOR

MAP 3, F9

(Nearby towns also listed: Acadia National Park, Bar Harbor, Cranberry Isles, Southwest Harbor)

This august, exclusive summer community, located on the eastern flank of Mt. Desert Island, has long been a favorite destination for the "haves." Shingle-style cottages date back to the Victorian tourist boom, and its sheltered harbor is crammed with yachts in the high season. A stroll in either of the two well-maintained public gardens and the water views, however, are within everyone's means.

Information: Mt. Desert Chamber of Commerce | Box 675, Sea St., Northeast Harbor, 04662 | 207/276–5040.

Attractions
Asticou and Thuya Gardens. Asticou, Maine's finest Japanese garden, was created from the remnants of gardens by renowned horticulturist and landscape architect Beatrix Ferrand, with azaleas dominating. It is best viewed in spring. Thuya garden, also in Northeast Harbor, has an excellent reference library and a massive perennial collection. | Rte. 198, entering Northeast Harbor | 207/276–5130 | Free | Daily 7–dusk.

Beal and Bunker Ferry service. This ferry service runs from Town Dock in Northeast Harbor to Islesford on the Cranberry Isles. | 207/244–3575 | $10 | Call for schedule.

ON THE CALENDAR
DEC.: *Mount Desert Christmas Festival.* Take a step into a Norman Rockwell painting with the folks of Northeast Harbor who gather in town every year to celebrate the holiday season with a bonfire, fire-truck rides, Santa, caroling, and a community production of *It's a Wonderful Life.* | Main St. | 207/276–5039.

Dining

Colonel's Deli and Bakery. American. This family-owned restaurant and bakery has been serving homemade meals and desserts since 1984. At the restaurant, you can order French toast for breakfast, and steak, pizza, quiche, or fresh fish for dinner or lunch. Sit inside and look at the pricey paintings for sale on the walls or sit outside on the patio. Kids' menu. | 142 Main St. | 207/276–5147 | Closed Oct.–Apr. | $5–$13 | No credit cards.

Docksider. Seafood. The lobster roll here was voted best in the nation by *USA Today*. There's open-air dining through the take-out window on the deck. Kids' menu. Beer and wine only. | Sea St. | 207/276–3965 | Closed mid-Oct.–mid-May | $8–$23 | MC, V.

Redfield's. Continental. An elegant bistro with white walls, white linens, and French art on the walls. The cuisine is light and healthy. Try the lobster and cucumber timbale, and the famous crab cakes served with a sherry-Cajun sauce made from a secret recipe. It has a well-known, extensive wine list. No smoking. | 129 Main St. | 207/276–5283 | fax 207/276–9838 | redfield@acadia.net | Reservations essential | Closed Sun. early May–Sept.; closed Sun.–Thurs. Oct.–early May. Closed Mar. | $18–$26 | AE, MC, V.

Lodging

Asticou Inn. This Victorian inn, 1 mi north of Northeast Habor, is on the harbor next to the public dock. Dining room, bar with entertainment, room service. No air-conditioning, some kitchenettes, TV in common area. Pool. Tennis. Business services. | Rte. 3 | 207/276–3344 or 800/258–3373 | fax 207/276–3373 | asticou@acadia.net | www.asticou.com | 31 rooms in inn, 16 rooms in 5 cottages, 11 suites | $302–$347, $332–$382 suites | Closed Nov.–late May | MC, V.

Grey Rock Inn. In a mansion on a hill overlooking the harbor, this inn has large Victorian rooms and access to Acadia National Park with the trails directly outside the front door. Wicker furniture, Oriental rugs, and hardwood floors add a fresh twist. Complimentary breakfast. | Rte. 198, Harborside Rd. | 207/276–9360 | www.quickpage.com/g/greyrockinn | 8 suites | $155–$325 | MC, V.

Harbourside Inn. This comfortable three-story inn no longer has the harborside cottages that gave it its name more than 100 years ago. Many rooms have fireplaces, king-size beds, kitchenettes, oriental rugs, and bright, airy sunporches overlooking the tall pines surrounding the property. Continental Breakfast. In-room fireplaces. Hiking. No smoking. No children under 10. In room telephone. Private bath. | Rte. 198 | 207/276–3272 | www.harboursideinn.com | 14 rooms | $125–$195 | Closed mid-Sept.–mid June | MC, V.

Kimball Terrace Inn. Established in 1970, this marina-view hostelry has many private balconies and patios. Restaurant, room service. No air-conditioning, cable TV. Pool. Business services. | 10 Huntington Rd. | 207/276–3383 or 800/454–6225 | fax 207/276–4102 | kimballterrace@adacia.net | www.acadia.net/kimball | 70 rooms | $118–$145 | Closed mid-Oct.–mid-Apr. | AE, D, MC, V.

Maison Suisse Inn. An elegant, shingle-style cottage that is filled with period furnishings, surrounded by gardens, and near the ocean. Complimentary breakfast. No air-conditioning, cable TV. No smoking. | 144 Main St. | 207/276–5223 or 800/624–7668 | maison@acadia.net | www.maisonsuisse.com | 10 rooms, 4 suites | $135–$195, $205–$255 suites | Closed Nov.–Apr. | MC, V.

NORWAY

MAP 3, B9

(Nearby town also listed: Poland Spring)

This town on the south end of Lake Pennesseewassee (more conveniently referred to as Norway Lake) first saw European settlement in the late 18th century. Norway is usually coupled with its neighboring town, South Paris, and traffic often creeps past these two towns' gas stations and strip malls on Route 26. (Cars from Sunday River Ski Resort clog things in winter.) Commerce aside, the downtown looks old-fashioned, with churches and brick storefronts, and a pleasant village green lies at the far end of town.

Information: Oxford Chamber of Commerce | Box 167, South Paris, 04281 | 207/743–2281 | www.oxfordhills.com.

Attractions

Carter's X-C Ski Center. This site, 6 mi south of town, has 15 mi of beginning and intermediate trails with views of the Little Androscoggin River. The Welchville Inn, built in 1820, offers lodging on premises. Ski shop on site. | Rte. 26, Oxford | 207/539–4848 | $10 per day | Oct.–May, daily (weather permitting).

McLaughlin Garden and Horticultural Center. Begun by Bernard McLaughlin in 1936 and taken over by a nonprofit organization in 1996 following his death, this garden has about 100 different cultivars of lilac and mature collections of Maine wildflowers, hosta, daylilies, phlox, and more. There's also a 19th-century barn and house on the site, 1 mi north of Norway. The gift shop and tearoom are open year-round. Tours leave at 5:30 PM on Thursdays. | 97 Main St. (Rte. 26), South Paris | 207/743–8820 | fax 207/743–3977 | www.dma.net/grden | Donation suggested | May–mid-Oct., daily 8–8.

Oxford Plains Speedway. This speedway, 3 mi south of Norway, has stock-car racing, with the biggest event the True Value 250 on the Fourth of July weekend. Most racing is Saturday nights, but special events are held on other days. | Rte. 26 | 207/539–8865 | www.oxford-plains.com | $10 | May–mid-Oct.

Pennesseewassee Lake. This lake has a picnic area, swimming area, marina rentals, and a boat launch. | Rte. 118 just west of town | May–Oct., daily.

ON THE CALENDAR
JULY: *Sidewalk Art Festival.* The town's main drag is filled with art for viewing and for sale. | Main St. | 207/743–2281.
AUG.: *Bluegrass Festival.* This annual festival features a full weekend of sweet strings and harmonies. | Rose-Beck Farm, South Paris | 207/743–2281.
SEPT.: *Oxford County Fair.* A classic county fair with loads of livestock, foods, and amusements. | Oxford County Fairgrounds in the town of Oxford | 207/743–2281.

Dining

Barjo Restaurant. American. A bright and cheery eatery that is known for fried haddock, shrimp dinners, and chicken potpie. Salad bar. Kids' menu. No liquor. No smoking. | 449 Main St. | 207/743–5784 | $10–$15 | MC, D, V.

Maurice. French. You'll find formal dining in a turn-of-the-20th-century home with French Provincial furnishings 1 mi north of town. Try the coquilles St. Jacques. Sunday brunch. No smoking. | 113 Main St. (Rte. 26), South Paris | 207/743–2532 | No lunch Sat. | $11–$18 | AE, D, DC, MC, V.

Trolley House. American. This building began housing trolleys in 1898. Today hundred-year-old pictures from around the area hang on the walls. The menu has fresh boiled lobsters, to pasta, steaks, and excellent desserts like bread pudding and cheesecake. | 110 Main St. | 207/743–2211 | Closed Sun. | $10–$16 | AE, MC, V.

Lodging

Bear Mountain Inn. This rural inn, 8 mi west of Norway, is on 50 acres between Bear Lake and Bear Mountain and has been in operation since 1820. No air-conditioning in some rooms, some microwaves, some refrigerators. Hiking, horseback riding, beach, boating, fishing. | South Waterford | 207/583–4404 | fax 207/583–4404 | www.bearmtninn.com | 10 rooms (4 with share bath), 1 suite, 1 cottage | $90–$125, $250 suite, $160 cottage | MC, V.

Goodwin's Motel. This downtown South Paris motel is mi west of Norway. Microwaves, cable TV. Cross-country skiing, downhill skiing. Pets allowed. | 191 Main St. (Rte. 26), South Paris | 207/743–5121, 800/424–8803 outside ME | fax 207/743–5121 | 25 rooms | $52 | AE, D, DC, MC, V.

Inn Town Motel. This family-run, one-story motel offers simple accommodation generally to families or businesspeople. Rooms have either queen or double beds. Complimentary Continental breakfast. In-room data ports. | 58 Paris St. | 207/743–7706 | fax 207/743–5849 | www.maineguide.com/norway/inntownmotel | 29 rooms | $59 | AE, D, MC, V.

King's Hill Inn. In 1811 this was the home of Horatio King, who became the U.S. Postmaster General. Today it houses a Victorian inn filled with antiques and crystals. Rooms have views of the White Mountains and perennial gardens, and are within walking distance of Streaked Mountain trailheads. It is totally handicap accessible and 10 minutes southwest of town. No air-conditioning, no room phones, no TV. | 56 King Hill Rd., South Paris | 207/744–0204 | 6 suite | $125 | AE, D, MC, V.

Waterford Inn. A converted 1825 farmhouse on 25 secluded acres that is 8 mi west of Norway. Dining room, complimentary breakfast. No room phones. Cross-country skiing. Library. Pets allowed (fee). | 258 Chadbourne Rd., Waterford | 207/583–4037 | inne@gwi.net | 9 rooms (2 with shared bath) | $75–$110 | AE.

OGUNQUIT

MAP 3, B12

(Nearby towns also listed: Wells, The Yorks)

Ogunquit was once a quiet fishing village, but that all changed around the turn of the 20th century with the advent of the artist colony. It began with Charles Woodbury and his genteel female students dressed in starched Victorian whites dabbling along the shore; shortly thereafter, Hamilton Easter Field showed up with his clutch of bohemians—and things have not been quite the same since. Artists still flock to the area, but they have to share the coast with tourists instead of fisherfolk at this popular beachfront resort. Ogunquit Beach is one of the most favored in the area; Shore Road is the primary shopping area; Marginal Way is a picturesque waterfront walk; and Perkins Cove is a lively mix of working port and jumbled shops and restaurants. The trick to enjoying the area is to ditch the car and use the town's trolley service.

PACKING IDEAS FOR HOT WEATHER

- ❑ Antifungal foot powder
- ❑ Bandanna
- ❑ Cooler
- ❑ Cotton clothing
- ❑ Day pack
- ❑ Film
- ❑ Hiking boots
- ❑ Insect repellent
- ❑ Rain jacket
- ❑ Sport sandals
- ❑ Sun hat
- ❑ Sunblock
- ❑ Synthetic ice
- ❑ Umbrella
- ❑ Water bottle

*Excerpted from *Fodor's: How to Pack: Experts Share Their Secrets*
© 1997, by Fodor's Travel Publications

Information: **Ogunquit Chamber of Commerce** | Box 2289, U.S. 1, Ogunquit, 03907 | 207/646–2939 | www.ogunquit.org.

Attractions

★ **Marginal Way Walk.** A mile-long oceanside footpath that hugs the shore of a rocky promontory called Israel's Head. There are magnificent ocean vistas, impressive summer homes, tidal pools, flowering bushes, and benches on which to rest and take it all in. | Off Shore Rd. | Free | Daily.

Ogunquit Beach. A 3-mi-wide stretch of sand at the mouth of the Ogunquit River. Families gravitate toward the ends of the beach, while gay and lesbian visitors tend to congregate in the center. The less crowded section to the north is accessible by footbridge. Rest rooms, snack bar, changing area are among the amenities. | At the mouth of the Ogunquit River | Free | Daily.

Ogunquit Museum of American Art. This oceanfront concrete, slate, and glass building has sculptured gardens and superb water views. Inside there is an excellent collection that includes works by Winslow Homer, Marsden Hartley, Edward Hopper, and Louise Nevelson. | 183 Shore Rd. | 207/646–4909 | $4 | July–mid-Sept., Mon.–Sat. 10:30–5, Sun. 2–5.

Ogunquit Playhouse. This professional summer-stock theater, 1 mi south of town, has been rolling out the perennial favorites to appreciative crowds since 1933. | U.S. 1 | 207/646–2402, 207/646–5511 box office | www.ogunquitplayhouse.org | $27 | Mid-June–Labor Day.

Perkins Cove. This neck of land is connected to the mainland by Oarweed Road and by a pedestrian bridge. Once the site of many fish houses, the cove now draws tourists for the shops and restaurants. It's 1 mi east of U.S. 1. | Free | Daily.

ON THE CALENDAR

AUG.: *Sand Building Contest.* Try your hand at sculpting a sand creation or simply examine the efforts of others. Prizes awarded to both adult and kids' teams. | Main Beach. | 207/646–2939.

SEPT.: *Capriccio.* A weeklong celebration of the performing arts with day and evening performances and events. | Townwide with performances at the Playhouse | 207/646–2939.

DEC.: *Christmas by the Sea.* Annual event ushering in the holiday season. Events include tree lighting, caroling, chowderfest, bonfire, live entertainment, and an appearance by you-know-who. Activities take place in the center of town. | 207/646–2939.

Dining

★ **Arrows Restaurant.** Contemporary. An 18th-century farmhouse with wide-board floors, period furnishings, and lovely views of the gardens that is 1¾ mi from the center of town. The imaginative menu changes daily and 80% of the produce is grown on the premises. Try the prosciutto cured on the premises or the sautéed foie gras. No smoking. Free parking. | Berwick Rd. | 207/361–1100 | www.arrowsrestaurant.com | Closed Mon. and mid-Dec.–Apr. | $37–$40 | MC, V.

Barnacle Billy's. Seafood. A half ton of lobster moves through this rustic eatery daily. Pine tables, fireplaces, and marine motifs predominate. Known for lobster and clams. Open-air dining on patio and two decks overlooking the water. Cafeteria service. Dock space. No smoking. | Perkins Cove, 1 mi east of U.S. 1 | 207/646–5575 | Closed mid-Oct.–Apr. | $15–$35 | AE, MC, V.

Billy's, Etc. Seafood. This offshoot of Barnacle Billy's (*see above*) has water views and is 1 mi south of town. Try the baked stuffed lobster. Open-air dining on the upper deck. Kids' menu. No smoking. | Oarweed Cove Rd. | 207/646–4711 | Closed Nov.–early May | $15–$35 | AE, MC, V.

Cafe Amore. American. Although you may see people lining up at the door to get in, they'll always say it was worth the wait to eat this unique gourmet breakfast and lunch food. Choose from 14 types of omelets, seven kinds of eggs Benedict, and an array of French toast and pancakes. For lunch try a panini sandwich or the clam chowder which Cafe Amore has down to a science. | 102 Shore Rd. | 207/646–6661 | Breakfast also available; closed mid-Dec.–mid-Mar. | $3–$10 | No credit cards.

Clay Hill Farm. Contemporary. This gracious 18th-century farmhouse, 2¼ mi southwest of Ogunquit, is on 30 acres and has Victorian furnishings, large bay windows overlooking the gardens, and a cocktail deck. Try the prime rib or lobster-stuffed haddock. Pianist nightly. Kids' menu. No smoking. Valet parking. | 226 Clay Hill Rd., Cape Neddick | 207/361–2272 | Closed Mon.–Wed. Nov.–Mar. No lunch | $20–$35 | AE, D, MC, V.

Cliff House. Contemporary. First established in 1872, this resort complex is perched at the head of Bald Cliff, with a window-lined, formal dining room and ocean views. Try the hazelnut-crusted lobster or bourbon-marinated lamb chops. Open-air dining on the terrace. Kids' menu. Sunday brunch. No smoking. | Shore Rd. | 207/361–1000 | Closed mid-Dec.–Apr. | $15–$35 | AE, D, DC, MC, V.

Demi's Santa Fe Grill. Eclectic. This festive place has live music several times a week and serves everything from burritos to steak and seafood. If that's not reason enough to convince you, it claims to have the best margaritas in Maine. Kids' menu and full bar and lounge. | 188 U.S. 1 | 207/646–4700 | $8–$13 | AE, D, MC, V.

Gypsy Sweethearts. Contemporary. An early-19th-century Cape with period furnishings, lovely flower gardens, local art, and a wraparound porch. Try the shrimp margarita, Jamaican jerk chicken, or rack of lamb. Open-air dining on the porch. No smoking. | 10 Shore Rd. | 207/646–7021 | Closed Dec.–Mar. No lunch | $14–$24 | AE, MC, V.

★ **Hurricane.** Contemporary. This retrofitted fishing shanty has an open, airy dining room, with a vintage bar and water views. There are wine-tasting dinners from January to April. Try the lobster chowder or baked stuffed lobster. Sunday jazz brunch off-season. No smoking. | 52 Oarweed Cove Rd. | 207/646–6348 | www.perkinscove.com | Closed 2 wks in Jan. | $16–$39 | AE, D, DC, MC, V.

Impastable Inn. Eclectic. Choose from an array of creative pasta dishes, like Greek pasta which has kalamata olives, feta cheese, and olive oil, or homemade ravioli. Leave just enough room for homemade ice cream or tiramisu. The comfort food here matches the cozy interior with a fireplace, and country feel. Full bar and kids' menu until 6:30. | 105 Shore Rd. | 207/646–3011 | Closed Tues.–Thurs in winter. No lunch | $8–$17 | AE, D, MC, V.

98 Provence. French. This restaurant has a French-country style with antiques, and provides intimate dining. Try the *soupe du pêcheur* (fisherman's soup). No smoking. | 104 Shore Rd. | 207/646–9898 | www.98provence.com | Reservations essential | Closed Tues. and mid-Dec.–Mar. No lunch | $25–$35 | AE, MC, V.

Ogunquit Lobster Pound. Seafood. This log cabin, ½ mi north of town, has mounted animal trophies, nautical paraphernalia, and fireplaces. You can also eat outside under the pines. You'll dine family-style here and can even select your own lobster from outdoor tanks. Try the steamed clams. Kids' menu. No smoking. | 256 U.S. 1 | 207/646–2516 | www.ogunquitlobsterpound.com | Closed Mon.–Thurs. Columbus Day–June | $15–$40 | AE, D, MC, V.

Old Village Inn. Contemporary. A casual three-story Victorian with five separate dining rooms, each with a unique style. Try the rack of lamb or shrimp and fillet teriyaki. Sunday brunch. No smoking. | 30 Main St. | 207/646–7088. | Closed Jan. No lunch | $14–$23 | AE, D, MC, V.

Poor Richard's Tavern. Contemporary. In this 18th-century building, the chef prepares traditional New England cooking with a French flair. Try the pot roast jardinière or the lobster pie. Pianist Friday and Saturday. No smoking. | 125 Shore Rd. | 207/646–4722 | Reservations essential | $15–$25 | AE, MC, V.

Lodging

Above Tide Inn. This inn with simple rooms is at the beach and central to the town and its attractions. Complimentary Continental breakfast. Refrigerators, cable TV, no room phones.

Massage. | 26 Beach St. | 207/646–7454 | info@abovetideinn.com | www.abovetideinn.com | 9 rooms (8 with shower only) | $130–$180 | Closed mid-Oct.–mid-May | MC, V.

Anchorage by the Sea. Near the Marginal Way coastal walk in busy Perkins Cove, this charming resort overlooks the ocean and is on the trolley route. Restaurant. Refrigerators, cable TV. 2 pools, wading pool. 2 hot tubs, sauna. | 55 Shore Dr. | 207/646–9384 | fax 207/646–6256 | www.mainesunshine.com/anchorby | 212 rooms | $140–$215 | D, MC, V.

Aspinquid Motel. This condo-style complex is just across the bridge from a white-sand beach. Some rooms have private balconies, and king-size beds are available. Take the trolley into town; it stops outside the front door. Pool, pond. Tennis court. Baby-sitting. | Beach St. | 207/646–7072 | fax 207/646–1187 | www.aspinquid.com | 50 rooms, 12 suites | $115–$230 | Closed end Oct.–end Mar. | AE, MC, V.

Beachmere Inn. A Victorian inn and motel on the water and near a beach. Picnic area, complimentary Continental breakfast. Kitchenettes, some microwaves, cable TV. Beach. Business services. | 12 Beachmere Pl. | 207/646–2021 or 800/336–3983 | fax 207/646–2231 | info@beachmereinn.com | www.beachmereinn.com | 53 rooms (1 with shared bath) in 6 buildings, 1 cottage | $130–$299, $195 cottage | Closed mid-Dec.–Mar. | AE, D, DC, MC, V.

Briarbrook Motor Inn. A quiet but convenient inn on the trolley route and minutes from the beach. It has landscaped gardens and is ¼ mi south of Ogunquit. Picnic area. Some kitchenettes, refrigerators, cable TV. Pool. | 42 U.S. 1 | 207/646–7571 | www.briarbrook.com | 18 rooms | $85–$93 | Closed mid-Oct.–early May | AE, D, MC, V.

Chestnut Tree Inn. This 1870 Victorian bed-and-breakfast has period antiques and a laid-back beach-house feel. Sit on one of the two porches after returning from the beach or downtown Ogunquit, both 10-minute walks. Some shared bathrooms. Complimentary Continental breakfast. | 93 Shore Rd. | 800/362–0757 or 207/646–4529 | www.chestnut-treeinn.com | 22 rooms | $70–$95 | Closed end Oct.–mid-May | AE, MC, V.

Cliff House. Fifteen miles from Interstate 95, atop Bald Head Cliff, Ogunquit's full-service resort has the most dramatic location around. The rooms, all with ocean views, lack character, but the facilities are relaxing and pleasant. 2 pools, 2 tennis courts. Hot tub. Gym. | Shore Rd. | 207/361–1000 | fax 207/361–2122 | www.cliffhousemaine.com | 149 rooms, 2 suites | $170–$240 | Closed Jan.–mid-Mar. | AE, D, MC, V.

Colonial Village Resort. This resort is on Tidal River and near the beach and downtown. Picnic area, complimentary Continental breakfast. Some kitchenettes, cable TV. 2 pools. Hot tubs. Tennis. Video games. Laundry facilities. | 266 Maine St. | 207/646–2794 or 800/422–3341 | fax 207/646–2463 | www.cybertours.com/~tooey | 67 rooms, 29 suites, 4 two-bedroom cottages | $126–$136, $182–$202 suites, $1,000–$1,200 cottages (7–day minimum stay) | Closed mid-Dec.–Mar. | D, MC, V.

Gorges Grant. A modern hotel and resort that is close to Ogunquit's beaches and shops. Restaurant. Refrigerators, cable TV. 2 pools. Hot tub. Exercise equipment. Business services. | 239 U.S. 1 | 207/646–7003 or 800/646–5001 | fax 207/646–0660 | gorgesgrant@ogunquit.com | www.ogunquit.com | 81 rooms | $127–$164 | AE, D, DC, MC, V.

Grand Hotel. A spacious, bright, and welcoming hotel, with a lobby at the bottom of a spectacular three-story atrium topped with skylights. It has intimate alcoves and the third-floor suites have large private decks and fireplaces. Complimentary Continental breakfast. Refrigerators, cable TV. Pool. | 108 Shore Rd. | 207/646–1231 | info@thegrandhotel.com | www.thegrandhotel.com | 28 suites | $150–$210 | Closed Dec.–Mar. | AE, D, MC, V.

Hartwell House Inn. A fine European-style country inn, furnished with antiques. Many rooms have balconies and views. Complimentary breakfast. Some kitchenettes, no in-room TVs, cable TV in common area. No kids under 14. | 118 Shore Rd. | 207/646–7210 | fax 207/646–6032 | hartwell@cybertours.com | www.hartwellhouseinn.com | 16 rooms, 3 suites | $125–$150, $170–$190 suites | AE, D, MC, V.

Juniper Hill Inn. This inn is on the beach and has a private, hickory-lined path that leads to the Ogunquit shore. It is also just a few minutes' walk from the shops, galleries, and restaurants. The rooms are spacious and contemporary, and there is also a garden. Refrigerators, cable TV. 3 pools. Hot tub, sauna. Exercise equipment. Laundry facilities. | 196 U.S. 1 | 207/646–4501 or 800/646–4544 | fax 207/646–4595 | juniperhill@ogunquit.com | www.ogunquit.com | 100 rooms | $99–$159 | AE, D, DC, MC, V.

Meadowmere. A comfortable, well-cared-for hotel that is a short walk from the beach and Perkins Cove. It's on the trolley route. Bar Refrigerators, cable TV, some room phones. 3 pools. No pets. | 56 U.S. 1 | 207/646–9661 or 800/633–8718 | www.meadowmere.com | 124 rooms | $159–$259 | AE, MC, V.

Milestone Inn. This central motel with attractive grounds is by Footbridge Beach. It has spacious, contemporary rooms. Refrigerators, cable TV. Pool. Hot tub. Exercise equipment. | 333 U.S. 1 | 207/646–4562 or 800/646–6453 | fax 207/646–1739 | milestone@ogunquit.com | www.ogunquit.com/milestone | 70 rooms | $99–$149 | Closed Nov.–Mar. | AE, D, DC, MC, V.

Norseman Motor Inn. A beachfront motel with many amenities, including balconies and decks. Restaurant. Refrigerators, cable TV. Beach. | 41 Beach St. | 207/646–7024 or 800/822–7024 | fax 207/646–0655 | 94 rooms | $99–$149 | Closed late Oct.–Mar. | AE, D, MC, V.

Pine Hill Inn. A Victorian hostelry within walking distance of the water. Complimentary breakfast. No room phones, no TV in guest rooms, cable TV in common area. No kids under 12 (in inn rooms). No smoking. | 14 Pine Hill Rd. | 207/361–1004 | fax 207/761–1815 | pine-hill@cybertours.com | www.pinehillinn.com | 8 rooms (4 with shower only), 1 suite, 1 cottage | $120–$175 | Closed Jan. | MC, V.

Pink Blossoms Resort. A shorefront family resort hotel with attractive grounds. Picnic area. Kitchenettes, microwaves, refrigerators, cable TV. Pool. Tennis. | 66 Shore Rd. | 207/646–7397 or 800/228–7465 | pinkb@concentric.net | www.pinkb.com | 26 rooms (8 with shower only), 11 suites | $135–$150, $195–$260 suites | Closed Oct.–Apr. | MC, V.

Puffin Inn. Built in 1888, this bed-and-breakfast also has a carriage house with adjoining rooms to form a suite. Some rooms have ocean views, and most have period antiques. It's a 10-minute walk to the beach and five minutes to downtown Ogunquit. Complimentary breakfast. No room phones. | 233 U.S. 1 | 207/646–5496 | fax 207/641–8764 | puffin@cybertours.com | www.puffininn.com | 9 rooms, 1 suite | $70–$145 | Closed mid-Oct.–mid-May | MC, V.

Riverside Motel. A mile south of Ogunquit, Riverside offers unsurpassed views of the busy fishing harbor of Perkins Cove. Modern rooms with ocean views. Complimentary Continental breakfast. Refrigerators, cable TV. | 159 Shore Rd. | 207/646–2741 | fax 207/646–0216 | riverside@cybertours.com | www.riversidemotel.com | 38 rooms | $125–$150 | Closed mid-Oct.–mid-Apr. | MC, V.

Rockmere Lodge. Restaurants and downtown are just ½ mi away from this 1899 Victorian B&B facing the ocean. Rooms, almost all on the corner and assuring ocean views, are furnished in high Victorian with antiques. The wraparound porch has wicker rocking chairs and hanging baskets of flowers. The living room is furnished with family antiques. Two-night minimum on weekends. Complimentary breakfast. No air-conditioning, no room phones. | 40 Stearns Rd. | 207/646–2985 | fax 207/646–6947 | www.rockmere.com | 8 rooms | $100–$200 | AE, D, MC, V.

Sea Chambers Motor Lodge. An attractive oceanfront hotel with access to fishing and other water sports with water views from many of its rooms. Complimentary Continental breakfast. Some refrigerators, cable TV. Pool. Tennis. Business services. | 25 Shore Rd. | 207/646–9311 | fax 207/646–0938 | info@seachambers.com | www.seachambers.com | 43 rooms | $124–$182 | Closed mid-Dec.–Mar. | AE, D, MC, V.

Sea View Motel. This central hotel, ¼ mi north of Ogunquit, has spacious rooms. Refrigerators, cable TV. Pool. Hot tub. Exercise equipment. | U.S. 1 | 207/646–7064 | 40 rooms | $59–$139 | Closed Dec.–Feb. | AE, D, DC, MC, V.

Sparhawk Motel. This 100-year-old hotel on the trolley route has elegantly furnished rooms that overlook the ocean. Complimentary Continental breakfast. Refrigerators, cable TV. Pool. Tennis. | 41 Shore Rd. | 207/646–5562 | 57 rooms, 30 suites, 5 apartments | $155–$165, $165–$250 suites, $170–$295 apartments | Closed late Oct.–mid-Apr. | MC, V.

Stage Run Motel. This motel is near the beach and the theater and has spacious rooms. Refrigerators, cable TV. Pool. Beach. | 238 U.S. 1 | 207/646–4823 | fax 207/641–2884 | staerun@cybertours.com | www.stagerunmotel.com | 24 rooms | $89–$129 | Closed Nov.–Mar. | D, MC, V.

Terrace by the Sea. A turn-of-the-20th-century inn with a modern motel. The elegant rooms overlook the ocean and have views of the rocky Maine coastline. Complimentary Continental breakfast. Some kitchenettes, refrigerators, cable TV. Pool. | 11 Wharf La. | 207/646–3232 | www.terracebythesea.com | 36 rooms | $124–$194 | Closed mid-Nov.–mid-Apr. | No credit cards.

Towne Lyne Motel. In the woods at the Wells town line, this motel 1½ mi north of town has attractive grounds. Some rooms have screened porches overlooking the river. Refrigerators, cable TV. | U.S. 1 | 207/646–2955 | 20 rooms | $115 | Closed mid-Nov.–Apr. | AE, D, MC, V.

Trellis House Bed and Breakfast. You'll find this a good value B&B just off Main Street with nice rooms and a full breakfast. The English Room has a separate sitting room with windows on three sides. Built in 1907, this New Englander beach home is so close to the center of town you'll forget you brought your car. Some rooms have fireplaces. Beds are either queen or king, and rooms accommodate two only. Complimentary breakfast. No air-conditioning, no room phones, no TV. | 2 Beachmere Pl. | 800/681–7909 or 207/646–7909 | www.trellishouse.com | 8 rooms | $110–$145 | MC, V.

Ye Old Perkins Place. This colonial home, 2 mi south of town, has been a bed-and-breakfast since the 1930s. Ocean views and some colonial antique furnishings at a reasonable price make for a pleasant stay. Complimentary breakfast. No air-conditioning, no room phones. | 749 Shore Rd., Cape Neddick | 207/361–1119 | 5 rooms | $60–$70 | Closed Labor Day–end June | No credit cards.

OLD ORCHARD
BEACH

INTRO
ATTRACTIONS
DINING
LODGING

OLD ORCHARD BEACH

MAP 3, C11

(Nearby towns also listed: Biddeford-Saco, Scarborough)

Maine's answer to Coney Island with cotton candy, arcades, T-shirt shops, amusement rides, and a sprawling 7-mi beach, where you'll jostle for space on a sultry summer day. The town's pier extends nearly 500 ft over the Atlantic. (Its first incarnation in 1898 stretched 1,770 ft out into the water.) This area has long been favored by Canadian visitors, but their numbers have recently decreased owing to the poor exchange rate. Brick sidewalks and Victorian streetlights have been installed downtown to create a family-friendly atmosphere.

Information: Old Orchard Beach Chamber of Commerce | Box 600, Old Orchard Beach, 04064 | 207/934–2500 or 800/365–9386 | fmly_fun@oldorchardbeachmaine.com | www.oldorchardbeachmaine.com.

Attractions
Ocean Park. This vacation community on the southwest side of town was founded in 1881 as a summer assembly, following the example of Chautauqua, New York. Today the community still has a wide range of cultural offerings, including movies, concerts, workshops, and religious services. Most are presented in the Temple, which is on the National Register of Historic Places. | 15 Colby Ave. | 207/934–9068.

Palace Playland. At Maine's biggest and bawdiest shorefront amusement park you'll find all the usual suspects: cotton candy, Maine's largest water slide, arcades, T-shirt shops, carnival rides—astride a sprawling 7-mi beach. | Old Orchard St. off Rte. 5 | 207/934–2001 | www.palaceplayland.com | Free | Memorial Day–Labor Day.

The Pier. Extending nearly 500 ft out into the Atlantic, the Pier has shops, games of skill and chance, and fast food, plus special events and live entertainment. It's on the beachfront, adjacent to Palace Playland, off Route 5. | Free | May–Sept., daily.

ON THE CALENDAR
AUG.: *Beach Olympics.* Competitions, music, displays, and lots of sandy fun at this event whose proceeds benefit the Maine Special Olympics. | Old Orchard Beach | 207/934–2500.

Dining
Bunny's Restaurant. American. This airy, bright place with skylights serves healthful breakfast and lunch fare, from omelets to banana pecan pancakes and fruit salad. It will accommodate private dinner parties. | 198 E. Grand Ave. | 207/934–3838 | Breakfast also available; no dinner | $2–$5 | No credit cards.

Danton's Restaurant. American. Open since 1946, this restaurant is the oldest eatery in Old Orchard. Steak and eggs are a specialty in the morning, while clam scallops or Italian sausage are favorites for lunch or dinner. Also try the hot subs or wraps. No alcohol, kids' menu. | 16 Orchard St. | 207/934–7701 | Breakfast also available; closed Sept. 15–May 15 | $5–$14 | D, MC, V.

Java Junction. American. Sit on the deck here, 1 mi from the center of town, and sip a chai tea or latte after you've tried a freshly baked breakfast muffin or sandwich for lunch. Come alone and read a book, or bring all your friends after visiting the beach. | 194 Saco Ave. | 207/934–0226 | Breakfast also available; no dinner | $1–$5 | No credit cards.

Joseph's by the Sea. French. Modern rendition of French cuisine has been served here since 1968, luring a mix of visitors and longtime residents. The two dining rooms have views of the ocean. The interior is trimmed with whitewashed birch, has a fireplace, mantle, and a terraced floor. For starters, try the lobster potato pancake with chipotle crème fraîche, and then move on to the crabmeat Napolean (halibut and crab in a puff pastry shell with carrot shellfish cream sauce) or the sea scallops seared with ham in balsamic vinegar over arugula. Try the lemon roulade or chocolate espresso torte for dessert. In season ask to sit at the surfside garden patio. | 55 W. Grand Ave. | 207/934–5044 | Breakfast also available; closed Mon.–Wed. Apr.–mid-May and Columbus Day–mid-Dec. Closed Jan.–Mar. No lunch | $15–$26 | AE, MC, V.

The Landmark. Continental. This restaurant in a 1910 Victorian house has gold pressed-tin ceilings, rock maple floors, fine woodwork, and burgundy and cream touches throughout. There's also a screened-in, wraparound porch and the tables are appointed with fine cloths and china. Try the roulade of pork tenderloin stuffed with spinach, pine nuts, chorizo sausage, and feta cheese or the roast duckling with raspberry glaze. Kids' menu. | 28 E. Grand Ave. | 207/934–0156 | Closed Mon. Labor Day–Jan. 1; Jan. 1–Apr. No lunch | $12–$18 | AE, D, MC, V.

Oceanside Grill. American. People come here to enjoy fresh seafood and steak while sitting on the deck overlooking the ocean. Try desserts like cheesecake, crème brulée, and carrot cake. Full bar and kids' menu. | 39 W. Grand Ave. | 207/934–0056 | $11–$19 | AE, D, MC, V.

Pier French Fries. American. This Old Orchard Beach landmark has been serving fresh, home-cut French fries since 1932. It used to be on the pier, but it's now right across from the fountain on Danton Square. | 4 Old Orchard St. | 207/934–2364 | Closed mid-Oct.–mid-May | $2–$5 | No credit cards.

ONE MAN'S TRASH

As we all know, the word *souvenir* is derived from the French "to remember," and no vacation is complete without bringing home something reminiscent of your stay. You can shop for that quintessential Maine thing—balsam pillows, Maine lobster or smoked salmon, festival T-shirts, handcrafted items from state fairs, blueberry products or, yes, even moose-dropping earrings—but if it is true that the best things in life are free, you might want to scavenge around for your own souvenirs. And there's no better place to do it than along the Maine coast.

Beachcombing is one of the most relaxing pursuits the Maine experience has to offer. And there's no end to the treasures you can find—from washed-up flotsam and jetsam to the many fascinating marine creatures that call the Maine coast home. (Please leave the live ones alone.) Think of each changing tide as bringing in a new inventory for your shopping pleasure.

Saco and Old Orchard Beach are especially good for finding sand dollars and razor clams; Castine for scallop shells; Dennysville for lava rocks. But perhaps the most rewarding find is beach glass. Although it can be found anywhere along the Maine coast, one of the best spots is way Down East, near Lubec and Eastport.

Beach glass (also known as sea glass, salt glass, rock glass, angel's tears, fairy glass, and mermaid's tears) is an elusive find, and that is perhaps why it's such a satisfying one. Purists will chuck back a piece that has even the slightest rough edge to it, claiming it is "not done." Beach glass with a frosted quality comes from pebbly beaches, smoother pieces from sandy ones. The glass can come in a variety of colors, ranging from hard-candy yellows and greens to ruby red and cobalt blue to soft pastels. The most common finds are white, brown, and green. Most people think brown beach glass comes strictly from beer bottles, but Clorox bleach, which was frequently used by fisherman to clean their boats, once came in brown jugs that went into the drink when they were empty.

Many pieces of beach glass are their own time capsules. Most glass produced prior to 1880 was Coke-bottle aqua-green. "Black glass" (which is actually a dark olive-green or olive-amber in color) was produced up to 1860, when iron slag was used in the manufacture of thick, dark bottles for beverages—bootleg liquor, for example—needing protection from light. Pastel-color pieces—peach and pale green—usually come from inexpensive 1930s Depression glass. True blue, green, and purple colors were produced by the use of metallic oxides. Cobalt was at one time added to make blue glass, which was used for medicine and poison bottles. A lot of purple glass started out clear. Between 1880 and 1914, most clear glass was made with manganese, which takes on a rich purple color when exposed to the ultraviolet rays of the sun. One of the most uncommon colors—red—was produced through the addition of copper or gold. Precious metals are still used today, making red a rare find—and wouldn't that just be a crowning trophy to your trip to Maine?

Lodging

Alouette Beach Resort. This friendly establishment is great for families. With four types of accommodations to choose from, you'll find a good fit. Just 10 minutes from downtown, and within walking distance to the beach, you can have an apartment or cottage with full kitchen and private porch or balcony. The main 100-year-old cottage has a dining room, two baths, and full kitchen, and sleeps eight. The motel-style rooms have kitchenettes and sleep four. Restaurant, bar, picnic area. No air-conditioning in some rooms, kitchenettes, some microwaves, cable TV. Beach. Pets allowed (fee). | 91 E. Grand Ave. | 207/934–4151 or 800/565–4151 | fax 207/934–9464 | info@alouettebeachresort.com | www.alouettebeachresort.com | 75 rooms | $77–$138 rooms, $116–$175 cottages and apartments | AE, DC, MC, V.

Aquarius Motel. Established in 1975, this motel has the ocean and beach right outside its door. You can picnic or barbecue while watching the kids in the sand, and then walk into town for ice cream. All beds are doubles, and the rooms have a nautical touch. Laundry facilities. | 1 Brown St. | 207/934–2626 | fax 207/934–0046 | aquarius@maine.rr.com | www.aquariusmotel.com | 16 rooms | $85–$145 | Closed Oct.–Apr. | MC, V, D.

Auberge by the Sea. A quaint bed-and-breakfast by the sea where breakfast is served on an airy sunporch. It's a 10-minute walk to downtown or the pier. There is a private path to the water, and some rooms have their own balconies. No room phones. | 103 E. Grand Ave. | 207/934–2355 | 4 rooms | $60–$129 | MC, V.

Carolina Motel. An old-style, oceanfront resort hotel. The rooms have a Mediterranean decor. Restaurant. No air-conditioning, kitchenettes, cable TV. Pool. | 1 Roussin St. | 207/934–4476 | 34 rooms | $130–$165 | Closed Nov.–mid-May | D, MC, V.

Deluxe Oceanfront Motel of Cottages. Families come here to relax on the beach, barbecue, and picnic. The center of town is a 15-minute walk so you are away from the hustle and bustle of it all. Some rooms have private porches or balconies. Pets allowed. | 187 E. Grand Ave. | 207/934–2460 | 12 rooms, 13 cottages | $135–$150 | MC, V.

The Edgewater. This attractively furnished and well-staffed hotel is on the water, adjacent to 7 mi of beach, and a short distance from downtown attractions. In-room data ports, some kitchenettes, refrigerators, cable TV. Pool. | 57 W. Grand Ave. (Rte. 9) | 207/934–2221 or 800/203–2034 | fax 207/934–3731 | edgelamb@janelle.com | www.janelle.com | 35 rooms | $120–$169 | Closed mid-Nov.–Mar. | AE, D, MC, V.

Flagship Motel. Just across the street from the ocean, near downtown attractions, this motel has small but pleasant knotty-pine rooms. Picnic area. Refrigerators, cable TV. Pool. Beach. Some pets allowed. | 54 W. Grand Ave. (Rte. 9) | 207/934–4866 or 800/486–1681 | www.flagshipmotel.com | 27 rooms, 8 suites, 1 cottage | $89–$109, $99–$119 suites, $675–$875/wk cottage | Closed mid-Oct.–mid-May | AE, D, MC, V.

Friendship Motor Inn. This attractive motel is on the beach and has a pleasant grass courtyard. Refrigerators, cable TV, some in-room VCRs. Pool. Beach. Laundry facilities. | 167 E. Grand Ave. (Rte. 9) | 207/934–4644 or 800/969–7100 | fax 207/934–7592 | fmi@lamere.net | www.friendshipmotorinn.com | 71 suites | $129–$179 | Closed Nov.–Apr. | AE, D, MC, V.

Grand Beach Inn. A gracious and spacious beachfront inn. Restaurant, picnic area. Some kitchenettes, cable TV. Pool. Playground. Laundry facilities. | 198 E. Grand Ave. (Rte. 9) | 207/934–3435 or 800/834–9696 | gbi@int.usa.net | www.oobme.com | 87 rooms | $99–$179 | AE, D, MC, V.

Gull Motel. This motel and cottage complex is by the beach and has comfortable, airy rooms. The cottages are right on the beach. Picnic area. Kitchenettes, some microwaves, cable TV. Pool. | 89 W. Grand Ave. (Rte. 9) | 207/934–4321 | www.gullmotel.com | 21 rooms, 4 cottages | $65–$115, $850 cottages (7–day minimum stay) | Closed mid-Oct.–Apr. | D, MC, V.

Island View. A small, older motel just a short walk to the beach. Refrigerators, cable TV, some in-room VCRs. Pool. Beach. Airport shuttle. | 174 E. Grand Ave. (Rte. 9) | 207/934–4262 | fax 207/934–3501 | islandview@lamere.net | 15 rooms | $75–$95 | AE, D, MC, V.

Neptune Motel. A small, convenient motel that is near downtown attractions and the beach. Picnic area. Kitchenettes, cable TV. | 82 E. Grand Ave. | 207/934–5753 or 800/624–6786 | 16 rooms, 12 suites | $68–$95, $95 suites | AE, D, MC, V.

Royal Anchor Resort. An oceanfront hotel on a quiet section of the beach. Complimentary Continental breakfast. No air-conditioning, refrigerators, cable TV. Pool. Tennis. | 203 E. Grand Ave. (Rte. 9) | 207/934–4521 or 800/934–4521 | www.royalanchor.com | 40 rooms | $119–$165 | Closed late Oct.–Apr. | AE, D, DC, MC, V.

Sandpiper Motel. This motel is on the ocean and convenient to downtown attractions. Picnic area, complimentary Continental breakfast. Some kitchenettes, refrigerators, cable TV. Beach. | 2 Cleaves St. | 207/934–2733 or 800/611–9921 | sandpipermotel@lamere.net | www.members.xoom.com/seavista/motel | 22 rooms | $95–$130 | AE, D, MC, V.

Sea Cliff House Motel. A family-oriented oceanfront hotel that has a modern look and central location. Some kitchenettes, refrigerators, cable TV. Pool. Beach. | 2 Sea Cliff Ave. | 207/934–4874 or 800/326–4589 | fax 207/934–1445 | seacliffmotel@cybertours.com | www.sea-cliffhouse.com | 35 rooms, 22 suites | $110–$140 | D, MC, V.

ORONO

MAP 3, F7

(Nearby town also listed: Bangor)

You can't swing a cat without hitting a coed in this home to the flagship campus of the University of Maine. A suburb of Bangor, Orono also enjoyed the benefits of the logging boom in the 19th century. There are a number of historic homes dating back to this period. The town is divided by the Stillwater River; the downtown lies on one side, the campus on the other.

Information: Bangor Region Chamber of Commerce | 519 Main St., Bangor, 04402-1443 | 207/947–0307 | chamber@bangorregion.com | www.bangorregion.com.

Attractions

Leonard's Mills. This 265-acre logging community is part of the Maine Forest and Logging Museum. The site, 8 mi northwest of Orono, includes a covered bridge, water-powered sawmill, nature trails, blacksmith shop, trapper line, and logging equipment. | Rte. 178, Bradley | 207/581–2871 | Donation suggested | Daily dawn–dusk.

Maine Center for the Arts. Included in this center is the 1,600-seat Hutchins Concert Hall. You can see musicals, plays, concerts, opera, and dance here. | College Ave. | 207/581–1755 | www.mainecenterforthearts.org | $35–$85 tickets | Daily 9–4.

Hudson Museum. Programs and exhibits explore anthropology and human culture. There are exhibits that stress Native American culture, pre-Columbian works, as well as items from Asia and Africa. | Maine Center for the Arts, College Ave. | 207/581–1901 | Free | Tues.–Fri. 9–4, weekends 11–4.

University of Maine. The state's land grant college and the flagship of the University of Maine system has a division I champion college hockey team, plus basketball, football, and other sports. It also has a planetarium, theater, and art museums. | College Ave. | 207/581–1110 or 207/581–1341 | www.umaine.edu | Daily.

Lyle E. Littlefield Ornamentals Trail Garden. A 6-acre garden containing a permanent collection of nearly 3,000 woody taxa. Major collections include crab apple, lilac, rhododendron, magnolia, holly, daylily, and hosta. | College Ave., hilltop section of campus | 207/581–2918 | Free | Daily.

SEPT.: *Orono Festival Day.* Come celebrate at this annual event filled with food, music, entertainment, a parade, and a kids' fair. Events take place throughout town. | Orono | 207/866–5056.

Dining

Bear Brew Pub. Eclectic. The beers are brewed on the premises of this college hangout, assuring you a refreshing cold drink to go with your exceptionally large burger. Healthy light fare is also available; try the fresh pesto or hummus accompanied with bread or local, organic vegetables. Live music three times a week, except in summer. Kids' menu. | 36 Main St. | 207/866–2739 | $6–$10 | AE, D, MC, V.

Margarita's. Tex-Mex. This cantina is popular with the college crowd. Try the fajitas. Live music in the lounge on weekends. Kids' menu. No smoking. | 15 Mill St. | 207/866–4863 | No lunch | $5–$15 | AE, D, MC, V.

Pat's Pizza. Pizza. This Orono landmark has been around since 1931. The interior has booths and wall-mounted jukeboxes. Try Pat's Combo or the loaded pizza, with everything—including pine nuts—on it. No smoking. | 11 Mill St. | 207/866–2111 | $5–$10 | MC, V.

Lodging

Best Western Black Bear Inn. Three miles from downtown Orono, this inn isn't within walking distance of anything. All rooms have two queen beds, and generally accommodate families visiting students at the University of Maine Orono. Less than half a mile from Interstate 95. Restaurant, complimentary Continental breakfast. Some microwaves, cable TV. Exercise equipment. Pets allowed. | 4 Godfrey Dr. | 207/866–7120 | fax 207/866–7433 | www.bestwestern.com | 68 rooms | $70–$99 | AE, D, DC, MC, V.

Highlawn Bed and Breakfast. This quiet, 1803 Greek Revival home is on 4 acres and is popular with families and professors visiting the University of Maine, which is five minutes away. Each room is individually furnished with period antiques like Victorian high-back and mahogany four-poster beds and marble dressers. There are two sitting areas, one a country den in the rear of the house with a Vermont Casting woodstove. Be sure to try the famous blueberry pancakes and muffins. Dining room, complimentary breakfast. No air-conditioning, some in-room data ports, cable TV, some room phones. No pets. No kids under 10. No smoking. | 193 Main St. | 207/866–2272 or 800/297–2272 | 6 rooms (3 with shared bath) | $55–$75 | MC, V.

Milford Motel. A riverfront motel in a small town, northwest of Orono picnic area. Kitchenettes, cable TV. Laundry facilities. Pets allowed. | 154 Main St. (U.S. 2), Milford | 207/827–3200 or 800/282–3330 | milford@mint.net | www.mint.net/milford.motel | 22 rooms (2 with shower only), 8 suites | $59–$84 | AE, D, MC, V.

University Motor Inn. This motel is within walking distance of the University and downtown. Complimentary Continental breakfast. Cable TV. Pool. Business services. Pets allowed. | 5 College Ave. | 207/866–4921 or 800/321–4921 | fax 207/866–4550 | www.universitymotorinn.com | 48 rooms | $56–$59 | AE, D, DC, MC, V.

PEMAQUID PENINSULA

MAP 3, D10

(Nearby towns also listed: Damariscotta, Newcastle)

The Pemaquid ("longest finger") Peninsula was settled in the early 17th century, and much of that history is still in evidence, particularly at the ongoing restoration project at the peninsula's point. A quiet calm prevails in its small fishing villages, wooded winding roads, and its majestic point that boldly juts out into the Atlantic and is home to the famed 1827 Pemaquid Lighthouse.

Information: **Damariscotta Region Chamber of Commerce** | Main St., Damariscotta, 04543 | 207/563–8340 | drcc@tidewater.net | www.drcc.org. **Pemaquid Area Association** | 301 Rte. 32, Chamberlain, 04541.

Attractions
Thomson Ice House. An early example of refrigeration, this is a double-walled barn lined with insulating sawdust, and it dates from 1826. Blocks of ice cut from frozen ponds could stay unmelted right through August. Take U.S. 1 to Damariscotta, then take Route 129, sign-posted after 3 mi. | 207/644–8551 | $1 suggested | July–Aug., Wed., Fri.–Sat. 1–4.

ON THE CALENDAR
AUG.: *Olde Bristol Days.* There are races, food, live entertainment, crafts, and fireworks at this largest family event on the Pemaquid peninsula. | Fort William Henry, Pemaquid | 207/563–3175.

Dining
Round Pond Lobsterman's Coop. American. Lobster doesn't get much rougher, fresher, or cheaper than served at this no-frills dockside takeout. The best deal is the dinner special: a 1-pound lobster, steamers, and corn-on-the-cob, with a bag of chips. Regulars often bring beer, wine, bread, and/or salads. Settle in at a picnic table and breathe in the fresh salt air while you drink in the view over dreamy Round Pond Harbor. | Round Pond Harbor, off Rte. 32 | 207/529–5725 | $10–$15 | MC, V.

Seagull Shop. Seafood. You'll find oceanfront dining at this restaurant adjacent to Pemaquid Peninsula Lighthouse and spectacular views. Seafood is a specialty in all its manifestations. Lobster and seafood platters and pies; also steaks and omelets. BYOB. | 3119 Bristol Rd. (last building before Pemaquid Point lighthouse) | 207/677–2374 | Closed Nov.–Apr. | $10–$20 | MC, V.

★ **Shaw's Fish and Lobster Wharf.** Seafood. This rustic lobster shack has a nautical look and views of a working harbor. There's an outdoor raw bar serving shellfish and jumbo shrimp. | Rte. 32, New Harbor | 207/677–2200 | Closed mid-Oct.–mid-May | $15–$20 | MC, V.

Lodging
Briar Rose. A turn-of-the-20th-century inn with country antiques and whimsies in its airy rooms. You'll find bookcases and views of Round Pond from any room. Complimentary breakfast. No air-conditioning, no room phones, no TV. | Rte. 32 | 207/529–5478 | briarose@tidewater.net | 2 rooms, 1 suite | $85 | No credit cards.

Gosnold Arms. On Pemaquid Neck, a rambling 1925 cottage colony where you have a view of New Harbor from your pine rooms. Breakfast is satisfying and sweet or savory with pancakes or eggs and fresh fruit juice. Complimentary breakfast. No air-conditioning, no room phones, no TV in some rooms. | Northside Rd. | 207/677–3727 | www.gosnold.com. | 11 rooms, 15 cottages | $75–$124 | Closed mid-Oct.–mid-May | MC, V.

Hotel Pemaquid. This 1888 farmhouse, 100 yards from Pemaquid Lighthouse and the ocean, was long ago converted to a country inn. The cottages were named after original families that built them and each is rented out weekly. You can hear and smell the ocean through the pines surrounding your room. In room TVs. No smoking. No pets. | 3098 Bristol Rd. | 207/677–2312 | www.hotelpemaquid.com | 28 rooms, 3 cottages | $60–$200 | No credit cards.

PEMAQUID PENINSULA

INTRO
ATTRACTIONS
DINING
LODGING

PHIPPSBURG

MAP 3, C10

(Nearby town also listed: Bath)

The expansive white sands of Popham Beach might be what first attracted the initial European settlers to Phippsburg in 1607. Had the winter not been so severe as to drive the settlers home (those it didn't kill), this settlement could have given Jamestown a run for its money as the first permanent English settlement in America. Winters aside, visitors have continued to return ever since—including film crews for two major motion pictures (*Message in a Bottle* and *Head Above Water*). This 18-mi, history-rich peninsula has sand beaches, authentic fishing villages, nature trails, a major resort, and craggy cliffs for exploring.

Information: Chamber of Commerce of Bath-Brunswick Region | 59 Pleasant St., Brunswick, 04011 | 207/725–8797 or 207/443–9751 | ccbbr@horton.col.k12.us | www.mid-coastmaine.com.

Attractions

Fort Popham. One of three forts built since 1607 at the mouth of the Kennebec River, 16 mi south of Bath, the current Fort Popham dates from the Civil War. Fort Baldwin, nearby and also open to the public, took over its military functions in 1905. | 10 Perkins Farm La. | 207/389–1335 | $1 | Apr.–Sept., daily 9–dusk.

© Artville

PEMAQUID PENINSULA

One could do worse than get lost on the Pemaquid peninsula. A wrong turn might land you on a dirt road you can't find on your map and that seems to lead nowhere, but before you panic, consider this: if you don't reconnect with Route 130, which bisects the peninsula, you will either end up back at U.S. 1 or at the peninsula's splendid shorefront. The beauty is, it's virtually impossible to get totally lost on a peninsula.

And the Pemaquid peninsula is the place to do it, if you're looking for an off-the-beaten-path destination. There are no theme parks, no outlet stores, no major tourist towns. (Although, if you get a hankering for one, Boothbay Harbor is right next door.) What you will find in this area is open countryside, a 17-mi lake, a craggy coast, tidy white clapboard homes and meetinghouses, rough-and-tumble fishing shanties and villages, one of the state's most picturesque lighthouses, authentic lobster shacks and farm stands, and heaps of history—in a word, the real Maine.

You can visit an ongoing colonial restoration project and a historic fort at the peninsula's point or explore the fishing villages of Round Pond, South Bristol, Christmas Cove, and New Harbor. Poke around in the tidal pools at the Rachel Carson Salt Pond Preserve, visit one of the peninsula's museums, or board an excursion boat for puffin, seal, or whale-watching.

If you wish to wander off the peninsula, the towns of Damariscotta and Newcastle at its head are ideal for exploring by foot. Or you can extend your boundaries with visits to the nearby towns of Wiscasset and Bath (gateway to Georgetown and Phippsburg) or travel east to the Rockland area, where you'll find plenty to keep you amused. There are pretty peninsulas in either direction worth exploring, but chances are, you'll be content to stay right where you are. You might even find yourself taking wrong turns—on purpose.

Popham Beach State Park. A spacious sand beach with bathwaters, freshwater rinse-off, showers, and charcoal grills. No pets between April 1 and October 1. | 10 Perkins Farm La. | 207/389–1335 | $2 | Daily 9–dusk.

ON THE CALENDAR

AUG.: *Fireman's Field Day.* This carnival at Chrisman Field on the first Sunday of the month has everything you'd expect, from dunk tanks and fried food to a display of fire trucks and equipment. Hose hookup competitions take place between regional firefighters. | Elementary School | 207/389–2653.

Dining

Spinney's. American. You can eat seafood, hamburgers, or even a goat-cheese sandwich on this closed-in deck on the ocean's edge. Desserts like ice-cream sundaes and strawberry shortcake make this a good place to take the kids. Portions and prices can be halved for kids. | 97 Popham Rd. | 207/389–1122 | $3–$28 | MC, V.

Water's Edge Restaurant. Seafood. Authentic fishing gear lines the walls of this family-run restaurant that's about a 10-minute drive from Phippsburg. The emphasis is on healthy preparation—steaming, broiling, grilling. Try the seafood, water's-edge salad plates, or steaks. No smoking. | 75 Black's Landing Rd., Sebasco | 207/389–1803 | Closed Sept.–May | $10–$26 | MC, V.

Lodging

Popham Beach Bed and Breakfast. The weathered exterior of this restored 1883 Coast Guard station gives little indication of its stylish interior. The Library, one of five guest rooms, is particularly spacious, with a bay window looking out on Popham Beach. So quiet is this little spot, you'll hear the waves breaking on the shore and a bell buoy clanging at sea. Two-night minimum required July–August. Complimentary breakfast. No room phones. | 4 Riverview Ave., Popham Beach | 207/389–2409 | 3 rooms | $80–$145 | Closed Nov.–Apr. | MC, V.

POLAND SPRING

INTRO
ATTRACTIONS
DINING
LODGING

POLAND SPRING

MAP 3, B10

(Nearby towns also listed: Lewiston-Auburn, Norway)

Amid scenic, rolling farmland, Poland Spring was once home to the grand 1875 Poland Spring Hotel, which attracted guests with its "curative" waters. (The hotel burned down in 1975.) Today Poland Spring is perhaps best known locally for its Sabbathday Lake Shaker Community and, internationally, as the home of the famous water that bears the town's name. (Those looking to make a pilgrimage to the font will be roundly disappointed; the plant is not open to the public.)

Information: **Oxford Chamber of Commerce** | Box 167, South Paris, 04281 | 207/743–2281.

Attractions

Shaker Museum. Part of the last active Shaker village in the United States, the museum has Shaker furniture, inventions, tools, tin and woodenware, textiles, tools, and fancy goods. A gift shops sells a variety of Shaker items, including herbs. Guided tours are available. Workshops and special events are held regularly. It is 1 mi south of town. | 707 Shaker Rd., New Gloucester | 207/926–4597 | www.shaker.lib.me.us | $6–$7.50 | Mon.–Sat. 10–4:30; tours at 10 and 3:25.

ON THE CALENDAR

DEC.: *Shaker Christmas.* Shaker furniture, musical instruments, dried herbs, baked goods, hot apple cider, displays, and tours are all featured at the Sabbathday Lake

Shaker Community. It sure beats shopping at the mall. It's 1 mi south of Poland Spring. | 707 Shaker Rd., New Gloucester | 207/926–4597.

Lodging

Country Abundance. This hotel on Tripp Lake is on an 11½-acre estate with a blacksmith forge. You can relax on the porch and enjoy the sunrise, sunset, and stars, and the wind in the giant Maine pines. Complimentary breakfast. No room phones, TV in common area. Hiking. Bicycles. Cross-country skiing. | 509 White Oak Hill Rd. | 207/998–2132 | www.countryabundance.com | 3 rooms | $80–$90 | AE, D, MC, V.

Wolf Cove Inn. A sturdy, white, turn-of-the-20th-century inn on 2½ wooded acres. Rooms have individual themes and furnishings, including easy chairs, wrought-iron and four-poster beds, fireplaces, hot tubs, and quilts. All have views of the lake or gardens. Complimentary breakfast. Some in-room hot tubs, some room phones, TV in common area. No pets. No kids under 6. No smoking. | 5 Jordan Shore Dr. | 207/998–4976 | wolfcove@exploremaine.com | www.wolfcoveinn.com | 10 rooms | $85–$250 | AE, MC, V.

PORTLAND

MAP 3, C11

(Nearby towns also listed: Cape Elizabeth, Chebeague Islands, Scarborough, Yarmouth)

Maine's largest city, on Casco Bay, offers up the best of many worlds. More large small town than city, Portland has been enjoying a revitalization over the past years. Home to a well-respected art museum, a symphony, a first-rate concert hall, numerous theater groups, a beautifully designed 28-store public market, and a ballpark—along with myriad nearby outdoor spaces—Portland distinguishes itself as the most happening town north of Boston.

The first European settlers arrived in the area in 1628, and the first home built on Machigonne (the Native American name for the neck that juts out into Casco Bay) went up in 1632. In 1658, Massachusetts commissioners renamed the greater Portland area Falmouth. Mills went up and families settled, living peaceably with the natives, until 1675, when King Philip, sachem of the Wampanoag tribe, declared war on the colonists. Nearly a century of bloody battles followed. A brief peace followed, bringing back settlers, creating a more compact village. When the second Indian War broke out, there were between 600 and 700 people living in Falmouth. Not long after, Falmouth was completely wiped out. In 1727, peace returned, and the colony got back to the business of colonizing. Fishing and lumbering were the prime occupations, and shortly thereafter shipbuilding followed. Falmouth began to prosper. Then troubles with England brewed up. After the War for Independence, the Neck separated from the rest of Falmouth in 1786 and took on the name Portland. In 1820, Maine was admitted into the Union, and Portland served as its first capital.

As the nation grew, so did demand for lumber and ships, and Portland rode the wave, becoming an important railway terminus. Then, shortly after the Civil War, devastation struck once again. The Great Fire of 1866 (started by a firecracker) leveled most of the city, but residents quickly rebuilt, earning once and for all Portland's motto, *resurgam* (I shall rise again). Evidence of this building boom can be seen in the proliferation of Victorian buildings that line the city streets.

Portland continued to flourish until after World War II, when it experienced a downswing. But in the early 1970s some enterprising individuals—largely artists and craftsmen—began taking up space and opening shops in the derelict Old Port, thus breathing new life into the city.

Today the Old Port is a booming commercial area, with tony shops, restaurants, and boutiques attracting year-round visitors. Congress Street, Portland's main artery and pre–Old Port heart of in-town Portland, has experienced its own recent resurgence. Not long ago, the street was lined with vacant storefronts. The relocation of Maine College of Art into a vacant department store in the center of town, the formation of an arts district, and the influx of businesses has revitalized this section of town.

The city can basically be broken into two sections: the peninsula and the 'burbs. While there are attractive residential areas on the other side of Interstate 295, which cuts the city in half, most of the action takes place on the peninsula. Peninsulites admit Portland extends beyond the highway—but only grudgingly. The highlights of the peninsula are:

NEIGHBORHOODS
West End. Situated 175 ft above sea level on the western end of the saddle of the Portland peninsula, the Western Promenade is the most distinguishing (and distinguished) feature of the West End neighborhood. Steeped in architectural history, the Western Prom is considered to be one of America's best-preserved Victorian residential neighborhoods. Styles range from Colonial Revival to Second Empire to Italianate to high Victorian Gothic, and include a great number of John Calvin Stevens designs.

Munjoy Hill. Commonly referred to as "The Hill," this somewhat scrappy neighborhood stretches from in-town Portland over a great lump of land down to the Eastern Promenade, with a grassy waterfront park and an eyeful of Casco Bay. The Hill, a tight-knit, working-class enclave, has seedy pockets here and there, but there is also a strong sense of community and history. Its famed landmark, the 1807 Portland Observatory, is currently being renovated, and a number of antiques shops have enlivened a small shopping district here.

The Old Port. The Old Port was nothing more than an assemblage of derelict warehouses until the early 1970s, when artists moved in, creating studio space and opening shops. Now it's action-central. Stretching north from Portland's working waterfront up to Congress Street, and sprawling both east and west, the Old Port is the hub of Portland's tourist activity and nightlife. Cobblestone streets, brick sidewalks, and Victorian architecture abound here, as do shops, restaurants, and people.

Congress Street. The Portland powers-that-be have been trying to reinvent Congress Street since the Maine Mall drew shoppers away from the city's center, starting in the 1970s, when the area went into decline. Most recently it's been dubbed the Downtown Arts District; the presence of Maine College of Art, numerous studios, and performance and arts spaces, including the lavishly restored Merrill Auditorium and the respected Portland Museum of Art, help it to fit the bill. There are also a number of historic buildings, a brand-new public market, coffeehouses, shops, and plenty of street life of all stripes.

Information: Convention and Visitors Bureau of Greater Portland | 305 Commercial St., Portland, | 207/772–5800 | www.visitportland.com.

TRANSPORTATION INFORMATION
Airports: Portland International Jetport | 1001 Westbrook St., just outside the city | 207/774–7301.
Bus Lines: Concord Trailways | 100 Sewall St. | 207/828–1151 or 800/639–3317.
Vermont Transit Lines | 950 Congress St. | 207/772–6587 or 800/5–BUSES.
Intracity Transit: Greater Portland Metro | 114 Valley St. | 207/774–0351.

Attractions

ART AND ARCHITECTURE
Portland City Hall. Completed in 1912, the city hall is an excellent example of Renaissance Revival architecture. | 389 Congress St. | 207/874–8300 | Free | Weekdays 8–4.

Tate House. Built astride the Stroudwater River on the outskirts of Portland, this 1755 house has period displays and gardens. | 1270 Westbrook St. | 207/774–9781. | $5 | Mid-June–Sept., Tues.–Sat. 10–4. Sun. 1–4. Open weekends in Oct.

Victoria Mansion. This Italianate villa, also known as the Morse-Libby house, was built between 1858 and 1860 by entrepreneur Ruggles Sylvester Morse. It is high Victorian—inside and out. A tour through this well-preserved manse might put you in the mood for a swoon. | 109 Danforth St. | 207/772–4841 | $7 | May–Oct., Tues.–Sat. 10–4, Sun. 1–5; special Christmas tours Dec.

Wadsworth-Longfellow House. The boyhood home of the famed poet, this 1785 colonial structure was the first brick house in Portland and today contains many original furnishings. There's also peaceful garden courtyard and 45-minute guided tours. | 489 Congress St. | 207/772–1807 or 207/774–1822 | www.mainehistory.org | $6 | June–Oct., daily 10–4.

KODAK'S TIPS FOR PHOTOGRAPHING THE CITY

Streets
- Take a bus or walking tour to get acclimated
- Explore markets, streets, and parks
- Travel light so you can shoot quickly

City Vistas
- Find high vantage points to reveal city views
- Shoot early or late in the day, for best light
- At twilight, use fast films and bracket exposures

Formal Gardens
- Exploit high angles to show garden design
- Use wide-angle lenses to exaggerate depth and distance
- Arrive early to beat crowds

Landmarks and Monuments
- Review postcard racks for traditional views
- Seek out distant or unusual views
- Look for interesting vignettes or details

Museums
- Call in advance regarding photo restrictions
- Match film to light source when color is critical
- Bring several lenses or a zoom

Houses of Worship
- Shoot exteriors from nearby with a wide-angle lens
- Move away and include surroundings
- Switch to a very fast film indoors

Stained-Glass Windows
- Bright indirect sunlight yields saturated colors
- Expose for the glass not the surroundings
- Switch off flash to avoid glare

Architectural Details
- Move close to isolate details
- For distant vignettes, use a telephoto lens
- Use side light to accent form and texture

In the Marketplace
- Get up early to catch peak activity
- Search out colorful displays and colorful characters
- Don't scrimp on film

Stage Shows and Events
- Never use flash
- Shoot with fast (ISO 400 to 1000) film
- Use telephoto lenses
- Focus manually if necessary

From *Kodak Guide to Shooting Great Travel Pictures* © 2000 by Fodor's Travel Publications

BEACHES, FORESTS, AND PARKS

Deering Oaks. A beautiful city park 2 mi south of Portland that was designed by William Goodwin with grants from the Olmsteds of Boston with a world-class rose circle. This is the site of regular concerts and performances by the Maine Summer Dramatic Institute. | Park Ave. | 207/874–8793 | Free | Daily.

Gilsland Farm. Headquarters of the Maine Audubon Society, the old farm on the Presumpscot River, 2 mi north of Portland, has hiking and cross-country skiing trails through meadows, woodlands, orchards, and marshes. Programs are offered throughout the year. | U.S. 1, Falmouth | 207/781–2330 | www.maineaudubon.org | Free. | Daily dawn–dusk.

Mackworth Island. A gift to the state from the same philanthropist who brought you Baxter State Park, Mackworth Island was once the summer retreat of the Baxter family and is now home to the Baxter School for the Deaf. Circling the island is a 1½-mi hiking trail; use the trail or walk the shorefront. | Falmouth Foreside, Andrews Ave. | Free | Daily dawn–dusk.

Smiling Hill Farm. This working dairy farm, 4 mi west of Portland, has more than 300 traditional and exotic farm animals from around the world. There are pony and hayrides, llama leading, and an ice-cream barn. It's a delight for toddlers. | 781 County Rd., Westbrook | 207/775–4818 | $5 | Daily 10–5.

CULTURE, EDUCATION, AND HISTORY

John Ford Memorial. The famous film producer grew up here and so Portland erected this memorial to him. This bronze statue is larger than life and shows Ford in his director's chair. | Pleasant and Center Sts. | Free | Daily.

Lady of Victories Monument. This 1891 memorial was erected in honor of those who served in the Civil War. | Monument Sq. at Congress St. | Free | Daily.

Merrill Auditorium in the Portland City Hall. The Merrill Auditorium is home to Portland Symphony Orchestra and hosts numerous musical and theatrical events. | 20 Myrtle St. | 207/874–8200.

Neal Dow Memorial. This brick federal mansion (1829) once belonged to Neal Dow (1804–97), an abolitionist and prohibitionist. It now operates as a museum, with period furnishings, grandfather clocks, and a silver collection. | 714 Congress St. | 207/773–7773 | Donations accepted | Weekdays 7–4.

Portland Stage Co. This first-class, 25-year-old company produces some traditional theater and some modern, thought-provoking dramas. | 25 Forest Ave. | 207/774–0465 | fax 207/774–0756 | Sept.–May, Tues.–Sun.

University of Southern Maine. The campus offers a planetarium, sporting events, theater, concert hall, and art museums. Events are held year-round. | Portland campus: I–295, exit 6; Gorham campus: Rte. 25 and College Ave. | 207/780–4200 or 207/780–4500 | www.usm.maine.edu | Daily.

Western Cemetery. This 12-acre cemetery was laid out in 1829. Today, it is a popular spot with dog walkers. | Off Western Promenade | Free | Daily.

MUSEUMS

Children's Museum of Maine. At this interactive, hands-on museum, kids can explore a space shuttle, try their hand at newscasting, and learn about lobstering. The museum's camera obscura is a highlight. | 142 Free St. | 207/828–1234 | childrensmuseumofme.org | $5 | Memorial Day–Labor Day, daily 10–5; Labor Day–Memorial Day, Wed.–Sat. 10–5, Sun. noon–5.

Maine Narrow Gauge Railroad Company and Museum. This museum displays antique railroad equipment dating back to 1880s. There are daily excursions along Casco Bay on original Maine narrow-gauge trains. | 58 Fore St. | 207/828–0814 | http://mngrr.rails.net | Museum free, $5 for round-trip train ride | Museum daily 10–4. Train rides mid-May–mid-

Oct., daily 11–4 (on the hr); last two wks Dec., daily 11–4 (on the hr); year-round, weekends 11–4 (on the hr); closed Jan.–mid-Feb.

★ **Portland Museum of Art.** This is Maine's largest and oldest museum. Its well-respected collections include works by Winslow Homer, Andrew Wyeth, and Marsden Hartley; the Impressionists are also represented. | 7 Congress Sq. | 207/775–6148 or 207/773–ARTS | www.portlandmuseum.org | $6 | Sat.–Wed. 10–5, Thurs.–Fri. 10–9.

Southworth Planetarium. You can enjoy laser-light shows, sometimes set to the music of Garth Brooks and others, at this site. There are also some astronomy shows. | 96 Falmouth St. | 207/780–4249 | www.usm.maine.edu/planet. | $3–$5.

RELIGION AND SPIRITUALITY

St. Lawrence Art and Community Center. An 1897 Queen Anne and Romanesque style church. | 207/775–5568 | Free | 76 Congress St.

SHOPPING

Old Port Exchange. This is Portland's shopping and dining hot spot. The bulk of the city's nightlife centers around this area. | Exchange St. | 207/761–4210 | Free | Daily.

Portland Public Market. The more than 20 locally owned businesses inside this market (which opened in 1998) specialize in fresh foods, organic produce, and imported specialty foods, including fresh-baked goods, soups and chowders, smoked seafood, rotisserie chicken, aged cheeses, and German meats. A skywalk connects the market to the third floor of a park-

MAINE HUMOR

"Does this road go to Portland?" "Nope. Stays right where it is."

Don't take offense if you encounter an exchange such as this while engaging in discourse with Mainers. It's the Maine wit—dry as driftwood, dripping in irony, and overabundant in understatement.

Maine humor has been popularized by numerous comics and storytellers, most notably the "Bert and I" recordings of Bob Bryan and Marshall Dodge, dating back to the 1950s. (Dodge was killed in a 1982 hit-and-run bicycle accident.) Maine humor is encountered in its rawest and purest form, however, in everyday conversation. Yes, people actually talk this way.

Recently, a bit of a controversy has bubbled up between Maine and Vermont over bragging rights to perhaps the quintessential Yankee punch line: "You can't get there from here." (This line generally follows a long, convoluted string of directions given by a local to a visitor.) The Vermont Board of Tourism has posted the line on its website as an example of a "classic Vermont joke." Mainers roundly dismiss the claim. Maine's Governor Angus King was quoted in response: "The next thing those Vermonters will be doing is claiming that lobsters are found in Lake Champlain." (Even though Governor King is "from away," note the irony in his response.)

The matter may never be settled, but there's one thing you can count on: you're unlikely to get a straight answer concerning it.

© Artville

ing garage on Elm Street; parking is free if you have a vendor stamp your ticket. | Exchange St. and Cumberland Ave. | 207/228–2000 | Free | Mon.–Sat. 9–7, Sun. 10–5.

SPORTS AND RECREATIONS

★ **Portland Sea Dogs.** The Sea Dogs are an AA affiliate of baseball's Florida Marlins, and an outing to one of their games will include minor league ball, a fuzzy and feisty mascot named Slugger, and souvenir and food booths. Tickets can be scarce, so call ahead. | Hadlock Field, 271 Park Ave. | 207/879–9500 | www.portlandseadogs.com | $2–$6 | Apr.–Sept.

OTHER POINTS OF INTEREST

Western Prom. One of the best-preserved Victorian neighborhoods in the United States, on the west end of Portland. This scenic area is full of old homes. From Interstate 295, Congress Street exit, head up the steep hill, past the Maine Medical Center, and make a right onto Brackett Street. | Free | Daily.

SIGHTSEEING TOURS/TOUR COMPANIES

Bay View Cruises. The *Bay View Lady* is a 66-ft passenger boat that holds 117. Scheduled and chartered cruises are available. | Fisherman's Wharf, 184 Commercial St. | 207/761–0496 | $10 | May–Oct.

Casco Bay Lines. One of the oldest continuously operated ferry services in the nation, this line serves both commuters and visitors. You can take a ferry to a specific island in Casco Bay, or ride the Mail Boat and hit them all. Charters and cruises are available. | 56 Commercial St. | 207/774–7871 | www.cascobaylines.com | $5.75–$10.75 | Daily.

Eagle Tours Inc. This outfit offers a number of excursions, including a seal-watch and a trip to Portland Head Light. Or make a day of it and take a trip to Eagle Island, the former summer home of Arctic explorer Admiral Robert Peary. | 1 Long Wharf, Commercial St. | 207/774–6498. | $8–$19 | June–Oct., Fri–Sun. Call for hours.

Olde Port Mariner Fleet, Inc. This outfit provides sightseeing, seal-watching, and lunchtime and evening harbor cruises, as well as offshore whale-watching and deep-sea fishing. | Long Wharf, 170 Commercial St. | 207/775–0727 or 800/437–3270 | fax 207/642–4926 | www.marinerfleet.com | $10–$50 | Memorial Day–July and Labor Day–Columbus Day, weekends; July–Aug., daily.

Palawan Sailing. This Coast Guard–certified outfit has been offering sailing excursions since 1989. | Long Wharf, Commercial St. | 207/773–2163 | fax 207/781–5530 | palawan@nlis.net.

M/S Scotia Prince. Overnight ferry service between Portland and Yarmouth, Nova Scotia, featuring full dining service, live entertainment, casino, and a duty-free shop. | 468 Commercial St. | 207/775–5616 or 800/341–7540. | www.princeoffundy.com | Call for details | May–Oct.

ON THE CALENDAR

MAR.: *Maine Boatbuilders Show.* Over 200 exhibitors will show you everything you want or need to know about the construction of watercraft. | Portland Company Complex, 58 Fore St. | 207/744–1067.
JUNE: *Old Port Festival.* Live music and entertainment, children's activities, and food booths fill every inch of the Old Port Exchange. | Exchange St. | 207/772–6828.
JUNE: *Back Cove Family Day.* Live entertainment, games, food vendors, and loads of family fun at Payson Park, overlooking Back Cove. | Baxter Blvd. | 207/874–8793.
JUNE: *Greek Heritage Festival.* A Greek food fest with live entertainment, arts, and crafts. | 133 Pleasant St. | 207/774–0281.
JULY: *OpSail Maine.* Formerly known as "Aucucisco," this celebration of the city's working waterfront features a number of marine-related activities and tall ships. | Portland Waterfront | 207/772–6828.
JULY–AUG.: *Summer Performance Series.* Free concerts by the area's top performers in various outdoor parks and public venues in Old Port and Arts District. | 207/772–6828.

AUG.: *Italian Street Festival.* A celebration of *la dolce vita,* with games, entertainment, and buckets of pasta sauce. | Federal St. | 207/773–0748.

AUG.: *Sidewalk Arts Festival.* Congress Street is lined with 350 booths, featuring artists from all over the country. | Congress St. | 207/828–6666.

SEPT.: *Cumberland Fair.* A large agricultural fair with exhibits, demonstrations, livestock, and harness racing at the Cumberland Fairgrounds. | Cumberland | 207/829–6647.

NOV.: *Maine Brewer's Festival.* You can sample wares from the best local breweries while enjoying live music and plenty of food at the Portland EXPO. | Park Ave. | 207/874–8200.

NOV.–DEC.: *Victorian Holiday.* Carolers, tree lighting, horse-drawn carriage rides, and special events fill the streets of Portland during the holiday season. | Old Port and Arts district | 207/772–5800.

DEC.: *New Year's Portland.* Chem-free citywide celebration with a parade, dance, music, performances, and fireworks. | Downtown Portland | 207/772–9012.

WALKING TOUR
Portland's West End
(approximately 2 hours without stops)

Begin on Congress Street, at Monument Square, which is punctuated by the 1891 **Lady of Victories Monument,** in honor of those who served in the Civil War. Proceed west on Congress Street and take a quick detour to your right on Preble Street to No. 25 and the **Portland Public Market,** where you will find fish-, flower-, and meat-mongers, housed in an attractive open-air market. Local products and produce are featured here. Return to Congress Street, turn right, and stop at No. 485 and the **Wadsworth-Longfellow House,** the boyhood home of the poet and an intriguing museum, with many original family artifacts and furnishings. Next go to 7 Congress Square. **The Portland Museum of Art** (PMA) is Maine's largest art museum, featuring works by Winslow Homer, Andrew Wyeth, and Marsden Hartley, plus collections of 18th- and 19th-century European and American art. Adjacent to PMA is the **Children's Museum of Maine,** 142 Free Street, with interactive and hands-on displays and exhibits. Both museums have gift shops and cafés. Continue on Congress Street, past Longfellow Square and the 1888 statue of the poet, at Congress and State Streets, to the **Neal Dow Memorial** at 714 Congress Street. This 1829 brick Federal mansion was once home to the father of prohibition and now is kept up as a museum, with fascinating period furnishings. Continue west and turn left onto Bramhall Street, past the Maine Medical Center with its high Victorian Gothic crested tower poking above the rest of the modern complex, to the **Western Prom,** considered one of the best-preserved Victorian neighborhoods in the country. Here grand mansions line this onetime walk- and carriage way, with views of the White Mountains (and the jetport, a strip mall, and oil tanks). Stick to the prom, or take time to wander around the neighborhood's wide streets. John Calvin Stevens fans will find 70 of his designs here. Continue along the Prom to the 1829 **Western Cemetery,** which is a popular dog run, where the who's who of Portland dog owners let their canines romp freely. At the junction of the Western Prom and Danforth Street, turn left, travel past Waynflete Academy, to No. 109 and the **Victoria Mansion.** The 1858 Italianate villa/museum features all things Victorian; the interior has ornate decorations and period furnishings. At the confluence of Danforth, York, Pleasant, and Fore streets, view the **John Ford Memorial,** a statue of the legendary filmmaker, who started life on Portland's Munjoy Hill. Go north on Center Street, which brings you back to Monument Square.

WALKING TOUR
Portland's Waterfront, Old Port, and East End

Start at 389 Congress Street and **Portland City Hall.** Built between 1909 and 1912, it's an excellent example of Renaissance Revival architecture. Head down Exchange Street into the heart of the Old Port Exchange district, where you'll find cobblestone streets, brick sidewalks, and tons of specialty shops and eateries housed in 19th-century brick buildings, built after the Great Fire of 1866. Many can (and do) spend hours here, but tear yourself away and proceed down to Commercial Street, where you can get a view of the working waterfront, marinas, and harbor cruises. Travel east on Commercial Street, past the imposing **U.S. Customs House,** a 1867–71 example of French Renaissance architecture, to the **Maine State Pier,** where you can take a walk out and watch the cheerful, chubby red-and-yellow ferryboats arrive and depart. In the harbor, you can see Fort Gorges, Spring Point Light, and Bug Light. At the eastern terminus of Commercial Street, the road gives way to a paved trail and brings you to the **Maine Narrow Gauge Railroad Company and Museum,** where you can ride the skinny rails on a 3-mi track. Those wishing to abbreviate their walk and avoid a large hill can circle back here. Those wishing to forge on should remain on the path, which winds below Fort Allen Park, astride East End Beach, to **Portland's Public Landing.** There are a couple of picnic tables here, and great views of Casco Bay. From the landing's parking lot, you will see a monolithic monument at the top of steep and grassy knoll. Ascend the hill to the monument, which puts you at the head of Congress Street, and head back toward town. At the corner of Congress and Munjoy Streets, note the 1897 Queen Anne and Romanesque **St. Lawrence Church,** which is being restored through a neighborhood, grassroots effort. At the crest of the hill, you will see the 1807 **Portland Observatory** at 138 Congress Street. This shingled, octagonal structure, which is the only remaining marine signal tower on the eastern seaboard, underwent a massive renovation project in 1999. As you descend the Hill, note the **Eastern Cemetery** at the corner of Congress and Mountfort Streets on your left. This cemetery, Portland's first, dates back to 1688 but is closed to the public. Across the street, there's an interesting stretch of junk and antiques shops and bookstores worth a peek. Continue down Congress Street, past Lincoln Park on your left, and you'll be back at City Hall.

Dining

INEXPENSIVE

Great Lost Bear. Contemporary. This cavernous, family-friendly restaurant has an extensive menu and vintage memorabilia on the walls. There are also more than 50 microbrews on tap. It's known for burgers, vegetarian items, and homemade desserts. Open-air dining on the patio. Kids' menu. No smoking. | 540 Forest Ave. | 207/772–0300. | $8–$13. | AE, D, DC, MC, V.

Gritty McDuff. English. The fish-and-chips and shepherd's pie keep Portland's original brewpub very English, and continue to attract people of all ages. Vegetarian fare like hummus wraps and veggie burgers is also available. There are ocean views from second floor. | 396 Fore St. | 207/772–2739 | $5–$9 | AE, D, MC, V.

Pepperclub. Eclectic. Half the menu is vegetarian, while the other half includes choices like free-range organic lamb and fresh seafood. Organic wines and microbrew beer are on the menu. Make sure you leave room for the peanut-butter roulade. | 78 Middle St. | 207/772–0531 | No lunch | $8–$13 | AE, D, MC, V.

Uncle Billy's. Barbecue. A roadhouse, anything-goes spot with low ceilings, swivel-stool counter, booths, and mismatched tables. There are lots of Elvis and porcine appointments as well as a jukebox and open kitchen. Known for jerk chicken, country-fried steak, and ribs. Open-air dining on the patio. Kids' menu. Beer and wine only. No smoking. | 69 Newbury St. | 207/871–5631 | No lunch | $6–$13 | No credit cards.

MODERATE

Back Bay Grill. Contemporary. This bistro in a Victorian drugstore has pressed-tin ceilings, original art, and an open kitchen. A five-course, prix fixe lobster tasting menu ($65) is offered in summer. Known for seafood, grill, and rack of lamb. No smoking. | 65 Portland St. | 207/772–8833 | www.backbaygrill.com | Closed Sun. No lunch | $18–$33 | AE, D, DC, MC, V.

Bella Cucina. Italian. This eatery has traditional country fare—the food is rustic, the portions are big, and the mood is intimate. Try the grilled fresh seafood, beef, or one of their two daily vegan and vegetarian entrées. Beer and wine only. | 653 Congress St. | 207/828–4033 | No lunch | $10–$19 | AE, D, DC, MC, V.

Cafe Uffa! Contemporary. This cheerful, funky restaurant has mismatched tables and chairs, tall windows, and original artwork on the walls. Sunday brunch is especially popular with locals. Known for fresh produce, vegetarian selections, grilled fish, and risotto. Live acoustic music on Sundays. Beer and wine only. No smoking. | 190 State St. | 207/775–3380 | Breakfast also available on weekends; closed Mon., Tues., and alternate Sun.; 1st wk Jan.; 1 wk in July. No lunch | $15–$20 | MC, V.

DiMillo's Floating Restaurant. Seafood. A sprawling restaurant on the water in a former coastal ferry. Known for lobster, pasta dishes. Open-air dining on two decks. Kids' menu, early-bird suppers. No smoking. | 25 Long Wharf | 207/772–2216 | www.dimillos.com | $15–$30 | AE, D, DC, MC, V.

Fore Street. Contemporary. This modern, industrial restaurant has an open kitchen. The menu features fresh and organic local produce. Try the spit-roasted pork. Kids' menu. No smoking. | 288 Fore St. | 207/775–2717 | No lunch | $13–$24. | AE, MC, V.

Joe's Boathouse. Contemporary. You'll find marina-side dining, with an open kitchen and water views here. Try the lobster fettuccine or beef tenderloin. Open-air dining on two decks. Kids' menu. Sunday brunch. No smoking. | 1 Spring Point Dr., South Portland | 207/741–2780 | www.joesboathouse.com | $12–$19 | AE, MC, V.

Perfetto. Mediterranean. This upscale bistro is in a restored late-19th-century jeweler's shop with original vaults, brick walls, bright colors, local artwork, and an open kitchen. Try the crispy shrimp ravioli or the North Beach cioppino. Sunday brunch. No smoking. | 28 Exchange St. | 207/828–0001 | $12–$18 | AE, MC, V.

Stone Coast Brewery. American. Beef and veggie burgers are found on this menu, where lobsters are also served in season. Leave room for their bourbon pecan pie. Live music makes this a lively spot. | 14 York St. | 207/773–2337 | $6–$22 | AE, D, DC, MC, V.

Street & Company. Seafood. A rustic bistro with an intimate, brick-lined interior and an open kitchen. Dried herbs hang from the exposed beams. Try the lobster diavolo or grilled tuna. Open-air café dining. Beer and wine only. No smoking. | 33 Wharf St. | 207/775–0887 | No lunch | $14–$24 | AE, MC, V.

Walter's Cafe. Contemporary. This eatery is in a 19th-century building, with much exposed brick. Try the crazy chicken or the calamari. No smoking. | 15 Exchange St. | 207/871–9258 | www.walterscafe.com | No lunch Sun. | $13–$22 | AE, MC, V.

EXPENSIVE

Aubergine. French. This restaurant in a former firehouse has a four-sided gallery that looks down on the main dining area and open kitchen. It is known for imaginative dishes from the southwest of France. Try the spiced duck with green peppercorns or the lobster medallions with mussels. Open-air dining by the front stoop. No smoking. | 555 Congress St. | 207/874–0680 | $18–$22 | MC, V.

Katahdin. American. Painted tables, flea-market artifacts, mismatched dinnerware, and a log-pile bar provide a fun and unpretentious place for dining on large portions of home-cooked New England fare. Try the chicken potpie, fried trout, crab cakes, or the nightly blue-plate special, and save room for the fruit cobbler. | 106 High St. | 207/774–1740 | Closed Sun. No lunch | $17–$25 | D, MC, V.

Wine Bar at Wharf Street Café. Eclectic. Tucked away on cobblestoned Wharf Street, an alley that runs parallel to Fore Street between Moulton and Union, this place is really two finds in one. The small, informal restaurant has a partially exposed kitchen, brick walls, and a painted floor. The menu changes seasonally, but the house specialty, lobster and brie ravioli with roasted grapes and caramelized onion sauce, is a mainstay. After dinner, head upstairs to the Wine Bar for dessert, wine, espresso, and drinks. | 38 Wharf St. | 207/772–6976, 207/773–6667 restaurant | No lunch | $20–$21 | AE, MC, V.

Lodging

INEXPENSIVE

Andrews Lodging Bed and Breakfast. You can breathe easy in this 1780 colonial built on a 1½-acre lot, 4½ mi from the Old Port. Some of the rooms share bathrooms. Complimentary breakfast. No air-conditioning, no room phones, no TV. | 417 Auburn St. | 207/797–9157 | www.travelguides.com/bb/andrews_lodging | 6 rooms (2 rooms baths) | $110–$165 | AE, D, MC, V.

Best Western Merry Manor Inn. This chain option is near the airport, the Maine Mall, and U.S. 1 and is 3½ south of the city. Restaurant. In-room data ports, some microwaves, some refrigerators, cable TV, some in-room VCRs. Pool. Laundry facilities. Business services. Free parking. Pets allowed. | 700 Main St., South Portland | 207/774–6151 | fax 207/871–0537 | www.bestwestern.com | 151 rooms | $107–$130 | AE, D, DC, MC, V.

Comfort Inn. This hotel near the Maine Mall and the airport is 2 mi south of Portland. Complimentary Continental breakfast. In-room data ports, some refrigerators, cable TV. Pool. Laundry facilities. Business services, airport shuttle, free parking. | 90 Maine Mall Rd., South Portland | 207/775–0409 | fax 207/775–1755 | 127 rooms | $90–$150 | AE, D, DC, MC, V.

Hampton Inn. A chain hotel south of Portland that is near the airport, at the center of the Maine Mall business area. Complimentary Continental breakfast. Some microwaves, some refrigerators, cable TV. Business services, airport shuttle, free parking. | 171 Philbrook Ave., South Portland | 207/773–4400 | fax 207/773–6786 | hinn0886@aol.com | maineguide.com/portland/hampton | 117 rooms | $109–$129 | AE, D, DC, MC, V.

Holiday Inn West. Near the turnpike, West Portland businesses, and shopping. Restaurant, bar, picnic area, room service. In-room data ports, some refrigerators, cable TV. Pool. Hot tub. Exercise equipment. Laundry facilities. Business services, airport shuttle. | 81 Riverside St. | 207/774–5601 | fax 207/774–2103 | www.portlandholidayinn.com | 200 rooms | $98–$130 | AE, D, DC, MC, V.

Howard Johnson. Near the turnpike and West Portland businesses. Restaurant, bar, room service. Some microwaves, some in-room hot tubs, cable TV. Pool. Hot tub. Exercise equipment. Video games. Laundry facilities. Business services, airport shuttle, free parking. Pets allowed (deposit). | 155 Riverside St. | 207/774–5861 | fax 207/774–5861 | www.hojoportland.com | 119 rooms | $110–$130 | AE, D, DC, MC, V.

Inn at St. John. An old-world turn-of-the-20th-century inn. Complimentary Continental breakfast. No air-conditioning in some rooms. Some microwaves, some refrigerators, cable TV. Laundry facilities. Business services, airport shuttle. Pets allowed. | 939 Congress St. | 207/773–6481 or 800/636–9127 | fax 207/756–7629 | www.innatstjohn.com | 37 rooms (15 with shared bath, 15 with shower only) | $55–$160 | AE, D, DC, MC, V.

Norman Brown House. A Victorian Italianate home in a quiet neighborhood. Rooms have antique heirloom furnishings, desks, and private sitting areas. Microwaves, refrigerators, cable TV. Business services. No pets. No smoking. | 135 Vaughan St. | 207/773–8529 or 877/897–8529 | www.mainewine.com/portland_maine | 2 rooms (share 1 bath) | $79 | MC, V.

Parkside Parrot Inn. A quiet 1894 home in a residential neighborhood that is within walking distance of Portland's major attractions. Rooms have simple colonial furnishings. The two woman owners make this a safe environment for guests of all persuasions. Complimentary Continental breakfast. No air-conditioning in some rooms, some room phones, TV in common area. Hot tub. No pets. No kids under 8. No smoking. | 273 State St. | 207/775–0224 | parpari@maine.rr.com | www.home.maine.rr.com/pparrot | 7 rooms (2 with shared bath) | $65–$85 | MC, V.

Sheraton South Portland. Distinctive round hotel at the Maine Mall, near the airport. Restaurant, bar. In-room data ports, some microwaves, cable TV. Pool. Gym. Business services, airport shuttle. | 363 Maine Mall Rd., South Portland | 207/775–6161 | fax 207/775–0196 | www.ittsheraton.com | 220 rooms | $109–$218 | AE, D, DC, MC, V.

Susse Chalet. Budget hotel near exit 8 of the Maine Turnpike. Complimentary Continental breakfast. In-room data ports, cable TV. Pool. Laundry facilities. | 1200 Brighton Ave. | 207/774–6101 | fax 207/772–8697 | 132 rooms | $65–$75 | AE, D, DC, MC, V.

MODERATE

Doubletree Hotel. This upscale hotel caters to businesspeople and kids alike. Chocolate-chip cookies wait for you on your arrival here in the center of town, just a few minutes' walk from shops and business and a five-minute drive to the Old Port. Restaurant. Pool. Hot tub. Exercise room. Free parking. | 1230 Congress St. | 800/222–TREE or 207/774–5611 | fax 207/761–1560 | www.hilton.com/doubletree/hotels/ | 149 rooms | $169 | AE, D, DC, MC, V.

The Eastland. A refurbished older hotel in the arts district, with an excellent view of the city, harbor, and mountains from lounge. Restaurant, bar with entertainment. Cable TV. Exercise equipment. Business services, airport shuttle. Pets allowed (deposit). | 157 High St. | 207/775–5411 | fax 207/775–2872 | 204 rooms | $169–$239 | AE, D, DC, MC, V.

Embassy Suites. This stylish modern hotel with all conveniences is about 500 yards from the airport. Restaurant, bar, complimentary breakfast. In-room data ports, microwaves, refrigerators, cable TV, VCR. Pool. Hot tub, sauna. Exercise equipment. Video games. Laundry facilities. Business services, airport shuttle. | 1050 Westbrook St. | 207/775–2200 | fax 207/775–4052 | www.embassyportland.com | 119 suites | $159–$219 | AE, D, DC, MC, V.

Holiday Inn by the Bay. Centrally located downtown hotel, across from the Civic Center with harbor views. Restaurant, bar with entertainment, room service. In-room data ports, cable TV. Pool. Exercise equipment. Laundry facilities. Business services, airport shuttle, free parking. | 88 Spring St. | 207/775–2311 or 800/345–5050 | fax 207/761–8224 | sales@innbythebay.com | www.innbythebay.com | 239 rooms | $141–$157 | AE, D, DC, MC, V.

Inn at Park Spring. This inn is in a lovely three-story, 1840 town house. It's a 10-minute walk to the Old Port. Complimentary breakfast. No TV. Free parking. | 135 Spring St. | 207/774–1059 | www.innatparkspring.com | 6 rooms | $130–$145 | AE, D, MC, V.

Inn on Carleton. A mid-19th-century town house with period furnishings. Complimentary breakfast. No room phones. Business services. No smoking. | 46 Carleton St. | 207/775–1910 or 800/639–1779 | fax 207/761–2160 | www.innnoncarleton.com | 6 rooms | $159–$199 | D, MC, V.

Marriott at Sable Oaks. Near the airport and Maine Mall businesses, on golf course. Restaurant, bar, room service. In-room data ports, cable TV, some in-room VCRs. Pool. Hot tub. Exercise equipment. Business services, free parking. Some pets allowed. | 200 Sable Oaks Dr., South Portland | 207/871–8000 | fax 207/871–7971 | www.marriott.com | 227 rooms | $149 | AE, D, DC, MC, V.

Pomegranate Inn. A late-19th-century mansion filled with antiques and art. There are fireplaces in some rooms. Complimentary breakfast. Cable TV. No kids under 16. No smoking. | 49 Neal St. | 207/772–1006 or 800/356–0408 | fax 207/773–4426 | www.pomegranateinn.com | 8 rooms (4 with shower only), 1 suite | $165–$195, $205 suite | AE, D, MC, V.

Portland Regency Hotel. A boutique hotel in a vintage redbrick building in the Old Port district. Restaurant, bar. In-room data ports, minibars, cable TV, some in-room VCRs. Hot tub, massage. Gym. Business services, airport shuttle. | 20 Milk St. | 207/774–4200 or 800/727–3436 | fax 207/775–2150 | www.theregency.com | 85 rooms, 10 suites | $199, $239–$249 suites | AE, D, DC, MC, V.

The Danforth. This beautiful, 1821 brick home has white columns, a cupola, and a prominent place in the Spring Street Historic District. Rooms have fireplaces and are plush with simple colonial furnishings and couches. There's a formal parlor and conference rooms for business meetings or weddings, and an efficiency unit with two fireplaces, a kitchen, and private entrance for longer-term guests. Dining room, complimentary breakfast, room service. In-room data ports, cable TV. Laundry service. Business services, free parking. No pets. No smoking. | 163 Danforth St. | 207/879–8755 or 800/991–6557 | fax 207/879–8754 | danforth@maine.rr.com | www.danforthmaine.com | 10 rooms (2 with shared bath) | $139–$329 | AE, MC, V.

Inn by the Sea. A deluxe inn on the ocean with a swimming beach nearby, it's 6 mi southeast of Portland. Restaurant, picnic area, room service. No air-conditioning, in-room data ports, kitchenettes, microwaves, cable TV, in-room VCRs. Pool. Bicycles. Tennis. Beach. Business services. Pets allowed. No smoking. | 40 Bowery Beach Rd., Cape Elizabeth | 207/799–3134 or 800/888–4287 | fax 207/799–4779 | innmaine@aol.com | www.innbythesea.com | 43 suites | $269–$549 | AE, D, MC, V.

PRESQUE ISLE

MAP 3, F3

(Nearby town also listed: Caribou)

Home to a branch of the University of Maine, and adjacent to the Canadian border, Presque Isle is the commercial and cultural center of Aroostook County. Permanent settlers first arrived in the early 19th century, but growth was slow. Presque Isle, incorporated in 1859, started as a logging town but is now known for potatoes. There are a number of parks and recreational areas, as well as historic sights, and winter sees a big influx of snowmobilers.

Information: **Presque Isle Area Chamber of Commerce** | 3 Houlton Rd., Presque Isle, 04769 | 207/764–6561 or 800/764–7420 | fax 207/764–6571 | www.mainerec.com.

Attractions
Aroostook Farm–Maine Agricultural Experiment Station. The farm, 2 mi south of Presque Isle, is part of the University of Maine. It explores improved methods of growing potatoes and other crops, and there are some displays as well as a guided tour. | Houlton Rd. | 207/762–8281 | Free | Weekdays 7:30–4:30.

Aroostook State Park. There are campsites, a beach with lifeguards, hiking, and mountain climbing at this state park, 4 mi southwest of Presque Isle. | State Park Rd. off U.S. 1 | 207/768–8341 | $1 | Daily dawn–dusk.

***Double Eagle II* Launch Site Monument.** The monument, 4 mi southwest of Presque Isle, marks the site of the start of the first successful trans-Atlantic balloon flight, which took place in 1978. | Spragueville Rd. | Free | Daily.

Presque Isle Historical Society. This 1850s Victorian home is a living museum filled with the original furnishings, historical photos, and memorabilia of the town and the home's original owners. | 16 3rd St. | 207/762–1151 | Free | Memorial Day–Labor Day, Tues. 9–noon, or by appointment.

ON THE CALENDAR
JULY: *Potato Blossom Festival.* When the hundreds of acres of potato fields come into blossom, the town celebrates with a festival; there's a parade, mashed-potato wrestling, the "Roostic River Raft Race," fireworks, and more. | Fort Fairfield | 207/472–3802.
AUG.: *Northern Maine Fair.* Established in 1854, this agricultural fair features the

largest midway in the county, exhibits, lumberjack roundup, and fireworks. | Presque Isle Fairgrounds | 207/764–6561.

Dining

Pat's Pizza. Pizza. This is one of several locations throughout the state. You can take your pizza out, have it delivered, or dine at the restaurant. | 9 North St. | 207/764–0367 | $8–$15 | MC, V.

Winnie's Restaurant & Dairy Bar. Seafood. This veteran restaurant has an Oldies look and Coca-Cola memorabilia. It's a popular hangout with the snowmobile crowd. Try the fresh seafood, Maine-potato French fries, burgers, or lobster stew. There's open-air dining on the patio. Kids' menu. No liquor. No smoking. | 79 Parsons St. | 207/769–4971 | $10–$15 | MC, V.

Lodging

Budget Traveler Motor Lodge. You'll find great views of Haystack Mountain from some of the rooms at this budget motel. Complimentary Continental breakfast. Some kitchenettes, some microwaves, refrigerators, cable TV, some in-room VCRs. Laundry facilities. Business services, airport shuttle. | 71 Main St. | 207/769–0111 or 800/958–0111 | fax 207/764–6836 | budgeth@bangornews.infi.net | 53 rooms | $39 | AE, D, DC, MC, V.

County View Inn. This business hotel 1 mi south of town has views of the hills. Cable TV. Pool. Sauna. | U.S. 1 | 207/764–3321 | fax 207/764–5167 | 144 rooms | $129–$229 | AE, D, DC, MC, V.

Northern Lights Motel. This family-run motel is business and family friendly. Picnic area. In-room data ports, microwaves, refrigerators, cable TV, some in-room VCRs. Laundry facilities. Business services. Pets allowed. | 72 Houlton Rd. | 207/764–4441 | northernlightsmotel@yahoo.com | www.northernlightsmotel.com | 13 rooms | $40–$50 | AE, D, MC, V.

RANGELEY

MAP 3, B7

(Nearby town also listed: Kingfield)

The heart of the Rangeley Lakes region, the town of Rangeley has something of a frontier feel, with its main street wrapping around the north shore of sprawling Rangeley Lake. The town was named for Squire Rangeley, who erected a grand British-style estate, built sawmills, gristmills, and a 10-mi road for area settlers and then promptly moved to Virginia. In winter Rangeley is snowmobile central. In summer things are a bit more laid back. You can hike along the numerous mountain trails, fish, boat, or swim. The breathtaking views from the Height of Land overlook lay your options out before you.

Information: **Rangeley Lakes Region Chamber of Commerce** | Box 317, Park Rd. off Main St., Rangeley, 04970 | 207/864–5364 or 800/MT–LAKES | fax 207/864–5366 | mtlakes@rangeley.org | www.rangeleymaine.com.

Attractions

Height of Land. On Route 17 between Rumford and Oquossoc, right next to the Appalachian Trail, this scenic overlook provides majestic views of the Rangeley Lakes and White Mountains. | Rte. 17 | Free | Daily.

★ **Rangeley Lake State Park.** In an area famous for trout and landlocked salmon fishing, this park, 9 mi southwest of town, offers some of the most beautiful scenery in the state. Amenities include a boat ramp with floats, swimming, snowmobile and hiking trails, and well-spaced campsites. | South Shore Dr. | 207/864–3858 | Call for prices | May–Sept.

Saddleback Ski Area. This is a big mountain that doesn't make a big production out of it. It operates in a friendly and casual manner. The base lodge, 7 mi east of Rangeley, is rustic but contains everything you need, and at reasonable prices. | Saddleback Rd. | 207/864–5671 or 207/864–3380 | Nov.–Apr., weekdays 9–4.

Wilhelm Reich Museum. This museum is on a 175-acre historic site called Orgonon, 4 mi west of town, and it represents and interprets the work of controversial Viennese scientist and psychoanalyst Wilhelm Reich, who believed he could treat diseases by trapping airborne sexual energy. The museum grounds incorporate a nature preserve, which can be visited. | Dodge Pond Rd. | 207/864–3443 | $3 | July–Aug., Tues.–Sun. 1–5; Sept., Sun. 1–5.

ON THE CALENDAR

JAN.: *Snodeo.* A roundup of sledders and their machines that includes activities, games, and fireworks. | Rte. 4 | 207/864–5364.

JULY: *Logging Museum Field Days.* Bean suppers, lumberjack contests and displays, as well as all things to do with the once-great logging days, comprise this event at the Rangeley Logging Museum. | Rte. 16 | 207/864–5364.

AUG.: *Blueberry Festival.* A one-day harvest celebration, where blueberry treats abound, in downtown Rangeley. | 207/864–5364.

Dining

Country Club Inn. Continental. The glassed-in dining room—open to nonguests by reservation only—has linen-draped tables set well apart and overlooking Rangeley Lake as well as the Western Mountains. The menu includes roast duck, veal, fresh fish, and filet mignon. Leave room for homemade treats like strawberry shortcake and fresh fruit pies. | Mingo Loop Rd. | 207/864–3831 | Closed Sun.–Wed; Apr.–mid-May; and mid-Oct.–late-Dec. | $14–$19 | AE, MC, V.

Gingerbread House. American. A big fieldstone fireplace, well-spaced tables, and an antique marble soda fountain, all with views to the woods beyond, make for a pleasant evening at this gingerbread-trim house. The ambitious dinner menu doesn't quite deliver, but the portions are huge. Reservations are essential on summer weekends. | Rtes. 17/4 | 207/864–3602 | Breakfast also available; closed Mon., Tues. No dinner Sun. | $18–$38 | AE, MC, V.

People's Choice. Steak. This casual eatery, 1 mi north of town, is anchored by a Paul Bunyan statue. It's known for seafood, steaks, and pasta. There's also a salad bar. Live music (rock) on Saturday. Kids' menu. No smoking. | Main St. (Rte. 4) | 207/864–5220 | $10–$20 | AE, D, MC, V.

Porter House Restaurant. Continental. This popular restaurant, 20 mi north of Rangeley, draws diners from Rangeley, Kingfield, and Canada with its good service and excellent food. Of the 1908 farmhouse's four dining rooms, the front one downstairs, which has a fireplace, is the most intimate and elegant. The broad menu includes entrées for diners with light appetites. On the heavier side are porterhouse steak and roast duckling. Try the boneless lamb loin and lobster Brittany casserole if they're on the menu. Reservations essential on weekends. | Rte. 27, Eustis | 207/246–7932 | Closed Mon., Tues. | $12–$29 | MC, V.

Rangeley Inn. Continental. The elegant restaurant of the vintage inn has elaborate woodwork and gleaming chandeliers. The adjacent pub has a separate menu. Try the rack of lamb or cedar-plank salmon. Extensive wine list. Open-air dining on the front porch. Kids' menu. No smoking. | 51 Main St. (Rte. 4) | 207/864–3341 or 800/666–3687 | www.rangeleyinn.com | Breakfast also available; no lunch | $18–$35 | AE, D, MC, V.

Lodging

Country Club Inn. An inn and a small motel 2½ mi north of town that is nearly at 2,000 ft above sea level. The lobby has fine views and the property is adjacent to an 18-hole golf course. All the rooms have views of the mountain lakes. Bar, dining room. No air-conditioning, no TV in rooms, TV in common area. Pool. Snowmobiling. Airport shuttle. | Country Club Dr. | 207/864–3831 | ccinn@rangeley.org | www.countryclubinnrangeley.com | 19 rooms in 3 buildings | $85–$110 | Closed Apr., Nov. | MAP | AE, MC, V.

Grant's Kennebago Camps. People rough it in comfort at this traditional Maine sporting camp on Kennebago Lake. "Sports" and families have been coming here since 1905, lured by the fresh water, mountain views, excellent fly-fishing, and hearty home-cooked meals. The wilderness setting, between the Kennebago Mountains, is nothing less than spectacular. The cabins, whose screened porches overlook the lake, have woodstoves and are finished in knotty pine. Meals (included in the price) are served in the cheerful waterfront dining room. Motorboats, canoes, sailboats, windsurfers, and mountain bikes are available. Float-plane rides and fly-fishing instruction can be arranged. Dining room. Lake. Hiking, boating, fishing, bicycles. Baby-sitting, playground. | Off Rte. 16 | 207/864–3608 in summer, 207/282–5264 in winter, 800/633–4815 all year. | 19 cabins | $110–$130 per person (meals included) | Closed Oct.–late May | MC, V.

Hunter Cove on Rangeley Lake. These lakeside cabins, which sleep from two to six people, provide all the comforts of home in a rustic setting. The interiors are unfinished knotty pine and include kitchens, full baths, and comfortable, if plain, living rooms. Cabin No. 1 has a fieldstone fireplace, and others have wood-burning stoves. Cabins No. 5 and No. 8 have hot tubs. In summer you can take advantage of a sand swimming beach, boat rentals, and a nearby golf course. In winter, snowmobile right to your door or ski nearby (cross-country and downhill). Beach, boating. | Mingo Loop Rd. | 207/864–3383 | 8 cabins | $110–$160 | AE.

North Camps. These rustic cottages on Rangeley Lake have woodstoves and screened porches with views of the lake. Lake. Boating. | North Camps Rd., near Oquossoc | 207/864–2247 | fax 207/882–9294. | 12 cottages | $75–$90 per cottage, $645/wk for 8–person cottage | AP during spring fishing and fall hunting seasons | AE, MC, V.

Rangeley Inn. This motel and lakeside cabin complex is downtown and near the lake and snowmobile trails. It has mountain views and a majestic setting. Restaurant, bar with entertainment. No air-conditioning, some kitchenettes, some in-room hot tubs, cable TV. Lake. Snowmobiling. | 51 Main St. (Rte. 4) | 207/864–3341 or 800/666–3687 | fax 207/864–3634 | rangeinn@rangeley.org | www.rangeleyinn.com | 50 rooms, 2 cabins | $69–$119, $120–$140 cabins | AE, D, MC, V.

ROCKLAND

MAP 3, E9

(Nearby towns also listed: Camden, Monhegan Island, Rockport)

The shire town of Knox County, Rockland was first settled in 1717 around a protected harbor. That harbor translated into a working waterfront based around shipbuilding, fishing, shipping, and, more recently, tourism. Numerous windjammer schooners call Rockland's port home, and the town claims dibs on being the "Lobster Capital of the World," celebrated by a giant summer festival. Rockland is also home to the Farnsworth Museum, which includes the Wyeth Wing, where you can view the works of three generations of Wyeths.

Information: Rockland-Thomaston Area Chamber of Commerce | Box 508, Harbor Park, Rockland, 04841-0508 | 207/596–0376 or 800/562–2529 | www.midcoast.com/~rtacc.

Attractions
Maine State Ferry Service. Trips to Vinalhaven and North Haven islands leave daily from 7 to 3:15. Vinalhaven trip is 15 mi and takes 1 hour and 15 minutes; North Haven, 12 mi and 1 hour. Both islands have basic facilities and rocky beaches. | 517A Main St. | 207/596–2202 | $9 | Daily.

Montpelier: General Henry Knox Museum. This museum just a few miles south of Rockland was built in 1930 as a replica of the late-18th-century mansion of Major General Henry Knox, a general in the Revolutionary War and Secretary of War in Washington's Cabinet.

Antiques and Knox family possessions fill the interior. Architectural features of note include an oval room and a double staircase. | U.S. 1 and Rte. 131, Thomaston | 207/354–8062 | www.generalknoxmuseum.org | $5 | Early June–early Oct., Tues.–Sat. 10–4.

A Morning in Maine Sailing Charters. Join Captain Bob Pratt for informative and relaxing sailing trips around Penobscot Bay and its environs. Captain Pratt is a marine biologist with many years of experience and his 55-ft ketch should keep even the landlubber feeling safe and sound. Ask about private dinner charters and overnight trips. Day trips are two hours and depart from the middle pier at Rockland Harbor. | Rockland Harbor | 207/563–8834 or 207/691–7245 | www.amorninginmaine.com | $25 | June–Oct., daily at 10 and 1; July–Aug., daily at 10, 1, 4, 6.

Owls Head Transportation Museum. This museum, 2 mi south of town, is recognized for its collection of pre-1930 aircraft, but it also has historically significant automobiles, carriages, bicycles, motorcycles, and more. A wide variety of special events are held all year long. | Rte. 73, Owls Head | 207/594–4418 | www.ohtm.org | $8 | Daily 10–5.

William A. Farnsworth Library and Art Museum. The museum houses a wide variety of American and European art, but with a decided emphasis on artists with Maine ties, including the Wyeths, Louise Nevelson, Fitz Hugh Lane, Winslow Homer, John Marin, and others. | 19 Elm St., off U.S. 1 | 207/596–6457 | $9 | June–Sept., daily 9–5; Oct.–May, Tues.–Sat., 10–5, Sun. 1–5.

Farnsworth Homestead. Built in 1849–50 in the Greek Revival style, the house has all original wallpaper, drapes, and carpets. There is also a kitchen with original stippled floor, and five bedrooms furnished in period style. | 356 Main St. | 207/596–6457 | Free with admission to the Farnsworth Art Museum | June–Sept., daily 10–5.

Olson House. This saltwater farmhouse belonged to the Olson and Hathorn families, frequent subjects of paintings by Andrew Wyeth. The home is seen clearly in *Christina's World*, one of Wyeth's best-known works. | Hathorn Point Rd., Cushing | 207/354–0102 | $3, free with admission to Farnsworth Museum | Daily 11–4.

Wyeth Center. With N. C., Andrew, and Jamie Wyeth such a large part of the Farnsworth collection, the museum opened this center in 1998 to house their art. | Union St. at Grace St. | 207/596–6457 | Free with admission to Farnsworth Art Museum | Memorial Day–Columbus Day, daily 9–5; Columbus Day–Memorial Day, Tues.–Sat. 10–5, Sun. 1–5.

Sailing trips. A variety of schooners operate out of Rockland, offering trips of anything from two hours to two weeks.

Schooner *J. and E. Riggin*. This 90-ft, 24-passenger schooner offers three- to six-day excursions. It departs from Rockland harbor. | 207/594–1875 or 800/869–0604 | www.riggin.com. | May–Oct.

Coasting schooners *American Eagle* and *Heritage*. These three schooners operate sailing vacations of three to 10 days from the North End Shipyard. They carry between 22 and 30 passengers. | North End Shipyard | 207/594–8007 or 800/648–4544 | www.midcoast.com/~schooner | *American Eagle* $795 for 6 days, *Heritage* $805 for 6 days | May–Oct.

Schooner *Stephen Taber*. This 68-ft, 22-passenger schooner offers three- and six-day cruises from Rockland Windjammer Wharf. | 207/236–3520 or 800/999–7352 | www.mainewindjammers.com or www.sailmainecoast.com | $446 3-day, $793–$838 6-day | Late May–Oct.

Friendship Sloop *Surprise*. This 33-ft, six-passenger sloop offers two- and three-hour sails from East Wind Dock in Tenants Harbor. | 207/372–6399 | May–Oct.

Schooner *Victory Chimes*. This 40-passenger, 132-ft, three-masted schooner offers four- and six-day cruises from Journey's End Marina. | 207/594–0755 or 800/745–5651 | www.victorychimes.com | May–Oct.

Schooner Yacht *Wendameen*. This 67-ft schooner yacht carries 14 passengers for one-night cruises and charters from the North End Shipyard. | 207/594–1751 | www.midcoast.com/wendameen | $170 per person | June–Sept.

Shore Village Museum. The museum, in a Grand Army of the Republic Hall, has an emphasis on lighthouses, with Coast Guard items including working horns, lights, bells, and other equipment. Civil War uniforms, weapons, and carved ivory are also displayed. | 104 Lime-rock St. | 207/594–0311 | Donation suggested | June–mid-Oct., daily 10–4; or by appointment.

ON THE CALENDAR

JULY: *Full Circle Summer Fair.* New Age themes, crafts, entertainment, and food (largely of the organic sort) are part of this annual celebration. | Union St. | 207/596–0376.

JULY: *Schooner Days and the North Atlantic Blues.* You'll find a sailboat parade, live entertainment, marine demonstrations, food vendors, and a daylong schooner race at this event. | Harbor Park | 207/596–0376.

AUG.: *Maine Lobster Festival.* This grande dame of Maine seafood festivals attracts thousands and includes a parade, craftspeople, entertainment, lobster-crate races, a Maine Sea Goddess Pageant, boat and train rides, and, of course, all the lobster you can eat. | Harbor Park | 207/596–0376.

Dining

★ **Cafe Miranda.** Continental. You can have an intimate dinner in this former men's gam-bling club near the Farnsworth Museum. The red-and-green-block tile floor dates from the 1940s and it has an Elvis shrine, open kitchen, and wood-fire brick oven. The expan-sive, 70-item menu changes daily. It's known for creative Thai, Chinese, Indian, Italian, and Polish preparations. Try grandma's spaghetti and sausage or the oven-roasted duckling. Kids' menu. Beer and wine only. No smoking. | 15 Oak St. | 207/594–2034 | Closed Sun.–Mon.; last 2 wks of Apr.; and last wk Oct. No lunch | $10–$18 | MC, V.

Harbor View Tavern. Contemporary. Enjoy the harbor views from this dining room 5 mi south of town while having steak, pasta, seafood, and prime rib. Open-air dining on the porch out the back. | Thomaston Landing, Thomaston | 207/354–8173 | Closed Sun.–Thurs. Nov.–Apr. | $15–$20 | AE, D, MC, V.

Jessica's European Bistro. Continental. This restaurant occupies four cozy rooms in a Vic-torian home on a hill at the southern end of Rockland. It's billed as a European bistro and lives up to this label with creative entrées that include veal Zurich, paella, and pork Portofino; other specialties of the Swiss chef are risottos, pastas, and focaccia. | 2 S. Main St. | 207/596–0770 | Closed Tues. in winter | $18–$22 | D, MC, V.

Waterworks. American. This restaurant in a brick building off Main Street serves light pub fare, including soups and home-style suppers like turkey and meat loaf. Maine microbrews are on tap, and the selection of single-malt Scotches is excellent. A wall of water decorates the small dining room, and a stone fireplace dominates the pub. Kids' menu. | Lindsey St. | 207/596–2753 | $12–$23 | AE, D, MC, V.

Lodging

Lakeshore Inn. This inn is in an 18th-century farmhouse. Complimentary breakfast. No room phones, no TV in rooms, TV in common area. Outdoor hot tub. Cross-country skiing. No kids under 12. No smoking. | 184 Lakeview Dr. | 207/594–4209 | fax 207/596–6407 | lakeshore@mid-coast.com | www.midcoast.come/~lakeshore | 4 rooms (1 with shower only) | $105–$125 | AE, MC, V.

Limerock Inn. You can walk to the Farnsworth and the Shore Village museums from this magnificent Queen Anne–style Victorian on a quiet residential street. The meticulously appointed rooms include Island Cottage, with a whirlpool tub and doors that open onto a private deck overlooking the backyard gargen, and Grand Manan, which has a fireplace, a whirlpool tub, and a four-poster, king-size bed. Bicycles. | 96 Limerock St. | 207/594–2257 or 800/546–3762 | fax 207/594–1846 | 9 rooms | $90–$180 | MC, V.

Navigator Motor Inn. This downtown hotel is near the ocean and close to state ferries. Restaurant, bar, room service. Some kitchenettes, refrigerators, cable TV. Laundry facilities. Business services. Pets allowed. | 520 Main St. | 207/594–2131 or 800/545–8026 | fax 207/594–7763 | 81 rooms | $75–$110 | AE, D, DC, MC, V.

ROCKPORT

(Nearby towns also listed: Camden, Rockland)

Tucked in a secluded harbor just minutes from the hubbub of Camden, Rockport is a more sedate version of its neighbor—but just barely. The two towns parted ways in 1891, but they still maintain a sister-city link. Lime kilns once fueled the town's major industry in the 19th century. Built on a high hill with exceptional harbor views, this trim little village now attracts music and art lovers, with concert series and galleries.

Information: Camden-Rockport-Lincolnville Chamber of Commerce | Box 919 Commercial St., Public Landing, Camden, 04843 | 207/236–4404 or 800/223–5459 | chamber@camdenme.org | www.camdenme.org.

Attractions

Bay Chamber Concerts. This group features weekly classical and jazz concerts in summer by internationally known musicians. There are monthly concerts from September through June at the Rockport Opera House. | Central St. | 207/236–2823 or 888/707–2770 | www.baychamberconcerts.org | $7–$20 | Call for schedule.

Maine Sports Outfitters. Stop in for a full selection of outdoor gear or inquire about sea-kayaking tours, expeditions, and guided fishing trips. Standard kayak tours last two hours and are suitable for beginners. | U.S. 1 | 207/236–8797 or 800/722–0826 | www.mainesport.com | Store 8 AM–9 PM, call for tour times.

Dining

The Helm. French. You can eat in either the dining room or the greenhouse—both have river views and a nautical theme. Try the steak au poivre, fresh seafood, or lamb shank. Extensive salad bar. Kids' menu. No smoking. | Commercial St. | 207/236–4337 | Closed Nov.–Mar. | $9–$16 | D, MC, V.

Marcel's. Continental. This restaurant in the Samoset Resort has views of the water to complement the menu, which has a New England flair. For appetizers try the clam chowder or butterflied lamb chops before moving on to the dijonnaise rack of lamb or the pancetta-wrapped filet mignon served over a spinach and artichoke pancake. There's an extensive wine list. | 220 Warrenton St. | 207/594–2511 | Breakfast also available | $18–$28 | AE, D, DC, MC, V.

Sail Loft. Seafood. This comfortable dining room overlooks the harbor. It has weathered-wood walls and a fireplace. Try the clam chowder and blueberry muffins. Kids' menu. Sunday brunch. Dock space. No smoking. | 1 Main St. | 207/236–2330 | $15–$30 | AE, MC, V.

Lodging

FeatherBed Bed and Breakfast and ChelTed Gallery. Your talented hosts run both a meticulously kept, romantic getaway and a high-end framing and photo restoration shop and art gallery out of the house. Rooms have sponge-painted pastel walls, stenciled ceilings, handmade soaps, candles, coffeemakers, fresh flowers, and air ionizers. Of course, cozy featherbeds are found in every room, along with down comforters and pillows. Dining room, complimentary breakfast. Refrigerators, cable TV, in-room VCRs. No pets. No kids under 10. No smoking. | 705 Commercial St. | 207/596–7230 | fax 207/596–7657 | chelted@midcoast.com | www.midcoast.com/~chelted/featherb | 2 rooms | $130–$175 | D, MC, V.

Samoset Resort. An extensive waterfront golf resort hotel that is ½ mi north of town. Dining room, bar with entertainment. In-room data ports, cable TV. 2 pools. Hot tub, massage. Driving range, 18-hole golf course, putting green, tennis. Gym, racquetball. Cross-country skiing. Video games. Children's programs (ages 3–12), playground. Business services, free parking. | 220 Warrenton St. | 207/594–2511, 800/341–1650 outside ME | fax 207/594–0722 | www.samoset.com | 153 rooms, 22 suites | $239–$339, $339–$389 suites | AE, D, DC, MC, V.

ROCKWOOD

MAP 3, C6

(Nearby towns also listed: Greenville, Moosehead Lake)

On the western shore of Moosehead Lake, the town of Rockwood has a front-row-center view of dramatic Mt. Kineo, particularly from the public boat landing. Once a rustic outpost, sometimes simply known as Kineo Station, it is now a major gateway to outdoor action adventure in the Moosehead region, with plenty of sports camps, hotels, and services to get you into the great outdoors.

Information: Moosehead Lake Region Chamber of Commerce | Box 581, Main St. (Rte. 15), Greenville, 04441 | 207/695–2702 or 207/695–2026 | moose@moosehead.net | www.mooseheadarea.com and www.mooseheadlake.org.

Attractions

Moose River. Outstanding fishing for landlocked salmon heading up from Moosehead Lake toward the Brassua Lake dam on Rte. 15.

Raft trips. White-water rafting is offered by about a dozen companies daily on the Kennebec and Penobscot rivers, several times a year on the Dead River. All trips are timed with dam releases to give the most exciting trip possible. Although they all travel the same water, the amenities vary, as do the locations. Rafting outfitters are in Rockwood, Millinocket, and along U.S. 201 between Bingham and Jackman, with the heaviest concentration in West Forks.

Magic Falls Rafting. This outfit includes the full complement of rafting trips, plus rock climbing, funyaks, and sport boats. | U.S. 201 | 207/663–2200 or 800/207–7238 | Apr.–Oct.

Moxie Outdoor Adventures. The full complement of rafting trips, plus canoes, inflatable kayaks, and overnight riverside camping. | The Forks, U.S. 201 | 800/866–6943 | $65–$85 | Apr.–Oct.

Northern Outdoors, Inc. This outfit offers a wide array of rafting trips, plus fishing, hunting, kayaking, a ropes course, and more. | U.S. 201 | 207/663–4466 or 800/765–RAFT | Apr.–Oct.

Raft Maine. This is the umbrella organization for white-water rafting in the state. If you want to find out who has vacancies, or to compare rates and offerings in one stop, give them a call. | Box 3, Bethel | 800/723–8633 | www.ncrivers.com | Apr.–Oct., 24 hrs. daily.

Unicorn Expeditions. A full complement of rafting trips, plus longer canoeing, hiking, camping, and other outdoor adventures. | U.S. 201 | 207/663–4466 or 800/765–RAFT | www.unicornraft.com | Apr.–Oct.

Wilderness Expeditions, Inc. Headquartered at The Birches resort in Rockwood, this outfitter offers an array of rafting trips as well as kayaking, cross-country skiing, ice fishing, ropes courses, and moose cruises. | Rte. 15 | 207/534–7305, 207/534–2242, or 800/825–9453 | www.birches.com | Year-round, daily.

ON THE CALENDAR

MAR.: *Moosehead Lake Ice Fishing Derby.* This weeklong event takes place on Moosehead Lake. Prizes are given for the largest salmon, trout, and so on, at the awards ceremony supper. Proceeds benefit local charities. | Moosehead Lake | 207/695–2702.

JULY: *Annual Rubber Duckie Race.* Sponsored by the Moosehead Lake Vacation and Sportsmen's Association, this race sends rubber duckies on a 3/4-mi cruise down Moose River, with proceeds going to local charities. You must purchase your duck from a local business. Winner gets a cash prize. The race starts at the Moose River Bridge on Route 15. | 207/695–2702.

Dining

The Birches Dining Room. American. This authentic log cabin dining room has a big fireplace at one end and a wall of windows overlooking Moosehead Lake with the mountains behind at the other. The baby back ribs are the selling point, but if you feel like something else try the seafood, chicken, or steak. Lunch is served at the Lakeside Grill, weather permitting. This deck overlooks the lake. | Birches Rd. | 207/534–2242, 207/534–7305, or 800/825–9453 | fax 207/534–8835 | wwld@aol.com | www.birches.com | Breakfast also available. Closed end Nov.–Christmas Day and Apr. | $14.95–$19.95 | AE, D, MC, V.

Lodging
Attean Lake Lodge. The Holden family has owned and operated this island lodge about an hour west of Rockwood since 1900. The 18 log cabins, which sleep from two to six people, provide a secluded environment. The tastefully appointed central lodge has a library and games. Beach, boating. Library. | Off Rte. 201 | 207/668–3792 | fax 207/668–4016 | 18 cabins | $225 | Closed Oct.–May | AE, MC, V.

Birches Resort. A log cabin resort on an 11,000-acre preserve along Moosehead Lake. Canoeing trips and moose-watching cruises are offered. Bar, dining room. No air-conditioning, some kitchenettes. Hot tub, sauna. Beach, boating, fishing, bicycles. Cross-country skiing, snowmobiling. Business services. Pets allowed (fee). | Birches Rd. | 207/534–7305 or 800/825–9453 | fax 207/534–8835 | wwld@aol.com | www.birches.com | 4 rooms (all with shared bath) in lodge, 20 cottages | $45–$75, $95–$185 cottages | AE, D, MC, V.

Rockwood Cottages. These eight cottages on Moosehead Lake near the center of Rockwood have screened porches and fully equipped kitchens and sleep from two to seven people. One-week minimum stay in July and August. Sauna. Dock, boating. | Rte. 15 | 207/534–7725 | 8 cottages | $65 | Closed Dec.–Apr. | D, MC, V.

RUMFORD

MAP 3, B8

(Nearby town also listed: Bethel)

Leashing the power of the turbulent Androscoggin Falls turned this town in the Oxford Hills into a thriving mill town during boom times. Paper mills still make a big statement here, with their smokestacks that tower over the town. Rumford is also the home town of noted politician Edmund S. Muskie. The area surrounding Rumford offers great hiking, scenic gorges, and winding country roads in the western Maine mountains.

Information: River Valley Chamber of Commerce | 23 Hartford St., Rumford, 04276 | 207/364–3241 | rvcc@agate.net | www.agate.net/~rvcc.

Attractions
Mt. Blue State Park. Swimming, fishing, hiking, boating, camping, and cross-country skiing are among the activities of this park on Lake Webb, 18 mi northeast of Rumford. | Rte. 142, Weld | 207/585–2347.

Swift River's Coos Canyon. This scenic gorge north of Rumford has been carved into the bedrock by the Swift River. You'll find picnic tables, rest areas, and viewpoints here. You can swim, fly-fish, pan for gold, or canoe while you enjoy the scenery. | Rte. 17 | Free | Daily.

ON THE CALENDAR
AUG.: *Dixfield Outdoor Market.* This annual town get-together turns downtown Dixfield, 5 mi east of Rumford, into an outdoor market. Feast on local treats like lobster rolls and fries, and check out the clowns, musicians, and local crafts for sale. | Main St. | 207/364–3241.

Dining
The Madison. American. A post-and-beam lounge and slightly more formal dining room inside the Madison Inn that serves regional fare like lobster rolls, sandwiches, and had-

dock. On the first Saturday of every month check out the Grand Buffet which has a sampling of soups, appetizers, salads, pasta, fish, meats, and dessert. | U.S. 2 | 207/364–7973 or 800/258–6234 | www.madisoninn.com | $8–$21 | AE, D, DC, MC, V.

Lodging

Andover Guest House. An 18th-century colonial home with Shaker-style furnishings that is popular with budget travelers and hikers. There's a dorm room with solid wood beds and ceiling fans and a large common room with a Ping-Pong table, darts, and a wood-burning stove. The kitchen is open for guest use. Dormers, bring your own blankets. The Andover Playground is across the street, with a picnic area and convenience store. Dining room. No air-conditioning, no room phones, TV in common area. Hiking. Cross-country skiing. Pets allowed. No smoking. | 28 S. Main St., Andover, about 15 mi from Rumford | 207/392–1209 | fax 508/653–7723 | info@andoverguesthouse.com | www.andoverguesthouse.com | 7 rooms, 1 dorm with 10 beds | $40–$55 rooms, $15 bunks | D, MC, V.

Blue Iris Motor Inn. A rural, roadside motel 5 mi west of town with attractive grounds. It's on the river and near Sunday River. Picnic area. Some kitchenettes, cable TV. Pool. | 1405 U.S. 2 | 207/364–4495 | www.sundayriveron~.com/blueirismotorinn | 14 rooms | $30–$70 | AE, MC, V.

Coos Canyon Cabins. This large, duplex cabin has two modern, fully equipped units with electricity, kitchen, satellite TV, and a loft and can sleep up to seven people. The property, 13 mi north of Rumford, is along the Swift River where you can pan for gold or jump off 32-ft cliffs into swimming holes. It is close to hiking, snowmobiling, skiing, and the Appalachian Trail. No air-conditioning, cable TV. Cross-country skiing, snowmobiling. Pets allowed. No smoking. | Byron Village Rd., Byron | 207/364–7446 | fax 207/369–9332 | coos_cabins@yahoo.com | www.geocities.com/coos_cabins/cooscanyoncabins | 2 units | $70 | No credit cards.

Linnell Motel and Rest Inn Conference Center. Open since 1954, this catch-all inn has accommodations and facilities for families and business travelers. King rooms have desks with a modem. Efficiencies have kitchenettes and are suitable for families or longer stays. There are conference facilities and a catering area on site. Restaurant, complimentary breakfast. Some in-room data ports, cable TV. | U.S. 2 W | 207/364–4511 or 800/446–9038 | fax 207/369–0800 | innkeeper@linnellmotel.com | www.linnellmotel.com | 49 rooms | $50–$75 | AE, D, MC, V.

The Madison. This large, four-season resort rests along the banks of the Androscoggin River. Choose from clean and modern motel-style suite, condominium, or guest-house accommodations. Condos and guest house have fully equipped kitchens and living rooms with couches. Many rooms have private balconies and river views. Restaurant, room service. In-room data ports, some kitchenettes, cable TV. Pool. Hot tub, sauna. Health club. Cross-country skiing, snowmobiling. Video games. | U.S. 2 | 207/364–7973 or 800/258–6234 | fax 207/369–0341 | innkeeper@madisoninn.com | www.madisoninn.com. | 57 rooms; 3 suites | $59–$99; suites $185 | AE, D, MC, V.

SCARBOROUGH

MAP 3, C11

(Nearby towns also listed: Biddeford-Saco, Cape Elizabeth, Old Orchard Beach, Portland)

A suburb of Portland, Scarborough is home to Maine's largest salt marsh, where you can rent a canoe and paddle at will or join a guided tour. There are also fine sand beaches, a harness racing track, and notable summer communities, one of which—Prouts Neck—was home to noted American painter Winslow Homer.

Information: Convention and Visitors Bureau of Greater Portland | 305 Commercial St., Scarborough, 04101 | 207/772–5800 | www.visitportland.com.

Attractions

Beech Ridge Motor Speedway. This track has four different classes of stock-car racing on a short track. | Holmes Rd. | 207/885–5800 | www.beechridge.com. | $9.75 | Mid-Apr.–mid-Sept., Fri.–Sat.; mid-June–mid-Aug., there's also Thurs. amateur races.

Harness Racing. Scarborough Downs Race Track offers harness horse racing with parimutuel throughout the season. | U.S. 1 | 207/883–4331 | $2 | Mar.–Dec.

Scarborough Marsh Nature Center. Operated by the Maine Audubon Society, this center has canoeing and tours through a marsh and wildlife preserve. | Pine Point Rd. | 207/883–5100 or 207/781–2330 | Hiking free, canoe rentals and tours $10 | Mid-June–Labor Day, daily.

ON THE CALENDAR

AUG.: *Scarborough Family Festival*. This annual event rounds up all the local non-profit organizations who put on the biggest fair of the year. Pony rides, face painting, live music and carnival games, food, and more, topped off with a huge fireworks show. Takes place at the Scarborough High School athletic field. | Rte. 114 | 207/883–4301.

Dining

Garofalo's Restaurant. Italian. Hardwood floors, a gas fireplace, and a screened-in sunporch describe this eatery in the Higgins Beach Inn. Try the appetizers like crab cakes with creamy dijon horseradish sauce and sweet corn relish or calamari, fried and tossed in red onions, lemon, Parmesan, and a balsamic vinaigrette. Then try the tournedos of beef with blue cheese and sautéed mushrooms and horseradish pancetta sauce or the baked stuffed lobster. Kids' menu. | 34 Ocean Ave. | 207/883–6684 | Breakfast also available | $14–$24 | AE, MC, V.

Lodging

Black Point Inn. A late-19th-century resort inn, 4 mi south of Scarborough, with its own beach and peaceful grounds. Don't miss the rose garden. Bar, dining room, room service. Cable TV. 2 pools. Barbershop, beauty salon, hot tubs, massage. Putting green. Gym. Bicycles. Business services, airport shuttle, free parking. | 510 Black Point Rd., Prouts Neck | 207/883–2500 or 800/258–0003 | fax 207/883–9976 | bpi@nlis.net | www.blackpointinn.com | 85 rooms, 4 cottages | $360–$500 | MAP | AE, D, MC, V.

Fairfield Inn by Marriott. A chain hotel that is near the airport and the Maine Mall. Complimentary Continental breakfast. In-room data ports, refrigerators, cable TV. Pool. Business services. | 2 Cummings Rd. | 207/883–0300 | fax 207/883–0300 | 120 rooms | $99–$140 | AE, D, DC, MC, V.

Higgins Beach Inn. This original 1897 Colonial Revival inn on Higgins Beach has modern additions in the same style. No room phones, TV in common area. No pets. No smoking. | 34 Ocean Ave. | 207/883–6684 or 800/836–2322 | fax 207/885–9570 | higgins@prodigy.net | www.higginsbeachinn.com | 24 rooms (10 with shared bath) | $109 | Closed mid-Oct.–mid-May | AE, MC, V.

Holiday House Inn and Motel. An oceanfront motel and inn near Old Orchard Beach's attractions. Picnic area. Refrigerators, cable TV. | 106 E. Grand Ave. | 207/883–4417 | fax 207/883–6987 | 24 rooms in 2 buildings | $125–$140 | Closed Nov.–Apr. | AE, MC, V.

Lighthouse Inn. A family-style, oceanfront resort in Pine Point Beach in Scarborough with 7 mi of sandy beach. Picnic area, complimentary Continental breakfast. No air-conditioning, refrigerators, cable TV. Beach. | 366 Pine Point Rd. | 207/883–3213 or 800/780–3213 | 22 rooms | $130–$225 | Closed mid-Oct.–late May | AE, D, MC, V.

SEARSPORT

MAP 3, E8

(Nearby towns also listed: Belfast, Bucksport)

The impressive array of ship captains' homes that line the streets of Searsport attests to the town's rich shipbuilding history. (Many of these manses have been turned into B&Bs.) Between 1810 and 1890, there were 11 shipyards, and one-tenth of the Merchant Marine captains called this small town home. Today, you can find a classic brick downtown, an excellent marine museum, and antiques shops galore.

Information: Waldo County Chamber of Commerce | Box 577, Unity, 04988 | 207/948–5050.

Attractions

Moose Point State Park. A place for easy day hikes and picnics with views of Penobscot Bay. | U.S. 1 | 207/338–5900 | Daily.

Penobscot Marine Museum. This museum depicts the life of a 19th-century seagoing community. There is a former sea captain's home, a display of different boats, marine paintings, and a library. | 5 Church St., off U.S. 1 | 207/548–2529 | www.penobscotmarinemuseum.org | $6 | Memorial Day–mid-Oct., Mon.–Sat. 10–5, Sun. 12–5.

ON THE CALENDAR

AUG.: *Lobster Boat Races*. Craft and food tables, games, and activities round out these popular races. | Penobscot Bay | 207/548–6302.

Dining

Jordan's Restaurant. Eclectic. The menu here includes everything from burritos, to steak and seafood, including a number of chowders and a veggie stir fry. Try the baked stuff haddock, and finish with a fresh berry pie. Takeout available. Kids' menu. | Main St. (U.S. 1) | 207/548–2555 | Breakfast also available | $7–$13 | AE, D, MC, V.

Rhumb Line. American. Local art adorns the walls of this 18th-century sea captain's home while big-band music plays in the dining room, which has oriental rugs and hardwood floors. Try the grilled rack of lamb with blackberry mint vinegar, and a lemon cream cake with berries for dessert. | 200 E. Main St. | 207/548–2600 | No lunch | $18–$24 | MC, V.

Seafarer's Tavern. Eclectic. Try the legendary crab cakes or opt for some Cajun crawfish or catfish. A 70-year canoe hangs over the bar where pizza, subs, and tavern fare are also available. | 23 E. Main St. | 207/548–2465 | $4–$10 | No credit cards.

Lodging

Brass Lantern Inn Bed & Breakfast. A mid-19th-century former sea captain's house, the Brass Lantern is a 10-minute walk from the harbor. The rooms are each named according to a theme, among them "Captain's Hideaway" and "Secret Garden," and are charmingly accented with quilts and four-poster beds. Complimentary breakfast. No air-conditioning, no room phones, cable TV in common area. No smoking. | 81 W. Main St. (U.S. 1) | 207/548–0150 or 800/691–0150 | fax 207/548–0304 | stay@brasslanternmaine.com | www.brasslanternmaine.com | 5 rooms (4 with shower only) | $85–$95 | D, MC, V.

Captain A. V. Nickels Inn. This 1874 early Victorian inn on 6½ acres is on the National Register of Historic Places. Named after a sea captain of great renown who raised his family on the property, the inn has two large parlors, a TV room, and a porch looking out over Penobscot Bay. Rooms are filled with period antiques. The apartment unit has a full kitchen, French doors opening to a porch, and can sleep four–five adults. Dining room, complimentary breakfast. No room phones, TV in common area. Pets allowed. No smoking. |

127 E. Atlantic Coast Hwy. | 207/548–6691 or 800/343–5001 | www.captavseaside.com | 9 rooms (4 with shared bath) | $55–$105 | Closed Nov.–Apr. | AE, D, MC, V.

Homeport. This former sea captain's house was built in 1863 and is on the National Historic Register. It has great views of Penobscot Bay. Complimentary breakfast. No air-conditioning, no room phones, cable TV in common area. Library. | 121 E. Main St. (U.S. 1/Rte. 3) | 207/548–2259 or 800/742–5814 | fax 978/443–6682 | hportinn@acadia.net | www.bnbcity.com/inns/20015 | 10 rooms (3 with shared bath), 2 cottages | $55–$90, $600–$750/wk for cottages | AE, D, MC, V.

Watchtide by the Sea. Since 1917, this colonial Cape house has been a resting spot for weary travelers along Route 1. Sit out on the sunporch overlooking Penobscot Bay while you eat an inventive breakfast, with treats like strawberry soup or crabmeat soufflé. Rooms all have king-size beds and antiques. The honeymoon suite has a skylight and a two-person Jacuzzi as well as hand-painted furniture. Complimentary breakfast. No air-conditioning, some in-room hot tubs, no room phones, no TV. | 190 W. Main St. | 207/548–0938 or 800/698–6575 | www.watchtide.com | 4 rooms | $95–$155 | DC, MC, V.

Yardarm. An attractive roadside motel, 1 mi northeast of Searsport, that was once owned by a master shipbuilder. It has quiet and spacious rooms. You can sit on the porch or under an apple tree and take in the Maine sea breezes. Complimentary Continental breakfast. Some air-conditioners, some refrigerators, cable TV. No pets. | 172 E. Main St. | 207/548–2404 | www.searsportmaine.com | 18 rooms | $48–$80 | Closed Nov.–Apr. | D, MC, V.

SEBAGO LAKE

MAP 3, B10

(Nearby town also listed: Bridgton)

Fifty lakes make up the Long Lakes Region, and Sebago is the largest (and second-largest in the state). A longtime tourist destination, the shores of Sebago Lake are crowded with summer homes, sunbathers, and children's camps. A 28-lock canal connected Sebago Lake with the Fore River in Portland from 1830 to 1870; now traffic between the two relies on the oft-congested U.S. 302. Water traffic can get nuts on the lake, so proceed with caution.

Information: **Greater Windham Chamber of Commerce** | 835 Roosevelt Trail (U.S. 302), Windham, 04062-1015 | 207/892–8265 | wincc@gwi.net | windhamchamber.sebago-lake.org/home.html. **Naples Business Association** | Box 412, U.S. 302, Naples, 04055 | 207/693–3285 | www.napleschamber.com.

Attractions

Jones Museum of Glass and Ceramics. This museum, 5 mi northwest of town, houses more than 7,000 pieces from ancient Egypt to the present. Special exhibits and programs are offered regularly. | 35 Douglas Mountain Rd., Sebago | 207/787–3370 | $5.

Marrett House and Garden. Owned by the Society for the Preservation of New England Antiquities, this house was built in 1789 and originally preserved in the 1880s, when the inhabitants held an elaborate family reunion. It is 2 mi south of Sebago Lake. | Rte. 25, Standish | 207/642–3032 or 617/227–3956 | $4 Donation suggested | June.–mid-Oct., weekends 11–4.

Point Sebago Resort. This impressive 13-acre golf resort and camping area occupies some of the nicest beach property on Sebago Lake. There's an 18-hole course, full hookup RV sites, and RVs you can rent while on the premises. There's also dining and a conference room. Sailing regattas and swim competitions take place in season. | Point Sebago Rd., Naples | 207/655–3821 or 800/655–1232 | Call for details | May 1—Oct. 31.

★ **Sebago Lake State Park.** This is one of Maine's most popular parks. The day-use area features extensive sand beaches on crystal clear Sebago Lake—the source of the Portland area's drinking water—and tables, boat ramps, and a playground. Songo Lock is nearby, and it allows for boat trips to Long Lake. | 11 Park Access Rd. | 207/693–6231 or 207/693–6613 | $2.50 | May–mid-Oct., daily dawn–dusk.

Songo River Queen. An old-fashioned riverboat takes 2½-hour cruises on Long Lake, the Brandy Pond area of Sebago Lake, and the Songo River, passing through the Songo River lock. There are also dinner-mystery cruises and concerts. | Rte. 302, Causway Naples | 207/693–6861 | $8–$11 | May–Oct.

ON THE CALENDAR
JUNE: *Windham Summer Fest.* A one-day celebration with parades, food, a carnival, games, and competitions. Takes place throughout town. | U.S. 302 | 207/892–8265.

Dining
Barnhouse Tavern. Contemporary. A late-19th-century post-and-beam charmer that's great for families. Try the prime rib or baked stuffed haddock. Open-air dining on the patio. Kids' menu, early-bird suppers. No smoking. | Rte. 35, North Windham | 207/892–2221 | $11–$25 | AE, D, MC, V.

Bray's Brewpub and Eatery. Contemporary. You'll dine casually in this Victorian house with a dining room, lounge, and on-premises brewery. It is known for chicken, pasta, ribs, and homemade beers. Open-air pub dining in the beer garden. Kids' menu. No smoking. | Rte. 302, Naples | 207/693–6806 | $11–$16 | AE, D, MC, V.

Chute's Cafe and Bakery. American. Five miles northwest of Sebago Lake, this spot serves breakfast all day. Order the French toast or pancakes or choose one of their combination platters. For lunch there are daily specials, often involving lobsters. Locals hang their mugs on the wall after they leave, because they're so sure to come back. | Rte. 302, Casco | 207/655–7111 | Breakfast also available; no dinner | $2–$6 | D, MC, V.

Lodging
Migis Lodge. A cottage resort with extensive grounds and more than ½ mi of waterfront on Lake Sebago. It is 8 mi north of Sebago Lake. Room prices include all meals. Dining room, room service. Refrigerators, cable TV. Tennis. Hiking, beach, dock, boating. Library. Playground. Airport shuttle, free parking. | Rte. 302, South Casco | 207/655–4524 | fax 207/655–2054 | www.migis.com | 6 rooms, 29 cottages | $180–$210 | Closed mid-Oct.–mid-June | No credit cards.

Suburban Pines Motel. A motel close to the lake that is 5 mi south of Sebago Lake and on U.S. 302. It has beautiful landscaped gardens. Picnic area. Some kitchenettes, cable TV. Laundry facilities. Pets allowed (deposit). | 322 Roosevelt Trail, Windham | 207/892–4834 | 18 rooms, 1 suite | $70–$80, $150 suite | D, MC, V.

SKOWHEGAN

MAP 3, D8

(Nearby town also listed: Waterville)

At the junction of U.S. 2 and 201, this "Crossroads of Maine" mill town is the shire town of Somerset County and a gateway to the North Woods. The name Skowhegan ("a place to watch for fish") reflects the penchant of the Indians, who came to catch Atlantic salmon at the falls here. Native daughter Margaret Chase Smith once said of her home: "There are eleven Bostons, many Londons, but only one Skowhegan."

Information: Skowhegan Area Chamber of Commerce | 10 Russell St., Skowhegan, 04976 | 207/474–3621 | fax 207/474–3306 | skowman@skowhegan.org | www.skowhegan-chamber.com.

Attractions

History House. Early local records, relics of the area, and Early American antiques are displayed here. | 40 Elm St. | 207/474–6632 | Donation suggested | Memorial Day–mid-Sept., Tues.–Fri. 1–5.

★ **Lakewood Theater.** Established in 1901 and on Wesserunsett Lake (6 mi north of Skowhegan), this is one of the oldest continuously operating summer theaters in the country. While the nationally known actors, who came here regularly in the 1960s and before, no longer perform, the theater still presents entertaining shows throughout the summer. The theater also runs a young performers' camp, which makes its own productions. | U.S. 201 | 207/474–7176 | Late May–mid-Sept., Thurs.–Sun.

Skowhegan Indian. The 62-ft wooden sculpture by Bernard Langlais sits in town in honor of the Abenaki tribe members who first watched the Kennebec River for salmon here. | Russell St. | 207/474–3621 | Free | Daily.

ON THE CALENDAR

JULY: *Skowhegan Log Days*. Brawny loggers test their skill at any number of lumber-related contests and demonstrations. There's also live entertainment, a golf tournament, a parade, craft show, public suppers, fireworks, and kids' stuff. | Downtown Skowhegan | 207/474–3621.

AUG.: *Skowhegan State Fair*. Ongoing for over 175 years, this may very well be the country's longest-running fair. Agricultural exhibits, carnival, food, family fun, live entertainment, and demolition derby are on offer at the Skowhegan Fairgrounds. | U.S. 201 | 207/474–3621.

DEC.: *Skowhegan Holiday Stroll*. This two-day event welcomes the holiday season with a bonfire, parade, refreshments, caroling, Santa, and local businesses keeping the doors open late for shopping. | Skowhegan | 207/474–3621.

SKOWHEGAN

INTRO
ATTRACTIONS
DINING
LODGING

Dining

Candlelight. Contemporary. Semiformal dining in a renovated storefront. Known for beef, seafood, pasta, and chicken. Salad bar. Kids' menu. No smoking. | 1 Madison Ave., at Water St. | 207/474–9724 | No dinner Sun.–Tues., Dec.–Mar. | $15–$20 | AE, D, DC, MC, V.

Charrier's. American. In downtown Skowhegan you'll find mostly seafood and steak on this menu. Try the sampler platter which includes provolone sticks, fried mushrooms, and fries or the garden salad with a fabulous dressing. Homemade pies and strawberry shortcake are the favored desserts. Full bar and kids' menu. Sit in the back and look out onto fountains and foliage on the premise. | 171 Madison Ave. | 207/474–9864 | Breakfast also available | $5–$20 | AE, D, MC, V.

Heritage House. Contemporary. This 18th-century house has three dining rooms. Try the apricot-glazed chicken or the cracked-pepper sirloin. Kids' menu. No smoking. | 260 Madison Ave. | 207/474–5100 | No lunch Sat.–Mon. | $15–$25 | AE, MC, V.

Lodging

Belmont Motel. A family hotel, near shopping and across from the Skowhegan fairgrounds. Picnic area. Some refrigerators, cable TV. Pool. | 425 Madison Ave. | 207/474–8315 or 800/235–6669 | www.belmontmotel.com | 36 rooms | $55–$85 | AE, D, DC, MC, V.

Breezy Acres Motel. This friendly, family-owned establishment has been open since 1979 and is 3 mi south of Skowhegan. The rooms are rustic but comfortable, with knotty-pine furniture. The big draw is the peaceful back yard, which opens up onto 8 acres of land and a pond. There's a picnic and barbecue area and a minigolf course. Picnic area. Cable TV. Lake. Miniature golf. Playground. No pets. | U.S. 201 S | 207/474–2703, phone/fax 207/474–2703 for reservations | www.skowhegan.maineusa.com/breezy | 14 rooms | $40–$58 | AE, MC, V.

Brewster Inn. A 1934 Colonial Revival house that was built by Portland architect John Calvin Stevens for former Governor Owen Brewster, who was later a Senator from Maine.

The rooms have floral wallpaper and brass beds, while the suites are large and have knotty pine finishings. An old hostelry with vintage fittings, a few fireplaces, and many gardens. Dining room, complimentary breakfast, cable TV, some in-room VCRs. No smoking. | 37 Zion's Hill Rd., Dexter | 207/924–3130 | fax 207/924–9768 | brewster@nconline.net | www.bbon-line.com/me/brewsterinn | 7 rooms, 2 suites | $59–$79, $79–$89 suites | D, MC, V.

Helen's Bed and Breakfast. This three-story, 1840 brick Empire rooms are filled with antiques. Complimentary breakfast. No room phones. | 2 Prospect St. | 207/474–0066 | 6 rooms | $45–$65 | D, MC, V.

Lovley's Motel. Centrally located, en route to Greenville and near Interstate 95. Picnic area. Some kitchenettes, cable TV. Pool. Hot tub. Laundry facilities. Business services. Pets allowed. | Rte. 2, Newport | 207/368–4311 or 800/666–6760 | 63 rooms | $59–$100 | AE, D, MC, V.

Towne Motel. A downtown hotel that is friendly and clean. Complimentary Continental breakfast. Some kitchenettes, cable TV. Pool. Laundry facilities. | 248 Madison Ave. | 207/474–5151 or 800/843–4405 | fax 207/474–6407 | 32 rooms | $55–$78 | AE, D, MC, V.

SOUTHWEST HARBOR

MAP 3, F9

(Nearby towns also listed: Acadia National Park, Bar Harbor, Cranberry Isles, Northeast Harbor)

The largest town on the west side of Mt. Desert Island, Southwest Harbor combines a working waterfront with the tourist trade. Boatyards and boatbuilders are as common as shops and eateries. The town is at Somes Sound, the only natural fjord on the East Coast.

Information: Southwest Harbor/Tremont Chamber of Commerce | Box 1143, Main St., Southwest Harbor, 04679 | 207/244–9264 or 800/423–9264 | swhtrcoc@acadia.net | www.acadia.net/swhtrcoc.

Attractions

Cranberry Cove Boating Co. The ferry runs from Southwest Harbor to Cranberry Island five times daily. On Cranberry Island, there are many sandy beaches and a restaurant. | Upper Town Dock, Clark Point Rd. | 207/244–5882 | $12 | Mid-June–Labor Day, by appointment after Labor Day–Christmas.

Flying Mountain Hiking Trail. This moderately difficult trail starts just off Route 102 south of town, and takes you along Somes Sound which was created by a fjord during the last ice age. This is the only fjord on the east coast and one of only three in the country. It's a great spot for kayaking, bird-watching, and picnicking. | Rte. 102 | 207/244–9264 | www.acadia.net/swhtrcoc | Free | Daily.

Maine State Ferry Service. The Captain Henry Lee makes 6-mi, 40-minute trips several times daily between Bass Harbor and Swans Island (4 mi south of Southwest Harbor), where visitors can take in the scenery, including the lighthouse. | Swans Island | 207/526–4273 or 207/244–3254 | $6.

Mt. Desert Oceanarium. This facility has a touch tank where visitors can hold sea animals while staff members discuss them. It also has more than 20 tanks of Maine sea life, a scallop tank, a whale exhibit, a fishing exhibit, and wheelhouse. Partner to the Oceanarium in Bar Harbor. | 172 Clark Point Rd. | 207/244–7330 | $6.95 | Mon.–Sat. 9–5.

Wendell Gilley Museum of Bird Carvings. This museum has bird carvings by Gilley (1904–83) in addition to changing exhibits by other historical and contemporary wildlife artists. Carving demonstrations are given daily. | Corner of Main St. and Herrick Rd. | 207/244–7555 | www.acadia.net/gilley | $3.25 | June–Oct., Tues.–Sun. 10–4; May and Nov.–Dec., Fri.–Sun.10–4.

JUNE: *Festival of the Kayak.* Paddling, race, demonstrations, lectures, and entertainment are available at this annual event. | Manset, on Wesley side of Mt. Desert Island | 207/244–9264 or 800/423–9264.

OCT.: *Mt. Desert Island's Acadia Octoberfest and Food Festival.* Fill your stein with beer from Maine's brewers at this international food festival for the whole family. There's also live music and entertainment, a display of Maine crafts and artists, a farmer's market and a food court. | Smuggler's Den Campground (Rte. 102) | 207/244–9264 or 800/423–9264.

Dining

Beal's Lobster Pier. Seafood. A popular lobster shack that has been in operation since 1930. All dining is outdoors on working wharf that overlooks Southwest Harbor. Cafeteria service. Beer and wine only. | Clark Point Rd., next to the Coast Guard base | 207/244–3202 | Closed Oct.–May | $10–$25 | AE, D, MC, V.

Preble Grill. Stained glass, original artwork, and a fireplace make this a warm, inviting, but casual place. The kitchen serves up mixed fare that has some fun with the standards (jalapeños in the chowder) and a strong Italian leaning. The risotto with Asiago cheese, roast duck, corn, jalapeños, and roast pumpkin seed is a favorite. | 14 Clark Point Rd. | 207/244–3034 | Closed Sun.–Wed., mid-Oct.–mid-May. No lunch | $11–$21 | D, MC, V.

Restaurant XYZ. Mexican. This restaurant has tables with white-linen tablecloths and green and red napkins, in a decorative take on the Mexican flag. There are excellent views of the harbor. Yucatán dishes are a speciality. | Shore Rd., Manset | 207/244–5221 | www.acadia.net/dockside/xyz | Closed mid-Oct.–May | $15 | MC, V.

Seawall Dining Room. Seafood. This eatery, 2½ mi east of town, has ocean views and artwork on the walls. This homey place attracts many families. Try the fried Maine shrimp in homemade batter or the baked stuffed lobster. Homemade desserts. Kids' menu. No smoking. | 566 Seawall Rd. | 207/244–3020. | Closed Dec.–Mar. | $10–$35 | AE, D, DC, MC, V.

Thurston's Lobster Pound. A bit off the beaten track and 4 mi southwest of Southwest Harbor, this no-frills lobster mecca is worth the trip. Locals come here to buy lobster, and many eat one on the spot. Lobsters are sold by the pound, and you can add on rolls, corn, and salad. | Steamboat Wharf Rd., Bernard | 207/244–7600 | Closed Columbus Day–Memorial Day | $4–$9; lobster dinners priced by the pound | MC, V.

Lodging

Birches Bed and Breakfast. This 1916 shingle-style home is on 5 peaceful acres in Acadia National Park. Two of the large rooms have ocean views from two rooms (and there are views of the garden and croquet court from the third). There's also a tree-shaded path to the water. Dining room, complimentary breakfast. No air-conditioning, no room phones, TV in common area. Dock. No pets. No smoking. | Fernald Point Rd. | 207/244–5182 | www.acadia.net/birches | 3 rooms | $105–$115 | MC, V.

Claremont Hotel. A vintage resort that is near the beach. It's famous for croquet. Restaurant, bar, picnic area. No air-conditioning, some kitchenettes. Tennis. Dock. Business services. | Claremont Rd. | 207/244–5036 or 800/244–5036 | fax 207/244–3512 | www.theclaremonthotel.com | 43 rooms, 12 cottages | $85–$220, $110–$200/day or $1,400–$2,500/wk for cottages | Closed mid-Oct.–late May | No credit cards.

Clark Point Inn. This antebellum captain's house was built in 1857 and has decks full of Adirondack chairs, where you can take in the water views and fresh ocean breezes. The grounds boast beautiful flower and herb gardens. Complimentary breakfast. No air-conditioning, cable TV. No kids under 8. No smoking. | 60 Clark Point Rd. | 207/244–9828 | fax 207/244–9924 | clarkpoint@acadia.net | www.clarkpointinn.com | 5 rooms (3 with shower only) | $85–$175 | D, MC, V.

SOUTHWEST HARBOR

INTRO
ATTRACTIONS
DINING
LODGING

Island House. Guest rooms in this small inn are full of air, light, and old white-painted furniture. There's a carriage house suite with loft bed, skylight, kitchenette, and serene tree-top view. Dining room, picnic area. No air-conditioning, some kitchenettes, no room phones, TV in common area. No pets. No kids under 5. No smoking. | 121 Clark Point Rd. | 207/244–5180 | islandab@acadia.net | www.acadia.net/island_house/ | 4 rooms, 1 suite | $95 rooms, $120 carriage house suite | No credit cards.

Kingsleigh Inn 1904. This harbor-view turn-of-the-20th-century hostelry is in the center of the village. It has a wraparound porch and a fireplace in the living room. Complimentary breakfast. No room phones, cable TV in some rooms, no TV in some rooms. Library. No kids under 12. No smoking. | 373 Main St. | 207/244–5302 | fax 207/244–7691 | info@kingsleigh-inn.com | www.kingsleighinn.com | 7 rooms, 1 suite | $95–$125, $190 suite | MC, V.

Moorings Inn. You can stay in the colonial inn, the motel, or in a cottage. All are on the water, with private screened decks. The property is 2 mi east of town. Picnic area, complimentary Continental breakfast. No air-conditioning, some kitchenettes, no TV in some rooms, cable TV in common area. Beach, dock, boating, bicycles. | Shore Rd. | 207/244–5523 | storrey@acadia.net | www.mooringsinn.com | 13 rooms in 2 buildings, 4 cottages | $65–$100, $110–$135 cottages | Closed Nov.–Apr. | No credit cards.

MAINE LIGHTHOUSES

More than 60 lighthouses, ranging from stubby "spark-plug" designs to soaring monoliths, dot the Maine coast and romance visitors. Maritime traffic has always been active around the treacherous Maine coast, and these lights served as both harbor markers and warnings. The earliest light is Portland Head, which was commissioned by George Washington and completed in 1791. Those wishing to meet a lighthouse keeper or climb a lonely tower will be disappointed, however. All Maine lighthouses are now automated and few allow access.

Still, lighthouses continue to have a distinct allure and appeal. Tons of books have been written on the subject (lighthouse ghost stories are especially popular), and PBS dedicated a series, *Legendary Lighthouses*, to them, in which Maine was featured. You can purchase lighthouse videos, lighthouse calendars, and all varieties of lighthouse knickknacks (including lighthouse toilet paper). Lighthouses, in a word, are big business.

But the best way to appreciate a lighthouse is in the up-close-and-personal way. Although many Maine lighthouses are not accessible from land, plenty are. Following is a list that will bring you right next to (or a stone's throw away) from some of Maine's most beloved lighthouses: Nubble Light, Cape Neddick; Spring Point Light, South Portland; Portland Head Light, Cape Elizabeth; Pemaquid Point Light, Pemaquid Point; Marshall Point Light, St. George; Rockland Breakwater Light, Rockland; Owls Head Light, Owls Head; Fort Point, Stockton Springs; Bass Harbor Head, Southwest Harbor; West Quoddy Head, Lubec.

(Those wishing for a taste of the light-keeping life might consider a memorable—albeit pricey—stay at the Keeper's House, located on Isle au Haut off the Deer Isle/Stonington coast. Those wishing to learn more about lighthouse lore should stop by the Lighthouse Depot in Wells, the largest lighthouse store in the world.)

© Artville

WATERVILLE

(Nearby towns also listed: Augusta, Belgrade Lakes, Hallowell, Skowhegan)

Colby College, sited on a stepped plain on the west bank of the Kennebec River, dominates this mill town, but it has to share honors as the hometown of former U.S. Senate Majority Leader George Mitchell. Waterville, incorporated in 1802, is the second-largest city in Kennebec County and a gateway to the Belgrade Lakes Region.

Information: Mid-Maine Chamber of Commerce | Box 142, 1 Post Office Sq, Waterville, 04903 | 207/873–3315 | mmcc@mint.net | www.mid-mainechamber.com. **Kennebec Valley Tourism Council** | 179 Main St., Waterville, 04901 | 207/877–7969 or 800/393–8629 | www.mint.net/mainevacation.

Attractions

Colby College. Founded in 1813, Colby is the 12th-oldest liberal arts college in the nation. The Georgian-style campus is known for its architectural and natural beauty. | 400 Mayflower Hill | 207/872–3000 | www.colby.edu | Daily.

North Street Playground and Pool. This community center has a picnic area with barbecues, a jungle gym, basketball and tennis courts, and kiddie and full-size swimming pools. | North St. | 207/877–7520 | $2 | Mid-June–Sept. 1, weekdays 1–5 and 6–8; weekends 1–5.

Old Fort Halifax. Built in 1754, this was the oldest blockhouse in the United States before it was destroyed by flood in 1987. A reconstructed blockhouse, using many timbers from the 1754 structure, stands at the original site at the confluence of the Sebasticook and Kennebec rivers. | Bay St., Winslow | Free | Daily.

Redington Museum. Formerly a 19th-century apothecary with soda fountain, this museum contains Civil War items, Indian relics, china, and silverware. | 64 Silver St. | 207/872–9439 | $3 | Memorial Day–Labor Day, Tues.–Sat. 10–2.

Two-Cent Footbridge. This pedestrian bridge was built to let workers get from Waterville to the paper mill across the river in Winslow. | Front St. | 207/873–7131 | Free | Daily.

ON THE CALENDAR

JUNE–AUG.: *New England Music Camp.* There are student orchestra, band, and choir performances on weekends and faculty recitals on Wednesdays at this camp 9 mi southwest of Waterville. | Pond Rd. | 207/465–3025.

SEPT.: *Common Ground Fair.* Whole and not-so-whole foods, artisans, crafters, animal demonstrations, and eco-friendly exhibits are on display at the Common Ground Fairgrounds. | Unity | 207/622–3118.

Dining

Big G's Deli. Delicatessen. Portraits of celebrities—from Lucille Ball to Elvis—line the walls in this casual eatery, 2 mi northeast of town. It is known for piled-high sandwiches, pasta dishes, and homemade soups. There's open-air dining at picnic tables with umbrellas. Cafeteria-style service. Kids' menu. No liquor. No smoking. | Rte. 4, Outer Benton Ave., Winslow | 207/873–7808 | $4–$6 | No credit cards.

Johann Sebastian B. German. This Victorian home has a fireplace, wraparound porch, and four separate dining rooms. It is known for upscale food, including schnitzels, sauerbraten, and bratwurst, as well as creative shrimp, veal, and chicken dishes. Open-air dining on the screened-in porch. Beer and wine only. No smoking. | 68 Fairfield St. (Rte. 23), Oakland | 207/465–3223 | Closed Sun.–Thurs. No lunch | $15–$23 | No credit cards.

John Martin's Manor Restaurant. Continental. The big draw at this local landmark is the 60-item, hot-and-cold buffet. You'll find everything from salads to seafood, pasta to meats, as well as a few vegetarian options. There's a regular menu with chicken cordon bleu, prime rib, fresh salmon, and lobster. There's also an OTB facility where you can place bets on horse races nationwide, and banquet facilities for 300 guests. Kids' menu. | 54 College Ave. | 207/873–5676 | $9–$17 | AE, D, DC, MC, V.

Weathervane. Seafood. You'll find family dining amid nautical artifacts and fireplaces and this eatery known for seafood. Raw bar. Kids' menu. | 470 Kennedy Memorial Dr. | 207/873–4522 | $5–$30 | MC, V.

Lodging

Best Western Inn. This chain option is near Interstate 95, but also has a wooded area at rear. Restaurant, bar. Some microwaves, refrigerators, cable TV, some in-room VCRs. Pool. Hot tub. Video games. Business services, free parking. Pets allowed. | 356 Main St. | 207/873–3335 | fax 207/873–3335 | bwwtun@mint.com | www.bestwestern.com/thisco/bw/20018/20018_b.html | 86 rooms | $85–$140 | AE, D, DC, MC, V.

Budget Host Inn. The clean, efficient rooms at this inn, as well as its proximity to local attractions, makes this a good choice. There's a diner on site remodeled in a 1950s style. Restaurant, picnic area, Continental breakfast. Cable TV. Laundry facilities. Pets allowed. | 400 Kennedy Memorial Dr. | 207/873–3366 or 800/BUD–HOST | www.budgethost.com | 45 rooms | $80–$100 | AE, D, MC, V.

Holiday Inn. A chain hotel with amenities for families that is near the interstate and Colby College. Restaurant, bar, room service. In-room data ports, refrigerators, cable TV. Pool. Hot tub. Exercise equipment. Video games. Laundry facilities. Business services. Pets allowed. | 375 Main St. | 207/873–0111 | fax 207/872–2310 | hiwlume@mint.net | www.acadia.net/hiwat-cm | 138 rooms | $95–$105 | AE, D, DC, MC, V.

WELLS

MAP 3, B11

(Nearby towns also listed: Kennebunk, Kennebunkport, Ogunquit, The Yorks)

Settled in 1640, Wells was especially tormented by the Indian conflicts between 1650 and 1730. It once covered a larger area, which included Kennebunk and Ogunquit (they were part of Wells until 1980). Farming was formerly a mainstay of this coastal village, but with 7 mi of sand beaches, two nature preserves, and heavy commerce along U.S. 1, tourism now defines this oceanfront community.

Information: Wells Chamber of Commerce | Box 356, 136 Post Rd., Wells, 04090 | 207/646–2451 or 800/943–5222 | fax 207/646–8104 | www.wellschamber.org.

Attractions

Historic Meeting House Museum. One of the oldest Congregational churches in Maine is now a museum filled with local lore and memorabilia. | U.S. 1 | 207/646–4775 | $2 | Memorial Day–Labor Day, Wed.–Thurs. 10–4.

Rachel Carson Preserve. Administered by the U.S. Fish and Wildlife Service, whose headquarters is in Wells, this reserve has 4,800 acres of marsh and upland habitat scattered from Kittery to Cape Elizabeth. The birding is exceptional along the mile-long loop through a salt marsh that borders the Little River. The white-pine forest attracts numerous species of birds. | 321 Port Rd. | Free | Trail open dawn–dusk.

Wells Auto Museum. This sprawling tribute to the motorcar includes 70 vintage automobiles, memorabilia, and an assortment of working arcade games, mutoscopes, and nickelodeons. | U.S. 1 | 207/646–9064 | $5 | Memorial Day–Columbus Day, daily 10–5.

Wells Natural Estuarine Research Reserve. Also known simply as Laudholm Farm, this 1,600-acre reserve is 1½ mi north of Wells and encompasses meadows, orchards, fields, salt marshes, and 9 mi of shorefront. There are also 7 mi of trails and guided tours are offered. | 342 Laudholm Farm Rd. | 207/646-1555 | www.wellsreserve.org. | $2 | Trails Open: mid-May–mid-Sept. 8-8; mid-Sept.–mid-May 8-5. Visitor Center: May - Oct.; M-S 10–4, Sun 12–4; Nov.–Apr., M-F 10-4.

ON THE CALENDAR

JULY: *Wells Week and Harbor Park Day.* Live concerts, booths, food, wooden boat launchings, and activities for the whole family are available at this event. | Wells Harbor Park | 207/646–2451.

SEPT.: *Laudholm Farm Nature Crafts Festival.* This juried craft fair at Laudholm Farm holds a solid reputation for fine works; there are also family and outdoor activities at this handsome farm and reserve. | 342 Laudholm Farm Rd. | 207/646–2451 or 207/646–1555.

Dining

Billy's Chowder House. Seafood. Visitors and locals head to this simple restaurant in a salt marsh for the generous lobster rolls, haddock sandwiches, and chowders. | 216 Mile Rd. | 520/394-2366 | Closed mid-Dec.–mid-Jan. | $13–$30 | AE, D, MC, V.

Grey Gull. American. You'll dine in a century-old inn on the water here. There are fine views from every table. Fresh seafood and traditional New England fare—prime rib, seafood, pasta, steak—are staples of the menu. Try the Yankee pot roast or the rack of lamb. Classical guitarist Sundays, strolling minstrel Tuesdays. Early-bird suppers. No smoking. | 475 Webhannet Dr. | 207/646-7501 | Closed Mon. Nov.–mid-Dec. and mid-Mar.–May; closed Mon.–Wed. mid-Dec.–mid-Mar. No lunch | $12–$24 | AE, D, MC, V.

The Hayloft. American. A farm motif prevails amid antique tools and poultry portraits. Kids are more than welcome. Known for fresh seafood, Angus beef, and homemade soups and chowders. Kids' menu. No smoking. | U.S. 1, next to Wells Information Center, Moody | 207/646-4400 | www.vhayloft.com | $9–$21 | AE, D, MC, V.

Litchfield's. Steak. This casual eatery 1 mi north of town has separate dining areas, including an atrium that overlooks flower gardens. Try the blackened swordfish or lobster stew. Open-air dining in the courtyard (lunch only). Raw bar. Pianist nightly in summer. Kids' menu. Sunday brunch. No smoking. | 2135 Post Rd. | 207/646-5711 | www.litchfields-restaurant.com | $9–$35 | AE, D, DC, MC, V.

Lord's Harborside. Seafood. This restaurant's window-lined dining room is on the harbor and has lobster tanks. Try the baked stuffed lobster. Kids' menu. No smoking. | 352 Harbor Rd. | 207/646-2651 | Closed Tues. and Nov.–mid-Apr. | $15–$30 | DC, MC, V.

Maine Diner. American. A classic diner, 1¾ mi north of Wells, with seating at the counter and in booths, filled with memorabilia and celebrity photos. Try the chowder, lobster pie, or chocolate cake. Kids' menu. Beer and wine only. No smoking. | 2265 Post Rd. | 207/646-4441 | www.mainediner.com | Breakfast also available; closed 1 wk in Jan. | $5–$16 | D, MC, V.

Lodging

Atlantic Motor Inn. On an ideal beachfront location between Portland and Portsmouth and 2 mi south of Wells, this motor inn has a variety of spacious rooms. Microwaves, refrigerators, cable TV. Pool. Beach. | 37 Atlantic Ave. | 207/646-7061 or 800/727-7061 | fax 207/641-0607 | am@cybertours.com | www.atlanticmotorinn.com | 35 rooms | $129–$169 | Closed Nov.–Mar. | AE, D, MC, V.

Elmwood Resort Motel. A family-oriented, all-suites, two-story motel with one-, two-, or three-bedroom units that can sleep up to six adults. All units have full kitchens and living rooms. Picnic area. Kitchenettes. 2 pools. Sauna. Exercise room. Video games. Playground.

Laundry facilities. No pets. No smoking. | U.S. 1 | 207/646–1038 | http://elmwood-resort.com/ | 54 units | $135–$185 | AE, D, DC, MC, V.

Garrison Suites. This property on U.S. 1 has an interesting mix of older cottages and a modern motel. The Garrison is on a grassy hill overlooking a panoramic view of the Atlantic Ocean on the horizon and the Rachel Carson Wildlife Refuge. Picnic area. Microwaves, refrigerators, cable TV. Pool. Playground. | 1099 Post Rd. (U.S. 1) | 207/646–3497 or 800/646–3497 | garrison@cybertours | www.garrisonsuites.com | 20 suites with full kitchens, 15 rooms, 11 cottages | $95–$150, $150 suites, $775/wk minimum cottages | Closed Nov.–Mar. | MC, V.

Grey Gull. A century-old Victorian inn that has views of the open sea and rocks on which seals like to sun themselves. Most of the unpretentious rooms have ocean views and all have queen-size beds. Restaurant, complimentary Continental breakfast. Cable TV, no rooms phones. No pets. No smoking. | 475 Webhannet Dr., at Moody Point | 207/646–7501 | fax 207/646–0938 | info@thegreygullinn.com | www.thegreygullinn.com | 5 rooms | $79–$129 | AE, D, MC, V.

Sea Mist Resort. A central motel on U.S. 1 with easy access to beaches. Picnic area. Kitchenettes, microwaves, cable TV. Pool. Hot tub. Playground. | 733 Post Rd. (U.S. 1) | 207/646–6044 or 800/448–0925 | fax 207/646–2199 | www.seamistresort.com | 66 rooms | $95 | Closed Jan.–Mar. | D, MC, V.

Seagull Motor Inn. A mix of cottages and motels on well-kept property ¼ mi south of Wells. It has screened-in porches and water views. Picnic area. No air-conditioning in some rooms, some microwaves, refrigerators, cable TV. Pool. Hot tub. Playground. | 1413 Post Rd. (U.S. 1) | 207/646–5164 or 800/573–2485 | seagull@vacations.com | www.seagullvacations.com | 24 rooms, 24 cottages | $92, $450–$840/wk for cottages | Closed mid-Oct.–late Apr. | AE, D, DC, MC, V.

Sleepytown Motel and Resort. A red-and-white, single-story farmhouse on 12 acres. The Wells trolley runs from the front door to town. The one- and two-bedroom cottages are fully furnished and have screened-in porches. Restaurant. Some kitchenettes, refrigerators, cable TV, some room phones. No pets. | U.S. 1 | 207/646–5545, 207/646–5545 reservations | www.sleepytown.com | 42 rooms, 38 cottages | $59–$99 rooms, $425–$750/wk cottages | Closed mid-Oct.–Apr. | AE, D, MC, V.

Super 8 Motel. This typical chain option is 12 mi north of Wells and is near the airport and businesses in Sanford. Some microwaves, refrigerators, cable TV. Business services. | 820 Main St., Sanford | 207/324–8823 | fax 207/324–8782 | www.super8.com | 49 rooms | $58–$63 | AE, D, DC, MC, V.

Victorian House Inn Bed and Breakfast. A turn-of-the-20th-century Victorian home with a wraparound porch. Rooms are filled with antiques and have hardwood floors, furniture, and beds. The fireplace room has a skylight. Dining room, complimentary breakfast. No room phones, no TV. No pets. No smoking. | 1616 Post Rd. | 207/646–5355 | fax 207/646–9814 | victhouse@cybertours.com | www.victorianhouse.com | 5 rooms | $100 | MC, V.

Village by the Sea. Spacious one- and two-bedroom hotel condominium suites on the coast, near Wells Beach overlooking the Rachel Carson Wildlife Refuge and tidal salt marsh. Picnic area. Kitchenettes, cable TV. 2 pools. Laundry facilities. | U.S. 1 S | 207/646–1100 or 800/444–8862 | fax 207/646–1401 | www.vbts.com | 72 suites | $179–$199 | AE, D, MC, V.

Village Green Motel and Cottages. An older but well-maintained mix of motel and cottages that is 2 mi south of Wells on U.S. 1 and convenient to beaches. There are screened porches in the cottages. Picnic area. No air-conditioning in some rooms, refrigerators, cable TV, no room phones. Pool. | 773 Post Rd. (U.S. 1) | 207/646–3285 | 10 rooms, 8 cottages | $45–$72 | Closed Nov.–Apr. | AE, D, MC, V.

Watercrest Cottages and Motel. A complex of motel and old-style cottages with screened porches that is ½ mi south of Wells. Picnic area. Some kitchenettes, some microwaves, cable TV. Pool. Hot tub. Playground, laundry facilities. | 1277 Post Rd. (U.S. 1) | 207/646–2202 or 800/

847–4693 | fax 207/646–7067 | wcrest@cybertours.com | www.watercrestcottages.com | 9 rooms, 50 cottages | $79–$84, $460–$775/wk for cottages | Closed Nov.–Mar. | D, MC, V.

WISCASSET

(Nearby towns also listed: Bath, Boothbay Harbor, Damariscotta, Newcastle)

Built astride the Sheepscot River, Wiscasset ("meeting of the three tides or rivers") was first settled in the mid-17th century. Known as Pownalborough until 1802, the town was a major port during the mid-19th century. It still has many fine examples of ship captains' homes, churches, and public buildings from this era. There are also a number of interesting shops and museums to mosey through in the compact downtown. Self-proclaimed as the "prettiest village in Maine," Wiscasset could very well be termed Maine's "prettiest bottleneck." U.S. 1 traffic creeps at a crawl through town in the high summer months.

Information: Bath-Brunswick Region Chamber of Commerce | 59 Pleasant St., Brunswick, 04011 | 207/725–8797 or 207/443–9751 | ccbbr@horton.col.k12.us | www.midcoast-maine.com. **Visitors Center** | U.S. 1 N, West Bath, 04530 | 207/725–8797 or 207/443–9751 | www.midcoastmaine.com.

Attractions

Castle Tucker. Built in 1807, this Georgian-style mansion includes Federal and Victorian furnishings and household items, as well as a freestanding elliptical staircase. | 2 Lee St. | 207/882–7364 | $4 | June–mid-Oct., Wed.–Sun. 11–4.

Fort Edgecomb. On Davis Island on the Sheepscot River, this fort was built in 1808 to protect Wiscasset, at the time the most important shipping port north of Boston. | 66 Fort Rd. | 207/882–7777 | $1 | Memorial Day–Labor Day, daily 9–5.

Maine Art Gallery. A wide range of exhibits and eclectic showings are imaginatively displayed, usually changing every month. It is in the Old Academy Building, which dates from 1807. | Warren St. | 207/882–7511 | Free | Mar.–Nov., Tues.–Sat. 10–4, Sun. 1–4; call to confirm.

Maine Coast Railroad. This railroad makes round-trip runs between Bath and Wiscasset and Bath and Newcastle. The train is reminiscent of 1930s coaches and has a diesel engine. It goes through tidal flats, marshes, and woodlands. | Waterfront Park | 207/882–8000 or 800/795–5404 | fax 207/882–7699 | $15 | Late June–early Sept., daily; late May–late June and early Sept.–mid-Oct., weekends.

Musical Wonder House–Music Museum. A showplace of mechanical musical instruments, with restored music boxes and player pianos that are used in rooms furnished with antiques of the period. The museum is in an 1852 sea captain's mansion. Inquire about evening concerts. | 16–18 High St. | 207/882–7163 or 800/336–3725 | www.musicalwonderhouse.com | $8–$15 | May–Oct., daily 10–5.

Nickels-Sortwell House. An outstanding example of Federal architecture, this house, built in 1807, was once the residence of Maine shipmaster William Nickels, whose fortune was made in the pine lumber trade. Today it contains Sortwell family furnishings, and an outstanding pinewood staircase. | Main and Federal Sts. (U.S. 1) | 207/882–6218 or 617/227–3956 | $4 | June–Oct., Wed.–Sun. 11–4.

ON THE CALENDAR

JUNE: *Annual Strawberry Festival and County Fair.* Berries (shortcakes and sundaes), crafts, and an auction in an old-fashioned setting at St. Phillip's Episcopal Church. | Hodge St. | 207/882–7184.

JUNE–AUG.: *St. Phillip's Chowder Suppers.* Homemade everything is available at St. Phillip's Episcopal Church. Reservations are strongly advised. | Hodge St. | 207/882–7184.

Dining

Le Garage. Seafood. This renovated turn-of-the-20th-century garage has exposed beams and harbor views from its upper and lower enclosed porches. It's within walking distance from the town dock. Try the charbroiled marinated lamb, the broiled seafood platter, or the Finnan Haddie. Sunday brunch. No smoking. | Water St. | 207/882–5409 | Closed Jan. and Mon. early Sept.–late May | $15–$30 | MC, V.

Sarah's Cafe. American/Casual. Harborside dining in a renovated hardware store that has water views and a country decor. You'll find lobster prepared in 13 different ways here; it is also known for regional cooking, fresh seafood, and lobster and crab rolls. It's a great place for the kids and has homemade baked goods and desserts. Open-air dining on the deck. Kids' menu. Beer and wine only. No smoking. | Main St. at Water St. | 207/882–7504 | www.sarahscafe.com | Breakfast also available weekends | $10–$25 | AE, D, MC, V.

Squire Tarbox. American. Midway between Bath and Wiscasset, the Federal-style dining room, part of an inn as well as a goat farm, serves a prix fixe menu which changes nightly but always includes a vegetarian entrée and a sampling of the inn's own goat cheese as well as entrées such as rack of lamb, duck breast, or lobster and crab cakes. Generally you can get your chocolate fix here to finish up, or try their berry tart. | Rte. 144 | 207/882–7693 | Closed Oct.–May. No lunch | $38 | AE, D, MC, V.

Lodging

Cod Cove Inn. A colonial-style inn overlooking the bay that is 1 mi southeast of Wiscasset. Complimentary Continental breakfast. In-room data ports, refrigerators, cable TV. Pool. Hot tub. Business services. No smoking. | 22 Cross Rd., Edgecomb | 207/882–9586 or 800/882–9586 | fax 207/882–9294 | codcovei@gwi.net | www.codcoveinn.com | 29 rooms | $119–$169 | Closed Dec.–Mar. | AE, MC, V.

Marston House. This hotel in the heart of Wiscasset is in a detached 19th-century carriage house. The rooms are small, but very private with Shaker and colonial furniture. One of the rooms overlooks a garden. Breakfast is delivered to your room and the tidal Sheepscot River is one block away. Complimentary Continental breakfast. No air-conditioning, no room phones, no TVs. | 101 Main St. | 800/852–4137 or 207/882–6010 | marstonhouse@nqi.net | 2 rooms | $90 | Closed Nov.–Apr. | AE, MC, V.

Squire Tarbox Inn. A restored 18th-century farmhouse on a working dairy goat farm that is 8½ mi south of Wiscasset. You can view dairy operations and sample the goats' distinctive cheese. Dining room, complimentary breakfast. No air-conditioning in some rooms, no room phones. Library. No smoking. | 1181 Main Rd., Westport | 207/882–7693 | fax 207/882–7107 | squiretarbox@ime.net | www.squiretarboxinn.com | 11 rooms | $112–$179 | Closed Nov.–Apr. | AE, D, MC, V.

Wiscasset Motor Lodge. Quiet, friendly motel in a secluded woodland that is 3 mi south of Wiscasset. No air-conditioning in some rooms, cable TV. | U.S. 1 | 207/882–7137 or 800/732–8168 | fax 207/882–7137 | www.wiscassetmotorlodge.com | 28 rooms, 7 cabins | $53–$72, $42 cabins | Closed mid-Nov.–mid-Apr. | D, MC, V.

YARMOUTH

MAP 3, C10

(Nearby towns also listed: Chebeague Islands, Freeport, Portland)

Just 11 mi from Portland, Yarmouth is all small-town Maine. Its shady main street is lined with white clapboard homes (some dating back to the 1700s) and includes a village green, steepled churches, and family-run shops. Well-sheltered Yarmouth Harbor is clustered with both pleasure and working craft. The Royal River Falls boils in spring, and there's a riverside park for picnicking and walking.

Information: Yarmouth Chamber of Commerce | 158 Maine St., Yarmouth, 04096-6712 | 207/846–3984 | fax 207/846–5419 | www.yarmouthmaine.org.

Attractions

★ **Maine Wildlife Park.** This park, run by the Maine Department of Inland Fisheries and Wildlife, holds native animals that are recuperating after being rescued in the wilderness. On view are moose, deer, mountain lions, lynx, bobcats, and more. Picnic grounds available. Great for toddlers. | Rte. 26 | 207/371–2303 | $3.50 | Daily 9–4.

Old Ledge School. This pre-Revolution one-room schoolhouse was reconstructed by the Yarmouth Historical Society in 1973. | W. Main St. | 207/846–6259 | Donation suggested | Sept.–June, Tues.–Sat.; July–Sept., weekdays.

Royal River Park. A town-owned park along the Royal River with paved hiking trails, waterfalls, and an area for concerts. | Elm St. | 207/846–2406 | Free | Daily.

Yarmouth Historical Society Museum. The museum's two galleries contain changing exhibits of town artifacts, photographs, and clothing that document local and maritime history. | Merrill Memorial Library, 3rd floor, 215 Main St. | 207/846–6259 | Donation suggested | July–Aug., weekdays 1–5; Sept.–June, Tues.–Fri 1–5, Sat. 10–5.

ON THE CALENDAR

JULY: *Yarmouth Clam Festival.* One of the state's biggest seafood events draws crowds for seafood treats, strawberry shortcake, crafts fair, parade, carnival, and live music. | Yarmouth | 207/846–3984.

Dining

The Cannery. Seafood. This eatery is in a renovated 1936 sardine cannery on the Royal River. It has a comfortable dining area, with lots of plants, wood carvings, and historical photographs. Try the fresh local seafood, vegetarian items, or organic beef. Open-air dining on the enclosed deck. Kids' menu. Sunday jazz brunch off-season. No smoking. | Rte. 88, Lower Falls Landing | 207/846–1226 | $9–$23 | AE, MC, V.

Muddy Rudder. This family-oriented restaurant has a view of Cousins River out back and is 1 mi from Interstate 95. The menu is varied and includes lots of comfort food like burgers. Some daily specials include sweet-and-sour steak and shrimp and the swordfish Santa Fe, which is pan-blackened and served with peppers, mushrooms, salsa, and sour cream. Kids' menu. | U.S. 1 | 207/846–3082 | $8–$18 | AE, D, MC, V.

Lodging

Down East Motel. One mile from the Maine Turnpike, and within walking distance of all the shops and restaurants of Yarmouth, this is a popular family place. Rooms have two double beds or a king or queen. Restaurant. Cable TV. Pool. | 705 U.S. 1 | 207/846–5161 | 31 rooms | $84–$99 | AE, D, DC, MC, V.

THE YORKS

MAP 3, B12

(Nearby towns also listed: Kittery, Ogunquit, Wells)

The Yorks, first settled in 1624 as Agamenticus, are made up of three small burgs, each with a distinct feel. York Beach, the most garrulous of the three, is a classic, old-time beach town, with a long stretch of sand beach, a zoo, and a carnivalesque downtown. York Harbor, dotted with imposing Victorian "cottages," is more reserved—more an exclusive enclave than a tourist spot. York Village is a splendidly preserved colonial village, which includes a seven-building historic museum.

Information: Yorks Chamber of Commerce | 571 U.S. 1, Yorks, 03909 | 207/363–4422 or 800/639–2442 | fax 207/363–7320 | york@gwi.net | www.yorkme.org.

Attractions

Long Sands Beach. Three miles of sandy beach, including the most photographed light-house in America, the Nubble Light. | U.S. 1A | Free | Daily.

Nubble Light. This 1879 lighthouse is on a rock-crop island. Its tidy Victorian cottages are best viewed from Sohier Park, where you'll find rest rooms, benches, and shore views. | Nubble Rd., Cape Neddick | 207/363–7608 | Free | Daily.

Old York Historical Society. Three centuries of maritime heritage and cultural history are housed in seven historic museum buildings: the Elizabeth Perkins House, the Emerson-Wilcox House, the George Marshall Store, Jefferds Tavern and Schoolhouse, John Hancock Warehouse, and Old Gaol. Live demonstrations, decorative arts, period schoolhouse, museum shop, Old Burying Ground, nature preserve, and tours round out the experience. | Lindsay Rd. (U.S. 1A), York Village | 207/363–4974 | www.oldyork.org | $7 for all 7 sites, $2 for individual sites | June–mid-Oct., Tues.–Sat. 10–5, Sun. 1–5.

Elizabeth Perkins House. A 1730 farmhouse with colonial-era antiques. | Sewall's Bridge | 207/363–4974 | June–Columbus Day, Tues.–Sat. 10–5, Sun. 1–5.

Emerson-Wilcox House. First constructed in the mid-1700s, this house has been added to over the years, resulting in an interesting mishmash of architectural styles. Costumed guides provide tours. | U.S. 1A | 207/363–4974 | June–Columbus Day, Tues.–Sat. 10–5, Sun. 1–5.

George Marshall Store. Originally a general store on the Hancock Wharf, this building now serves as a gallery for revolving historical exhibits. | 140 Lindsay Rd. | 207/363–4974 | June–Columbus Day, Tues.–Sat. 10–5, Sun. 1–5.

Jefferds Tavern. This colonial hostelry features cooking demonstrations and an introductory video tour of Old York. It also serves as a visitors center and you can purchase your tickets to the seven museum buildings here. | Lindsay Rd. | 207/363–4974 | $7 for all seven buildings | June–Columbus Day, Tues.–Sat. 10–5, Sun. 1–5.

John Hancock Warehouse. This site captures the early seafaring days of this coastal community and is part of a museum complex. | Lindsay Rd. | 207/363–4974 | June–Columbus Day, Tues.–Sat. 10–5, Sun. 1–5.

★ **Old Gaol.** This is one of the oldest public buildings (1719) in North America and is equipped with old dungeons and cells. Costumed guides chill the young and not so young. | U.S. 1A | 207/363–4974 | June–Columbus Day, Tues.–Sat. 10–5, Sun. 1–5.

Sayward-Wheeler House. This early-18th-century home has original antique Queen Anne and Chippendale furnishings. | 79 Barrell La. Extention, York Harbor | www.spnea.org | 603/436–3205 | $4 | June–mid-Oct., weekends 11–4.

York's Wild Kingdom. This zoo houses a collection of animals, ranging from llamas to lions. There are animal events and shows, amusement park rides, and food vendors. | 102 Railroad Ave., York Beach | 207/363–4911 or 800/465–4911 | www.yorkzoo.com | $14.75. | Memorial Day–Labor Day, daily 10–5.

ON THE CALENDAR

JULY–AUG.: *York Days Celebration.* This annual summer event features concerts, tournaments, crafts fair, parade, and fireworks. | 207/363–1040.

OCT.: *Harvest Fest.* A festival with a colonial theme. There are hayrides, apple pressing, food vendors, art show and sale, kids' activities, and live entertainment. | 207/363–4422.

DEC.: *York Village Festival of Lights.* Open houses, caroling, parade, church suppers, and craft fairs are part of this annual event. | 207/363–4974.

Dining

Cafe Shelton. American. This perky restaurant with blue-and-white color scheme sits across from Short Sands Beach. Lunch fare includes soups, sandwiches, and salads. Dinner is more elaborate, with entrées such as Grand Marnier salmon and lobster ravioli sharing the menu with linguine and meatballs. Kids' menu. | 1 Ocean Ave. | 207/363–0708 | Closed Oct. 15–Apr. 15 | $10–$35 | MC, V.

Cape Neddick Inn. Contemporary. The dining room is in an upscale country inn and is fronted by woods and lawn. There's original artwork by local and regional artists on the walls. Try the smoked seafood sampler appetizer or rack of lamb. Sunday brunch (fall and winter only). Kids' menu. No smoking. | 1233 U.S. 1, Cape Neddick | 207/363–2899. | No lunch | $17–$28 | AE, MC, V.

Dockside. Seafood. With windows on three of four walls, this eatery is open and breezy. You'll have views of the ocean channel and harbor while dining in this nautical spot. Try the lobster bouillabaisse. Open-air dining on the screened-in porch. Salad bar. Kids' menu. Dock space. No smoking. | Harris Island Rd., York | 207/363–2722 | Closed Mon. and Columbus Day–Memorial Day | $15–$20 | MC, V.

Fazio's Italian Restaurant. Italian. You'll find family-friendly dining in this homey, comfortable spot. Family photos from the 1920s–40s deck the walls. It is known for steak, seafood, and homemade pasta. Try the seafood tecchia—scallops, shrimp, and pasta with wine, garlic, lemon, and tomato butter—or the chicken français. Open-air dining on the deck. Kids' menu, early-bird suppers. No smoking. | 38 Woodbridge Rd., York Village | 207/363–7019 | No lunch | $9–$17 | AE, D, MC, V.

The Goldenrod. American. A York Beach landmark, where saltwater taffy kisses are pulled in the window. This is a great family spot with American-style lunches. The paneled dining room is dominated by a fieldstone fireplace and there's an old-fashioned soda fountain. Homemade ice cream. | 2 Railroad Ave., York Beach | 207/363–2621 | Closed Columbus Day–Memorial Day | $4–$8 | MC, V.

York Harbor Inn. Continental. This inn has four separate dining areas, the earliest of which dates back to the early 1800s. It has wainscoting and ocean and harbor views. Try the lobster-stuffed breast of chicken or the baked stuffed lobster. Live music on weekends in the adjacent pub. Kids' menu, early-bird suppers. Sunday brunch. No smoking. | U.S. 1A, York Harbor | 207/363–5119 | www.yorkharborinn.com | Closed Mon.–Thurs., Jan.–Apr. | $26–$34 | AE, DC, MC, V.

Lodging

Anchorage Inn. A family resort convenient to York's many beaches. Bar. Refrigerators, cable TV. 3 pools. Hot tub. Exercise equipment. Business services. | 265 Long Beach Ave. (U.S. 1A), York Beach | 207/363–5112 | fax 207/363–6753 | www.anchorageinn.com | 179 rooms | $124–$275 | MC, V.

Cutty Sark Motel. Rooms here are standard motel fare, but you can't beat being right on the ocean by Long Sands Beach. Every room has an ocean view. Complimentary Continental breakfast. | 58 Long Beach Ave. | 800/543–5131 or 207/363–5131 | fax 207/351–1335 | 42 rooms | $125–$145 | D, MC, V.

Dockside Guest Quarters. You can enjoy waterfront views from this wooded island resort. Restaurant, picnic area. No air-conditioning, some kitchenettes, cable TV. Dock, boating. Playground. No smoking. | Harris Island Rd. | 207/363–2868 | fax 207/363–1977 | info@docksidegq.com | www.docksidegq.com | 25 rooms (4 with shower only, 2 with shared bath) in 5 buildings, 6 suites | $78–$142, $189–$199 suites | Closed weekdays Nov.–Apr. | D, MC, V.

Edward's Harborside Inn. Turn-of-the-20th-century house on the beach that is 1 mi east of York. Picnic area, complimentary Continental breakfast. Cable TV. Dock. No smoking. | Stageneck Rd., York Harbor | 207/363–3037 or 800/273–2686 | fax 207/363–1544 | www.edwardsharborside.com | 10 rooms (8 with shower only, 2 with shared bath), 2 suites | $110–$260, $230 suites | MC, V.

Homestead Inn. The rooms of this inn, 4 mi east of York, are comfortable and sea breezes come through the double windows. Complimentary Continental breakfast. No air-condi-

tioning, no room phones. No kids under 12. No smoking. | 8 S. Main St. (U.S. 1A), York Beach | 207/363–8952 | fax 207/363–8952 | http://members.aol.com/homstedbb | 4 rooms (2 with shared bath) | $59–$69 | Closed mid-Oct.–Mar. | No credit cards.

Riverbank on the Harbor. This white clapboard, shingle-style cottage, built in 1890, sits on the edge of York Harbor in a neighborhood of expansive homes, shade trees, and flowering gardens. All rooms have king-size beds and tasteful turn-of-the-20th-century furnishings. Complimentary breakfast. | 11 Harmon Park Rd. | 207/363–8333 | fax 207/363–3684 | 5 rooms | $120–$150 | MC, V.

Stageneck Inn. This beachfront hotel offers a wide variety of services and is within walking distance of York Harbor center. 2 restaurants, bar with entertainment, room service. Refrigerators, cable TV. 2 pools. Hot tub. Tennis. Exercise equipment. Beach. Laundry facilities. Business services. No smoking. | 22 Stageneck Rd., York Harbor | 207/363–3850 or 800/222–3238 | fax 207/363–2221 | stageneck@aol.com | www.stageneck.com | 60 rooms | $195–$285 | AE, D, MC, V.

Union Bluff. Five miles from Interstate 95, this fortresslike, modern, white structure, with balconies across the front and turrets on the ends, is right across from Short Sands Beach with views to forever. The best rooms are in the front of the inn, but many on the north side, which cost less, also have ocean views. The front rooms in the adjacent motel have ocean views, but the motel has fewer services. Restaurant, bar. | 8 Beach St. | 207/363–1333 or 800/833–0721 | fax 207/363–1381 | sales@unionbluff.com | www.unionbluff.com | 36 rooms, 4 suites | $99–$219 | AE, D, MC, V.

York Commons Inn. This inn is on U.S. 1 and is near beaches and shopping. It has modern, landscaped grounds. Complimentary Continental breakfast. Some refrigerators, cable TV. Pool. Business services. Some pets allowed. | 362 U.S. 1 | 207/363–8903, 800/537–5515 New York and New England | fax 207/363–1130 | 90 rooms | $95–$120 | AE, D, DC, MC, V.

York Harbor Inn. This inn is across the street from the ocean. A section from the original, 1637 house is now the sitting room. Restaurant, picnic area, complimentary Continental breakfast. Cable TV. Hot tub. Business services. | U.S. 1A, York Harbor | 207/363–5119 or 800/343–3869 | fax 207/363–7151 | garyinkeep@aol.com | www.yorkharborinn.com | 33 rooms (23 with shower only) | $99–$239 | AE, DC, MC, V.

Pack an easy way to reach the world.

Wherever you travel, the MCI WorldCom Card℠ is the easiest way to stay in touch. You can use it to call to and from more than 125 countries worldwide. And you can earn bonus miles every time you use your card. So go ahead, travel the world. MCI WorldCom℠ makes it even more rewarding. For additional access codes, visit **www.wcom.com/worldphone**.

EASY TO CALL WORLDWIDE

1. Just dial the WorldPhone® access number of the country you're calling from.
2. Dial or give the operator your MCI WorldCom Card number.
3. Dial or give the number you're calling.

Canada	1-800-888-8000
Mexico	01-800-021-8000
United States	1-800-888-8000

EARN FREQUENT FLIER MILES

6 "I'm thirsty"s, 9 "Are we there yet"s, 3 "I don't feel good"s,
1 car class upgrade.
At least something's going your way.

Hertz rents Fords and other fine cars. ® REG. U.S. PAT. OFF. © HERTZ SYSTEM INC., 2000/005-00

Make your next road trip more comfortable with a free one-class upgrade from Hertz.

(L)et's face it, a long road trip isn't always sunshine and roses. But with Hertz, you get a free one car class upgrade to make things a little more bearable. You'll also choose from a variety of vehicles with child seats, Optional Protection Plans, 24-Hour Emergency Roadside Assistance, and the convenience of NeverLost® the in-car navigation system that provides visual and audio prompts to give you turn-by-turn guidance to your destination. In a word: it's everything you need for your next road trip. Call your travel agent or Hertz at **1-800-654-2210** and mention PC# **906404** or check us out at **hertz.com** or AOL Keyword: **hertz**. Peace of mind. Another reason nobody does it exactly like Hertz.

exactly.®

TOP TIPS FOR TRAVELERS

Smart Sightseeings

Don't plan your visit in your hotel room. Don't wait until you pull into town to decide how to spend your days. It's inevitable that there will be much more to see and do than you'll have time for: choose sights in advance.

Organize your touring. Note the places that most interest you on a map, and visit places that are near each other during the same morning or afternoon.

Start the day well equipped. Leave your hotel in the morning with everything you need for the day—maps, medicines, extra film, your guidebook, rain gear, and another layer of clothing in case the weather turns cooler.

Tour museums early. If you're there when the doors open you'll have an intimate experience of the collection.

Easy does it. See museums in the mornings, when you're fresh, and visit sit-down attractions later on. Take breaks before you need them.

Strike up a conversation. Only curmudgeons don't respond to a smile and a polite request for information. Most people appreciate your interest in their home town. And your conversations may end up being your most vivid memories.

Get lost. When you do, you never know what you'll find—but you can count on it being memorable. Use your guidebook to help you get back on track. Build wandering-around time into every day.

Quit before you're tired. There's no point in seeing that one extra sight if you're too exhausted to enjoy it.

Take your mother's advice. Go to the bathroom when you have the chance. You never know what lies ahead.

Hotel How-Tos

How to get a deal. After you've chosen a likely candidate or two, phone them directly and price a room for your travel dates. Then call the hotel's toll-free number and ask the same questions. Also try consolidators and hotel-room discounters. You won't hear the same rates twice. On the spot, make a reservation as soon as you are quoted a price you want to pay.

Promises, promises. If you have special requests, make them when you reserve. Get written confirmation of any promises.

Settle in. Upon arriving, make sure everything works—lights and lamps, TV and radio, sink, tub, shower, and anything else that matters. Report any problems immediately. And don't wait until you need extra pillows or blankets or an ironing board to call housekeeping. Also check out the fire emergency instructions. Know where to find the fire exits, and make sure your companions do, too.

If you need to complain. Be polite but firm. Explain the problem to the person in charge. Suggest a course of action. If you aren't satisfied, repeat your requests to the manager. Document everything: Take pictures and keep a written record of who you've spoken with, when, and what was said. Contact your travel agent, if he made the reservations.

Know the score. When you go out, take your hotel's business cards (one for everyone in your party). If you have extras, you can give them out to new acquaintants who want to call you.

Tip up front. For special services, a tip or partial tip in advance can work wonders.

Use all the hotel resources A concierge can make difficult things easy. But a desk clerk, bellhop, or other hotel employee who's friendly, smart, and ambitious can often steer you straight as well. A gratuity is in order if the advice is helpful.

© Artville

New Hampshire

For a small state, New Hampshire packs a big punch. It has stunning scenery, a long and varied history as one of the original 13 colonies, and friendly people. There's good skiing, hiking, snowmobiling, and fishing. Indoor pleasures aren't ignored either: quality restaurants and luxurious lodgings can be found even in the most rural sections of the state. Most museums are small but well done, concentrating on the state's unique heritage and history. The state is as welcoming to the bikers who come for Motorcycle Week in June as to the RVers who cruise the back roads during foliage season.

While New Hampshire remains focused on tourism, it is nonetheless a state in transition. Once heavily rural, with only a handful of small cities, it has seen steady growth in its southern tier during the last two decades. Much of the state's industry is in that area and accessible interstates also make commuting to jobs in Massachusetts easy. New Hampshire's lower housing prices and lack of income and sales taxes often make that commute worthwhile.

With growth, however, comes change. The family farms that once dotted the landscape around Londonderry, Hampton Falls, Salem, and other towns have sprouted bumper crops of three- and four-bedroom houses on culs-de-sac with cute names. In the southern towns this suburbanization has triggered a switch from the traditional town meeting/board of selectman form of government, beloved to longtime natives. Professional town managers now cope with rapidly growing school enrollments, roads too narrow for heavy traffic, and increases in crime.

Growth has been slow in towns without easy access to major roads or that lie too far north for easy commuting. Consequently, two distinct ways of life are developing in New Hampshire. In the south, coffeehouses, warehouse stores, and fast-food chains have replaced the corner stores, local hardware stores, and diners that are still very much a part of life north of Concord and in the western part of the state.

CAPITAL: CONCORD	POPULATION: 1,109,300	AREA: 9,024 SQUARE MI
BORDERS: ME, MA, VT, CANADA, ATLANTIC OCEAN		
TIME ZONE: EASTERN	POSTAL ABBREVIATION: NH	WEB SITE: WWW.VISITNH.GOV

For visitors, the changes have mostly been either invisible or for the better. Except for Portsmouth and Hampton Beach, the state's heavily visited areas are removed from this development. And those towns, being among the oldest in the state, have had more experience handling growth. Portsmouth, in particular, has a large historic district and an active commission working to preserve the character of the city. Infrastructure changes, like the expansion of Manchester's airport and improvements to the highways and secondary roads, generally benefit tourists.

Throughout the Lakes Region, the White Mountains, and the western half of the state, you'll find family-run businesses that go back generations, as well as new enterprises started with that same entrepreneurial spirit. In fact, the sheer number of family-run businesses is one of the things that makes New Hampshire a great place for visitors. The woman behind the cash register is as likely to be the owner of the store as she is to be an employee. And, as such, she cares not just about the purchases you make, but about your whole experience visiting her town. Her business depends on people like you who return over and over again.

Taken as a whole, New Hampshirites are an independent lot. It may seem that nearly everyone you meet is self-employed or aspires to be. Although wary of outsiders who try to change their way of life, the folks here welcome visitors.

If a tourist laughs about the state's quirks when he gets home, that's OK. After all, since New Hampshire began holding the first-in-the-nation presidential primary in 1952, the state has been the focus of media stories that poke fun at the role such a small state plays in the country's political future. New Hampshirites argue that the state's size is its greatest asset when it comes to presidential politics. Let California or Texas hold the first primary and only those candidates with plenty of money to spend on TV advertising could afford to compete. In New Hampshire, candidates can travel the length and breadth of the state in one day. Folks here expect them to make their pitch in person—and no gathering is deemed too small. Both well-known and obscure candidates go to Rotary Clubs, church dinners, and small gatherings in people's homes. Campaigning here is up close and personal. As the old joke goes: when a reporter asked a crusty New Hampshire voter what he thought of a particular candidate. He replied, "I don't know yet, I've only met him three times."

While politics is a popular hobby in New Hampshire, the money it generates doesn't hurt either. Without a state income tax or sales tax (although one or both are on the horizon), dollars from visiting candidates, media, and campaign personnel not only keep businesses flourishing, they contribute directly to the state coffers through taxes on hotel rooms and restaurant meals. Tourist dollars fill in the gaps between presidential elections.

In general, the New Hampshire way is to tax sin (through cheap state-run liquor stores, cigarettes, and state lotteries) and out-of-staters. Of course, locals pay their share through town property taxes, and if you want to see a native sputter, just say that you don't think property taxes are all that high in New Hampshire, or suggest adding the dreaded income tax.

History

New Hampshire had long been home to Abenaki and Pennacook branches of the Algonquin Indians when Europeans began to arrive in 1623. Expanding colonial settlements soon came into conflict with the Native Americans, resulting in a series of bloody raids and counter raids that reached their height during King Philip's War in 1675 and the fighting continued well into the 18th century. During this time, New Hampshire settlers prospered by supplying mast pines to the Royal Navy, and through farming, fishing, and boatbuilding.

New Hampshire was quick to declare independence from Great Britain during the Revolution. Its militia was well seasoned from skirmishes with Native Americans, and soldiers from the fledgling state were involved in all of the war's major campaigns. New Hampshire, though, was the only one of the original 13 colonies on whose soil no battles with the British took place.

Following the Revolution, New Hampshire saw the rise of mills along its many rivers, an influx of immigrants to work those mills, and the beginnings of a tourist industry as wealthy industrialists and artsy bohemians began to "summer" in the state. It was in the 19th century, too, that New Hampshire produced its only U.S. president, Franklin Pierce. The mills closed in the 20th century, so now tourism plays an increasingly important role in the state's economy.

INTRODUCTION
HISTORY
REGIONS
WHEN TO VISIT
STATE'S GREATS
RULES OF THE ROAD
DRIVING TOURS

Regions

1. SEACOAST REGION

New Hampshire boasts only 18 mi of seacoast—a minuscule distance compared to neighbors Maine and Massachusetts. Despite its small extent, New Hampshire's seacoast has a rich heritage as a fishing and boating region. A series of tidal rivers combine to create an inland estuary called the Great Bay, so most of the towns here either border water, have rivers running through them, or both.

The region extends from the border with Massachusetts at Seabrook to the border with Maine at Portsmouth and inland to Rochester, Dover, and Exeter. The towns are the oldest in the state and they retain a strong sense of history. Portsmouth is a favorite spot for shopping, dining, and theater. There are a number of ocean beaches and riverfront parks to enjoy as well.

Towns listed: Dover, Durham, Exeter, Hampton, Hampton Beach, Portsmouth, Rye

2. LAKES REGION

Beginning just above Rochester and continuing north through Wolfeboro and Madison, New Hampshire is blessed with an abundance of lakes. The region is bounded on the east by the Maine border and on the west by Newfound Lake and the towns of Plymouth and Franklin. In many ways, this is the state's summer playground. The largest and most heavily used of the lakes is Lake Winnipesaukee, but the smaller lakes also have something special to offer visitors.

The Lakes Region is filled with small bed-and-breakfasts, charming inns, and cottages on the lakefronts. Many are seasonal and close for the winter. Others stay open and cater to visitors who come to ski at Gunstock Ski Area, to snowmobile, or to ice-fish.

Towns listed: Center Harbor, Center Sandwich, Gilford, Holderness, Laconia, Madison, Meredith, Moultonborough, Tamworth, Weirs Beach, Wolfeboro

NH Timeline

1600	1603	1622	1623
Native American tribes have inhabited the area for several thousand years. Algonquin Indian tribes have spread throughout New England, including the Abenaki and the Pennacook in New Hampshire.	Martin Pring explores the mouth of the Piscataqua River.	John Mason and Fernando Gorges are given the first British land grant in New Hampshire.	The first permanent English settlement is established at Odiorne Point in what is now Rye.

3. MERRIMACK VALLEY

The Merrimack Valley refers to the river valley formed by the Merrimack River, roughly paralleled by U.S. 3, Interstate 93, and the Everett Turnpike. It begins just north of Concord and continues south to the Massachusetts border. It is bounded by Hollis and Nashua on the west and Salem on the east.

This is the state's commercial beltway and its most heavily populated area. Nearly all the state's cities—Concord, Manchester, and Nashua—as well as the large towns of Salem, Derry, and Londonderry are found here.

Towns listed: Canterbury, Concord, Franklin, Manchester, Merrimack, Milford, Nashua, Salem

4. MONADNOCK REGION

New Hampshire's western corner, from Hollis west to the Connecticut River (the Vermont border) and from the Massachusetts border north to Hillsborough, remains quiet and rural. Keene, home of Keene State College, is the largest city in the region. It is a great place for hiking, relaxing, or spending a romantic weekend, antiquing, and shunpiking. Most towns are small, and many have a distinctly colonial air with white houses bordering village greens. This, combined with rolling hills, small mountains, and numerous small lakes and streams, gives the Monadnock Region its great visual appeal.

Towns listed: Fitzwilliam, Hillsborough, Jaffrey, Keene, Peterborough

5. LAKE SUNAPEE AND THE UPPER CONNECTICUT RIVER VALLEY

West of Interstate 93 and north of Hillsborough, stretched out along Interstate 89 to the Vermont border, are a string of small towns set against the backdrop of the region's lakes and mountains. The Connecticut River, designated one of the nation's "wild and scenic" rivers, sparkles along the western edge. Cultural events at several colleges in the region, including Dartmouth, lend an air of sophistication to the otherwise quiet countryside. Outdoor sports such as alpine and cross-country skiing, fishing, and boating are popular pastimes.

Towns listed: Charlestown, Cornish, Enfield, Grafton, Hanover, Henniker, Lyme, New London, Newport, Sunapee, Warner

6. THE WHITE MOUNTAINS

The White Mountain National Forest extends over much of this region that runs the width of the state from Waterville Valley north to Jefferson and Gorham. As its name implies, the rugged mountains are the area's focus. Placement of roads is determined by the notches, or passes, through the mountain range, and towns cluster in the valleys. This is one of the most heavily visited sections of the state and it has year-round

---

1642

Darby Field becomes the first man to climb Mt. Washington. Although several Native American tribes have lived in the region for centuries, they believe the Great Spirit lives on the mountain, making it off-limits to mortals.

1675–1730

King Philip's War begins as the New England Indian tribes recognize the European threat to their land as settlements move farther into the wilderness. The French take advantage of this unrest, inciting the Abenaki and Pennacook Indians to conduct repeated raids against white settlements at Portsmouth, Dover, Exeter, and other areas. The colonial government places a high bounty on Native scalps, leading to the virtual extermination of the tribes in the region.

INTRODUCTION
HISTORY
REGIONS
WHEN TO VISIT
STATE'S GREATS
RULES OF THE ROAD
DRIVING TOURS

attractions, which helps keep it from being overburdened. During foliage season, though, it is best not to arrive without a reservation. In summer, people hike, fish, mountain bike, and visit the area's museums and other attractions. In winter, skiing is the main draw.

Towns listed: Bartlett, Bretton Woods, Conway, Franconia, Glen, Gorham, Intervale, Jackson, Jefferson, Lincoln and North Woodstock area, Littleton, North Conway, Pinkham Notch and Mt. Washington, Plymouth, Sugar Hill, Waterville Valley

7. THE GREAT NORTH WOODS

The quietest and least populated section of the state is north of all the White Mountain notches except Dixville Notch. From Berlin north to the Canadian border and running the narrow width of the state is an area where moose can outnumber people. Towns are small and friendly, but services for visitors may be limited in some areas.

Towns listed: Colebrook, Dixville Notch

When to Visit

New Hampshire's seasons are fairly consistent throughout the state, although winter comes earlier and spring later to the White Mountains. It is not a state with either extreme heat or cold. Mt. Washington is the exception that proves the rule. The highest winds ever recorded—231 mph—were experienced there in April 1934. And the peak can see snow in any month of the year. As for the rest of the state, the first snow arrives in November (early in the month to the north and around Thanksgiving in the south) and wintry weather continues through March. Snowfalls vary widely from year to year, with no one area guaranteed to have heavy snows. The White Mountains can usually count on enough to make winter sports enjoyable, and, of course, the ski areas make their own snow even when nature is generous. Spring begins arriving in the southern parts of the state in April and slowly works its way north. Snow melt, spring rains, and black flies combine to make April and May perhaps the least pleasant time to visit. Summer brings warm days but rarely any long stretches of really hot weather. In the north country, nights can be cool, even in July. Fall is a special season in New Hampshire with some warm days, crisp evenings, and brilliant foliage.

CLIMATE CHART
Average High/Low Temperatures (F) and Monthly Precipitation (in inches)

	JAN.	FEB.	MAR.	APR.	MAY	JUNE
CONCORD	32/11	34/12	42/22	56/32	69/42	78/51
	2.51	2.53	2.72	2.91	3.14	3.15

	JULY	AUG.	SEPT.	OCT.	NOV.	DEC.
	83/56	81/54	72/46	62/36	48/27	35/15
	3.23	3.32	2.81	3.23	3.66	3.16

1769
Eleazar Wheelock founds Hanover's Dartmouth College to educate Native American youth.

1774
A band of rebel patriots raids Fort William and Mary (now Fort Constitution) in New Castle and steals gunpowder and cannons that are later used against the British in the Battle of Bunker Hill.

1775
New Hampshire becomes the first state to declare independence from Great Britain. A year later, New Hampshire is the first of the colonies to adopt a state constitution.

1782
General John Stark of Derryfield (now Manchester) leads the patriot forces to victory at the crucial Battle of Bennington during the Revolutionary War. His letter, celebrating the 20th anniversary of that victory, gives New Hampshire its state motto: Live Free or Die.

	JAN.	FEB.	MAR.	APR.	MAY	JUNE
PORTSMOUTH	32/15	33/16	41/27	53/36	65/46	75/55
	2.3	2.3	3.2	4.0	3.7	3.5

	JULY	AUG.	SEPT.	OCT.	NOV.	DEC.
	79/61	78/59	70/52	61/42	48/34	35/21
	3.5	4.3	3.8	3.3	4.5	3.1

ON THE STATE CALENDAR

WINTER

Dec. **Annual Strawbery Banke Museum Candlelight Stroll** in Portsmouth. Normally closed in winter, the museum opens in the evenings for two weekends to celebrate traditional winter activities and holidays that would have taken place at various times in Portsmouth's history. The museum's Victorian-era mansion is decked out in Christmas splendor, while in the colonial-era home, a hearth-cooking demonstration reenacts preparations for a long winter. Luminarias light the walkways between the buildings, carolers stroll the grounds. Hot cider and other refreshments are served. | 603/433–1106.

SUMMER

June **Motorcycle Rally and Race Week** in Laconia and other areas around the state. Motorcycle riders come from all over the country and gather for a week of races, hill climbs, riding tours, and other events. | 603/366–2000.

Aug. **Annual League of New Hampshire Craftsmen Fair,** Sunapee. This juried weeklong crafts festival, the oldest such crafts fair in the nation, showcases contemporary and traditional crafts made by members of the League. These works are displayed under tents outdoors at Mt. Sunapee Ski Area. There are demonstrations and exhibits in addition to the sale. | 603/224–3375.

Festival of Fireworks in Jaffrey. The largest fireworks display is put on by one of the country's leading fireworks companies. | 603/532–4549.

AUTUMN

Sept. **Annual New Hampshire Highland Games** at Loon Mountain Park in Lincoln. This weekend festival presents traditional Scottish Highland games with competitions, bagpipes, traditional dancing, and crafts. | 603/358–7208.

1782	1788	1808	1833	1850
Daniel Webster is born in Franklin, New Hampshire. He goes on to become a United States Congressman, a Senator, and Secretary of State.	The convention of delegates from 175 New Hampshire towns approves the proposed federal Constitution, making New Hampshire the ninth and deciding state to ratify the document.	Salmon P. Chase, future Secretary of the Treasury under Abraham Lincoln and Chief Justice of the Supreme Court from 1864 to 1873, is born in Cornish.	The nation's first free public library opens in Peterborough.	The Amoskeag Mills in Manchester produce nearly 5 million yards of cloth per week, making them the world's largest textile mills and attracting a wave of foreign immigrants, partic-

State's Greats

Not only does the state boast mountains, lakes, and beaches, but it also has large tracts of protected and preserved land. Of particular note are the 770,000 acres of forested mountains, valleys, and notches in the northern part of the state that make up the White Mountain National Forest. Long popular with hikers, campers, and skiers, and easily accessible to Bostonians and New Yorkers, it is one of the most heavily used of the nation's forests.

Still, with so much land available, some areas see fewer visitors than others, so it is still quite possible to get away from it all. The Kancamagus Highway that runs from Lincoln to Conway and the trails off it tend to be among the most crowded. Majestic Mt. Washington gets more than its share of visitors as well.

The Outdoors

Although many people like the honky-tonk atmosphere at **Hampton Beach, Wallis Sands State Beach** in Rye is quieter and more sheltered for swimming. There's a lifeguard on duty, plenty of parking (fee), and a bathhouse as well.

When it comes to forests, it is hard to beat the 770,000-acre **White Mountain National Forest.** Hiking trails crisscross it, including a section of the Appalachian Trail. Rugged mountains, cascading streams, and panoramic views combined with accessibility make this perhaps the best forested area in the northeast.

New Hampshire has more than 60 state parks and scenic areas. Two of the nicest are within the White Mountain National Forest: **Franconia Notch State Park** and **Crawford Notch State Park. Monadnock State Park** is another favorite. **Rhododendron State Park,** south of Keene in Fitzwilliam, blooms each year with hundreds of wild rhododendrons. For a city park, try Portsmouth's **Prescott Park,** which runs along the Piscataqua River. A popular venue for outdoor theater in summer, it has lovely gardens.

Participatory sports get people outside. The White Mountains, which slice across the center of the state, are great for skiing and snowboarding. With 20 or so alpine areas, there's something for everyone. **Attitash Bear Peak** is one of the largest, with a wide variety of terrain. **Wildcat Mountain** trails challenge even the experts. Smaller, family-run areas like **Pats Peak** and **Black Mountain** are friendly, fun, and varied.

Jackson Ski Touring Foundation, in the town of Jackson, remains one of the top cross-country ski destinations in the country, but cross-country trails can be found elsewhere as well. In summer, mountain biking takes over the trails in many ski areas. The White Mountains are full of hikers through fall.

History and Culture

As one of the original 13 colonies, with settlements that date back to 1623, New Hampshire is full of history. In addition to historic buildings and well-known museums, every small town seems to have its own historical museum, sometimes just one room, with fascinating tidbits about the past. For an overview, stop in at the **Museum of New Hamp-**

INTRODUCTION
HISTORY
REGIONS
WHEN TO VISIT
STATE'S GREATS
RULES OF THE ROAD
DRIVING TOURS

	1852	1854	1876	1911
ularly French Canadians.	Franklin Pierce, born in Hillsborough and living in Concord, is elected 14th President of the United States.	The Republican Party is formed in Exeter.	The Appalachian Mountain Club is formed.	The Weeks Law, sponsored by John Wingate Weeks of New Hampshire, allows for the creation of the White Mountain National Forest, the first national forest in the United States.

shire **History** in Concord. Also, don't miss **Strawbery Banke Museum,** a living history museum in Portsmouth that uses costumed interpreters, and skilled craftspeople to demonstrate what life has been like in Portsmouth during the last 300 years. **Canterbury Shaker Village** is another important stop.

While history is important in New Hampshire, the arts, too, have played a significant role in shaping the state. Scores of writers and artists have worked here. The **Saint-Gaudens National Historic Site** displays the heroic bronzes for which this sculptor is known. The **Barnstormers Summer Theater** in Tamworth was founded by the son of U.S. president Grover Cleveland. **Portsmouth** is another center for theater in the state, with several groups presenting works both traditional and cutting edge.

Rules of the Road

License Requirements: To drive in New Hampshire you must be at least 16 years old and have a valid driver's license from your home state or country.

Right Turn on Red: Everywhere in the state, you can make a right turn at a red light after a complete stop unless the intersection is posted to the contrary.

Seat belt and Helmet Laws: There is no requirement for seat belts in New Hampshire; however, restraints are required for children under 12. Motorcycle helmets are required for riders under 18.

Speed Limits: Most interstates have speed limits of 65 mph, except in congested areas where the limit is 55 mph. Secondary roads rarely have speed limits over 50 mph.

For More Information: Contact the New Hampshire Department of Safety | 10 Hazen Dr., Concord, NH | 603/271–2333.

White Mountains Loop Driving Tour
THROUGH THE WHITE MOUNTAINS NATIONAL FOREST

Distance: 108 mi   Time: 2 days

Breaks: Stop overnight in Jackson, approximately midway on the tour. The village is scenic, and there are lots of lodging options from which to choose.

This tour takes you through the heart of the White Mountain National Forest and covers some of New Hampshire's most spectacular scenery. Only a small section of the tour is on the highway—and that stretch is only two lanes in each direction. For the rest of the tour, winding roads cut through rugged mountain passes and deep forests. The last section of the tour traverses the Kancamagus Highway, nationally known for its fall splendor. In early summer, wildflowers mix with the trees at

1929	1944		1952	1961
Katharine Peckett opens the country's first organized ski school in Sugar Hill.	The World Monetary Fund conference is held at the Mt. Washington Hotel in Bretton Woods and establishes the price of gold at $35 an ounce, stabilizing post–World War II Western economy	and making the American dollar an important unit of exchange in international finance markets.	New Hampshire holds its first "First in the Nation" presidential primary.	Astronaut Alan Shepard of Derry makes the first U.S. space flight.

the edges of the roads. Winter brings lots of snow, and it seems that every other car carries a ski rack. Spring, which tends to be wet and muddy, is the least desirable time to visit.

INTRODUCTION
HISTORY
REGIONS
WHEN TO VISIT
STATE'S GREATS
RULES OF THE ROAD
DRIVING TOURS

① Begin your tour at **Franconia Notch State Park** (access from Franconia Notch State Pkwy., Exits 1–3). This narrow notch through the White Mountains is one of the state's prettiest state parks. The **Flume Gorge and Park Information Center** (Exit 1) has information and trail maps for visitors and is also the access point for the **Flume,** one of the park's natural wonders. Be sure to stop for a look at the **Old Man of the Mountain** (Exit 2), a natural rock profile that has become the state's symbol. In summer, a trip to the top of **Cannon Mountain Ski Area** on a tram offers a panoramic view of the White Mountains.

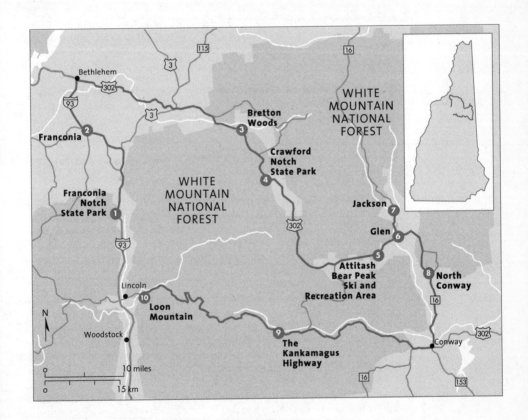

1986
Concord teacher Christa McAuliffe, the first civilian chosen to go into space, is killed when the space shuttle *Challenger* explodes.

1996
Jeanne Shaheen becomes the first woman to be elected Governor of New Hampshire.

2000
John Irving, one of New Hampshire's most successful writers, wins the Academy Award for the Best Adapted Screenplay for *The Cider House Rules*.

❷ Continue north along Interstate 93 to **Franconia,** where you'll find **Frost Place** (I–93 Exit 38, 1 mi south on Rte. 116 to Bickford Hill Rd., right over bridge, left at fork onto Ridge Rd.). Poet Robert Frost lived here from 1915 to 1920.

❸ Continue north on Interstate 93 to Exit 40, where you'll pick up U.S. 302 heading east. In **Bretton Woods,** stop at the historic marker in front of the **Mount Washington Hotel** (U.S. 302) to read about the role this grand resort played in the International Monetary Conference of 1944. If you visit in summer or fall, you may want to take a ride to the top of **Mt. Washington,** the highest mountain in the northeast, aboard the **Cog Railway** (Base Station Rd., 4 mi east of junction U.S. 3 and U.S. 302). This steam-powered railway provides a scenic trip to the top of the mountain. Mt. Washington is known for its extreme weather and high winds, so a jacket is advisable no matter what the temperature is at the base.

❹ **Crawford Notch State Park** (U.S. 302, beginning about 6 mi from the Mount Washington Hotel and continuing for another 6 mi) is the second of the mountain passes, or "notches," you travel through on this tour. Hiking trails from either side of U.S. 302 lead to several waterfalls.

❺ **Attitash Bear Peak Ski and Recreation Area** (U.S. 302 W) in Bartlett has nearly year-round activities. Winter, naturally, is devoted to alpine and cross-country skiing and snowshoeing. In summer and fall, try the water slides or dry alpine slide or go horseback riding.

❻ Continue on U.S. 302 to **Glen. Story Land** (Rte. 16) and **Heritage New Hampshire** (Rte. 16) provide entertainment for families.

❼ Head north on Route 16 to **Jackson** (Rte. 16A), perhaps the most charming of the White Mountain towns. The **Honeymoon Covered Bridge** spanning the Ellis River marks the entrance to the village off Route 16, and the White Mountains surround the town, giving it a sheltered and timeless air. Activities are geared toward the outdoors, as Jackson is one of the nation's top cross-country skiing destinations. Hiking, golfing, and tennis are popular in summer.

❽ From Jackson, take Route 16 south to **North Conway. Shopping** is one of the primary activities in North Conway. Outlet stores line both sides of Route 16. You'll also find some nice shops with local and regional crafts and sporting goods in the town center, also on Route 16. **Conway Scenic Railroad** (38 Norcross Circle; off Rte. 16 in the center of town, look for the Victorian train station) uses vintage coaches, including a dome observation coach, for scenic trips through the White Mountain National Forest.

❾ Continue south on Route 16 to Conway, where you'll pick up the **Kancamagus Highway** (Route 112, between Conway and Lincoln), probably the state's best-known roadway. It cuts through the **White Mountain National Forest** for 32 mi, paralleling the Swift River. Although the trip is beautiful any time of year, traffic is horrendous on weekends during foliage season and snow can cause closings in winter. You can get hiking information and check on winter road conditions at the **Saco Ranger Station,** at the Conway end of the route (Rte. 112). There are a number of scenic overlooks and other stopping points along the road.

❿ In Lincoln and North Woodstock, **Loon Mountain** (Rte. 112) is a year-round resort area with skiing in winter and activities that range from mountain biking to a wildlife theater in summer. This is also a popular base from which to hike in the surrounding White Mountain National Forest.

New Hampshire's Waterfront Driving Tour

FROM EXETER TO WOLFEBORO

INTRODUCTION
HISTORY
REGIONS
WHEN TO VISIT
STATE'S GREATS
RULES OF THE ROAD
DRIVING TOURS

Distance: 95 mi　　　　Time: 3 days

Breaks: Take your first break in Portsmouth, one of the state's liveliest cities. In fact, you may find you'd like to spend an extra day shopping and enjoying the historic district and restaurants. Either Meredith or Center Harbor makes a good choice for the next stop. Both are on the shore of Lake Winnipesaukee and have a selection of lodgings and restaurants.

This tour takes you along New Hampshire's short but lovely seacoast and around the largest of the state's many lakes. You'll also see some of the smaller lakes and the rivers that feed them. In addition, many of the towns along the way have museums that highlight New Hampshire's long and varied history. Summer and fall are the best times to make this drive since many of the attractions are closed in winter and spring. Around the lakes, in particular, even restaurants and lodgings close in the off-season. Summer is the best choice if you want to swim or sunbathe, but fall ushers in cool sunny days, crisp nights, and colorful foliage that make driving a delight.

❶ Begin at colonial Exeter, on the Swamscott River. One of the state's earliest towns, it was the capital before the political center was moved inland to Concord. The **American Independence Museum** (1 Governors La.) explains the state's early history with exhibits such as a draft of the U.S. Constitution. Nearby, the **Gilman Garrison House** (12 Water St.) was built around 1690 as a fortified garrison.

❷ From Exeter, head north on Route 108 until you reach Route 101. Then take Route 101 southeast to **Hampton Beach,** where you'll find the state's longest beach, weekly fireworks throughout the summer, arcades, shops, ice-cream stands, and other traditional seacoast fun. **Fuller Gardens** (10 Willow Ave.; 4 mi northeast of Hampton Beach via Rte. 1A) blooms all summer long with 2,000 rosebushes of every shade and type.

❸ Head north along Route 1A and stop at **Odiorne Point State Park** (Rte. 1A) in Rye to walk along the rocks at the water's edge and examine tide pools or visit the **Seacoast Science Center.** The Science Center has guided nature walks and exhibits on the area's natural history and marine life.

❹ Follow Route 1A north to **Portsmouth.** Enjoy a walk through Portsmouth's historic district and be sure to stop in at least one or two of the half dozen or so historic houses open for visitors. The **Moffatt-Ladd House** (154 Market St.) and the **John Paul Jones House** (43 Middle St.) are both good choices. You can pick up a brochure for a walking tour and information on multiple-house tickets at any of the houses. For a more comprehensive look at Portsmouth's history, be sure to spend some time at **Strawbery Banke Museum** (Marcy St.), where a series of renovated and furnished houses provide a peek at 300 years of history in one neighborhood. To see what's playing around town, stop at the **kiosk in Market Square** or check with the **Chamber of Commerce** (500 Market St.). If you have a little longer to spend in Portsmouth, consider a cruise to the **Isles of Shoals.** These nine islands (eight at high tide) are divided between New Hampshire and Maine. Two companies offer harbor tours and island cruises from the waterfront near the center of town: **Isles of Shoals Steamship Co.** (315 Market St.) and **Portsmouth Harbor Cruises** (64 Ceres St.).

❺ From Portsmouth, take the **Spaulding Turnpike** north to Route 11 (at Exit 15). This route leads first through small towns and countryside as it heads toward **Lake Winnipesaukee,**

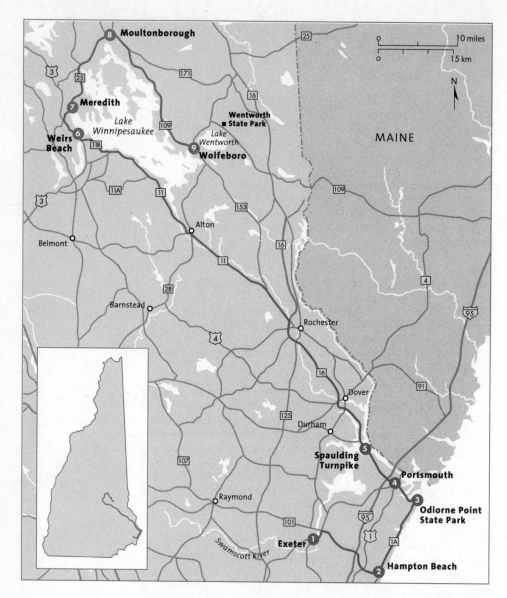

the state's largest lake, which covers 72 square mi and has 274 islands. Routes 11 and 11B follow the shoreline, offering both quick glimpses of the water between the trees and wide open vistas from higher points.

❻ Off Route 11B is **Weirs Beach,** the lakefront equivalent of Hampton Beach. You'll find a public beach; **Surf Coaster** (Rte. 11B), a water park with seven slides; and two lake cruise boats, including the **M/S *Mount Washington*** (at Lakeside Ave.). There's no shortage of arcades, miniature golf, and other such things.

❼ Take U.S. 3 north to **Meredith.** There you'll find one end of the **Winnipesaukee Scenic Railroad** (U.S. 3), which runs along the lakeshore. You can board either here or in Weirs Beach.

8 From Meredith, take Route 25 northeast to **Moultonborough.** The **Loon Center** (Lees Mills Rd. follow signs from Rte. 25 to Blake Rd. to Lees Mills Rd.) is a great place to learn about the pretty black-and-white birds whose haunting calls drift across New Hampshire's lakes in the evening and early morning. The view alone is reason enough to visit **Castle in the Clouds** (Rte. 171). This odd, elaborate mansion took three years to build and cost nearly $7 million in 1911.

9 Head southeast on Route 109 to **Wolfeboro,** a pretty Lake Winnipesaukee resort town, with a main street that runs along the waterfront, as well as nice shops and restaurants, and a lovely atmosphere. Wolfeboro also has shoreline on **Lake Wentworth,** named for an early governor, where you'll find **Wentworth State Park** (Rte. 109; 6 mi east of town). The park has a beach, picnic areas, and a bathhouse. Also worth a stop is the **Wright Museum** (77 Center St.), which overflows with artifacts illustrating the contributions of those on the home front to World War II.

BARTLETT

(Nearby towns also listed: Bretton Woods, Glen, Intervale, Jackson, North Conway)

Bartlett is primarily a ski town, particularly since the purchase and expansion of Attitash Bear Peak. In summer, Bear Notch Road, which terminates in Bartlett, offers the only midpoint access to the Kancamagus Highway (*see* White Mountain National Forest *in* Lincoln and North Woodstock). The surrounding mountains—Bear Peak, Mt. Parker, and Mt. Cardigan—and the Saco River make a scenic backdrop for the town, incorporated in 1790.

Information: Mt. Washington Valley Chamber of Commerce | Box 2300, Rte. 16, North Conway, 03860 | 603/356–3171 | fax 603/356–7069 | www.mtwashingtonvalley.org.

Attractions

★ **Attitash Bear Peak Ski Area.** This high-profile American Skiing Company resort hosts many special events and ski races. Its skiable terrain covers two peaks and has options for every level of skier and snowboarder. Summer activities include water slides, an alpine slide, a golf driving range, and horseback riding. A golf course is planned. | U.S. 302 | 603/374–2368, 800/223–7669 snow conditions | www.attitash.com.

Bear Notch Ski Touring Center. This cross-country ski area adjacent to Attitash Bear Peak has more than 42 mi of cross-country trails and unlimited backcountry skiing. | U.S. 302 | 603/374–2277 | www.attitash.com | Mid-Dec.–mid-Mar., daily, weather permitting.

White Mountain National Forest. Bartlett is bordered on the north and south by the White Mountain National Forest, which has many recreational opportunities. *See* Lincoln and North Woodstock.

ON THE CALENDAR
AUG.: *Attitash Bear Peak Equine Festival.* World-class riders and horses compete in this annual show-jumping event. | Equine Center at Attitash Bear Peak | 603/374–2368.

Dining
Crawford's Pub and Grill. American/Casual. Tucked inside the Grand Summit Hotel and Conference Center, this casual, family-style restaurant serves up pub-style fare and wood-fired pizzas. | U.S. 302 | 603/374–1900 or 800/554–1900 | fax 603/374–3040 | www.attitash.com | $8–$15 | AE, D, MC, V.

Lodging

Attitash Mountain Village. A sprawling condominium complex across the street from the ski resort. Restaurant, bar, picnic area. Refrigerators, cable TV, some in-room VCRs. 3 pools (1 indoor). Hot tub, sauna. Tennis. Hiking. Ice-skating. Cross-country skiing, downhill skiing. Video games. Playground, laundry facilities. Business services. | U.S. 302 | 603/374–6500 or 800/862–1600 | fax 603/374–6509 | www.attitashmtvillage.com | 300 rooms | $160–$220 | AE, D, MC, V.

Grand Summit Hotel & Conference Center. A contemporary resort hotel at the base of Attitash Bear Peak. Restaurant. Kitchenettes, cable TV, in-room VCRs. Outdoor pool. 2 hot tubs, massage, sauna. Health club. Cross-country skiing, downhill skiing. | U.S. 302 | 603/374–1900 or 800/554–1900 | fax 603/374–3040 | www.attitash.com | 143 rooms | $139–$199 | AE, D, MC, V.

North Colony Motel. A modern, single level motel on Route 302 with beautiful views of the nearby mountains, right at the base of Attitash Mountain and the entrance to Bear Peak Ski Area. Some microwaves, refrigerators, cable TV. Outdoor pool. Playground. No pets. | U.S. 302, | 603/374–6679 or 800/685–4895 | fax 603/374–6216 | www.northcolonymotel.com | 16 rooms | $49–$129 | D, MC, V.

Seasons Condominium Resort. Fully furnished condominium accommodations 1 mi east of Attitash Bear Peak Ski Area. Units have full kitchens with dining room, washer-dryer, and woodstoves. Picnic area. Cable TV. Indoor pool. 2 tennis courts. Hot tub, sauna. Exercise room, hiking. Video games. Playground. No pets. | U.S. 302, | 603/374–2361 or 800/332–6636 | fax 603/374–2414 | www.seasonsattitash.com | 70 units | $135–$199 | AE, MC, V.

BRETTON WOODS

MAP 7, F5

(Nearby town also listed: Bartlett)

Bretton Woods is still dominated by the Mount Washington Hotel, just as it was 100 years ago when as many as 50 private trains a day brought wealthy summer visitors to the foot of Mt. Washington. Then, as now, those so inclined could ride Sylvester Marsh's steam railway to the peak for a view of the White Mountains' entire Presidential

PACKING IDEAS FOR COLD WEATHER

- ❑ Driving gloves
- ❑ Earmuffs
- ❑ Fanny pack
- ❑ Fleece neck gaiter
- ❑ Fleece parka
- ❑ Hats
- ❑ Lip balm
- ❑ Long underwear
- ❑ Scarf
- ❑ Shoes to wear indoors
- ❑ Ski gloves or mittens
- ❑ Ski hat
- ❑ Ski parka
- ❑ Snow boots
- ❑ Snow goggles
- ❑ Snow pants
- ❑ Sweaters
- ❑ Thermal socks
- ❑ Tissues, handkerchief
- ❑ Turtlenecks
- ❑ Wool or corduroy pants

Range. When Marsh applied to the state legislature in 1858 for permission to build the railway, one legislator responded he'd have better luck building a railroad to the moon. Marsh persevered, however, and the Cog Railway remains a fixture on the New Hampshire landscape.

Information: **Mt. Washington Valley Chamber of Commerce** | Box 2300, Rte. 16, North Conway, 03860 | 603/356–3171 | fax 603/356–7069 | www.mtwashingtonvalley.org.

Attractions

Bretton Woods Ski Area. The pristine setting of this ski area 25 mi north of Bretton Woods and its lack of crowds make it popular among families. Most slopes are rated for beginners and intermediates, with a few steeper sections near the peak. | U.S. 302 | 603/278–5000 or 800/232–2792 | www.brettonwoods.com | Mid-Dec.–late Mar., daily.

Crawford Notch State Park. This state park 8 mi southeast of Bretton Woods encompasses the 6-mi mountain pass that is one of the most scenic in the state. Hiking trails offer views of the Presidential mountain range and lead to several waterfalls. | U.S. 302 | 603/374–2272 | www.nhparks.state.nh.us | $2.50 | Daily dawn–dusk.

Arethusa Falls. This waterfall, 6 mi north of Bartlett and accessible by hiking trail, is one of the highest in New Hampshire. Frankenstein Cliff, near the falls, is named for artist George L. Frankenstein, whose paintings of the White Mountains were once well known.

Silver Cascade. One of several waterfalls in Crawford Notch State Park, these cascades vary in intensity as the water level changes over the course of the year. | U.S. 302 at the north end of Crawford Notch.

★ **Mt. Washington Cog Railway.** The Cog Railway went up on the great mountain's western flank in 1869 and has been providing a thrilling alternative to climbing or driving to the top of Mt. Washington ever since. | Base Station Rd. | 603/846–5404 or 800/922–8825 | www.thecog.com | $44 round-trip | call for hrs; closed Nov–late Apr.

ON THE CALENDAR

MAR.: *Annual Mt. Washington Cup.* A 10K freestyle cross-country ski race with several age categories. | Bretton Woods Cross-Country Ski Touring Center at Mt. Washington Hotel | 603/278–3300.

Dining

Cold Mountain Cafe. Eclectic. Slick halogens highlight the rotating art exhibits gracing the frescoed walls of this friendly, popular local hangout 15 mi west of Bretton Woods. The menu is as diverse as its clientele, serving up ethnic lunch favorites like Thai noodle salad and hummus plates to complete nightly dinners such as Thai chicken curry and flounder stuffed with scallops and asparagus in a béarnaise sauce. | 2015 Main St., Bethlehem | 603/869–2500 | $10 | No credit cards.

Fabyan's Station. American. Railroading mementos decorate this former train station that's a good bet for hamburgers. Kids' menu. | U.S. 302 at Cog Railway Base Rd. | 603/278–2222 | Closed late Apr.–mid-June and Oct.–late Dec. | $12–$29 | AE, D, MC, V.

Mary's Malt Shop. American. This old-time ice-cream parlor in Bethlehem town center, 15 mi west of Bretton Woods, is decked out with pinball machines, penny candy, original fixtures, and TVs showing 1950s reruns. Malteds, shakes, cones, and toppings of every kind are available, as are light sandwiches, like roast beef, turkey, and egg salad. | 2111 Main St., Bethlehem | 603/869–9789 | Columbus Day–May | $3 | No credit cards.

Munroe's Family Restaurant. American. A restaurant has been serving here since 1954. This family-style incarnation specializes in breakfast, with hearty three-egg omelets, home fries, and toast. The lunch menu has a full range of club sandwiches, burgers, soups, and salads. Kids' menu. | 633 U.S. 3 S | 603/846–5542 | Breakfast also available. No dinner | $3–$5 | No credit cards.

Pizza Pub Family Restaurant. Italian. A cast-iron woodstove is the centerpiece for this homey, wood post-and-beam dining room 6 mi west of Bretton Woods. The house specialty is pizza, but the homemade vegetable lasagna, subs, and pastas are equally good. Try the Supreme pizza with your choice of 10 fresh toppings. Kids' menu; screened-in porch for outdoor dining. | U.S. 3, Twin Mountain | 603/846–5003 | Closed weeknights Columbus Day–Christmas and Apr.–Memorial Day | $7–$12 | No credit cards.

Lodging

Above the Notch Motor Inn. A simple, single- story inn with beautiful mountain views and sports-club access. The rooms are clean with standard, modern furnishings. Picnic area. Cable TV. Playground. No pets. | 2058 Rte. 302, | 603/846–5156 | fax 603/846–2183 | www.abovethenotch.com | 13 rooms | $63–$77 | D, MC, V.

Angel of the Mountains. A towering pastel, storybook Victorian inn with classical hardwood floors, ornate wainscotting, and bright, simple rooms trimmed in lace, 20 mi northwest of Bretton Woods. The Carriage House, a separate, fully furnished unit with a porch and kitchen, is suitable for up to four adults. The Mystery Lantern Tour, complimentary for guests of the inn, takes you on a nighttime, lantern-guided historical walk through the streets of Bethlehem in summer. Complimentary breakfast. No air-conditioning in some rooms, no smoking. No room phones, TV in common room. Outdoor pool. No kids under 12. No pets. | 2007 Main St., Bethlehem | 603/869–6473 or 888/704–4004 | fax 603/869–5409 | info@angelofthemountains.com | www.angelofthemountains.com | 3 rooms, 1 cottage | $89–$160 | MC, V.

Bretton Arms Inn. A turn-of-the-20th-century Victorian inn with period furnishings. Dining room. Cable TV. 2 pools (1 indoor). Cross-country skiing, sleigh rides. Children's programs (ages 5–12), playground. Business services. Airport shuttle. | U.S. 302 | 603/278–1000, 800/258–0330 outside NH | fax 603/278–8858 | www.mtwashington.com | 31 rooms, 3 suites | $119–$189 | AE, D, MC, V.

Bretton Woods Motor Inn. A contemporary motor inn with views of the White Mountains. Restaurant. Indoor pool. Sauna. | U.S. 302 | 603/278–1504 or 800/258–0330 | fax 603/278–8838 | www.mtwashington.com | 50 rooms | $70–$139 | AE, D, MC, V.

Four Seasons Motor Inn. A modern motor inn with views of Mt. Washington and the Presidential Range. Picnic area. Some refrigerators, cable TV. Pool. Video games. Playground. | U.S. 3 | 603/846–5708 or 800/228–5708 | www.4seasonsmotorinn.com | 24 rooms | $50–$70 | D, MC, V.

★ **Mount Washington Hotel.** The sparkling white facade of this historic turn-of-the-20th-century grande dame is breathtaking against the backdrop of Mt. Washington. The hotel was the meeting place for the International Monetary Conference of 1944 that set the American dollar as the standard currency for international exchange. The endless porch is the best place the contemplate the view. Rate includes breakfast and dinner. 5 restaurants w/bars with entertainment. No air-conditioning, cable TV, some in-room VCRs. 2 pools (1 indoor). Sauna. Driving range, golf courses, putting green, tennis. Hiking. Bicycles. Cross-country skiing, downhill skiing. Video games. Children's programs (ages 5–12), playground. Business services. | U.S. 302 | 603/278–1000, 800/258–0330 outside NH | fax 603/278–8838 | www.mtwashington.com | 200 rooms | $219–$419 | MAP | AE, D, MC, V.

Northern Zermatt Inn. A turn-of-the-20th-century vintage boardinghouse. Picnic area, complimentary Continental breakfast. No air-conditioning in some rooms, some kitchenettes, cable TV in some rooms, no room phones. Pool. Playground. | U.S. 3 | 603/846–5533 or 800/535–3214 | fax 603/846–5664 | 17 rooms | $40–$79 | D, MC, V.

Notchland Inn. This Civil War–era granite mansion 12 mi south of Bretton Woods in Harts Location anchors 100 spectacular acres in Crawford Notch. The front parlor is by the arts-and-crafts movement's Gustav Stickley. Dining room. No smoking, some in-room hot tubs, no room phones. Outdoor hot tub. | U.S. 302, Harts Location | 603/374–6131 or 800/866–

6131 | fax 603/374–6168 | notchland@aol.com | www.notchland.com | 7 rooms, 5 suites | $175–$235, $235–$350 suites | MAP; B&B;B rates available | AE, D, MC, V.

Paquette's Motor Inn. A simple motel at base of White Mountains. Restaurant, bar. Cable TV. Pool. Tennis. | U.S. 3 | 603/846–5562 | 33 rooms | $45–$65 | Closed Apr.–May and Oct.–Dec. | AE, MC, V.

Profile Deluxe. A basic, single-story motel, 10 mi south of Loon Mountain on Route 3. Some refrigerators, no smoking, cable TV. No pets. | U.S. 3 S, | 603/846–5522 or 800/682–7222 | profiledeluxe@aol.com | 13 rooms | $55–$80 | D, MC, V.

CANTERBURY

(Nearby towns also listed: Concord, Franklin)

Although only a short drive from Concord, the state's capital, Canterbury remains a small, quiet town with fewer than 2,000 residents. It is best known for the community of Shakers who founded a village here in 1792.

Information: Chamber of Commerce | 244 N. Main St., Concord, 03301 | 603/224–2508 | fax 603/224–8128. | www.concordnhchamber.com.

Attractions

Canterbury Shaker Village. This outdoor museum and National Historic Landmark has a large shop with Shaker reproductions. A religious community, the Canterbury village, founded in 1792, flourished here and practiced equality of the sexes and races, common ownership, celibacy, and pacifism. Shakers invented household items such as the clothespin and the flat broom and were known for the simplicity and integrity of their designs. Members of the sect lived here until 1992 when the 694-acre property was left in trust as a museum. Tours are 90 minutes. | 288 Shaker Rd. | 603/783–9511 or 800/982–9511 | www.shakers.org | $10 for 2 consecutive days | May–Oct., daily 10–5; Apr., Nov.–Dec., Sat.–Sun. 10–5; Fri. and Sat. 6:45 candlelight dinner and tour (reservations essential).

ON THE CALENDAR
JULY: *Canterbury Fair.* This fair includes a chicken barbecue, children's activities, road races, arts, crafts and antiques. | 603/783–0335.
AUG.: *Mother Ann Day.* A celebration of the traditional Shaker holiday commemorating the arrival of Ann Lee, Shakerism's founder in America. | Canterbury Shaker Village | 603/783–9511.

Dining
Creamery Restaurant. Contemporary. Diners sit communally at long wooden tables and feast upon hearty Shaker-inspired cuisine. Try the four-course prix fixe candlelight dinner with a seasonally changing menu. Maine crab bisque with roasted corn and applewood smoked loin of pork with hard cider–sage gravy are a couple of past choices, and the meal may be followed by a tour of the Shaker Village Center. | 288 Shaker Rd. | 603/783–9511 or 800/982–9511 | www.shakers.org | Lunch 11:30–2:30 daily; candlelight dinners Fri.–Sat. 6:45 by reservation only | Closed weekdays in Apr., Nov., and Dec. Closed Jan.–Mar. | $6.95–$8.95 | AE, MC, V.

Lodging
Shaker Woods Farm. This unique inn, located on a working farm with animals and herb gardens, offers comfortable, spacious rooms, decorated with artifacts collected from years of the owner's Air Force travel. Complimentary breakfast. No air-conditioning. Kitchenette shared by both rooms. TV and VCR in common area. Cross-country skiing. No pets. | 30 Lower

Smith Rd., Sanbornton | 603/528–1990 | fax 530/481–5153 | www.shakerwoodsfarm.com | 2 rooms | $85 | D, MC, V.

CENTER HARBOR

MAP 7, F8

(Nearby towns also listed: Center Sandwich, Holderness, Meredith, Moultonborough, Wolfeboro)

Center Harbor borders three bays at the northern end of Lake Winnipesaukee, as well as Lakes Squam, Waukewan, and Winona. As such, it is a commercial center for smaller towns surrounding the lakes and for boaters who spend summer weekends on the water.

Information: Center Harbor-Moultonborough Chamber of Commerce | Box 824, Center Harbor, 03226. | 603/253–4582.

Attractions

Center Harbor Town Beach. A small public beach in the middle of the town shopping area with a picnic area, pavilion, and boat launch. | Lake St. | 603/279–6121 | Free | Daily.

ON THE CALENDAR

JUNE: *Strawberry Festival.* A festival featuring lots of strawberry shortcake. | 603/253–7698.

JULY: *Annual Flea Market & Crafts Sale.* More than 85 vendors come here to sell a wide variety of crafts and merchandise. | 603/253–7698.

Dining

Red Hill Inn. Contemporary. Cozy dining rooms with fireplaces and floral print wallpaper set the mood for dishes like roast pheasant, venison, and jumbo shrimp scampi, and an extensive wine list. Save room for the Kentucky High Pie for dessert. Sunday brunch in summer. | Rte. 25B | 603/279–7001 or 800/573–4455 | fax 603/279–7003 | www.redhillinn.com | No lunch Sun.–Fri. | $15–$20 | AE, D, DC, MC, V.

Lodging

Meadows Lakeside Lodging. A motel on the shore of Lake Winnipesaukee. Picnic area. No room phones. Lake. Beach, dock, boating. Playground. Pets allowed (fee). | Rte. 25, | 603/253–4347 | 39 rooms | $46–$119 | Closed Nov.–Apr. | AE, D, MC, V.

Red Hill Inn. Only 3 mi west of Center Harbor, this 1904 mansion with a view of Squam Lake is warmed by fireplaces and period furnishings. Dining room, bar, complimentary Continental breakfast. No air-conditioning, no TV in rooms, cable TV in common area. Hot tubs. Cross-country skiing. Business services. | Rte. 25B | 603/279–7001 or 800/573–3445 | fax 603/279–7003 | www.redhillinn.com | 18 rooms, 8 suites | $105–$175 | AE, D, DC, MC, V.

Watch Hill Bed and Breakfast. This 1772 colonial inn has views of Lake Winnepesaukee and a wood-burning stove in the dining room. Rooms are comfortable and fitted with period antiques. Complimentary breakfast. No air-conditioning, no smoking, no room phones, TV in common room. No pets. | Old Meredith Rd., | 603/253–4334 | fax 603/253–8560 | 4 rooms (2 with shared bath) | $65–$70. | MC, V.

CENTER SANDWICH

(Nearby towns also listed: Center Harbor, Holderness, Moultonborough, Wolfeboro)

Bordered by Squam Lake to the west and the Sandwich Mountains to the north, Center Sandwich has one of the prettiest settings of any town in the Lakes Region. The town center is a cluster of well-kept 18th- and 19th-century houses, mostly painted white. The town was a favorite with poet John Greenleaf Whittier and his poem "Sunset on the Bearcamp" refers to the region's Bearcamp River. Center Sandwich's location off the main roads has helped to maintain its sense of timelessness and has also attracted many artisans who have homes and workshops in the town.

Information: **Squam Lakes Area Chamber of Commerce** | Box 65, Ashland, 03217 | 603/968–4494.

Attractions

Durgin Covered Bridge. The current bridge, built in 1869, is the fourth on the site. Over the space of 25 years, floods washed away three previous bridges. Jacob Berry, who built this one (a link in the Underground Railroad), claimed it was so strong it wouldn't collapse even if it were filled up with wood. No one has ever tested his claim, however. | Durgin Rd., spanning the Cold River; 1½ mi north of Rte. 113.

Historical Society Museum. A local museum dedicated to the history of Center Sandwich and its residents. You can view works by local artists and photographers, tools, textiles, and antique furnishings. | Maple St. | 603/284–6269 | Free | Mid-June–Sept., Tues.–Sat. 11–5.

League of New Hampshire Craftsmen Sandwich Home Industries. This store is one of seven that exhibit and sell the contemporary and traditional crafts made by its members. In fact, it was this store and the concentration of artisans in the Sandwich area that gave birth to the League of New Hampshire Craftsmen. | Main St. | 603/284–6831 | Mid-May–mid-Oct., Mon.–Sat. 10–5, Sun. 12–5.

ON THE CALENDAR

FEB.: *Sandwich Notch Sled Dog Races.* International distance sled-dog races. | 603/929–3508.

OCT.: *Sandwich Fair.* A country fair dedicated to supporting agriculture through education and entertainment for the whole family. | 603/284–7062.

Dining

Corner House Inn. Continental. This restaurant has two dining rooms—one a mid-19th-century former harness shop with exposed beams and wood-burning stove; the other in a Victorian home replete with marble fireplace. Try the Lobster and Mushroom Bisque or sautéed shellfish in a light sherry sauce. Early-bird suppers. No smoking. | 22 Main St. (Rte. 113) | 603/284–6219 | fax 603/284–6220 | Breakfast also available. Closed Mon.–Tues. | $11–$21 | AE, D, MC, V.

Lodging

Overlook Farm Bed and Breakfast. A 1783 colonial farmhouse on 15 rolling acres with views of the nearby mountains. The rooms are rustic, warm and filled with period antiques and handmade pottery crafted by the proprietor. Complimentary breakfast. No smoking, no room phones, TV in common area. Library. No kids under 5. | 14 Mountain Rd., | 603/284–6485 | b.b.farm@juno.com | 4 rooms (2 with shared bath) | $75–$85 | Closed mid-Oct.–mid-May | No credit cards.

CHARLESTOWN

(Nearby town also listed: Cornish)

This town on the Connecticut River was a stockaded outpost during the French and Indian War and withstood an attack by 400 French soldiers in 1747. Its main street, laid out in 1763, is 1 mi long with 63 Federal, Greek Revival, and Gothic Revival homes—10 of which were built before 1800—that together make up the state's largest historic district.

Information: Greater Claremont Chamber of Commerce | Moody Building, Tremont Sq., Claremont, 03743 | 603/543–1296 | fax 603/542–1469.

Attractions

Fort at No. 4. This fort was a lonely outpost on the periphery of colonial civilization in 1747, the year it was attacked by the French. Costumed interpreters demonstrate cooking over an open hearth, weaving, gardening, and candle making. Each year, the museum holds full reenactments of militia musters and battles of the French and Indian War. | 267 Springfield Rd. (Rte. 11) | 603/826–5700 | www.chesulwind.com/fortatno4/ | $6 | Late May–Aug., Wed.–Mon. 10–4; first two weeks Sept., Sat., Sun. 10–4; mid-Sept.–mid-Oct., Wed.–Mon. 10–4.

Morningside Flight Park. A hang-gliding, paragliding, and ultralight flight school. There is both a camping site and a training facility on the premises. | 357 Morningside La. | 603/542–4416 | fax 603/543–9577 | www.flymorningside.com | Daily.

ON THE CALENDAR

JULY: *Yard Sale Day.* The entire population collaborates on this town-wide yard sale. | Look for signs at houses all around town | 603/826–3814.

JULY: *Sutler's Market.* A two-day gathering and reenactment of a traditional, early colonial market at Fort at No. 4, the reconstructed colonial fortified town of Charlestown. Handcrafted wares for sale include moccasins, soap, candles, pottery, and antique pistols. | 267 Springfield Rd. (Rte. 11) | 603/826–5700 | $8 | Sat. 10–4, Sun. 10–3.

AUG.: *French and Indian War Weekend.* History buffs gather at the Fort at No. 4 for a reenactment of the battles between Native Americans, and French and British armies. | 267 Springfield Rd. (Rte. 11) | 603/826–5799 | $8 | Sat. 10–4, Sun. 10–3.

Dining

Charlestown Heritage Restaurant, Diner and Tavern. American. A 1924, red, white, and blue Wooster Railroad lunch car that has been restored to its original function now houses one of the region's most unique dining establishments. Attached to an 1820s Federal brick building that's now a tavern, the boxcar has homemade raspberry and apple pies, delicious soups, burgers and, during breakfast, hearty omelets. Kids' menu. | 122 Main St. | 603/826–3110 | Breakfast also available. No dinner | $3.50–$6 | AE, D, MC, V.

Lodging

Maplehedge Bed and Breakfast. This 1820 colonial is on the National Historic Register. In the Connecticut River Valley, the hotel has bright, large rooms with period antiques. It is next door to the Foundation for Biblical Research. Complimentary breakfast. Air-conditioning, no smoking, no room phones, no TV. No kids under 12. No pets. | Main St. (Rte. 12), | 603/826–5237 or 800/9–MAPLE9 | debrine@fmis.net | www.maplehedge.com | 5 rooms | $90–$105 | Closed Jan.–Mar. | MC, V.

COLEBROOK

(Nearby town also listed: Dixville Notch)

In the 1700s, when people spoke of the area now called Colebrook, they called it "a place up back of New Hampshire." That description still fits this small town on the border with Vermont and only a few miles from Canada.

Information: **North Country Chamber of Commerce** | Box 1, Colebrook | 603/237–8939 | fax 603/237–4573 | www.northcountrychamber.org.

Attractions
Beaver Brook Falls. Beaver Brook Falls, 2 mi north of Colebrook, is one of the region's most photographed natural sights. There are picnic tables at the wayside area. | Rte. 145 | Free | Daily.

Coleman State Park. The northernmost of New Hampshire's state parks is 12 mi northeast of Colebrook and has fishing, photography, hiking, and wildlife-watching. | Diamond Pond Rd. | 603/538–6965 | www.nhparks.state.nh.us | $2.50 | Daily.

Columbia Covered Bridge. This is the northernmost bridge connecting New Hampshire and Vermont. It was built in 1912 to replace an earlier bridge over the Connecticut River that was destroyed by fire. | Columbia Bridge Rd. off U.S. 3.

Shrine of Our Lady of Grace. Fifty religious monuments depicting the Way of the Cross nestle between the White and the Green Mountains 1 mi south of Colebrook. | U.S. 3 | 603/ 237–5511 | Free | Mid-May–mid-Oct., Daily 9–5.

ON THE CALENDAR
JUNE: *Blessing of the Motorcycles.* A weekend of motorcycle-related events is capped off by a blessing of the motorcycles at the Shrine of Our Lady of Grace. | 603/237–5511.

Dining
Colebrook Country Club. Continental. With views of the golf course and the town of Colebrook, this cozy dining room is a nice place to enjoy a shrimp scampi or filet mignon. Kids' menu. Sunday brunch. | Rte. 26 | 603/237–5566 | fax 603/237–5009 | $7.95–$15.95 | D, MC, V.

Lodging
Colebrook Country Club. A four-season resort with plenty of activities for the outdoor-lover nearby. The simple rooms are in a plain, single-story building. Restaurant, bar. Cable TV. 9-hole golf course. Cross-country skiing, snowmobiling. | Rte. 26 | 603/237–5566 | fax 603/ 237–5009 | www.colebrookcountryclub.com | 18 rooms | $50. | D, MC, V.

The Glen. This onetime fishing lodge, 29 mi north of Colebrook, on First Connecticut Lake still retains its outdoorsy, informal air. Now a B&B, the accommodations are rustic and simple with maple floors, antique chests, and individually decorated rooms. Cabins are well suited to families. Dining room, complimentary breakfast. Kitchenettes in some rooms, some refrigerators, no room phones, TV in common area. Lake. Dock, boating. Fishing. Ice-skating. Library. Pets allowed. | 77 The Glen Rd., Pittsburgh | 603/538–6500 or 800/445–4536 | fax 603/538–7121 | 6 rooms, 10 cabins | $77–$96 | Closed mid-Oct.–mid-May | MAP included | No credit cards.

Northern Comfort. Knotty-pine interiors and spacious well-maintained rooms in a hotel 1 mi south of Colebrook. No air-conditioning in some rooms, some kitchenettes, cable TV. Pool. Basketball. Playground. Pets allowed. | U.S. 3 | 603/237–4440 | 19 rooms | $54–$72 | AE, D, MC, V.

CONCORD

MAP 7, F10

(Nearby towns also listed: Canterbury, Manchester)

Although Concord is New Hampshire's capital, it remains a quiet city with a stable population of less than 38,000. Politics and the business of running the state are the city's principal interests, which seems even quieter when the legislature isn't in session. Of course, since New Hampshire's House of Representatives has 400 members—said to be the fourth-largest deliberative body in the world—the legislators are numerous enough to make their collective presence felt.

Although a trading post from 1660 and a settlement from 1725, Concord was not an influential city in the early days of the state's history, when most of the wealth and political power was concentrated in the southern part of the state. Until the 1800s, Concord was best known as the spot where Hannah Dustin, stolen from Haverhill, Massachusetts, by the Pennacook Indians, scalped her attackers and escaped. Concord first became the state's capital in 1808, when northern and western towns complained that the southern cities of Portsmouth and Exeter had too much influence on the state's business. Moving the legislative sessions from Exeter north to Concord appeased them.

Soon thereafter, Concord made history once again when wheelwright Louis Downing and coach builder J. Stephens Abbot teamed up to create the Concord Coach. Wells Fargo and other coach companies were quick to adopt the high-wheeled coach

USEFUL EXTRAS YOU MAY WANT TO PACK

- ❏ Adapters, converter
- ❏ Alarm clock
- ❏ Batteries
- ❏ Binoculars
- ❏ Blankets, pillows, sleeping bags
- ❏ Books and magazines
- ❏ Bottled water, soda
- ❏ Calculator
- ❏ Camera, lenses, film
- ❏ Can/bottle opener
- ❏ Cassette tapes, CDs, and players
- ❏ Cell phone
- ❏ Change purse with $10 in quarters, dimes, and nickels for tollbooths and parking meters
- ❏ Citronella candle
- ❏ Compass
- ❏ Earplugs
- ❏ Flashlight
- ❏ Folding chairs
- ❏ Guidebooks
- ❏ Luggage tags and locks
- ❏ Maps
- ❏ Matches
- ❏ Money belt
- ❏ Pens, pencils
- ❏ Plastic trash bags
- ❏ Portable TV
- ❏ Radio
- ❏ Self-seal plastic bags
- ❏ Snack foods
- ❏ Spare set of keys, not carried by driver
- ❏ Travel iron
- ❏ Travel journal
- ❏ Video recorder, blank tapes
- ❏ Water bottle
- ❏ Water-purification tablets

for use on the rapidly expanding stage lines in the West. More than 3,000 were built in Concord, causing some to refer to them as the coach that won the west.

The gold dome of the State House, built in 1819, dominates Concord's skyline and its Main Street. The city itself is compact, bounded by the Merrimack River and Interstate 93. Although suburban sprawl has brought the inevitable malls and plazas to the outskirts of town, the presence of the State House has ensured that Main Street continues to thrive.

Information: Chamber of Commerce | 244 N. Main St., Concord, 03301 | 603/224–2508 | fax 603/224–8128. | www.concordnhchamber.com.

TRANSPORTATION

Airport: Manchester Airport. Approximately 20 minutes from Concord, the airport has scheduled daily flights by many major airlines. | Airport Rd. | 603/624–6539.
Bus lines: C & J Transportation. | 603/742–5111. **Concord Trailways.** | 603/228–3300 or 800/639–3317. **Greyhound Bus Lines.** | 603/436–0163 or 800/231–2222.
Driving Around Town: Driving in and around Concord should be a pleasure. Roads are generally in good repair and are easy to navigate with modern, clearly marked signs. Traffic, though increasing, is rarely snarled; bottlenecks are uncommon. Some congestion, however, is likely on major highways around rush hour and at the intersection of Louden Road and Interstate 93.

Downtown Concord's streets are easy to drive and wide enough for RVs. The layout is a simple, irregularly spaced grid with most streets running parallel and perpendicular to each other. One way streets are plentiful and clearly marked. Right turns on red are permitted, except where noted or when pedestrians are in the adjacent walkway.

Parking generally isn't a problem between July and December. From January through June, however, when the legislature is in session, parking can be more difficult. If you can't find a spot on the street, use the public garages on School or North State streets, both of which are a short walk from the town center. Twenty-five cents per hour covers any meter in town. Fines are $3 for an expired meter and $5 for a no-parking zone infraction. The Concord police use "boots" on repeat offenders or if your fines are more than $100 in arrears.

The two interstate toll roads in Concord are north/south I–93, which links you to Boston, and the roughly east/west I–89, which takes you to Montpelier, Vermont. Route 9 runs east/west to Portsmouth.

CONCORD

INTRO
ATTRACTIONS
DINING
LODGING

Attractions

ART AND ARCHITECTURE

Kimball Jenkins Estate. This late-Victorian home is now the campus of the Community Arts School, offering classes and summer workshops. The beautiful, large gardens are open to visitors. | 266 N. Main St. | 603/225–3932 | www.kimballjenkins.com | Free | Daily.

Pierce Manse. Franklin Pierce lived in this Greek Revival home before becoming the 14th U.S. president. | 14 Penacook St. | 603/224–7668 | $3 | Mid-June–Labor Day, weekdays 11–3.

CULTURE, EDUCATION, AND HISTORY

Capitol Center for the Performing Arts. New Hampshire's premiere cultural and art center, with live Broadway productions, concerts, galleries, and children's programs. | 44 S. Main St. | 603/225–1111 | www.ccanh.com.

State House New Hampshire's well-known legislature still meets in this gold-domed building, built in 1819. Tours daily. | 107 N. Main St. | 603/271–1110 | Free | Weekdays 8–4:30.

MUSEUMS

Museum of New Hampshire History. Among the artifacts in this museum is an original Concord Coach. During the 19th century, when more than 3,000 of them were built in Concord, this was about as technologically perfect a vehicle as you could find. Other exhibits provide an overview of New Hampshire's history, from the Abenaki Indians to the settlers of Portsmouth to the current residents. | 6 Eagle Sq. | 603/226–3189 | www.nhhistory.org | $5 | Tues.–Sat. 9:35–5, Sun. 12–5; July 1–mid Oct., also open Mon.

OTHER POINTS OF INTEREST

Christa McAuliffe Planetarium. The high-tech Christa McAuliffe Planetarium was named for the Concord teacher and first civilian on a space mission, who was killed in the 1986 *Challenger* space shuttle explosion. Shows in the 40-ft dome theater focus on the solar system, constellations, and space exploration by incorporating computer graphics, sound, and special effects. | 3 Institute Dr. | 603/271–7827 | www.starhap.com | Exhibit area free, shows $6 | Mon.–Wed. 9–2, Thurs.–Fri. 9–5, Sat. 10–5, Sun. 12–5.

League of New Hampshire Craftsmen. The foundation runs seven stores around the state and organizes a number of crafts fairs, including the Annual Craftsmen's Fair at Mt. Sunapee State Park each August. Exhibits are shown throughout the year in the gallery. | 205 N. Main St. | 603/224–3375 | Weekdays 8:30–4:30.

Concord Arts & Crafts. This store exhibits and sells traditional and contemporary crafts made by League of New Hampshire Craftsmen members. | 36 N. Main St. | 603/228–8171 | Weekdays 9:30–5:30, Sat. 9–5.

ON THE CALENDAR

MAY: *Kiwanis Annual Spring Fair.* A fair including a carnival, games, and fireworks. | 603/226–8016.

MAY: *Astronomy Day.* There are exhibits, rides, and family activities designed both to educate and entertain. | 603/271–7827.

AUG.: *Annual Downtown Concord Fiddle Championship.* Fiddlers from throughout New England compete under the stars for cash prizes and trophies. | 603/225–5512.

Dining

Franklin Pierce Dining Room. American. This open, functional, dining room, set in the Centennial Inn, is ideal for banquets and conferences. Try the grilled salmon or filet mignon. | 96 Pleasant St. | 603/225–7012 or 800/360–4839 | fax 603/225–5031 | www.someplaces-different.com | $15–$24 | AE, D, DC, MC, V.

Grist Mill. Contemporary. You'll have a fine view of the Turkey River from this former mill 3 mi south of Concord. In season, there's open-air dining. The menu has pasta and seafood, the Turkey River special dinners are recommended. Kids' menu. Lounge and gaming room. | 520 South St., Bow | 603/226–1922 | $7–$19 | AE, MC, V.

★ **Hermano's Cocina Mexicana.** Mexican. A casual place full of plants, with Aztec and Mayan murals. The menu includes many vegetarian options—and the margaritas are great. Live jazz weekend nights. No-smoking. | 11 Hills St. | 603/224–5669 | No lunch Sun. | $8–$12 | D, MC, V.

Margaritas. Mexican. The prison cells in this former police station have been turned into a dining room. The lounge bar has couches in front of a large fireplace. Live guitar music on Tuesday, Thursday. Kids' menu. | 1 Bicentennial Sq. | 603/224–2821 | No lunch | $6–$12 | AE, D, MC, V.

Lodging

Centennial Inn. A sturdy brick Victorian with period furnishings and porches on some rooms. Restaurant. In-room data ports, some in-room hot tubs, cable TV, some in-room VCRs. | 96 Pleasant St. | 603/225–7102 or 800/360–4839 | fax 603/225–5031 | centennialinn@nh.interwebb.com | www.someplacesdifferent.com | 32 rooms | $110–$149 | AE, D, DC, MC, V.

Comfort Inn. Part of the chain that is close to downtown. Complimentary Continental breakfast. In-room data ports, some refrigerators, some in-room hot tubs, cable TV. Indoor pool. Hot tub, sauna. Business services. Free parking. Pets allowed (fee). | 71 Hall St. | 603/226–4100 or 800/228–5150 | fax 603/228–2106 | www.comfortinn.com | 100 rooms | $59–$130 | AE, D, DC, MC, V.

Days Inn. A two-story chain motel 1 mi north of the city center. Complimentary Continental breakfast. Cable TV. Pool. Playground. Business services. | 406 S. Main St. | 603/224–2511 | www.daysinn.com | fax 603/224–6032 | 40 rooms | $59–$150 | AE, DC, D, MC, V.

Fairfield Inn Concord. A three-floor, centrally located member of the hotel chain. Restaurant, bar, complimentary Continental breakfast. In-room data ports, cable TV. Laundry facilities. Business services. Free parking. No pets. | 4 Gulf St.; U.S. 3 exit 13 | 603/225–0303 | fax 603/228–3353 | www.fairfieldinn.com | 105 rooms, 4 suites | $99–$139 | AE, D, MC, V.

Hampton Inn. This motor inn near the junction of Interstates 89 and 93 is typical of the chain. Picnic area, complimentary Continental breakfast. Some refrigerators, some hot tubs, cable TV, some in-room VCRs. Indoor pool. Hot tub. Laundry facilities. | 515 South St., Bow | 603/224–5322 | fax 603/224–4282 | 145 rooms | $110 | AE, D, DC, MC, V.

Holiday Inn. This modern member of the chain has clean rooms with standard furnishings. Restaurant, bar. In-room data ports, cable TV. Indoor pool. Hot tub, sauna. Exercise equipment. Laundry facilities. Business services. Free parking. Pets allowed. | 172 N. Main St. | 603/224–9534 | fax 603/224–8266 | hotelconc@aol.com | www.holidayinn.com/concordnh | 122 rooms | $105 | AE, D, DC, MC, V.

CONWAY

INTRO
ATTRACTIONS
DINING
LODGING

CONWAY

MAP 7, G7

(Nearby towns also listed: Glen, Intervale, Jackson, Madison, North Conway)

Long a popular gateway to the White Mountains, Conway had five inns by 1825. Although neighboring North Conway surged to shopping-outlet prominence during the 1980s and early '90s, Conway remains a busy town catering to visitors and providing necessities to residents of the smaller surrounding towns.

Information: **Chamber of Commerce** | Box 1019, Main St. (Rte. 16), Conway, 03818 | 603/447–2639. | fax 603/447–3692 | www.conwaychamber.com.

Attractions
Saco Bound & Rapid River Rafting. This company 2 mi east of Conway offers you a choice of adventures. For gentle family fun, Saco Bound provides canoe rentals and a shuttle service for canoeing the crystal-clear, sandy Saco River. | U.S. 302 | 603/447–2177 | www.sacobound.com | Fees vary | May–Oct., daily.

Saco River Bridge. There have been three covered bridges on this site just north of Route 16. The first, built in 1850, was swept away in an 1869 flood when the Swift River Bridge crashed into it. The second was destroyed by fire in 1890. The current bridge was built that same year and remains in use. | Rte. 153.

Swift River Bridge. Heavy rains flooded the Swift River in 1869, lifting this bridge from its foundations and sending it crashing into the Saco River Bridge. Thrifty townspeople salvaged much of the old bridge's lumber and used it to build the current bridge. It has been closed to vehicular traffic since 1974 when a concrete and steel bridge was built over the river. | ½ mi north of Rte. 16 off Washington St.

★ **White Mountain National Forest.** The Kancamagus Highway (Route 112) between Conway and Lincoln is a popular route through the southern part of the White Mountain National

Forest, especially during fall foliage season. A number of hiking trails have trailheads on the Kancamagus. The Saco Ranger Station, at the Conway end of the Kancamagus, has maps and information. You can also buy the $5 recreation pass needed for parking in National Forest lots there. *See* Lincoln and North Woodstock. | 603/447–5448 | Daily.

ON THE CALENDAR

SEPT.: *White Mountain National Forest Festival.* You'll find special events at the stopping points along the Kancamagus Highway. | Kancamagus Hwy. between Conway and Lincoln (Rte. 112) | 603/447–2166.

Dining

Darby Field Inn and Restaurant. Continental. A spectacular mountain view and a warm interior with wood furnishings and linen-draped tables make for a delightful setting. Try the New Zealand rack of lamb with a Dijon burgundy wine sauce or the White Mountain Chicken, baked in an apple, with cheddar stuffing, and topped with a maple brandy glaze. | 185 Chase Hill Rd., Albany | 603/447–2181 or 800/426–4147 | fax 603/447–5726 | www.darbyfield.com | Closed Apr. No lunch July–Oct. daily, and weekends and some weekdays Nov.–June | $19–$23 | AE, MC, V.

Snowvillage Inn. French. A cozy, candlelit dining room with polished wood, fine linens, and beautiful views of the surrounding mountains that is 6 mi south of Conway. Try the cranberry duck a l'orange and the pan-seared scallops putanesca. | Stuart Rd., Snowville | 603/447–2818 or 800/447–4345 | fax 603/447–5268 | No lunch | $17–$24 | AE, D, DC, MC, V.

Lodging

Albert B. Lester Memorial Hostel. If you're on a budget or are just looking for an interesting stay, this old farmhouse has bunkhouse dorms for up to 45 people and a community kitchen. Private rooms are available. Picnic area, complimentary Continental breakfast. No smoking, no room phones, TV in common area. Volleyball. Cross-country skiing. Pets allowed (fee). | 36 Washington St., Conway | 603/447–1001 or 800/909–4776 | fax 603/447–1001 | hiconway@nxi.com | www.angel.net/~hostel | 34 bunks, 4 private rooms | $18 bunks, $45 private rooms | MC, V.

Darby Field Inn. A former farmhouse with fine mountain views 2 mi northwest of Conway. Dining room, complimentary breakfast. No air-conditioning in some rooms, no smoking, some in-room hot tubs, no room phones, no TV in some rooms, cable TV in common area. Pool. Hot tub. Cross-country skiing. Library. No kids under 2. | 185 Chase Hill Rd., Albany | 603/447–2181, 800/426–4147 outside NH | fax 603/447–5726 | marc@darbyfield.com | www.darbyfield.com | 14 rooms | $120–$230 | Closed Apr. | MAP available (required during foliage season and Christmas week) | AE, MC, V.

Lavender Flower Inn. A quaint, restored 1850s farmhouse painted throughout in five shades of lavender. Restored antiques, mahogany beds. Complimentary breakfast. No smoking, cable TV in common area, no room phones. No pets. | 1657 Main St. | 603/447–3794 or 800/729–0106 | lfi@landmarknet.net | 7 rooms (4 with shared bath) | $75–$95 | AE, D, MC, V.

★ **Snowvillage Inn.** The inn's 10 acres in Snowville, 6 mi south of Conway, are very private with quintessential White Mountain views. Dining room, complimentary Continental breakfast. No air-conditioning, no smoking, no room phones. Sauna. Hiking. Cross-country skiing. Business services. | Stuart Rd., Snowville | 603/447–2818 or 800/447–4345 | fax 603/447–5268 | www.snowvillageinn.com | 18 rooms | $99–$229 | MAP available | AE, D, DC, MC, V.

CORNISH

(Nearby towns also listed: Charlestown; Windsor, VT)

At the start of the 20th century, Cornish was known as the home of hugely popular novelist, Winston Churchill. No relation to the British prime minister and almost forgotten today, Churchill was such a celebrity that he hosted Teddy Roosevelt during the president's 1902 visit. Nor was Churchill the only creative person to call Cornish home during that period—painter Maxfield Parrish lived and worked here and sculptor Augustus Saint-Gaudens set up his studio in the town. Today, reclusive author J. D. Salinger makes his home in Cornish.

Information: Greater Claremont Chamber of Commerce | Moody Building, Tremont Sq, Claremont, 03743 | 603/543–1296 | fax 603/542–1469.

Attractions

Covered Bridges. Cornish has four covered bridges, all built by James Tasker between 1866 and 1882. He is known to have built 11 bridges in the area.
Blacksmith Shop Bridge. Built in 1881, this 91-ft-long bridge over Mill Brook, 2 mi east of Route 12A, was named for a blacksmith shop that once stood nearby. The bridge is closed to cars and can only be used by pedestrians. | Town House Rd., spanning Mill Brook.
Blow Me Down Bridge. James Tasker built this bridge in 1877 to span a deep gorge on Blow Me Down Brook. | Mill Rd.; 1/2 mi southwest of Plainfield Village off Rte. 12A.
Cornish Windsor Covered Bridge. At 449 1/2 ft, this bridge spanning Connecticut River is the longest wooden covered bridge in the United States and is listed on the National Register of Historic Places. The bridge was built in 1866 to replace bridges destroyed by floods. Tasker and Bela Fletcher first framed the bridge on a nearby meadow and later moved it to its present location over the Connecticut River. | Cornish Toll Bridge Rd.
Dingleton Hill Bridge. Only passenger cars can use this 1882 covered bridge spanning Mill Brook that is 1 mi east of Route 12A, at the foot of Dingleton Hill. | Root Hill Rd.

★ **Saint-Gaudens National Historic Site.** From 1885 to 1907, sculptor Augustus Saint-Gaudens lived and worked in the house and studio on this site off Route 12A, across the river from Windsor, Vermont. Full-size casts of the heroic bronzes for which he is known are scattered throughout the 150 acres of grounds and lovely gardens. | Saint-Gaudens Rd. | 603/675–2175 | www.sgnhs.org | $4 | Memorial Day–Oct., daily 9–4:30; grounds open until dusk, tours at 2 PM.

ON THE CALENDAR
JULY–AUG.: *Saint-Gaudens Summer Concert Series.* An annual concert series featuring chamber music, vocal ensembles, and ethnic groups. | 603/675–2175.
AUG.: *Cornish Fair.* A local agricultural fair. | 603/543–1296.

Dining
Home Hill Country Inn. French. French owners, nouvelle cuisine, and an extensive wine list, in a 19th-century mansion on 25 acres make for a delicious, authentic meal. Try the lobster with fois gras or the fricassee of veal sweetbreads with asparagus and baby onions. There is a vegetarian prix fixe menu available. Sunday brunch. | 703 River Rd., Plainfield | 603/675–6165 | $24–$36 | MC, V.

Lodging
Chase House Bed & Breakfast. This 1779 Federal-style house and property with 11 riverfront acres, 1/2 mi south of the Cornish Windsor Covered Bridge, was the birthplace of Salmon P. Chase, Abraham Lincoln's secretary of the treasury and a chief justice of the Supreme Court. Complimentary breakfast. No smoking. Gym, hiking. Cross-country skiing. No kids

under 12. | R.R. 2, Box 909, Rte. 12A | 603/675–5391 or 800/401–9455 | fax 603/675–5010 | www.chasehouse.com | 6 rooms, 3 suites | $105–$150 | Closed Nov. | MC, V | Reservations required.

Home Hill Country Inn. This Federal-style brick mansion built in 1818 in Plainfield, 5 mi north of Cornish, has Victorian-decorated rooms, many of which have fireplaces. The restaurant features French cuisine. Restaurant. No air-conditioning, no smoking, no room phones. Pool. Tennis. Cross-country skiing. No kids under 14. | 703 River Rd., Plainfield | 603/675–6165 | 6 rooms, 2 suites, 1 cottage | $150–$225.

DIXVILLE NOTCH

MAP 7, F3

(Nearby town also listed: Colebrook)

Dixville Notch, the northernmost and perhaps most beautiful of the White Mountain notches, is synonymous with the Balsams Grand Resort. The tiny town has fewer than 30 residents, most of whom work at the resort. Every four years, the town makes the national news when the residents gather in the resort's Ballot Room shortly after midnight on primary day to cast the first-in-the-nation votes for president.

Information: **Northern White Mountains Chamber of Commerce** | Box 298, 164 Main St., Berlin, 03570 | 603/752–6060 | fax 603/752–1002 | www.northernwhitemtn-chamber.org.

Attractions

Balsams Grand Resort. The slopes at this small ski area, mainly for guests of the Balsams Resort, have tough-sounding names like Umbagog and Magalloway, but the 12 trails and four glades are only moderately difficult. The resort's out-of-the-way location, although spectacularly scenic, means the slopes are never crowded. | Rte. 26 | 603/255–3400 or 800/255–0600, 800/255–0800 in NH for reservations | www.thebalsams.com | Dec.–Mar. and May–Oct., daily.

Dixville Notch State Park. This park, in New Hampshire's northernmost White Mountain notch 1 mi from town, has picnic areas, a waterfall, and many hiking trails. Peregrine falcons inhabit some of the cliffs, and moose are often spotted in the area. | Rte. 26 | 603/823–9959 | www.nhparks.state.nh.us | $2.50 | Daily.

Table Rock. A narrow, flat ledge jutting out of the southern wall of Dixville Notch about 800 ft above the road bears the name Table Rock. Two hiking trails lead to it, one of which is best suited for rock climbers, as it rises at a slope of about 60 degrees. While the other has some steep sections, it is not as difficult. Either way, the view is spectacular and makes the effort worthwhile. Both trailheads are off Route 26 near the Balsams resort. The easier trail begins just past the hotel, at the entrance to its ski area. The climbing trail begins almost directly across from hotel entrance. | Rte. 26.

ON THE CALENDAR

AUG.: *Umbagog Wildlife Festival.* A one-day event celebrating the natural heritage of the Umbagog Lake Wildlife Refuge. Informative talks are available as are guided hikes and canoe and pontoon trips for an additional charge. The Errol town center and the U.S. Fish and Wildlife Service Headquarters, 3 mi to the south, are the centers of action. | Junction Rtes. 16 and 26, Errol | 10–6 | 603/482–3906 | www.umbagogchambercommerce.com.

Dining

★ **Balsams Grand Resort Hotel.** Continental. The grand air of this resort carries into its turn-of-the-20th-century dining room replete with linen and china. Try the famous 100-ft luncheon buffet or more formal dinner dishes such as veal medallions and seared scallops with sun-dried tomato cream sauce. | Rte. 26 | 603/255–3400 or 800/255–0600 | fax 603/255–4221 | www.thebalsams.com | Jackets required after 6 PM | Closed early Apr.–mid-May, mid-Oct.–Christmas | $14–$22 | AE, D, MC, V.

Lodging

Balsams Grand Resort Hotel. This gleaming white, one-of-a-kind resort dating from the turn of the 20th century is stunning against its lush green backdrop of forests and mountains. On the 15,000-acre property you'll find all manner of activities, both indoor (dancing, lectures, movies, theater, shopping) and out (angling for trout in a stocked pond, naturalist programs, swimming, and more). 5 Bars, dining room. No air-conditioning, in-room data ports, room service, no TV, cable TV in common area. Pool, lake. Golf courses, 2 putting greens, 6 tennis courts. Hiking, boating. Bicycles, ice-skating. Cross-country skiing, downhill skiing, snowmobiling. Video games. Children's programs (ages 5–13). Business services. | Rte. 26 | 603/255–3400, 800/255–0600 outside NH, 800/255–0800 in NH | fax 603/255–4221 | www.thebalsams.com | 202 rooms | $210–$460 | Closed late Mar.–mid-May and mid-Oct.–mid-Dec. | MAP in winter, AP in summer | AE, D, MC, V.

Magalloway River Inn. This early 1800s outpost is right in the heart of moose country. Rooms are modest and simple, and reflect well the overall mood of the surroundings. The common areas are fixed with plants, knickknacks, and a warm, welcoming air. The larger rooms sleep up to four adults and are suitable for families. Complimentary breakfast. No air-conditioning, no smoking, no room phones, TV in common area. Hiking. Fishing. Cross-country skiing, snowmobiling. Pets allowed (no fee). | Rte. 16, Errol | 603/482–9883 | www.magriverinn.com | 6 rooms | $65 | MC, V.

DOVER

INTRO
ATTRACTIONS
DINING
LODGING

DOVER

MAP 7, H10

(Nearby towns also listed: Durham, Portsmouth)

Dover was founded in 1623 by fishermen drawn to the area by the plentiful waters of the Great Bay. As industry learned to harness the power generated by the falls on the Cocheco River, the town shifted from a fishing community to a mill town with grist, saw, and cotton mills. Today, Dover is a business hub for the seacoast area. Recent renovations have turned the mill buildings in the downtown area into shops and restaurants, returning vitality to Central Avenue, Dover's main street.

Information: Chamber of Commerce | 299 Central Ave., Dover, 03820 | 603/742–2218 | www.dovernh.org.

Attractions

Woodman Institute. These three buildings tell the story of Dover's early history. The 1675 Damme Garrison House has early-American cooking utensils, clothing, and furniture. Portholes allowed early settlers to fire guns on Indian attackers. The 1818 Woodman House has a Civil War room, as well as natural history and science exhibits. The 1813 Hale House is best known for the period from 1840 to 1873, when abolitionist Senator John P. Hale lived there. | 182–190 Central Ave. | 603/742–1038 | Free | Apr.–Jan., Tues.–Sat. 2–5; Feb.–Mar., Sat. 2–5.

ON THE CALENDAR

JULY–AUG.: *Cocheco Arts Festival.* A festival including Friday concerts, children's shows, and lunchtime performances downtown. | 603/742–2218.
OCT.: *Apple Harvest Day.* Dover's main street is closed to traffic as craft booths, entertainment, food, and other activities fill the street. | Central Ave. | 603/742–2218.
NOV.: *Holiday Parade.* A Christmas parade with marching bands, floats, and the arrival of Santa Claus. | Central Ave. | 603/742–2218.

Dining

Barn Tavern. American. This fully restored barn, replete with real farm fixtures and horse stalls, is now a watering hole for local folks, serving up a nice selection of steaks, seafood, and sandwiches. Try the St. Louis–style ribs in a bourbon barbecue sauce or the scampi schooner: baked seafood and stuffed shrimp over a bed of linguine with a creamy white wine sauce. | 17 Portland Ave. | 603/743–4489 | $9–$15 | AE, MC, V.

Garrison City Tavern Firehouse One Restaurant. American. Comfy chairs and Victorian antiques fill this mid-19th-century former firehouse. Open-air dining. Kids' menu. Sunday brunch. | 1 Orchard St. | 603/749–2220 | No lunch Sat., Sun. | $10–$23 | AE, D, DC, MC, V.

Governor's Inn. Continental. Wood trim, fine linens, and a crackling fireplace make fine company for your meal of Australian rack of lamb with tropical fruit chutney or the *Coquille St. Jacques*, shrimp, scallops, and mushrooms baked in pastry with a sweet wine sauce at this inn 10 mi north of Dover. Patio dining and entertainment in summer. | 78 Wakefield St., Rochester | 603/332–0107 | fax 603/335–1984 | $14–$22 | AE, D, MC, V.

Newick's Lobster House. Seafood. This very casual restaurant has a view of Great Bay and often exceptional sunsets as well as a seafood market. | 431 Dover Point Rd. | 603/742–3205 | $6–$24 | AE, D, MC, V.

Vegetarian Café. Vegetarian. Tucked inside the Dover Natural Foods store, this small café has an organic salad bar, homemade breads, and daily specials for the health-conscious traveler. Grab some takeout for a picnic along the Cocheco River just next door. | 24 Chestnut St. | 603/749–9999 | $4–$9 | AE, D, MC, V.

Lodging

Days Inn. A chain motel in the center of town. Complimentary Continental breakfast. Some kitchenettes, cable TV. Indoor pool. Hot tub. Laundry facilities. Business services. | 481 Central Ave. | 603/742–0400 | fax 603/742–7790 | www.dover-durham-daysinn.com | 50 rooms, 13 suites | $62–$100 | AE, D, DC, MC, V.

Highland Farm Bed and Breakfast. An 1850, three-story, brick Victorian farmhouse on 5 acres on the Cocheco River with large, comfortable rooms and lots of antiques. Complimentary breakfast. In-room data ports, no smoking, cable TV in common area. Cross-country skiing. Library. No pets. | 148 County Farm Rd., | 603/743–3399 | www.highlandfarms.com | 4 rooms (2 with shared bath) | $90–$120 | MC, V.

Silver Street Inn. In an old Victorian home. Complimentary breakfast. Cable TV. Business services. | 103 Silver St. | 603/743–3000 | fax 603/749–5673 | 10 rooms (1 with shared bath) | $79–$129 | AE, D, DC, MC, V.

DURHAM

MAP 7, H10

(Nearby towns also listed: Dover, Portsmouth)

More than 50% of the land and buildings in Durham are owned by the University of New Hampshire, including much of Main Street. Since many of the remaining buildings are occupied by businesses catering to students, you could be fooled into thinking that this is nothing more than a college town. But Durham's roots predate the college.

Settled in 1635, Durham was an active fishing and boatbuilding community at the time of the Revolutionary War, when John Sullivan and a group of Durham patriots attacked Fort William and Mary in New Castle. The gunpowder and cannons taken in the attack were first stored in Durham and then used by the patriots at the Battle of Bunker Hill. John Sullivan went on to become a three-term governor of New Hampshire.

Information: **Dover Chamber of Commerce** | 299 Central Ave., Dover | 603/742–2218 | fax 603/749–6317 | www.ci.durham.nh.us.

Attractions

Emery Farm. Established in 1655, this 12-acre farm has pick-your-own fruit, fresh baked goods, and local crafts in the country store, and a small petting zoo, summer reading hours, and activites for kids. It's across from Wagonhill Farm. | U.S. 4 | 603/742–8495 | www.nhagri-culture.com/emeryfarm | Apr.–Jan., daily 9–6.

Little Bay Buffalo Farm. Come visit this 40-acre prairie to view and learn about the legendary American bison. Viewing tours are conducted in a covered wagon. Gift shop. | 50 Langley Rd. | 603/868–3300 | Free entry, $10 tours | Daily.

Misty Meadows Herbal Center. A 160-acre herb farm and holistic education center with plant identification tours, classes in herbology, yoga, and tai chi and an apothecary with homemade tinctures. | 185 Wednesday Hill Rd. off Rte. 155, Lee | 603/659–7211 | fax 603/659–8582 | www.mistymeadows.org | Wed.–Sat. 10–5, Sun. 12–5.

The University of New Hampshire. Founded in 1866, UNH is a state university with over 12,000 undergraduates. | 603/862–1360 | www.unh.edu | Daily.

The Art Gallery. The University of New Hampshire's Art Gallery occasionally exhibits items from a permanent collection of about 1,800 pieces but generally uses its space to host traveling exhibits of contemporary and historic art. Noted items in the collection include 19th-century Japanese woodblock prints and American landscape paintings. | Paul Creative Arts Center, 30 College Rd. | 603/862–3712 | Free | Sept.–May, Mon.–Wed. 10–4, Thurs. 10–8, Sat.–Sun. 1–5.

New England Ecological Garden. An ongoing project, the 200 acres of the University of New Hampshire–Durham campus are being transformed into an ecologically sustainable community. Low-maintenance wildlife and community gardens, wild meadows, and native plant projects aid in making the campus in harmony with the surrounding landscape. | Main St. | 603/862–1091 | www.sustainableunh.unh.edu | Free.

ON THE CALENDAR

MAR.: *Seacoast Flower, Home, and Garden Show.* This regional home show runs concurrently with UNH's greenhouse open house. | 603/356–7750.

AUG.: *Llama and Alpaca Fall Festival.* Llamas and alpacas are on display and for sale at this festival. | 603/654–2161.

SEPT.–MAY: *Faculty Concert Series.* Free concerts are given by members of the UNH Department of Music. | 603/862–2404.

SEPT.–MAY: *UNH Celebrity Series.* Occasional concerts, lectures, and performances by visiting artists. | 603/862–2418.

Dining

Acorns Restaurant. Café. This restaurant within the formal New England Conference Center has a casual menu with lite fare such as a Cajun duck salad and Mexican quesadillas. | 15 Strafford Ave. | 603/862–2801 or 800/590–4334 | fax 603/862–4897 | $8–$15 | AE, MC, V.

Three Chimneys Inn. American. Four fireplaces, Georgian decor, hand-hewn beams, and warm wood tones make a nice setting for your meal that can include dishes such as the sesame crusted yellowfin tuna with a red wine and wild mushroom vinaigrette or the oven-roasted Australian rack of lamb with a pistachio mango crust. You can enjoy an outdoor meal in a grape arbor on the Conservatory terrace. Sunday brunch. | 17 Newmarket Rd. (Rte. 108) | 603/868–7800 or 800/399–9777 | fax 603/868–2964 | $10–$25 | AE, D, MC, V.

Lodging

Hickory Pond Inn and Golf Course. A comfortable inn with a 9-hole golf course on the premises. Rooms are individually decorated. Complimentary Continental breakfast. No smoking, cable TV, VCR available. Golf. Cross-country skiing. Pets allowed. | 1 Stagecoach Rd. | 603/

659–2227 or 800/658–0065 | fax 603/659–7910 | www.hickorypond.com | 18 rooms (4 with shared bath) | $69–$99 | AE, MC, V.

New England Conference Center and Hotel. A modern hotel with woodsy grounds on the UNH campus. Guests have indoor-outdoor pool privileges. Restaurant, bar. Cable TV. Business services. | 15 Strafford Ave. | 603/862–2801 or 800/590–4334 | fax 603/862–4897 | 115 rooms | $94–$151 | AE, MC, V.

Pines Guest House. A charming yellow 1870 Georgian Victorian farmhouse inn on 15 acres with frontage on the Oyster River and Beards Creek, ½ mi from the University of New Hampshire on Route 108. Complimentary Continental breakfast. No smoking, cable TV, in-room VCRs and movies. Pond. Hiking, dock. Fishing. No pets. | 47 Dover Rd. | 603/868–3361 | coescorner@aol.com | www.newenglandinns.com/inns/pines | 4 rooms (1 with shared bath) | $55–$105 | AE, D, DC, MC, V.

Three Chimneys Inn. This house overlooking the Oyster River and Old Mill Falls dates from the mid-17th century. There are guest rooms in both the mansion and the carriage house, which are furnished with fine Georgian mahogany, Edwardian drapes, polished wood floors, and oriental rugs. Most of them have fireplaces. 2 restaurants, complimentary breakfast. In-room data ports, some in-room hot tubs. No kids under 6. Business services. | 17 Newmarket Rd. (Rte. 108) | 603/868–7800 or 888/399–9777 | fax 603/868–2964 | www.threechimneysinn.com | 23 rooms | $119–$329 | AE, D, MC, V.

University Guest House. Built in 1938, this guest house is next to the University of New Hampshire campus. Complimentary Continental breakfast. No smoking, no room phones. | 47 Mill Rd. | 603/868–2728 | fax 603/868–2744 | 4 rooms (2 with shower only, 3 with shared bath) | $79 | AE, D, MC, V.

ENFIELD

MAP 7, C8

(Nearby towns also listed: Grafton, Hanover)

In 1782, two Shaker brothers from Mount Lebanon, New York, arrived at a community on the northeastern side of Mascoma Lake. Moving to the lake's southern shore around 1800, they founded Enfield, the ninth of 18 Shaker communities in this country.

Information: | 23 Main St., Box 373, Enfield, 03748 | 603/632–4201 | fax 603/632–5182 | www.enfield.nh.us.

Attractions

Enfield Shaker Museum. A self-guided walking tour takes you through 13 of the remaining buildings constructed by Enfield's Shaker community. The Great Stone Dwelling, now housing the Shaker Inn, is the largest Shaker structure ever built. The museum preserves and explains Shaker artifacts, and skilled craftspeople demonstrate Shaker techniques. | 24 Caleb Dyer La. | 603/632–4346 | www.shakermuseum.org | $7 | Memorial Day–end Oct., Mon.–Sat. 10–5, Sun. 12–5; Oct. 31–Memorial Day, Sat. 10–4, Sun. 12–4.

Whaleback Ski Area. There are 30 trails and 65 skiable acres at this ski area overlooking Interstate 89. The trails are mainly intermediates with a few steep pitches. There is also a tubing park and snowshoeing is available. | 160 Whaleback Mt. Rd., I–89 Exit 16 | 603/448–1489 | www.whaleback.com | $29 | Mid-Dec.–mid-Mar., daily.

ON THE CALENDAR

JUNE: *Summer Solstice Crafts and Garden Fair.* Come celebrate the longest day of the year and shop for locally hewn crafts, garden ornaments, plants, and homemade food on the grounds of the Enfield Shaker Museum. | 24 Caleb Dyer La. | 10–5 | 603/632–4346.

Dining

Baited Hook. Seafood. A great place to settle down for a beer and burger or fried seafood platter. The restaurant's interior is fitted with nautical knickknacks and has open views of Lake Mascoma. Eight miles west of Enfield. Outdoor patio dining. Kids' selections. | U.S. 4, Lebanon | 603/448–1133 | Closed Labor Day–Memorial Day | $8–$12 | MC, V.

Shaker Inn. Continental. Part of the Shaker Inn on the shores of Lake Mascoma, this restaurant serves fine regional and Shaker-influenced dishes like roast duckling with raspberry maple glaze and seasonally inspired whole foods. | Rte. 4A | 603/632–7810 or 888/707–4257 | $14–$24 | AE, D, DC, MC, V.

Lodging

Mary Keane House. The views of Lake Mascoma and the adjoining 1,200 acres of field and woodlands add to this pleasant 1929 Victorian Inn with antique furnishings that is next door to the Shaker Museum. Complimentary breakfast. Some kitchenettes, some refrigerators, no smoking, cable TV, no room phones. Lake. Hiking, volleyball, beach, dock, boating. Fishing. Ice-skating. Pets allowed (fee). | 93 Chosen Vale La. | 603/632–4241 or 888/239–2153 | mary.keane.house@valley.net | www.marykeanehouse.com | 2 room, 2 suites | $95–$145 | AE, D, MC, V.

Shaker Inn. Reproduction Shaker furnishings fill this immense stone structure overlooking Lake Mascoma on the grounds of the Enfield Shaker Museum. Restaurant, complimentary breakfast. No air-conditioning, no smoking, no room phones. | 447 Rte. 4A | 603/632–7810 or 888/707–4257 | info@theshakerinn.com | www.theshakerinn.com | 24 rooms | $85–$165 | AE, D, MC, V.

EXETER

MAP 7, H11

(Nearby towns also listed: Hampton, Hampton Beach, Portsmouth, Rye)

During the Revolutionary War and up until 1808, Exeter was the capital of New Hampshire. It was here that the Republican party was formed and the first state constitution—first in the original 13 states—and the first declaration of independence from Great Britain were written. Although no longer the center of New Hampshire politics, Exeter remains a vibrant town with many shopping and cultural opportunities.

Information: **Chamber of Commerce** | 120 Water St., Exeter, 03833 | 603/772–2411. | fax 603/772–9965.

Attractions

American Independence Museum. The story of the American Revolution unfolds during each tour of the Ladd Gilman House. Drafts of the U.S. Constitution and the first Purple Heart are some of the items on display. The house served as the state treasury from 1775 to 1789 and as the governor's mansion during the 14-year term of John Taylor Gilman. | 1 Governors La. | 603/772–2622 | www.independencemuseum.org | $5 | May–Oct., Wed.–Sun. 12–5 | Guided tours only, no walk-thrus.

Gilman Garrison House. This historic house, built around 1690 as a fortified garrison, is one of the oldest remaining structures in Exeter. Massive logs form the walls and a portcullis was installed behind the main door. | 12 Water St. | 603/436–3205 | www.spnea.org | $4 | June–mid-Oct., Tues., Thurs., Sat., Sun., 12–5.

Kingston State Park. Relax by Great Pond or take a leisurely dip in this 44-acre park southwest of Exeter. No pets. | Rte. 125, Kingston | 603/642–5471 | $2.50 | May–Sept., daily.

League of New Hampshire Craftsmen. One of seven stores that exhibit and sell the contemporary and traditional crafts made by the members of the League. | 61 Water St. | 603/778–8282 | Mon.–Sat. 10–5:30, Sun. 12–4.

Phillips Exeter Academy. This prep school opened its doors in 1783 and has gone on to become one of the most esteemed in the nation. The buildings, with architectural styles spanning several centuries, are mainly along Front Street in the historic district. Tours are offered year-round by appointment. | Front St. | 603/777–3437 | www.exeter.edu.

ON THE CALENDAR

JULY: *Revolutionary War Festival.* This annual event celebrates independence from British rule with battle reenactments, music, and other festivities. | Downtown Exeter | 603/772–2411.

Dining

Inn of Exeter's Terrace Restaurant. Continental. Quintessential New England furnishings and food befitting the history and renown of the Inn make for an authentic dining experience. Try the house-special chateaubriand served on a sizzling oak plank with dutchess potatoes and a béarnaise sauce or the grilled, lime-marinated chicken. Sunday brunch. | 90 Front St. | 603/772–5901 or 800/782–8444 | fax 603/778–8757 | Reservations not accepted | $15.95–$24.95 | AE, D, DC, MC, V.

Loaf and Ladle. Cafés. A bustling, family-style spot with cafeteria service on the Exeter River serving hearty fresh breads, stews, chowders, and sandwiches. Outdoor dining by the riverside. | 9 Water St. | 603/778–8955 | $2.50–$7.75 | AE, D, MC, V.

Sal and Anthony's. Italian. Slate, stone, and wood-burning ovens fill the two levels of this elegant restaurant with views of the Exeter River. It has old-world specialties like veal rollotini and seafood parmigiana. | 69 Water St. | 603/778–1949 | fax 603/772–5001 | $12–$20 | AE, MC, V.

Lodging

Governor Jeremiah Smith House Inn. This bright, two-story, 1730s colonial inn, listed in the National Historic Register, was the home of New Hampshire Governor Jeremiah Smith, known for his eulogy at George Washington's funeral. Original period furnishings and fixtures, from gas-fired cast-iron stoves and woven quilts to open-beamed cathedral ceilings and custom lace draperies, spin an authentic old-world feel. Dining room, complimentary breakfast. In-room data ports, no smoking, cable TV, room phones. | 41 Front St., | 603/778–7770 | fax 603/778–7771 | jeremiahsmithinn@aol.com | www.portsmouthnh.com/jeremiahsmithinn | 8 rooms | $89–$139 | MC, V.

Inn by the Bandstand. This 1809 Federal-style town house is listed on the National Register of Historic Places. Most rooms lean to the romantic with fireplaces and gracious furnishings. Bar. Complimentary Continental breakfast. No smoking. In room TVs. Library. No pets. | 4 Front St. | 603/772–6352 or 877/239–3837 | fax 603/778–0212 | info@innbythebandstand.com | www.innbythebandstand.com | 8 rooms | $110–$200 | AC, D, MC, V.

Inn of Exeter. Antiques and period furnishings fill this brick Georgian-style building on the Phillips Exeter grounds. Restaurant (*see* The Inn of Exeter's Terrace Restaurant), bar. In-room data ports, cable TV. Business services, free parking. | 90 Front St. | 603/772–5901 or 800/782–8444 | fax 603/778–8757 | www.exeterinn.com | 43 rooms, 3 suites | $140–$169 | AE, D, DC, MC, V.

FITZWILLIAM

(Nearby towns also listed: Jaffrey, Keene, Peterborough)

At the southern edge of New Hampshire is the postcard New England village of Fitzwilliam. It was founded as Stoddardtown in 1752 and renamed in 1773 in honor of nobleman and Earl, William Fitzwilliam, one of England's wealthiest landowners and kinsman of then New Hampshire Governor John Wentworth. It was the hub of New Hampshire's granite industry from the time the railroad arrived in 1849 through the 19th century. Today, Fitzwilliam is a well-preserved colonial town with a population of 2,100, many whom commute to nearby Keene and Peterborough for work. Though growing, Fitzwilliam maintains its small-town flavor, still conducting town business in the 1817 Meeting House.

Information: **Greater Peterborough Chamber of Commerce** | Box 401, 10-B Wilton Rd., Peterborough, 03458 | 603/924–7234 | fax 603–924–7235 | www.peterboroughchamber.com.

Attractions

Fitzwilliam Historical Society–Amos J. Parker House. A small museum in the mid-1800s home of renowned New Hampshire legislator, lawyer, and Fitzwilliam town resident, the late Amos J. Blake. The exhibits include antiques, paintings, furniture, and period memorabilia. | On the Common, Rte. 119 | 603/585–7742 | Memorial Day–Columbus Day, Sat. 10–4.

Rhododendron State Park. This 300-acre park is renowned for its 16-acre stand of wild *rhododendron maximus*, which bloom during July. The local Garden Club also maintains a wheelchair-accessible wildflower walking trail. Call for blooming time updates. | Rhododendron Rd. (Rte. 119) | 603/532–8862 | $2.50 | Daily.

ON THE CALENDAR

JUNE: *Fitzwilliam Annual Strawberry Festival.* Held on the town common, this old-time event is sponsored by the Historical Society. There are plenty of fresh berries as well as whipped cream, shortcake, and more. | On the Common | 1–4 | 603/924–7234.
JUNE: *Charlie Wallace Memorial 5K Road Race.* Starting at the Emerson School, this race and kids Fun Run raises money for the local sports field and is followed by music, food, swimming, and a raffle on the lawn of the Fitzwilliam Inn. | Rhododendron Rd. | 603/924–7234.

Dining

Fitzwilliam Inn. Continental. This old-English-style pub and adjoining dining room are dimly lit and cozy. House specials are the broiled scallops in brandy butter and the Saturday- and Sunday-night prime rib. Lunches are more modest with sandwiches, quiche, and their famous pumpkin bread. Kids' menu. | On the Common, Rte. 119 | 603/585–9000 | Breakfast also available | $10–$20 | D, MC, V.

Lodging

Fitzwilliam Inn. The doors of this stately home have been open to guests since 1796. The Town Common, a National Historic Register site, is visible from the rooms and the front porch. Rooms are individually fashioned with antiques and period furnishings. Restaurant, bar. TV in common room. Outdoor pool. | On the Common, Rte. 119, | 603/585–9000 | fax 603/585–3495 | www.fitzwilliaminn.com | 23 rooms (7 with shared bath) | $50–$70 | D, MC, V.

★ **Hannah Davis House.** A pleasant, laid-back bed-and-breakfast experience in a meticulously maintained and decorated home, built in 1820. The suites and one of the rooms have wood-burning fireplaces. The wraparound deck has a view of a pond. The common area and pantries have homemade crafts, recipes, treats, jellies, and teddy bears for sale. Complimentary breakfast. No smoking, no room phones, TV in common area. | 106 Rte. 119 W, | 603/585–3344 | 3 rooms, 3 suites | $70–$95, $120–$140 suites | D, MC, V.

FRANCONIA

MAP 7, D6

(Nearby towns also listed: Lincoln and North Woodstock Area, Littleton, Sugar Hill)

The town of Franconia is north of the notch of the same name, which provides a north–south route through the White Mountains. Robert Frost wrote one of his most remembered poems, "Stopping by Woods on a Snowy Evening," while living in Franconia. Other literary visitors have included Washington Irving, Henry Wadsworth Longfellow, and Nathaniel Hawthorne, who wrote a short story about the Old Man of the Mountain. Today, Franconia is a destination for alpine and cross-country skiers, hikers, mountain bikers, and rock climbers.

Just as in Hawthorne's day, many of these outdoor sports–minded visitors spend at least part of their time in 6,440-acre Franconia Notch State Park, where a footpath from the notch to the top of Mt. Lafayette is said to have been in existence since 1825. The path soon became a full-fledged trail as visitors arrived from Boston and New York to enjoy the scenic wonders and clear air of Franconia Notch. A local rock formation, called the Old Man of the Mountain, has become a beloved state symbol. The park also includes Cannon Mountain Ski Area and Aerial Tramway, the Flume, Echo Lake, and numerous hiking trails.

Information: Franconia-Sugar Hill-Easton Chamber of Commerce | Box 780, Franconia, 03580. | 603/823–5661 | www.franconianotch.com.

Attractions

Franconia Iron Furnace Interpretive Center. Take an outdoor, self-guided tour of the remains of this iron-blast furnace built in 1805. Informative plaques explain the history of the furnace, the bellows, and the tools on display. | Junction Rtes. 18 and 117 | 603/823–5000 | Free | Daily dawn–dusk.

© Artville

THE OLD MAN OF THE MOUNTAIN

Twelve hundred feet above Profile Lake in Franconia Notch State Park, five separate ledges jut out of a sheer cliff. Individually, they are nothing more than craggy outcroppings, like hundreds of others found throughout the rocky, glacier-carved White Mountains. Together, though, they form the distinct profile of a man's face, weather-beaten and dignified, perhaps quietly pleased with what he surveys from his lofty perch.

That stone face has long captured visitors' imaginations. Nathaniel Hawthorne wrote a short story about it. Painters have tried to capture its spirit. Native son and orator Daniel Webster said of the Old Man: "Men hang out their signs indicative of their respective trades: shoemakers hang out a gigantic shoe; jewelers a monster watch . . . but up in the mountains of New Hampshire, God Almighty has hung out a sign to show that there he makes men."

Today's New Hampshirites don't pin such lofty claims on the Old Man of the Mountain, but they love him nonetheless. His image appears on license plates and state road signs, on tourist brochures, and on T-shirts as well. It is a symbol of endurance and of the mountains that surround it.

★ **Franconia Notch State Park.** Franconia Notch State Park, 7 mi south of Franconia, contains a few of New Hampshire's best-loved attractions, including the granite profile of the Old Man of the Mountain, the icon of New Hampshire. | Rte. 18 or the Franconia Notch Pkwy. (I–93) | 603/823–5563, 603/271–3628 for camping reservations statewide | Free | Daily.

The Basin. One of several interesting natural features in Franconia Notch State Park, the Basin is a deep glacial pothole, 20 ft in diameter, at the base of a waterfall. South of Profile Lake, below the Basin, the Pemigewasset River splashes through a gorge that is a smaller version of the Flume (*see below*). The Basin is reached from the Basin Cascades hiking trail. | Franconia Notch Pkwy. (I–93) exit 1 | 603/823–5563 | Daily.

Cannon Mountain Ski Area. This state-owned and -operated ski area 5 mi south of Franconia is one of the most rugged and scenic ski mountains in New Hampshire. The narrow trails wind down 2,145 vertical ft, in a thoroughly New England style. | Franconia Notch State Pkwy. (I–93) exit 2 or 3 | 603/823–8800 | Dec.–Mar., daily.

The Flume. A chasm at the southern end of Franconia Notch, 15 mi south of Franconia, extends 800 ft at the base of Mt. Liberty. Granite walls that rise 70 to 90 ft are only 12 to 20 ft apart and a mountain stream flows between them. A boardwalk takes you through the Flume, which remains cool even on the hottest day of the year. | Franconia Notch State Pkwy. (I–93) exit 1 | 603/745–8391 | $7 | Mid-May–late Oct., daily 9:30–4:30.

Flume Bridge. One of two covered bridges in Franconia Notch State Park. This structure is used both by hikers and by buses bringing visitors to the Flume. The shingles that roofed the bridge when it was built in 1871 were replaced in 1951. | Rte. 175 at U.S. 3, spanning the Pemigewasset River.

Flume Gorge & Park Information Center. Interpretive films explain the geology and history of the area in this center 15 mi south of Franconia. | Franconia Notch State Pkwy. (I–93) Exit 1 | 603/745–8391 | Free | Mid-May–late Oct., daily 9:30–4:30.

Lafayette Campground. This campground in Franconia Notch State Park, 9 mi south of Franconia Village, has hiking and biking trails, 97 tent sites, showers, and easy access to the Appalachian Trail. | Franconia Notch State Pkwy. (I–93) Exit 1 | 603/823–9513, 603/271–3628 reservations | $14 per site.

New England Ski Museum. This member-owned and -operated museum is in Franconia Notch State Park at the foot of the Cannon Mountain Tramway, 5 mi southeast of Franconia. Old photos, trophies, skis and bindings, and clothing dating from the late 1800s are on display. | Franconia Notch State Pkwy. (I–93) Exit 2 | 603/823–7177 | www.skimuseum.org | Free | Dec.–Mar., Fri.–Tues. 12–5; Memorial Day–Columbus Day, daily 12–5.

Old Man of the Mountain. This naturally formed granite profile juts from a sheer cliff 1,200 ft above Profile Lake. Five separate ledges form the profile that measures 40 ft from forehead to chin. | Franconia Notch State Pkwy. (I–93) Exit 2 | Free | Daily.

Sentinel Pine Bridge. The Society for the Protection of New Hampshire Forests built this footbridge in 1939 over the pool in the Flume Gorge. The year before the bridge was built, a major hurricane blew down the pine tree that stood near the rear of the pool like a sentinel. A 60-ft section of the tree was built into the base of the bridge. | Franconia Notch State Pkwy. (I–93) Exit 1.

Frost Place. This small farm about a mile south of town was Robert Frost's home from 1915 to 1920. A short film describes the writer's life in Franconia. Two rooms in the house contain memorabilia and signed copies of his books. Short hiking trails are marked with lines from his poetry. | Ridge Rd. | 603/823–5510 | www.frostplace.com | $3 | Memorial Day–June 30, Sat., Sun. 1–5; July–mid-Oct., Wed.–Mon. 1–5.

White Mountain National Forest. Franconia and Franconia Notch State Park are entirely within the White Mountain National Forest. *See* Lincoln and North Woodstock. | Accessible via Rte. 18 or the Franconia Notch Pkwy. | 603/447–1989.

ON THE CALENDAR

JUNE: *Annual Fields of Lupine Festival.* Events at area inns in Franconia, Sugar Hill, and Bethlehem celebrate the blooming of wild lupines. | 603/823–5661.

FRANCONIA

INTRO
ATTRACTIONS
DINING
LODGING

FEB.: *Frostbite Follies.* Includes fireworks, sliding, and other events at Cannon Mountain Ski Area. | 603/823–5563.
OCT.: *Fall Foliage Walk.* A 7- to 14-mi walk during foliage season sponsored by the American Lung Association of New Hampshire. | Cannon Mountain | 603/669–2411 or 800/83–LUNGS.

Dining

Franconia Inn. Contemporary. The setting is casually elegant, and the unusual dining room features a lofted ceiling. Try the Maine crabcakes with a chipolte mayonnaise and gaufrette or the Sauteed Tournedo of Atlantic Salmon served with black linguini and lemon-coriander butter. Kids' menu. No smoking. | 1300 Easton Rd. (Rte. 116) | 603/823–5542 or 800/473–5299 | Closed Apr.–mid-May. Lunch served on weekends Dec.-Feb. only. Hrs vary off-season | $14–$21 | AE, MC, V.

Horse & Hound. Continental. The seafood is a standout in this upscale pine-paneled dining room. Kids' menu. No smoking. | 205 Wells Rd. | 603/823–5501 | Mid-May–June, first 3 weeks of Sept., and Thanksgiving–Mar., closed Sun.–Wed.; July–Aug., closed Mon.–Tues.; closed mid-Oct.–Thanksgiving. No lunch | $12–$21 | AE, D, DC, MC, V.

Lloyd Hill's Restaurant. Eclectic. With a menu sure to suit any taste, this popular restaurant in an 1880s Victorian-style building has a casual country feel. The menu is a combination of pastas, sandwiches, seafood, and steaks, and the daily specials feature hits from their vast repertoire of styles and dishes, including 75 types of eggs benedict. Outdoor seating. | 2061 Main St., Bethlehem | 603/869–2141 | Breakfast available Sat.–Sun. | $6–$21 | D, MC, V.

Lovett's Inn by Lafayette Brook. American. The inn occupies a late-18th-century farmhouse and there are views of Cannon Mountain from the dining room. Try the Chicken Florentine. | 1474 Profile Rd. | 603/823–7761 | Reservations essential | Closed Apr. No lunch | $13–$21 | AE, D, MC, V.

Lodging

Bungay Jar B and B Inn. A cozy 18th-century barn on 12 secluded and wooded acres. The rooms are delightfully furnished and have views of the surrounding mountains and gardens, which are worth a visit in themselves. Gardening workshops available. Complimentary breakfast. Some kitchenettes, no smoking, some in-room hot tubs, some room phones, no TV. Sauna. Hiking. No pets. | Easton Valley Rd. (Rte. 116), | 603/823–7775 or 800/421–0701 | info@bungayjar.com | www.bungayjar.com | 6 rooms, 1 cottage | $105–$225 | AE, D, MC, V.

Franconia Inn. This country inn just south of Franconia has great views of the mountains and many activities, including swimming in the river. Restaurant, bar. No air-conditioning, cable TV in common area, no room phones, no TV. Pool. Hot tub. Tennis. Horseback riding. Ice-skating. Cross-country skiing, sleigh rides. Video games, library. | 1300 Easton Rd. (Rte. 116) | 603/823–5542 or 800/473–5299 | fax 603/823–8078 | info@franconiainn.com | www.franconiainn.com | 34 rooms | $81–$156 | Closed Apr.–mid-May | MAP available | AE, MC, V.

Gale River Motel. Just a short walk from a river with mountain views. Picnic area. No air-conditioning, refrigerators, cable TV. Pool. Hot tub, outdoor hot tub. Playground. | 1 Main St. | 603/823–5655 or 800/255–7989 | 10 rooms, 2 cottages | $50–$82 | AE, D, MC, V.

Hillwinds Lodge. A rustic lodge on the Gale River with beautiful views and simple but comfortable accommodations. Restaurant, Continental breakfast. Pool. Sauna. Bicycling. Library. No pets. | Dow Ave. | 603/823–5551 or 800/473–5299 | hillwinds@franconiainn.com | www.franconiainn.com | 29 rooms, 3 suites | $55–$75 | AE, MC, V.

Horse & Hound. A cozy country inn not far from Cannon Mt. Restaurant, complimentary breakfast. No air-conditioning, no TV, TV in common area. Pets allowed (fee). | 205 Wells Rd. | 603/823–5501 or 800/450–5501 | 10 rooms (2 with shared bath) | $86 | Closed Apr. and Nov. | AE, D, DC, MC, V.

Inn at Forest Hills. This inn in a turn-of-the-20th-century home has a huge front porch set with chairs overlooking Cannon and Lafayette. Complimentary breakfast. No air-conditioning, no smoking, cable TV, some in-room VCRs, no room phones. Tennis. Cross-country skiing. No kids under 11. | Rte. 142 | 603/823–9550 or 800/280–9550 | fax 603/823–8701 | nhhg@innfhills.com | www.innatforesthills.com | 8 rooms (1 with shower only, 3 with shared bath) | $85–$145 | AE, D, MC, V.

Lovett's Inn by Lafayette Brook. There are fireplaces in some of the cottages in this late-18th-century inn on 10 stream-crossed acres. Restaurant, bar. No air-conditioning in some rooms, no smoking, no room phones, no TV in some rooms, TV in common area. Pool. Hot tub. Cross-country skiing. | 1474 Profile Rd. (Rte. 18) | 603/823–7761, 800/356–3802 outside NH | 21 rooms | $110–$160 | Closed Apr. and Nov. | MAP | AE, MC, V.

Red Coach Inn. A resort with Cannon Mountain views. Restaurant. Room service, cable TV, some in-room VCRs. Indoor pool. Beauty salon, hot tub. Exercise equipment. Video games. Business services. | Box 861, Wallace Hill Rd. | 603/823–7422 or 800/262–2493 | fax 603/823–5638 | redcoachinn@connriver.net | 60 rooms | $60–$120 | D, MC, V.

Rustic Log Cabins. Fully furnished, comfortable log cabins on 16 acres along Salmon Hole Brook, 7 mi north of Franconia. All the units have porches, charcoal grills, wood-burning fireplaces, wall-to-wall carpeting, and full kitchens. Picnic area. No air-conditioning, kitchenettes, some microwaves, refrigerators, no TV, no room phones. Hiking. | 1450 Sugar Hill Rd., Lisbon | 603/838–6731 | info@rusticlogcabins.com | www.rusticlogcabins.com | 7 cabins | $80 | AE, D, MC, V.

Stonybrook Motel & Lodge. On 8 acres just south of town, with mountain views and a pretty brook. Picnic area. Some refrigerators, cable TV. 2 heated pools (1 indoor). Video games. Playground. | Rte. 18 | 603/823–8192 or 800/722–3552 | fax 603/823–8196 | www.stonybrook-motel.com | 23 rooms | $48–$92 | D, MC, V.

FRANKLIN

MAP 7, E9

(Nearby towns also listed: Canterbury, Laconia)

Although not exactly on the beaten path today, Franklin was the birthplace of one of New Hampshire's most famous citizens, Daniel Webster. This orator represented New Hampshire in Congress from 1813 to 1817 and Massachusetts in the Senate from 1827 to 1841. The bust of Webster in front of the Congregational Church was sculpted by Daniel Chester French, who also sculpted the seated figure of Abraham Lincoln in the Lincoln Memorial in Washington, D.C.

Information: **Greater Franklin/Tilton Chamber of Commerce** | Box 464, Franklin, 03235 | 603/934–6909 | www.franklin.nh.us/chamber.

Attractions

Congregational Christian Church. This church, built in 1820, was Franklin's first. The bust of Daniel Webster in front of the church is the work of Daniel Chester French, the sculptor who created the seated version of Abraham Lincoln for the Lincoln Memorial in Washington, D.C. | 47 S. Main St. (U.S. 3) | 603/934–4242 | Wed., Thurs., Sun.; call for hours.

Daniel Webster Birthplace Living History Project. Daniel Webster, one of the country's most distinguished orators and statesmen, was born in this 1782 two-room frame house 4 mi south of Franklin. Here people in costume recreate the era and bring forth its lively history. | Rte. 127 | 603/934–5057 | $2.50 | Mid-June–Labor Day, Sat., Sun. 10–6.

SEPT.: *Annual Frontier Days.* The festival includes cowboys, Indian teepees, dancing, Civil War reenactment, and crafts demonstrations. | 603/934–6909.

Dining

Le Chalet Rouge. French. The small dining rooms in this 19th-century Greek Revival house 3 mi east of Franklin are decorated with French lithographs. Specialties include duckling prepared with home-grown fruit and herbs according to season, and flaming pepper steak. | 385 W. Main St., Tilton | 603/286–4035 | No lunch | $13–$21 | MC, V.

Mr. D's. American. Family-style service and vintage photos are the hallmarks of this West Franklin restaurant. Kids' menu. | 428 N. Main St., West Franklin | 603/934–3142 | Breakfast also available | $7–$13 | AE, D, DC, MC, V.

Oliver's. American. Period furnishings make for an elegant setting for sophisticated meals in Tilton, 3 mi from Franklin. Try the pastry-baked chicken with cranberry glaze. Entertainment. Kids' menu. Sunday brunch buffet. | 4 Sandborn Rd., Tilton | 603/286–7379 | $7–$21. | AE, D, MC, V.

Lodging

Atwood Inn. Antiques fill this newly restored 1830 charmer in nearby West Franklin. Some rooms have their own fireplaces. Complimentary breakfast. No smoking, no TV in some rooms, cable TV in common area. | 71 Hill Rd. (Rte. 3A) | 603/934–3666 | atwoddinn@cyber-portal.net | www.atwoodinn.com | 7 rooms | $80 | AE, D, DC, MC, V.

Englewood Bed and Breakfast. A meticulously maintained 1890 Queen Anne Victorian with hardwood floors, wraparound porch, and individually decorated rooms with antiques and nice touches like bathrobes and a night-time pillow treat. The Southwestern-style room is a nice change of pace. Complimentary breakfast. No smoking, no room phones, TV in common area. No pets. | 69 Cheney St., | 603/934–1017 or 888/207–2545 | info@englewoodbnb.com | www.englewoodbnb.com | 4 rooms | $65–$75 | AE, MC, V.

Highland Lake Inn. In an 18th-century former farmhouse in East Andover, 5 mi west of Franklin, with lake and mountain views. Picnic area, complimentary breakfast. No smoking, cable TV in common area, no room phones, no TV. Lake. Beach. No kids under 8. | 32 Maple St., East Andover | 603/735–6426 | fax 603/735–5355 | www.highlandlakeinn.com | 10 rooms | $85–$125 | AE, D, MC, V.

Super 8. This typical example of the chain is in nearby Tilton. Cable TV, some in-room VCRs. Business services. | U.S. 3, Tilton; I–93 Exit 20 | 603/286–8882 | fax 603/286–8788 | 63 rooms | $65–$95 | AE, D, DC, MC, V.

GILFORD

MAP 7, F9

(Nearby towns also listed: Laconia, Wiers Beach)

Gilford is one of the least commercial of the towns surrounding busy Lake Winnipesaukee. When the town was incorporated, the oldest resident was asked to name it. A veteran of the Battle of the Guilford Courthouse in North Carolina, he borrowed that town's name. Apparently, though, he didn't know how to spell it.

Information: **Laconia–Weirs Beach Chamber of Commerce** | 11 Veterans Sq, Laconia, 03246 | 603/524–5531 | fax 603/524–5534 | www.laconia-weirs.org.

Attractions

Ellacoya State Beach. This small park is a good place for a swim, picnic, or view of the surrounding mountain ranges. | Rte. 11 | 603/293–7821 | $2.50 | Daily.

Gunstock Recreation Area and Ski Area. The recreation area at Gunstock, 5 mi south of Gilford, has an Olympic-size pool, a children's playground, hiking trails, mountain bike rentals, and trails, horses, paddleboats, and a campground. In winter, visitors come to ski (both down-hill and cross-country) and snowboard. The ski area, which dates from the 1930s, is best for beginners and intermediates. A tubing park with 10 runs and multipassenger tubes and the 15 trails for night skiing and boarding make Gunstock a favorite with families. | Rte. 11A | 603/293–4341 or 800/486–7862 | www.gunstock.com | Daily. Activities are seasonal, call for information.

Gunstock Campground. A full-service campground with 275 sites, amenities, and activi-ties including horseback riding, paddleboats, mountain biking, a playground, picnic area, and rec center. | Rte. 11A | 603/293–4341 or 800/486–7862 | fax 603/293–4318 | www.gun-stock.com | $24–$30 | Mid-May–mid-Oct. and Dec.–Mar.

Meadowbrook Farm Musical Arts Center. The largest musical venue in the lakes region that has big name acts in summertime. | Meadowbrook La. | 603/293–4700 | fax 603/293–0269 | www.meadowbrookevents.com.

ON THE CALENDAR
JULY–AUG.: *New Hampshire Music Festival.* A classical music concert series that has been in existence since 1952. | Gilford Middle/High School | 603/524–1000.
OCT.: *Annual Gunstock Octoberfest.* Includes German food, beer, live entertainment, and children's activities. | Gunstock Recreation Area | 603/293–4341.

Dining
Patricks Pub and Eatery. American. The bronze statue of the restaurant founder's father holding a beer stein at the entrance let's you know you're in for a fun meal. The pub area has eight TVs for the 350 or so "Sports Club" members whose custom beer mugs hang around the bar. The smoke-free Emerald Room is a bit more refined, but still relaxed and known for the legendary seafood chowder and the rotisserie cooked lamb, turkey, and prime rib. Live music, comedy shows, and talent nights. Outdoor dining. Kids' menu. | Junction Rtes. 11 and 11B | 603/293–0841 | $8–$16 | AE, D, MC, V.

Lodging
B. Mae's Resort Inn & Suites. A modern two-story motel with large rooms. Restaurant, bar. Cable TV, some in-room VCRs. 2 pools (1 indoor). Hot tub. Exercise equipment. Video games. | 17 Harris Shore Rd. | 603/293–7526 or 800/458–3877 | fax 603/293–4340 | 59 rooms, 24 suites | $99–$185 | AE, D, DC, MC, V.

Bay Side Inn. A quaint two-story lodge with 300 ft of waterfront in Alton, 16 mi south of Gilford. Each room has a balcony with views of Lake Winnepesaukee and the White Moun-tains. Cottage units have full kitchens. Complimentary Continental breakfast. No air-con-ditioning, some kitchenettes, some microwaves, some refrigerators, no smoking, cable TV. Lake. Beach, dock, water sports, boating. Fishing. No pets. | Rte. 11D, Alton Bay | 603/875–5005 | fax 603/875–1040 | info@bayside–inn.com | www.bayside–inn.com | 18 rooms, 5 cot-tages | $125 | Closed Oct.–Apr. | MC, V.

Belknap Point Motel. This motel is on a lake and has views of the water and Mt. Wash-ington. Picnic area. Some kitchenettes, cable TV. Beach, dock, boating. | Rte. 11, 1 mi east of Rte. 11B | 603/293–7511 | fax 603/528–3552 | hblinn@cyberportal.net | www.bpmotel.com | 16 rooms | $58–$108 | AE, D, MC, V.

Gunstock Inn, Tavern and Fitness Center. A country-style resort near the Gunstock recre-ation area. Some rooms have views of Lake Winnipeesaukee. Restaurant, bar, compli-mentary Continental breakfast. Cable TV. Indoor pool. Sauna, steam room. Health club. No pets. | 580 Cherry Valley Rd. (Rte. 11A) | 603/293–2021 or 800/654–0180 | fax 603/293–2050 | www.gunstockinn.com | 21 rooms, 4 suites | $79–$140 | D, MC, V.

GILFORD

INTRO
ATTRACTIONS
DINING
LODGING

GLEN

(Nearby towns also listed: Bartlett, Conway, Intervale, Jackson, Mt. Washington, North Conway, Pinkham Notch)

Although little more than a crossroads, busy Glen is the link between North Conway, Jackson, Franconia, and Bartlett. As such, it has become home to a few of the man-made attractions in the Mt. Washington Valley, as well as a number of restaurants and lodgings.

Information: Mt. Washington Valley Chamber of Commerce | Box 2300, Rte. 16, North Conway, 03860 | 603/356–3171 | fax 603/356–7069 | www.mtwashingtonvalley.org.

Attractions

Heritage New Hampshire. A trip to Heritage New Hampshire is as close as you may ever come to experiencing time travel. Special effects usher you aboard the HMS *Reliance* and carry you from a village in 1634 England over tossing seas to the New World. You'll saunter along Portsmouth's streets in the late 1700s, hear a speech by George Washington, then continue on to the present day. | Rte. 16 | 603/383–9776 | www.heritagenh.com | $10 | Mid-June–mid-Oct., daily 9–5.

Story Land. Stroll through this children's theme park, which has life-size storybook and nursery-rhyme characters. High points include the 16 rides and four shows, the Victorian-theme river-raft ride, farm family variety show, and simulated voyage to the moon, among others. | Rte. 16 at U.S. 302 | 603/383–4186 | www.storylandnh.com | $17 | Mid-June–Labor Day, daily 9–6; Labor Day–mid. Oct., Sat., Sun. 10–5.

Dining

Prince Place Restaurant at Bernerhof Inn. Continental. White linen tablecloths, a fireplace, and lots of stained glass set the scene. Try the Wiener schnitzel—veal sautéed in bread crumbs. Kids' menu. | U.S. 302 | 603/383–4414 | No lunch Nov.–June | $17–$22 | AE, D, MC, V.

Red Parka Pub. American. A comfortable, unpretentious steak house where you can sit in a World War I–era train car. Try the ribs. Open-air dining. Salad bar. Entertainment week-ends. Kids' menu. | U.S. 302 | 603/383–4344 | No lunch | $10–$20 | AE, D, DC, MC, V.

Lodging

Bernerhof Inn. Period furnishings embellish this Victorian 1890s-era home with original woodwork, 1 mi west of Glen. Restaurant, complimentary breakfast. Room service, some in-room hot tubs, cable TV. | U.S. 302 | 603/383–9132 or 800/548–8007 | fax 603/383–0809 | www.bernerhofinn.com | 9 rooms | $95–$140 | AE, D, MC, V.

Covered Bridge House Bed and Breakfast. Perched on the banks of the Saco River, this inn is named for the 1850s covered bridge on the property. Rooms are filled with quilts and colonial antiques. Picnic area, complimentary breakfast. No smoking, cable TV in common area. Hot tub. Beach. Fishing. Playground. No pets. | U.S. 302 | 603/383–9109 or 800/232–9109 | cbhouse@landmarknet.net | www.coveredbridgehouse.com | 6 rooms (2 with shared bath) | $79–$89 | Closed Apr. | AE, D, MC, V.

Red Apple Inn. A motor inn, in a rustic wooded setting close to local attractions. Picnic area. Refrigerators, no smoking, cable TV. Pool. Game room w/pool table, video games, large screen TV. Playground. | U.S. 302, 1½ mi. west of junction U.S. 302 and Rte. 16 junction | 603/383–9680 | www.redapple.com | 16 rooms | $49–$130 | Closed 1st wk Nov. | AE, D, MC, V.

Storybook Resort Inn. A motor inn that's great for families. Restaurant, bar, picnic area. Some refrigerators, cable TV, some in-room VCRs. 2 pools (1 indoor). 2 hot tubs (1 outdoor). Tennis. Exercise equipment. Video games. Playground, laundry facilities. | Junction U.S. 302

and Rte. 16 | 603/383–6800 | fax 603/383–4678 | www.storybookresort.com | 78 rooms | $89–$149 | AE, D, DC, MC, V.

GORHAM

(Nearby town also listed: Jefferson, Mt. Washington, Pinkham Notch)

During the heyday of the railroads, Gorham was an important White Mountains entry point for tourists who came via the Atlantic and St. Lawrence Railroad from Portland, Maine. Although Gorham's importance declined with the advent of the automobile, recent interest in watchable wildlife, specifically moose, has put Gorham back on the map.

Information: Town of Gorham Information Center | 69 Main St., Gorham, 03581 | 603/466–3103. **Northern White Mountains Chamber of Commerce** | 164 Main St., Box 298, Berlin, 03570 | 603/752–6060 or 800/992–7480 | fax 603/752–1002 | www.northern-whitemountains.com.

Attractions

Gorham Historical Society. This restored 1907 railroad station is as much a monument to the history of rails in New England as it is a local museum. The baggage rooms, ticket and telegraph rooms, and men's and women's waiting rooms house local memorabilia. Two locomotives (one steam, one diesel) and two boxcars, mostly predating 1930, are on display. | 25 Railroad St. | 603/466–5570 | Free | Memorial Day–Nov., call for hrs.

Libby Memorial Pool & Recreation Area. This town area, open to nonresidents, has an outdoor pool and softball and field-hockey areas. | Rte. 16 | 603/466–2101 | Daily dawn–dusk.

Moose Brook State Park. This park, 2 mi west of Gorham, is popular with anglers and hikers. The park campground has 42 tent sites nestled amid spruce and birch trees. | U.S. 2 | 603/466–3860 | www.nhparks.state.nh.us | $2.50 | Daily.

Mt. Washington. Gorham is the largest town in the vicinity of Mt. Washington, which is only 10 mi south of Gorham. *See* Mt. Washington | Rte. 16.

Northern Forest Moose Tours. One of the favorite pastimes in this region is looking for moose. Although you may spot one of these large, ungainly, and elusive members of the deer family on your own, these bus tours are an almost sure bet. | 164 Main St., Berlin | 603/466–3103 or 603/752–6060 | www.northernwhitemountains.com | $15 | Memorial Day thru Columbus Day; Call for hrs.

ON THE CALENDAR
JULY: *July 4th Celebration Week.* The Independence Day events include concessions, rides, parades, and fireworks. | Gorham Common | 603/752–6060.

Dining
Birches Grill. American. Relax with a drink by the lounge fireplace before moving into the main dining room, which is well suited to large groups. Settle in to a home-style breakfast of waffles and omelets, or try the Maine crab cakes and the hand-cut sirloin selections from the dinner menu. | 128 Main St. | 603/466–5424 | No lunch | $9–$15 | AE, MC, V.

Town and Country Motor Inn Dining Room. Continental. This large banquet hall and dining room serves up house specials like the prime rib dinner, seafood Newburg, and filet mignon and is suitable for large groups. Live entertainment. Kids' menu. | U.S. 2, Shelburne | 603/466–3315 or 800/325–4386 | fax 603/466–3315 | $11–$17 | AE, D, DC, MC, V.

Wilfred's. American. Serving up hearty fare to locals and tourists since 1971, this local landmark is just across the street from Gorham High School and is known for roast turkey dinner with mashed potatoes, gravy, vegetables, cranberry sauce, and traditional Indian pudding, served warm with ice cream. | 117 Main St. | 603/466–2380 | $9–$12 | AE, D, MC, V.

Lodging

Gorham Motor Inn. Modern motel. Bar. Some refrigerators, cable TV. Pool. Some pets allowed (fee). | 324 Main St. | 603/466–3381 or 800/445–0913 | 39 rooms | $40–$86 | AE, D, MC, V.

Mount Madison Motel. A nicely landscaped motor inn. Some refrigerators, cable TV. Pool. Playground. | 365 Main St. | 603/466–3622 or 800/851–1136 | www.mtmadisonmotel.com | 33 rooms | $56–$78 | Closed Nov.–mid-Apr. | AE, D, MC, V.

Philbrook Farm Inn. The country's oldest inn continuously run by the same family (since 1861), this vintage inn sits on 900 acres of fields and forests in nearby Shelburne. Dining room, complimentary breakfast. No air-conditioning, no room phones. Pool. Cross-country skiing. | 881 North Rd., Shelburne | 603/466–3831 | www.innbook.com | 18 rooms (9 with shared bath), 7 cottages | $115–$145 | Closed Nov. 1–Christmas and Apr. | MAP | No credit cards.

Royalty Inn. A large, family-owned motor inn. Restaurant, bar. Some refrigerators, cable TV, in-room VCRs. 2 pools (1 indoor). Hot tub, sauna. Health club. Video games. Laundry facilities. Business services. Pets allowed (fee). | 130 Main St. | 603/466–3312 or 800/437–3529 | fax 603/466–5802 | innkeeper@royaltyinn.com | www.royaltyinn.com | 90 rooms | $58–$78 | AE, D, DC, MC, V.

Top Notch Motor Inn. Spacious motel-style accommodations in a clean, friendly, setting. There are larger rooms for families or groups. Refrigerators, cable TV. Outdoor pool. Hot tub. Laundry facilities. Pets allowed (deposit). | 265 Main St. (Rte. 16) | 603/466–5496 | www.top-notch.com | 36 rooms | $44–$89 | Closed mid-Oct.–mid.-May | MC, V.

Town and Country Motor Inn. A family owned, two-story inn in the heart of the White Mountains that has large guest rooms. Restaurant, bar with entertainment. Indoor pool. Hot tub, sauna, steam room. Health club. Video games. | U.S. 2, Shelburne | 603/466–3315 or 800/325–4386 | fax 603/466–3315 | labnon@townandcountryinn.com | www.townandcountryinn.com | 156 rooms, 4 suites | $50–$100 | AE, D, DC, MC, V.

GRAFTON

MAP 7, D8

(Nearby town also listed: Enfield)

Commercial production of mica in this country began here in 1803 when Sam Ruggles put his large family to work mining the mica that was used for lamp chimneys and stove windows. As demand for his product grew, Ruggles kept the location of his mine a secret, some say only making the trip to it at night. Although commercial mining ended in 1959, visitors enjoy exploring the caves on Isinglass Mountain.

Attractions

Ruggles Mine. You are allowed to collect the more than 150 minerals found in this mine at the top of Isinglass Mountain. Opened in 1803, it's an open-pit mine that also includes arched tunnels and giant rooms. | Off U.S. 4 | 603/523–4275 | $15 | June 15–Oct.–15, daily 9–6; Oct. 15–June 15, weekends only 9–5.

ON THE CALENDAR

AUG.: *Old Home Days.* You can watch as area residents pull out all the stops and celebrate their hometown spirit at this three-day festival of dining, races, music food, and local crafts. The main events take place in Canaan, 8 mi west of Grafton. | The Town Green, Canaan | 603/523–7310.

Lodging

Inn on Canaan Street. One of the first planned communities in New England was on Canaan Street, 8 mi northwest of Grafton. Much of the area, including this hospitable Federal inn, is on the National Register of Historic Places. Fourteen wooded acres with frontage on Canaan Street Lake, three fireplaces, and wraparound porches with views make this a nice place to stay. Rooms are quaint and furnished with wicker, antiques, and oriental ornaments. Complimentary breakfast. No air-conditioning, no smoking, no room phones, TV in common area. Lake. Hiking, dock. Fishing. Cross-country skiing. Library. No pets. | 92 Canaan St., Canaan | 603/523–7310 | theinnoncanaanst@endor.com | 4 rooms | $85–$100 | MC, V.

HAMPTON

(Nearby towns also listed: Exeter, Hampton Beach, Rye)

In the 17th century, Hampton was called Winnacunnet, which means "beautiful place of pines." The center of the early town was Meeting House Green, where 42 stones still represent the town's founding families. Today, Hampton is mainly residential.

Information: Hampton Beach Area Chamber of Commerce | 490 Lafayette Rd., Hampton, 03842 | 603/926–8717 | www.hamptonbeach.org.

Attractions

Applecrest Farm Orchards. A pick-your-own fruit orchard, 4 mi south of Hampton, with seasonal activites including hay rides, pumpkin picking, and live music on weekends. | 133 Exeter Rd. (Rte. 88), Hampton Falls | 603/926–3721 | fax 603/926–0666 | www.applecrest.com | Daily 10–dusk.

Meeting House Green. Here in the center of Hampton, you will find 42 stones commemorating the families who founded the city in 1638. | 40 Park Ave. | 603/929–0781.

Raspberry Farm. Choose from eight varieties of berries at this pick-your-own berry farm 8 mi southeast of Hampton. Jams, sauces, and home-baked treats can be found in the farm store. | Rte. 84, Hampton Falls | 603/926–6604 | Early June–mid-Oct., weekdays 12–5, weekends 9–5 | Call for picking conditions.

Tidewater Campground. A good place for family camping, with picnic area, swimming pool and basketball court. Choose from 230 camping sites, 180 with full RV hookup. | 160 Lafayette Rd. | 603/926–5474 | $25–$30 | Mid-May–mid-Oct.

Tuck Memorial Museum. This small museum has displays on the town's early history, farm implements, and early fire-fighting equipment. | 40 Park Ave. | 603/929–0781 | Free | June–Sept., Wed.–Fri. and Sun. 1–4, or by appointment.

ON THE CALENDAR

JUNE–SEPT.: *New Playhouse at Hampton.* A summer theater festival and live performances. | 603/926–3073.

Dining

Galley Hatch Restaurant & Bakery. Seafood. A local landmark since 1970, this restaurant is known for fried clams, haddock, and shrimp. It's next to Hampton Cinemas, and dinner-and-movie packages are available. | 325 Lafayette Rd. | 603/926–6152 | $9–$18 | AE, D, DC, MC, V.

Newick's Fisherman's Landing. Seafood. A casual spot with many marine motifs, including detailed ship models. Kids' menu. | 845 Lafayette Rd. | 603/926–7646 | $12–$35 | AE, D, MC, V.

99 Restaurant. American. A family-oriented, New England pub–style restaurant fixed with local memorabilia, serving a host of appetizers, pasta, chicken, and steaks. Try the house-special broiled sirloin tips or the New England roast turkey dinner. | 831 Lafayette Rd., Seabrook | 603/474–5999 | $8–$11 | AE, D, DC, MC, V.

Old Salt Eating and Drinking Place. American. The ocean views, nautical knickknacks, and plenty of fresh seafood make this a favorite landmark among locals. There is an expanded outdoor deck with live music and seating for large groups. House specialties include fried clams, oysters, chowders, steaks, fish, and late-night pizza menu. Don't miss the Friday-Night Fish Fry. Kids' menu. | 83 Ocean Blvd. | 603/926–8322 | $6–$13 | AE, MC, V.

Lodging

Curtis Field House. Ten lovely acres surround this antiques-filled B&B. Complimentary breakfast. No smoking, no room phones. | 735 Exeter Rd. | 603/929–0082 | 3 rooms | $75 | Closed Nov.–May | No credit cards.

Hampton Falls Inn. A modern motel whose individually decorated rooms have views of the neighboring farmland from private balconies. Restaurant. In-room data ports, microwaves, refrigerators. Indoor pool. Hot tub. Video games. Laundry facilities. Business services. Pets allowed (free). | 11 Lafayette Rd. (U.S. 1), Hampton Falls | 603/926–9545 or 800/356–1729 | www.hamptonfallsinn.com | 33 rooms, 15 suites | $99–$169 | AE, D, DC, MC, V.

Hampton Village Resort. Complimentary Continental breakfast. Microwaves, refrigerators, cable TV. Indoor pool. Hot tub, sauna. | 660 Lafayette Rd. (U.S. 1) | 603/926–6775 or 800/292–9990 | fax 603/929–7332 | 40 rooms | $89–$155 | AE, MC, V.

Inn of Hampton. A modern motel with a glass-paneled facade and large rooms. Restaurant. In-room data ports, some kitchenettes, microwaves, refrigerators, cable TV, some in-room VCRs. Indoor pool. Hot tub. Gym. Video games. Laundry facilities. Business services. | 815 Lafayette Rd. (U.S. 1) | 603/926–6771 or 800/423–4561 | fax 603/929–2160 | www.theinnofhampton.com | 71 rooms | $119–$139; suites $169–$189 | AE, D, DC, MC, V.

Lamie's Inn. A country inn in the center of town. Restaurant, bar with entertainment. Cable TV. Business services. Airport shuttle, free parking. | 490 Lafayette Rd. (U.S. 1) | 603/926–0330 | fax 603/929–0017 | www.lamiesinn.com | 32 rooms, 1 suite | $79–$125 | AE, DC, MC, V.

Victoria Inn. A quiet B&B in a 19th-century carriage house that is ½ mi from the beach. There are antique furnishings, a gazebo, and a wraparound porch. Complimentary breakfast. No smoking, cable TV. Bicycles. | 430 High St. | 603/929–1437 | fax 603/929–0747 | www.thevictoriainn.com | 6 rooms | $95–$130 | MC, V.

HAMPTON BEACH

MAP 7, H11

(Nearby towns also listed: Exeter, Hampton, Rye)

Hampton Beach is New Hampshire's longest beach. The 3-mi strand is lined with arcades, T-shirt shops, ice-cream vendors, and fried-dough stands. Nearly deserted in winter, the town attracts an estimated 200,000 people on the 4th of July and on busy weekends in summer.

Information: **Chamber of Commerce** | 490 Lafayette Rd., Hampton, 03842 | 603/926–8717 | fax 603/964–7293 | www.hamptonbeach.org.

Attractions

Al Gauron's Deep Sea Fishing and Whale Watching. A private three-boat charter with fireworks cruises and seasonal fishing and whale expeditions. | 1 Ocean Blvd. | 603/926–2469 or 800/985–7820 | www.deepseafishing-nh.com | Apr.–Oct., daily. Call for departure schedules.

Fuller Gardens. Arthur Shurtleff designed this turn-of-the-20th-century estate garden in the Colonial Revival style. In the 1930s, the Olmsted brothers added to it. Now, the garden blooms all summer long, with 2,000 rosebushes of every shade and type. Other plantings include a hosta display garden and a serenity-inspiring Japanese garden. | 10 Willow Ave., North Hampton | 603/964–5414 | www.fullergardens.org | $5 | May–mid-Oct., daily 10–6.

Hampton Beach Casino Ballroom. On summer evenings, this live performance venue is packed with vacationers and locals who come to see name entertainers. Tina Turner, Jay Leno, and Loretta Lynn are just a few who have played here. | 169 Ocean Beach Blvd. | 603/926–4541, 603/929–4201 event hot line | www.casinoballroom.com | June–Oct.

Hampton Beach State Park. The state park 3 mi south of Hampton Beach has lifeguards, a bathhouse, and a sandy beach. | Rte. 1A | 603/926–3784 | Parking fee | Daily.

ON THE CALENDAR

MAY–AUG.: *Nightly Concert Series at the Sea Shell Stage.* Over 80 free outdoor concerts with everything from bluegrass to big band. | The Sea Shell Stage at Hampton Beach | 603/926–8718 | fax 603/964–7293 | www.hamptonbeach.org.

JUNE: *Annual Hampton Beach Hobie Cat Regatta.* A regatta of catamaran races. | 603/926–8718.

JULY–AUG.: *Fireworks at Hampton Beach.* There are fireworks each Wednesday evening in summer. | 603/926–8718.

JULY–AUG.: *Karaoke on the Seashell Stage.* Friday-evening karaoke sing-alongs on an outdoor stage. | 603/926–8718.

JULY–AUG.: *Talent Show on the Seashell Stage.* A weekly talent show on an outdoor stage on Monday evenings. | 603/926–8718.

AUG.: *Children's Festival.* Five days of free activities for families, including sand-castle contests, costume parades, magic shows, and other events. | 603/926–8718.

SEPT.: *Hampton Beach Annual Seafood Festival and Sidewalk Fair.* A three-day festival on Ocean Boulevard and the Hampton Beach boardwalk with three stages of live music, 60 restaurants serving up their best fare, entertainment, fireworks, a skydiving show, local crafts, and more. | Ocean Blvd. | 603/926–8718 | fax 603/964–7293 | www.hamptonbeach.org.

Dining

Ashworth by the Sea. American. Enjoy views of the sea beyond Hampton Beach while sampling from an eclectic menu of casual café cuisine, elaborate buffets, and gourmet seafood dinners, including several versions of lobster. | 295 Ocean Ave. | 603/926–6762 or 800/345–6736 | fax 603/926–2002 | $11–$25 | AE, D, DC, MC, V.

Cat in the Custard Cup. American. The setting of this 18th-century building takes you straight back to colonial America. Try the Mile High Seafood combo and the porterhouse steak. Happy hour 4-6 PM. Kids' menu. | 490 Lafayette Rd. | 603/929–2020 | $9–$13 | AE, MC, V.

Ron's Landing at Rocky Point. Contemporary. In an oceanfront setting with a view of Hampton Beach, this restaurant serves seafood, pasta, veal, and beef. Try the veal and lobster pistachio in a Frangelico creme sauce. Sunday brunch. | 379 Ocean Blvd. | 603/929–2122 | No lunch | $16–$25 | AE, D, DC, MC, V.

Lodging

Ashworth by the Sea. A family-owned four-story hotel on the beach with a sundeck and many balconies. Restaurant, bar with entertainment, dining room. In-room data ports, cable TV, some in-room VCRs. Indoor-outdoor pool. Beauty salon. Business services. | 295 Ocean Blvd. | 603/926–6762 or 800/345–6736 | fax 603/926–2002 | www.ashworthhotel.com | 105 rooms | $130–$210 | AE, D, DC, MC, V.

D.W.'s Oceanside Inn. A late-19th-century beach-house inn across the street from the ocean. Complimentary breakfast. No smoking, cable TV in common area. Beach. | 365 Ocean Blvd. | 603/926–3542 | fax 603/926–3549 | oceansid@nh.ultranet.com | www.nh.ultranet.com/~oceansid | 10 rooms | $110–$160 | Closed mid-Oct.–mid-May | AE, D, MC, V.

Hampshire Inn. This three-story motel with nicely decorated suites is in nearby Seabrook. Complimentary Continental breakfast. In-room data ports, microwaves, refrigerators, some in-room hot tubs, cable TV. Indoor pool. Hot tub. Gym. Laundry facilities. Business services. Airport shuttle, free parking. | Rte. 107 | 603/474–5700 or 800/932–8520 | fax 603/474–2886 | www.hamphshireinn.com | 35 rooms | $115–$159 | AE, D, DC, MC, V.

Jonathan's Motel. A friendly beachfront getaway perfect for families with kids. All rooms have private balconies and pull-out couches. Complimentary Continental breakfast. Microwaves, refrigerators, cable TV. | 415 Ocean Blvd. | 603/926–6631 or 800/634–8243 | fax 603/926–6088 | 32 rooms | $115–$135 | D, MC, V.

Regal Inn of Hampton Beach. Clean, basic hotel rooms, one block from the waterfront and beach. The kitchenette suites are good for families. Complimentary Continental breakfast. Refrigerators, some in-room hot tubs, cable TV. Outdoor pool. Hot tub. Video games. No pets. | 162 Ashworth Ave. | 603/926–7758 or 800/445–6782 | fax 603/926–7957 | info@regalinn.com | www.regalinn.com | 36 rooms | $85–$189 | AE, D, MC, V.

Sands Resort at Hampton Beach. Modern, fully furnished three-room suites with pull-out couches, dinette sets, and private balconies. Restaurant, bar. Kitchenettes, microwaves, refrigerators, cable TV. Hot tub, sauna. Exercise room. No pets. | 32 Ashworth Ave. | 603/929–0685 | 84 rooms | $99–$129 | AE, D, MC, V.

HANOVER

MAP 7, C8

(Nearby towns also listed: Enfield, Lyme; Norwich, VT)

It was in 1769 that Eleazar Wheelock founded Hanover's Dartmouth College, the northernmost Ivy League school, to educate Abenaki Indians "and other youth." When he arrived, the town consisted of about 20 families, making Dartmouth's motto, *Vox Clamantis in Deserto* (a voice crying in the wilderness), especially apt. The college and the town grew symbiotically, though, and today Hanover is synonymous with Dartmouth. But it also has a respected medical center and is the cultural center for the Upper Valley region.

Information: Chamber of Commerce | 216 Nugget Building, Box 5105, Hanover, 03755 | 603/643–3115 | fax 603/643–5606 | www.hanoverchamber.org.

Attractions

Ava Gallery and Arts Center. Year-round exhibits by renowned New Hampshire and Vermont artists, 6 mi south of Hanover. Art education classes for all ages. | 11 Bank St., Lebanon | 603/448–3117 | Free | Tues.–Sat. 11–5.

Dartmouth College. The center of Hanover has a decidedly collegiate atmosphere due to the presence of the northernmost Ivy League college, founded by Reverend Eleazar Wheelock in 1769. | Main and Wheelock Sts. | 603/646–1110 | www.dartmouth.edu.

Dartmouth Row. The first building built by Reverend Eleazar Wheelock for the fledgling Dartmouth College was a simple log hut. Today, the college's buildings are in many architectural styles. The four classroom buildings on Dartmouth Row, one of which dates from 1784, are among the oldest. | East side of Green.

Baker Memorial Library. Among the buildings clustered around the Green is the college library, which houses literary treasures including 17th-century editions of Shakespeare's works. Murals painted by José Clemente Orozco depict the story of civilization on the American continents. | 1 Elm St. | 603/646–2560 | Free | Daily 8–8 when college is in session.

Hood Museum of Art. The Hood Museum has exhibits on African, Peruvian, Oceanic, Asian, European, and American art. Among its notable holdings are the Picasso painting *Guitar on a Table*, silver made by Paul Revere, and a set of Assyrian reliefs from the 9th century BC. | E. Wheelock St. | 603/646–2808 | Free | Tues.–Sat. 10–5, Wed. 10–9, Sun. 12–5.

Hopkins Center for the Arts. The Hopkins Center, which is connected to the Hood Museum, will appear familiar to anyone who has visited the Metropolitan Opera House at Lincoln Center in New York City: architect Wallace K. Harrison designed the two buildings at about the same time. Some say the Hopkins Center was the prototype for the Metropolitan. The complex includes a 900-seat theater for film and music, a 400-seat theater for plays, and a black box theater for new plays. | E. Wheelock St. | 603/646–2422.

Dartmouth Skiway. This small ski area about 3 mi east in Lyme has 30 trails, a vertical drop of 968 ft, and a base lodge. Three-quarters of the terrain is rated for beginners and intermediates. | Grafton Tpk. | 603/795–2143 | www.dartmouth.edu/~skiway/ | Mid-Dec.–Mar., daily.

League of New Hampshire Craftsmen. One of seven stores that exhibit and sell contemporary and traditional crafts made by members of the League. | 13 Lebanon St. | 603/643–5050 | www.nhcrafts.org | Mon.–Sat. 10–5.

Webster Cottage. This cottage is named for statesman Daniel Webster, who lived here while an undergraduate at Dartmouth. It is furnished with Shaker items and Webster memorabilia. | 32 N. Main St. | 603/646–3371 | Free | June–mid-Oct., Wed., Sat., Sun. 2:30–4:30.

ON THE CALENDAR
FEB.: *Dartmouth Winter Carnival*. Ice sculptures, ski races, and other events are features of this carnival. | 603/643–1110.

Dining
★ **Hanover Inn.** Contemporary. With its Palladian windows, columns, and moldings, the elegant dining room evokes the feeling of a grand hotel. Try the rack of lamb. | Corner of Main and E. Wheelock Sts. | 603/646–8000 | Closed Sun., Mon. No lunch | $19–$27 | AE, D, DC, MC, V.

Jesse's. American. A casual spot with Victorian motifs that is known for steak and seafood. Open-air dining. Salad bar. Kids' menu. | Rte. 120 | 603/643–4111. | No lunch | $9–$22 | AE, MC, V.

Molly's Balloon. American. This restaurant has lots of glass and brass, plus open-air dining in warm weather. It is known for its burgers and brick-oven pizza. No smoking. | 43 S. Main St. | 603/643–2570 | $9–$15 | AE, MC, V.

Ramunto's Brick and Brew. Pizza. The centerpiece of this very casual restaurant is a wood-fired, brick pizza oven. You can watch food being prepared and pizza dough being tossed. Sandwiches are also served. | 68 S. Main St. | 603/643–9500 | $10–$18 | AE, MC, V.

Lodging
Chieftain. You can see the Connecticut River from your room in this small motel. Picnic area, complimentary Continental breakfast. | 84 Lyme Rd. (Rte. 10) | 603/643–2550 or 800/845–3557 | fax 603/643–5265 | 22 rooms | $89 | AE, D, DC, MC, V.

Hanover Inn at Dartmouth College. This late-18th-century redbrick building feels very much a part of the college, which owns it. Restaurant, bar. Room service, cable TV, some in-room VCRs. Sauna. Driving range, putting green. Exercise equipment. Business services. Airport shuttle, parking (fee). Pets allowed. | Main and Wheelock Sts. | 603/643–4300 or 800/443–7024 | fax 603/646–3744 | hanover.inn@dartmouth.edu | www.dartmouth.edu/inn | 92 rooms, 22 suites | $250–$310 | AE, D, DC, MC, V.

Moose Mountain Lodge. This secluded country lodge in nearby Etna was built as a ski lodge in the 1930s. It sits on 350 acres with views of the Connecticut River valley and the Green Mountains. Rate includes breakfast and dinner. No air-conditioning, no smoking, no room phones. Cross-country skiing. | Box 272, 33 Moose Mountain Lodge Rd., Etna | 603/643–3529 | fax 603/643–4119 | meeze@aol.com | www.moosemountainlodge.com | 12 rooms (using 5 shared baths) | $160–$190 | Closed Nov.–mid-Dec. and Apr.–May | AP or MAP | MC, V.

HANOVER

INTRO
ATTRACTIONS
DINING
LODGING

Trumbull House Bed & Breakfast. A white colonial-style house on 16 acres 4 mi east of Hanover. Complimentary breakfast. In-room data ports, no smoking, some in-room hot tubs, cable TV. Pond. Cross-country skiing. Business services. | 40 Etna Rd. | 603/643–2370 or 800/651–5141 | fax 603/643–2430 | bnb@valley.net | www.trumbullhouse.com | 4 rooms, 1 suite | $125–$250, $250 suite | AE, D, DC, MC, V.

White Goose Inn. The smaller part of this charming Federal-Colonial-style inn was built in 1770, with a beautiful brick extension added in 1833. A large porch affords views of the rural scenery. Complimentary breakfast. No smoking, no room phones, no TV. Kids by arrangement only. | Rte. 10, Orford | 603/353–4812 or 800/358–4267 | fax 603/353–4543 | www.whitegooseinn.com | 10 rooms (2 with shared bath) | $105–$125 | MC, V.

HENNIKER

MAP 7, D10

(Nearby towns also listed: Hillsborough, Warner)

Once a mill town producing bicycle rims and other goods, Henniker is now the home of New England College and Pats Peak Ski Area. The unusual town name was bestowed by Governor Wentworth, who chose it to honor his friend, London merchant and member of Parliament John Henniker. Residents are proud to be from "the only Henniker in the world."

Attractions

Pats Peak Ski Area. With 710 vertical ft and 20 winding trails and slopes, Pats Peak (3 mi south of Henniker) feels friendly with an old-time New England flavor. | Flanders Rd. off Rte. 114 | 603/428–3245, 800/742–7287 for snow conditions | www.patspeak.com | Dec.–late Mar., daily.

ON THE CALENDAR

JUNE: *Festival New Hampshire.* New Hampshire's unique history is the focus of this five-day event 20 mi northeast of Henniker. More than 150 "tradition bearers" demonstrate their know-how in crafts, music, politics, food, and culture. There are also interactive workshops, programs, and exhibits. | Hopkinton State Fairgrounds, Contoocook | 603/224–1777 or 800/215–5181 | www.festivalnh.org.

Dining

Colby Hill Inn. Continental. Built in 1800, this property was once a working farm. The tavern, now serving as the dining room, has a glass wall overlooking the garden. Try Chicken Colby Hill, stuffed with lobster and leeks, or the Cajun Swordfish. No smoking. No kids under 8. | 3 The Oaks, off Western Ave. | 603/428–3281 | Closed 1 wk in Mar. No lunch | $10–$22 | AE, D, DC, MC, V.

Meeting House Inn and Restaurant. Continental. High ceilings and Christmas lights adorn this popular barn–turned–dining room. Hearty gourmet regional dishes include beef Wellington and the brandied seafood beurre blanc with lobster, shrimp, and scallops in a cream sauce. | 35 Flanders Rd. | 603/428–3228 | fax 603/428–6334 | $15–$26 | AE, MC, V.

Lodging

Colby Hill Inn. This historic farmhouse (circa 1800) has been used as tavern, church, meeting house, and private school. The inn sits on 5 acres and is filled with antiques and reproductions. Restaurant, complimentary breakfast. In-room data ports, no smoking, cable TV in common area, no TV. Pool. Ice-skating. Business services. No kids under 8. | 3 The Oaks, off Western Ave. | 603/428–3281 or 800/531–0330 | fax 603/428–9218 | info@colbyhillinn.com | www.colbyhillinn.com | 16 rooms (11 with shower only) | $95–$195 | AE, D, DC, MC, V.

Meeting House Inn and Restaurant. A late-1700s farmhouse with views of Pat's Peak ski area. The individually decorated rooms contain family antiques and books. Check out the hot tub and sauna in the greenhouse. Restaurant, bar, complimentary breakfast. No smoking. Hot tub, sauna. No pets. | 35 Flanders Rd., | 603/428–3228 | fax 603/428–6334 | meetinghouse@conknet.com | www.meetinghouseinn.com | 4 rooms, 2 suites | $65–$105 | AE, D, MC, V.

HILLSBOROUGH

(Nearby town also listed: Henniker)

Of the four villages that make up Hillsborough, Hillsborough Center is the oldest and most picturesque. Eighteenth-century houses surround its Green, many still occupied by descendants of the original settlers who founded the town in 1769. The road leading to it is winding and lined with farms. The whole village feels solid and timeless.

Not too far from the center is the Pierce Homestead, where Franklin Pierce, 14th president of the United States, was born and raised. His father, Benjamin Pierce, was a Revolutionary War hero and twice governor of New Hampshire. Franklin Pierce first entered politics as a state legislator while his father was governor.

Information: Chamber of Commerce | Box 541, Hillsborough, 03244 | 603/484–5858.

NEW HAMPSHIRE'S MONADNOCK REGION

The southwestern corner of New Hampshire has no major highways. Instead, country roads and rural routes wind around rolling hills and along scenic rivers. It is the quietest part of the state and its pleasures are the state's subtlest. Every town seems to have a pretty Common and at least one inviting country inn or romantic bed-and-breakfast. Antiques shops and craft studios far outnumber chain stores, and only Keene has anything that remotely resembles a mall.

Don't worry about finding enough to do, though. There are nice museums, including the Pierce Homestead in Hillsborough and the Fort at No. 4 in Charlestown. The Connecticut River, which forms the western boundary of the state and the region, has been designated as one of the nation's wild and scenic rivers. Canoeing is popular, but be sure to get advice from a local outfitter because parts of the river can be dangerous.

There are nice hikes here, like the one to the top of Mt. Monadnock, considered the most-climbed mountain in the world. Several state parks protect areas of particularly scenic beauty and offer additional opportunities for hiking, swimming, fishing, and boating. In winter, cross-country skiing is popular, and toward spring a visit to a maple-sugar producer is a must. The fall foliage in this part of the state equals that of the White Mountains, although the vistas are softer and more serene.

Related towns: Charlestown, Cornish, Hillsborough, Jaffrey, Keene, Peterborough

© Artville

Attractions

Fox State Forest. Hikers and cross-country skiers enjoy the 20 mi of trails here. There's an observation tower as well. | Center Rd. | 603/464–3453 | www.nhparks.state.nh.us | $2.50 | Daily.

Pierce Homestead. Franklin Pierce, the country's 14th president, was born in Hillsborough and lived in this house until he married. It is still decorated much as it was during Pierce's life. Members of the Hillsborough Historical Society provide guided tours. | Rte. 31 | 603/478–3165 | $2.50 | June and Sept.–Columbus Day, Sat. 10–4, Sun. 1–4; July–Aug., Mon.–Sat. 10–4, Sun. 1–4.

ON THE CALENDAR

JULY: *Hillsborough Balloon Festival & Fair.* This event includes a carnival, balloon rides, live entertainment, a pancake breakfast, and a 5K road race. | 603/464–5858.

Dining

German John's Bakery. Café. This authentic German takeout has traditional breads, South German pretzels, crusty rolls, and pastries—all made from scratch. Check out the animal sculptures and decorations made of bread. | 5 West Main St. | 603/464–5079 | Jan.–May, Thurs.–Sat.; Mid May–Christmas, Tues.–Sat (Open Sundays in July) | $2–$4 | No credit cards.

Lodging

Stonewall Farm Bed and Breakfast. A relaxed country air fills this 1785 Federal farmhouse inn on 7 peaceful acres. The 100 lilac trees and views of the surrounding farm are a real treat and complement the warm, simple rooms with wide pine floors and antiques. Dining room, picnic area, complimentary breakfast. No air-conditioning, no smoking, no room phones, TV in common area. Hiking. Cross-country skiing. Library. Playground. No kids under 8. No pets. | 235 Windsor Rd. | 603/478–1947 or 888/870–1947 | fax 603/478–5227 | stonewall_farm@hotmail.com | www.stonewallfarm.com | 5 rooms | $95–$125 | D, MC, V.

Weare House Bed and Breakfast. An 1809 colonial farmhouse on 12 acres of rolling hills 20 mi east of Hillsborough with a simple, old-world feeling. Exposed brick, hardwood floors and beams, and modest furnishings fill the common areas. Rooms are crisp and airy with antique beds, floral print stencils, and down comforters. There's also a barn full of farm animals. Complimentary breakfast. No smoking, no room phones, no TV. Hiking. Cross-country skiing. | 76 Quaker St., Weare | 603/529–2660 | information@thewearehouse.com | www.thewearehouse.com | 4 rooms (2 with shared bath) | $65–$85 | D, MC, V.

HOLDERNESS

MAP 7, E8

(Nearby towns also listed: Center Harbor, Center Sandwich, Plymouth)

Holderness's calm and quiet are a reflection of the peacefulness of Squam Lake, which the town borders. The setting for the movie *On Golden Pond,* starring Henry Fonda and Katharine Hepburn, Squam is currently the subject of a controversy between state legislators, who want to make it accessible to power boaters from other areas, and residents, who prefer to limit visiting boaters to canoes and other similar watercraft.

Information: Squam Lakes Area Chamber of Commerce | Box 665, Ashland, 03217 | 603/964–4494.

Attractions

Original Golden Pond Scenic Tours. Take a guided, entertaining boat tour of Squam Lake, setting for the film *On Golden Pond.* You can see the locations for the movie while learning about the natural history of this pristine lake and its most famous inhabitants, the loons. | 603/279–4405 | $12 | Memorial Day–Oct.

Squam Lakes Natural Science Center. The several trails at the 200-acre nature center include one where you will encounter black bears, bobcats, otters, and other native wildlife in trailside enclosures. Educational events at the center include the Up Close to Animals series in July and August, at which you can study such species as the red-shouldered hawk. The Children's Activity Center has interactive exhibits. | Rte. 113/25 | 603/968-7194 | $8 | May–Oct., daily 9:30–4:30.

Yogi Bear's Jellystone Park. A member of the Yogi Bear campground network on Route 32 N, 10 mi southeast of Holderness. Choose from 261 sites and cabin accommodations. The park has a general store, laundromat, rec hall, pool, hot tub, miniature golf, playground, and video games. | R.R. 1, Box 396, Ashland | 603/968-9000 | fax 603/968-7349 | www.yogibearnh.com | $6 | Daily 8-6; Mid-May–Columbus Day.

Dining

Common Man. Continental. This restaurant has old wood beams, chintz curtains, and period furnishings, plus a lounge furnished with comfy couches and chairs. Try the quiche of the day or the Nightmare casserole of ham, turkey, and broccoli with cheese. Open-air dining. Kids' menu. | 25 Main St., Ashland | 603/968-7030 | $9–$20 | AE, D, MC, V.

Manor on Golden Pond. Contemporary. This formal, circa-1900 English manor sits on 14 acres with a view of Squam Lake and the White Mountains. Tables are set with silver and white linen and the menu changes daily. Excellent wine cellar. No smoking. | Shepard Hill Rd. (U.S. 3) | 603/968-3348 | Reservations essential | No lunch | 3–course prix fixe $38, 5–course prix fixe $50 | AE, MC, V.

Walter's Basin. American. This casual restaurant, perched on the edge of Squam Lake, is named after Walter the prized trout in the film *On Golden Pond*. A nautical theme prevails throughout but is kept classy with granite tabletops, hardwood chairs and floors, and a beautiful view of the lake. The home-smoked trout is a local specialty as is the *Trafalgar*—a New York sirloin steak served with shrimp scampi. Kids' menu. Sunday brunch with live music. | Main St. (U.S. 3) | 603/968-4412 | $10–$24 | AE, MC, V.

Lodging

Glynn House Inn. A turn-of-the-20th-century Victorian inn 4 mi from Holderness in Ashland that offers complimentary sherry and chocolates. Picnic area, complimentary breakfast. No smoking, some in-room hot tubs, cable TV, no room phones. No kids under 7. | 43 Highland St., Ashland | 603/968-3775 or 800/637-9599 | fax 603/968-3129 | glynnhse@lr.net | www.new-hampshire-lodging.com | 9 rooms, 4 suites | $89–$159 | AE, MC, V.

KODAK'S TIPS FOR USING LIGHTING

Daylight
· Use the changing color of daylight to establish mood
· Use light direction to enhance subjects' properties
· Match light quality to specific subjects

Dramatic Lighting
· Anticipate dramatic lighting events
· Explore before and after storms

Sunrise, Sunset, and Afterglow
· Include a simple foreground
· Exclude the sun when setting your exposure
· After sunset, wait for the afterglow to color the sky

From *Kodak Guide to Shooting Great Travel Pictures* © 2000 by Fodor's Travel Publications

Inn on Golden Pond. A late-19th-century hideaway in the woods near Squam Lake. Complimentary breakfast. No smoking, cable TV in common area, no room phones, no TV. Hiking. No kids under 12. | U.S. 3 | 603/968–7269 | fax 603/968–9226 | innongp@lr.net | www.innongoldenpond.com | 8 rooms, 1 suite | $120–$145 | AE, MC, V.

★ **Manor on Golden Pond.** A turn-of-the-20th-century English manor overlooking Squam Lake and the White Mountains. Restaurant, bar, picnic area, complimentary breakfast. No smoking, some in-room hot tubs, cable TV, some in-room VCRs. Pool, lake. Tennis, beach. No kids under 12 in the inn. Business services, free parking. | Shepard Hill Rd. (U.S. 3) | 603/968–3348 or 800/545–2141 | fax 603/968–2116 | www.manorongoldenpond.com | 25 rooms in 4 buildings, 2 cottages | $150–$350 | AE, MC, V.

Mary Chase Inn. An 1895 country Victorian inn on 13 acres with period furnishings, hardwood floors, fireplaces, and views of Little Squam Lake. The inn is on a precipice overlooking the lake and has a 70-ft wraparound porch. Complimentary breakfast. No smoking, no room phones, TV in common room. Library. No kids under 12. No pets. | U.S. 3 | 603/968–9454 | mcinnb-b@worldpath.net | www.marychaseinn.com | 4 rooms (with 2 shared baths), 1 suite | $85–$125 | AE, D, DC, MC, V.

Pressed Petals Inn. An ornate, 1875 Victorian farmhouse inn with a wraparound porch. The common areas have wood floors and conversation nooks; the guest rooms are filled with antiques, oriental rugs, and quilts. The suites have gas fireplaces. Complimentary breakfast. No smoking, no room phones, no TV. Library. No kids under 10. | Shepard Hill Rd. | 603/968–4417 or 800/839–6205 | fax 603/968–3661 | pressedpetalsinn@fcgnetworks.com | www.pressedpetalsinn.com | 6 rooms, 2 suites | $115–$150 | D, MC, V.

INTERVALE

MAP 7, G6

(Nearby towns also listed: Bartlett, Conway, Glen, Jackson, North Conway)

To most visitors, Intervale is simply an extension of North Conway, because it straddles Route 16 to the north of that shopping mecca. Intervale, though, has the advantage of being slightly quieter than North Conway while still offering many amenities to visitors.

Information: **Mt. Washington Valley Chamber of Commerce** | Box 2300, Rte. 16, North Conway, 03860 | 603/356–3171 or 800/367–3364.

Attractions

Hartmann Model Railroad Museum. Railroad buffs marvel at the 2,000 engines, 5,000-plus cars and coaches, and 54 operating layouts (from G to Z scales). A café, crafts store, hobby shop, and outdoor train ride are also on the property. | 302 Town Hall Rd. | 603/356–9922 | www.hartmannrr.com | $5 | Daily 10–5.

Dining

New England Inn. Continental. Lots of polished wood and a big fireplace set the tone for dishes like the Sirloin steak au Poivre, with cracked peppercorns and mushrooms in a cognac sauce, or the Seafood Imperial—shrimp, lobster, and scallops in a champagne sauce. | Rte. 16A | 800/826–3466 | $13–19 | AE, D, MC, V.

Tuckerman's Tavern. American. You'll find a laid-back, après-ski attitude in the comfortable, wooded dining room of the New England Inn. You can enjoy light snacks at the bar or burgers, quesadillas, and shrimp alfredo at your fireside table. Live entertainment. Kids' menu. | Rte. 16A | 603/356–5541 or 800/826–3466 | www.tuckermanstavern.com | $6–$15 | AE, D, MC, V.

Lodging

The Forest: A Country Inn. This 1890 B&B sits on 25 acres. Complimentary breakfast. No smoking, no TV, TV in common area. Pool. | Rte. 16A | 603/356–9772 or 800/448–3534 | fax 603/356–5652 | forest@ncia.net | www.forest-inn.com | 8 rooms, 2 cottage rooms | $80–$160 | AE, D, MC, V.

New England Inn. A huge, 1809 farmhouse with B&B and cottage accommodations. The cottages are fully furnished and perfect for families or romantic getaways. 2 restaurants, bar, complimentary breakfast. Some kitchenettes, some in-room hot tubs, some room phones, no TV in some rooms. No pets. | Rte. 16A | 603/826–3466 or 800/826–3466 | inquiries@newenglandinn.com | www.newenglandinn.com | 11 rooms, 4 cottages | $90–$130, $135–$246 cottages | MAP available | AE, D, MC, V.

Perry's Motel and Cottages. Five minutes from Storyland on Route 16A, this motel has furnished cottages with grills and rooms with pull-out beds. There is also a large playground and resident llamas. Picnic area. No air-conditioning in some rooms, some kitchenettes, some refrigerators, no smoking, no cable TV in some rooms. Outdoor pool. Hot tub. Playground. No pets. | Rte. 16A | 603/356–2214 | fax 603/356–7049 | perrymotel@aol.com | www.perrysmotel.com | 23 rooms | $49–$99 | Closed Nov.–Apr. | D, MC, V.

Swiss Chalets Village Inn. There's an alpine motif to this hostelry. Picnic area, complimentary Continental breakfast. Refrigerators, no smoking, some in-room hot tubs, cable TV, in-room VCRs (and movies). Pool. 2 hot tubs (1 outdoor). Video games. Pets allowed (fee). | Rte. 16A, 2½ mi north of North Conway Scenic Vista | 603/356–2232 or 800/831–2727 | stay@swisschaletsvillage.com | www.swisschaletsvillage.com | 42 rooms | $49–$169 | AE, D, MC, V.

JACKSON

INTRO
ATTRACTIONS
DINING
LODGING

JACKSON

MAP 7, G6

(Nearby towns also listed: Bartlett, Conway, Glen, Intervale, North Conway, Pinkham Notch/Mt. Washington)

Jackson has a national reputation for its cross-country skiing. Trails start from the center of town, and most inns have connector trails right from the door. With one downhill ski area in town and three others just minutes away, the town is ideally situated for alpine skiers too.

Unlike neighboring North Conway, Jackson retains a New England village feeling that attracts both families and those looking for romantic getaways. The covered bridge leading into town and the river that flows through the center, the Ellis, are just two of the features that charm visitors in all seasons. In summer, skiing gives way to golf, tennis, and hiking. And, of course, fall brings spectacular foliage.

Information: Chamber of Commerce | Box 304, Jackson, 03846 | 603/383–9356 or 800/866–3334 | www.jacksonnh.com.

Attractions

Black Mountain. The atmosphere is fun, friendly, and informal at this ski area 2½ mi from Jackson. The mountain's 38 trails and two glades have good sections for beginners and intermediates, as well as a number of trails that keep experts happy. The southern exposure is welcome on cold days, and the view of Mt. Washington from the top of the double chair is breathtaking. | Rte. 16B | 603/383–4490 or 800/698–4490 | www.blackmt.com | Mid-Dec.–Mar., daily.

Honeymoon Covered Bridge. This bridge across the Ellis River, built around 1876, is the first thing that most visitors to Jackson see. A pedestrian sidewalk was added in 1930. | Rte. 16A/16.

★ **Jackson Ski Touring Foundation.** Rated as one of the nation's top cross-country skiing areas and by far the largest in New Hampshire, Jackson offers 98 mi of trails. Sixty miles are track groomed, 53 mi are skate groomed, and there are 38½ mi of marked and mapped backcountry trails. Right in the center of Jackson, the new headquarters, which serves skiers in winter and golfers in summer, is easy to find and well designed. Trails leave from the door. | Main St. (Rte. 16A) | 603/383–9355 or 800/927–6697 | www.jacksonxc.com | Dec.–mid-Apr., daily.

White Mountain National Forest. The town of Jackson is surrounded by the White Mountain National Forest. *See* Lincoln and North Woodstock. | Rte. 16 | www.fs.fed.us.

Wildcat Mountain Gondola. A round-trip gondola journey to the 4,100-ft peak of Wildcat Mountain with views of the White Mountain area that starts 10 mi north of Jackson. | Rte. 16 | 603/466–3326 | $8 | Mid-May–July 4, weekends, 10–4; July 4–Columbus Day, daily 10–4.

Dining

★ **Christmas Farm Inn.** Contemporary. The cuisine is truly sophisticated at this casual spot in an 18th-century inn. Try the Seafood Diane or stop by for a hearty breakfast. There is a harpist on Saturday evenings. | Rte. 16B | 603/383–4313 | Breakfast also available. No lunch | $17–$27 | AE, D, MC, V.

Inn at Thorn Hill. Contemporary. Candlelit and intimate, the dining room of this vintage inn mirrors the elegance of the food. Try the hazelnut-herb-crusted rack of lamb or the grilled swordfish with thyme and truffle oil. | Thorn Hill Rd. | 603/383–4242 or 800/289–8990 | fax 603/383–8062 | $20–$25 | AE, D, DC, MC, V.

Thompson House Eatery. American. Chef-owned since 1977, this busy local legend is in a late 1700s farmhouse. The food is hearty and homemade with a rustic Italian slant. Special dishes include the seafood *Francesca*, shrimp, scallops, and haddock sautéed in onions, garlic, and tomatoes in a white wine sauce over linguine, or the chicken *San Remo*, sautéed with tomatoes, peppers, and prosciutto in a chicken broth over vegetable rice. | Rte. 16A | 603/383–9341 | $7–$22 | AE, D, DC, MC, V.

The Wentworth. Continental. Hurricane lamps, hardwood floors, and an air of casual opulence set the tone for gourmet dinners like the almond-crusted rainbow trout with roasted oyster mushrooms and the cider-poached salmon. The wine list has more than 300 titles. | Rte. 16A | 603/383–9700 or 800/637–0013 | fax 603/383–4265 | $17–$25 | AE, D, DC, MC, V.

Wildcat Tavern. Contemporary. A cozy place in Jackson Village decorated with antiques. The tavern is known for fresh seafood and the Wildcat Chicken. Open-air dining. Kids' menu. | Rte. 16A | 603/383–4245 | $15–$24 | AE, MC, V.

Yesterday's Restaurant. American. Breakfast is king in this family-style restaurant. At other times, go for the clam chowder or the soup of the day. Kids' menu. | Rte. 16 | 603/383–4457 | Breakfast also available. No dinner | $3–$7 | No credit cards.

Lodging

Christmas Farm Inn. No two rooms are alike in this quirky complex of antique buildings, which number among them a jail and Jackson's first church. Breakfast and dinner included. Restaurant, bar. Some in-room hot tubs, some cable TV. Pool. Hot tub, sauna. Putting green. Cross-country skiing. Playground. Business services. | Rte. 16B | 603/383–4313 or 800/443–5837 | fax 603/383–6495 | info@christmasfarminn.com | www.christmasfarminn.com | 29 rooms, 5 cottages | $178–$400 | MAP | AE, D, MC, V.

Dana Place Inn. A late-1800s colonial country inn at the base of Mt. Washington. The 300 acres are surrounded by the White Mountain National Forest and border the Ellis River. Rooms are individually designed and many have private patios and views of the gardens, river, or Presidential Range. Restaurant, bar, picnic area, complimentary breakfast. No smoking. Indoor pool. Hot tub. 2 tennis courts. Hiking. Fishing. Cross-country skiing. Library. Pets allowed. | Rte. 16 | 603/383–6822 or 800/537–9276 | fax 603/383–6022 | contact@danaplace.com | www.danaplace.com | 35 rooms | $155–$225 | MAP | AE, D, DC, MC, V.

Eagle Mountain House. You see trees and mountains from your window at this establishment 1 mi north of town. Dining room, bar. No air-conditioning, cable TV, some in-room VCRs. Pool. Hot tub. 9-hole golf, tennis. Exercise equipment. Cross-country skiing. Video games. Playground. | Carter Notch Rd. (Rte. 16B) | 603/383–9111 or 800/966–5779 | fax 603/383–0854 | www.eaglemt.com | 93 rooms, 30 suites | $89–$169 | AE, D, DC, MC, V.

Ellis River House. A romantic country inn with a sundeck overlooking the Ellis River. Some of the rooms have fireplaces. Dining room, complimentary breakfast. No smoking, some in-room hot tubs, cable TV. Pool. Hot tub, sauna. Hiking. Cross-country skiing. | Rte. 16 | 603/383–9339 or 800/233–8309 | fax 603/383–4142 | innkeeper@erhinn.com | www.erhinn.com | 17 rooms, 3 suites, 1 cottage | $99–$199, $189–$259 suites, $159–$199 cottage | AE, D, DC, MC, V.

★ **Inn at Thorn Hill.** Architect Stanford White designed this old home in 1895, and it's full of vintage charm today. You can stay in the main building or in a cozy cottage for two. Bar, dining room. No smoking, no cable TV in some rooms. Pool. Hot tub. Cross-country skiing. No kids under 8. Business services. | Thorn Hill Rd. | 603/383–4242 or 800/289–8990 | fax 603/383–8062 | 16 rooms in 2 buildings, 3 cottages | $190–$300 | MAP | AE, D, MC, V.

Windy Hill Bed and Breakfast. This secluded inn, built in 1923, is tucked in a quiet valley has the air of a remote country home. Rooms are clean and simple with modest antique furnishings and views of the nearby mountains. Complimentary breakfast, picnic area. No smoking, no TV, no room phones. Hot tub. Hiking. Cross-country skiing. Laundry facilities. | Black Mountain Rd., Jackson | 603/383–8917 or 877/728–8927 | windyhill@compuserve.com | www.windyhillbandb.com | 3 rooms | $65–$80 | Closed May and Nov. | AE, MC, V.

Lodge at Jackson Village. Overlooking the Ellis River. Refrigerators, some in-room hot tubs, cable TV. Pool. Tennis. Cross-country skiing. Laundry facilities. | Rte. 16 | 603/383–0999 or 800/233–5634 | fax 603/383–6104 | www.lodgeatjacksonvillage.com | 32 rooms | $99–$229 | AE, D, MC, V.

Luxury Mountain Getaways. One-, two-, and three-bedroom luxury condominium, villa, and town-house accommodations on 100 acres with mountain views. Units are fully furnished with kitchen, washer/dryer, and fireplace. Picnic area. Some in-room hot tubs. 3 pools. 2 hot tubs, steam room. Tennis. Basketball, hiking. Bicycles. Video games. Playground. | Rte. 16 | 603/383–9101 or 800 472–5207 | fax 603/383–9823 | www.luxurymountaingetaways.com | 198 units | $119–$549 | AE, D, MC, V.

Nestlenook Farm. A restored Victorian building filled with antiques on 65 acres. There is a screened gazebo, animal barn, open-air chapel, apple orchard, gardens, and pond. The common area has a river-stone fireplace. Picnic area, complimentary breakfast. No air-conditioning in some rooms, no smoking, some in-room hot tubs, cable TV in common area. Pool. Ice-skating. Sleigh rides. No kids under 12. | Dinsmore Rd. | 603/383–9443 or 800/659–9443 | fax 603/383–4515 | www.nestlenookfarm.com | 7 rooms, 2 suites | $125–$185, $175–$230 suites | D, MC, V.

The Wentworth. Restored antiques fill this homey historic inn on beautifully manicured grounds. Restaurant, bar with entertainment. In-room hot tubs, cable TV. Pool. Tennis. Ice-skating. | Junction Rtes. 16A and 16B | 603/383–9700 or 800/637–0013 | fax 603/383–4265 | wentwort@nxi.com | www.thewentworth.com | 57 rooms | $155–$265 | MAP (B&B rates available) | AE, D, DC, MC, V.

JAFFREY

MAP 7, C12

(Nearby towns also listed: Fitzwilliam, Peterborough)

Mt. Monadnock is Jaffrey's main draw. The 3,165-ft mountain attracts plenty of people who want to enjoy a view of three states from the top. Ralph Waldo Emerson even wrote a poem, "Monadnoc," after he climbed it. In fact, residents claim it is perhaps the world's most climbed mountain now that the summit on Japan's Mt. Fuji is accessible by car.

In 1801, Amos Fortune, a former slave who became prosperous by establishing a tannery here, willed his money to the district school. When the school closed 126 years later, residents voted to use the money to fund an ongoing summer lecture series and public speaking contest called the Amos Fortune Forum.

Jaffrey's other literary claim to fame is that Willa Cather wrote two of her best-known books, *My Antonia* and *Death Comes to the Archbishop*, while summering here. Cather is buried in Jaffrey's cemetery.

Information: Chamber of Commerce | Box 2, Jaffrey, 03452 | 603/532–4549.

Attractions

Barrett House "Forest Hall." This impressive Federal house, built around 1800 in New Ipswich 10 mi southeast of Jaffrey, has a ballroom on the third floor and is filled with period furniture. | Main St., New Ipswich | 603/878–2517 | $5 | June–mid-Oct., Thurs.–Sun. 12–4.

Cathedral of the Pines. An outdoor memorial to American men and women, both civilian and military, who sacrificed their lives in service to their country, Cathedral of the Pines has an inspiring view of Mt. Monadnock and Mt. Kearsarge and is 6 mi southeast of Jaffrey in Rindge. The Altar of the Nation is composed of rock from every U.S. state and territory, and all faiths are welcome to hold services here. The memorial Bell Tower is built of native stone, and the bronze tablets over the four arches were designed by Norman Rockwell. | 75 Cathedral Entrance Rd., Rindge | 603/899–3300 | www.cathedralpines.com | Free | May–Oct., daily 9–5.

Melville Academy Museum. A Greek Revival schoolhouse built in 1833 and listed on the National Register of Historic Places. Small placards give a bit of history. | Thorndike Pond Rd. | 603/532–7455 | Free | June–Aug.

Monadnock State Park. Mt. Monadnock is the focal point of Monadnock State Park. In addition to more than a two dozen trails to the summit from five different trailheads, the park maintains picnic grounds and some tent campsites. Trail maps are available for $2. Exhibits in the visitor's center document the mountain's history. | Off Rte. 124 | 603/532–8862 | www.nhparks.state.nh.us | $2.50 | Daily | No pets.

ON THE CALENDAR

AUG.: *Festival of Fireworks.* The largest fireworks display in the Northeast. | 603/532–4549.

Dining

Delrossi's. Italian. This 1785 colonial farmhouse, 7 mi north of Jaffrey, has been transformed into a popular local destination for pasta, seafood, and house specials like the chicken in a Gorgonzola creme sauce over a bed of cheese tortelloni. The original wood floors, walls, and exposed beams make for a nice country feel, and the 100-plus title wine list will warm you up even further. Kids' menu. | Rte. 137 N | 603/563–7195 | www.delrossi.com | $9–$18 | AE, D, MC, V.

Lodging

Benjamin Prescott Inn. An 1853 colonial farmhouse with antiques-filled rooms, surrounded by acres of farmland, 2.3 mi east of Jaffrey. Complimentary breakfast. No air-conditioning in some rooms, in-room data ports, TV in common area. | 433 Turnpike Rd. (Rte. 124) | 603/532–6637 | bprescottinn@aol.com | www.benjaminprescottinn.com | 7 rooms, 3 suites | $75–$150 | AE, MC, V.

Woodbound Inn. Open to the public since 1892 this full-service, four-season resort on 165 acres on Lake Contoocook has bed-and-breakfast, hotel-style, or cabin accommodations. Cabins are fully furnished and can sleep four to six adults and have fireplaces or woodstoves. Picnic area. Cable TV. Lake. 9-hole golf course, tennis. Hiking, volleyball, beach, water sports, boating. Fishing. Cross-country skiing. Some pets allowed. | 62 Woodbound Rd., Rindge | 603/532–8341 or 800/688–7770 | fax 603/532–8341 | info@woodboundinn.com | www.woodboundinn.com | 36 rooms, 10 cabins | $50–$70 | AE, MC, V.

JEFFERSON

(Nearby town also listed: Gorham)

Primarily a summer resort town on the northern edge of the White Mountains' Presidential Range, Jefferson has attractions for families with young children and plenty of scenic beauty. A marker on the outskirts of town commemorates the birthplace of pioneer aeronaut Thaddeus S. C. Lowe, who led a Union balloon force during the Civil War.

Information: Northern White Mountains Chamber of Commerce | Box 298, 164 Main St., Berlin, 03570 | 603/752–1002.

Attractions

Santa's Village. This theme park, 1 mi outside town, has rides and shows with a Christmas motif. Children can feed Santa's reindeer, ride the "Santa's Skyway Sleigh" monorail, and get wet on the Yule log flume ride. | U.S. 2 | 603/586–4445 | www.santas.village.com | $16 | Mid-June–Labor Day, daily 9:30–6:30; Labor Day–Columbus Day, weekends 9:30–5.

Six Gun City. This combination theme park and museum 4 mi east of Jefferson has 35 buildings in a frontier setting, including a blacksmith shop, a schoolhouse, and a carriage and sleigh museum. The theme-park portion has a raft ride, water slides, a petting zoo, bumper boats, and miniature golf. | U.S. 2 | 603/586–4592 | www.sixguncity.com | $13.45 | Memorial Day–mid-June, weekends only 10–4:30; mid-June–Labor Day, daily 9–6.

Twin Maples Antiques. Tucked behind the Twin Maples B&B, this busy little shop 7 mi north of Jefferson deals exclusively in Depression-era glass, china, pottery, and flatware. | 185 Main St., Lancaster | 603/788–3936 | fax 603/788–3936 | www.greatnorthwoods.org/twinmaples | May–Oct., Wed.–Sat. 11–5.

ON THE CALENDAR
AUG. OR SEPT.: *Lancaster Fair.* A traditional country fair 7 mi north of town with games, rides, and exhibits. | Lancaster Fair Grounds | 603/746–4531.

Dining
Seasonings. American. This casual snack bar–style restaurant has mountain views. There's a buffet three meals a day and you can get burgers, sandwiches, and seafood as well. Kids' menu. | U.S. 2 | 603/586–7133 | Closed Columbus Day–Memorial Day | $5–$12 | No credit cards.

Lodging
Applebrook Bed and Breakfast. Stained glass, a wood-fired hot tub, and 35 acres with views of the White Mountains add to the charm of the beautiful, antiques-filled rooms of this Victorian guest house. Some rooms can be adjoined for family suites. Complimentary breakfast. No smoking, some in-room hot tubs, no room phones, TV in common area. No pets. | Rte. 115A | 603/586–7713 or 800/545–6504 | vacation@applebrook.com | www.applebrook.com | 14 rooms (6 with shared bath) | $55–$180 | MC, V.

Jefferson Inn. This hostelry occupies an old Victorian inn with the obligatory immense veranda. Complimentary breakfast. No air-conditioning, some refrigerators, no smoking, some room phones, no TV, TV in common area. Business services. | U.S. 2 | 603/586–7998 or 800/729–7908 | fax 603/586–7808 | 11 rooms, 2 suites | $80–$120, $100–$175 suites | Closed Apr. | AE, D, MC, V.

Lantern Resort. A woodsy place across from Santa's Village with campsites next door. Cable TV. Pool. Hot tub. Video games. Playground, laundry facilities. | U.S. 2 | 603/586–7151 | www.thelanternresort.com | 30 rooms | $59–$69 | Closed Nov.–Apr. | AE, D, MC, V.

Twin Maples Bed and Breakfast and Antiques Shop. This 19th-century Victorian inn 7 mi north of Jefferson in the town of Lancaster has rooms loaded with antiques and an old-time air with quilts, rockers, and lace curtains. There's an antiques store in the back of the house. Complimentary breakfast. No smoking, no room phones, TV in common area. No pets. | 185 Main St., Lancaster | 603/788–3936 | fax 603/788–3936 | twinmaple@ncia.net | www.greatnorthwoods.org/twinmaples/ | 3 rooms with shared bath | $45–$65 | MC, V.

KEENE

MAP 7, C11

(Nearby town also listed: Fitzwilliam)

Keene is the largest city in the southwest corner of the state, often called "the quiet corner." Parts of the Robin Williams movie *Jumanji* were filmed on Main Street. Once known for the production of glass and pottery, it is now home to Keene State College and is the place local residents come for shopping or a movie. Keene is a good base for exploring the back roads winding through the quiet Monadnock region.

Information: **Chamber of Commerce** | 48 Central Sq, Keene, 03431 | 603/352–1303 | www.keenechamber.com.

Attractions

Bretwood Golf Course. *Golf Digest* subscribers rate this course as one of the best values in U.S. golf courses. | E. Surry Rd. | 603/352–7626 | Apr.–Nov.

The Colonial Theater. First opened in 1924, this old-time vaudeville house now hosts plays and folk, classical, and jazz concerts. | 95 Main St. | 603/352–2033 | www.thecolonial.org | Call for show times.

Colony Mill Marketplace. This old mill building is now a shopping center with 30-plus stores. | 222 West St. | 603/357–1240 | Daily.

Horatio Colony House Museum. Horatio Colony, grandson and namesake of Keene's first mayor, lived in this 1806 Federal-era home. Many items he collected from around the world are on display. | 199 Main St. | 603/352–0460 | Free | June–mid-Oct., Tues.–Sat. 11–4; mid-Oct.–June, Sat. 11–4.

Keene State College. Established in 1909, this small school is the hub of the local arts community. Take a tour of the 4,700-student campus for a good look at the architecture and history. | Main St. | 603/352–1909 | www.keene.edu | Tours Mon.–Fri. 11 and 2. Call for availability.

Redfern Arts Center on Brickyard Pond. Three theaters and eight art studios host year-round music, theater, and dance performances. | 229 Main St., Keene State College | 603/358–2168 | www.keene.edu | No performances May–Aug.

Thorne-Sagendorph Art Gallery. Nationally known musicians perform among art exhibits, including George Ridici's *Landscape*. | Wyman Way, Keene State College | 603/358–2720 | www.keene.edu/tshe | Mon.–Wed. and Sat. noon–4, Thurs.–Fri. noon–7.

The Moving Company Dance Center. A movement center with classes in yoga, drumming, dance, and fitness, which also has an in-house performance company. In summer there are nature and dance programs for kids. | 76 Railroad St. | 603/357–2100 | fax 603/357–2100 | www.moco.org | Call for schedule.

Swanzey Lake Camping Area. A full-service campground on Swanzey Lake with boat rentals, convenience store, rec hall, and laundry. | 88 E. Shore Rd., West Swanzey | 603/352–9880 | fax 603/357–8995 | www.swanzeylake.com | $18–$24 | May–Nov.

ON THE CALENDAR

JUNE: *Annual Monadnock Valley Indian Festival.* This Native American pow wow, 6 mi southeast of Keene in Swanzey, includes dancing, singing, arts, and crafts. | 978/297–0272.

JUNE–AUG.: *Apple Hill Chamber Players.* Chamber music students from around the world join the summer intensive program. The faculty performs concerts on Tuesdays in summer. | Apple Hill Rd., Nelson | 603/847–3371 | www.applehill.org.

JULY: *Old Homestead.* This annual dramatic history of early townsfolk takes place in a natural amphitheater 6 mi southeast of Keene in Swanzey. | Potash Bowl, Swanzey Center | 603/352–0697.

JULY OR AUG.: *Cheshire Fair.* This traditional country agricultural fair 3½ mi south of Keene features demonstrations, exhibits, and games. | Cheshire Fair Grounds on Rte. 12, Swanzey | 603/357–4740.

OCT.: *Pumpkin Festival.* Thousands of carved and lighted jack-o'-lanterns line Main Street in an attempt to break the world record of 17,693 set in 1998. Forty-foot-high scaffoldings covered with pumpkins, children's Halloween parade, carving contests, food. You must bring a pumpkin! | Main St. | 603/358–5344 | www.centerstagenh.com.

Dining

Margarita's. Mexican. A casual and festive restaurant with all the traditional regalia, including custom-made crafts and a California-style hand in the kitchen. Try the sizzling fajitas and the chimichanga—a stuffed, fried burrito topped with enchilada sauce and cheese. Kids' menu. | 77–81 Main St. | 603/357–4492 | fax 603/357–9642 | No lunch | $9–$14 | AE, D, MC, V.

Nicola's Trattoria. Italian. Intimate, elegant, and cosmopolitan, this restaurant showcases work by local artists. | 39 Central Sq | 603/355–5242 | Closed Sun., Mon. No lunch Fri., Sat. | $19–$38 | MC, V.

176 Main. Eclectic. The menu runs the gamut from Mexican to Italian to seafood dishes in this tavernlike eatery. Open-air dining. Kids' menu. | 176 Main St. | 603/357–3100 | $12–$19 | AE, D, DC, MC, V.

Thai Garden. Thai. Reservations on weekends are a necessity at this popular restaurant which places an emphasis on traditional Thai food; the chefs try to prepare the dishes as their mother did. | 118 Main St. | 603/357–4567 | fax 603/357–0449 | $7–$13 | AE, D, MC, V.

Timoleon's. American. No-frills New England comfort food is what keeps this diner-style joint packed from breakfast through dinner. The family feel, hearty menu, and congenial staff, combined with dishes like creamed chipped beef on toast, shepherd's pie, and roast pork dinners with stuffing make this a local landmark for diners from across the region. | 81 Main St. | 603/357–4230 | $5–$8 | No credit cards.

★ **Tony Clamato's Ristorante.** Italian. Martinis are the specialty of the bar in this restaurant, which feels like something straight out of Boston's North End. Try the vitello saltimbocca. | 15 Court St. | 603/357–4345 | Closed Mon. No lunch | $10–$20 | AE, D, MC, V.

Lodging

Best Western Sovereign Hotel. A standard member of the chain with quiet, comfortable rooms. Restaurant, bar with entertainment, picnic area, complimentary breakfast. In-room data ports, some microwaves, some refrigerators, cable TV. Indoor pool. Video games. Business services. Pets allowed. | 401 Winchester St. | 603/357–3038 | fax 603/357–4776 | 131 rooms | $59–$140 | AE, D, DC, MC, V.

KEENE

INTRO
ATTRACTIONS
DINING
LODGING

Carriage Barn Bed and Breakfast. A charming bed-and-breakfast with lots of exposed wood and lace curtains, across the street from Keene State College. Rooms are decorated with locally collected antiques. Complimentary breakfast. No smoking, no room phones, TV in common area. No kids under 5. No pets. | 358 Main St., | 603/357–3812 | carriage@carriagebarn.com | www.carriagebarn.com | 4 rooms | $75–$100 | AE, D, MC, V.

★ **Chesterfield Inn.** Gardens surround this 18th-century former farmhouse and barn 10 mi west of Keene. It has a view of the mountains and the Connecticut River. Dining room, complimentary breakfast. In-room data ports, refrigerators, no smoking, cable TV. Business services. | Rte. 9, Chesterfield | 603/256–3211 or 800/365–5515 | fax 603/256–6131 | www.chesterfieldinn.com | 15 rooms | $150–$250 | AE, DC, MC, V.

LACONIA

MAP 7, F9

(Nearby towns also listed: Franklin, Gilford, Weirs Beach)

Now a busy entry point to the Lakes region, Laconia was a sleepy little town until the railroad reached it in 1848. The community quickly became a center for manufacturing and trading. Although Laconia is generally busy all summer long, Motorcycle Week in mid-June is especially loud and boisterous. The first such gathering of motorcycling enthusiasts from all over the country took place in 1939. With the exception of 1965, when riots between locals and riders broke out, the week usually passes without major mishap.

Information: **Laconia–Weirs Beach Chamber of Commerce** | 11 Veterans Sq, Laconia, 03246 | 603/524–5531 | fax 603/524–5534 | www.laconia-weirs.org.

Attractions

Bartlett Beach. Bring the family for a picnic or swim at this beach on Lake Winnisquam. There are lifeguards on duty. | 150 Winnisquam Ave. | 603/524–5046 | Free | Memorial Day–Labor Day.

Belknap Mill Society. The Belknap Mill is the oldest unaltered brick textile mill in America. It contains a knitting museum and a year-round cultural center. | The Mill Plaza | 603/524–8813 | Free | Weekdays 9–5.

Lakes Region Factory Stores. This cluster of factory outlet stores includes Eddie Bauer, Brooks Brothers, and Black & Decker. | U.S. 3, Tilton | 603/286–7880 | www.shoplakesregion.com | Jan.–Apr., Sun.–Thurs. 10–6, Fri.–Sat. 10–8; May–Dec., Mon.–Sat. 10–9, Sun. 10–6.

Opechee Park. A 32-acre park on Lake Opechee with two beaches, a track, baseball fields, picnic area, and bathhouses. | 915 N. Main St. | 603/524–5046 | Free | Daily.

ON THE CALENDAR
JUNE: *Motorcycle Rally and Race Week.* Motorcycle races, hill climbs, riding tours, and other motorcycle-related events. | 603/366–2000.
JULY–AUG.: *Riverside Concert Series.* Thursday-evening concerts of local pop, bluegrass, and so on at the bandstand in Riverside Park. | 603/524–8813.

Dining
Hickory Stick Farm. Contemporary. In an early-American farmhouse with garden views in sleepy Belmont, 4 mi south of Laconia, this restaurant is known for its slow-roasted duck with orange sherry sauce. Open-air dining. Sunday brunch. No smoking. | 66 Bean Hill Rd., Belmont | 603/524–3333. | Closed Mon. No lunch in Dec., Jan., and Feb. Call for hrs | $13–$22 | AE, D, MC, V.

When it Comes to Getting Cash at an ATM, Same Thing.

Whether you're in Yosemite or Yemen, using your Visa® card or ATM card with the PLUS symbol is the easiest and most convenient way to get cash. Even if your bank is in Minneapolis and you're in Miami, Visa/PLUS ATMs make getting cash so easy, you'll feel right at home. After all, Visa/PLUS ATMs are open 24 hours a day, 7 days a week, rain or shine. And if you need help finding one of Visa's 627,000 ATMs in 127 countries worldwide, visit **visa.com/pd/atm**. We'll make finding an ATM as easy as finding the Eiffel Tower, the Pyramids or even the Grand Canyon.

It's Everywhere You Want To Be®

Find America *with a Compass*

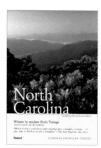

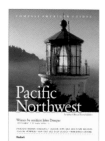

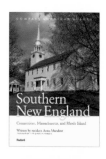

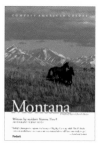

Written by local authors and illustrated throughout with images from regional photographers, Compass American Guides reveal the character and culture of America's most spectacular destinations. Covering more than 35 states and regions across the country, Compass guides are perfect for residents who want to explore their own backyards, and for visitors seeking an insider's perspective on all there is to see and do.

Fodor's Compass American Guides

At bookstores everywhere.

Las Piñatas Mexican Restaurant. Mexican. Tucked in an old stone railway station at the edge of Laconia's downtown, this restaurant serves up familiar Mexican/margarita fare. Try the enchiladas de mole, sizzling fajitas, and chiles rellenos. | 9 Veteran's Sq | 603/528–1405 | fax 603/524–8861 | Closed on Tues. Columbus Day–May. No lunch Sun. | $11–$16 | AE, D, MC, V.

Victorian House. French. Set in an 1831 Victorian home, this formal dining room bares antique furniture and candle–lit tables fixed with individual china sets. The food is country-style and regal, including dishes like beef Wellington, rack of lamb, veal, oysters and escargot. | Lake Shore Rd. (Rte. 11) | 603/293–8155 | No lunch | $17–$23 | AE, D, DC, MC, V.

Lodging

Barton's Motel. A motel with cottages and 600 ft on the lake. Some kitchenettes, cable TV, some room phones. Pool, lake. Beach, dock, boating. Air conditioning. | 1330 Union Ave. (U.S. 3) | 603/524–5674 | www.bartonsmotel.com | 37 rooms, 4 cottages | $65–$90, $140–$160 cottages | Closed late Nov.–Mar. | AE, MC, V.

Ferry Point House B& B. A gracious Victorian home on Lake Winnisquam that was built in the early 1800s as a summer retreat for the Pillsbury family. Complimentary breakfast. No air-conditioning, no smoking, no room phones, no TV, cable TV in common area. Lake. Beach, boating. | 100 Lower Bay Rd., Sanbornton | 603/524–0087 | fax 603/524–0959 | ferrypt@together.net | www.new-hampshire-inn.com | 7 rooms | $95–$125 | Closed Nov.–Apr. | No credit cards.

★ **Hickory Stick Farm.** This late-18th-century Cape-style inn on 17 secluded acres 4 mi south of Laconia has comfortable, antique-furnished rooms. Restaurant, complimentary breakfast. No smoking, no room phones, TV in common area. Hiking. Cross-country skiing. No pets. | 66 Bean Hill Rd., Belmont | 603/524–3333 | fax 603/524–4472 | brian@hickorystickfarm.com | www.hickorystickfarm.com | 2 rooms | $85 | AE, D, DC, MC, V.

Hi-Spot Motor Court. Clean motel-style rooms and fully furnished cottages on Lake Winnipesaukee. The motor court has been family owned and operated since 1962. In room refrigerators and TVs. Beach, boating. No Pets. | 277 Weirs Blvd., | 603/524–3281 | 10 rooms, 10 cottages | $65–$150 | Closed Mid Oct.–Apr. | MC, V.

Lord Hampshire Motel. A motel and cottages on 600 ft of lakefront with its own beach 5 mi west of Laconia in Winnisquam. Picnic area. Some kitchenettes, cable TV. Boating. | 885 Laconia Rd., Winnisquam | 603/524–4331 | www.lordhampshire.com | 8 rooms, 12 cottages | $95–$175, $500–$1,095 wk cottages | Closed Nov.–Apr. | AE, MC, V.

Margate on Winnipesaukee. A large hotel overlooking Lake Winnipesaukee. Restaurant. Cable TV. 2 pools (1 indoor). Hot tub, sauna. Tennis. Gym, boating. | 76 Lake St. | 603/524–5210 or 800/627–4283 | fax 603/528–4485 | reservations@themargate.com | www.themargate.com | 146 rooms | $119–$289 | AE, D, DC, MC, V.

LINCOLN AND NORTH WOODSTOCK AREA

MAP 7, E6

(Nearby towns also listed: Franconia, Waterville Valley)

Around the turn of the 20th century, Lincoln was a thriving company town built and owned by lumber baron J. E. Henry. Neighboring North Woodstock, just a mile away, catered to tourists who came to summer with a view of Franconia and Kinsman notches. By the time the lumber mills closed in the 1970s, Lincoln boasted Loon Ski Area, and, as summer visitors dwindled in North Woodstock, the numbers of skiers skyrocketed. Franconia Notch State Park, located half in Lincoln and half in Franconia, is another draw.

LINCOLN
AND NORTH
WOODSTOCK
AREA

INTRO
ATTRACTIONS
DINING
LODGING

Today Lincoln is a busy resort town with year-round activities, and North Woodstock retains a quieter, village feeling but with equal access to area attractions.

Most land surrounding Lincoln is part of the 770,000-acre White Mountain National Forest. The Kancamagus Highway that runs from Lincoln to Conway is considered one of New Hampshire's most scenic drives. Several popular hiking trails are accessible from the road.

Information: Chamber of Commerce | Box 358, Lincoln, 03251 | 603/745–6621.

Attractions

Clark's Trading Post. Florence Clark, the first woman to reach the summit of Mt. Washington by dogsled, opened this trading post in the 1920s as a dog ranch. Still run by the Clark family, today the trading post is known for its trained black bears. Other attractions include a train ride, the Clark Museum, an 1884 fire station, and bumper boats. | U.S. 3, Lincoln | 603/745–8913 | www.clarkstradingpost.com | $10 | Late May–late June, weekends 10–6; late June–Labor Day, daily 10–5.

Franconia Notch State Park. Franconia Notch State Park is half in Lincoln and half in Franconia, on either side of the Franconia Notch State Parkway. The park has a number of recreational opportunities. *See* Franconia. | U.S. 3.

Hobo Railroad. One hour and 20 minute narrated excursions along the Pemigewasset River with views of the White Mountain National Forest. | Railroad St. | 603/745–2135 | $8 | June–Labor Day, daily; May and Sept.–Oct., Sat. and Sun.

★ **Kancamagus Highway.** The Kancamagus Highway (Route 112) through the southern part of the White Mountain National Forest is especially popular during fall foliage season. There are a number of hiking trails from trailheads that begin at the Kancamagus. The Lincoln Woods Visitor Center, 4 mi east of Lincoln, has maps and trail information as well as the recreation pass you need for parking in National Forest lots ($5 per vehicle, good for seven consecutive days). | Rte. 112 | Daily.

Loon Mt. Recreation Area. This four-season resort hosts numerous special events in addition to the full slate of activities on site. In winter, skiing and snowboarding are the main activities. Trails are mainly for intermediates, but there are sections for beginners and experts as well. In warm weather, take the gondola to the summit for a panoramic view of the White Mountain National Forest, watch lumberjack shows, listen to storytelling by a mountain man, or attend performances at the popular wildlife theater. In-line skating, mountain biking, and hiking are also popular. | Rte. 112 (Kancamagus Hwy.), Lincoln | 603/745–8111, 800/227–4191 for lodging | www.loonmtn.com | Daily; activities are seasonal.

Lost River Gorge. Lost River appears and disappears as it tumbles its way through a narrow gorge with crevasses, caverns, and waterfalls 6 mi north of North Woodstock. The self-guided tour is marked with information on local natural history, ecology, and plant life. Walkways and bridges make the trip easier, and caves can be bypassed. | Rte. 112, Kinsman Notch | 603/745–8031 | www.findlostriver.com | $8.50 | Last two wks May and Sept.–mid-Oct., daily 9–5; June–Aug., daily 9–6.

Rail 'N River Forest Trail. A simple ½-mi self-guided tour exhibiting the history of logging and geology in the White Mountain area that starts at the Russell Colbath historic house in Albany, 15 mi east of Lincoln. | Rte. 112 (Kancamagus Hwy.), Albany | 603/528–8721 | Free | Daily.

Whale's Tale Water Park. Float on an inner tube along a gentle river, careen down giant water slides, or body-surf in the large wave pool. | U.S. 3, North Lincoln | 603/745 8810 | $16.50 | Mid-June–Labor Day, daily 10–6.

White Mountain National Forest. With nearly 800,000 acres, the White Mountain National Forest is slightly larger than the state of Rhode Island. Eight peaks rise more than a mile above sea level, including Mt. Washington (6,288 ft). There are more than 100 roads, over 1,128-ft trails, and 20 campgrounds with over 900 campsites. Deer, bear, moose, and bobcats roam the forest, and trout inhabit the clear streams. | 603/745–8720 or 800/346–3687 | www.fs.fed.us | Daily.

ON THE CALENDAR
FEB.: *Annual Mountain Dew Grandparent/Grandchild Race.* A ski race with grand-parents teaming up with their grandchildren. | Loon Mountain Recreation Area | 603/745–8111.

EASTER WEEKEND: *Annual Easter Egg Hunt.* Four thousand eggs hidden, prizes for three age groups, children's movie. | Mill at Loon Mountain | 603/745–2245.

SEPT.: *Annual New Hampshire Highland Games.* Competitions, music, Scottish danc-ing and crafts. | Loon Mountain Park | 603/229–1975 or 800/358–7208.

Dining
Clement Room Grille. Contemporary. Fine dining in the Woodstock Inn. Try the seafood and special Bison pot roast. | 135 Main St., North Woodstock | 603/745–3951 | Breakfast also available. No lunch | $18–$35 | AE, D, MC, V.

Gordi's Fish and Steak House. American. Skiing is a theme in this family-owned restau-rant with Loon Mountain views and a steak-and-seafood menu. Salad bar. Kids' menu. | 112 Main St. (Kancamagus Hwy.), Lincoln | 603/745–6635 | No lunch | $9–$24 | AE, D, MC, V.

Govoni's. Italian. Given the New England clapboards, you'd never guess that the menu is strictly old world. Kids' menu. | Lost River Rd. (Rte. 112), North Woodstock | 603/745–8042 | Closed Labor Day–Memorial Day and Mon.–Wed. in June. No lunch | $12–$30 | MC, V.

Indian Head Resort. Continental. Relaxed family dining with views of the White Moun-tains. Try the gulf shrimp with garlic, white wine, and feta cheese over pasta, or the Yan-kee pot roast. Save room for the hot Indian pudding dessert. | U.S. 3 | 603/745–8000 or 800/343–8000 | fax 603/745–8414 | $12–$20 | AE, D, DC, MC, V.

Old Timber Mill Restaurant and Pub. Contemporary. This converted mill drying shed close to hotels and ski areas in the Millfront Marketplace dates from 1926 and has a fancy din-ing room downstairs and a pub upstairs with a separate menu. There are many windows with views of the nearby mountains. Open-air dining. | Rte. 112, Lincoln; I-93 Exit 32 | 603/745–3603 | $6–$21 | AE, D, MC, V.

Station Brewery. American. A casual restaurant in the Woodstock Inn with over 100 items on the menu from burgers to sandwiches. There is weekend entertainment in season. Kids' menu. Sunday brunch. | 135 Main St., North Woodstock | 603/745–3951 | Breakfast also available. No lunch | $10–$25 | AE, D, MC, V.

Sunny Day Diner. American. A classic country diner serving up hearty helpings of Amer-icana and with an in-house bakery. Look for the daily specials. | U.S. 3 | 603/745–4833 | fax 603/745–3914 | Closed Tues. No dinner Sat.–Wed. | $4–$11 | MC, V.

Truants Taverne. American. The bar and tables in this casual family-owned restaurant are made from school desks. It is known for its prime rib. Kids' menu. | 96 Main St (U.S. 3), North Woodstock | 603/745–2239. | $9–$15 | AE, D, MC, V.

Lodging
Beacon Resort. A good-size family resort with many amenities. Restaurant, bar with enter-tainment. Some kitchenettes, in-room hot tubs, cable TV. 4 pools (2 indoor w/saunas), wad-ing pool. All suites and some rooms have hot tubs. Putting green. Game room. Laundry facilities. | U.S. 3, Lincoln | 603/745–8118, 800/258–8934 outside NH | fax 603/745–3783 | www.beaconresort.com | 132 rooms, 26 suites, 24 cottages | $89–$119, $175 suites, $89 cot-tages | MAP | AE, D, MC, V.

Cozy Cabins. These simple, rustic cabins with stocked kitchenettes are perfect for extended forays into the surrounding wilderness. Picnic area. No air-conditioning, some kitch-

LINCOLN
AND NORTH
WOODSTOCK
AREA

INTRO
ATTRACTIONS
DINING
LODGING

enettes. Playground. | Box 486, U.S. 3 | 603/745–8713 | cozycabins@linwoodnet.com | www.cozycabins.com | 9 cabins | $44–$86 | Closed mid-Oct.–mid-May | MC, V.

Drummer Boy Motor Inn. A two-story motor inn with varied rooms, near area attractions. Picnic area. Some kitchenettes, some refrigerators, some in-room hot tubs, cable TV, some in-room VCRs. 2 pools (1 indoor). Hot tub, sauna. Playground, laundry facilities. | U.S. 3, Lincoln | 603/745–3661 or 800/762–7275 outside NH | fax 603/745–9829 | www.drummerboymotorinn.com | 51 rooms, 2 cottages, 4-bedroom house | $68–$170, $72–$112 cottages, $250 per day/$1200 per week house | AE, D, MC, V.

Franconia Notch Motel. A quaint, single-story motel on the Pemigewasset River, ½ mi south of Franconia Notch State Park. The screened-porch cottages are good for families. Some kitchenettes, cable TV. No pets. | U.S. 3, | 603/745–2229 or 800/323–7829 | www.franconianotch.com | 12 rooms, 6 cottages | $57–$75 | AE, D, MC, V.

Indian Head Resort. A 180-acre hostelry that looks out on the White Mountains. Restaurant, bar. Refrigerators, some in-room hot tubs, cable TV. 2 pools (1 indoor), lake. 2 hot tubs (1 outdoor). Tennis. Fishing. Bicycles, ice-skating. Video games. Laundry facilities. | U.S. 3, North Lincoln; I–93 Exit 33 | 603/745–8000 or 800/343–8000 | fax 603/745–8414 | info@indianheadresort.com | www.indianheadresort.com | 98 rooms, 40 cottages | $89–$169 | AE, D, DC, MC, V.

Jack O'Lantern. A family-oriented resort with extensive grounds flanking the Pemigewasset River. Dining room, bar with entertainment. Cable TV, some in-room VCRs. 2 pools (1 indoor), wading pool. Hot tub, sauna. 18-hole golf course, tennis. Playground. | U.S. 3, Woodstock; I–93 Exit 30 | 603/745–8121, 800/227–4454 outside NH | fax 603/745–8197 | info@jackolanternresort.com | www.jackolanternresort.com | 23 rooms, 20 apartments, 30 cottages | $99–$109 | Closed late Oct.–mid-May | MAP | AE, D, MC, V.

Kancamagus Motor Lodge. You come to this area for views and you get them at this simple, two-story property. Restaurant. Cable TV. Pool. Laundry facilities. | Kancamagus Hwy. (Rte. 112), Lincoln | 603/745–3365 or 800/346–4205 | fax 603/745–6691 | www.kancmotorlodge.com | 34 rooms | $49–$79 | AE, D, MC, V.

Lincoln Motel. A small, comfortable motel right in the town of Lincoln. Family suite with kitchenette available. Refrigerators, cable TV, no room phones. No pets. | Rte. 112 | 603/745–2780 | fax 603/745–6112 | lincolnmotel@earthlink.net | 7 rooms | $55 | D, MC, V.

Mill House Inn. A rustic, innlike hotel. Restaurant. Cable TV, some in-room VCRs. 2 pools (1 indoor). 2 hot tubs (1 outdoor). Tennis. Exercise equipment. | Kancamagus Hwy. (Rte. 112), Lincoln; I–93 Exit 32 | 603/745–6261 or 800/654–6183 | fax 603/745–6896 | www.millatloon.com | 96 rooms | $70–$129 | AE, D, DC, MC, V.

Mount Coolidge Motel. The rooms are a good size at this simple, streamside lodge. Cable TV. Pool. | U.S. 3, Lincoln; I–93 Exit 33 | 603/745–8052 | www.mtcoolidgemotel.com | 20 rooms | $42–$72 | Closed Nov.–Mar. | D, MC, V.

Mountain Club on Loon. A slope-side resort hotel with mountain views and a nature trail. Dining room, bar with entertainment, picnic area. Some kitchenettes, some in-room hot tubs, cable TV. 2 pools (1 indoor). Hot tub, massage, saunas, steam rooms. Tennis. Gym, racquetball, squash. Bicycles. Cross-country skiing, downhill skiing. Video games. Children's programs (ages 5–12), laundry facilities. | Kancamagus Hwy. (Rte. 112), Lincoln | 603/745–2244 or 800/229–7829 | fax 603/745–2317 | www.mtnclubonloon.com | 234 rooms, 117 suites | $169, $259 suites | AE, D, MC, V.

Mountaineer Motel. A two-story inn with modern rooms with views, right on the Corridor 11 Snowmobile Trail. Restaurant, bar. Some in-room hot tubs, cable TV. Indoor pool. Hot tub, sauna. Exercise room. Laundry facilities. | U.S. 3 | 603/745–2235 or 800/356–0046 | fax 603/745–2640 | mtneermt@aol.com | www.mountaineermotel.com | 56 rooms, 2 suites | $59–$89 | AE, D, DC, MC, V.

Nordic Inn. Comfortable and simply furnished studio, and one-, two-, and three-bedroom condominiums with full kitchens, fireplaces, and private balconies that are well suited for families. Microwaves, refrigerators, cable TV. 2 pools. Hot tub, sauna. Tennis. Gym. Laundry facilities. | Rte. 112 E, Lincoln | 603/745–2727 or 888/883–2305 | 12 units | $59–$249 | AE, D, MC, V.

Red Doors Motel. A family motel close to attractions with a view of the White Mountains. Rooms vary in size and quality. Picnic area. Cable TV. Pool. Video games. Playground, laundry facilities. | U.S. 3, Lincoln; I–93 exit 33 | 603/745–2267 or 800/527–7596 | www.red-doorsmotel.com | fax 603/745–3647 | 30 rooms | $42–$79 | AE, D, MC, V.

Riverbank Motel and Cabins. This family-owned and -operated motel on the Pemigwasset River has clean, simple rooms and fully furnished cabins ideal for families. Some kitchenettes, cable TV. Outdoor pool. No pets. | Connector Rd. (Rte. 3A), Lincoln | 603/745–3374 or 800/633–5624 | www.musar.com/riverbank | 11 rooms, 4 cabins | $40–$90 | No credit cards.

Wilderness Inn. A small wood-shingled inn, built in 1912 by an area lumber baron, with comfortable rooms and family suites. It is known for its elaborate breakfast. Three miles east of Loon Mountain on Route 112 and 5 mi south of Franconia Notch Park on Route 3. Complimentary breakfast. No smoking, no room phones, cable TV. No pets. | Rte. 112 and U.S. 3, North Woodstock | 603/745–3890, 800/200–9453, or 888/777–7813 | fax 603/745–6367 | info@thewildernessinn.com | www.thewildernessinn.com | 7 rooms, 1 cottage | $60–$150 | AE, MC, V.

Woodstock Inn. A turn-of-the-20th-century mansion anchors this three-building inn complex in North Woodstock with varied rooms and period furnishings throughout. 2 restaurants, 2 bars, complimentary breakfast. Some refrigerators, some in-room hot tubs, cable TV, some in-room VCRs. Hot tub. | 80 Main St., North Woodstock | 603/745–3951 or 800/321–3985 | fax 603/745–3701 | relax@woodstockinnnh.com | www.woodstockinnnh.com | 21 rooms (8 with shared bath) | $62–$150 | AE, D, MC, V.

Woodward's Resort. The grounds are nicely landscaped and crossed by a pretty stream at this hostelry 2 mi south of the entrance to Franconia Notch State Park. Kids are drawn to the duck pond like magnets. Restaurant, bar. Cable TV. 2 pools (1 indoor). Hot tub, sauna. Tennis. Racquetball. Playground, laundry facilities. | U.S. 3, Lincoln | 603/745–8141 or 800/635–8968 | fax 603/745–3408 | www.woodwardsresort.com | 88 rooms | $66–$112 | AE, D, DC, MC, V.

LITTLETON

MAP 7, E5

(Nearby towns also listed: Franconia, Sugar Hill)

A commercial center for people living in the western part of the White Mountains, Littleton was a stop on the Underground Railroad in the years leading up to the Civil War. The town also produced most of the Victorian era's stereoscopes (double picture viewers).

Information: **Chamber of Commerce** | Box 105, Littleton 03561 | 603/444–6581 | chamber@moose.ncia.net | www.littletonareachamber.com.

Attractions
Littleton Grist Mill. A 1798 waterwheel-powered gristmill with a museum and upscale gift gallery with Peacock glass, Lillyraye Collectibles, pewter, maple syrup, and organic stone-ground flours and grains. | 18 Mill St. | 603/444–7478 or 888/284–7478 | www.littletongristmill.com | Free | Mon.–Thurs. 10–5, Fri. 10–8, Sat. 10–4, Sun. 11–3.

Littleton Historical Museum. Located in the old town firehouse, this little museum has items of local interest and a large collection of stereoscopic slides. | 2 Union St. | 603/444–6435 | July–Sept., Wed., Sat. 1:30–4:30; Oct.–June, call for hrs.

Main Street. A ½-mi walking tour of 12 Littleton buildings of historic and architectural renown. You can pick up a map at any of the houses open to the public or at the Chamber of Commerce booth on Main Street. | Main St. | 603/444–6561 | Free | Daily.

Samuel C. Moore Station. The Ammonoosuc River descends 235 ft as it travels through Littleton. At Moore Station, 8 mi west of town, water power is harnessed to create electricity. A visitor's center explains the process. You can also hike or picnic around Moore Reservoir. | Rte. 18 | 603/638–2327 | Free | Memorial Day–Columbus Day, daily.

ON THE CALENDAR
JUNE: *Littleton Trout Tournament.* A three-day fishing tournament. | Moore Dam Lake | 603/444–6561.

SEPT.: *Annual Sidewalk Art Show and Sale.* Started in 1969, this yearly sale attracts artists from throughout New England. The lobster boil, antique car show, and delicious food are definite highlights. | Main St. | 9–6 | 603/444–6561.

OCT.: *Annual Model Railroad Show.* Exhibits and displays of model railroads. | National Guard Armory | 603/869–3928.

Dining
Burrito Alley. Mexican. A festive, family-style place decked with full Mexican regalia. Dishes run the gamut from burritos, fajitas, and quesadillas to the vegetarian "flat ugly," a three-layer tortilla dish with refried beans, grilled vegetables, salsa, and cheese. | 30 Main St. | 603/444–2200 | Closed Mon. Sept.–May | $5–$7 | AE, D, MC, V.

Clam Shell. American/Casual. Service is family style in this vintage eatery decorated with nautical artifacts, news clippings, and Tiffany-style lamps. The popular lounge often offers special activities such as trivia games. Try the steak and scallops. Salad bar. Kids' menu. | U.S. 302; U.S. 93 Exit 42 | 603/444–6445 | $11–$17 | AE, D, MC, V.

Eastgate. Continental. The restaurant's modern decor is enhanced by a gazebo with a fountain, and diners enjoy views of Mt. Eustis. It is known for seafood, chicken, and prime rib au jus. | 335 Cottage St. | 603/444–3971 | No lunch | $6–$17 | AE, D, MC, V.

Italian Oasis. Italian. A microbrewery is at the heart of this old Victorian inn and marketplace. There's open-air dining and live entertainment on Friday in summer. Look for steak and seafood as well as pasta dishes. | 106 Main St., in Parker's Marketplace | 603/444–6995 | $6–$16. | AE, D, MC, V.

Lodging
Adair Country Inn. This gracious Georgian revival home in Bethlehem, 5 mi north of Littleton, dates from 1927. The interiors are as spacious as the 200-acre wooded grounds, which include perennial gardens. Complimentary breakfast. No smoking, no room phones, no TV, TV in common area. Tennis. | 80 Guider La., Bethlehem | 603/444–2600 or 888/444–2600 | fax 603/444–4823 | www.adairinn.com | 8 rooms, 2 suite, 1 cottage | $145–$185, $250–$285 suites, $295 cottage | AE, MC, V.

Beal House Inn. Built in 1833, this beautiful colonial inn on Main Street is within walking distance to town. Antiques-filled rooms have four-poster canopy beds, claw-foot bathtubs, and fireplaces. Restaurant, bar, complimentary breakfast. No smoking, cable TV, some room phones, TV in common area. No pets. | 2 W. Main St. | 603/444–2661 or 888/616–2325 | fax 603/444–6224 | beal.house.inn@connriver.net | www.bealhouseinn.com | 4 rooms, 3 suites | $95–$150 | AE, D, MC, V.

Eastgate Motor Inn. A simple motel with large modern rooms just off Interstate 93 Exit 41. Restaurant, bar, complimentary Continental breakfast. Cable TV. Pool, wading pool. Playground. Business services. Pets allowed. | 335 Cottage St. | 603/444–3971 | fax 603/444–3971 | www.eastgatemotorinn.com | 55 rooms | $50–$70 | AE, D, DC, MC, V.

Edencroft Inn. This former family estate is now a romantic bed-and-breakfast with cozy nooks and antique furnishings. Some rooms have canopy beds and fireplaces. The five-course candlelit breakfast is a definite highlight. Complimentary breakfast. No smoking, some in-room hot tubs. No kids under 12. No pets. | 120 Littleton Rd. | 603/444–1158 | fax 603/444–5671 | stay@edencroftinn.com | www.edencroftinn.com | 7 | $85–$140 | AE, D, MC, V.

Mulburn Inn. The dime store king, F. W. Woolworth, spared no expense when he built this restored Bethlehem mansion, 4 mi north of Littleton, as a summer getaway spot in 1908. Check out the 100-year-old croquet court. Complimentary breakfast. No smoking, no room phones, no TV, TV in common area. | 2370 Main St. (U.S. 302), Bethlehem | 603/869–3389 or 800/457–9440 | the.mulburn.inn@onnriver.net | www.mulburninn.com | 7 rooms | $70–$125 | AE, MC, V.

Thayers Inn. A cupola-topped, mid-19th-century inn with great views of Mt. Washington. Complimentary Continental breakfast. Some refrigerators, cable TV. | 116 Main St. | 603/444–6469 or 800/634–8179 | fax 603/444–6469 | don@thayersinn.com | www.thayersinn.com | 40 rooms (16 with shared bath), 6 suites | $49–$99 | AE, D, DC, MC, V.

Wayside Inn. Franklin Pierce's family lived in the early-19th-century section of this Bethlehem hostelry, 4 mi north of Littleton, on the Ammonoosuc River. Dining room, bar. Some refrigerators, no cable TV in some rooms. Beach. Cross-country skiing. | U.S. 302 at Pierce Bridge, Bethlehem | 603/869–3364 or 800/448–9557 | fax 603/869–5765 | www.thewaysideinn.com | 26 rooms | $59–$129 | Closed Nov. and Apr. | AE, D, MC, V.

LYME

MAP 7, C7

(Nearby town also listed: Hanover)

This small town on the Connecticut River is dominated by a splendid 1812 Congregational Church with Palladian windows, a tower with an octagonal dome, and horse sheds with 27 numbered stalls. Each year the church holds crafts fairs using the horse sheds as the venue.

Information: Hanover Area Chamber of Commerce | Box 5105, Hanover, 03775 | 603/643–3115 | www.hanoverchamber.com.

Attractions

Lyme Edgell Covered Bridge. This bridge, which crosses Clay Brook, 2 mi south of Orford off Route 10, was built on the Lyme Common in 1885 and then transported complete to the river. The builder, Warren Piper, was only 18 years old. | River Rd.

ON THE CALENDAR

OCT.: *Artists Studio Tour.* Take the rare opportunity to visit the working studios of more than 25 artists, writers, and sculptors in the surrounding area. The ticket price includes a driving map, tour, and an evening wine-and-cheese gathering. | On the Common | 10–5 | 603/795–2773.

Dining

Alden Country Inn. Continental. This simple dining room has hardwood floors and fireplace and a menu reflecting its history, with dishes like the Shaker cranberry pot roast and the roast beef tenderloin with cabernet Stilton cheese sauce. | On the Common | 603/795–2222 or 800/794–2296 | fax 603/795–9436 | $14–$22 | AC, D, DC, MC, V.

Lodging

Alden Country Inn. This beautiful, classic New England inn has been open since 1809. The rooms have antiques, four-poster beds, and handmade quilts. Restaurant, complimentary breakfast. In-room data ports, no smoking, cable TV. Laundry facilities. No pets. | On the Common | 800/795–2222 or 800/794–2296 | fax 603/795–9436 | info@aldencountryinn.com | www.aldencountryinn.com | 15 rooms | $165 | AE, D, DC, MC, V.

Dowds' Country Inn. A charming colonial home built in 1780 on 6 acres on the Common in Lyme. Complimentary breakfast. No smoking, no TV, TV in common area. Business services. | On the Common, | 603/795–4712 or 800/482–4712 | fax 603/795–4220 | www.dowdscountryinn.com | 22 rooms | $135–$165 | D, DC, MC, V.

Loch Lyme Lodge. Summer cabins flank the main lodge built in 1784 on 120 wooded acres with a pond. Cabins are open Memorial Day to Labor Day. Complimentary breakfast. No air-conditioning, some kitchenettes, some refrigerators, no room phones, no TV. Beach, boating. Playground. Pets allowed. | 70 Orford Rd. | 603/795–2141 or 800/423–2141 | www.dartbook.com | 4 rooms (with shared baths), 24 cabins | $68, $90 cabins | No credit cards.

MADISON

(Nearby towns also listed: Conway, Tamworth)

Madison is one of several small towns surrounding the lakes on the northern edge of New Hampshire's Lakes Region. Although Ossipee Lake is the largest of these, Silver, Purity, and Conway lakes and Long Pond are also beautiful. These lakes see much less traffic than the larger lakes to the south and are prized by those who prefer peace and quiet to boisterous summer fun.

Information: Mt. Washington Valley Chamber of Commerce | Box 2300, Rte. 16, North Conway, 03860 | 603/356–3171 or 800/367–3364 | www.mtwashingtonvalley.org.

Attractions

King Pine Ski Area. This small ski area and resort west of town has been in the same family for seven generations. It is great for families and anyone else who wants a break from the fast pace of larger resorts. | Rte. 153 | 603/367–8896 or 800/367–8897 | www.kingpine.com | Dec.–Mar., daily.

ON THE CALENDAR

FEB.: *Winter Carnival at King Pine Ski Area.* Family games and activities plus fireworks. | 603/367–8896.

Lodging

Mt. Chocorua View House. A modest but cheery inn with individually decorated rooms, turn-of-the-20th-century antiques, and a guest kitchen. You can have a cup of tea on the enclosed porch and look at the view of the Chocorua River. Complimentary breakfast. No air-conditioning in some rooms, no smoking, no room phones, TV in common room. Gym. Library. No kids under 10. No pets. | 201 White Mountain Hwy. (Rte. 16) | 603/323–8350 or 888/323–8350 | fax 603/323–3319 | fbhomes@landmark.net | www.mtchocorua.com | 7 rooms | $60–$100 | Closed Apr. | AE, D, MC, V.

Purity Spring Resort. A 100-year-old resort for families that's perfect in every season. Bar, dining room, picnic area. Some microwaves, some refrigerators, no TV in some rooms, TV in common area. Indoor pool. Hot tub. Tennis. Exercise equipment, beach, water sports, boating. Ice-skating. Cross-country skiing. downhill skiing. Video games. Children's program (ages infant–6), playground, laundry facilities. Business services. | Rte. 153, East Madison | 603/367–8896 or 800/373–3754 | fax 603/367–8664 | www.purityspring.com | 55 rooms, 14 suites (2 with shared bath), 3 cottages, 4 condos | $80–$116 per person | AP or MAP | AE, D, MC, V.

MANCHESTER

(Nearby towns also listed: Concord, Merrimack, Milford, Nashua, Salem)

Like its English namesake, Manchester is a mill town. The first of many mills was operating in 1810, and by mid-century they were producing nearly 5 million yards of cloth per week. Although the mills are now silent, Manchester remains the largest city in the state, with nearly 10% of its population. Recent years have brought new businesses to the mill buildings, and Manchester is enjoying a revitalized riverfront and a happy era of economic diversification. It is the state's financial and banking center and home to the state's largest and busiest airport.

Manchester also claims Revolutionary General John Stark as one of its native sons. Stark was born in Derryfield, now a part of Manchester. In an 1809 letter commemorating his troops' victory at the Battle of Bennington, Stark said, "Live free or die, death is not the worst of evils." More than 100 years later, his words—live free or die—became the state motto.

Information: Chamber of Commerce | 889 Elm St., Manchester 03101 | 603/666–6600 | www.manchester-chamber.org.

MANCHESTER

INTRO
ATTRACTIONS
DINING
LODGING

Attractions

Amoskeag Fishways. From an underwater viewing window you can watch the shad and river herring climb the fish ladder near the Amoskeag Dam during the migration period in May and June. The visitor's center has year-round interactive exhibits and programs as well as a hydroelectric station viewing area. | Fletcher St. | 603/626–3474 | www.amoskeag-fishways.com | Free | May–June, daily 9–5; July–Apr., Mon.–Sat. 9:30–5.

Currier Gallery of Art. This 1929 Beaux Arts building houses a collection of European and American paintings, sculpture, and decorative arts from the Renaissance to the 20th century. Works by Monet, Picasso, Hopper, and O'Keeffe are among its prizes. Also part of the museum is the Frank Lloyd Wright–designed Zimmerman House, built in 1950. Wright called this sparse, utterly functional style living space "Usonian." The house is New England's only Wright-designed residence open to the public. | 201 Myrtle Way | 603/669–6144, 603/626–4158 for Zimmerman House tours | www.currier.org | Museum $5 (free Sat. 10–1), Zimmerman House $7 (reservations required) | Sun.–Mon. and Wed.–Thurs. 11–5, Fri. 11–9, Sat. 10–5.

Lawrence L. Lee Scouting Museums & Max I. Silber Library. The world's finest collection of Scouting memorabilia and books displays rare items from the collection of the founder of scouting, Lord Baden-Powell. | Camp Carpenter, Bodwell Rd. | 603/669–8919 | www.scoutingmuseum.org | Free | July–Aug., daily 10–4; Sept.–June, Sat. 10–4.

Manchester Historic Association. This museum houses exhibits, collections, and a research library on Manchester and the textile mills that made the city famous during the Industrial Revolution. | 129 Amherst St. | 603/622–7531 | www.manchesterhistoric.org | Free | Tues.–Fri. 9–4, Sat. 10–4.

Science Enrichment Encounters (SEE) Center. This hands-on discovery center features more than 65 exhibits demonstrating basic principles of science. | 200 Bedford St. | 603/669–0400 | www.see-sciencecenter.org | $4 | Mon.–Fri. 10–3, Sat.–Sun. 12–5.

ON THE CALENDAR

JULY–AUG.: *Manchester Summer Concert Series.* Free outdoor concerts each Thursday evening featuring regional performers. | Veteran's Park | 603/645–6825.
AUG.: *New Hampshire Antique Dealers Association Annual Show.* An antiques show and sale by New Hampshire dealers. | 603/286–7506.

Dining

★ **Bedford Village Inn.** American. In this 18th-century clapboard structure, most of the eight intimate dining rooms have fireplaces and are furnished with antiques. Try the rack of lamb. Sunday brunch. | 2 Village Inn La., Bedford | 603/472–2001 | Breakfast also available | $16–$30 | AE, DC, MC, V.

La Carreta. Mexican. Large pictures evoke Mexico in this informal restaurant that serves great margaritas in its popular bar. Try the *pollo ranchero*, marinated chicken breast with ranchero sauce and cheese on top. | 545 Daniel Webster Hwy., Maple Tree Mall | 603/628–6899 | fax 603/628–6890 | $7–$11 | AE, D, MC, V.

Lakorn Thai. Thai. You'll find a variety of spicy and nonspicy dishes in this restaurant redolent of Thailand. | 470 S. Main St. | 603/626–4545 | No lunch Sat.–Sun. | $6–$12 | D, MC, V.

Puritan Backroom. American. This dining room is a clubby place with oak furniture and Tiffany lamps. Try the grilled baby back ribs. Kids' menu. | 245 Hooksett Rd. | 603/669–6890 | $9–$21 | AE, D, DC, MC, V.

Lodging

Bedford Village Inn. Rooms vary in this Federal-style inn in Bedford village, but luxury is a constant. Restaurant. Some refrigerators, cable TV. Hot tubs. Business services. | 2 Village Inn La., Bedford | 603/472–2001 or 800/852–1166 | fax 603/472–2379 | www.bedfordvillageinn.com | 14 rooms | $195–$295 | AE, DC, MC, V.

Comfort Inn & Conference Center. A modern five-story hotel in downtown within walking distance to attractions. Complimentary Continental breakfast. In-room data ports, some refrigerators, cable TV. Indoor pool. Saunas. Exercise equipment. Laundry facilities. Business services. Airport shuttle. Pets allowed. | 298 Queen City Ave. | 800/228–5150 | 603/668–2600 | www.hotelchoice.com | 104 rooms | $65–$126 | AE, D, DC, MC, V.

Econo Lodge. A chain motel in a converted mill building overlooking the Merrimack River. Some microwaves, refrigerators, cable TV. Laundry facilities. Business services. Pets allowed (fee). | 75 W. Hancock St. | 603/624–0111 or 800/553–2666 | fax 603/623–0268 | 120 rooms | $40–$80 | AE, D, DC, MC, V.

Four Points By Sheraton. Less than a mile from the Mall of New Hampshire. Restaurant, bar. Some refrigerators, room service, cable TV. Indoor pool. Hot tub. Business services. Airport shuttle, free parking. | 55 John Devine Dr. | 603/668–6110 or 800/325–3535 | fax 603/668–0408 | www.sheraton.com | 120 rooms | $89–$170 | AE, D, DC, MC, V.

Holiday Inn The Center of New Hampshire. A 12-story hotel and conference center in the heart of the city. Restaurant, bar with entertainment. In-room data ports, room service, cable TV. Indoor pool. Hot tub. Exercise equipment. Business services. Airport shuttle, free parking. | 700 Elm St. | 603/625–1000 or 800/465–4329 | fax 603/625–4595 | www.thecenteratcnhhi.grolen.com | 250 rooms | $109–$139 | AE, D, DC, MC, V.

Super 8. A basic four-story hotel just off Route 293. Some refrigerators, some in-room hot tubs, cable TV. Airport shuttle, free parking. | 2301 Brown Ave. | 603/623–0883 or 800/800–8000 | fax 603/624–9303 | www.super8.com | 93 rooms | $59–$149 | AE, D, DC, MC, V.

Susse Chalet Inn. A typical property in the chain, just off Route 293 Exit 1. Complimentary Continental breakfast. In-room data ports, some refrigerators, cable TV. Pool. Business services. Free parking. | 860 S. Porter St. | 603/625–2020 or 800/524–2538 | fax 603/623–7562 | www.sussechalet.com | 102 rooms | $59–$79 | AE, D, DC, MC, V.

Wayfarer Inn. With a river, waterfall, covered bridge, and restored gristmill, this modern inn lends a real touch of New England. Restaurant, bar with entertainment. In-room data ports, no-smoking rooms, some refrigerators, room service, cable TV. 2 pools (1 indoor). Hot tub. Exercise equipment. Business services. Airport shuttle, Free parking. | 121 S. River Rd., Bedford | 603/622–3766 | fax 603/625–1126 | www.wayfarerinn.com | 194 rooms | $95–$109 | AE, D, DC, MC, V.

MEREDITH

(Nearby towns also listed: Center Harbor, Moultonborough, Weirs Beach)

Meredith is a popular resort town on the western end of Lake Winnipesaukee, the sixth-largest lake completely inside U.S. borders.

Information: Chamber of Commerce | 272 Daniel Webster Hwy., Meredith, 03253 | 603/279–6121 | www.meredithcc.org.

Attractions

Annalee's Doll Museum. Come see the world's largest collection of Annalee dolls at this museum with over 800 pieces spanning the creative career of Annalee Thorndike, the doll's creator and museum curator. | 50 Reservoir Rd. | 603/279–4144 | www.annalee.com | Free | Mid-June–Labor Day, daily 9–5, closed mid-Oct.–mid-June.

Lakes Region Symphony Orchestra. A community-based teaching orchestra with three winter concerts per year performed at the Inner Lakes Community Auditorium. | Rte. 25 | 603/279–5900.

League of New Hampshire Craftsmen. This store is one of seven that exhibit and sell contemporary and traditional crafts made by members of the League. | 279 Daniel Webster Hwy. (U.S. 3) | 603/279–7920 | Daily 10–5; sun 12–5.

Meredith Marina. This is the place to rent a powerboat to explore Lake Winnipesaukee. | Bay Shore Dr. | 603/279–7921 | June–Sept., daily.

Mill Falls Marketplace. Just a stone's throw from 40-ft Mill Falls, this delightful set of shops has 15 boutiques, restaurants, galleries, and an ice-cream parlor. | Junction Rtes. 3 and 25, Lake Winnepesaukee | 603/279–7006 or 800/622–6455 | Free | Mon.–Thurs. 10–5:30, Fri.–Sat. 10–8, Sun. 10–4.

Wellington State Beach. A ½-mi stretch of beach on Newfound Lake, ideal for swimming, sunning, or picnics, 4 mi north of Meredith in Bristol. | Rte. 3A, Bristol | 603/744–2197 | $2.50 | Daily.

Winnipesaukee Scenic Railroad. Early-19th-century railroad cars carry passengers along the shore of Lake Winnipesaukee on one- to two-hour rides. Passengers can board at Weirs Beach or Meredith. | U.S. 3 | 603/745–2135 | www.hoborr.com | $8.50 | June 24–Labor Day, daily; Labor Day–Oct., weekends only; call for departure and ride times.

ON THE CALENDAR

JUNE–AUG.: *Lakes Region Summer Theater.* Broadway musical productions six nights a week in summer. | Lakes Region Theater, Rte. 25 | Wed.–Thurs. at 2, Tues.–Sat. at 8, Sun. at 7 | 603/279–9933 | www.lrst.com | $18.

AUG.: *Lakes Region Fine Arts and Crafts Festival.* An annual event with over 100 artists and craftspeople. | 603/279–6121.

SEPT.: *Altrusa Annual Antiques Show and Sale.* Another opportunity to test your acquisitive mettle. | 603/279–6121.

Dining

Hart's Turkey Farm Restaurant. American. Founded in 1954, this family-style restaurant grew out of a turkey farm and turkey is still its specialty, along with seafood and prime rib. Kids' menu. | 233 Daniel Webster Hwy.; at Rte. 104 | 603/279–6212 | $5–$19 | AE, D, DC, MC, V.

Mame's. Continental. An 1825 brick village home, just a two-minute walk from the Millsfalls Marketplace, that has six dining rooms with exposed beams, antiques, and a tavern

MEREDITH

INTRO
ATTRACTIONS
DINING
LODGING

with light fare in evening. Try the prime rib. Kids' menu. Sunday brunch with entrées. | 8 Plymouth St. | 603/279–4631 | $10–$20 | AE, D, MC, V.

Meredith Bay Bakery and Cafe. American/Casual. A small eatery favored by locals who stop in for a hearty breakfast or lunchtime sandwich made on fresh, homemade bread. | 7 Main St. | 603/279–2279 | Breakfast also available. No dinner | $3–$6 | D, DC, MC, V.

Lodging

Inn at Bay Point. A country inn on Lake Winnipesaukee. Restaurant, bar, picnic area, complimentary Continental breakfast. Some refrigerators, room service, cable TV, some in-room VCRs. Hot tub, sauna. Exercise equipment, beach, dock. Business services. | Rte. 25 | 603/279–7006 or 800/622–6455 | fax 603/279–6797 | www.millsfalls.com | 24 rooms | $129–$259 | AE, D, DC, MC, V.

Inn at Mill Falls. Next to Mill Falls Marketplace. Refrigerators available, room service, cable TV, some in-room VCRs. Indoor pool. Hot tub, sauna, gym. Business services. | 312 Daniel Webster Hwy. (U.S. 3) | 603/279–7006 or 800/622–6455 | fax 603/279–6797 | www.mills-falls.com | 55 rooms | $69–$189 | AE, D, DC, MC, V.

Nutmeg Inn. This 1763 home was built by a sea captain who dismantled his ship for the lumber. It was also a part of the Underground Railroad. The rooms are named with spice themes. Complimentary breakfast. No smoking, TV and VCR in common room. Pool. No kids under 6. No pets. | 80 Pease Rd. | 603/279–8811 | nutmeginn@aol.com | www.bbhost.cpm/nutmeginn | 8 rooms | $85–$105 | Closed Nov.–mid May (except open weekends Dec.–Feb.) | MC, V.

MERRIMACK

MAP 7, E11

(Nearby towns also listed: Manchester, Milford, Nashua)

This suburb halfway between Manchester and Nashua, the state's two largest cities, is known primarily today as the regional home of Anheuser-Busch. It was also the home of Matthew Thornton, who presided over the Provincial Congress in 1775 and signed the Declaration of Independence.

Information: **Chamber of Commerce** | Box 254, 301 Daniel Webster Hwy., Merrimack, 03054 | 603/424–3669 | fax 603/429–4325 | www.merrimackchamber.org.

Attractions

Anheuser Busch, Inc. Tours of the brewery where Michelob and Busch beers are made end in the tasting room, where adults can sample the brews. Some of the famous Anheuser Busch Clydesdale horses are stabled on the grounds and are reached by a short walk through the gardens. On the first Saturday of each month, you can have your picture taken with one of these famous horses if you bring your camera. | 221 Daniel Webster Hwy., U.S. 3 Exit 10 | 603/595–1202 | www.budweisertours.com | Free | May–Oct., daily 9:30–5; Nov.–May, Wed.–Sun. 10–4.

Dining

Chez Gilly. American. A Gallic mood prevails in this rustic restaurant and bakery. You'll find everything from shrimp scampi and filet mignon to deli sandwiches and French pastry. | 32 Daniel Webster Hwy. | 603/880–3635 | Breakfast also available. No supper Sun.–Wed. | $5–$8 | AE, MC, V.

Country Gourmet. Continental. An upscale and casually elegant restaurant that specializes in seafood. | 438 Daniel Webster Hwy. | 603/424–2755 | No lunch. | $14–$22 | AE, D, DC, MC, V.

Stormy Monday's. American. This restaurant serves light café fare with Cajun hints in a laid-back blues bar. Live music Wednesday–Monday. Kids' menu. | 438 Daniel Webster Hwy. | 603/424–2755 | www.stormymonday.com | No lunch | $6–$12 | AE, D, DC, MC, V.

Ya Mama's. Italian. A casual, cozy place for food that your mother would have made, if your mother were Italian. Try the chicken carcioffo, made with artichoke hearts, shrimp, and provolone cheese. | 75 Daniel Webster Hwy. | 603/883–2264 | No lunch Sat.–Sun. | $7–$17 | AE, D, DC, MC, V.

Lodging
Merrimack Days Inn. A simple, two-story member of the chain with standard furnishings. In-room data ports, cable TV, room phones. Laundry facilities. Business services. Pets allowed. | 242 Daniel Webster Hwy. | 603/429–4600 or 800/544–8313 (reservations) | fax 603/424–3804 | www.daysinn.com | 69 rooms | $55–$99 | AE, D, DC, MC, V.

Residence Inn by Marriott. A very comfortable all-suite hotel. Complimentary Continental breakfast. In-room data ports, kitchenettes, cable TV. Pool. Hot tub. Laundry facilities. Business services. Free parking. Pets allowed (fee). | 246 Daniel Webster Hwy. (Rte. 3) | 603/424–8100 or 800/331–3131 | fax 603/424–3128 | www.residenceinn.com/ashmh | 129 suites | $105–$155 | AE, D, DC, MC, V.

MILFORD

MAP 7, E12

(Nearby towns also listed: Manchester, Merrimack, Nashua)

From 1810 to the mid-1900s, Milford was known as the "Granite Town in the Granite State" because of the monument-quality stone quarried there. The arrival of the railroad in 1850 made transportation of the granite easier and local economy boomed. By 1912 there were eight granite companies. Today, the quarries are silent, but Milford remains a thriving residential community.

Information: Chamber of Commerce | 52 Nashua St., Milford, 03055 | 603/673–4360.

Attractions
The Toadstool Bookshop. A full-service, independently owned bookshop with monthly readings and other special events. A good place to find New Hampshire–related books and maps. In the Lourden's Plaza Mall. | Rte. 101A | 603/673–1734 | Mon.–Sat. 9–9, Sun. 11–5.

Dining
Lucille's Dinette. American. Old-fashioned home-style cooking is the hallmark of this cozy, brick-lined local hangout. Fresh, homemade breads and the peachy creamy French toast are the house specialties. Lunches include hearty soups, shepherd's pie, and bison burgers. | 241 Union Sq | 603/673–8599 | No dinner | $4–$6 | No credit cards.

Parker's Maple House. American. Next to a sugarhouse, where you can watch and learn about the history and making of maple syrup, this old-world restaurant has home-style meals in a rustic setting. Try the maple-glazed baby back pork ribs or the hearty breakfast, while buying some wood-fired maple syrup at the gift shop. | 1313 Brookline Rd., Mason | 603/878–2308 or 800/832–2308 | www.parkersmaplebarn.com | Breakfast also available. Valentine's Day–mid-Dec., open daily. No dinner Mon.–Fri. | $10–$17 | AE, D, DC, MC, V.

Lodging
Zahn's Alpine Guest House. Tucked into the woods off Route 113 is this Austrian-style chalet with a Bavarian tile oven, Alpine carpets, regional antiques, and balconies. Complimentary Continental breakfast. In-room data ports, no smoking, cable TV, in-room VCRs.

No pets. | 97 S. Main St., Mount Vernon | 603/673–2334 | fax 603/673–8415 | www.inter-condesign.com/zahns | 8 rooms | $65 | AE, D, MC, V.

MOULTONBOROUGH

MAP 7, F8

(Nearby towns also listed: Center Harbor, Center Sandwich, Meredith, Wolfeboro)

With miles of shoreline on Lakes Kanasatka, Winnipesaukee, and Squam, Moultonborough is full of vacation homes owned by out-of-staters. The rolling hills to the northeast of Lake Winnipesaukee, the Ossipee Mountains, offer outstanding views. Thomas Gustave Plant spent three years and several million dollars building his mansion on top of one of those hills. Today, the Castle in the Clouds, as it is called, is the town's main attraction.

Information: **Squam Lakes Area Chamber of Commerce** | Box 665, Ashland, 03217 | 603/968–4494.

Attractions

Castle in the Clouds. The odd, elaborate stone mansion high in the Ossipee Mountains was built by Thomas Gustave Plant between 1911 and 1914. Plant spent $7 million, the bulk of his fortune, to build the 16-room house. The nearly 6,000-acre estate is now a recreation area. Tours are given of the house, the Castle Springs Microbrewery, and the Castle Springs water-bottling facility. You can also ride a paddleboat, picnic, or take a guided horseback ride. | Rte. 171 | 603/476–2352 or 800/729–2468 | $10 with tour, $4 without tour | Mid-May–mid-June, Sat., Sun. 10–4; mid-June–mid-Oct., daily 9–5.

The Loon Center. The headquarters for the Loon Preservation Committee of the New Hampshire Audubon Society has changing exhibits about these popular black-and-white birds, whose calls haunt New Hampshire's lakes. Two nature trails wind through the 200-acre property. Vantage points on the Loon Nest Trail overlook the spot resident loons sometimes occupy in June. | Lees Mills Rd. off Rte. 25 | 603/476–5666 | www.loon.org | Free | July 4–mid-Oct., daily 9–5; mid-Oct.–July 4, Mon.–Sat. 9–5.

Old Country Store and Museum. This local landmark has been selling everything from penny candy and homemade jams to coonskin caps and weather vanes since it opened in 1781. The upstairs museum is filled with old-time farming equipment. | 1101 Whittier Hwy. | 603/476–5750 | www.nhcountrystore.com | Daily 10–5.

ON THE CALENDAR
AUG.: *Lakes Region Folk Festival.* An all-day folk festival. | 603/253–4366.

Dining
The Woodshed. American. Tucked ½ mi down a quiet country road that is 1 mi south of town, this 1860s barn and farmhouse has become a local legend, serving delicious fare to a steady stream of celebrities and local folks alike. The interior is charmed and rustic with old farm implements on the walls. The home-cured, heavy-aged western beef makes for a mouthwatering prime rib, and the grilled or blackened swordfish and lobster are of equal renown. Kids' menu. | 128 Lee Rd., off Rte. 109 | 603/476–2311 | Closed Mon. No lunch | $12–$21 | AE, D, DC, MC, V.

Lodging
Matterhorn Motor Lodge. A friendly, two-story Swiss chalet–style motel set just off Route 25. Most rooms have two double beds and are suitable for families. Picnic area. No smoking, cable TV. Cross-country skiing, Snowmobiling. No pets. | Rte. 25 at Moultonborough Neck Rd. | 603/253–4314 | 28 rooms | $85–$125 | AE, D, DC, MC, V.

Olde Orchard Inn. A Federal-style inn in Moultonborough on 12 acres. Picnic area, complimentary breakfast. No smoking, some in-room hot tubs, no room phones, cable TV, TV in common area. Cross-country skiing. | 108 Lee Rd. | 603/476–5004 or 800/598–5845 | fax 603/476–5419 | www.oldeorchardinn.com | 9 rooms | $75–$140 | D, MC, V.

MT. WASHINGTON AND PINKHAM NOTCH

(Nearby towns also listed: Glen, Gorham, Jackson)

The crowning jewel of the Presidential Range of the White Mountains, Mt. Washington is the highest peak in the northeast at 6,288 ft. It is said to experience some of the most severe weather in the world; in fact, the yearly average temperature is below freezing. A wind velocity of 231 mph—the highest ever recorded—was registered here in April 1934. That weather gives Mt. Washington the reputation as the most dangerous small mountain in the world. In spite of all that, on a clear day the view is spectacular. The first person known to climb it was Darby Field in 1642, and it has been attracting visitors ever since. With 8 square mi above tree line, Mt. Washington has the largest area of alpine tundra east of the Rocky Mountains. The tiny alpine flowers that bloom near the summit are at their peak in late June. When weather permits, it is possible to reach the summit on foot, by railway (from Bretton Woods), or by automobile.

Most of the access to Mt. Washington is from Pinkham Notch, on the east side of the mountain. It is said that in 1790 Joseph Pinkham, for whom the notch is named, used a pig-drawn sled to reach his new home at the base of Mt. Washington. Whether he employed pigs or not, the route Pinkham forged is now scenic Route 16. Nearly all of this area is within the White Mountain National Forest, and the visitor's center is a joint venture between the Forest Service and the Appalachian Mountain Club. The White Mountain headquarters of this venerable hiking and outdoor sporting association is there as well.

MT. WASHINGTON
AND PINKHAM
NOTCH

INTRO
ATTRACTIONS
DINING
LODGING

KODAK'S TIPS FOR PHOTOGRAPHING WEATHER

Rainbows
- Find rainbows by facing away from the sun after a storm
- Use your auto-exposure mode
- With an SLR, use a polarizing filter to deepen colors

Fog and Mist
- Use bold shapes as focal points
- Add extra exposure manually or use exposure compensation
- Choose long lenses to heighten fog and mist effects

In the Rain
- Look for abstract designs in puddles and wet pavement
- Control rain-streaking with shutter speed
- Protect cameras with plastic bags or waterproof housings

Lightning
- Photograph from a safe location
- In daylight, expose for existing light
- At night, leave the shutter open during several flashes

From Kodak Guide to Shooting Great Travel Pictures © 2000 by Fodor's Travel Publications

Information: **Mt. Washington Valley Chamber of Commerce** | Box 2300, North Conway, 03860 | 603/356–3171 or 800/367–3364 | fax 603/356–7069 | www.mtwashingtonvalley.org.

Attractions

★ **Auto road.** This toll road opened in 1861 and is said to be the nation's first manufactured tourist attraction. The road is 8 mi long, with an average grade of 12%. In summer, you can drive your own vehicle to the top or take a guided van tour. In winter, a specially equipped van takes you to just above the tree line for a spectacular view of the snow-covered mountains. Winter tours begin from Great Glen Trails (*see below*). Access is from Glen House, with a rest stop in Pinkham Notch, 8 mi south of Gorham and 17 mi north of Jackson. | Rte. 16, Pinkham Notch | 603/466–3988 | www.mt-washington.com | Prices vary, call for specifics | Mid-May–mid-Oct., daily 7–6, weather permitting.

Glen Ellis Falls Scenic Area. The falls on the Ellis River are one of the most easily accessible scenic spots in the Pinkham Notch area. The parking area is just beyond the top of the notch. From there, a tunnel leads under Route 16. The trail to the falls is short and well marked. There's a picnic area here as well, and the Glen Boulder hiking trail begins at the parking area. | Rte. 16 | Free | Daily.

Dolly Copp Campground. This campground, north of Mt. Washington, is one of several in the White Mountain National Forest and the closest one to Mt. Washington. There are 170 sites. | Rte. 16 | 603/466–3984 or 877/444–6777 (reservations) | July–Columbus Day, daily.

Hiking trails. Hiking is one of the most popular activities in the White Mountains. Numerous trails lead to the summit of Mt. Washington from Pinkham Notch and to the summits of other peaks in the Presidential Range. The Tuckerman Ravine Trail, which leaves from the Pinkham Notch Visitor Center (*see below*), is one of the most popular. The Appalachian Trail, which runs through the White Mountains, can be accessed from Pinkham Notch. The Pinkham Notch Visitor Center provides information on hiking, weather conditions, and equipment to Appalachian Mountain Club members and the public alike. AMC lodges and huts are popular among hikers planning trips of more than one day. | Rte. 16 | 603/466–2725 trail information, 603/466–2727 lodging reservations | www.outdoors.org | Fee for special programs, guided hikes, and use of huts or lodges | Daily.

Mt. Washington Cog Railway. *See* Bretton Woods.

Mt. Washington Summit Museum and Observatory. The Sherman Adams Summit building contains a museum of memorabilia from each of the three hotels that have stood at the peak and a display of native plant life and alpine flowers. With approximately 8 square mi of mountain above tree line, Mt. Washington has an alpine tundra environment unique in New England. The glassed-in viewing area provides a warm spot to enjoy the White Mountains panorama even when the famed Mt. Washington wind is howling. | Top of Mt. Washington | 603/466–3388 | www.mountwashington.org | $1 | Memorial Day–mid-Oct., Daily: 9–5.

Pinkham Notch Visitor Center. The Appalachian Mountain Club operates the Pinkham Notch Visitor Center in conjunction with the White Mountain National Forest where displays describe current weather conditions and explain equipment needs for outdoor activities in the White Mountains. You can get hiking information and browse through the excellent selection of books on the region. The dining room in the center serves three meals a day. | Rte. 16 | 603/466–2725 trail information, 603/466–2727 lodging reservations | www.outdoors.org | Fee for special programs, guided hikes, and lodging | Daily.

Skiing. There are both alpine and Nordic skiing opportunities in Pinkham Notch.
Great Glen Trails. This outdoor sports company a mile north of the Pinkham Notch Visitor Center has 24 mi of groomed cross-country trails and more than 1,100 acres of backcountry skiing. You can even ski the lower half of the Mt. Washington Auto Road. Snowshoeing is another popular winter activity. In summer, you can mountain-bike, go fly-fishing, or

learn how to canoe or kayak. | Rte. 16 | 603/466–2333 | www.mt-washington.com | Daily.

Tuckerman Ravine. It's a 3-plus-mi hike, and not for beginners or the faint of heart. But each spring dedicated skiers make the trip carrying their gear in order to ski down from the top of the headwall at Tuckerman's Ravine. Over the winter, winds blow snow from Mt. Washington into the ravine, sometimes reaching depths of 75 ft. By early spring, conditions are usually right for skiing and the fun continues at least until June even as the snow melts, exposing the rocks below. Check with the Appalachian Mountain Club at the Pinkham Notch Visitor Center for avalanche warnings and conditions. | Starts at Pinkham Notch Visitor Center (*see above*) | Free.

Wildcat Ski & Recreation Area. Advanced skiers and glade skiers flock to Wildcat when the weather turns snowy. The ski area, which is totally in the White Mountain National Forest, was the home of off-piste skiing before glades became trendy. Although there are official glade trails, nothing's really off-limits. Marked trails include some stunning double black diamonds, and all the trails are narrow and winding. But there are trails for beginners as well, including the 2³⁄₄-mi Polecat. Snowboarders have several terrain parks and the run of the mountain. And on a clear day, views of Mt. Washington and Tuckerman Ravine are a bonus. | Rte. 16 | 603/466–3326 | www.skiwildcat.com | $39 midweek, $49 weekends and holidays | Dec.–mid-Apr., daily.

White Mountain National Forest. Mt. Washington and all of Pinkham Notch are in the White Mountain National Forest. *See* Lincoln and North Woodstock.

ON THE CALENDAR

MAR.: *Annual Audi Sun 'n' Ski Weekend.* A beach party in the snow with limbo contests, beach wear, and snow golf. | Great Glen Trails | 603/466–2333.

MAR.: *Annual "Ski to the Clouds" Cross-Country Race.* Competitors race 4 mi up the Mt. Washington Auto Road on either cross-country skis or snowshoes. | Mt. Washington Auto Rd. in Pinkham Notch | 603/466–2333.

JUNE: *Annual Mt. Washington Road Race.* In this event, competitors run up the Mt. Washington Auto Road, one of the country's toughest footraces. | Mt. Washington Auto Rd. in Pinkham Notch | 603/863–2537 | www.gsrs.com.

AUG.: *Mt. Washington Bicycle Hillclimb.* One of the world's most difficult bicycle hill climbs goes up the Mt. Washington Auto Road. | Mt. Washington Auto Rd. in Pinkham Notch | 603/447–6991 | www.tinmtn.com.

DEC.: *Country Inns in the White Mountains Holiday Inn-to-Inn Cookie Tour.* Once a year two-days are set aside at all the inns in the area for a self-guided walking tour. The inns are decked out in their holiday finest, sponsored by the local association of innkeepers. Compare ornaments and sample homemade cookies at each stop. Call for maps, date, and locations. | 603/356–9460 | $15.

Lodging

Joe Dodge Lodge. This hikers' lodge at the foot of Mt. Washington is next to the Pickham Notch Visitors Center and has private or single-sex dorm rooms. Restaurant. No air-conditioning, no room phones, no TV. Hiking. Cross-country skiing. | Rte. 16 | 603/466–2727 | fax 603/466–3871 | www.outdoors.org | 35 rooms to accomodate up to 100 guests | $30 per person in the dorm, $65 for private room.

NASHUA

MAP 7, F12

(Nearby towns also listed: Manchester, Merrimack, Milford, Salem)

Once a fur-trading post, Nashua became a mill town when the opening of the Middlesex Canal in 1804 gave businesses direct access to Boston markets. The town soon became one of the state's centers of business and industry. Although it is New Hampshire's second-largest city with much commercial activity, many residents commute to jobs in Massachusetts' high-technology beltway.

Information: Chamber of Commerce | City Plaza, 146 Main St., Nashua, 03060 | 603/881–8333 | www.nashua.com.

Attractions

American Stage Festival. The state's largest professional theater company presents shows in two locations. The season runs from March through October and includes five Broadway plays, one new work, and a children's theater series. | 14 Court St. | 603/886–7000 | www.americanstagefestival.com | June–Aug.

Nashua Historical Society. The collections of the Nashua Historical Society are housed in the modern Florence Hyde Spear Memorial Building behind the Abbot Spalding House. | 5 Abbot St. | 603/883–0015 | Free | Tues.–Thurs. 10–4, Sat. 1–4.

Silver Lake State Park. The eponymous small lake has a nice beach, a raft, a bathhouse, and more than 100 picnic sites scattered among the pines at this state park about 10 minutes from Nashua. | Off Rte. 122 | 603/271–3556 | www.nhparks.state.nh.us | $2.50 | Daily.

ON THE CALENDAR

JULY: *Nashua's 4th of July Celebration.* A festive Independence Day celebration at Holman Stadium, replete with a drum and bugle corps, road race, children's activities, food vendors, and a fireworks display to top it off. | Amherst St. | 10–9:30 | 603/881–8333.
SEPT.: *Twisting the Night Away.* The Nashua Downtown Association hosts this busy little fair right on Main St. It's filled with entertainment, food, vendors, kids activities, and a vintage car collection. | Main St. | 4:30–10 | 603/881–8333.
OCT.: *Nashua River Harvest Festival.* An annual gathering on the banks of the Nashua River, honoring the heritage and culture of Nashua. There is live music, entertainment, food, and water-related activites. | Water St. | 603/886–2900 | Free.

Dining

Chen Yang Li. Asian. Service is superb and decor upscale here and the menu offers dishes ranging from Peking duck to the special Yan Brothers filet mignon with black pepper sauce. | 337 Amherst St. | 603/883–6800 | $8–$15 | AE, D, DC, MC, V.

Michael Timothy's Urban Bistro. Continental. This intimate, upscale bistro has a wine and jazz bar. Try the tournedos of beef in puff pastry. Sunday brunch. | 212 Main St. | 603/595–9334 | No lunch Sat. | $13–$23 | AE, D, MC, V.

Modern Restaurant. American. A casual, country-style place that's good for steak, seafood, and chicken. Kids' menu. | 116 W. Pearl St. | 603/883–8422 | $6–$17 | AE, D, DC, MC, V.

Ninety Nine Restaurant. Steak. A down-to-earth steak house popular with families. Known for fresh seafood, steak, and fajitas. Kids' menu. | 10 Laurent St. | 603/883–9998 | $6–$9 | AE, D, DC, MC, V.

Pine Street Eatery. American. A local institution established in 1998, this restaurant is casual and homey—a large mural depicting the neighborhood adorns one wall, and old photos depict a little of Nashua's history. Prime rib, fresh seafood on weekends. | 136 Pine St. | 603/886–3501 | Breakfast also available | $8–$21 | MC, V.

Lodging

Comfort Inn. This two-floor property is just off Route 3 Exit 7 E. The rooms have standard furnishings, though some rooms are larger with pull-out couches and coffeemakers and are suitable for families. Complimentary Continental breakfast, restaurant. In-room data ports, some microwaves, some refrigerators, cable TV. Outdoor pool. Laundry facilities. Business services. No pets. | 10 St. Laurent St. | 603/883–7700 | fax 603/595–2107 | www.comfortinn.com | 104 rooms | $99–$109 | AE, D, DC, MC, V.

Crowne Plaza. A comfortable eight-story member of the chain. Restaurant, bar, dining room. In-room data ports, some refrigerators, some in-room hot tubs, cable TV. Indoor pool. Beauty salon, hot tub. Tennis. Health club. Business services. Airport shuttle. | 2 Somerset Pkwy. | 603/886–1200 or 800/962–7482 | fax 603/595–4199 | www.crowneplazanashua.com | 226 rooms | $95–$160 | AE, D, DC, MC, V.

Holiday Inn. A nicely landscaped, standard member of the chain. Restaurant, bar with entertainment. Some kitchenettes, room service, cable TV, no VCRs. Pool. Exercise equipment. Laundry facilities. Business services. Free parking. Pets allowed. | 9 Northeastern Blvd. | 603/888–1551 | fax 603/888–7193 | www.holidayinn.com | 215 rooms, 34 suites | $69–$109, $109–$139 suites | AE, D, DC, MC, V.

Howard Johnson's. This well-maintained member of the chain has a nice air, with plenty of wood trim and clean, modern rooms. Restaurant. In-room data ports, cable TV. Indoor pool. Golf. Laundry service. Business services. No pets. | 170 Main Dunstable Rd. | 603/889–0173 | www.hojo.com | 72 rooms | $49–$84 | AE, D, DC, MC, V.

Marriott. Chandeliers and Asian art add some panache to this large hotel. Restaurant, bar. In-room data ports, some refrigerators, room service, cable TV. Indoor pool. Hot tub. Health club. Playground. Business services. Pets allowed. | 2200 Southwood Dr. | 603/880–9100 or 800/228–9290 | fax 603/886–9489 | www.marriott.com | 245 rooms | $89–$119 | AE, D, DC, MC, V.

Red Roof Inn. A part of the chain that is located 50 ft off Highway 3. Picnic area. In-room data ports, cable TV. Laundry facilities. Business services. Pets allowed. | 77 Spit Brook Rd. | 603/888–1893 or 800/733–7663 | fax 603/888–5889 | 115 rooms | $49–$80 | AE, D, DC, MC, V.

Sheraton Tara. An imitation Tudor castle. Restaurant, bar with entertainment. In-room data ports, some refrigerators, cable TV. 2 pools (1 indoor). Sauna. Tennis. Gym. Children's programs (ages infant–15). Business services. Airport shuttle. | 11 Tara Blvd. | 603/888–9970 or 800/325–3535 | fax 603/888–4112 | 337 rooms | $89–$121 | AE, D, DC, MC, V.

NEW LONDON

MAP 7, D9

(Nearby towns also listed: Newport, Sunapee, Warner)

New London, home of Colby-Sawyer College, is a good base for exploring the Lake Sunapee region. The college dates from 1837, and its redbrick buildings contrast pleasingly with white colonial-era homes in the center of town.

Information: New London & Lake Sunapee Region Chamber of Commerce | Box 532, New London, 03257 | 603/526–6575.

Attractions

Colby-Sawyer College. This small, independent college opened in 1837 is the hub of the local arts and intellectual community. Campus tours are given five days a week. | 100 Main St. | 603/526–3000 | www.colby-sawyer.edu | Tours: Mon., Wed., Fri. 10:30, 11:30, 2, 3; Tues. and Thurs. 10, 11, 2, 3; Sat. 9, 9:30, 10, 10:30, 11.

Ragged Mountain. This ski area, 20 mi northeast of New London, has 35 trails spread over 160 acres and a 1,250-ft vertical drop. The trails are pretty evenly split among beginner, intermediate, and expert. Eight lifts shuttle skiers up the mountain. | Ragged Mountain Rd., Danbury | 603/768–3475, 603/768–3971 ski conditions | www.raggedmt.com | $38 | Mid-Dec.–Mar., daily.

JUNE–SEPT. *Barn Playhouse.* In existence since the 1820s, this barn hosts the oldest continuously operated theater in New Hampshire, which puts on musicals and productions of Broadway shows. | Main St. off Rte. 11 | 603/526–4631 or 603/526–6710.

Dining

Four Corners Grille and Flying Goose Brew Pub. American. This wooden chalet-style restaurant with exposed beams, lofted ceilings, and fireplace has 18 microbrewed beers on tap as well as a variety of burgers, from Cajun to Chicago style with sautéed mushrooms and blue cheese. It also serves soups, and steaks, chicken, and the combination plate of spareribs, rotisserie chicken, and brisket. Live entertainment. There is seasonal outdoor dining with a view of the mountains. Kids' menu. | Junction Rtes. 11 and 114 | 603/526–6899 | www.flyinggoose.com | $7–$21 | AE, MC, V.

Inn at Pleasant Lake. Continental. A simple but elegant dining room with linen cloths, candles, and wood trim. The nightly prix fixe dinner menu changes according to season and the chef's inspiration. Past menu items have included wild mushroom bisque with parsley oil and grilled Chilean sea bass with a basil beurre blanc. | 125 Pleasant St. | 603/526–6271 or 800/626–4907 | $46 | D, MC, V.

Millstone. Continental. This elegant restaurant has garden views, candlelight, and fresh flowers on every table. The veal, seafood, and pasta are all good; the duck is excellent. Kids' menu. Sunday brunch. | New Port Rd. | 603/526–4201 | $10–$22 | AE, D, DC, MC, V.

New London Inn. Contemporary. The dining room of this late-18th-century inn on the Village Green serves an excellent garlic-scented New York strip steak, grilled vegetables and shiitake mushroom sampler, and herb-crusted Atlantic salmon. Kids' menu. Sunday brunch. No smoking. | 140 Main St. | 603/526–2791 | No breakfast Mon., Tues. | $13–$24 | AE, MC, V.

Potter Place Inn. Continental. The dining room is recently renovated in this 18th-century inn in Andover, 8 mi northeast of New London, has a New England feel with its rough plaster walls. The wine cellar is good and the kitchen is known for its renditions of roast duckling, fresh seafood, and game. | 88 Depot St., Andover | 603/735–5141 | Restaurant Closed on Mondays. No lunch | $15–$24 | AE, MC, V.

Lodging

Fairway Motel. A tiny motel at the Lake Sunapee Country Club. Restaurant. Cable TV. Pool. Cross-country skiing. | 100 Country Club La. | 603/526–6040 | fax 603/526–9622 | 12 rooms | $70 | D, MC, V.

Follansbee Inn. A vintage farmhouse-turned-inn on the edge of a lake that is about 4 mi southeast of New London in North Sutton. Complimentary breakfast. No smoking, no room phones. Beach, dock, boating. Bicycles. Cross-country skiing. No kids under 10. | Rte. 114, North Sutton | 603/927–4221 or 800/626–4221 | www.follansbeeinn.com | 23 rooms (12 with shared bath) | $90–$120 | MC, V.

Inn at Pleasant Lake. This 1790 Cape farmhouse was converted into summer resort in the late 1800s. The inn has a country-antiques decor. Dining room (by reservation only), picnic area, complimentary breakfast. No smoking, no room phones, no TV, TV in common area. Beach. | 125 Pleasant St. | 603/526–6271 or 800/626–4907 | fax 603/526–4111 | www.innatpleasantlake.com | 11 rooms | $110–$165 | D, MC, V.

Lamplighter Motor Inn. A motel with spacious rooms right in the middle of New London. You'll find complimentary coffee and doughnuts in the lobby each morning. Some kitchenettes, some refrigerators, cable TV, some in-room VCRs. Business services. No pets. | 6 Newport Rd. | 603/526–6484 | 14 rooms | $55–$70 | AE, D, DC, MC, V.

New London Inn. A rambling late-18th-century hostelry on Main St. Restaurant, bar, complimentary breakfast. No air-conditioning in some rooms, no smoking, no TV, some in-room VCRs, TV in common area. Business services. | 140 Main St. (Rte. 114) | 603/526–2791 or 800/

526–2791 | fax 603/526–2749 | nlinn@kear.com | www.newlondoninn.com | 25 rooms (6 with shower only) | $110–$150 | AE, MC, V.

NEWPORT

(Nearby towns also listed: New London, Sunapee)

Sarah Hale, who rose to prominence as editor of *Ladies Magazine* and *Godey's Lady's Book*, came from the mill town of Newport. She's also remembered as the author of "Mary Had a Little Lamb" and for urging President Lincoln to adopt Thanksgiving as a national holiday.

Information: Chamber of Commerce | 2 N. Main St., Newport, 03773 | 603/863–1510 | fax 603/863–9486 | www.chamber.newport.nh.us.

Attractions

Claremont Historical Society Museum. A small collection of Claremont memorabilia, with photos, antiques, and books covering original settlers and prominent citizens and town history, 10 mi west of Newport. | 26 Mulberry St., Claremont | 603/543–1400 | Free.

Library Arts Center. The center has rotating exhibits of fine crafts, paintings and sculptures by local artisans, as well as classes, workshops, and performances. | 58 N. Main St. | 603/863–3040 | Free | Tues.–Sat. 11–4.

ON THE CALENDAR
FEB.: *Newport Winter Carnival.* A carnival queen contest, sliding, ski jumping, skating, and other winter activities take place all over Newport on the second weekend of the month. | 603/863–1510.

Lodging

Cutter's Loft Bed and Breakfast. A restored 1796 colonial farmhouse set among lush gardens and within walking distance to Gunnison Lake. Handmade quilts and antiques adorn the rooms. Complimentary breakfast. No smoking, no room phones, TV in common area. No pets. | 686 Washington Rd. (Rte. 31) | 603/863–1019 | fax 603/863–9227 | bryantw@cyberportal.net | www.angelfire.com/nh/cuttersloftbb | 2 rooms | $70 | Closed Thanksgiving and Christmas | No credit cards.

Newport Motel. A basic motel with clean, comfortable rooms. Some refrigerators, cable TV. Pool. No pets. | 467 Sunapee St. | 603/863–1440 or 800/741–2619 | 18 rooms | $53–$75 | AE, MC, V.

Soo Nipi Lodge. This fully restored 140-year-old dairy barn on 5 acres is now a unique lodging experience for groups. Up to 20 people gather for retreats, reunions, and outdoor excursions and have exclusive run of the facilities which include 4,000 square ft of floor space, floor-to-ceiling windows with views of Mt. Sunapee and Sunapee Lake, a living room with fireplace and cathedral ceilings, and five communal bedrooms. Picnic area. No smoking, no room phones, TV in common area. Hiking, volleyball. Cross-country skiing. No pets. | 5 Schoolhouse Rd. | 603/863–7509 | fax 603/863–7509 | www.soo-nipi-lodge.com | 5 rooms with shared bath | $600 | MC, V.

NORTH CONWAY

MAP 7, G6

(Nearby towns also listed: Bartlett, Conway, Glen, Intervale, Jackson)

North Conway has long been the commercial center of the Mt. Washington Valley recreation area. People came to ski, hike, bicycle, and enjoy scenery so captivating that in 1850 artist Benjamin Champney set up his easel in the middle of the road to paint the view of Mt. Washington. Skiing became the primary focus in the latter half of the 20th century. The Cranmore Skimobile was built in 1938 and Austrian ski instructor Hannes Schneider arrived a year later. Although many visitors still come for these reasons, the 150 or more outlet stores built during the 1980s bring busloads of shoppers in all seasons and weather. Everyone complains about the traffic, but people keep coming all the same.

Information: Mt. Washington Valley Chamber of Commerce | Box 2300, North Conway, 03860 | 603/356–3171 or 800/367–3364 | www.mtwashingtonvalley.org.

Attractions

Conway Scenic Railroad. Vintage coaches pulled by steam or diesel engines, including a dome observation coach, travel through some of the finest scenery in the Northeast. The trip through Crawford Notch is especially scenic. The 1874 Victorian train station has displays of railroad artifacts, lanterns, and old tickets and timetables. Foliage-season trains and special December trains sell out early, sometimes months in advance. | 38 Norcross Circle, just behind Schouler Park | 603/356–5251 or 800/232–5251 | www.conwayscenic.com | $9.50–$48 depending on trip | Mid-May–late Oct., daily 9–6; Apr.–mid-May and Nov.–late Dec., Sat., Sun. 10–3; call or check Web site for departure times.

Cranmore Mt. Resort. This ski area on the outskirts of North Conway opened in 1938. The mountain's 38 trails are well laid out and fun to ski. Snowboarders have a terrain park and a halfpipe. There's also outdoor skating, snowshoeing, and, on Fridays and Saturdays until 9 and Sundays until 4, snow tubing. | 1 Skimobile Rd., 1 mi east of U.S. 302 (Rte. 16) | 603/356–5543, 603/356–8516 snow conditions, 800/786–6754 lodging | www.cranmore.com | Mid-Dec.–Mar., daily.

YOUR CAR'S FIRST-AID KIT

- ❏ Bungee cords or rope to tie down trunk if necessary
- ❏ Club soda to remove stains from upholstery
- ❏ Cooler with bottled water
- ❏ Extra coolant
- ❏ Extra windshield-washer fluid
- ❏ Flares and/or reflectors
- ❏ Flashlight and extra batteries
- ❏ Hand wipes to clean hands after roadside repair
- ❏ Hose tape
- ❏ Jack and fully inflated spare
- ❏ Jumper cables
- ❏ Lug wrench
- ❏ Owner's manual
- ❏ Plastic poncho—in case you need to do roadside repairs in the rain
- ❏ Quart of oil and quart of transmission fluid
- ❏ Spare fan belts
- ❏ Spare fuses
- ❏ Tire-pressure gauge

Echo Lake State Park. A paved road 2 mi west of North Conway leads to the top of scenic White Horse Ledge. From there you'll have a panoramic view of the White Mountains, the Saco River valley, and Echo Lake at the base of the ledge. Swimming is allowed in the lake and there are picnic sites scattered throughout the park. | Off U.S. 302 | 603/356–2672 | www.nhparks.state.nh.us | $2.50 | Daily.

Factory outlet stores. North Conway is famous among outlet shoppers. The more than 150 stores include Anne Klein, Reebok, L. L. Bean, and Dansk. | Rte. 16 | Daily.

Kayak Jack Fun Yak Rentals. Full and half-day kayak and canoe trips on the Saco River. Transportation to the launching point is available, and the trip terminates at your car. Double-wide kayaks are suitable for beginners. | 558 White Mountain Hwy. (Rte. 16) | 603/447–5571 | $25–$35 | Memorial Day–Labor Day.

League of New Hampshire Craftsmen. This store is one of seven that exhibit and sell contemporary and traditional crafts made by members of the League. | 2526 Main St. (Rte. 16) | 603/356–2441 | www.nhcrafts.org | Daily 9:30–5:30.

Zeb's General Store. Named after local sea legend Captain Zebulon Northrup Tilton, this store has become legendary in its own right with nearly 5,000 items in its inventory of New England's finest food and crafts. | 2675 Main St. | 603/356–9294 or 800/676–9294 | www.zebs.com. | Mid-June–Christmas, Daily 9–10. Christmas–mid-June, Daily 9–8.

NORTH CONWAY

INTRO
ATTRACTIONS
DINING
LODGING

ON THE CALENDAR

EASTER WEEKEND: *Bunny Express and Easter Parade.* The Easter Bunny arrives by train and leads an Easter parade. | 603/356–8776.

JUNE–SEPT.: *Eastern Slope Playhouse.* | On the grounds of Eastern Slope Inn Resort, Main St. | 603/356–5776.

JULY–AUG.: *Arts Jubilee.* An outdoor, free summer concert series geared to family audiences. Shows, including jazz, folk, swing, and Celtic performances, are held on Friday nights in Schouler Park in North Conway Village, 8 mi south of Glen. | Rte. 16 | Show times 6 and 7:30 | 603/356–9393 | www.monarchenterprises.com/artsjubilee.

OCT.: *Annual Rail Fan's Weekend.* A flea market, equipment demonstrations, special train rides, and other railroad-related events. | Conway Scenic Railroad | 603/356–5251.

Dining

Bellini's. Italian. Victorian on the outside, this town-center restaurant feels like something straight out of Tuscany on the inside, with copper-topped tables and vintage posters to burnish the effect. Try the rigatoni broccoli chicken or veal Marsala. Open-air patio. Kids' menu. | 33 Seavey St. | 603/356–7000 | Closed Tues. No lunch | $12–$24 | AE, D, DC, MC, V.

Cafe Chimes. Vegetarian. A funky basement hangout for local health-conscious souls. All of the food is homemade, including the veggie burgers and the curried tofu sandwich. Try the natural soups, salads, breads, and cookies. | Norcross Center | 603/356–5500 | No dinner | $3–$7 | MC, V.

Elvio's Pizza. Pizza. A warm, casual eatery with exposed brick walls where you can order a variety of pizzas or dishes like shrimp scampi and veal Marsala at the counter. There is outdoor dining in summer, a nice wine list, and combinations of Italian and American cuisines. | Main St. | 603/356–3307 | $4–$10 | MC, V.

Horsefeathers. American. Touted as "The greatest neighborhood eatery in the known universe," this eccentric local hangout fosters a lighthearted spirit with local microbrewed beers and good eats. Try the apple-smoked bacon cheddar burger or the pork tenderloin with spicy red beans and green rice. Live music on weekends. | Main St. | 603/356–2687 | fax 603/356–9368 | www.horsefeathers.com | $6–$18 | AE, MC, V.

Ledges Dining Room at the White Mountain Hotel and Resort. American. A simple dining room with wide-open views of the surrounding mountains. Try the New Hampshire apple chicken with a caramelized apple sauce, farm-raised venison with roasted shallots in a cranberry currant sauce, or the Friday-night seafood buffet. Live entertainment. Sunday brunch. | Hales Location, West Side Rd. | 603/356–8732 or 800/533–6301 | fax 603/356–8732 | $15–$24 | AE, D, MC, V.

Moat Mountains Smokehouse and Brewery. American. This restaurant is in an early-1800s late-colonial building with great views of Mt. Washington. There's an in-house brewery and a patio. Try the smoked salmon with black beans, rice with roasted garlic aoili, or the Texas-style pecan-smoked brisket. Vegetarian menu. Kids' menu. Sunday brunch. | 3378 White Mountain Hwy. | 603/356–6381 | $6–$20 | D, DC, MC, V.

Muddy Moose. American. This wilderness lodge–cum–restaurant is rustic and casual, fitted with antler chandeliers, exposed wood, and an outdoor deck over Cathedral Ledge with views of the White Mountains. Try the Muddy Moose spareribs in a blackberry barbecue sauce or the Cajun catfish sandwich. | Rte. 16 | 603/356–6381 | fax 603/356–7696 | $9–$16 | AE, D, MC, V.

Peach's. Contemporary. This turn-of-the-20th-century house has an expansive front porch and five small dining rooms. Try the homemade corned-beef hash and homemade soups. | Main St. | 603/356–5860 | Breakfast also available. No dinner | $3–$9 | No credit cards.

Pinkham's Pub. American. This laid-back, hardy pub in the Eastern Slope Inn has a hardwood bar, copper mantle fireplace, and an enclosed courtyard and dance floor. The menu features fare from basic bar snacks to grilled burgers, deluxe sandwiches, and nightly specials. You can choose from over 70 brands of microbrewed beers. Live entertainment on summer weekends. | Main St. | 603/356–6321 or 800/258–4708 | fax 603/356–8732 | No breakfast | $7–$14 | AE, D, DC, MC, V.

1785 Inn. French. You can see Mt. Washington from this lovely restaurant in a late-18th-century home 1½ mi north of North Conway. Meals are served in a formal dining room and a glass-enclosed porch. Try the rack of lamb and venison. No smoking. Kids' portions available. | Rte. 16 | 603/356–9025 | Breakfast also available. No lunch | $16–$29 | AE, D, DC, MC, V.

Stonehurst Manor. Pizza. An 1876 mansion with four dining rooms that serves up a host of creative pizzas from its wood-fired oven. The oak-smoked, aged prime rib and the salmon, dill-cured and cooked on a cedar shingle, are equally popular. | Rte. 16 | 800/525–9100 | No lunch | $9–$22 | AE, D, DC, MC, V.

Lodging

Best Western Red Jacket Mountain View Hotel. A chain motel on 40 acres on top of Sunset Hill with panoramic mountain views. 2 Restaurants/bars and entertainment. Some kitchenettes, refrigerators, room service, some in-room hot tubs, cable TV. 2 pools (1 indoor). Sauna. Tennis. Gym, hiking. Video games. Children's programs (ages 4–12), playground, laundry facilities. Business services. | 2251 White Mt. Hwy. (Rte. 16) | 603/356–5411 or 800/752–2538 | fax 603/356–3842 | rjacket@landmark.net | www.redjacketinns.com | 154 rooms, 12 town houses | $129–$279 | AE, D, DC, MC, V.

Buttonwood Inn. Shaker-style furnishings, stenciling, and murals fill this early-19th-century inn on 17 wooded hillside acres 2 mi north of North Conway. Complimentary breakfast. No smoking, some in-room hot tubs, cable TV in common area. Pool. Hiking. Cross-country skiing. | Mt. Surprise Rd. (Rte. 16) | 603/356–2625 or 800/258–2625 | fax 603/356–3140 | innkeeper@buttonwoodinn.com | www.buttonwoodinn.com | 10 rooms | $95–$225 | AE, D, MC, V.

Cranmore Inn. A Civil War–era (1863) hostelry within walking distance of the North Conway town center. Complimentary breakfast. No air-conditioning, cable TV in common area. Pool. | 80 Kearsarge St. | 603/356–5502 or 800/526–5502 | www.cranmooreinn.com | 18 rooms, 2 studios with kitchen | $69–$83. | AE, MC, V.

Cranmore Mountain Lodge. Babe Ruth's daughter is among those who have owned this vintage hostelry on 8 acres complete with pond and farm animals. Dining room, picnic area, complimentary breakfast. No air-conditioning in some rooms, some room phones, TV in some rooms. Pool. Hot tub. Tennis. Ice-skating. Cross-country skiing. Playground. | Kearsarge Rd. | 603/356–2044 or 800/356–3596 | fax 603/356–8963 | cu@cml1.com | www.cml1.com | 28 rooms in 3 buildings, 40 bunks in hostel, 4 suites | $105–$136, $145–$300 suites., $17 bunk in hostel | AE, D, DC, MC, V.

Eastern Slope Inn Resort. In operation since 1925, this inn is on 40 acres and is within walking distance of the center of North Conway. Restaurant, bar with entertainment, picnic area. Cable TV, some in-room VCRs. Indoor pool, pond. Hot tub, sauna. Tennis. Laundry facilities. | 2760 Main St. (Rte. 16) | 603/356–6321 or 800/862–1600 | fax 603/356–8732 | www.easternslopeinn.com | 145 rooms, 20 condos, 4 cottages | $89–139, $179–$309 condos | AE, D, MC, V.

Eastman Inn. The furnishings are all period pieces in this late-18th-century charmer with a sprawling porch and a fireplace-warmed common area. Complimentary breakfast. No smoking, cable TV. | Rte. 16 | 603/356–6707 or 800/626–5855 | eastman@eastmaninn.com | www.eastmaninn.com | 14 rooms | $79–$199 | D, MC, V.

Four Points by Sheraton. A large resort hotel with outlet shopping on the grounds. Restaurant, bar. In-room data ports, some minibars, some refrigerators, cable TV. Indoor pool. Hot tub, sauna. Tennis. Ice-skating. Gym. Video games. Playground, laundry facilities. Business services. | Settlers' Green | 603/356–9300 or 800/648–4397 | fax 603/356–6028 | www.4pointsnconway.com | 200 rooms, 10 suites | $99–$179, $199 suites | AE, D, DC, MC, V.

Fox Ridge Motor Inn. A family resort on 300 acres with fine mountain views. Restaurant, picnic area. Some refrigerators, cable TV. 2 pools (1 indoor). Hot tub. Tennis. Video games. Children's programs (ages 4–12), playground. | Rte. 16 | 603/356–3151 or 800/343–1804 | fax 603/356–0096 | www.foxridgeresort.com | 136 rooms | $67–$175 | Closed Nov.–mid-May | AE, MC, V.

Golden Gables Inn. A standard one- and two-story independent motel. Some microwaves, some refrigerators, cable TV. Pool. Hot tub. | Rte. 16 | 603/356–2878 | fax 603/356–9094 | www.goldengablesinn.com | 40 rooms | $69–$129 | AE, D, DC, MC, V.

Green Granite Inn & Conference Center. A two-story motor inn near the outlet shops. Picnic area, complimentary Continental breakfast. Some refrigerators, some in-room hot tubs, cable TV, some in-room VCRs. 2 pools (1 indoor). Hot tub. Gym. Playground. | Rte. 302 E/16 S | 603/356–6901 or 800/468–3666 | fax 603/356–6980 | granite@nxi.com | www.greengranite.com | 86 rooms, 5 suites | $59–$169 rooms, $129–229 suites | AE, D, MC, V.

Junge's Motel. A small resort hotel on trail-covered 35 acres bordering the Saco River, 1½ mi. south of N. Conway. Picnic area. Cable TV. Pool. Playground. | 1858 White Mountain Hwy. (Rte. 16) | 603/356–2886 | www.jungesmotel.com | 28 rooms | $75–$125 | AE, D, MC, V.

Merrill Farm Resort. The Saco River runs through the grounds of this late-18th-century former farmhouse. Picnic area, complimentary Continental breakfast. Some kitchenettes, some refrigerators, cable TV. Pool. Hot tub, sauna. Laundry facilities. | 428 White Mountain Hwy. (Rte. 16) | 603/447–3866 or 800/445–1017 | fax 603/447–3867 | merril2@ncia.net | www.merrillfarm.com | 63 rooms, 17 suites, 11 cottages | $99–$159 | AE, D, DC, MC, V.

North Conway Mountain Inn. An attractive, nicely furnished two-story motel. No smoking, cable TV. | Rte. 16 | 603/356–2803 | www.mountaininn.com | 32 rooms | $69–$159 | MC, V.

Old Red Inn and Cottages. An 1810 candy-apple-red farmhouse with quintessential New England furnishings like four-poster and canopy beds and handmade quilts in each room. Cottages have gas-log fireplaces and are suitable for families. Complimentary breakfast. Some kitchenettes, some refrigerators, cable TV, no room phones. Outdoor pool. No pets. | 2406 White Mountain Hwy. (Rte. 16) | 603/356–2642 or 800/338–1356 | fax 603/356–6626 | oldredinn@nxi.com | www.oldredinn.com | 7 rooms (2 with shared bath), 10 cottages | $58–$178 | AE, D, MC, V.

Oxen Yoke Inn. Choose from motel, B&B, or cottage accommodations at this quiet colonial house and barn. Guests have access to all facilities at the Eastern Slope Inn. Complimentary breakfast. Some kitchenettes, some refrigerators, no smoking, some in-room hot tubs, cable TV. Video games. Library. Children's programs, playground. Pets allowed. | Kearsage St. | 603/356–6321 or 800/258–4706 | www.easternslopeinn.com | 15 rooms, 5 cottages | $80–$177 | AE, D, MC, V.

Purity Spring Resort. A family run, 100-year-old, four-season resort with an on-premise ski area (King Pine), lodge, and lakeside cottages. Choose from B&B, lodge, or condominium accommodations. Restaurant. No air-conditioning in some rooms, some refrigerators, no TV in some rooms, TV in common area. Indoor pool. Hot tub. Tennis. Hiking, volleyball. Fishing. | Rte. 153, East Madison | 603/367–8896 or 800/373–3754 | www.purityspring.com | 74 rooms (13 with shared bath) | $53–$113 rooms, $120–$252 cottages | MAP available | AC, D, MC, V.

1785 Inn. Fireplaces keep things cozy in this early American former farmhouse on the Saco River, with rooms looking out onto Mt. Washington. Restaurant, bar, picnic area, complimentary breakfast. No air-conditioning in some rooms, some refrigerators, room service, no smoking, no room phones, no TV in some rooms, TV in the common area. Pool. Cross-country skiing. | Rte. 16 | 603/356–9025 or 800/421–1785 | fax 603/356–6081 | 17 rooms (5 with shared bath) | $99–$219 | AE, D, DC, MC, V.

Stonehurst Manor. A stunning 1876 Victorian mansion inn 1.2 mi north of Conway catering to a mixed crowd of younger adventure/sports oriented travelers and romantic getaway seekers. Rooms are elegant and warm, with colonial furnishings and finished wood trim. Complimentary breakfast. Cable TV. Outdoor pool. Hot tub. Tennis. Hiking. Cross-country skiing. Pets allowed (fee). | Rte. 16 | 603/356–3113 or 800/525–9100 | fax 603/356–3217 | smanor@aol.com | www.stonehurstmanor.com | 24 rooms (2 with shared bath) | $80–$140 | MAP | AE, MC, V.

White Mountain Hotel & Resort. The White Mountain National Forest and Echo Lake State Park abut the grounds of this resort 2 mi from North Conway, so it feels quite secluded. Dining room, bar with entertainment. Room service, cable TV. Pool. Hot tub, sauna. 9-hole golf course, putting green, tennis. Gym. Cross-country skiing. Video games. Laundry facilities. Business services. | West Side Rd., Hales Location | 603/356–7100 or 800/533–6301 | fax 603/356–7100 | www.whitemountainhotel.com | 80 rooms, 13 suites | $149–$179 | MAP available | AE, D, MC, V.

White Trellis Motel. This is one of the nicer looking motels as it does not seem out of place nestled away in the mountains; with a great view of Cathedral Edge and White Horse Mountain. Cable TV. | 3245 N. Main St. (Rte. 16) | 603/356–2492 | 22 rooms | $40–$135 | D, MC, V | wtm@ncia.net | www.whitetrellismotel.com.

Wyatt House Country Inn. An 1880 Victorian inn on the banks of the Saco River that is packed with antiques and comfortable nooks. The rooms are furnished with four-poster beds and lace trim. Afternoon English tea is a highlight. Complimentary breakfast. No smoking, cable TV, no room phones. Hiking. Cross-country skiing. No kids under 12. No pets. | Main St. (Rte. 16) | 603/356–7977 or 800/527–7978 | fax 603/356–2183 | wyatthouse@webtv.net | www.wyatthouseinn.com | 7 rooms (2 with shared bath), 3 suites | $89–$159 | AE, D, MC, V.

PETERBOROUGH

MAP 7, D11

(Nearby town also listed: Jaffrey)

The nation's first free public library opened in Peterborough in 1833. The town, incorporated in 1760, is both a commercial and cultural hub for the region. In 1907, composer Edward MacDowell founded a colony that still bears his name as an artists' retreat, and Thornton Wilder was in residence when he wrote *Our Town*. Peterborough's resemblance to the play's Grover's Corners is thus no coincidence. Only a small part of the artists' colony is open to the public. In addition to the colony, the town hosts a theater group and an arts center.

Information: **Chamber of Commerce** | Box 401, Rte. 101/202, Peterborough, 03458 | 603/924–7234 | www.peterboroughchamber.com.

Attractions
Greenfield State Park. This somewhat off-the-beaten-path state park 9 mi north of Peterborough has ½ mi of frontage on Otter Lake for swimming. There are separate areas for campers and day-trippers. In winter, you can snowmobile or cross-country ski on the hiking trails. | Forest Rd. off Rte. 136, Greenfield | 603/547–3497 | www.nhparks.state.nh.us | $2.50 | May–Oct., daily.

MacDowell Colony. Founded in 1907 as an artists' retreat, this colony, the oldest of its kind in the country, has supported the works of Thornton Wilder and Willa Cather. Artists still reside here so some areas are not open to the public. | 100 High St. | 603/924–3886 | fax 603/924–9142 | www.macdowellcolony.org | Free | Daily.

Miller State Park. This park 3 mi east of Peterborough was established in 1891 as a memorial to General James Miller, hero of the Battle of Lundy's Lane during the War of 1812. An auto road leads to a parking lot a short hike below the summit of Pack Monadnock Mt. (elevation 2,290 ft). | Rte. 101 | 603/924–3672 | www.nhparks.state.nh.us | $2.50 | May.–Oct., daily; Apr. and Nov., Sat. and Sun.

Peterborough Historical Society. The local history museum has a colonial kitchen, a country store, a mill worker's house, and exhibits of toys and tools. | 19 Grove St. | 603/924–3235 | Free | Mon.–Fri. 1–4.

Sharon Arts Center. A combination gallery and school 5 mi southeast of Peterborough, the Arts Center sells exceptional fine crafts and offers classes year-round. | 457 Rte. 123, Sharon | 603/924–7256 | www.sharonarts.org | Mon.–Sat. 10–5, Sun. 12–5.

Temple Mt. Ski Area. Temple, 4 mi east of Peterborough, is a good place for young families and learners. There are 16 trails, the majority of them for beginners and intermediates. | Rte. 101, Temple | 603/924–6949 | Dec.–mid-Mar., daily.

ON THE CALENDAR
MAY: *Children and the Arts Festival.* Celebrates children's artistic, musical, dance, and theatrical accomplishments and has a parade with giant puppets. | 603/924–7234.
JUNE–AUG. OR SEPT.: *Peterborough Players Summer Season.* Six main plays and two children's shows are presented over the summer season. | 603/924–7585 | www.peterboroughplayers.com.
JULY–AUG.: *Monadnock Music Festival.* Chamber music, piano recitals, orchestra concerts, and other musical events at various locations. | 603/868–9613.
JULY–AUG.: *TGIF Concert Series.* A Friday-night concert series in Depot Square Park with bluegrass, entertainment, and a variety of musical acts. | 603/924–7234.

Dining
Birchwood Inn. Continental. Murals painted by New England's famous wandering artist, Rufus Porter, from 1825 to 1833 fill the walls of this intimate dining room 8 mi southeast of Peterborough. Choose from one of the complete dinners which reflect seasonal tastes; the slow-roasted duckling in a Grand Marnier sauce is a Saturday-night tradition. Fresh breads and cobblers are baked daily. | Rte. 45, Temple | 603/878–3285 | Reservation essential | No lunch | $18–$24 | No credit cards.

Hancock Inn. American. New Hampshire's oldest (1789) continuously run inn, this traditional village landmark 3 mi west of Peterborough has served the likes of Daniel Webster. Try the Shaker cranberry pot roast and the Seafood Stew. No smoking. | 33 Main St., Hancock | 603/525–3318 | Reservations essential | No lunch | $18–$28 | AE, D, DC, MC, V.

Latacarta. Vegetarian. Using only organic ingredients, the students of the Monadnock School for Natural Cooking and Philosophy prepare gourmet, health-conscious, one-of-a-kind meals for private parties. *Kaiseki,* a 12-course traditional Japanese meal prepared by one of the few qualified chefs in the country, is available for $100–$200 per head. | 77 Rte. 137 | 603/924–6878 | fax 603/924–6953 | latacarta@pop.monad.net | www.pagepeople.com/lat-acar | Reservations essential | No dinner | No credit cards.

Lodging

Applegate Bed & Breakfast. A small but charming B&B named for the 90 acres of apple orchards surrounding it. Your room is in a farmhouse that dates from 1832. Complimentary breakfast. No air-conditioning, no room phones, TV in common area. | 199 Upland Farm Rd. | 603/924–6543 | fax 603/924–6543 | 4 rooms | $65–$85 | MC, V.

Birchwood Inn. This 1775 inn in Temple, 8 mi southeast of Peterborough, is listed in the National Register of Historic Places and was a layover spot for Henry David Thoreau. It has also served as the town post office and meeting hall, an antiques shop, and a general store. Rooms look much the way they did centuries ago. Restaurant, complimentary breakfast. No smoking, no room phones, TV in common room. No kids under 11. | Rte. 45, Temple | 603/878–3285 | fax 603/878–2159 | wolfe@birchwood.mv.com | 7 rooms (2 with shared bath) | $60–$79 | No credit cards.

Greenfield Bed and Breakfast Inn. Built in 1817, this Victorian-style mountain village B&B is located on 3 wooded acres 3 mi north of Peterborough. Complimentary breakfast. Cable TV, some in-room VCRs. Business services. | Forest Rd. (Rte. 31 N), Greenfield | 603/547–6327 or 800/678–4144 | fax 603/547–2418 | www.greenfieldinn.com | 9 rooms (3 with shared bath), 1 suite, 1 cottage | $49–$79, $119–$129 suite, $139 cottage | AE, MC, V.

Hancock Inn. Moses Eaton and Rufus Porter are the early-American artists responsible for the murals and painting that are one of the distinguishing features of this venerable inn in a late-18th-century clapboard house 3 mi west of Peterborough. Antiques and fireplaces add just the right note. Restaurant, complimentary breakfast. In-room data ports, No smoking, cable TV. No kids under 12. Business services. | 33 Main St., Hancock | 603/525–3318 or 800/525–1789 | fax 603/525–9301 | inkeeper@hancockinn.com | www.hancock-inn.com | 11 rooms, 4 suites | $106–$210 | AE, D, DC, MC, V.

Inn at Crotched Mountain. A cozy 1822 colonial farmhouse, 15 mi northeast of Peterborough, on 65 acres with nine fireplaces and views of the Piscatagoug Valley. Rooms are comfortable and filled with antiques or colonial reproductions; some have fireplaces. Restaurant, bar. Complimentary breakfast. No smoking, no room phones, TV in common area. Outdoor pool. Tennis. Hiking. Ice-skating. Cross-country skiing. Pets allowed. | 534 Mountain Rd., Francestown | 603/588–6840 | fax 603/588–6623 | perry-inncm@conknet.com | 13 rooms (5 with shared bath) | $100–$120 | Closed Apr. and Nov. | No credit cards.

PLYMOUTH

MAP 7, E8

(Nearby town also listed: Holderness)

Another former mill town, this one on the Pemigewasset River (known to locals as the "Pemi"), Plymouth produced everything from mattresses to shoe trees. Today, it is a college town, home to Plymouth State College and 4,000 or so students.

Information: Chamber of Commerce | Box 65, Plymouth, 03264 | 603/536–1001 | www.plymouthnh.org.

Attractions

Mary Baker Eddy Historic House. Mary Baker Eddy, who founded the Christian Science Church, lived here from 1860 to 1862. Be sure to take the second half of the tour (included in price) to the Mary Baker Eddy Historic House in Groton where she lived from 1855 to 1860. Both sites are restored with pre–Civil War furnishings. Tours start at house in Rumney, 10 mi west of Plymouth. | 58 Stinson Lake Rd., Rumney | 603/786–9943 or 800/277–8943 | www.longyears.org | $3 | May–Oct., Tues.–Sat. 10–5, Sun. 2–5.

Pauline E. Glidden Toy Museum. Five rooms 6 mi south of Plymouth filled with antique toys, dolls and dollhouses, and penny and lithographed tin toys from the late 1800s. | Main St., Ashland | 603/968–7289 | $1 | July 4–Aug., Wed.–Sat. 1–4.

Plymouth State College. The town of Plymouth and the college are wrapped around one another. College buildings dot the town center and many residents are involved with the college in one way or another. Arrange for campus tours through the Office of Admissions. | 17 High St., | 603/535–2237 | www.plymouth.edu.

Polar Caves Park. These paths 5 mi west of town lead through a series of caves created by glaciers 14,000 years ago. Granite boulders and mineral formations of quartz, beryl, mica, and garnet decorate the passages. | Tenney Mt. Hwy. (Rte. 25) | 603/536–1888 or 800/273–1886 | www.polarcaves.com | $10 | Mid-May–mid-Oct., daily 9–5.

ON THE CALENDAR

JUNE–AUG.: *Keniston-Freeman Summer Concert Series.* A family-oriented outdoor concert series on the town common with live jazz, blues, big band, and more. | The Common | Wed. 7–9 PM | 603/536–2700.

AUG.: *Plymouth State Fair.* A traditional country agricultural fair. | Plymouth State Fairgrounds | 603/536–1001.

OCT.: *Annual Plymouth Art Show.* New England artists display their work on the Plymouth Common. | 603/536–8946.

Dining

Jigger Johnson's. Contemporary. You're served family-style in this lively, casual restaurant. Try the candied garlic steak. Kids' menu. | 75 Main St. | 603/536–4386. | $8–$15 | AE, D, MC, V.

Tree House Restaurant. Continental. The tank full of tropical fish draws kids' attention in this homey restaurant filled with antique farm tools, hand-pegged beams, and an immense stone fireplace. Try the homemade schnitzel, grilled teriyaki plate, or vegetarian selections. Kids' menu. | 3 S. Main St. | 603/536–4084 | No lunch | $8–$18 | AE, D, DC, MC, V.

Lodging

Deep River Motor Inn. A clean, two-story motor lodge with some efficiency units on 6 wooded acres. Cottage units are fully furnished with kitchens and utensils. Picnic area. Some kitchenettes, some refrigerators, cable TV. Outdoor pool. | 166 Highland St. | 603/536–2155 or 800/445–6809 | 22 rooms, 5 cottages | $65–$75 | AE, D, MC, V.

Susse Chalet. A member of the chain, 1 mi north of Portsmouth. Picnic area, complimentary Continental breakfast. In-room data ports, some refrigerators, cable TV, VCR in some rooms. Pool. Laundry facilities. Business services. Pets allowed. | U.S. 3; I–93 Exit 26 | 603/536–2330 | fax 603/536–2686 | 38 rooms | $62–$80 | AE, D, DC, MC, V.

PORTSMOUTH

MAP 7, I11

(Nearby towns also listed: Dover, Durham, Exeter, Rye)

Settled in 1623 as Strawbery Banke, Portsmouth became a prosperous port before the Revolutionary War. The long, straight logs prized by the Royal Navy as masts were among the first products sent from the port. Shipbuilding and fishing were active area trades as well.

Many houses from that pre-Revolutionary era still stand in the historic district, including the boardinghouse where John Paul Jones lived while supervising the outfitting of two ships for the Continental Navy. Tugboats, oil tankers, and cargo ships regularly cruise into the turbulent Piscataqua River, sharing space in summer with pleasure boaters and year-round with the submarines at the Portsmouth Naval Shipyard.

In addition to remaining an active port, Portsmouth is the cultural center of the coast with restaurants, theater, and art galleries for every taste. Shopping is a popular pastime too, with crafts galleries, bookstores, antiques shops, and boutiques lining the streets around Market Square. The square itself is a great place to grab a cappuccino or other beverage from any one of several cafés, pull up some space on one of the benches, and people-watch.

Information: Chamber of Commerce | 500 Market St. Portsmouth 03802 | 603/436–1118 | www.portsmouthchamber.org; www.seacoastnh.com for extensive historical information on entire seacoast area.

NEW HAMPSHIRE'S FURNITURE MASTERS

Back in the 1700s and early 1800s, New Hampshire, and especially Portsmouth, had a reputation for producing fine furniture equaling that of larger, wealthier areas such as Boston and Philadelphia. Over time, as mass-produced furniture replaced custom-made, New Hampshire became just a footnote in the history of furniture production. Today, though, there has been a resurgence both in the appreciation of fine, handmade furniture and in the number of craftspeople who create it.

Not only can you find a surprising number of extraordinary craftspeople making furniture throughout New Hampshire, but since 1995, they have been organized into a guildlike organization called the New Hampshire Furniture Masters. The tiered system works like a Renaissance patron-artist guild and artists must be invited to join, thus ensuring the quality of the workmanship.

The support of groups like the New Hampshire Historical Society, the League of New Hampshire Craftsmen, and the Guild of New Hampshire Woodworkers has helped create a pool of talented woodworkers in the state by providing outlets for the sale of their work. The New Hampshire Furniture Masters, though, have taken the system to a new level, gathering national acclaim for their members' wares. Some members are traditionalists who specialize in museum-quality reproductions of Federalist and other styles. Loran Smith of New Durham melds Federal and Shaker styles to create furniture with clean lines and incredible detail. Still others prefer to create contemporary pieces.

If you are interested in viewing fine New Hampshire–made furniture, you will find examples at the League of New Hampshire Craftsmen shops around the state or you can contact the New Hampshire Furniture Masters through the New Hampshire Historical Society (603/225–0420) or on line at www.furnituremasters.org.

© Artville

Attractions

Children's Museum of Portsmouth. Eighteen hands-on exhibits explore subjects ranging from lobstering to space travel. | 280 Marcy St. | 603/436–3853 | www.childrensmuseum.org | $4 | Labor Day–mid-June, Tues.–Sat. 10–5, Sun. 1–5; mid-June–Labor Day, Mon.–Sat. 10–5, Sun. 1–5.

Ft. Constitution. Originally called Ft. William and Mary, this National Historic Site 4 mi east of Portsmouth was once a British stronghold overlooking Portsmouth Harbor. Rebel patriots raided the fort in 1774 in one of revolutionary America's first overt acts of defiance against the King of England. The rebels later used the captured munitions against the British at the Battle of Bunker Hill. Only the base of the walls remains. Interpretive panels give the site's history. | Rte. 1B at the Coast Guard Station, New Castle | 603/436–1552 | Free | Daily.

Ft. Stark State Historic Site. This 10-acre site 5 mi east of Portsmouth overlooks Little Harbor and was first used for defensive purposes in 1746. It was an active fortification in every war from the Revolutionary War through World War II. | Wild Rose La., New Castle | 603/436–1552 | $2.50 | Daily.

Great Bay Estuary. The Great Bay Estuary and its 4,471-acre nature preserve of shallow tidal flats and grassland is well known for its winter eagle population. Osprey, herons, and snowy egrets, among others, stop here during migrations. There's lots of hiking trails and canoeing. Head to the Sandy Point Discovery Center for information and details. | Depot Rd. off Rte. 101, Greenland | 603/778–0015 | www.greatbay.org | Free | Grounds dawn–dusk, center Wed.–Sun. 10–4, closed in winter (Nov.-Apr.).

Sandy Point Discovery Center. In the Great Bay Estuary, this center has interactive exhibits, walking tours, and a boat launch for kayaks and canoes. This is the best place for information and maps for the Great Bay Estuary. | Depot Rd. off Rte. 101, Greenland | 603/778–0015 | www.greatbay.org | Free | Grounds dawn–dusk, center Wed.–Sun. 10–4, closed in winter (Nov.-Apr.).

Harbor Cruises. Tours of the harbor, the ocean off Portsmouth's coast, and the inland Great Bay estuary system are good ways to get a sense of the importance of water to the development of this area.

Isles of Shoals Steamship Co. Isles of Shoals cruises, river trips, and whale-watching expeditions are among the offerings of this cruise company. Captain Jeremy Bell sails a replica Victorian steamship. Some trips include a stopover and historic walking tour on Star Island, the Five Lighthouse cruise, and foliage excursions on Great Bay may include tours of Durham's Little Bay Buffalo Farm. Watch for holiday and special-event cruises. | Barker Wharf, 315 Market St. | 603/431–5500 or 800/441–4620 | www.islesofshoals.com | Mid–June–Labor Day, daily. Call or check Web for off-season schedules and reservations.

Portsmouth Harbor Cruises. Sunset cruises, foliage trips, and trips to the Isles of Shoals and Portsmouth Harbor, aboard the MV *Heritage* are among the popular offerings of this cruise company. | 64 Ceres St., Old Harbor District | 603/436–8084 or 800/776–0915 | www.portsmouthharbor.com | Mid-May–mid-Oct., daily; call for cruise times.

★ **Historic District.** The first white settlers arrived here in 1623, making Portsmouth one of the oldest cities in New Hampshire, or even in the United States. As such, Portsmouth boasts a large historic district that has been broken into several adjoining areas. The Old Harbor area, along Bow and Ceres streets, was once the focus of this thriving seaport. Shops and restaurants now occupy its chandleries and warehouses, but the tugboats and container ships are a reminder that this is still a busy port. The Market Square section, always the bustling heart of the city, is the center for shopping and dining in today's Portsmouth. Fourteen Federal and Georgian houses on The Hill at Deer and High streets have all been refurbished and are mainly used as office spaces. Each has a plaque with the date it was built. Marcy Street, Prescott Park, and the narrow streets surrounding the Strawbery Banke Museum (*see below*) are in the oldest part of the city. Point of Graves, the city's oldest cemetery, has graves dating from 1682. | Take Exit 7 from I–95 and follow signs for historic district.

PORTSMOUTH

INTRO
ATTRACTIONS
DINING
LODGING

Isles of Shoals. The Isles of Shoals are nine small islands (eight at high tide) off the coast of Portsmouth. The islands were divvied up after a border dispute: five belong to Maine and four to New Hampshire. Many, like Hog Island, Smuttynose, and Star Island, retain the earthy names given them by the transient fishermen who visited them in the early 17th century. A colorful history of piracy, murder, and ghosts surrounds the archipelago, long populated by an independent lot who, according to one writer, hadn't the sense to winter on the mainland. Celia Thaxter, a native islander, romanticized these islands with her poetry in "Among the Isles of Shoals "(1873). In the late 19th century, Appledore Island became an offshore retreat for her coterie of writers, musicians, and artists. Star Island has a nondenominational conference center and is open to those on guided tours. For information about visiting the Isles of Shoals, *see* Harbor Cruises, *above*.

Portsmouth Historic Homes. With such a long history, Portsmouth naturally has a number of historic homes. The Society for the Preservation of New England Architecture runs tours at a number of Portsmouth's restored homes.

Governor John Langdon House. John Langdon was a three-time governor of the state, a signer of the Constitution, and the first president of the Senate. His 1784 Georgian mansion, which George Washington described in 1789 as "the finest house in Portsmouth," contains ornate woodwork and period furniture. | 143 Pleasant St. | 603/436–3205 | www.spnea.org | $5 | June–mid-Oct., Wed.–Sun. 11–5 | Visits by hourly tour only.

Jackson House. This home was built in 1664 and is one of the oldest examples of plank-frame construction in the region. | 50 Mechanic St. | 603/436–3205 | www.spnea.org | $5 | June–mid-Oct., Sat. and Sun. 11-5(tours on the hour, last tour at 4).

John Paul Jones House. Costumed guides conduct tours of the 1758 boardinghouse that John Paul Jones called home while supervising the outfitting of two ships for the Continental Navy. The yellow, hip-roof house is the headquarters of the Portsmouth Historical Society. Exhibits include costumes, glass, guns, portraits, and late-18th-century documents. | 43 Middle St. | 603/436–8420 | www.seacoastnh.com/jpj | $5 | Mid-May–mid-Oct., Sat. 10–4, Sun. 12–4.

Moffatt-Ladd House. The house was built in 1763 by wealthy sea merchant John Moffatt, whose son-in-law William Whipple was one of the signers of the Declaration of Independence. The Moffatt-Ladd House tells the story of Portsmouth's merchant class through portraits, letters, and furnishings. | 154 Market St. | 603/436–8221 | $5 | June–mid-Oct., Mon.–Sat. 10–4, Sun. 1–4.

Rundlet May House. This three-story 1807 Federal mansion was built by textile merchant James Rundlet. The house reflects the lifestyles of several successive generations of the family and contains several pieces of furniture made by Portsmouth craftsmen. | 364 Middle St. | 603/436–3205 | www.spnea.org | $5 | June–mid-Oct., Sat.–Sun. 1–5 | Visits by hourly tour only.

Warner House. The murals lining the hall staircase of the 1716 Warner House might be the oldest-known murals still in their original place in the United States. The house itself is a noted example of Georgian architecture with 18-inch-thick brick walls. The west wall lightning rod is believed to have been installed in 1762 under the supervision of Benjamin Franklin. | Daniel St. at Chapel St. | 603/436–5909 | www.warnerhouse.org | $5 | June–Oct. 31, Tues.–Sat. 10–4, Sun. 1–4 | Visits by tour only.

Wentworth Coolidge Mansion. This National Historic Landmark was originally the home of Benning Wentworth, New Hampshire's first Royal Governor (1753–70). Notable among the period furnishings is the carved pine mantelpiece in the council chamber. Wentworth's imported lilac trees, believed to be the oldest in North America, bloom each May. Contemporary arts exhibits and gift shop in the visitor's center. | 375 Little Harbor Rd. | 603/436–6607 | $2.50 | June–Oct., Tues., Thurs., Fri., Sat. 10–3, Sun. 1–5.

Wentworth Gardner House. This lovely blocked-front 1760 house is said to rank among the finest Georgian-style buildings in the country. Its wood carvings are one of its best features. | 50 Mechanic St. | 603/436–4406 | $4 | Mid-June–mid-Oct., Tues.–Sun. 1–4.

Portsmouth Livery Co. Clip-clop your way through colonial Portsmouth and Strawbery Banke on these narrated horse-and-carriage tours. Look for carriages at stand in Market Sq. | 603/427–0044 | Memorial Day–Labor Day, daily; Labor Day–mid-Oct., Sat., Sun.

Portsmouth Trail. A great way to view the historic homes of Portsmouth, this walking trail can be followed with an informative map and audio guide, purchased at the information kiosk at Market Square, the Chamber of Commerce, or from homes on the tour route. Local expert guided tours are also available. | 20 Highland St. | 603/436–3988 | www.seacoastnh.com | Daily.

Prescott Park. Located between the Strawbery Banke and the Piscataqua River is this public park filled with fountains, gardens, and places to picnic. | Marcy St. | 603/436–3988 | www.seacoastnh.com | Free.

Red Hook Ale Brewery. Come for an informative tour and tasting of this popular microbrewed beer. | 35 Corporate Dr., Pease International Tradeport | 603/430–8600 | www.redhook.com | $1 | Tours Mon.–Fri. at 2 and 4, Sat.–Sun. at 1, 3, 5.

★ **Strawbery Banke Museum.** The first English settlers named the area around what's now called Portsmouth for the abundant wild strawberries they found along the bank of the Piscataqua River. The city's outdoor living history museum now uses the name. The award-winning 10-acre museum with period gardens, exhibits, and craftspeople holds 46 buildings that date from 1695 to 1820. Ten furnished homes represent 300 years of history in one continuously occupied neighborhood. The Drisco House, built in 1795, was first used as a dry-goods store, and half the house still depicts this history; the living room and kitchen, on the other hand, are decorated just as they were in the 1950s. The Shapiro House has been restored to reflect the life of the Russian Jewish immigrant family who lived in the home in the early 1900s. Perhaps the most opulent home is the 1860 Goodwin Mansion, former home of Governor Ichabod Goodwin, decorated in period Victorian style. | Marcy St., across from Prescott Park | 603/433–1100 | www.strawberybanke.org | $12 pass good for 2 consecutive days | Mid-Apr.–Oct., daily 10–5; 1st 2 weekends in Dec. 4–9 for candlelight stroll.

Urban Forestry Center. A 180-acre nature preserve, tree farm, wildlife sanctuary, and learning center. An extensive trail system with interpretive signs takes you through salt-marsh habitat and describes tree and landscape variations. | 45 Elwyn Rd. | 603/431–6774 | Free | Daily.

U.S.S. Albacore Museum. The *AGSS Albacore*, a prototype submarine built here in 1952 as a floating laboratory, and the Memorial Garden for submariners can be seen here in Albacore Park. | 600 Market St. | 603/436–3680 | www.portsmouthnh.com | Memorial Day–Columbus Day, daily 9:30–5:30; Columbus Day–Memorial Day, Thurs.–Mon. 9:30–5:30.

Water Country. A river tube ride, a large wave pool, white-water rapids, and 12 large water slides are a few of the amusements at New Hampshire's largest water park, 3 mi south of Downtown Portsmouth. | Rte. 1 | 603/436–3556 | www.watercountry.com | $28 | Memorial Day–Labor Day, daily 10–6.

ON THE CALENDAR

MAY: *Annual Heritage Plant Sale.* Antique plant varieties cultivated by the landscape department at Strawbery Banke Museum are for sale. | 603/433–1106.

JULY: *Bow Street Fair.* Portsmouth's oldest crafts festival is a two-day fair held along the waterfront in the historic district. Also includes performances by musicians and theater groups. | Bow and Ceres Sts. | 603/433–4793.

AUG.: *Portsmouth Blues Festival.* National and local blues musicians, craftspeople, and artists perform here. | Strawbery Banke Museum | 603/436–1106.

SEPT.: *Annual Grand Old Portsmouth Brewers' Festival.* Sample New England microbrews at this event. | Strawbery Banke Museum | 603/433–1106.

DEC.: *Annual Strawbery Banke Museum Candlelight Stroll.* A yearly festival celebrating winter activities and holidays through 300 years of Portsmouth history. Luminaries light the pathways between the buildings at the Strawbery Banke Museum. | 603/433–1106.

DEC.: *First Night Portsmouth.* The annual New Year's eve celebration with artists, theater groups, musicians, and other events. | Various locations around downtown | 603/436–1118.

Dining

B.G.'s Boathouse Restaurant. Seafood. It might look like an old bait shack on the outside, but this busy spot serves up surprisingly large portions of fresh seafood such as lobster and fried clams. | Rte. 1B | 603/431–1074 | Closed Nov.–Mar. | $7–$14 | AE, D, MC, V.

Blue Mermaid World Grill. Jamaican. A favorite with locals and tourists, this lively restaurant serves up Jamaican-style dishes and eclectic ethnic fare, fired up on the wood-burning grill. Try the slow-roasted BBQ platter or the lobster and shrimp pad Thai. Vie for a table with a view of Portsmouth's *Hill* neighborhood. Outdoor dining in season. Kids' menu and vegetarian entrées. Live music. | The Hill at Hanover and High Sts. | 603/427–2583 | www.blue-mermaid.com | $7–$20 | AE, D, DC, MC, V.

Ciento. Spanish. Local artists' work is displayed in the dining room, where tapas is the specialty. | 100 Market St. | 603/766–8272. | $15–$20 | AE, MC, V.

Dolphin Striker. Contemporary. The motif is marine and the tables and chairs are hand-crafted in this post-and-beam structure. Try the lobster ravioli or the filet mignon with chèvre cheese and chipotle pepper sauce. | 15 Bow St., at Penhallow St. | 603/431–5222 | $14–$24 | AE, D, DC, MC, V.

Dunfrey's Aboard the *John Wanamaker*. Contemporary. Fine harborside dining in a unique setting aboard America's last steam-operated tugboat, built in 1923. Try the pan-seared lobster tail or grilled black Angus steak with roasted shallot cabernet sauce and haricot vert. Casual dining and cocktails on the upper deck at the Smokestack Grill. | 1 Harbor Pl. | 603/433–3111 | $12–$33 | AE, D, DC, MC, V.

Karen's. Continental. The small dining room replete with fireplace, red-painted walls, wooden floors, and big picture windows is a favorite local hangout. The ever-changing menu brims with pastas, sandwiches, fresh seafood, and daily specials. There is outdoor dining on an enclosed brick patio in season. Brunch on weekends. | 105 Daniel St. | 603/431–1948 | $15–$25 | AE, D, MC, V.

★ **Library Restaurant.** Contemporary. At the turn of the 20th century, the Russo-Japanese peace treaty was signed in this building, which today feels like a fine gentlemen's club, with its shelves of books, hand-carved mahogany, and pressed-linen ceiling. Try the veal Marsala or the baked stuffed haddock. Live music. | 401 State St. | 603/431–5202 | $16–$26 | AE, D, DC, MC, V.

Lindbergh's Crossing. French. This late-18th-century warehouse with brick walls and massive beams overhead has a view of the tugboats on the Piscataqua River. Signature dishes include moules marinière—Prince Edward Island mussels sautéed in butter, shallots and parsley—and salmon roulade. | 29 Ceres St. | 603/431–0887 | No lunch | $12–$24 | AE, D, DC, MC, V.

Metro. Contemporary. Decorated in dark wood and stained glass, the dining room is set with white tablecloths and candles. Try the award-winning clam chowder, the panfried Maine crab cakes, or the Atlantic salmon with potato and goat cheese crust. Live jazz Friday and Saturday. | 20 High St. | 603/436–0521 | Closed Sun. | $13–$24 | AE, D, DC, MC, V.

Pier II. Seafood. A casual classic seafood eatery with open-air dining in summer. Salad bar. Kids' menu. Dock space. | 10 State St. | 603/436–0669. | Closed mid-Oct.–mid-Apr. and Mon., Tues. mid-Apr.–Memorial Day | $13–$19 | AE, D, DC, MC, V.

Porto Bello. Italian. This second-floor bistro has views of Portsmouth Harbor and serves Italian specialties like grilled Portobello mushrooms and homemade ravioli stuffed with eggplant, walnuts, and Parmesan cheese. | 67 Bow St. | 603/431–2989 | Closed Mon.–Tues. No lunch | $11–$22 | AE, D, DC, MC, V.

Sakura. Japanese. In this intimate restaurant and sushi bar you can sit on the floor, Japanese style, or opt for Western seating. Try the Dynamite Tuna—Japanese peppercorn crusted and pan-seared fresh tuna fillet. | 40 Pleasant St. | 603/431–2721 | Reservations not accepted

| Sun.–Thurs. 5–9:30, Fri.–Sat. 5–10:30; lunch 11:30–2:30 daily. Call for seasonal hrs variations | $10–$25 | AE, D, MC, V.

Shalamar. Indian. A casual atmosphere and Indian decor. Try the *tikka saagwala* (chicken with spinach) or the tandoori dishes. | 80 Hanover St. | 603/427–2959 | $9–$19 | D, MC, V.

Yoken's Thar She Blows Restaurant. Seafood. This fun, family-style fish place has the dubious distinction of being the home of a gift shop that's said to be the largest in New England. Kids' menu. | 1390 Lafayette Rd. (U.S. 1). | 603/436–8224 | $8–$19 | AE, D, DC, MC, V.

Lodging

Comfort Inn. A six-story motor inn on U.S. 1 with an adjacent restaurant. Complimentary Continental breakfast. Some refrigerators, cable TV. Indoor pool. Hot tub. Exercise equipment. Laundry facilities. Business services. | 1390 Lafayette Rd. | 603/433–3338 | fax 603/431–1639 | www.comfortinn.com | 121 rooms | $60–$115 | AE, D, DC, MC, V.

Holiday Inn. A standard example of the chain with six stories. Restaurant. Some refrigerators, room service, cable TV. Indoor pool. Exercise equipment. Video games. Free parking. | 300 Woodbury Ave. | 603/431–8000 | fax 603/431–2065 | 130 rooms | $95–$160 | AE, D, DC, MC, V.

Inn at Christian Shore. A charming early-1800s Federal-style inn just a short stroll from Portsmouth Harbor. Complimentary breakfast. No smoking, no room phones, cable TV. No kids. | 335 Maplewood Ave. | 603/431–6770 | fax 603/431–7743 | 5 rooms (2 with private baths across hall) | $65–$85 | AE, MC, V.

Martin Hill Inn. Two Greek Revival homes within walking distance of the historic district, with lovely gardens and antique furnishings. Complimentary breakfast. No smoking, no room phones, no TV. No kids under 16. | 404 Islington St. | 603/436–2287 | www.portsmouthnh.com/martinhillinn | 7 rooms | $105–$125 | MC, V.

Meadowbrook Inn. A sprawling, three-building complex with clean, quiet, modest rooms right off the highway. Complimentary Continental breakfast, restaurant, bar. Some microwaves, some refrigerators, cable TV. Outdoor pool. Laundry facilities. Pets allowed (no fee). | 549 Hwy. 1 Bypass | 603/436–2700 or 800/370–2727 | fax 603/433–2700 | info@meadowbrookinn.com | www.meadowbrookinn.com | 122 rooms | $60–$89 | AE, D, MC, V.

Oracle House Inn. A meticulously restored 1702 inn, known as the publishing house of the state's first newspaper, "The Oracle of the Day." All rooms have fireplaces and views of Prescott Park and the waterfront. Complimentary breakfast. In-room data ports, No smoking, some in-room hot tubs, no TV. No pets. | 38 Marcy St. | 603/433–8827 | fax 603/433–3591 | oraclehouseinn@aol.com | www.oraclehouseinn.com | 3 rooms | $150 | AE, MC, V.

Port Motor Inn. A motor inn with an old New England feel. While the building looks like an inn, all the rooms are off an exterior corridor. If you choose to go into the lobby, you can relax by the fireplace. The grounds are well-maintained and landscaped. Complimentary Continental breakfast, picnic area. Some microwaves, some refrigerators, cable TV. Pool. | 505 U.S. 1 Bypass; I–95 Exit 5, 100 yards south on Rte. 1 bypass | 603/436–4378 or 800/282–7678 | fax 603/436–4378 | www.theportinn.com | 33 rooms, 20 studios, 4 suites | $109 Mon.–Thurs., $129 weekends; studios: $119 Mon.–Thurs., $139 weekends; discounts for stays longer than 7 days | AE, D, DC, MC, V.

Sheraton Harborside. A full-service hotel in the historic district overlooking the Piscataqua River. 2 restaurants, bar. In-room data ports, minibars, some refrigerators, room service, cable TV. Indoor pool. Sauna. Gym. Business center. Airport shuttle, valet parking. | 250 Market St. | 603/431–2300 or 800/325–3535 | fax 603/433–5649 | 176 rooms, 24 suites | $135–$165 | AE, D, DC, MC, V.

★ **Sise Inn.** Built in 1881, this Queen Anne–style inn is located in the historic district. Complimentary Continental breakfast. No smoking, some in-room hot tubs, cable TV, in-room VCRs. Business services. | 40 Court St. | 603/433–1200 or 888/SISEINN | fax 603/433–1200 | 25 rooms, 9 suites | $145 rooms, $175–$225 suites | AE, DC, MC, V.

Susse Chalet. Basic digs in a four-story building. Complimentary Continental breakfast. Cable TV. Pool. Business services. | 650 Borthwik Ave. | 603/436–6363 or 800/524–2538 | fax 603/436–1621 | www.sussechalet.com | 105 rooms | $82–$87 | AE, D, DC, MC, V.

Wynwood Hotel & Suites. The three buildings of this sprawling complex, 2 mi south of Portsmouth, have accommodations ranging from basic motel to deluxe suite rooms, suitable for families, with full kitchens and living and dining rooms. Restaurant, bar with entertainment. In-room data ports, refrigerators, some in-room hot tubs, cable TV. 2 pools. Hot tub. Exercise equipment. Laundry service. Business services. No pets. | Interstate Traffic Circle, | 603/436–7600 or 800/654–2000 | fax 603/436–7600 | 135 rooms, 29 suites | $80–$200 rooms, $165–$350 suites | AE, D, DC, MC, V.

RYE

MAP 7, H11

(Nearby towns also listed: Exeter, Hampton, Hampton Beach, Portsmouth)

In 1623 the first European settlers landed at Odiorne Point and built the first house in the state. Today the main reason for visiting Rye is its beaches. There are two oceanfront state parks in Rye and views of crashing surf from Route 1A.

Information: **Greater Portsmouth Chamber of Commerce** | Box 239, 500 Market St., Portsmouth, 03802 | www.portsmouthchamber.org | fax 603/436–5118 | 603/436–1118.

Attractions

★ **Odiorne Point State Park.** In 1623, the first European settlers landed at Odiorne Point in what is now Rye, making it the birthplace of New Hampshire. During World War II, Fort Dearborn was built on the point to protect Portsmouth Harbor from enemy submarines off the coast. The park encompasses 350 acres of protected land. There are several nature trails for strolling and wonderful views of the Isles of Shoals. The tidal pools shelter crabs, periwinkles, and sea urchins. | Rte. 1A north of Wallis Sands State Park | 603/271–3556 | www.nhparks.state.nh.us | Free weekdays Columbus Day–May 1, $2.50 May–Oct.

Seacoast Science Center. The Seacoast Science Center conducts guided nature walks and interpretive programs at Odiorne Point State Park. The center also has exhibits on the area's natural history, and traces the history of Odiorne Point back to the Ice Age. Kids love the tide pool touch tank and the 1,000-gallon Gulf of Maine deep-water aquarium. | Odiorne Point State Park, Rte. 1A | 603/436–8043 | www.seacenter.org | $1 plus park admission ($2.50) | Daily 10–5.

Wallis Sands State Beach. This 700-ft sandy beach is one of the nicest along New Hampshire's coast. In addition, there's plenty of parking, a bathhouse with showers, and lifeguards in summer. | Rte. 1A | 603/436–9404 | www.nhparks.state.nh.us | Mon.–Fri. $5 per car, $8 weekends | Memorial Day–Labor Day, daily; Labor Day–Memorial Day, weekends.

ON THE CALENDAR

JULY: *Stratham Fair.* A three-day agricultural festival with rides, games, contests, food, and live entertainment, 15 mi west of Rye on Route 33. | Stratham Fairgrounds | 603/772–4977.

Dining

Paul's Carriage House Restaurant. Mediterranean. An eclectic choice of food, served in a seaside colonial with lots of polished wood and views of the sea. Ethnic flares from around the world include the French-style Island Lady Navarin de Homard (pan-roasted lobster, sea scallops, and vegetables flamed and served in a tomato basil beurre blanc) or the veal pasquale (rolled with proscuitto, spinach, and provolone in an anise cream sauce). | 2263 Ocean Blvd. | 603/964–8251 | No lunch | $12–$32 | AE, MC, V.

Lodging

Hoyt's Lodges. Rustic beachside one- and two-bedroom housekeeping cottages, family owned and operated since the 1950s. All units are fully furnished and have kitchens, private decks, and barbecue grills. Picnic area. Air-conditioning in some rooms, kitchenettes, some microwaves, refrigerators, cable TV, no room phones. | 891 Ocean Blvd. | 603/436–5350 | 891rye@mediaone.net | www.hoytslodges.com | 10 cottages | $400–$825 wk | Closed Nov.–May | D, MC, V.

Rock Ledge Manor. A mid-19th-century summerhouse built out on a point with a sweeping view of the ocean and a large porch. Complimentary breakfast. No smoking, no room phones, no TV. | 1413 Ocean Blvd. (Rte. 1A) | 603/431–1413 | www.rockledgemanor.com | 4 rooms, 2 with private half baths and shared shower | $125–$225 | No credit cards.

SALEM

(Nearby towns also listed: Manchester, Nashua)

The area that now makes up the town of Salem was once fought over by New Hampshire and Massachusetts as the colonies struggled to agree on their borders. Today Salem is the first town you reach after crossing into New Hampshire from Massachusetts on Interstate 93. For that reason and the absence of a sales tax in New Hampshire, Salem has become home to malls and stores looking to sell to border crossers from Massachusetts. In return, many of Salem's residents make the trek south to jobs in Massachusetts.

Information: **Greater Salem Chamber of Commerce** | Box 304, 220 N. Broadway, Salem, 03079 | 603/893–3177 | www.salemnhchamber.org.

Attractions

America's Stonehenge. Although no one knows who built this arrangement of megaliths, chambers, and tunnels, archaeological research has demonstrated that it can be used to chart the seasons and the course of the stars. | 105 Haverhill Rd., North Salem | 603/893–8300 | www.stonehengeusa.com | $8 | Daily.

Canobie Lake Park. This full-scale amusement park has rides and games for all age groups. There are four roller coasters, including a wooden one, a Ferris wheel, and an 1890s carrousel with hand-carved horses. | 1 mi east of I–93 Exit 2 | 603/893–3506 | www.canobie.com | $20 | Mid-June–Labor Day, daily 12–10; mid-Apr.–mid-June and Sept., Sat.–Sun. Call ahead for updated and special event hrs.

Robert Frost Farm. Poet Robert Frost lived on this farm 1 mi southeast of Salem from 1901 to 1909. Now restored, it contains original family furnishings as well as other furnishings appropriate to the period. A ½-mi poetry trail winds through the property. | Rte. 28, Derry | 603/432–3091 | www.nhparks.state.nh.us | $2.50 | Late May–late June and Labor Day–Columbus Day, weekends 10–5; late June–Labor Day, daily 10–5.

Rockingham Park. There is live thoroughbred and simulcast horse racing at this track and fairgrounds opened in 1906. | I–93 Exit 1 | 603/898–2311 | $3.50 clubhouse, $2.50 grandstand | Live racing June–Sept. (call for post times); year-round for simulcasting.

Searles Castle at Windham. Completed in 1915 at a cost of $1,250,00, this English-style castle, 10 minutes northwest of Salem, was built by interior decorator and antique collector Edward F. Searles. Now owned by the New Hampshire Sisters of Mercy, it is open to the public as a meeting house, conference center, or for private functions. | 21 Searles Rd., Windham | 603/898–6597 | www.searlescastlewindham.org | Closed Jan.–Feb.

Dining

Loafers American Restaurant and Bake Shop. American. Lots of exposed brick and simple colonial wood furnishings make a modest yet classy setting for dishes like the pepper-crusted yellow fin tuna with sautéed baby greens and shiitake mushrooms or the lobster ravioli in a ginger and basil cream sauce. Cakes, sticky buns, pastries, cookies, and breads are available for takeout from the bakery. | 43 Pelham Rd. | 603/890–6363 | www.loafers-nh.com | $13–$25 | MC, V.

Lodging

Park View Inn. This inn with well-landscaped grounds and large rooms is just a short walk from downtown and a shopping mall. Complimentary Continental breakfast. In-room data ports, some kitchenettes, refrigerators, cable TV. Laundry facilities. | 109 S. Broadway, I–93 Exit 1 | 603/898–5632 | fax 603/894–6579 | www.parkviewinn.com | 58 rooms | $50–$70 | AE, D, DC, MC, V.

Salem Holiday Inn. A modern facility, about five minutes from Salem. Restaurant, complimentary Continental breakfast. In-room data ports, refrigerator available, no-smoking rooms, cable TV. Pool. Business services. | 1 Keewaydin Dr., I–93 Exit 2 | 603/893–5511 | fax 603/894–6728 | 83 rooms | $89–$119 | AE, D, DC, MC, V.

Stillmeadow Bed and Breakfast. An 1850s Greek Renaissance Italianate home, 8 mi east of Salem, on 2 peaceful acres with original hardwood floors and crown moldings. Rooms are individually decorated and fitted with mahogany four-post or brass beds and period antiques. One of the rooms has a crib, two queen beds and a sitting room and is suitable for families. Complimentary breakfast. Refrigerators, no smoking, cable TV, no room phones. Hiking. Cross-country skiing. Business services. No pets. | 545 Main St., Hampstead | 603/329–8381 | fax 603/329–0137 | stillmeadowb@yahoo.com | 4 rooms | $65–$90 | AE, D, MC, V.

Susse Chalet. Just off Interstate 95 exit 2 and 1 mi from Salem's main attractions, this hotel is typical of the chain. Complimentary Continental breakfast. In-room data ports, cable TV. Pool. Laundry facilities. Business services. | 8 Keewaydin Dr. | 603/893–4722 or 800/524–2538 | fax 603/893–2898 | www.sussechalet.com | 103 rooms | $49–$70 | AE, D, DC, MC, V.

SUGAR HILL

MAP 7, D6

(Nearby towns also listed: Franconia, Littleton)

Set on a ridge above Franconia, Sugar Hill has a stunning view of Franconia Notch and the surrounding mountains. Originally a hunting ground for Abenaki Indians, it was settled by white farmers but soon turned to mining and lumbering. Like many towns in the White Mountains, Sugar Hill flourished as a resort community around the beginning of the 20th century. (It claims the country's first organized ski school.) When the era of the grand hotels faded away, Sugar Hill settled into rural village life with residents who prize its pristine setting and heritage. It has recently been rediscovered by vacationers who appreciate its quiet beauty.

Information: Franconia–Sugar Hill–Easton Chamber of Commerce | Box 780, Franconia, 03580 | 603/823–5661 | www.franconianotch.org.

Attractions

Sugar Hill Historical Museum. Sugar Hill may have only 500 residents, but it boasts an historical museum better than those of many larger towns. The exhibits, both changing and permanent, focus on the history of the area from settlement through the resort era. | Rte. 117 | 603/823–5336 | $2 | July–Oct. 15, Thurs., Sat., Sun. 1–4.

JUNE: *Annual Fields of Lupine Festival.* Celebration of the blooming of the wild lupines. Special events at area inns. Festival covers Franconia, Sugar Hill, and Bethlehem. | Various locations | 603/823–5661.

Dining

Polly's Pancake Parlor. American. This restaurant, under the same family ownership since 1938, is in a mid-19th-century carriage house with charm to spare. It offers a selection of whole-wheat pancakes, waffles, and fresh-baked breads made from grain ground on the premises. Kids' menu. No smoking. | Rte. 117 | 603/823–5575 | Breakfast also available. Closed Nov.–Apr. and weekdays in May. No dinner | $6–$12 | AE, D, MC, V.

Sugar Hill Inn. Contemporary. Located in the 1789 Sugar Hill farmhouse inn, you can dine on the prix fixe menu of delicious regional cuisine like New England clam chowder, roast duck, and homemade desserts. | 116 Scenic Rte. 117 | 603/823–5621 or 800/548–4748 | fax 603/823–5639 | Breakfast also available. Closed Sun.–Thurs. from mid-Feb.–May, closed Sun.–Wed. from June–mid-Feb. No lunch | $35 | AE, MC, V.

Sunset Hill House Dining Room. French. The five, intimate, upscale dining rooms, replete with linen, orchids, fine china, and fireplaces, are enhanced by the views of the White Mountains. Special dishes include duckling Bombay with almond chutney and brandy sauce and the grilled game hen with herbed shiitake mushrooms. | 231 Sunset Hill Rd. | 603/823–5522 | Reservations essential | No lunch | $15–$27 | AE, D, MC, V.

Sunset Hill House Tavern. American. A casual, welcoming pub and dining room with extensive sunset views of Vermont's Green Mountains. The in-house smoked seafood and the grilled half baby back ribs are local favorites. | 231 Sunset Hill Rd. | 603/823–5522 | $5–$15 | AE, D, MC, V.

Lodging

Foxglove: A Country Inn. A charming Victorian inn with period furnishings and extensive gardens with outstanding views of the White Mountains. Complimentary breakfast. No smoking, cable TV, VCR available on request. No kids under 12. Business services. | Rte. 117 at Lover's La. | 603/823–8840 or 888/343–2220 | fax 603/823–5755 | foxgloveinn@compuserve.com | www.foxgloveinn.com | 6 rooms | $85–$165 | MC, V.

Hilltop Inn. Sparkling white turn-of-the-20th-century farmhouse filled with hand-pieced quilts and vintage furniture. Complimentary breakfast. No air-conditioning, room service, no smoking, no room phones, cable TV in common area. Pets allowed (fee). | Main St. (Rte. 117) | 603/823–5695 or 800/770–5695 | fax 603/823–5518 | aaa@hilltopinn.com | www.hilltopinn.com | 5 rooms, 1 cottage | $70–$150, $200–$250 cottage | D, MC, V.

Homestead Inn. Family antiques and heirlooms spanning seven generations fill this 1802 inn, one of the oldest family operated inns in America. Founded by Sugar Hill's first permanent settlers and constructed with material gathered from the property, including hand-hewn beams and hardwood floors, this inn gives an authentic look at early days of New England innkeeping. Rooms are filled with crafts and quilts and have views of the White Mountains. A two-bedroom 1917 stone-and-log chalet has a fireplace and kitchen and is suitable for families. Complimentary breakfast. No smoking, no room phones, TV in common area. Hiking. Cross-country skiing. Pets allowed. | 10 Sunset Hill Rd., | 603/823–5564 or 800/823–5564 | fax 603/823–9599 | homestead@together.net | www.thehomestead1802.com | 19 rooms (10 with shared bath), 1 cottage | $70–$125 | AE, D, MC, V.

Sugar Hill Inn. A 1789 clapboard inn with a rambling veranda on 16 acres of lawns and perennial gardens. Dining room, complimentary breakfast, afternoon refreshments. No air-conditioning, no smoking, hot tubs in suites. | 116 Scenic Rte. 117, Sugar Hill | 603/823–5621 or 800/548–4748 | fax 603/823–5639 | www.sugarhillinn.com | 10 inn rooms, 2 suites, 6 cottages | $100–$195, $225–$325 suites, $135–$235 cottages | Closed Apr. | AE, MC, V.

Sunset Hill House. A grand inn, built in 1880, on a 1,700-ft ridge with extensive mountain views just a few miles from Sugar Hill. Dining room, complimentary breakfast. No air-conditioning, no smoking, no TV, cable TV in common area. Pool. 9-hole golf course with complimentary greens fees for guests. Cross-country skiing. Business services. | 231 Sugar Hill Rd. | 603/823–5522 or 800/786–4455 | fax 603/823–5738 | www.sunsethillhouse.com | 22 rooms, 5 suites | $100–$250 | AE, D, MC, V.

SUNAPEE

MAP 7, C9

(Nearby towns also listed: New London, Newport)

Sunapee is one of several resort communities around sparkling Lake Sunapee, one of New Hampshire's finest recreational lakes. The lake is the draw in summer, while winter snows attract skiers and snowmobilers.

Information: New London & Lake Sunapee Region Chamber of Commerce | Box 532, New London, 03257 | 603/526–6575.

Attractions

Lake cruises. Sightseeing tours of Lake Sunapee are a popular way to enjoy its scenic setting.

Sunapee Cruises. Narrated lake cruises aboard the MV *Mt. Sunapee II* cover the region's history and geology. There are also fall foliage tours. | Lake Ave. off Rte. 11, Sunapee Harbor | 603/763–4030 | www.sunapeecruises.com | $12 | Mid-June–Labor Day, daily; mid-May–mid-June and Labor Day–mid-Oct., Sat.–Sun.

Sunapee Dinner Cruises. Dine buffet-style aboard the MV *Kearsarge* while you cruise on Lake Sunapee. | Steamboat Landing, Sunapee Harbor | 603/763–5477 | $25 | May–Labor Day, Tues.–Sun. departures 5:30, 7:45; Mon. 5:30 only.

Mt. Sunapee State Park. Mt. Sunapee rises to an elevation of nearly 3,000 ft and overlooks Lake Sunapee. Although the state owns the mountain and a slice of lakefront, the mountain has been leased to Vermont's Okemo Ski Area. The state still operates a beach on Lake Sunapee with lifeguards, picnic areas, and a bathhouse. | Rte. 103 | 603/763–3149 | $2.50 | Daily.

Skiing. The Sunapee area has both downhill and cross-country skiing.

Eastman Cross Country Center. The trails that wind around the lake at this quiet community include 12 mi of groomed trails and 6 mi of backcountry trails. Ice skating pond, snowshoeing, and sledding hill. | I–89 Exit 13, Grantham | 603/863–4500 | www.eastmannh.com | $9 | Dec.–Apr. 1, daily.

Mt. Sunapee Ski Area. The area's 51 mostly intermediate trails are spread out over 210 acres, with a 1,510-ft vertical drop. There are now nine Black diamond slopes—including Goosebumps, a double black diamond—so experts have some challenges. There are also hiking trails and a new halfpipe and snowboard park extends the options for snowboarders. | Rte. 103 | 603/763–2356, 603/763–4020 snow conditions, 877/687–8627 lodging | www.mtsunapee.com | $47 weekends, $42 midweek | Nov.–mid-Apr., daily.

ON THE CALENDAR

JUNE: *Annual Eastman Crafts Fair.* More than 30 New England artisans gather for one day at the Southcove Activities Center on Eastman Lake, 20 mi north of Sunapee, to display and sell their wares including homespun clothing and quilts, handmade furniture, brassworks, dolls, and beeswax candles. Local charities also host benefit plant and art sales. | Road Round the Lake | 603/863–6772 | Free | 10–4.

AUG.: *Annual League of New Hampshire Craftsmen Fair.* League members sell contemporary and traditional fine crafts in this state-juried, nine-day sale event. There are also workshops and demonstrations. | Mt. Sunapee Ski Area | 603/224–3375 | www.nhcrafts.com | $6 | 10–5 during fair.

Dining

Anchorage at Sunapee Harbor. American. Plenty of parking, a premiere lakeside location, a casual air, and a family-oriented menu make this a favorite spot for locals. Try the Anchorage Chowdah, with fresh clams, potatoes, bacon, and cream, or the Harbor Barbecued Chicken topped with pepper-jack cheese, fried onions, and peppers over a bed of rice. There is lakeside dining on the deck in season. Boat parking available. Live entertainment. Kids' menu. | 1 Garden St. | 603/763–3334 | Closed mid-Oct.–mid-May | $7–$15 | MC, V.

Appleseed Restaurant. American. This inn and tavern on Lake Todd, 6 mi south of Sunapee, serves up hearty pub fare and plenty of seafood. House specials are the Dutchess cheese soup and the Appleseed chicken breast with maple sauce, cheddar cheese, and sliced apples. There's prime rib Saturday nights and outdoor dining in season. Kids' menu. Sunday breakfast buffet. | 63 High St., Bradford | 603/938–2100 | No lunch | $8–$16 | MC, V.

Lodging

Best Western Sunapee Lake Lodge. A standard, modern member of the chain, four minutes' walk from Mt. Sunapee State Park and ¼ mi from the Mt. Sunapee Ski area on Route 103. Restaurant, bar, complimentary Continental breakfast. In-room data ports, some microwaves, some refrigerators, cable TV. Indoor pool. Exercise equipment, volleyball. Ice-skating. Tobogganing. Laundry facilites. Business services. Pets allowed. | 1403 Rte. 103 | 603/763–2010 or 800/606–5253 | fax 603/763–3314 | info@sunapeelakelodge.com | www.sunapee-lakelodge.com | 53 rooms, 2 suites | $99–$229 | AE, D, DC MC, V.

Blue Goose Inn Bed and Breakfast. A 19th-century farmhouse on 3½ acres, adjacent to Mt. Sunapee State Park. Some rooms have a private porch. Picnic area, complimentary breakfast. No air-conditioning, no smoking, no room phones, no TV. Lake. Bicycles. No pets. | 24 Rte. 103B | 603/763–5519 | fax 603/763–8720 | 5 rooms | $65–$75 | MC, V.

Burkehaven Motel. This motel is within walking distance of Sunapee Harbor and has rooms overlooking Mt. Sunapee. Some refrigerators. Pool. Hot tub. Tennis. Business services. Pets allowed. | 179 Burkehaven Hill Rd. | 603/763–2788 or 800/567–2788 | fax 603/763–9065 | www.burkehavenatsunapee.com | 10 rooms (all with showers only) | $74–$84 | AE, D, MC, V.

Candlelite Inn. This white clapboard 1897 Victorian decorated with quilts and tole paintings is 10 mi southeast of Sunapee. You can contemplate the surrounding countryside from the gazebo-like extension of the porch. Complimentary breakfast. No smoking, no room phones, no TV. | 5 Greenhouse La., Bradford | 603/938–5571 or 888/812–5571 | fax 603/938–2564 | www.virtualcities.com/nh/candlelightinn.htm | 6 rooms (2 with shower only) | $80–$110 | AE, D, DC, MC, V.

Dexter's Inn and Tennis Club. Built as a farmhouse in 1801, and remodeled in 1930 into a summer estate of author and economist Samuel Crowther, this polished inn on 20 acres has beautifully manicured gardens and rolling-hill views. The two-floor Holly House is perfect for family rentals. Dining room, bar, complimentary breakfast. Room service, no smoking, no room phones, no TV in rooms, TV and VCR in common area. Pool. Tennis. Library. Business services. | 258 Stagecoach Rd., | 603/763–5571 or 800/232–5571 | dexters@kear.tds.net | www.bbhost.com/dextersinn | 17 rooms, 1 cottage | $95–$165, $195–$350 cottage | Closed Nov.–Apr. | MAP | D, MC, V.

TAMWORTH

MAP 7, F7

(Nearby town also listed: Madison)

A quiet town on the northern edge of the Lakes Region, Tamworth has been a place to "summer" since at least the latter part of the 1800s, when President Grover Cleveland brought his family each year. His son, Francis, returned to stay and founded the Barnstormers Theater. The town of Tamworth is made up of several villages, including the pretty Chocorua. Mt. Chocorua is a popular hike.

Information: Greater Ossipee Chamber of Commerce | Box 577, West Ossipee, 03890 | 603/539–6201.

SUMMER THEATER

You won't catch many touring productions of the latest Broadway offerings in New Hampshire and there's no defined theater district, but for small theater the state can't be beat. Although some of the local theaters, especially in Portsmouth, offer performances in winter, summer is really when the scene heats up.

Don't expect offerings to be limited to New Hampshire's cities. In fact, one of the state's best summer theaters is in the small town of Tamworth, in the northern part of the Lakes Region. Barnstormers (603/323–8500) is New Hampshire's oldest professional summer theater, founded by Francis Cleveland, son of President Grover Cleveland. The Cleveland family summered in Tamworth and when Francis returned to the area as an adult, he brought his love of the theater with him.

Nashua is home to the American Stage Festival (603/886–7000), the state's largest professional theater group. They put on five Broadway plays and one new work in two locations each summer. In Peterborough, which was the inspiration for Thornton Wilder's Grover's Corners in *Our Town,* the Peterborough Players (603/924–7585) have presented their performances in a converted barn for more than 60 years. In North Conway, the Mt. Washington Valley Theater Company at the Eastern Slope Playhouse (603/356–5776) keeps locals and visitors entertained.

The choices are almost dizzying in the lively seacoast community of Portsmouth. The centerpiece of each summer's Prescott Park Arts Festival (603/436–2848) is a musical presented outdoors in the park on a stage built for the occasion. The Pontine Movement Theater (603/436–6660) concentrates on dance, the Players Ring (603/436–8123) is the place to look for touring theater groups, and the Seacoast Repertory Theatre (603/433–4472) runs the gamut from musicals to works by up-and-coming playwrights.

Whether you're looking for a light comedy, a serious drama, or a new production of an old classic, you'll surely find it in New Hampshire.

© Artville

Attractions

Remick Country Doctor Museum and Farm. A museum and hands-on working farm with views of Mt. Chocorua, New England's most photographed mountain. The exhibits document the life and work of Edwin and Edwin C. Remick, father and son country doctors who practiced consecutively from 1894 to 1993. There is a barn with animals, a working woodcrafts shop, and a milk-house display. There are also special events, a fishing derby, and a farm fest. | 58 Cleveland Hill Rd. | 603/323–7591 or 800/686–6117 | www.remickmuseum.org | Free | July–Oct., Mon.–Sat. 10–4; Nov.–June, weekdays 10–4.

White Lake State Park. This beautiful beach on White Lake is one of the region's most popular. The 72-acre stand of pitch pine is a National Natural Landmark. Amenities include two campgrounds, picnic areas, canoe rentals, and hiking trails. | Rte. 16 | 603/323–7350 | $2.50 | Daily.

ON THE CALENDAR

FEB.: *Winter Carnival.* Sledding, cross-country skiing, skating, sleigh rides, and other winter activities. | Remick Country Doctors Museum | 603/323–7591.
JULY–AUG.: *Barnstormers Summer Theater.* New Hampshire's oldest professional summer theater, Barnstormers was founded by Francis Cleveland, son of President Grover Cleveland. | Main St. | 603/323–8500 or 603/323–8661.

Dining

★ **Tamworth Inn.** Continental. This restaurant is adorned with fine china and antiques and has views of the Swift River and a large wine list. Try the house salad of mixed greens tossed in a poached garlic vinaigrette or the pan-seared seafood pasta with pine nuts and roasted garlic chardonnay butter sauce. | 15 Cleveland Hill Rd. | 603/323–7721 or 800/NH2RELAX | fax 603/323–2026 | Closed Sun.–Mon. Mar.–Nov.; Sun.–Wed. Dec.–Mar. No lunch | $13–$22 | AE, D, MC, V.

Lodging

Chocorua Camping Village and Wabanaki Lodge. A 158-acre, full-service, lakeside property with camping sites and cottage accommodations. Primitive and full hookups are available for RVs. The cottages are private, simple, and electricity-free. They also have outdoor toilets and sleep from four to eight adults. No vehicles are allowed in the cottage area, but the golf-cart shuttle will transport you and your bags. There is a rec hall, movie theater, and general store on the premise. Picnic area. No air-conditioning, no room phones, TV in common area. Pond. Hiking, beach, dock, boating. Fishing. Video games. Children's programs, laundry facilities. Pets allowed. | 893 White Mountain Hwy. (Rte. 16) | 603/323–8536 or 888/237–8642 | info@chocoruacamping.com | www.chocoruacamping.com | 175 sites, 6 cabins | $24–$34 camping, $69–$98 cottages | Closed Nov.–Apr. | MC, V.

Mount Whittier Motel. A charming single-story motel with comfortable, well-appointed rooms, ½ mi from Ossipee Lake and 18 mi from Lake Winnepeesaukee. Some kitchenettes, cable TV. Outdoor pool. No pets. | 1695 Rte. 16, Ossipee | 603/539–4951 | fax 603/539–8107 | whittier@worldpath.net | www.mountwhittiermotel.com | 20 rooms | $61–$78 | AE, D, MC, V.

Tamworth Inn. A 19th-century Victorian inn in the center of the village, on the Swift River near Hemenway State Forest. The inn is on 3 acres with landscaped gardens and views. Restaurant, bar, complimentary breakfast. No room phones, no TV, TV in common area. Pool. Hiking. Cross-country skiing. | 15 Cleveland Hill Rd. | 603/323–7721 or 800/642–7352 | fax 603/323–2026 | inn@tamworth.com | www.tamworth.com | 9 rooms, 6 suites, 1 family suite | $135–$225 | MAP available | MC, V.

WARNER

(Nearby towns also listed: Henniker, New London)

Three New Hampshire governors were born in this quiet agricultural community just off Interstate 89. Mt. Kearsarge, in Rollins State Park, provides the backdrop for the town's main street, which has buildings dating from the late 1700s and early 1800s.

Information: New London & Lake Sunapee Region Chamber of Commerce | Box 532, (Rte. 49 exit 28), New London, 03257 | 603/526–6575.

Attractions

Dalton Bridge. Built around 1853, this is one of the oldest covered bridges still in use. It is also known as the Joppa Road Bridge. | Joppa Rd. off Rte. 301, spanning the Warner River.

★ **Mt. Kearsarge Indian Museum.** Guided tours of the extensive collection of moccasins embroidered with moose hair, intricately woven baskets, quillwork, beaded tunics, and so on illustrate the artistry of Native American tribes. Outside, signs on the self-guided Medicine Woods trail identify plants and explain how each was used. | Kearsarge Mountain Rd. | 603/456–2600 | www.indianmuseum.org | $6 | May–Oct., Mon–Sat. 10–5, Sun. 12–5; Nov.–Dec., Sat. 10–5, Sun. 12–5.

Rollins State Park. A scenic auto road snakes nearly 3,000 ft up the southern slope of Mt. Kearsarge, where you can tackle the ½-mi trail to the summit on foot. A fire tower offers an even more impressive view of the region. | Kearsarge Mountain Rd. | 603/456–3803 | www.nhparks.state.nh.us | $2.50 | Daily.

Waterloo Bridge. Although this bridge 2 mi west of Warner was built in 1840, making it older than the Dalton Bridge, it was completely rebuilt in 1857. | New Market Rd., spanning the Warner River.

ON THE CALENDAR

JULY: *Powwow.* Native American gathering open to the public. Celebrate Native American music, dance and storytelling. | Mt. Kearsarge Indian Museum | 603/456–3244 | www.indianmuseum.org.

OCT.: *Harvest Moon Festival.* Native American drumming, flute playing, and storytelling. Exhibits and museum tour. Children's games and crafts. | Mt. Kearsarge Indian Museum | 603/456–3244 | www.indianmuseum.org.

Dining

Roter's Dining Room. Contemporary. This restaurant in the Thistle and Shamrock Inn, 15 mi west of Warner, is a cozy spot with a collection of artist Carl Roter's works. It serves roast duck a l'orange and farfalle with artichokes and shrimp. Kids' menu. | 11 W. Main St., Bradford | 603/938–5553 or 888/938–5553 | fax 603/938–5554 | www.thistleandshamrock.com | No lunch | $11–$18 | AE, D, MC, V.

Lodging

Rosewood Country Inn. New Hampshire's 1999 Inn of the Year is a stunning 1860 Country Victorian on 12 landscaped acres with individually decorated rooms, 15 mi west of Warner. Some rooms have fireplaces and hot tubs. Complimentary breakfast. No smoking, no room phones, no TV in some rooms, TV in common area. No kids under 10. | 67 Pleasant View Rd., Bradford | 603/938–5253 or 800/938–5273 | rosewood@conknet.com | www.rosewoodcountryinn.com | 11 rooms | $95–$175 | AE, D, DC, MC, V.

Thistle and Shamrock Inn and Restaurant. A late-19th-century Federal-style inn 15 mi west of Warner, with a large parlor, fireplace, and comfortable rooms. Family suites available. Restaurant, pub, complimentary breakfast. No air-conditioning, no smoking, no room phones, TV in common area. | 11 W. Main St., Bradford | 603/938–5553 or 888/938–5553 | fax 603/938–5554 | stay@thistleandshamrock.com | www.thistleandshamrock.com | 10 rooms | $75–$120 | AE, D, MC, V.

WATERVILLE VALLEY

(Nearby town also listed: Lincoln and North Woodstock Area)

Visitors began arriving in Waterville Valley in 1835, coming at first for summer recreation in the 10-mi-long valley that was cut by one of New England's many Mad Rivers and surrounded by 4,000-ft mountains. In the middle of the 20th century, summer visitors were surpassed by skiers drawn to the slopes of Mt. Tecumseh. The resort that exists today was developed first for the skiers and then became a year-round venue, bringing Waterville Valley full circle.

Information: Chamber of Commerce | R.R. 1, Box 1067, Waterville Valley, 03215 | 800/237–2307.

Attractions

New Hampshire Homecraft Cooperative. A nonprofit cooperative selling local crafts out of a converted 1878 one-room schoolhouse, 15 mi southeast of Waterville Valley. | Rte. 3, West Campton | 603/726–8626 | Mid-June–mid-Oct., daily 9:30–4:30.

Waterville Valley Resort. Former U.S. ski team star Tom Corcoran designed this family-oriented resort. The lodgings and other resort amenities are laid out around a town square about a mile from the ski slopes. This gives the resort a more relaxed feeling than the typical cluttered buildings at the base of a mountain, and a shuttle makes a car unnecessary. Although it began as a winter resort, the addition of a golf course, tennis courts, hiking trails, mountain biking, a pond for swimming and boating, and a sports center with indoor and outdoor pools have made this a year-round destination. Winter guests enjoy 52 trails that are long, wide, and generally intermediate. But this ski area has also hosted more World Cup races than any other in the east, so advanced skiers and boarders will be adequately challenged. A 7-acre ski treeing area adds variety. | Rte. 49 | 603/236–8311, 603/236–4144 for snow conditions, 800/468–2553 for lodging | www.waterville.com | $40 weekdays, $47 weekends | Nov.–Apr., daily.

The Adventure Center and the Nodric Center. In-line skates and bicycle rentals are available according to the season. | Town Square, Waterville Valley Resort | 603/236–4666 | fax 603/236–4344 | www.waterville.com | Call for rates.

ON THE CALENDAR
MAR.: *Jack Williams' Ski Race for Wednesday's Child.* Yearly celebrity ski-race to raise funds for special-needs children in New England. | 603/236–8311.

Dining
Chile Peppers Restaurant. Tex-Mex. This restaurant serves a mix of Mexican and American fare right in the middle of Town Square. Patio dining in nice weather gives you views of the mountains and Snows Brook waterfall. Try the sizzling fajitas and barbecued ribs. | Town Square | 603/236–4646 | $7–$15 | AE, D, DC, MC, V.

Wild Coyote Grill. American. Perched on the second floor of the White Mountain Athletic Club, this rustic, log-framed restaurant has beautiful views of Mt. Tecumseh. Try the potato-crusted salmon or the wild mushroom ravioli. | Rte. 49 | 603/236–4919 | www.wildcoyotegrill.com | No lunch | $12–$18 | D, MC, V.

William Tell. Swiss. This rustic, wood-beam and stucco restaurant with fireplace is about 3 mi east of town in Thornton. It serves traditional schnitzels and fondues as well as venison and veal dishes. Open-air dining. Kids' menu. Sunday brunch. | Waterville Valley Rd. (Rte. 49), Thornton | 603/726–3618 | Closed late Oct.–late Nov., mid-Apr.–Memorial Day, and Wed. No lunch | $6–$24 | AE, D, MC, V.

Lodging

Black Bear Lodge. A family-oriented, individually owned condominium all-suites hotel complex. No air-conditioning in some rooms, in-room data ports, kitchenettes, cable TV. Indoor-outdoor pool. Hot tub, sauna. Health Club. Video games. Laundry facilities. Business services. | 3 Village Rd. | 603/236–4501 or 800/349–2327 | fax 603/236–4114 | www.black-bear-lodge.com | 107 kitchen suites | $100–$250 | AE, D, DC, MC, V.

Golden Eagle Lodge. An all-suite condominium resort on the Waterville Valley Ski Resort property. All units have full kitchens and the price includes use of all facilities. Restaurant, bar. In-room data ports, microwave, refrigerators, some in-room hot tubs, cable TV. 2 pools, pond. Hot tub, sauna, steam room. 9-hole golf course, 18 tennis courts. Health club, water sports, boating. Bicycles. Ice-skating. Cross-country skiing, downhill skiing. Video games. Playground, laundry facilities. Business services. | 6 Snow's Brook Rd. | 603/236–4600 or 800/910–4499 | fax 603/236–4947 | www.goldeneaglelodge.com | 110 suites | $108–$168 plus 13% resort fee | AE, D, DC, MC, V.

Silver Fox Inn. Comfortable, unpretentious lodge accommodations in the middle of the Waterville Valley resort. Complimentary Continental breakfast. In-room data ports, cable TV. Hot tub, sauna, steam room. 9-hole golf course, 18 tennis courts. Health club, water sports, boating. Bicycles. Ice-skating. Cross-country skiing, downhill skiing. Video games. Playground, laundry facilities. Business services. | 14 Snow's Brook Rd. | 603/236–8325 or 800/468–2553 | wvlodges@together.net | www.silverfoxinn.com | 32 rooms | $89 plus 15% resort fee | AE, D, DC, MC, V.

Snowy Owl Inn. With four fireplaces, three hot tubs, and a nightly wine-and-cheese social, this is a great place to relax. Complimentary Continental breakfast. No air-conditioning in some rooms, minibars, in-room data ports, some in-room hot tubs, cable TV. 2 pools (1 indoor). 3 hot tubs. Video games. Laundry facilities. Business services. | 4 Village Rd. | 603/236–8383 or 800/766–9969 | fax 603/236–4890 | www.snowyowlinn.com | 85 rooms | $63–$170 | AE, D, MC, V.

Valley Inn. A well-appointed five-story hotel with a variety of room styles. Dining room, bar with entertainment. In-room data ports, refrigerators, room service, cable TV. Indoor-outdoor pool. Hot tub. Video games. Laundry facilities. Business services. | 17 Tecumseh Rd., Waterville | 603/236–8336 or 800/343–0969 | fax 603/236–4294 | www.valleyinn.com | 52 rooms | $69–$289 | AE, D, DC, MC, V.

Village Condominium. Two- to five-bedroom attached condominiums with fully equipped kitchens, washer/dryer, and fireplaces. Your stay entitles you to free access at the White Mountain Athletic Club and activites at the Waterville Valley Recreation center Cable TV, TV in common area. Sauna. No pets. | Rte. 49 | 603/236–8301 or 800/532–6630 | fax 603/236–3363 | villagecondo@cyberportal.net | www.waterville.com | $125–$306 | AE, D, DC, MC, V.

WEIRS BEACH

MAP 7, F8

(Nearby towns also listed: Center Harbor, Gilford, Laconia, Meredith)

This summer community is one of the prime destinations on Lake Winnipesaukee. In addition to a nice beach and access to the lake, the town offers lots of family activities, such as miniature golf and waterslides. Before the arrival of Europeans, Native

Americans set up their weirs at this spot to catch fish and eventually built a permanent settlement. Weekly fireworks light up the lake in summer.

Information: **Laconia-Weirs Beach Chamber of Commerce** | 11 Veterans Sq., Laconia, 03246 | 603/524–5531 | www.lanconia-weirs.org.

Attractions

Funspot. With miniature golf, bowling, more than 500 video and fun games, and an indoor golf driving range, this a great place for kids and families. | Rte. 11B | 603/366–4377 | www.funspotnh.com | Mid-May–Labor Day, daily 9 AM–1 AM; Labor Day–mid May, Sun.–Thurs. 10–10, Fri.–Sat. 10–11.

Lake Winnipesaukee Cruises. Lake Winnipesaukee is the largest of New Hampshire's lakes, with 183 mi of shoreline and 274 islands. Taking a tour of the lake is a popular summer pastime. Sunset cruises are especially nice.
M/S Mount Washington. A 230-ft motor cruiser with space for 1,250 passengers with scenic and evening dinner dance cruises. | 211 Lakeside Ave. | 603/366–5531 or 888/843–6686 | www.cruisenh.com | $13 and up | Late May–late Oct., call for cruise times.

Old Burlwood Country Store. This old-time shop is packed with a wide selection of country gifts, gourmet food, penny candy, and handmade crafts. | Rte. 3 | 603/279–3021 | www.burlwoodcountrystore.com | Daily 10–5.

Surf Coaster. Seven slides, a wave pool, and a large aquatic play area for young children make up this water park near Lake Winnipesaukee. | Rte. 11B | 603/366–4991 | $18.99 | July, daily 10–8; mid-June–late June and Aug., daily 10–7.

Winnipesaukee Scenic Railroad. *See* Meredith. | U.S. 3 | 603/745–2135.

ON THE CALENDAR
MAY: *Winni Derby.* An annual fishing derby for landlocked salmon and lake trout on Lake Winnipesaukee. | 603/253–8689.
JULY: *Lake Winnipesaukee Antique & Classic Boat Show.* A judged show of antique and classic boats. | Weirs Beach Public Docks | 603/524–0348 or 603/544–2015.
JULY–AUG.: *Music at the Marketplace.* Free outdoor concerts on the Wiers Beach Pier, including barbershop quartets, jazz, folk, and big band. | Wiers Beach Pier | Wed., Fri., and Sun. | 603/524–5531.

Dining
Nothin Fancy Mexican Bar and Grill. Mexican. This friendly, hopping joint is popular with boaters and motorcyclists and is just a quick walk from the public docks. Try the deep-fried chimichanga or the steak-and-cheese burrito. The canning jar margarita is a local legend. | 306 Lakeside Ave. | 603/366–5764 | $8–$12 | AE, D, MC, V.

Lodging
Abakee Cottages. Comfortable, simply furnished cottages on Lake Winnipesaukee. Picnic area. Kitchenettes, refrigerators, cable TV. Beach, dock. Fishing. No pets. | 603/366–4405 | fax 603/366–4399 | info@abakeecottages.com | www.abakeecottages.com | 13 cottages | $70–$125 | Closed Oct.–May | No credit cards.

Birch Knoll Motel. Roadside motel 1 mi from Weirs Beach. Picnic area. Refrigerators, cable TV. Pool. Beach, boating. | 867 Weirs Blvd. | 603/366–4958 | fax 603/366–4081 | www.birch-knollmotel.com | 24 rooms | $52–$99 | Closed Nov.–Apr. | AE, D, MC, V.

St. Moritz Terrance Motel & Chalet. You can stay in a motel or housekeeping chalet with a lake view. There's a private beach. Picnic area. Refrigerators, no-smoking rooms, cable TV. Pool. | 937 Weirs Blvd. | 603/366–4482 | 17 rooms, 7 chalets (with showers only) | $55–$68, $600–$700 per wk chalets | Closed mid-Oct.–mid-May | MC, V.

WOLFEBORO

MAP 7, G8

(Nearby towns also listed: Center Sandwich, Moultonborourgh)

In 1768, John Wentworth, the state's last royal governor, built a summer home here and a road linking the east side of Lake Winnipesaukee to Portsmouth. Although the Wentworths fled the colonies at the start of the Revolution and their house burned in 1820, a marker at Wentworth State Park commemorates the country's first summer home. The road led other wealthy families to build summer homes in the area, and Wolfeboro became perhaps the nation's first summer resort town.

Today's visitors, who come by boat or by car, enjoy the fact that downtown Wolfeboro is right on the edge of Lake Winnipesaukee. You can take lake cruises, and a pleasant shopping district and several good restaurants add to the charm.

Information: **Chamber of Commerce** | Box 547, 32 Central Ave., Wolfeboro, 03894 | 603/569–2200 or 603/516–5324 | www.wolfeborochamber.com.

Attractions

Clark House Museum Complex. This cluster of three buildings on the Village Green includes an 1820 one-room schoolhouse, a replica of an 1862 firehouse, and a typical colonial-period farmhouse. | S. Main St. | 603/569–4997 | Free | July–Aug., Mon.–Sat. 10–4.

Libby House. A small natural-history museum, chartered and collected by Dr. Henry Forrest Libby in 1912, 3 mi north of Wolfeboro. Exhibits include animal and insect specimens as well as Abenaki Indian artifacts. | Rte. 109 | 603/569–1035 | $2 | June–Labor Day, Tues.–Sun. 10–4.

MV *Winnipesaukee Bell*. Although most Lake Winnipesaukee cruises are based around Weirs Beach, Wolfeboro has one cruise boat of its own, a 1½-hour tour of the southern portion of the lake. There are dinner cruises on Thursdays and private charters. | Off Main St. from the town docks | 603/569–3016 | www.wolfboroinn.com | $10 | Mid-may–mid-June, 1 cruise per day, weekends only 10:30 AM; mid-June–Sept., 3 cruises per day (10:30, 12:30, 2:30) closed Tues.; Sept. 3–Oct. 8, weekends only, 1 cruise per day 10:30am.

Wentworth State Park. This park 6 mi east of Wolfeboro has a beach on Lake Wentworth with good swimming, picnic areas, and a bathhouse. | Rte. 109 | 603/271–3556 | www.visitnh.gov | $2.50 | Daily.

Wright Museum. Uniforms, vehicles, period advertisements, and other artifacts illustrate the contributions of those on the home front to America's World War II effort. Exhibits cover major events and the impact of the war as well as details of life at home. | 77 Center St. | 603/569–1212 | www.wrightmuseum.org | $6 | May–Oct., daily 10–4; Nov.–Apr., Sat. 10–4, Sun. 12–4 (call ahead to confirm hrs).

ON THE CALENDAR

JULY: *Annual Lakes Region Open Waterski Tournament*. A waterskiing competition with variety of age groups that includes both slalom and jumping. | 603/569–2200.

JULY: *Annual Wolfeboro Antiques Fair*. Sixty exhibitors offering antiques of all kinds at this event. | 603/569–2200.

AUG.: *Annual New Hampshire Water Ski Championship*. A waterskiing competition for all age groups that included slalom, jumping, and tricks. | 603/569–2200.

AUG.: *Annual Granite Man Triathlon*. A race event with a ¾-mi swim, a 15-mi bike ride, and a 4.2-mi run. | 603/569–2200.

OCT.: *Antique and Classic Boat Society and Car Rendezvous*. A gathering of antique and classic boats and antique and classic cars. Not judged. | 603/544–2200.

Dining

The Bittersweet. American. Two levels of antiques, crafts, and quilts convert this barn into a cozy restaurant that serves lobster pie and slow-roasted prime rib. | Rte. 28 | 603/569–3636 | Closed Thurs.–Mon. No lunch | $7.95–$20.00 | AE, D, MC, V.

Love's Quay. Eclectic. The lakeside patio and enclosed gazebo and two main dining rooms are busy with boating enthusiasts who pack the tables of this classy, renowned establishment in summertime. The menu culls from several ethnicities, but the house specialty is seafood. Try the *zarzuella*, Portuguese-style lobster, shrimp, scallops, clams, and mussels in a brandy garlic, sherry olive oil, and tomato sauce. Everything, from the butter and ice cream to the white chocolate mints, is homemade. Kids' menu. Live entertainment. | 51 Mill St. | 603/569–3303 | $12–$27 | AE, MC, V.

Strawberry Patch. American. This cozy, local favorite restaurant and gift shop is fashioned like an English tea house with fresh flowers, wooden tables, and a menu filled with fresh treats made from scratch. Try the pecan almond French toast or, from the lunch menu, the baked quiche or cashew chicken. Kids' menu. | 30 N. Main St. | 603/569–5523 | No dinner | $3–$8 | No credit cards.

Wolfetrap Grill and Raw Bar. Seafood. Next to the Back Bay Marina, this summer spot is known for its raw specialties like oysters, clams, steamers, and the New England–style lobster boils. Burgers, fried-fish sandwiches, and seasonal, free boat trips make for a suitable family destination. Boat parking. Live music. | 19 Bay St. | 603/569–1047 | Closed Labor Day–Memorial Day | $6–$22 | AE, D, MC, V.

Lodging

Allen 'A' Motor Inn. A small, family-owned inn set on 7 acres, with comfortable accommodations. There is beach access on the property. Cable TV. Outdoor pool. Beach. Playground. No pets. | Rte. 28, | 603/569–1700 or 800/732–8507 | 43 rooms | $69–$89 | AE, D, MC, V.

Brook and Bridle Summer Homes. Bed-and-breakfast and deluxe home accommodations on 30 quiet, lakeside acres, 4 mi south of Wolfeboro on Route 28. The polished common rooms show off views of the nearby mountains. Home units are fully furnished with a kitchen, fireplace, wood floors, and screened-in porch. Complimentary breakfast, picnic area. No air-conditioning in some rooms, some kitchenettes, some microwaves, no TV in some rooms. Lake. Hiking, volleyball, beach, dock, water sports, boating. Fishing. Cross-country skiing. Playground, laundry facilities. | R.R. 1, Box 87 A, Alton | 603/569–2707 | fax 603/569–6949 | www.brookbridle.com | 7 rooms, 1 suite, 10 units | $145–$165 inn, $1,200–$1,975 a wk homes | AE, D, MC, V.

Lake Motel. This vacation motel is in a secluded area off Route 28, just south of downtown Wolfeboro. It has 650 ft. of lake-front and beach and is next to a golf course. Restaurant. Some kitchenettes, cable TV. Tennis. Beach, dock, boating. | 280 S. Main St. (Rte. 28) | 603/569–1100 or 888/569–1110 | fax 603/569–1620 | thelake@worldpath.net | www.thelakemotel.com | 30 rooms, 5 apartments | $105–$115, $715 per week for apartments | Closed mid-Oct.–mid-May | D, MC, V.

Lakeview Inn & Motor Lodge. You can stay in a vintage inn or in modern motel units here. Restaurant, bar with entertainment, complimentary Continental breakfast. Some kitchenettes, cable TV. Business services. | 200 N. Main St. (Rte. 109) | 603/569–1335 | fax 603/569–9426 | 17 rooms | $45–$90 | AE, MC, V.

Museum Lodges. Private, fully equipped and furnished cottages on Lake Winnepesaukee in a relaxed, no-frills setting. Picnic area. No air-conditioning, kitchenettes, refrigerators, no room phones, no TV. Lake. Beach, dock, water sports, boating. Fishing. Ice-skating. Pets allowed (seasonally). | 32 Governor Wentworth Hwy. (Route 109) | 603/569–1551 | rsmuseum@worldpath.net | www.museumlodges.com | 10 cottages | $690–$940 wk | Closed mid-Oct.–mid-May | No credit cards.

Pine View Lodge. Rooms in this small motel 7 mi north of Wolfboro all have Winnipesaukee views (but no bathtubs, only showers). Picnic area. Cable TV, no room phones. | Rte. 109, Melvin Village | 603/544–3800 | 12 rooms | $59–$85 | D, MC, V.

Wolfeboro Inn. The landscaping is lovely at this antique inn on the edge of Lake Winnipesaukee. Dining room, bar, complimentary Continental breakfast. Some kitchenettes, room service, cable TV. Lake. Beach. Cross-country skiing. Business services. Free parking. | 90 N. Main St. (Rte. 109) | 603/569–3016 or 800/451–2389 | fax 603/569–5375 | 44 rooms, 3 suites | $109–$229 | AE, MC.

Eating Well is the Best Revenge

Start at the top By all means take in a really good restaurant or two while you're on the road. A trip is a time to kick back and savor the pleasures of the palate. Read up on the culinary scene before you leave home. Check out representative menus on the Web—some chefs have gone electronic. And ask friends who have just come back. For big-city dining, reserve a table as far in advance as you can, remembering that the best establishments book up months ahead. Remember that some good restaurants require you to reconfirm the day before or the day of your meal. Then again, some really good places will call you, so make sure to leave a number where you can be reached.

Adventures in eating A trip is the perfect opportunity to try food you can't get at home. So leave yourself open to try an ethnic food that's not represented where you live or to eat fruits and vegetables you've never heard of. One of them may become your next favorite food.

Beyond guidebooks You can rely on the restaurants you find in these pages. But also look for restaurants on your own. When you're ready for lunch, ask people you meet where they eat. Look for tiny holes-in-the-wall with a loyal following and the best burgers or crispiest pizza crust. Find out about local chains whose fame rests upon a single memorable dish. There's hardly a food-lover who doesn't relish the chance to share a favorite place. It's fun to come up with your own special find—and asking about food is a great way to start a conversation.

Sample local flavors Do check out the specialties. Is there a special brand of ice cream or a special dish that you simply must try?

Have a picnic Every so often eat al fresco. Grocery shopping gives you a whole different view of a place.

Beyond T-Shirts and Key Chains

Budget for a major purchase If souvenirs are all about keeping the memories alive in the long haul, plan ahead to shop for something really special—a work of art, a rug or something else hand-crafted, or a major accessory for your home. One major purchase will stay with you far longer than a dozen tourist trinkets, and you'll have all the wonderful memories associated with shopping for it besides.

Add to your collection Whether antiques, used books, salt and pepper shakers, or ceramic frogs are your thing, start looking in the first day or two. Chances are you'll want to scout around and then go back to some of the first shops you visited before you hand over your credit card.

Get guarantees in writing Is the vendor making promises? Ask him to put them in writing.

Anticipate a shopping spree If you think you might buy breakables, bring along a length of bubble wrap. Pack a large tote bag in your suitcase in case you need extra space. Don't fill your suitcase to bursting before you leave home. Or include some old clothing that you can leave behind to make room for new acquisitions.

Know before you go Study prices at home on items you might consider buying while you're away. Otherwise you won't recognize a bargain when you see one.

Plastic, please Especially if your purchase is pricey and you're looking for authenticity, it's always smart to pay with a credit card. If a problem arises later on and the merchant can't or won't resolve it, the credit-card company may help you out.

© Artville

Vermont

Second smallest of all states in population, Vermont looms at least as large as Texas in that corner of the popular imagination where icons are minted. Anyone who has ever heard "Moonlight in Vermont," looked at the bucolic scene on a can of maple syrup, or has a mind's-eye picture of a covered bridge surrounded by flame-red autumn maples has felt the hold that the Green Mountain State has on our national consciousness.

Based on the percentage of its population that lives in cities, Vermont is the most rural state in the Union. But what counts more than the Census Bureau's assessment is the extent to which Vermonters have traded on their image as a hidden land of yeomen farmers and villagers, even in an age when the number of dairy operations in the state has dipped well below 2,000 (one-tenth as many as there were 50 years ago) and a good number of those villagers are "flatlander" transplants playing the stock market on the Internet. Vermont secured its popular image back when the legend really was fact—when 10 cows made a farm and you couldn't get the buggy to town during mud season—and kept it alive by sheer force of will and a Yankee's sense of what sells.

Nevertheless, these Yankees are selling something real. If Vermont retains a particularly strong upcountry New England flavor, it's because the state remained in relative isolation far longer than its neighbors. For one thing, Vermont is the only New England state without a seacoast. Lacking the equivalent of a Newport or a Boston—or even a Portsmouth, New Hampshire—Vermont never developed the same cosmopolitan attitude as these coastal cities. (It would develop one eventually, but that had to wait for the building of the interstate highways.)

The state's terrain also helped Vermont stay isolated. Unlike New Hampshire, whose northern mountains, in the words of Robert Frost, "curl up in a coil," Vermont's Green Mountains run north and south for the length of the state, creating a series of

STATE CAPITAL: MONTPELIER	POPULATION: 590,883	AREA: 9,609 SQUARE MI
BORDERS: NH, MA, NY, CANADA	TIME ZONE: EASTERN	POSTAL ABBREVIATION: VT
WEB SITE: WWW.TRAVEL-VERMONT.COM (TRAVEL), WWW.STATE.VT.US (GENERAL)		

valleys whose old-time inhabitants didn't see much of each other, let alone the outside world. The railroads came along in the mid-19th century, but mostly left the hill towns alone. They never converged on a great manufacturing center, the way they did on Manchester, New Hampshire; for a long time, manufacturing in Vermont, outside of Burlington, meant the machine-tool factories of the Connecticut River valley and a scattering of industries largely related to forest products. Vermont was farm country, stony steep-sloped farm country, a place where, as Ethan Allen said, "the gods of the valleys are not the gods of the hills."

Life as it was lived in old-time Vermont—Arcadian or hardscrabble, depending on how you look at it—gave a certain cast to the land and to the character of the inhabitants. Much of the farmland was, to put it mildly, a challenge to human mettle, as is the generous helping of weather served over four heroically distinct seasons. The net result of years of expanding and then receding agriculture has left a landscape in which meadow and forest stand in splendid counterpoint; years of strong attachment to community have created villages and towns with distinct identities. There is only one big city—Burlington—and it is only big by local standards, suffering the country folks' jibe that it has the advantage of "being close to Vermont." There is also a big and beautiful lake, Champlain.

All this has helped create the legend of the flinty, plainspoken Yankee, most popularly exemplified by President and Vermont native Calvin "Silent Cal" Coolidge, but even better represented by the late governor and senator, George Aiken, famous for remarking that the United States ought simply to declare victory in Vietnam and pull out, and for spending a total of $17 on his last reelection campaign. (He won by a landslide.) Vermont also produced George Perkins Marsh, who was one of the first to philosophize on the proper relation of human beings to the land and its resources. In this state, a vest-pocket domain whose resources largely amounted to dirt, granite, water, and wood, Marsh has plenty of latter-day apostles who fight the good fight for sound land-use policies, and against suburban sprawl. Many of them are transplants—but then again, Ethan Allen himself was a flatlander from Connecticut.

For most outsiders—the ones who haven't moved here yet—it all boils down, like sap into maple syrup, to elements of that old Vermont mystique: happy Holsteins, working for Ben and Jerry, with maybe a little milk left over for hot cocoa in the lodge after the day's last run; autumn colors; great white spires rising high above the villages of a peaceable kingdom. Of course that's all surface, but it runs pretty deep, and people worked hard to make it, not make it up.

History

Before the advent of European settlement, Vermont was the home of the Abenaki, members of the Algonkian group of Native Americans, who were allied with the French during the early days of European exploration and settlement. In 1609 Samuel de Champlain became the first white man to look upon the Green Mountains and paddle the waters of the great lake that now bears his name. The French established a fort

VT Timeline

1200–1790

The Abenakis, an Algonquian Native America subgroup, include northern Vermont within a range that spreads across the upper portions of New Hampshire and Maine. They were preceded by Pre- and Old Algonkian cultures that dated back to at least 2000 BC.

1609

Samuel de Champlain, traveling south from the St. Lawrence valley, discovers the lake that will bear his name.

1666

The French establish the first white settlement in what will become Vermont, on Isle La Motte in the Champlain Islands.

INTRODUCTION
HISTORY
REGIONS
WHEN TO VISIT
STATE'S GREATS
RULES OF THE ROAD
DRIVING TOURS

in the Champlain Islands as early as 1666; the English, arriving by way of their colony in Massachusetts, did not follow suit until they built Fort Dummer, near modern-day Brattleboro, in 1724. Unlike the French, the New Englanders came to stay—although few settlers cared to call Vermont home during most of the 18th century, when the region was a wilderness corridor between the two colonizing powers for the struggles that culminated in the French and Indian Wars.

Even after the French had been routed, Vermont was a bone of contention between settlers claiming rights under the "New Hampshire Grants" and New York authorities trying to enforce boundaries that extended as far east as the Connecticut River. This was the era of Ethan Allen and his Green Mountain Boys, a paramilitary band bent on evicting the "Yorkers" for good. Allen and his men later fought for independence from the British, paving the way for the Republic of Vermont, a sovereign state that survived until its willing assimilation into the United States in 1791. This incorporation paved the way for a flood of settlers, mostly from Connecticut and Massachusetts, who ushered in the early 19th-century golden age of self-sufficient agriculture and small-town life.

After the Civil War, in which officers and men from this staunchly abolitionist state fought and died in numbers out of all proportion to Vermont's size, the farm population gradually diminished, without any accompanying rush to industrialization. Vermont's few industrial centers never achieved the prowess of their more populous New England neighbors, who had easier access to markets. But during the latter half of the 20th century, Vermont discovered its most saleable commodity: Vermont itself. Primed by the phenomenal postwar growth of the ski industry and the building of the interstate highways, tourism became one of the state's principal economic engines. Each year more and more of the tourists stay, fueling the growth of the education, high technology, and "electronic cottage" industries that best suit this still-pastoral landscape.

Regions

1. SOUTHERN VERMONT

Southern Vermont was the site of the state's first permanent settlement, near Brattleboro, and it was also the region first extensively affected by tourism. Well over a century ago, Manchester and environs were already an outpost of fashionable society: Abraham Lincoln's family sojourned here, and his son, Robert Todd Lincoln, liked the area so much that he built a grand summer estate on the outskirts of town. The polished villages along Route 30, a tradition of summer theater, and exclusive Bennington College are all reminders that the southern part of the state has long appealed to outsiders. Industry, too, found southern Vermont early on: along the Connecticut River valley, Yankee industrialists made Vermont famous as a center for machine-tool manufacture.

1724	1749		1764	1770–71
Ft. Dummer, near present-day Brattleboro, is established by the colony of Massachusetts; it is the first permanent white settlement on Vermont soil.	New Hampshire governor Benning Wentworth makes his first grants of Vermont townships; these "New Hampshire Grants" will become the focus of controversy between Vermont	settlers and surveyors from colonial New York.	New York, acting on royal decree, states its claim to the lands between Lake Champlain and the Connecticut River.	Ethan Allen organizes the Green Mountain Boys, dedicated to disputing New York claims and driving that colony's surveyors from Vermont territory.

But southern Vermont still has plenty of rough edges, thanks in part to the huge swath of land given over to the Green Mountain National Forest. Here, as in the far north, there are towns with almost no residents and vast tracts of woodland traversed only by primitive gravel roads—or perhaps only by the tortuous footpath called the Long Trail, which links the loftiest peaks of the Green Mountains. The state's ski industry got an early start and is well represented in the south, where farsighted Vermonters first saw the need for enacting landmark legislation to control sprawl around the booming resorts.

Towns listed: Arlington, Bellows Falls, Bennington, Brattleboro, Chester, Dorset, Grafton, Londonderry, Ludlow, Manchester, Marlboro, Newfane, Peru, Putney, Rockingham, Springfield, Stratton Mountain, West Dover, Weston, Wilmington.

2. CENTRAL VERMONT

North of a line running roughly from Mount Ascutney in the east to Lake St. Catherine in the west, Vermont broadens both in terms of sheer distance and the scope of its landscape. Near the southern reaches of Lake Champlain, which resembles a wide, lazy river this far south, some of the state's best dairy country stretches across a rolling plain that nestles against the forested massif of the Green Mountains. The mountains themselves, mostly within the boundaries of the Green Mountain National Forest's northern unit, are riven by a series of narrow gaps treasured by motorists who find occasional hairpin turns a small price to pay for spectacular lake and valley views. In the middle of it all is Rutland, Vermont's second-largest city, and the bustle of Killington, its biggest ski resort.

To the east is a patchwork of farmland and forest and a delightfully confusing scramble of back roads and postcard villages that tumble down toward the valley of New England's longest river, the Connecticut. Here workaday towns such as White River Junction and Bradford still seem dressed for the traffic of river and railroad, while elegant Woodstock sets the tone for its manicured surrounding shire.

Towns listed: Barnard, Brandon, Bridgewater, Bristol, Fairlee, Killington, Middlebury, Norwich, Plymouth, Randolph, Rutland, Waitsfield, White River Junction, Vergennes, Warren, Windsor, Woodstock.

3. NORTHERN VERMONT

The twin cities of Barre and Montpelier—one the world's granite capital, the other the capital of Vermont—mark the fringes of northern Vermont. Here vistas broaden—Mt. Mansfield, Vermont's highest peak, is visible across much of the state's northern tier of counties—and many small towns and villages look as if they spend more effort preparing for the onslaught of winter than the onslaught of tourists. Yet there are a few places where tourism reigns supreme, such as Stowe, Vermont's legendary winter sports capital, and towns like Peacham and Craftsbury Common, which each autumn must be responsible for a good portion of all the color film purchased in the United States.

1775	**1777**		**1791**	**1800**
Ethan Allen crosses Lake Champlain and takes Fort Ticonderoga from the British.	Town delegates meet in a constitutional convention at Windsor and establish the Republic of Vermont. Vermont troops join in defeating a British drive to seize military stores at	Bennington; the "Battle of Bennington" is fought just across the border in New York State.	The University of Vermont is established at Burlington by Ira Allen. Vermont joins the Union as the 14th state.	Middlebury College is established as a religious alternative to the University of Vermont.

INTRODUCTION
HISTORY
REGIONS
WHEN TO VISIT
STATE'S GREATS
RULES OF THE ROAD
DRIVING TOURS

Northern Vermont is where Lake Champlain is broadest and most inviting for boaters and anglers—and for those who just want to stroll along Burlington's cosmopolitan waterfront and enjoy what has been called the world's most beautiful sunset. Burlington itself is a lively, arts-conscious college town, offering a remarkable contrast to the solemnly beautiful, lake-strewn forest vastness that lies to its northeast. This quarter, called the Northeast Kingdom, stands out as one of New England's last frontiers, a place so enormous that more than 130,000 acres recently changed hands in a single timber-company transaction. Fortunately much of that land will be preserved, and the rest kept in sustainable logging.

Towns listed: Barre, Burlington, Charlotte, Craftsbury Common, Highgate Springs, Island Pond, Jeffersonville, Lyndonville, Montgomery Center, Montpelier, Morrisville, Newport, North Hero, St. Albans, St. Johnsbury, Shelburne, Stowe, Waterbury.

When to Visit

Along with the other northern New England states, Vermont shares a climate of extremes, especially in winter. The state's high temperature record was set on the Fourth of July in 1911, when the mercury reached 105°F at Vernon, near the Massachusetts border. Such temperatures are unusual; in 1998 Burlington, which lies at the state's lowest altitude of 95 ft, did not experience any 90°F days. Vermont's all-time low of −50°F was reached in Bloomfield, in the far north of the Connecticut River valley, on December 30, 1933. Mountain locations and cold valley pockets will often register double-digit negative temperatures in midwinter; however, daytime highs are nearly always warm enough for comfortable enjoyment of winter sports. The average annual rainfall is in the 40-inch range, with the 24-hour record belonging to Somerset: on November 3 and 4, during the 1927 flood (the state's worst), when that southern Vermont town was drenched with 8.77 inches. St. Johnsbury, in the northeast, holds the one-day snowfall record: 33 inches on February 25, 1969. Annual snowfall is difficult to average, because of considerable differences from one region to the next. Statewide figures range from 80 and 90 inches, with 150 inches or more not uncommon in the higher Green Mountains and less than 50 inches likely in the southern Connecticut River valley.

Of all Vermont seasons, spring is the most difficult to learn to appreciate. Spring skiing can be terrific right into April, although that month is best known for its notorious "mud season," when melting snows can transform dirt roads into impassable morasses. Especially at higher elevations, spring really doesn't begin until May. Summer in Vermont is short and glorious. The 10 weeks between mid-June and late August offer fine weather for hiking, bicycling, and water sports, with oppressive heat a rarity and evenings often cool enough for a light sweater. (Just keep the bug repellent handy in rural areas, especially during early summer.) Vermont seems to own the copyright on autumn, when the state's hardwood forests achieve a dazzling palette of reds, yellows, oranges, and a thousand other shades between purple and gold. The foliage display

1805	1814	1848	1861–65	
Montpelier becomes Vermont's capital.	A Vermont-based Lake Champlain fleet wins the battle of Plattsburgh against the British in the War of 1812.	Vermont's first passenger train travels between White River Junction and Bethel.	Vermont supplies more than 34,000 men to the Union army, suffering the highest casualty rate of any Northern state. Vermonters break Pickett's charge at Gettysburg and are victors	at the Battle of Cedar Creek.

begins in the northeast and at the upper altitudes of the Green Mountains in mid-September and lasts well into October in the south and along the Champlain Valley. Then, after a cold, brown and somber November, the snows of winter usher in the East's best skiing—alpine and cross-country—and snowshoeing. There's usually a January thaw; but don't look for bare ground until well into March or even April.

CLIMATE CHART
Average High/Low Temperatures (°F) and Monthly Precipitation (in inches)

	JAN.	FEB.	MAR.	APR.	MAY	JUNE
BURLINGTON	25/8	27/9	38/21	53/33	66/44	76/54
	1.9	1.7	2.2	2.8	3.0	3.6

	JULY	AUG.	SEPT.	OCT.	NOV.	DEC.
	80/59	78/57	69/49	57/39	44/30	30/15
	3.4	3.9	3.2	2.8	2.8	2.4

FESTIVALS AND SEASONAL EVENTS
WINTER

Dec. **First Night** in Burlington. Beginning in mid-afternoon on New Year's Eve, dozens of Burlington venues host music, story-telling, dance, comedy, and kid's performances; there are fireworks over the Lake Champlain waterfront early in the evening and again at midnight. Purchase of a button allows admission to all events. | 802/863–6005.

Jan. **Winter Carnival** in Stowe. Vermont's oldest winter fest, with a hockey tournament, snowshoe race, cross-country race, snow golf and volleyball, and more. | 802/253–7321.

SPRING

Apr. **Maple Festival** in St. Albans. The annual running of the sap in thousands of maple trees—and its transformation by heat and hard work into Vermont's signature elixir—is a carnival-like celebration in the streets of "St. A." Here's the place to try sugar on snow, a taffylike treat traditionally served with pickles and doughnuts. | 802/524–2444.

SUMMER

June **Discover Jazz Festival** in Burlington. At indoor and outdoor locations all over the Queen City, local and out-of-town soloists and ensembles—from amateurs to international big names—perform all week from noon until well past dark. | 802/863–7992.

1864	**1866–70**	**1910**	**1923**	**1933**
Confederate infiltrators stage the St. Albans Raid, robbing the city's banks.	Vermont is the staging area for the Fenian Raids, unsuccessful attempts by Irish nationalists to seize Canada from Britain.	The Green Mountain Club is established to build and maintain the 260-mi Long Trail, America's first planned recreational footpath running the length of an entire state.	Upon the death of Warren G. Harding, Calvin Coolidge is sworn in as president of the United States by his father, John Coolidge, at his Plymouth Notch family home.	The Civilian Conservation Corps cuts the first ski trails on Mt. Mansfield, marking the beginning of Stowe's emergence as an alpine mecca.

INTRODUCTION
HISTORY
REGIONS
WHEN TO VISIT
STATE'S GREATS
RULES OF THE ROAD
DRIVING TOURS

Aug. **Champlain Valley Exposition,** Route 15, Essex Junction. Vermont's biggest end-of-summer extravaganza combines the traditional elements of a country fair—the biggest pumpkin, the best pickles, the most handsome livestock—with all the glitter of a midway and first-class amusement rides. The food stands are a fairground traditionalist's delight, and the worst nightmare of the food police. | 802/878–5545.

AUTUMN

Sept. **Tunbridge World's Fair,** Route 110, Tunbridge. What other World's Fair has been held every year since the mid-1800s? Tiny Tunbridge (pop. 1,000) puts on quite the annual show, with tractor and draft-horse pulls, judging of the harvest's bounty, and plenty to eat. It's toned down in some ways, though: it's said that years ago wardens rounded up the sober at 3 PM and evicted them from the fairgrounds. | 902/889–5555.

State's Greats

Most visitors to Vermont think of the Green Mountain State in terms of outdoor activities, set amid a panorama of mountain, farmland, and lake scenery that is scarcely rivaled in the northeastern United States. More than a dozen major ski resorts dot the slopes of the Green Mountains, while forests and meadows are liberally laced with cross-country skiing, snowshoe, and snowmobile trails. When the snows melt, the Vermont countryside is no less alluring. Most travelers choose to meander from village to village by car (and increasingly by bicycle), seeking out cozy inns, intriguing antiques and craft shops, and informal country restaurants.

Although it is the only New England state without ocean frontage, Vermont boasts a coastline, the region's "west coast," along the 125-mi-long Lake Champlain. In conjunction with a scattering of smaller lakes, Champlain offers superb fishing, boating, and swimming, as well as historic sites from the American Revolution and the War of 1812.

Vermont's only metropolitan area is Burlington, with fewer than 150,000 people in the city and its environs. The "Queen City" hosts a lively, college-influenced café, shopping, and arts scene that's reflected in smaller cities and towns throughout the state.

Beaches, Forests, and Parks

The crown jewel among Vermont's public lands is the nearly 600,000-acre **Green Mountain National Forest,** a federally managed woodland divided into northern and southern components that straddle the Green Mountain range. The National Forest is well supplied with picnicking and primitive campsites, as well as hiking trails connected to the Massachusetts-to-Quebec Long Trail. There is one national park—500-acre

---

1934
A group of Woodstock ski enthusiasts powers an endless loop of rope with an old Model-T engine to create America's first mechanical ski tow.

1939
Robert Frost, Vermont's poet laureate, begins a 34-year residence in Ripton. Of his earlier home state, New Hampshire, he once said, "It's one of the two best states in the Union. The other's Vermont."

1957
International Business Machines (IBM) begins operations in Essex Junction, near Burlington. The company's chip-making plant becomes Vermont's largest private-sector employer and ushers in the state's modern industrial era.

1964
The first segments of interstate highway open in Vermont. The interstates eventually transform the state's transportation and growth patterns, while fueling the growth of the tourist economy.

Marsh-Billings, dedicated to the conservation and land-use principles of Vermonters George Perkins Marsh and Frederick Billings, in Woodstock—and some 50 state parks and forests, most providing camping facilities. The majority of state parks on larger bodies of water have unsupervised swimming beaches and boat access; notably **Elmore, Little River,** and **Lake Carmi** in the north; **Lake St. Catherine** in central Vermont; and **Emerald Lake** in the south. The best parks for swimming and other water sports, though, are those along Lake Champlain, especially in the **Champlain Islands.** Because of its proximity to Burlington, spectacular views, and gentle drop-off, the best of these for families is **Sand Bar,** in Milton.

Culture, History, and the Arts

Vermont's role in the Revolutionary War era is highlighted at **Mt. Independence** on Lake Champlain; the **Hubbardton Battlefield** in the southern Green Mountains; the **Bennington Battle Monument;** and the **Ethan Allen Homestead** in Burlington. The life of Vermont-born president **Calvin Coolidge** is recalled at his birthplace in Plymouth. The founder of the Mormon religion is commemorated at the **Joseph Smith Birthplace** in Sharon. The state's premier trove of Americana is the **Shelburne Museum,** just south of Burlington; one of the best family attractions in Vermont, it comprises 45 acres of period buildings, working old-time artisans, folk art, and even a dry-moored steamboat. Other fine historical museums include Montpelier's **Vermont Museum,** on the ground floor of the Vermont Historical Society; the **Bennington Museum,** with its Grandma Moses collection; and the **Fairbanks Museum,** a St. Johnsbury institution with ethnographic and natural science exhibits, as well as a small planetarium. Among the state's art museums, the University of Vermont's small but comprehensive **Fleming Museum** and the Victorian gallery at the **St. Johnsbury Athenaeum** are standouts.

Vermont's most celebrated series of musical events is the **Mozart Festival,** with summer and winter schedules taking place at a variety of locations. The **Marlboro Music Festival** is a respected institution based at Marlboro College in southern Vermont. **Summer theater** takes the boards at a number of venues, most notably in Dorset.

Sports

Vermonters head for the outdoors in all seasons, and the state attracts visitors who take the same hearty approach to the invigorating climate and challenging landscape of water and woods. Extending along the backbone of the Green Mountains for some 265 mi, the **Long Trail** has been Vermont's "Footpath in the Wilderness" since its route was first cut in 1910. Bookstores and outdoor suppliers throughout the state sell the Green Mountain Club's guide to the trail and its overnight huts, along with tips for shorter treks on an intricate system of trails throughout the state. Mountain bikers also have their favorite Green Mountain trails, and an increasing number of ski areas, such as **Stowe** and **Jay Peak,** offer mountain bike routes.

1970
Act 250, Vermont's landmark land-use and planning law, is passed by the legislature. The legislation is a response to unregulated subdivision and growth, particularly near resort areas, and is

credited with preserving much of the state's rural character.

1978
Ben Cohen and Jerry Greenfield begin selling homemade ice cream in a converted Burlington gas station. Ben and Jerry's Inc. gains an international following, largely because of

its identification with the wholesome Vermont image.

1990
Vermont sends former Burlington mayor Bernard Sanders, a socialist, to Washington as the nation's only Independent congressman.

INTRODUCTION
HISTORY
REGIONS
WHEN TO VISIT
STATE'S GREATS
RULES OF THE ROAD
DRIVING TOURS

Anglers come to Vermont to go after lake trout, landlocked salmon, and other game fish on big lakes such as **Champlain, Memphremagog,** and **Willoughby.** One of America's most renowned trout streams, the **Battenkill,** flows through the southwestern portion of the state; farther north, the **Missisquoi** and **Lamoille** rivers also challenge the fly-casting crowd. And in winter, the bays of Lake Champlain and smaller lakes and ponds across the state are favored for ice fishing.

Sailing and power-boating enthusiasts have a range of opportunities, from the challenge of Lake Champlain to small, tranquil ponds. Canoeists ply the waters of **Missisquoi National Wildlife Refuge, Otter Creek,** and the **Winooski, Lamoille,** and **Missisquoi** rivers; in spring, fast waters fed by melting snows bring kayakers to these and smaller streams.

There are 55 public golf courses in Vermont. Some of the most challenging—and most spectacularly located—are at ski resorts such as **Stratton** and **Sugarbush,** which have become year-round playgrounds, and at the **Equinox Hotel** in Manchester. The big resorts also draw tennis buffs to courts where, as at the golf courses, the scenery is a major distraction.

Winter, of course, means skiing in the state that gave America its first powered lift. Fifteen major downhill areas are strung along the Green Mountains and on the outlying peaks. Cross-country skiing opportunities range from self-contained resorts with dozens of miles of groomed trails, to bushwhacking through woodlands where Vermont's increasing army of snowshoers join in the fun. For snowmobilers, there is a 3,100-mi network of trails maintained by the **Vermont Association of Snow Travelers** (VAST).

Rules of the Road

License requirements: Valid licenses issued by other state and national jurisdictions are recognized in Vermont. The legal driving age is 16.

Right turn on red: Permitted unless posted otherwise.

Seat belt and helmet laws: Vermont law requires all vehicle occupants to be secured with seat belts; children under the age of five must be secured in a federally approved child safety seat. Motorcycle operators and passengers are required to wear helmets.

Speed limits: The limit on Vermont highways is 50 mph, except as posted otherwise in settled areas; on interstate highways, a 65-mph speed limit is observed unless posted otherwise.

For More Information: Vermont Department of Motor Vehicles | 120 State St., Montpelier | 802/828–2014.

1998
Vermont's first national park, Marsh-Billings, opens on a 500-acre Woodstock tract donated by Laurance Rockefeller.

Lake Champlain Islands Driving Tour

FROM MILTON TO THE MISSISQUOI NATIONAL WILDLIFE REFUGE

Distance: 87 mi round-trip from Burlington   Time: 1–2 days
Break: North Hero makes a good overnight stop; there are several lodging places overlooking
Lake Champlain.

Florida has its keys, and Vermont has the Lake Champlain Islands—a bucolic archipelago
running north to south just north of Burlington, in the broadest part of the lake.
Although the islands mostly consist of gently rolling terrain, their situation affords
spectacular views of both Vermont's Green Mountains, to the east, and the Adiron-

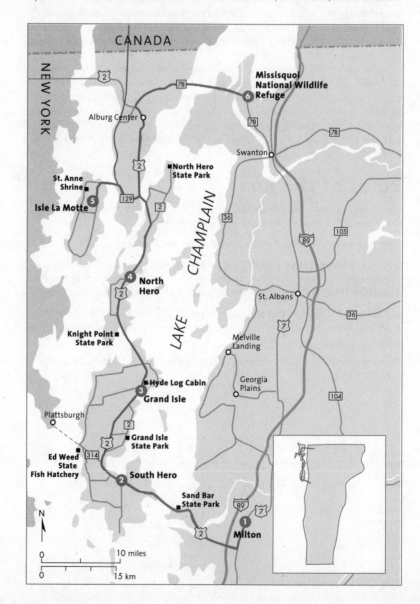

INTRODUCTION
HISTORY
REGIONS
WHEN TO VISIT
STATE'S GREATS
RULES OF THE ROAD
DRIVING TOURS

dacks of New York State, to the west. This is a tour for any time of the year—winter brings a stark beauty to the lake, with bays and inlets sheathed in ice and dotted with ice-fishing shacks—but the island scenery is at its prettiest between late spring and mid-autumn. Given the climate-moderating influence of the lake, foliage season comes a bit later and lasts a little longer in this part of Vermont.

❶ In **Milton** (8 mi north of Burlington, I–89 Exit 17 onto U.S. 2 W). Just before you reach the U.S. 2 causeway (4 mi from I–89) over the eastern portion of Lake Champlain, a right-hand turnoff leads to **Sand Bar State Park** (Rte. 2), which boasts one of Vermont's finest swimming beaches. The drop-off is so gentle that it seems almost as if you could wade across to the islands; the lake and mountain views are sublime. There are picnic facilities, a nearby boat launching ramp, and windsurfer rentals in summer.

❷ South Hero (2 mi west of causeway on U.S. 2) is the southernmost of the Lake Champlain Islands. According to legend, this island and its companion, North Hero, were named for Ethan Allen and his brother Ira, two heroes of Vermont's early struggle for independence from New York. At South Hero village, turn left on South Street to reach two of the islands' remaining apple orchards, **Hackett's** (86 South St.) and **Allenholm Farm** (South St.). This was once prime apple country, although development has taken its toll.

❸ At **Grand Isle** (2 mi north on U.S. 2, then 2 mi west on Rte. 314), the **ferry to Plattsburgh, New York** (Rte. 314) is the only Lake Champlain boat crossing operating all year. Just opposite the ferry dock is the **Ed Weed State Fish Hatchery** (Rte. 314), which has exhibits on Lake Champlain's fish species and offers a look at a state-of-the-art trout hatching operation. To the right (east) of U.S. 2 (4 mi north of South Hero) is **Grand Isle State Park** (Rte. 2), with tent sites, lean-tos, and swimming (registered campers only). Also on Route 2 in Grand Isle is the **Hyde Log Cabin,** believed to be the oldest log cabin in the United States. The 1783 structure was built by one of the islands' earliest settlers, and houses artifacts of pioneer life.

❹ **North Hero** (4 mi north on U.S. 2) is a separate island, with a town of the same name, lying across a causeway—in summer, the drawbridge may be open to allow tall-masted sailboats to pass through. **Knight Point State Park** (Rte. 2) is on the left, just past the causeway. The day-use park has a swimming beach and rowboat rentals. Up ahead, the village of North Hero clusters around the handsome 1824 **Grande Isle County Court House,** built of local marble. The little town faces City Bay (there's nothing remotely like a city in sight), where you can rent a canoe or kayak to enjoy the calm lake waters and magnificent views of the northernmost Green Mountains. To the north, beyond a narrow isthmus across which Indians once portaged their canoes, bear east off Route 2 to reach North Hero State Park (Rte. 2), with attractive campsites and beaches occupying the island's northern tip.

❺ Isle La Motte (Follow U.S. 2 across a bridge leading to the Alburg peninsula—connected by land only to the Canadian mainland—then west onto Route 129 and across another bridge; 9 mi total from North Hero) is the smallest of the Champlain Islands. Near the island's northern tip is the **St. Anne Shrine** (W. Shore Rd.), run by the Edmundite fathers to mark the spot where the first Catholic Mass in Vermont was celebrated, in 1666. On Isle La Motte several of the world's only black marble quarries once turned out stone used in the U.S. Capitol and in New York City's Radio City Music Hall. At a now-unused quarry on the island's southwest shore and in other outcroppings on Isle La Motte are remnants of the world's oldest **fossil reef,** formed some 400 million years ago when this entire area was submerged beneath warm ocean waters.

❻ The **Missisquoi National Wildlife Refuge** (Return over the Isle La Motte Causeway to Alburg, then east on Route 129 and north on U.S. 2 and east on Route 78 and the causeway leading to the Vermont mainland; 15 mi total from Isle La Motte) encompasses a 6,300-acre tract of marshland and forest at the mouth of the Missisquoi River, where nearly 300 species of birds have been recorded, and where the canoeing and fishing are superb (Rte. 78). From the refuge, drive 10 mi east on Route 78 to pick up Interstate 89 at Exit 21 in Swanton for the return to Burlington (27 mi south).

Middlebury and the Lower Champlain Valley Driving Tour

FROM SHELBURNE TO LARABEES POINT

Distance: 167 mi round-trip from Burlington   Time: 2 days
Break: Given the number of things to do and see between Burlington and Middlebury, Middlebury—with its several fine inns—makes a good overnight stop.

Although just about every Vermont town once had its dairy farms, most of the state's milk production is now centered on the rich bottomlands of the Champlain Valley. South of Burlington, the land that hugs the big lake offers a different type of Vermont scenery—broad and expansive, with the Green Mountains as a distant backdrop. The unofficial capital of this land of milk and apples is a college town right out of central casting.

❶ Shelburne (7 mi south of Burlington on U.S. 7) is a suburban community boasting two prime attractions that are both the legacy of a single remarkable family. The Shelburne Museum (Shelburne Rd.) is a 45-acre New England village made up of historic and architecturally representative structures moved to the site. On a side road leading to Shelburne Point is Shelburne Farms (Harbor Rd.), which comprises the core of the estate developed by Dr. William Seward Webb, father of Shelburne Museum donor Electra Havemeyer Webb. The Webb heirs have established a model demonstration farm and cheese-making operation.

❷ The approach to **Charlotte** (5 mi south on U.S. 7, 2 mi east on local Rte. F5 from Charlotte if taking ferry) is characterized by magnificent views of Lake Champlain and the Adirondacks on the opposite shore. The tiny village serves as the eastern terminus for the **ferry to Essex, New York** (Ferry Rd.).

❸ At **Ferrisburgh** (5 mi south on U.S. 7), 19th-century writer Rowland Robinson's farmstead **Rokeby** (Rte. 7) illuminates the days when Robinson, like many Vermonters, sheltered runaway slaves heading north to Canada and freedom.

❹ **Vergennes** (3 mi south on U.S. 7, then 1 mi east on Rte. 22A) is a vest-pocket community of Victorian homes and public buildings. In this unlikeliest of naval ports a fleet was constructed on the banks of Otter Creek to assault the British in the 1814 Battle of Plattsburgh. This story and much of the rest of Lake Champlain's history in peace and war is told at the nearby **Lake Champlain Maritime Museum** (7 mi east on Basin Harbor Rd., Ferrisburgh). Just south of the museum, off a road that follows the lake shore, stop at **Button Bay State Park** to look for the tiny, perforated pebbles that gave the bay its name.

❺ **Middlebury** (16 mi south of Vergennes turnoff on U.S. 7) is the home of **Middlebury College.** Founded in 1800, the college is highly regarded for its liberal arts programs.

Middlebury's compact downtown surrounds the falls of Otter Creek; within a short walk are the **Vermont State Craft Center** at Frog Hollow (1 Mill St.); the **Sheldon Museum** (1 Park St.) of local 19th-century Americana; the **Vermont Folklife Center** (2 Court St.), devoted to regional folklore and the everyday life of times past; and the gracious old **Middlebury Inn** (14 Courthouse Sq). The 136-ft tower of the 1809 **Congregational Church** is perhaps Vermont's finest; on the college campus, just west of downtown, look for the 1816 **Painter Hall** and the college's Museum of Art. Two side trips from Middlebury are particularly worthwhile. Head 11 mi east on Route 125 to reach the **Robert Frost Interpretive Trail,** an easy path through woods and meadows, marked with quotations from works influenced by the poet's long residence nearby. Drive 3 mi north of Middle-

INTRODUCTION
HISTORY
REGIONS
WHEN TO VISIT
STATE'S GREATS
RULES OF THE ROAD
DRIVING TOURS

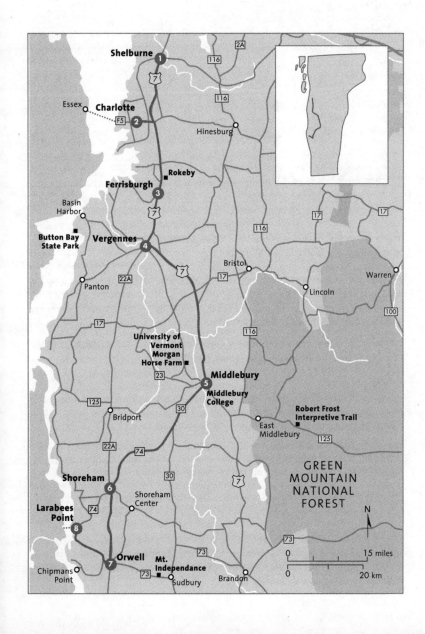

bury via Route 23 and a side road to visit the **University of Vermont Morgan Horse Farm** (74 Battell Dr.), which showcases Vermont's state animal, the sturdily graceful Morgan.

6 Along the way to **Shoreham** (12 mi southwest of Middlebury via Rte. 30 and Rte. 74), you will head deep into the dairy country of the lower Champlain Valley. This is also one of Vermont's prime apple-producing regions; several farms run pick-your-own operations in early fall.

7 At Orwell (6 mi south of Shoreham on Rte. 22A), head west 6 mi via Route 73 and 73A to reach **Mt. Independence** (Rte. 73A), where interpretive displays and self-guided paths explain the site's Revolutionary War importance in securing this narrow portion of Lake Champlain.

8 At Larabees Point (6 mi north from Orwell via Rte. 73), the oldest (1799) continually operating **Lake Champlain ferry** (Rte. 74, Shoreham, May through Oct., blow horn if the ferry is on the other side) takes passengers to Ticonderoga, New York, site of the fortress, now restored, that was captured by Ethan Allen in 1775. From Larabees Point, take Route 74 8 mi northeast to Shoreham and follow Route 22A 20 mi north to Vergennes and U.S. 7, taking in views of both the Adirondacks and Green Mountains as well as some of Vermont's most picturesque dairy country. From Vergennes, it is 22 mi north to Burlington via U.S. 7.

ARLINGTON

MAP 11, C10

(Nearby towns also listed: Bennington, Manchester, Manchester Center)

Arlington, settled in 1763, was the onetime residence of Ethan Allen and many of his cohorts from the fabled Green Mountain Boys. In more recent times the handsome little village has perhaps best been known as the home of Norman Rockwell, who chose many of his subjects for magazine covers and other illustrations from among his Arlington neighbors. The Battenkill River, which runs through the city, has long been famous among fishermen for its abundance of trout. Today, it offers tranquil scenery and a locus for a range of outdoor activities.

Information: Arlington Area Chamber of Commerce | Box 245, Rte. 7A, Arlington, 05250 | 802/375–2800 | fax 802/442–5494 | www.arlingtonvt.com.

Attractions

Candle Mill Village. Dip your own candles at Vermont's oldest candle shop; there are also dining and craft and antiques shops. | 316 Old Mill Rd. | 802/375–6068 | fax 802/375–9521 | www.candlemillvillage.com | Free | Mon.–Sat., 9–5:30, Sun. 10–5:30.

Norman Rockwell Exhibition. Rockwell (1894–1978) is perhaps America's favorite illustrator, and he once called Arlington home. This museum in a gallery that was once a church displays his printed works and there are discussions by some of the over 200 locals who once posed for him. (*See* also Norman Rockwell Museum *under* Rutland.) | 3772 Rte. 7A | 802/375–6423 | fax 802/375–6489 | www.normanrockwellexhibit.com | $2 | May–Oct., daily 9–5; Nov.–Dec. and Feb.–Apr., daily 10–4.

ON THE CALENDAR

JUNE: *Ethan Allen Days.* Performers reenact famous skirmishes from the Revolutionary War and fire cannons. Mock encampments illustrate the day-to-day life of the soldiers. | Rte. 7A, Sunderland | 802/375–2800.

Dining

Arlington Inn. Continental. This colonnaded Greek Revival structure is now a superb country inn with a romantic, candlelit main dining room and a country greenhouse eating area that looks out onto the gardens. Try the snails in a puff pastry, the Maine crab cakes, or the roasted duckling in a pear and port wine sauce. No smoking. | Historic Rte. 7A | 802/375–6532 | fax 802/375–6534 | www.arlingtoninn.com | Closed Sun.–Mon. No lunch | $35 | AE, D, DC, MC, V.

Green River Inn. Contemporary. Formerly the Evergreen Inn and 7 mi northwest of Arlington, this historic property is relaxed and pleasant. The back deck, on the banks of the Green River, has serene views of Mt. Equinox. Try the crab cakes in Cajun rémoulade sauce or the sesame-crusted tuna marinated in soy-ginger, both local legends. | 2480 Sandgate Rd., Sandgate | 802/375–2272 or 888/648–2212 | fax 802/375–2272 | www.greenriverinn.com | Reservations essential | Closed Tues. Off-season hrs Thurs.–Sun. 6–8:30 | $20 | AE, D, MC, V.

West Mountain Inn. Contemporary. The six-course, prix fixe dinner is served in a low-beamed, candlelit dining room. Swedish rye and other delectable breads, not to mention desserts, are all baked on the premises. Try to get a table by a window. | 144 W. Mountain Inn Rd. | 802/375–6516 | $35 prix fixe | AE, D, MC, V.

Lodging

Arlington Inn. Full of mid-19th century charm, rooms in the century-old carriage house annex have country French or Queen Anne furnishings. Restaurant, bar, picnic area, complimentary breakfast. Some in-room VCRs, some room phones. Tennis. Cross-country skiing, downhill skiing. Business services. | Rte. 7A | 802/375–6532 or 800/443–9442 | fax 802/375–1528 | www.arlingtoninn.com | 22 rooms, 5 suites | $115, $265 suites | AE, D, DC, MC, V.

Candlelight. A nonchain motel alternative, on the Battenkill River with a pleasant fireside lounge. Picnic area, complimentary Continental breakfast. Refrigerators, cable TV. Pool. | Rte. 7A | 802/375–6647 or 800/348–5294 | fax 802/375–2655 | www.candlelightmotel.com | 17 rooms | $60–$95 | AE, MC, V.

Country Willows Bed and Breakfast. A wraparound porch, landscaped lawns, and a mountain view complement the colonial charms of this Arlington historic landmark. Complimentary breakfast. Some refrigerators, no smoking, some in-room VCRs, no room phones. No pets. | 332 E. Arlington Rd. | 802/375–0019 or 800/796–2585 | cw@sover.net | www.countrywillows.com | 5 rooms | $95–$145 | AE, MC, V.

Cutleaf Maples Motel. Near the Battenkill River, golf, and tennis courts, this Victorian motel offers clean, affordable accommodations. A wraparound porch has been converted into a lounge and contains a fireplace and web-TV. A full breakfast is available for an extra charge. Cable TV. Pets allowed. | Rte. 7A | 802/375–2725 | cutleafsandy@webtv.net | www.virtualvermont.com/cutleafmaples | 9 rooms | $55–$75 | AE, D, MC, V.

Hill Farm Inn. The two buildings on 50 riverfront acres, 4 mi north of Arlington, date from 1830 and 1972. Room 7 is a standout, with views of Mt. Equinox. Dining room, complimentary breakfast. Cable TV in common area, no room phones, no TV in some rooms. Cross-country skiing, downhill skiing. Playground. Library. | 458 Hill Farm Rd. | 802/375–2269 or 800/882–2545 | fax 802/375–9918 | www.hillfarminn.com | 13 rooms, 5 suites, 4 cabins | $80–$150 | Cabins closed late Oct.–late May | AE, D, MC, V.

★ **West Mountain Inn.** Llamas live on this 150-acre riverfront property. Some rooms have fireplaces, and dinners are prix fixe with six courses. Dining room, bar. Some kitchenettes, some refrigerators, no smoking, cable TV in common area. Hiking. Cross-country skiing. Playground. | 144 W. Mountain Inn Rd. | 802/375–6516 | fax 802/375–6553 | www.westmountaininn.com | 13 rooms, 5 suites (all suites with fireplaces) | $209–$255, $249 suites (includes breakfast and dinner) | AE, D, MC, V.

BARNARD

MAP 11, E7

(Nearby town also listed: Woodstock)

Once a community of sleepy hill farms, Barnard has over the past half century become more of an exclusive vacation home community, reflecting the cachet of nearby Woodstock. In the 1930s Sinclair Lewis and his wife, journalist Dorothy Thompson, lived here; their home is now part of Vermont's most sumptuous inn.

Information: Woodstock Area Chamber of Commerce | Box 486, 18 Central St., Woodstock, 05091 | 802/457–3555 or 888/496–6378 | fax 802/457–1601 | www.woodstockvt.com.

Attractions
Silver Lake State Park. Fishing, swimming, picnicking, and boating are available at this scenic park. | Rte. 12 | 802/234–9451 or 800/299–3071 | $2 | Mid-May–Columbus Day.

ON THE CALENDAR
AUG.: *Barnard Street Dance.* Hosted by the Barnard General Store and enthusiastically supported by the community, the annual street dance is an exciting celebration of local color. | Rte. 12 | 802/ 234–9688.

Dining
Barnard Inn. French. Gas lamps and glowing fires illuminate this cozy restaurant. Built in 1796 as a farmhouse, this inn has small, intimate dining rooms. Try the rabbit tenderloin, served with wild, fresh mushrooms on a phyllo dish. | Rte. 12 | 802/ 234–9961 | Closed Mon. | $21–$27 | AE, DC, MC, V.

Lodging
The Inn at Chelsea Farm. Surrounded by beautiful formal gardens and adjacent to a lush forest, this bed-and-breakfast is a rural oasis. The rooms overlook meadows where pet sheep graze. Complimentary breakfast. No air-conditioning, no smoking, no room phones, TV in common area. Hiking. Pets allowed. | Rte. 12 | 802/234–9888 | fax 802/234–5629 | emmy@sover.net | www.innatchelseafarm.com | 3 rooms | $95–$130 | AE, MC, V.

Maple Leaf Inn. A replica of a Victorian farmhouse, this antiques-filled inn has a wraparound porch and sits on 16 wooded acres. The rooms are large and have wood-burning fireplaces. Ideal for romantic getaways. Complimentary breakfast. No air-conditioning, no smoking, some in-room hot tubs, cable TV, in-room VCRs (and movies). Cross-country skiing, downhill skiing. Business services. | Rte. 12 | 802/234–5342 or 800/516–2753 | www.mapleleafinn.com | 7 rooms | $115–$190 | AE, D, DC, MC, V.

Twin Farms. Vermont's most sumptuous and expensive inn is in novelist Sinclair Lewis's former residence. Rooms are in the 1795 house and its outbuildings on 300 acres. Every room has a fireplace and is suberbly decorated with antiques. Dining room. In-room data ports, room service, no smoking. Massage. 2 tennis courts. Gym, hiking. Cross-country skiing, downhill skiing. No kids. Business services. | Stage Rd. | 802/234–9999 or 800/894–6327 | fax 802/234–9990 | www.twinfarms.com | 4 rooms, 9 cottages | $900–$1,600 per night | Closed Apr. | AE, MC, V.

KODAK'S TIPS FOR TAKING GREAT PICTURES

Get Closer
- Fill the frame tightly for maximum impact
- Move closer physically or use a long lens
- Continually check the viewfinder for wasted space

Choosing a Format
- Add variety by mixing horizontal and vertical shots
- Choose the format that gives the subject greatest drama

The Rule of Thirds
- Mentally divide the frame into vertical and horizontal thirds
- Place important subjects at thirds' intersections
- Use thirds' divisions to place the horizon

Lines
- Take time to notice lines
- Let lines lead the eye to a main subject
- Use the shape of lines to establish mood

Taking Pictures Through Frames
- Use foreground frames to draw attention to a subject
- Look for frames that complement the subject
- Expose for the subject, and let the frame go dark

Patterns
- Find patterns in repeated shapes, colors, and lines
- Try close-ups or overviews
- Isolate patterns for maximum impact (use a telephoto lens)

Textures that Touch the Eyes
- Exploit the tangible qualities of subjects
- Use oblique lighting to heighten surface textures
- Compare a variety of textures within a shot

Dramatic Angles
- Try dramatic angles to make ordinary subjects exciting
- Use high angles to help organize chaos and uncover patterns, and low angles to exaggerate height

Silhouettes
- Silhouette bold shapes against bright backgrounds
- Meter and expose for the background illumination
- Don't let conflicting shapes converge

Abstract Composition
- Don't restrict yourself to realistic renderings
- Look for ideas in reflections, shapes, and colors
- Keep designs simple

Establishing Size
- Include objects of known size
- Use people for scale, where possible
- Experiment with false or misleading scale

Color
- Accentuate mood through color
- Highlight subjects or create designs through color contrasts
- Study the effects of weather and lighting

From *Kodak Guide to Shooting Great Travel Pictures* © 2000 by Fodor's Travel Publications

BARRE

(Nearby towns also listed: Montpelier, Waterbury)

Barre is Vermont's granite capital. The vast quarries on the city's outskirts have been worked since the early years of the 19th century and are estimated to contain enough stone to keep Barre's signature industry humming for another 800 years.

Barre's reliance on the granite industry resulted in the development of social and economic patterns that were markedly different from those that characterized most other communities in this most rural of American states. The demand for skilled labor in quarries and workshops led to reliance on foreign immigration; the Scots, and later the Italians, moved to Barre, bringing with them their old-world stonecutters' skills. The granite workers also made Barre the capital of Vermont's labor movement in the early years of the 20th century.

Barre's downtown offers two eloquent monuments to its principal immigrant groups—a statue of Robert Burns, its plinth decorated with carved scenes from his poetry; and another of a typical Italian stonecutter, with cap, apron, hammer, and heroic mustache. Both statues are, of course, executed in Barre granite.

Barre is one of only a handful of Vermont communities with an actual urban down-town. In defiance of suburban sprawl, a clutch of independent retailers keep Main Street vibrant, and the restored Barre Opera House—upstairs from the city's municipal offices—is a busy venue for music, dance, and theater.

Information: Central Vermont Chamber of Commerce | Box 336, Beaulieu Pl., Stewart Rd., Barre, 05641 | 802/229–4619 | fax 802/229–5713 | www.central/vt.com.

Attractions

Floating Bridge. The nation's only surviving floating bridge and the seventh in a series dating from the early 1800s, rests on 400 barrels on the surface of a pond in the tiny village of Brookfield, 15 mi south of Barre. It opened to automobile traffic in summer 2000. | 802/276–3352 | Free | Closed to traffic in winter.

Goddard College. A small, progressive liberal arts college. | 123 Pitkin Rd., Plainfield | 802/454–8311 | www.goddard.edu | Free | Daily.

Groton State Forest. This forest, 19 mi east of Barre, is a Northeast Kingdom jewel encompassing much of Lake Groton, with good bass fishing, as well as Ricker Pond. There are several campgrounds and picnic areas. | 126 Boulder Beach Rd. | 802/584–3822 | www.vtstateparks.com | $13 per night | Daily 9–9.

Hope Cemetery. Barre's stonecutters did some of their finest work here—mostly for each other. Look for the easy chair, the soccer ball, and the touching statue of labor leader Elia Corti. | Rte. 141 mi. N. of Barre | 802/476–6245 | Free | Daily, dawn–dusk.

Rock of Ages. At the world's largest dimension granite quarries, a guided tour offers views of stonecutting operations on sheer rock cliffs. | From I–89, take Exit 6, then follow signs for 4 mi | 802/476–3119 | www.rockofages.com | Free, $4 for tours | June–Oct., Mon.–Fri. 9:15–3, Sat. and Sun. call for hours; tours weekdays.

ON THE CALENDAR

MAY: *Vermont Square and Round Dance Convention.* Squares and rounds are supplemented by cloggers and line dancers at this annual event in the Spaulding High School Auditorium. $16 per couple from 1:30 to 11. | Ayer St. | 802/563–2777 or 802/748–8538 | fax 802/748–4742 | www.squaredancevt.org.

Dining

Autumn Harvest Inn. Contemporary. Sitting atop a mountain plateau, the dining room of this 18th-century inn, 7 mi southwest of Barre, affords scenic panoramic views of mountains. The filet mignon au poivre served with a brandy peppercorn sauce is one of the inn's specialties. | Clark Rd., Williamstown | 802/433–1355 | $9–$17 | AE, MC, V.

Hill Top Restaurant. American. A wide array of classic dishes are on the menu of this family restaurant. Try the "Veal Fly-Away-Bird," thin slices of veal rolled in stuffing and seasoning, cooked in wine and chicken broth. | 241 Quarry Rd. | 802/479–2129 | $8–$17 | AE, MC, V.

A Single Pebble. Chinese. One of the best values in Vermont. A party of four can dine like emperors for well under $100, and leave not just satisfied but sated—doggie bags in tow. The inventive menu blends traditional Szechuan favorites with modern variations. Try the silky and spicy Three River Soup, the dry-fried green beans, or the mock eel, made from braised shiitake mushrooms, in a ginger sauce. | 135 Barre Montpelier Rd. | 802/476–9700 | fax 802/476–9702 | Closed early Jan., late Apr., late Aug., and Sun.–Mon. No lunch | $20 | MC, V.

Soup N' Greens. American. The floral pattern tablecloths and potted plants that fill this restaurant's dining area create a casual, fresh environment in which to enjoy the variety of homemade soups, salads, and entrées. The chicken cacciatore is a favorite main course, while the clam and corn chowders and the most popular soups. | 325 N. Main St. | 802/479–9862 | Breakfast also available | $3–$13 | AE, D, MC, V.

Lodging

Autumn Harvest Inn. Standing atop a knoll 7 mi southwest of Barre, this inn overlooks a 46-acre workhorse farm, the valley, and the surrounding mountains. Five rooms are part of the original farmhouse and feature wide-board wooden floors. A porch graces the front of the inn and the living room has a brick fireplace. Restaurant, bar. No smoking. Cable TV, in-room VCRs. Pond. Horseback riding. Cross-country skiing. Pets allowed. | Clark Rd., Williamstown | 802/433–1355 | fax 802/433–5501 | autumnharv@aol.com | central-vt.com/web/autumn | 18 rooms | $89 | AE, MC, V.

Days Inn. A full-service member of the chain, with a convenient in-town location. Restaurant, bar. Some refrigerators, cable TV. Indoor pool. Hot tub. Business services. | 173 S. Main St. | 802/476–6678 | fax 802/476–6678 | 42 rooms | $39–$89 | AE, D, DC, MC, V.

Green Trails Inn. This inn is in the center of Brookfield, 15 mi south of Barre, and just across the road from the famous Floating Bridge. The public rooms are filled with antique clocks, most of which are for sale. Dining room, complimentary breakfast. No air-conditioning, no room phones, TV in common area. Lake. Fishing. Cross-country skiing. No kids under 10. Airport shuttle. | Stone Rd., off Rte. 65, Brookfield | 802/276–3412 or 800/243–3412 | www.greentrailsinn.com | 13 rooms (4 with shared bath) | $79–$130 | D, MC, V.

Hollow Inn. This inn has motel convenience with inn ambience. It is near heart of town. Picnic area, complimentary Continental breakfast. Some kitchenettes, some refrigerators, cable TV, in-room VCRs (and movies). Pool. Hot tubs. Exercise equipment. Business services. | 278 S Main St. | 802/479–9313 or 800/998–9444 | fax 802/476–5242 | 41 rooms in 2 buildings | $90–$110 inn rooms, $90 motel rooms | AE, D, DC, MC, V.

Motel Pierre. This Vermonter-run motel is just off Exit 7 of Interstate 89 and only footsteps from shopping and restaurants. Complimentary Continental breakfast. Some refrigerators, cable TV. Pool. | 362 N. Main St. | 802/476–318 | fax 802/476–3189 | 20 rooms | $45–$95 | AE, D, MC, V.

Vermonter Motel. Four miles northwest of Barre, this two-story, brick motel has comfortable, clean rooms at an affordable price. No room phones. No pets. | 509 Barre Mountpelier Rd. | 802/476–8541 | 27 rooms | $43–$68 | D, MC, V.

BARRE

INTRO
ATTRACTIONS
DINING
LODGING

BELLOWS FALLS

(Nearby towns also listed: Grafton, Putney, Rockingham)

Bellows Falls, not a municipality in its own right but actually the main settlement in the town of Rockingham, is an old railroad and industrial community clinging to the banks of the Connecticut River. The waterfall, named like the town for colonial proprietor Benjamin Bellows, is the most prominent on this portion of New England's longest river and provided power for early industries, most notably paper mills. Bellows Falls' factory days are mostly a memory, but the compact downtown—now a gateway to the resort communities of southern Vermont—retains a workaday atmosphere.

When the light is just right, Native American petroglyphs are visible on the rocks downstream from the Vilas Bridge.

Information: **Great Falls Region Chamber of Commerce** | Box 554, Village Sq, Bellows Falls, 05101 | 802/463–4280 | www.gfrcc.org.

Attractions

Adams Gristmill. A classic Yankee farmstand, offering Vermont-made foodstuffs and locally grown produce in season. | End of Mill St. | 802/463–3734 | Free | July–Oct., weekends 1–4 and by appointment.

Green Mountain Railroad. You can hop aboard the "Flyer," ¼ mi north of Bellows Falls, for a scenic 22-mi, two-hour round-trip to Chester. | Depot St. (at Amtrak station) | 802/463–3069 | $11 | 2 trips Tues.–Sun., leaving at 11 and 2.

Native American Petroglyphs. Visible only in certain light, these carvings long predate European settlement. | On riverbanks near Vilas Bridge. Further information from Bellows Falls Chamber of Commerce, The Square, Bellows Falls | 802/463–4280 Bellows Falls Chamber of Commerce | www.gfrcc.org | Free | Daily.

Rockingham Meetinghouse. A graceful if severe building, this 1787 structure is a model of early American church architecture. Inside are period box pews. There is a festival during the first week of August. | Old Rockingham Rd. | 802/463–3426 | www.ramp-vt.org | Free | Mon.–Sat. 2–4.

ON THE CALENDAR

AUG.: *Rockingham Old Home Days.* Rockingham's annual celebration opens with a pilgrimage to Rockingham Meetinghouse (1787), Vermont's oldest church building, followed by fireworks and other attractions in the locality. | Downtown Bellows Falls, Exit 5 from I-91 | 1st weekend in Aug. | 802/463–4280 | www.ramp–vt.org.

Dining

Joy Wah. Chinese. One of a few excellent Chinese restaurants in Vermont. Hunan and Szechuan cuisines are served in a Victorian farmhouse overlooking the Connecticut River. Try the Satay Chicken to start and follow with the imperial duck or the Hunan trio—sautéed jumbo shrimp, chicken, beef, and broccoli. The inside porch, open all year, offers spectacular views of the river below. No smoking. | Rte. 5 N | 802/463–9761 | $7–$17 | MC, V.

Miss Bellows Falls Diner. American. This 1920s Worcester Diner Car has original oak booths and stained-glass windows. The restaurant serves traditional diner fare. | Rockingham St. | 802/463–9800 | Breakfast also available | $4–$10 | AE, D, V.

Lodging

Horsefeathers Inn. Sitting atop its own "little mountain," this cozy bed-and-breakfast has its own pond and a garden. From your room, you can gaze upon the magnificent Connecticut

River and its picturesque environs. Each morning you will be treated to a two-course gourmet breakfast. Complimentary breakfast. No air-conditioning, no smoking, TV in common room. Pond. Hiking. Ice-skating, cross-country skiing. No kids under 10. | 16 Webb Terr | 802/463–9776 or 800/299–9776 | fax 802/463–4928 | info@horsefeathersinn.com | www.horsefeathersinn.com | 6 rooms | $75–$120 | AE, MC, V.

BENNINGTON

MAP 11, C11

(Nearby towns also listed: Arlington, Wilmington)

Bennington is most closely associated with a battle that didn't occur here, and a college. The August 16, 1777, Battle of Bennington was fought just across the border in Walloomsac, New York, but is commemorated in Bennington by a 306-ft granite monument that stands near the site of the military storehouse that the British attempted—unsuccessfully—to capture that day.

Along with Bennington College, a highly regarded liberal arts institution, the town is known for Bennington pottery, a locally produced stoneware. Prominent Vermonters associated with Bennington include Ethan Allen, who met with his Green Mountain Boys at the long-vanished Catamount Tavern; and Robert Frost, who is buried in the graveyard of the exquisite 1806 First Congregational Church.

Information: Bennington Area Chamber of Commerce | Veterans Memorial Dr., Bennington, 05201 | 802/447–3311 | fax 802/447–1163 | www.bennington.com.

Attractions

Bennington Battle Monument. Still the tallest structure in Vermont, this granite shaft, 1½ mi west of downtown Bennington, commemorates the American victory over the British in the 1777 battle. | 15 Monument Circle, Old Bennington | 802/447–0550 | $1.50; special rates for children | Mid-Apr.–Oct. 31, daily 9–5.

Bennington College. A small, progressive liberal arts college. | Rte. 67A | 802/442–5401 | www.bennington.edu | Free | Daily 9–5.

Bennington Museum. This museum has exhibits on local history and military artifacts. Its highlight is the world's largest collection of original Grandma Moses paintings. | W. Main St. | 802/447–1571 | www.benningtonmuseum.com | $6 | Daily 9–5.

Bennington Potters, Inc. This pottery manufacturer has been making and selling ceramics since 1948. They are perhaps best known for their line of blue agate cookware and table settings. An outlet store offers their ware at a fraction of the retail price. | 324 County St. | 802/447–7531 | Store daily 9:30–6; factory May–Oct., weekdays 9:30–6.

Long Trail. This footpath runs for some 270 mi through the Green Mountains, from Massachusetts to the Canadian border. The oldest long-distance hiking trail in the country, it was completed in 1930, and crosses Route 9 about 5 mi east of Bennington. | 4711 Waterbury Store Rd., Waterbury Center | 802/244–7037 | www.greenmountainclub.org | Free | May–Oct. 9–5; call for details and weather reports.

Old Burying Ground. Robert Frost, Vermont's late poet laureate, lies in this cemetery behind the Old First Church beneath a simple stone inscribed with his words, "I had a lover's quarrel with the world." | Monument Ave. | 802/467–8696 | Free | Daily.

Old First Church. A superb 1806 structure with notable Palladian windows and a graceful spire. | Monument Ave. | 802/447–1223 | Memorial Day–June, weekends only; July–Columbus Day, daily 10–noon and 1–4, Sun. 1–4; Sun. service 9:30 in July–Aug. and 11 year-round.

Park-McCullough House Museum. This large, ornate Victorian structure was the home of John McCullough, a turn-of-the-20th-century Vermont governor. | Corner of Park and West

BENNINGTON

INTRO
ATTRACTIONS
DINING
LODGING

Sts., North Bennington | 802/442–5441 | fax 802/442–5442 | www.parkmccullough.org | $6 | Late May–mid-Oct., Thurs.–Mon. 9–5.

Shaftsbury State Park. This pretty little park on tiny Lake Shaftsbury is 10½ mi north of town. There is also a bathing beach and a picnic area. | U.S. 7A, Shaftsbury | 802/375–9978 or 802/483–2001 | Memorial Day–Labor Day, daily 10–8.

Valley View Horses and Tack Shop, Inc. Trail and pony rides, horse sales, and a well-stocked tack and western-wear shop in a town with a racing tradition. | Northwest Hill Rd. | 802/823–4649 | $15 | May–Oct. daily 10:30–5 (reservations essential).

Woodford State Park. Tent sites, swimming, and nature trails, just off the Molly Stark Trail (Route 9) 10 mi east of Bennington. | 317 Sanitorium Rd. | 802/447–7169 or 802/483–2001 | www.vtstateparks.com | $2 | May–oct., daily 10–9.

ON THE CALENDAR

MAY: *Mayfest.* Held on the Saturday of each Memorial Day weekend, Mayfest is a celebration of craft art from all around the Northeast. Booths and vendors completely fill Main Street. | Main St. | 802/442–5758 | www.bennington.com/attraction/events/mayfest.html.

SEPT. *Antique and Classic Car Show.* The Bennington Antique and Classic Car Show is held every September. Admission is $5. | Willow Park | 802/447–3311 | www.bennington.com/carshow/ | Fri.–Sun. 9–4.

Dining

Alldays and Onions. Contemporary. This popular Bennington eatery serves savory dishes such as roast chicken layered with blue cheese in a roasted red pepper sauce. The homemade herb bread is not to be missed. The restaurant doubles as a delicatessen. Sunday brunch. No smoking. | 519 Main St. | 802/447–0043 | Closed Mon.–Tues. No dinner Sun. | $12–$23 | AE, D, DC, MC, V.

Belly's Deli. Delicatessen. This Bennington establishment has been serving homemade soups, quiches and gourmet sandwiches since 1979. The lounge, located above the deli, provides a convenient and relaxed spot to enjoy your meal. | 100 Pleasant St. | 802/442–3653 | $5 | D, MC, V.

Bennington Station. American/Casual. The old mahogany walls of this turn-of-the-20th-century railroad station are illuminated by globed gas lamps hanging from the vaulted ceiling. The cuisine itself is not exceptional, but it's a fun place to gather. Stick with basic, uncomplicated dishes and reserve your high expectations for the architecture. Kids' menu, early-bird supper. Sunday brunch. No smoking. | 150 Depot St. | 802/447–1080 | $8–$22 | AE, DC, MC, V.

Blue Benn Diner. American/Casual. Serving breakfast all day, this authentic diner offers such favorites as turkey hash and breakfast burritos with scrambled eggs, sausage, and chilies. The menu includes all kinds of pancakes as well as many vegetarian selections. Lines may be long on the weekends. | 100 Hunt St. | 802/442–5140 | $2–$11 | No credit cards.

Four Chimneys. Continental. A historic Georgian mansion on 11 acres. Four Chimneys enjoys a well-deserved reputation for excellent sweetbreads. Try the the Beef Wellington with chestnut stuffing. Don't miss the crème brûlée flamed with cognac for dessert. No smoking. | 21 West Rd. | 802/447–3500 or 800/649–3503 | www.fourchimneys.com | Closed Mon. No lunch | $19–$30 | AE, DC, MC, V.

Publyk House. American/Casual. A good bet for road-weary families or large get-togethers. The converted barn boasts a huge stone fireplace and panoramic views of the Bennington Monument and the basic comfort food will not disappoint. Try the hefty steaks or the fresh seafood. Salad bar. Kids' menu. Open-air dining in summer. | 783 Harwood Hill | 802/442–8301 | $10–$17 | AE, MC, V.

Lodging

Alexandra Bed-and-Breakfast. Built in 1859 as a farmhouse, this property sits on a 2-acre lot, minutes away from shopping, dining, and historic Old Bennington. Some rooms have fireplaces. Complimentary breakfast. In-room hot tubs, cable TV, some in-room VCRs. | Historic Rte. 7A | 802/442–5619 or 888/207–9386 | alexandr@sover.net | www.alexandrainn.com | 12 rooms | $75–$150 | AE, D, MC, V.

Bennington Motor Inn. A clean, quiet independent motel close to Bennington and Old Bennington village. Some refrigerators, cable TV. | 143 W. Main St. (Rte. 9) | 802/442–5479 or 800/359–9900 | 16 rooms | $66–$88 | AE, D, DC, MC, V.

Best Western New Englander. A chain motel on Bennington's northern outskirts and near the Battle Monument, Old Bennington, Bennington College. Restaurant, picnic area, complimentary Continental breakfast. Refrigerators, in-room hot tubs, cable TV. Pool. Cross-country skiing, downhill skiing. Playground. Business services. | 220 Northside Dr., off Historic Rte. 7A | 802/442–6311 | fax 802/442–6311 | 58 rooms | $95–$102 | AE, D, DC, MC, V.

Catamount. Small independent motel south of town center. Picnic area. Cable TV. Pool. | 500 South St. | 802/442–5977 or 800/213–3608 | fax 802/447–8765 | 17 rooms | $49–$92 | D, MC, V.

The Fife 'n Drum Motel. Picnic areas, lawns, and a playground surround this affordable motor lodge with views of the majestic Green Mountains. The proprietors speak German and manufacture small clocks that they sell in a gift shop adjacent to the motel. Some microwaves, refrigerators, no smoking, cable TV. Pool. Pets allowed (fee). | 693 Rte. 7 S | 802/442–4074 or 802/442–4730 | fax 802/442–8471 | toberua@sover.net | www.sover.net/~toberua | 18 rooms | $95 | AE, D, MC, V.

Four Chimneys. Lovely landscaped grounds surround this sparkling white 1915 Georgian Revival mansion named for the four chimneys that dominate the roofline. The restaurant is renowned for its Continental cuisine. Restaurant, complimentary Continental breakfast. Business services. | 21 West Rd. | 802/447–3500 or 800/649–3503 | fax 802/447–3692 | www.fourchimneys.com | 11 rooms | $125–$195 | AE, DC, MC, V.

Governor's Rock Motel. A small motel with lovely views, on the "old road" (Historic Route 7A), 7 mi north of Bennington. Picnic area, complimentary Continental breakfast. Refrigerators, cable TV. | Rte. 7A, Shaftsbury | 802/442–4734 | govrock1@sover.net | www.sover.net/govrock1/ | 9 rooms (all with shower only) | $45–$69 | Closed Nov.–Apr. | MC, V.

The Henry House. Nestled in the sleepy village of North Bennington, just 5 mi north of the city, this bed-and-breakfast evokes the colonial era with its many fine antiques, exposed wood floors, and handmade quilts. Some rooms have fireplaces while others have a view of the meandering Walloomsac River. Complimentary Continental breakfast. No air-conditioning, no smoking, some room phones, TV in common area. No kids under 12. | Murphy Rd., North Bennington | 802/442–7045 or 888/442–7045 | fax 802/442–3045 | www.henryhouseinn.com/index.html | 5 rooms | $85–$135 | MC, V.

Kirkside Motor Lodge. This charming lodge steps away from restaurants and stores has clean, affordable rooms. Personal heirlooms give each room its distinctive character. No smoking, cable TV. | 25 W. Main St. | 802/447–7596 | fax 802/447–7596 | bennbear@sover.net | www.thisisvermont.com/kirkside/index.html | 25 rooms | $49–$115 | AE, D, DC, MC, V.

Knotty Pine. A nice, quiet option on the road north out of Bennington. Picnic area. Some kitchenettes, refrigerators, cable TV. Pool. Business services. | 130 Northside Dr., Historic Rte. 7A | 802/442–5487 | kpine@sover.net | www.bennington.com | 21 rooms | $64–$82 | AE, D, DC, MC, V.

Molly Stark. An antiques-filled, country-casual 1860 inn with homey ambience. The rooms in back and separate cottage are quietest. "Molly's Room" in the main house has an oval hot tub. The cottage has a 16-ft ceiling and king-size brass bed. Complimentary breakfast. | 1067 E. Main St. (Rte. 9) | 802/442–9631 or 800/356–3076 | fax 802/442–5224 | mollyinn@vermontel.com | www.mollystark.com | 6 rooms, 1 cottage | $70–$95, $145 cottage | AE, D, MC, V.

Serenity. Cottages with inviting porches, 7 mi north of Bennington. Picnic area. Cable TV, refrigerators. Pets allowed. | 4379 Rte. 7A, Shaftsbury | 802/442–6490 or 800/644–6490 | www.thisisvermont.com/pages/serenity | 8 units (all with shower only) | $55–$75 | Closed Nov.–Apr. | AE, DC, MC, V.

South Shire Inn. Built in 1870, this inn, a Victorian showpiece, has a mahogany-paneled library with an ornate mantel over the fireplace and bedrooms furnished with antiques. Complimentary breakfast. No smoking, no TV in some rooms. No kids under 12. Business services. | 124 Elm St. | 802/447–3839 | fax 802/442–3547 | www.southshire.com | 9 rooms | $125–$180 | AE, MC, V.

Vermonter Motor Lodge. A pleasant motel with cabins, 3 mi west of Bennington near the New York border. Restaurant. Some refrigerators, cable TV. Pond. Business services. | Rte. 9, West Rd. | 802/442–2529 | www.sugarmapleinne.com | 32 rooms (18 rooms in winter), 14 cottages | $55–$90 | AE, D, MC, V.

BRANDON

MAP 11, C7

(Nearby towns also listed: Middlebury, Rutland)

Brandon straddles busy Route 7, halfway between Rutland and Middlebury. Its rambling 1786 Brandon Inn is often the only sight passersby take note of—unless they get off the main drag and discover broad, quiet Park Street with its gracious Victorian homes. "Little Giant" Stephen A. Douglas, Abraham Lincoln's opponent in the 1860 presidential contest, was born in a Brandon cottage that is open to visitors.

Information: Brandon Area Chamber of Commerce | Box 267, Brandon, 05733 | 802/247–6401 | fax 802/247–6401 | www.brandon.org.

Attractions

Branbury State Park. Here you can camp, picnic, swim, and fish on one of central Vermont's largest lakes, 3 mi northeast of Brandon. | 3570 Lake Dunmore Rd. | 802/247–5925 or 802/483–2001 | $2 | End of May–mid-Oct., daily 10–sunset.

Green Mountain & Single Lakes National Forests. Sprawling over 350,000 acres in two separate units, the GMNF has hiking trails, primitive campsites, and many miles of forest roads to explore. | 231 N. Main St., Rutland | 802/747–6700 | fax 802/747–6766 | www.fs.fed.us | Daily 8–4:30.

Mt. Independence. During the American Revolution, thousands of Continental soldiers manned—then abandoned—this Lake Champlain redoubt. Some foundations of the original structure survive at this site 6 mi west of town. | Rte. 73A, Orwell | 802/948–2000 | www.cit.state.vt.us/dca/historic/hp_sights.htm | $2 | End of May–mid-Oct., daily 9:30–5:30.

New England Maple Museum and Gift Shop. Murals, exhibits, and a slide show explain the history and process of transforming maple sap into syrup at this museum, 9 mi south of Brandon | Rte. 7 | 802/483–9414 | $1.75 | May–Oct., daily 8:30–5:30; Mar.–Apr. and Nov.–Dec., daily 10–4.

Stephen A. Douglas Birthplace. The "Little Giant" of Lincoln debate fame was born here in 1813. Douglas (1813–61) was U.S. Secretary of State and a Supreme Court justice, dying shortly after he lost to Lincoln in the 1860 Presidential campaign. The house is now operated by the Daughters of the American Revolution and furnished with period pieces. | 2 Grove St., at U.S. 7 | 802/247–6332 | www.virtualvermont.com | By appointment only.

OCT.: *Harvest Fest.* The focus of this festival is the construction of scarecrows, or as the locals say "leaf people." Clothing and construction material are all provided free, and afterwards you can take your creations home. | Central Park | 802/ 247–6401.

Dining

Blueberry Hill Inn. Contemporary. Composed primarily of local, organically grown foods, this restaurant's cuisine strikes a pleasing balance between gourmet and down-home. The menu offers such dishes as venison fillet with cherry sauce and chilled, steamed asparagus with maple strawberry vinaigrette. It is 10 mi northeast of town. | Forest Service Rd. #32, Goshen | 802/247–6735 or 800/448–0707 | fax 802/247–3983 | info@blueberryhill.com | www.blueberryhillinn.com | Closed Apr. | $35 | MC, V.

Brandon Inn. Contemporary. The dining room of this Queen Anne–style building evokes the rustic air of the colonial era. Try the rack of lamb, served with a mint demi-glace and rosemary red potatoes. | 20 Park St. | 802/247–5766 | fax 802/247–5768 | www.brandoninn.com | $14–$27 | AE, D, MC, V.

Lilac Inn. Contemporary. This stunning 1909 Georgian Revival mansion is in the middle of one of Vermont's most beautiful blocks of classic Gilded Age architecture. The small menu of excellent food doesn't endeavor to be too gourmet. Try the rack of lamb with garlic rosemary cream sauce. The fresh-baked breads are delicious. | 53 Park St. | 802/247–5463 | www.lilacinn.com | Closed Wed.–Sun. No lunch | $15–$28 | AE, DC, MC, V.

Lodging

Adams. One mile south of Brandon. Charming cottages set on wooded grounds. A fireplace in the lobby and in some rooms make this a welcoming place to be. Restaurant, bar. No air-conditioning. Pool, pond. Miniature golf. Fishing. | 1246 Franklin St. | 802/247–6644 or 800/759–6537 | 20 cottages | $60–$80 | Closed mid-Oct.–mid-May | MC, V.

Blueberry Hill Inn. This blue clapboard structure, 10 mi northeast of Brandon, is one of Vermont's most secluded inns, with a well-organized cross-country ski center. The homemade chocolate-chip cookies are famous, and rooms are furnished with handmade quilts on the beds. Dining room. No air-conditioning, no smoking, no room phones. Sauna. Hiking. Cross-country skiing. Library. Business services. | Box 3338, Goshen Rd., Ripton | 802/247–6735 or 800/448–0707 | fax 802/247–3983 | info@blueberryhill.com | www.blueberryhillinn.com | 12 rooms | $80–$130 | MAP | AE, MC, V.

Brandon Inn. This big, gambrel-roof inn in a building that dates from 1786 has the feel of a small-town hotel from another era. The rooms in back are quieter. Dining room, bar. Pool. Business services. | 20 Park St. | 802/247–5766 | fax 802/247–5768 | www.historicbrandoninn.com | 35 rooms | $115–$150 | AE, D, MC, V.

Churchill House Inn. Originally built as a stopover point for farmers in transit to the mills, this 19th-century structure is nestled in the Green Mountains, 4 mi east of Brandon, and has easy access to all kinds of outdoor recreation. Complimentary breakfast. No air-conditioning, no room phones. Pool. Hiking. Bicycles. Cross-country skiing. | 3128 Forest Dale Rd. | 802/247–3078 or 877/248–7444 | fax 802/247–0113 | www.churchillhouseinn.com | 9 rooms | $85–$190 | MAP | AE, MC, V.

Lilac Inn. The early-20th-century mansion that houses this inn has been stunningly restored, with antiques-filled rooms and luxurious baths. The bridal suite, which has a pewter canopy bed, is spectacular, and there are lovely gardens outside. Restaurant, complimentary breakfast. In-room data ports, no smoking, cable TV, some in-room VCRs. Putting green. Downhill skiing. Library. Business services. | 53 Park St. | 802/247–5463 or 800/221–0720 | fax 802/247–5499 | lilacinn@sover.net | www.lilacinn.com | 9 rooms | $195 | AE, D, MC, V.

Moffett House. A handsome Victorian home on Brandon's finest residential street. Complimentary breakfast. No air-conditioning in some rooms, no smoking, some in-room hot tubs, no room phones. Pets allowed (fee). | 69 Park St. | 802/247–3843 or 800/394–7239 | 6 rooms (3 with shared bath) | $90–$200 | Closed Apr. | MC, V.

Rosebelle's Victorian Inn. This early-19th-century manor in Brandon village has a flower garden with swing set and picnic table, a lounge with fireplace, and a porch. Rooms evoke the Victorian era with period furniture and antiques. A gift shop within the inn sells Vermont collectibles. Complimentary breakfast. No air-conditioning, no smoking, no room phones, TV in common area. Library. No kids under 12. | 31 Franklin St., at Rte. 7 | 802/247–0098 or 888/ROSEBEL | fax 802/247–4552 | rosebel@together.net | www.rosebelles.com | 5 rooms | $95 | AE, D, MC, V.

BRATTLEBORO

MAP 11, E11

(Nearby towns also listed: Marlboro, Newfane, Wilmington)

Brattleboro, a Connecticut River town with a lively center worthy of a small city, stands near the site of Vermont's first permanent settlement (1724). Like many Connecticut River valley towns, Brattleboro cast its lot with industry—by the late 19th century, it was home to paper mills, printing plants, and the Estey company, America's largest organ manufacturer.

Brattleboro also produced two leading artistic lights of the Gilded Age, architect Richard Morris Hunt and his brother, painter William Morris Hunt. Although the Hunts left their hometown to pursue their careers, another creative genius moved to Brattleboro and did some of his best work here. While living at his country house, Naulakha, which still stands on the outskirts of town, Rudyard Kipling wrote *The Jungle Book* and *Captains Courageous*.

The area around Brattleboro was especially popular with late 1960s counterculture types, who moved to Vermont as part of the era's "back-to-the-land" migrations. The '60s influence, laced with entrepreneurial capitalism, survives in the downtown restaurant, café, and bookstore scene. And, anachronistically, in the middle of it all stands the restored 1930s Latchis Hotel, one of only two true Art Deco buildings in Vermont (the other is an office building in Rutland).

Information: Brattleboro Area Chamber of Commerce | 180 Main St., Brattleboro, 05301 | 802/254–4565 | fax 802/254–5675 | www.brattleboro.com.

Attractions

Brattleboro Museum and Art Center. A restored railroad station, exhibiting Brattleboro art and historical mementos, including locally made Estey parlor organs. | 10 Vernon St. | 802/257–0124 | www.brattleboromuseum.org | $3 | Mid-May–Nov., Tues.–Sun. 12–6.

Brooks Memorial Library. This library features a collection of 19th-century art by the likes of Daniel Chester French and William Morris Hunt. The library also exhibits works by local Vermont artists. | 224 Main St. | 802/254–5290 | brattlib@brooks.lib.vt.us | www.state.vt.us/b733/libraries/brookslibrary | Labor Day–Memorial Day, Mon.–Wed. 9–9, Thurs.–Fri. 9–6, Sat. 9–5; Memorial Day–Labor Day, Sat. 9–noon.

Creamery Bridge. Built in 1879, this 80-ft-long covered bridge, 3 mi west of Brattleboro, has a "Town Lattice" frame and passes over the Whetstone Brook. | Exit 2, Rte. 9 | 802/254–4565 | Daily.

Fort Dummer State Park. Two miles west of Brattleboro, the park has numerous hiking trails along the scenic Connecticut River. | S. Main St. | 802/254–2610 | Closed in winter.

Harlow's Sugar House. Learn how maple sap is transformed into syrup 3 mi north of Brattleboro. Stop by in April, when the new crop is in. | 556 Bellows Falls Rd., Putney | 802/387–5852 | Free | Mon.–Sun. 9–5. Open all year, but sugar boiling takes place only Feb.–Mar.

Santa's Land. A deer park and petting zoo, train rides, Christmas shops—and Santa is always on hand. | 655 Bellows Fall Rd. | 802/387–5550 | www.santasland.com | $9.75 | July 4–Labor Day, daily 10–6; late May–July 4 and Labor Day–late Dec., weekends 10–5.

ON THE CALENDAR
FEB.: *Winter Carnival.* A family festival, over 50 events including a parade, snow sugar eating, winter queen pageant, skiing, skating, sleighing, ski jumping. | 802/254–4565.
JULY–AUG.: *Yellow Barn Music Festival.* A 30-year-old chamber music school presenting its annual five-week summer festival, 10 mi north of Brattleboro. Thirty concerts in Putney and on tour throughout Vermont. | 91 Old Rte. 5, Putney | $5–$20 | Opens in July, call for details | 802/387–6637 or 800/639–3819 | www.yellowbarn.com.

Dining
Back Side Café. American/Casual. An intimate café with views of Brattleboro. The menu has Tex-Mex overtones and is known for burgers, sandwiches, omelets, and salads. A deck behind the restaurant provides open-air seating with views of the downtown and mountain peaks. No smoking. | 24 High St. | 802/257–5056 | Breakfast also available. No dinner Sat.–Thurs. | $5–$8 | AE, D, MC, V.

The Café Beyond. American/Casual. This industrial chic café, displaying the work of local artists, is in the Collected Works bookstore, Brattleboro's literati landmark. There are sidewalk tables and a wall of windows for observing local color. Known for creative sandwiches, panini, and roll-ups. No smoking. | 29 High St. | 802/254–2920 or 258–4900 | Breakfast also available. No dinner | $5–$7 | AE, D, MC, V.

Common Ground. Vegetarian. This staff-owned restaurant has mostly organic vegetarian dishes such as a marinated sea vegetable salad, served with organic marinated tofu with lemon tahini sauce. The dining rooms are upstairs in large, loftlike spaces. | 25 Eliot St. | 802/257–0855 | Closed Tues. and Wed. | $4–$13 | No credit cards.

Jolly Butcher's. Steak. This reliable restaurant enjoys a good local reputation. With its comfortable dining room and charming bar area, Jolly Butcher's makes a great spot for early-bird travelers or for business meetings. Known for steaks, seafood, and fresh lobsters. | 254 Marlboro Rd., W. Brattleboro | 802/254–6043 | $15–$25 | AE, DC, MC, V.

Latchis Grille. American/Casual. Home to the Windham Brewery, this restaurant serves traditional pub fare as well as more creative dishes like chicken and watercress roulade. The Grille is in the Latchis Hotel. | 50 Main St. | 802/254–6300 | Closed Mon.–Tues. No lunch Mon.–Thurs. | $7–$20 | AE, MC, V.

Marina on the Water. American/Casual. Dock your boat and enjoy views of the West River while indulging in one of the many delicious sandwiches, salads, or reasonably priced entrées. Try the roasted Garlic Bulv or fresh bruschetta as an appetizer and then have the fresh seafood, a 16-ounce porterhouse, or Teriyaki chicken. Outdoor smoking sections provided. | Putney Rd. | 802/257–7563 | No dinner Sun. | $8–$24 | AE, D, MC, V.

Peter Havens. Contemporary. This chic 10-table bistro serves entrées such as house-cured gravlax made with lemon vodka. Seasonal fresh fish and a superb wine list complement the menu. | 32 Eliot St. | 802/257–3333 | Closed Sun. and Mon. | $18–$25 | MC, V.

Sarkis Market. Middle Eastern. Family recipes are the basis for much of the food at this popular eatery. Try the *kibbe*—layered meat loaf stuffed with ground lamb, pine nuts, and onions. Bring your own bottle of wine. | 50 Eliot St. | 802/258–4906 | Closed Sun. (except in Oct.) | $4–$9 | No credit cards.

Lodging
Crosby House 1868. The rooms of this Victorian bed-and-breakfast have antiques and heirlooms, evoking 19th-century life, and a full range of modern amenities, including gas fireplaces. Complimentary breakfast. In-room data ports, cable TV, in-room VCRs. Library.

No kids. Business services. | 175 Western Ave. | 802/257–4914 or 800/528–1868 | www.crosbyhouse.com | 3 rooms | $110–$140 | Closed Apr. | AE, D, MC, V.

40 Putney Road Bed & Breakfast. This antiques-filled mansion, ½ mi north from center of Brattleboro, is styled after a French chateau and has landscaped grounds with fountains along the West River. There is breakfast on the patio in season. Complimentary breakfast. No smoking. | 40 Putney Rd. | 802/254–6268 or 800/941–2413 | frytyptny@sover.net | www.putney.net/40putneyrd/htm | 3 rooms, 1 suite | $110–$170, $170 suite | AE, D, MC, V.

Latchis Hotel. A 1938, restored Art Deco hotel in downtown. Rooms are on the small side and those facing Main Street can be noisy. The adjacent movie palace is in the same Deco style, and the Windham Brewery, a brewpub, is on the premises. Restaurant, complimentary Continental breakfast. | 50 Main St. | 802/254–6300 | fax 802/254–6304 | www.brattleboro.com/latchis | 27 rooms, 3 suites | $85–$95 | AE, MC, V.

Quality Inn. A representative of the reliable chain, convenient to the Interstate. Restaurant, bar. In-room data ports, room service, cable TV. 2 pools (1 indoor). Hot tub, sauna. Business services. Pets allowed. | 1380 Putney Rd. (Rte. 5 N) | 802/254–8701 | fax 802/257–4727 | 104 rooms | $129 | AE, D, DC, MC, V.

Super 8. Budget accommodations just off the Interstate. Cable TV. | 1043 Putney Rd. | 802/254–8889 | fax 802/254–8323 | 64 rooms | $52–$76 | AE, D, DC, MC, V.

BRIDGEWATER

MAP 11, E8

(Nearby towns also listed: Killington, Plymouth, Woodstock)

Bridgewater, 8 mi west of Woodstock, is the creature of the Ottauquechee River. The town grew up around the river's woolen mills, powered by the swiftly flowing water. The mills are no more, but their premises are partially occupied by an indoor boutique mall and a microbrewery.

Information: Woodstock Area Chamber of Commerce | Box 486, 18 Central St., Woodstock, 05091 | 802/457–3555 or 888/496–6378 | fax 802/457–1601 | www.woodstockvt.com.

Attractions

Charles Shackleton Furniture and Miranda Thomas Pottery. Artisans craft individual pieces of furniture and ceramics at these twin workshops. There are free daily tours (at 11, 1, and 3) and the store, adjacent to the factory, sells the wares. | The Mill, Rte. 4 | 802/672–5175 | www.shackletonfurniture.com | Daily 10–5:30.

Dining

Corners Inn and Restaurant. Contemporary. A fieldstone fireplace is at the center of this inn's dining room, which overlooks the Ottauquechee River valley. The creative cuisine has Italian flares. Try the pine nut–encrusted rack of lamb with wild blueberry sauce. | Upper Rd./Rte. 4, Bridgewater Corners | 802/672–9968 or 877/672–9968 | fax 802/672–5200 | Closed Mon.–Tues. | $15–$24 | AE, MC, V.

Lodging

Corners Inn and Restaurant. This Victorian farmhouse overlooks the mountains and Ottauquechee River. The simple rooms have a warm, country charm. During the warmer seasons you can relax in the perennial gardens or on the deck. Dining room, complimentary Continental breakfast. No smoking. No room phones, TV in common area. | Upper Rd./Rte. 4, Bridgewater Corners | 802/672–9968 or 877/672–9968 | fax 802/672–5200 | pirkey1@vermontel.com | www.cornersinn.com | 5 rooms | $75–$135 | AE, MC, V.

October Country Inn. A cozy bed-and-breakfast known for the sincere hospitality of its pro-prietors, its warm, welcoming environment, and complimentary breakfasts and dinners. The living room has a fireplace and a potbellied stove. No air-conditioning, no smoking, no room phones, no TV. Pool. Hiking. Library. | Upper Rd. | 802/672–3412 or 800/648–8421 | fax 802/672–3412 | oci@vermontel.com | www.octobercountryinn.com | 10 rooms | $129–$154 | Closed Apr. and 1st 2 wks Nov. | MAP | AE, MC, V.

BRISTOL

(Nearby towns also listed: Middlebury, Vergennes)

Nestled at the the juncture of the Green Mountain National Forest and the Cham-plain Valley's lush farm country, Bristol possesses an archetypal New England village green, around which stand modest rows of brick commercial structures and a fine Romanesque Revival town hall. Once known for its woodworking industries, Bristol is increasingly a bedroom community for Middlebury and bustling Chittenden County. The population of Bristol is 3,982, and Middlebury is home to 8,403.

Information: Addison County Chamber of Commerce | 2 Court St., Middlebury, 05753 | 802/388–7951 | fax 802/388–8066 | www.midvermont.com.

Attractions

The Lord's Prayer Rock. In the mid-1800s a former logger etched The Lord's Prayer into this mammoth stone. The rock was a signal to loggers traveling across treacherous peaks that their trip to the Mill was almost at an end. | Rte. 116.

ON THE CALENDAR

JULY: *Fourth of July Celebration.* The focus of Bristol's Independence Day celebration is the "Outhouse Race," in which outhouses of all variety are pushed, pulled, and dragged to a finish line, each with its own patron sitting inside. | Rte. 116.

Dining

Mary's at Baldwin Creek. Contemporary. Built as a farmhouse in the late 18th century, this restaurant has a rustic country charm. The chef serves inspired, innovative dishes like Ver-mont rack of lamb with a rosemary-mustard sauce. The "summer kitchen" contains a fire-

CAR RENTAL TIPS

- ❏ Review auto insurance policy to find out what it covers when you're away from home.
- ❏ Know the local traffic laws.
- ❏ Jot down make, model, color, and license plate number of rental car and carry the information with you.
- ❏ Locate gas tank—make sure gas cap is on and can be opened.

- ❏ Check trunk for spare and jack.
- ❏ Test the ignition—make sure you know how to remove the key.
- ❏ Test the horn, headlights, blinkers, and windshield wipers.

*Excerpted from *Fodor's: How to Pack: Experts Share Their Secrets*
© 1997, by Fodor's Travel Publications

place and rough-hewn barn boards while the main dining room is colored in pastels. | Rte. 116 | 802/453–2432 | fax 802/453–4825 | marys@together.net | www.marysatbc.com | Closed Mon.–Tues. No lunch | $14–$23 | AE, DC, MC, V.

Lodging

Mary's at Baldwin Creek. Built as a farmhouse in 1796, this inn's individually decorated rooms offer simple, comfortable accommodations with views of the Green Mountains. Restaurant, complimentary breakfast. No air-conditioning, some in-room data ports, no smoking, no room phones, no TV. Outdoor hot tub. Hiking. Fishing. | Rte. 116 | 802/453–2432 | fax 802/453–4825 | marys@together.net | www.marysatbc.com | 4 rooms | $75–$185 | AE, DC, MC, V.

BURLINGTON

MAP 11, C4

(Nearby town also listed: Shelburne)

Burlington, Vermont's largest city, is a community whose personality increasingly reflects its service-oriented, post-industrial economy. This is not to say that Burlington has no traditional industries: meatpacking, brewing, munitions manufacturing, printing, and computer chips are all a part of the economic mix in and around the "Queen City," which began life as a Lake Champlain lumber-shipping port and grew prosperous in the era of railroads and steamboats. But modern Burlington comes across first and foremost as a college town, with four major institutions of higher learning—the University of Vermont and St. Michael's, Champlain, and Trinity colleges—and a large teaching hospital, in or close to the city.

This educational matrix, combined with Burlington's closeness to northern Vermont's tourist attractions and outdoor recreation opportunities, gives the city a festive, youth-oriented air. Downtown's Church Street, which 20 years ago hosted a typical midcentury mix of clothing, stationery, and department stores, was transformed during the early 1980s into a pedestrian mall, complete with boutiques, chic bistros, and outposts of national casual-wear retailers such as Banana Republic and Eddie Bauer. (The fight to keep mainstream retailing from migrating entirely to the suburbs goes on, however, with Burlington's recent capture of a brand-new Filene's department store.)

Even business and politics have gotten trendy in Burlington. The two companies for which the city is perhaps best known are Ben and Jerry's, the ice-cream empire that began here in the late 1970s; and Burton Snowboards, the emblem of Youth Hitting the Slopes. And it was with a big push from the college community that Bernie Sanders, an independent socialist, captured the Burlington mayoralty in 1981 and founded a Progressive Party dynasty that lasts to this day. (Sanders himself is now Vermont's lone congressman.)

Beyond the snowboards and sushi, the microbrews and street musicians—beyond even the sparklingly restored waterfront and lakeside bike path—Burlington is still a handsome, old-fashioned city worth a few hours' leisurely walk. Rising above the Church Street bustle is a severely elegant 1816 Unitarian church with a Paul Revere bell in its spire; rising above the entire city is the elm-studded campus of the University of Vermont, its broad green faced by a row of august structures including the cupola-crowned 1825 Old Mill and H. H. Richardson's masterful Romanesque Revival library, now a student center. And once you've headed down to one of the waterside parks or climbed past the palatial wooden houses near the top of the hill, the views of Lake Champlain and the distant Adirondacks are exquisite.

Information: Lake Champlain Regional Chamber of Commerce | 60 Main St., Suite 100, Burlington, 05401 | 802/863–3489 | fax 802/863–1538 | www.vermont.org.

TRANSPORTATION INFORMATION

Airports: Burlington and the surrounding area are served by the **Burlington International Airport,** which is 4 mi east of Burlington, off U.S. 2 (Airport Dr., Box 1, S. Burlington | 802/863–1889). Major commercial airlines offer regularly scheduled flights.

Bus Lines: Vermont Transit serves Burlington, with a terminal at 245 Pine Street. Call | 802/864–6811 or 800/552–8737. for fares and schedules.

Driving Around Town: Although the cold weather does have an impact on the roads, they are, as a whole, well maintained and free of potholes. Driving is made easy by the numerous two-way thoroughfares; one-ways are not very common here. When you want to stop and get out, there are parking spots galore on the street and parking lots are plentiful. You should keep in mind that the first two hours of parking in municipal lots are free and that parking fines are not that steep. Also, because many of Burlington's office buildings are adjacent to the sight-seeing destinations, it is harder to find parking during the weekdays. The only rush hour traffic to speak of occurs in the evening on Route 7, heading south out of town. The speed limit throughout the city, with the occasional exception of school zones, is 30 mph. Right on red is permitted except where noted.

Attractions

BEACHES, PARKS, AND NATURAL SIGHTS

Battery Park. This is the best spot in Burlington to watch the sun set over the Adirondacks, with Lake Champlain burnished gold in the foreground. | Rte. 127 at North Ave. | 802/863–3489 | Free | Daily dawn to dusk, pedestrians only.

Champlain Islands. Dotting the northern expanses of Lake Champlain, these islands are a hub for water recreation in summer and ice fishing in winter. | 802/372–5683.

Green Mountain Audubon Nature Center. Trails meander through meadows and woodland and along ponds on over 200 pristine acres. The center, 20 mi southeast of Burlington, has maple sugaring in spring. | Sherman Hollow Rd., Huntington | 802/434–3068 | Donations accepted | Daily dawn–dusk.

Jay Peak. Popular with Montrealers, Jay Peak is actually two mountains with 64 trails for downhill and cross-country skiers. | Rte. 242, Jay | 802/988–2611 or 800/451–4449 | www.jaypeakresort.com | $49 | Daily 9–4.

Missisquoi National Wildlife Refuge. Bird-watching, canoeing, and hiking are popular activities on these 6,300 acres of federally protected wetlands, meadows, and forests 36 mi north of Burlington. | 371 N. River St., Swanton | 802/868–4781 | Daily; offices weekdays 8–4:30.

Sand Bar State Park. One of Lake Champlain's best swimming beaches is 1 mi north of Burlington. There's a gentle drop-off for kids, picnic tables, changing facilities, and windsurfer rentals. | Rte. 2, Milton | 802/372–8240 | $3 | Mid-May–Labor Day, daily 10–dusk.

CULTURE, EDUCATION, AND HISTORY

Ethan Allen Homestead. Vermont's founding father spent the last years of his tempestuous life at this house, 2 mi north of Burlington. The furnishings illustrate life in pioneer days. | 61 Colchester Ave. | 802/865–4556 | $4 | May–mid-Oct., Mon.–Sat. 10–5, Sun. 1–5, or by appointment.

St. Michael's College. St. Mike's, 7 mi northeast of Burlington, is the home of a respected summer theater series. | 1 Winooski Park, Colchester | 802/654–2000 or 802/654–2535 | www.smcvt.edu | Daily.

University of Vermont. Vermont's state university occupies a fine hilltop campus. There are outstanding buildings facing the Green on University Row, including an H. H. Richardson library, now a student center, said by the architect to be "the best thing I've done." | Waterman Building, S. Prospect St. | 802/656–3480 | www.uvm.edu | Free | Daily 8–4.

MUSEUMS

Lake Champlain Basin Science Center. The science center focuses on the ecology of Lake Champlain and its surroundings. Aquarium tanks display the lake's many fish species; hands-on exhibits introduce kids to subjects such as fossils and wetlands species. | 1 College St. | 802/864–1848 | www.lakechamplaincenter.org | $3, $30 yearly pass | Mid-June–Labor Day, daily 11–5; Labor Day–mid-June, weekends 12:30–4:30.

Robert Hull Fleming Museum. Small but comprehensive, the Fleming has centuries of American and European art, Vermont artists, and an Egyptian mummy. | 61 Colchester Ave. | 802/656–0750 | www.smcvt.edu | $3 | May–Aug., Tues.–Fri. noon–4, weekends 1–5; Sept.–Apr., Tues.–Fri. 9–4, weekends 1–5.

SHOPPING

Church Street Marketplace. Intriguing boutiques, restaurants, sidewalk cafés, craft vendors, and street performers fill this downtown pedestrian mall, a focal point of the community. | Church Street Marketplace.

Lake Champlain Chocolates. These chocolates are rich and delicious—made with Vermont milk and other local ingredients. | 750 Pine St. | 802/864–1807 | www.lakechamplain-chocolates.com | Mon.–Sat. 9–6, Sun. 11–5.

SPORTS AND RECREATION

Cochran Ski Area. One of the last small independent ski areas, this site 9 mi east of Burlington is run by the Cochran ski family of Olympic fame. Ski trails and a ski school make this a great place to introduce kids to the sport. | 910 Cochran Rd., Richmond | 802/434–2479 | $12 | Closed Mon. and Wed., call for seasonal information.

Vermont Expos. Vermont's baseball team is a Single-A farm club for the Montreal Expos. Home games are at the University of Vermont's Centennial Field, an intimate, old-time park. | Colchester Ave., near the UVM campus | 802/655–4200 | $1–$5 | Mid-June–early Sept.

OTHER POINTS OF INTEREST

Burlington Ferry. It's an hour each way between Burlington and Port Kent, New York, and worth the trip just for the scenery even if you're coming right back. The still-operating ferry *Adirondack* was built in 1913. | King Street Ferry Dock | 802/864–9804 | fax 802/864–6830 | www.ferries.com | Driver and automobile $12.75 one way, $23 round-trip; passengers $3.25 one way, $5.75 round-trip | Mid-May–mid-Oct., departures daily 7:45–7:30.

Excursion Cruises. Narrated scenic cruises aboard the new *Spirit of Ethan Allen II*; also dinner and brunch cruises. Wedding party packages also available; fully accessible to mobility-impaired guests. | Burlington Boathouse, College St. | 802/862–8300 | www.soea.com | Reservations essential | $8.95, lunch cruises $16.99, dinner cruises $26.95 | May–Oct., daily cruises lasting 1½ hrs; dinner cruises lasting 2½ hrs.

ON THE CALENDAR

JUNE: *Discover Jazz Festival.* Every second week in June, six days of free and ticketed all-jazz events, attracting crowds of up to 40,000, and famous names as well as local talent. Swing, blues, gospel as well. | Throughout Burlington, in bars, tents, concert halls, and outdoors | All day through 2 AM | 802/863–7992 | www.discoverjazz.com.

JUNE–AUG.: *St. Michael's Playhouse Professional Summer Theater.* Four summer productions, a musical, drama, comedy and "wild card" show. Each show runs for two weeks, using professional actors from around the United States. Advance tickets recommended. | McCarthy Arts Center, St. Michael's College | June–Aug., Tues.–Sat. 8 PM | 802/654–2535 | $16–$22.

JULY–AUG.: *Vermont Mozart Festival.* A three-week annual summer festival, with nine venues in northwestern Vermont. Mozart and other classical composers; tickets $20, advance booking recommended | 110 Main St. | Weekdays 9–5 | 802/862–7352 | www.vtmozart.com.

AUG.: Champlain Valley Exposition, Route 15, Essex Junction. Vermont's biggest end-of-summer extravaganza combines the traditional elements of a country fair—the biggest pumpkin, the best pickles, the most handsome livestock—with all the glitter of a midway and first-class amusement rides. The food stands are a fairground traditionalist's delight, and the worst nightmare of the food police. | 802/878–5545.

DEC.: First Night in Burlington. Beginning in mid-afternoon on New Year's Eve, dozens of Burlington venues host music, storytelling, dance, comedy, and kids' performances; there are fireworks over the Lake Champlain waterfront early in the evening and again at midnight. Purchase of a button allows admission to all events. | 802/863–6005.

WALKING TOUR

Burlington Walking Tour (approximately 2 ½ hours without stops)
Begin at the head of Church Street, downtown Burlington's pedestrians-only main drag. At Pearl Street is the 1816 First Unitarian Church, a white-steepled late-Georgian gem. Paul Revere's foundry cast the church's original bell. Walk the four-block **Church Street Marketplace,** a great place for boutique browsing and people-watching at sidewalk cafés. Worthwhile stops include **Lake Champlain Chocolates** (No. 63), home of rich locally-made treats; Vermont State Craft Center (No. 85), which exhibits and sells work by Vermont's finest artisans; and the Fire House Gallery (No. 135), featuring rotating exhibits of paintings and sculpture. At Main Street, turn right and head four blocks to the Lake Champlain waterfront. One block to the left, at King Street, is the dock for **Lake Champlain Transportation Company** ferries to Port Kent, NY. The scenic crossing takes one hour each way, with fine lake and mountain views. Facing the lake, turn right and walk two blocks to College Street, where the **Spirit of Ethan Allen II** offers narrated lake cruises departing from the Community Boathouse. The nearby **Lake Champlain Basin Science Center** (1 College St.) features exhibits on lake ecology, including aquarium tanks and hands-on kid's activities. Turn left from College Street onto Battery Street and head two blocks to **Battery Park,** with its playground and splendid lake views. Sunsets here are spectacular. From Battery Park, follow Pearl Street for 10 uphill blocks to the **University of Vermont (UVM)** campus. (If the walk seems daunting, take a free shuttle bus, leaving every 15 minutes from Main and Battery streets and heading up College Street to the university.) The handsome row of buildings facing the Green includes the 1886 Billings Student Center, designed by H.H. Richardson in his Romanesque Revival style. Behind Ira Allen Chapel on Colchester Avenue is the **Robert Hull Fleming Museum,** which has a fine collection of European and American paintings, works by Vermont artists, and an Egyptian mummy. Return to downtown via Pearl, College, or Main streets, or take the College Street shuttle bus.

BURLINGTON

INTRO
ATTRACTIONS
DINING
LODGING

Dining

INEXPENSIVE

Libby's Blue Line Diner. American/Casual. This popular local eatery 2 mi north of Burlington has a diverse menu, ranging from classic diner cuisine to more upscale offerings such as eggplant burgers and brook trout. Try to go between mealtimes since lines can be long. | 46 Highpoint Center/Rte. 7, Colchester | 802/655–0343 | fax 802/654–3910 | No dinner Sun.–Tues. | $5–$12 | AE, DC, MC, V.

The Tavern. American/Casual. This pub is part of the Inn at Essex and serves traditional pub food, including burgers, meat loaf, and chicken potpie. The wooden tables and long, L-shape bar are the perfect complement to the pub fare. | 70 Essex Rd./Rte. 15 | 802/878–1100 or 800/727–4295 | $6–$10 | AE, D, DC, MC, V.

MODERATE

Butler's Restaurant. Contemporary. The dining rooms, which overlook the herb garden and green meadows, are suffused with sunlight during the day. The restaurant is run by the New England Culinary Institute and has such dishes as sweet dumpling squash with ginger-garlic basmati rice. | 70 Essex Rd./Rte. 15 | 802/878–1100 or 800/727–4295 | Breakfast also available | $15–$25 | AE, D, DC, MC, V.

Daily Planet. Contemporary. Energetic and fun, this eatery is distinguished by modern art and a superb mural on the brick facade. The creative, eclectic fare proves that the artistry is not just on the walls. Choose from Asian stir fries, Italian risottos, or Moroccan Chicken Charmoula on couscous. | 15 Center St. | 802/862–9647 | No lunch | $12–$20 | AE, DC, MC, V.

Five Spice Café. Pan-Asian. Notably good dim sum in Vermont? Yes! This cozy bi-level eatery combines Burmese, Vietnamese, Thai, Chinese, and Indonesian cuisine and employs locally grown and organic products whenever possible. Try the dim sum sampler entrée, the Burmese Mt. Ruby chicken, or any of the vegetarian offerings. Excellent desserts. | 175 Church St. | 802/864–4045 | $8–$18 | AE, DC, MC, V.

Leunig's Bistro. Contemporary. Old-world European charm, marble bar, tile floors, and curbside tables make you feel as though you are strolling along the Left Bank. It's not Paris, but Burlington's Church Street Marketplace is the best people-watching spot in town. Excellent bistro menu includes a delicious French onion soup, innovative pastas and salads, and creative entrées. There's live jazz a few nights a week. | 115 Church St. | 802/863–3759 | Breakfast available weekends | $8–$25 | AE, DC, MC, V.

NECI Commons. American/Casual. The New England Culinary Institute runs this all-in-one café, bakery, market, restaurant, and bar. Items at the deli counter can get a little pricey, but everything is fresh and tasty. | 25 Church St. | 802/862–6324 | fax 802/863–5129 | Breakfast also available | $11–$18 | AE, D, MC, V.

Perry's Fish House. Seafood. The weathered wood fish house adorned with driftwood, nets, and lobster traps puts you in a nautical mood. You can't go wrong with steamed lobster or the Cajun blackened versions of daily specials. Steaks and prime rib are also a good bet. Kids' menu. Sunday brunch. | 1080 Shelburne Rd., S. Burlington | 802/862–1300 | www.perrysfishhouse.com | No lunch | $10–$19 | AE, DC, MC, V.

Saigon Café. Vietnamese. One of Burlington's best bargains. The high-ceiling, garage-door facade setting feels spacious and comfortable, despite what is often a hub of activity. Try the traditional beef soup, the marinated grilled chicken appetizer, or To Thuang, with fresh bean sprouts and tropical hot chili. | 133 Bank St. | 802/863–5637 | No lunch Sun. | $7–$14 | AE, D, MC, V.

Sweetwaters. Contemporary. This regal converted 19th-century bank, updated with murals, is a great hangout and fun place to dine alfresco. Try the Bison Burger or the almond-encrusted, deep-fried chicken fingers with horseradish sauce. Kids' menu. Sunday brunch. | 120 Church St. | 802/864–9800 | www.sweetwatersbistro.com | $9–$20 | AE, D, DC, MC, V.

EXPENSIVE

Carbur's. American/Casual. Fun, casual ambience accented with Vermont relics and antiques. The bustling never seems to dampen the staff's cheery service. Choose from unique burgers named after local celebs, traditional entrées, Tex-Mex treats, and salads. If you have time (and aren't driving), go around the world in 80 beers. An open deck provides comfortable outdoor seating beneath the sun. Kids' menu. No smoking. | 115 St. Paul St. | 802/862–4106 | $23 | AE, D, DC, MC, V.

Ice House. Seafood. At this former icehouse overlooking the lake, the cuisine takes second place to the setting. Order a fresh seafood special or steak. Sunsets across the lake and Adirondacks are particularly spectacular from one of the two outdoor decks. Kids' menu. Sunday brunch. | 171 Battery St. | 802/864–1800 | $14–$23 | AE, DC, MC, V.

Isabel's. Contemporary. The best bet for dining on Burlington's waterfront, this historic, restored 19th-century lumber mill has outdoor dining with lake views or cozy indoor seating by the fireplace in colder months. Try the Gibraltar Shrimp (stuffed with spinach, Portobello mushrooms, and feta cheese), salmon-and-artichoke pasta, beef tenderloin, or

Pesto Lamb. Sunday brunch. | 112 Lake St. | 802/865–2522 | Closed Mon. No lunch Sat. | $13–$24 | AE, D, DC, MC, V.

Opaline. French. This sophisticated eatery serves rustic bistro and country dishes from the south of France. The menu is distinguished by a superb wine list and aperitif menu. For starters, try the lobster bisque or salmon rosettes, and for entrées try the Seafood Champagne, or Roasted Duck Opaline. A courtyard on the side of the restaurant offers a charming, secluded spot for outdoor dining. No smoking. | One Lawson La. | 802/660–8875 | Closed Sun.–Mon. No lunch | $14–$24 | AE, MC, V.

Pauline's. Continental. Two distinct dining experiences have set a regional standard for the past two decades. The elegant upstairs dining room, decorated in muted tones with original oil paintings and plush seating, offers the more elaborate (and more expensive) menu. The lively downstairs bistro with its warm wood paneling offers a café menu, early-bird specials, and reasonably priced prix fixe selections. Whichever you choose, be assured of lots of crisp vegetables, heart-healthy options, and fresh local ingredients. Try the Maine crab cakes. The upper-level terrace provides cozy, private open-air dining. Early-bird suppers. No smoking. | 1834 Shelburne Rd. (U.S. 7) | 802/862—1081, 800/491–1281 in VT | Café $12–$15, upstairs dining $15–$23 | AE, D, DC, MC, V.

Sirloin Saloon. Steak. This full-service steak house serves consistently good, traditional American cuisine. Also try wood-grilled fresh seafood or chicken. Salad bar. Kids' menu. No smoking. | 1912 Shelburne Rd., Shelburne | 802/985–2200 | No lunch | $9–$22 | AE, D, DC, MC, V.

Smokejacks. Contemporary. A central bistro with bold American food and a great bar, where you can choose from myriad olives for your martini. Small, reasonably priced plates allow you to sample a number of dishes, such as Cambozola cheese with garlic and hot herbed bread, maple-smoked salmon, rare grilled yellowfin tuna, or spicy steak salad with Asian noodles in a peanut sauce. Known for unusual cheeses. Saturday and Sunday brunch. No smoking. | 156 Church St. | 802/658–1119 | www.smokejacks.com | $28 | AE, D, DC, MC, V.

Sweet Tomatoes. Italian. Tile floors and brick arches enhance this downstairs trattoria. The prominent wood-fired ovens and charcoal grills produce terrific thin-crust pizzas, grilled chicken, seafood, beef, veal, and lamb. An excellent selection of Italian wines available by the glass. The outdoor patio sits in the front of the restaurant amid street lanterns and entertainers. | Church St. Marketplace | 802/660–9533 | No lunch Sun. | $12–$14 | AE, MC, V.

Trattoria Delia. Italian. A cozy, authentic trattoria with lots of wood paneling, a coffered ceiling, a tile-backed bar, and a fireplace. The restaurant has won the Wine Spectator Award each year since 1995. All the pasta dishes are guaranteed to be great, however if you're adventurous, you might want try the wild boar. No smoking. | 152 St. Paul St. | 802/864–5253 | No lunch | $10–$28 | DC, MC, V.

Lodging

MODERATE

Bel-Aire Motel. A homey motel set back from the busy road. The family suite has fine lake views and there is a recreational park at the rear of the motel. Complimentary Continental breakfast. Microwaves, refrigerators, cable TV. | 111 Shelburne Rd. (Rte. 7) | 802/863–3116 | 14 rooms | $65–$75, $75–$85 weekends | AE, D, DC, MC, V.

Days Inn. An expanded chain representative, directly opposite St. Michael's College, 7 mi northeast of town. Complimentary Continental breakfast. Refrigerators, some in-room hot tubs, cable TV. Indoor pool. Business services. Pets allowed (fee). | 23 College Pkwy., Colchester | 802/655–0900 | fax 802/655–6851 | www.daysinn.com | 73 rooms | $69–$125 | AE, D, DC, MC, V.

Hartwell House Bed-and-Breakfast. Chinese silkscreens, feather mattresses, and an eclectic assortment of antiques decorate this colonial-style B&B. One room, the Benedict Arnold room, has memorabilia from the general's last battle. Swimming in the pool and lounging in the garden provide relaxation in summer. Complimentary Continental breakfast. No smoking, no room phones, TV in common area. Pool.|170 Ferguson Ave.|802/658–9242 or 888/658–9242 | fax 802/865–1090 | hartwell@together.net or hartwellhouse@vermontbedandbreakfast.com | www.members.aol.com/hartwellbb or www.vermontbedandbreakfast.com |3 rooms | $45–$65 | No credit cards.

Ho-Hum Motel. A Burlington area landmark that is small and old-fashioned but clean and convenient to airport. It is 3 mi east of town. Cable TV. Pool.|1660 Williston Rd., S. Burlington | 802/863–4551 | 36 rooms | $55 | AE, D, MC, V.

Sunset House Bed-and-Breakfast. Built as a boardinghouse in 1854, this Queen Anne–style house has high ceilings, carpeted floors, and a comfortable, homey charm. Family heirlooms contribute to the appeal of this B&B, which has been owned by the same family since 1915. Complimentary Continental breakfast. No smoking, TV in common area.| 78 Main St. | 802/864–3790 | www.sunsethousebb.com | 4 rooms | $79–$89 | No credit cards.

Tetreault House. "Just like going home to Mom" is the proprietor's motto. This pink house, 3 mi north of the city, is close to the lake and only ½ mi from Leddy Park and Beach. It has a screened-in gazebo porch, perfect for enjoying late-spring evenings when the lilac aroma wafts from the yard. Complimentary breakfast. No air-conditioning, no smoking, cable TV, no room phones. | 251 Staniford Rd. | 802/862–2781 |3 rooms | $40–$60 | No credit cards.

EXPENSIVE

The Artful Lodger Bed-and-Breakfast. Once a carriage barn, this small B&B has a 22-ft ceiling in the living space. Hardwood and marble floors complement the modern furnishings. The property is only steps away from shops and restaurants. Complimentary breakfast. No smoking, no room phones, no TV. Pool. | 15 Lafayette Pl | 802/658–2046 | www.theartfullodger.com | 2 rooms | $100 | No credit cards.

Best Western Windjammer Inn and Conference Center. A handy chain option for airport travelers. The Windjammer restaurant is on site. Restaurant, complimentary Continental breakfast. Cable TV. Pool. Hot tub. Exercise equipment. Laundry facilities. Business services. Airport shuttle. Pets allowed (fee). | 1076 Williston Rd. | 802/863–1125 | fax 802/658–1296 | www.bestwestern.com | 173 rooms | $89–$179 | AE, D, DC, MC, V.

Burlington Red Stone Bed-and-Breakfast. Built of native Vermont red stone, this three-story Greek Revival–style B&B has spectacular views of the lake and mountains even from its first floor. Coffee and tea are served before breakfast in the "Lake Room," one of the three sitting rooms. The property also has two porches, a patio, and a two-tier garden. Complimentary breakfast. No air-conditioning in some rooms, no smoking, TV in common area. No kids under 13. | 497 S. Willard St. | 802/862–0508 | burlingtonredstone.com | 3 rooms | $90–$125 | No credit cards.

Clarion Hotel & Conference. Right on Williston Road, this hotel is 2 mi east of Burlington. The rear rooms are quieter. Trader Duke restaurant is on the premises. Restaurant, bar. In-room data ports, refrigerators, room service, cable TV, some in-room VCRs. Pool, wading pool. Hot tub. Business services. Airport shuttle. |1117 Williston Rd., S. Burlington | 802/658–0250 | fax 802/863–0376 | 130 rooms | $119–$139 | AE, D, DC, MC, V.

Comfort Inn. A chain operation on a busy thoroughfare that is very convenient to airport. Complimentary Continental breakfast. In-room data ports, some refrigerators, cable TV. Pool. Exercise equipment. Business services. Free parking. | 1285 Williston Rd., S. Burlington | 802/865–3400 | fax 802/865–3400 | www.selectvermont.com/comfortinn | 105 rooms | $90–$120 | AE, D, DC, MC, V.

Hampton Inn and Conference Center. A large, full-service hotel just off Interstate 89 on Burlington's northern outskirts. You'll need to drive to downtown from here. Restaurant, complimentary Continental breakfast. In-room data ports, some refrigerators, cable TV, some in-room VCRs. Indoor pool. Hot tub. Exercise equipment. Laundry facilities. Business services.

Airport shuttle. Pets allowed. | 42 Lower Mountain View Dr., Colchester | 802/655–6177 | fax 802/655–4962 | www.hampton-inn.com | 188 rooms | $94–$109 | AE, D, DC, MC, V.

Holiday Inn. One of the area's largest hotels is 1¹/₂mi from the city, halfway between downtown and the airport. Restaurant, bar with entertainment. In-room data ports, room service. Cable TV. 2 pools (1 indoor). Sauna. Exercise equipment. Business services. Airport shuttle. Pets allowed. | 1068 Williston Rd., S. Burlington | 802/863–6363 | fax 802/863–3061 | www.holiday-inn.com/hotels/btvvt | 174 rooms | $100 | AE, D, DC, MC, V.

Howard Johnson. This chain option is on busy Shelburne Road 3 mi south of downtown Burlington and near Shelburne Museum. The popular What's Your Beef restaurant is on the premises. Restaurant, bar, complimentary breakfast. In-room data ports. Indoor pool. Hot tub. Exercise equipment. Laundry facilities. Business services. Airport shuttle. | 1720 Shelburne Rd., S. Burlington | 802/860–6000 | fax 802/864–9919 | 121 rooms | $99–$110 | AE, D, DC, MC, V.

Howard Street Guest House. The one, spacious suite of this house is in the second story of a carriage house and has its own kitchenette, refrigerator, and microwave. A private, secluded deck provides views of a garden and the lake. Kitchenettes, microwaves, refrigerators, no smoking, cable TV. No pets. | 170 Ferguson Ave. | 802/864–4668 | agray@together.net | www.together.net/~agray | 1 suite | $110 | No credit cards.

Willard Street. Burlington's only luxury bed-and-breakfast is in a turn-of-the-20th-century mansion in the historic hill section. A marble outdoor staircase provides formal elegance as do the paneled public rooms. There is also bright solarium filled with plants and views of Lake Champlain. The rooms have down comforters. Complimentary breakfast. | 349 S. Willard St. | 802/651–8710 or 800/577–8712 | fax 802/651–8714 | wstinn@vermontel.com | www.willard-streetinn.com | 14 rooms (2 have bath across the hall) | $115–$225 | AE, D, MC, V.

Wilson Inn. An all-suite hotel 5 mi north of the city that is close to the IBM complex in Essex Junction. Complimentary breakfast buffet. In-room data ports, kitchenettes, microwaves, cable TV, some in-room VCRs. Pool. Cross-country skiing. Playground, laundry facilities. Business services. | 10 Kellogg Rd., Essex Junction | 802/879–1515, 800/521–2334 outside VT | fax 802/878–7950 | www.wilsoninn.com | 32 suites | $124–$144 | AE, D, DC, MC, V.

VERY EXPENSIVE

Holiday Inn Express. The big chain's other Burlington entry is 3 mi south of Burlington and handy if you're visiting the Shelburne Museum or other sites south of downtown or the airport. Complimentary Continental breakfast. Pool. Cross-country skiing. Laundry facilities. Business services. Airport shuttle. Free parking. | 1712 Shelburne Rd., S. Burlington | 802/860–1112 | fax 802/860–1112 | www.hiexpress.com | 6 rooms, 78 suites | $125–$185 | AE, D, DC, MC, V.

Inn at Essex. This hotel, 15 minutes' drive from downtown, feels like a country inn, with its one-of-a-kind rooms furnished with reproductions of 18th-century pieces and wood-burning fireplaces in some. But the amenities are those of a big hotel. Trainee chefs at the New England Culinary Institute do the cooking for the restaurant. Room service. In-room data ports, some kitchenettes, some in-room hot tubs, cable TV. Bicycles. Business services. Airport shuttle. | 70 Essex Way, Essex Junction | 802/878–1100, 800/727–4295 outside VT | fax 802/878–0063 | www.innatessex.com | 120 rooms, 20 suites | $169–$189, $209–$229 suites, $399–$499 premier suites | AE, D, DC, MC, V.

Radisson. Downtown Burlington's only hotel is a short walk from Church Street Marketplace. The west-side, upper-story rooms have spectacular lake views. 2 restaurants, bar with entertainment. Cable TV. Indoor pool. Hot tub. Exercise equipment. Business services. Airport shuttle. | 60 Battery St. | 802/658–6500 | fax 802/658–4659 | radisson@together.net | www.radisson.com/burlingtonvt | 256 rooms | $179–$219 | AE, D, DC, MC, V.

Residence Inn by Marriott. A chain option that is near the airport and Interstate 89 and is popular with business travelers. It's a 10-minute drive to downtown. Some rooms with fireplaces. Complimentary Continental breakfast. In-room data ports, kitchenettes, cable

TV. Indoor pool. Hot tub. Exercise equipment. Playground. Laundry facilities. Business services. Airport shuttle, free parking. Pets allowed (fee). | One Hurricane La., Williston 05495 | 802/878–2001 | 96 suites | $159–$175 | AE, D, DC, MC, V.

Sheraton Hotel and Conference Center. The area's largest hotel is 1½ mi east of Burlington and frequently hosts major functions. Restaurant, bar with entertainment, room service. In-room data ports, some refrigerators, cable TV, some in-room VCRs. Indoor pool. Hot tub. Gym. Video games. Business services. Airport shuttle. Pets allowed. | 870 Williston Rd., S. Burlington | 802/865–6600 | fax 802/865–6670 | www.sheraton.com/burlington | 309 rooms | $145–$195 | AE, D, DC, MC, V.

CHARLOTTE

MAP 11, C4

(Nearby towns also listed: Shelburne, Vergennes)

Charlotte typefies the transition of many small Vermont towns from agriculture to suburbanization. As recently as the 1970s, it was securely in the Addison County dairy-farming orbit—but its proximity to growing Burlington has resulted in farmland being subdivided and dotted with upscale commuters' homes. Charlotte is the Vermont terminus of car ferry service across Lake Champlain to Essex, New York.

Information: **Lake Champlain Regional Chamber of Commerce** | 60 Main St., Suite 100, Burlington, 05401 | 802/863–3489 | fax 802/863–1538 | www.vermont.org.

Attractions

Charlotte Beach. Drive west from Route 7 on Ferry Road, then north on Lake Road and cross the covered bridge to reach this secluded beach with spectacular, picture-perfect views of Lake Champlain and the Adirondacks. | Lake Rd. | 802/863–1538.

Mt. Philo State Park. Easy trails up 980-ft Mt. Philo lead to terrific Lake Champlain views. There is also a campsite with hot showers and facilities. | 5425 Mt. Philo Rd. | 802/425–2390 or 802/483–2001 | $2, tent sites $11, shelters $15, cabins $75 | Memorial Day–Columbus Day, Daily 10–dusk.

Vermont Wildflower Farm. Stroll through 6 acres of wildflowers and woodlands, or buy seed mixes for any U.S. growing conditions at this farm. | Rte. 7 | 802/425–3500 | www.americanmeadows.com | $3 | May–late Oct., daily 10–5.

Lodging

Inn at Charlotte. The sliding-glass doors of this rural inn overlook a perennial garden, a pool, and in the distance Mt. Philo State Park, which is just a walk away. Complimentary breakfast. No smoking, no room phones. Pool. Tennis court. No kids under 5. No pets. | 32 State Park Rd. | 802/425–2934 or 800/425–2934 | leticiae@aol.com | www.virtualcities.com/ons/vt/j/vtjc801.htm | 6 rooms | $85–$115 | Closed Jan.–Apr. | AE, MC, V.

CHESTER

MAP 11, E9

(Nearby towns also listed: Grafton, Rockingham, Springfield)

Known for its elongated town green dividing Main Street, Chester is also unusual among Vermont towns for its large number of stone houses, clustered at the north end of the village. Chester is the home of the National Survey, which stocks a vast assortment of topographical and other maps; just off Main Street is the terminal serving the Green Mountain Flyer, a tourist train that runs to Bellows Falls.

Information: Chester Area Chamber of Commerce | Box 623, Main St., Chester, 05143 | 802/875–2939 | www.vacationinvermont.com.

Attractions

The Stone Village. Constructed from quarried stone in the early 1800s, these historic buildings are said to have been part of the Underground Railroad. Today they serve as residences, bed-and-breakfasts, and a doll shop. | North St./Rte. 103 N.

ON THE CALENDAR

SEPT.: *Fall Craft Fair.* Held on the Village Green, the fair features handmade Vermont products from around the area. | The Village Green | 802/875–2939.

Dining

Raspberries and Thyme. American/Casual. One of the area's most popular spots, this restaurant offers a variety of breakfast specials, homemade soups, a large selection of salads, homemade desserts, and more than 40 sandwiches. At dinner, the steak, encrusted in a five-peppercorn medley and dijon mustard sauce, is a favorite. | On the Village Green | 802/875–4486 | No dinner Mon.–Tues. | $11–$23 | AE, D, DC, MC, V.

Ye Old Bradford Tavern at the Fullerton Inn. Contemporary. This double-porched Victorian presides over the town green. Wide-board floors, antique furniture, and a large fieldstone fireplace enhance the main dining room. Fare includes steaks and chops, seafood, and salads. Live music on Saturday. | 40 The Common, On the Village Green | 802/875–2444 | Closed Wed. No lunch | $11–$18 | AE, MC, V.

Lodging

Fullerton Inn. A big, handsome inn on the village green, more like a small hotel, formerly known as Inn at Long Last. The rooms are distinctively furnished with country quilts and lace curtains throughout. Restaurant. No air-conditioning in some rooms. Cross-country skiing, downhill skiing. No kids under 12. | 40 The Common, On the Village Green | 802/875–2444 | fax 802/875–6414 | getaway@fullertoninn.com | www.fullertoninn.com | 18 rooms, 3 suites | $109, $149 suites | AE, D, MC, V.

Inn Victoria. A converted high Victorian mansion, this bed-and-breakfast features rooms with period furniture, yet with up-to-date amenities. The front porch and rear deck are perfect places to unwind and soak in the village's summer evenings. Complimentary breakfast. No smoking, some in-room hot tubs, no room phones, no TV in some rooms, TV in common area. No kids. No pets. | On the Village Green at Main St. | 802/875–4288 or 800/732–4288 | fax 802/875–2504 | innkeeper@innvictoria.com | www.innvictoria.com | 7 rooms | $110–$195 | MC, V.

CRAFTSBURY COMMON

MAP 11, F3

(Nearby town also listed: Morrisville)

Considered by many aficionados of upcountry Yankee architecture and town design to be one of Vermont's most beautiful villages, Craftsbury Common stands on a lofty plateau, with views of surrounding valleys and distant mountains in nearly every direction. The name says it all—the settlement is built around a great grassy common, stitched in place by a neat fence painted the same snow white as the surrounding homes and public buildings. The village is home to the sumptuous Inn on the Common, and to small, environmentally oriented Sterling College.

Information: Hardwick Area Chamber of Commerce | Box 111, Hardwick, 05843 | 802/472–5906 | fax 802/472–6865 | www.hardwickvtarea.com.

CRAFTSBURY
COMMON

INTRO
ATTRACTIONS
DINING
LODGING

Attractions

Sterling College. Eight white clapboard buildings make up the campus of this college specializing in environmental studies. The administrative building was originally an inn. | On the Common | 802/586–7711 | admissions@sterlingcollege.edu | www.sterlingcollege.edu.

ON THE CALENDAR

JULY: *Antiques and Uniques.* Rain or shine, over one hundred vendors come to the Common to sell their high-end antique furniture and crafts. | On the Common | 802/655–0006.

Lodging

Craftsbury Outdoor Center. Lakes and hills surround this haven for outdoor enthusiasts. The center has terrific cross-country skiing on its 160 km (99 mi) of trails, which also go through the local farmland. Dining room, complimentary breakfast. No air-conditioning, no smoking, no room phones, TV in common area. Tennis court. Hiking, beach, boating. Bicycles, ice-skating. Cross-country skiing. Library. Pets allowed (in cottages only). | Lost Nation Rd. | 802/586–7767 or 800/729–7751 | fax 802/586–7768 | crafts@sover.net | www.craftsbury.com | 29 rooms (26 share bath), 3 cottages, 2 efficiencies | $118–$215 | AP | MC, V.

Highland Lodge. This casual, unfussy, down-home rambling 19th-century farmhouse, an inn since the 1920s, stands above Caspian Lake, 8 mi south of Craftsbury. There is dining on the veranda in season and a supervised playroom. Most rooms have lake views. Restaurant. No room phones. Tennis. Hiking, beach, boating. Cross-country skiing. | 1608 Craftsbury Rd., Greensboro | 802/533–2647 | fax 802/533–7494 | hlodge@connriver.net | www.highlandlodge.com | 11 rooms, 11 cottages (4 cottages in winter) | $189–$250 | Closed mid Oct.–late Dec., mid-Mar.–late May | MAP | D, MC, V.

Inn on the Common. Set on 10 acres, this picturesque Federal-style inn has tastefully appointed rooms with handcrafted country furnishings and quilts. Five-course dinners are served at communal tables in the dining room, overlooking the gardens. Excellent cross-country skiing is available. Dining room, complimentary breakfast. Pool. Tennis court. Library. TV in common area. Pets allowed (fee). | N. Craftsbury Rd. | 802/586–9619 or 800/521–2233 | fax 802/586–2249 | 16 rooms | $250–$300 | MAP | AE, MC, V. .

DORSET

(Nearby towns also listed: Manchester, Manchester Center, Peru)

Dorset, along with nearby Manchester, was one of the first southern Vermont towns to appeal to wealthy out-of-staters, more than 100 years ago. Still au courant with the weekend crowd but without Manchester's shopping bustle, Dorset remains everyone's vision of the picture-book Vermont village, with its two-century-old Dorset Inn, omnium-gatherum general store (with fine wines), and summer playhouse.

Information: Dorset Chamber of Commerce | Box 121, Dorset, 05251 | 802/867–0132 | fax 802/867–5753 | www.dorsetvt.com.

Attractions

Lake St. Catherine. This picturesque lake, 12 mi north of Dorset, is a splendid location for picnics. A state park lies just off the highway as it flanks the lake's east shore. | Rte. 30.

ON THE CALENDAR

JUNE–SEPT.: *Dorset Theatre Festival.* Professional actors perform with apprentices in three months of diverse productions. | Cheney La. | Tickets $22–$35 | Tues–Sun. at 8; matinees Wed. at 2, Sat. at 4 | 802/867–5777 and 802/867–2223.

Dining

Barrows House Inn. Contemporary. Majestically set on 11 landscaped acres, this historic 1804 country inn has restored stencilled walls and charmingly creaky floorboards. Before dinner take a stroll through the perennial gardens. Try the Maine Crab Cakes Chesapeake Style or the grilled Portobello mushroom appetizer with Gorgonzola cheese, artichoke hearts, and roasted red pepper puree over seasonal greens. No smoking. | Rte. 30 | 802/867–4455 or 800/639–1620 | www.barrowshouse.com | Breakfast also available. No lunch | $11–$27 | AE, D, MC, V.

Chantecleer. Contemporary. A rustic remodelled dairy barn, 3½ mi north of Dorset, with exposed beams, enormous fieldstone fireplace, and folk art decor. Try the onion soup, prepared with leeks, Spanish and white onions, and Gruyère and Emmenthal cheese. Or try the superb Black Angus Fillet with Chanterelle Mushrooms and Rosemary Peppercorn Spaetzle. The substantial wine list offers only a few moderately priced selections, but certain labels are available in half bottles. | Rte. 7A, E. Dorset | 802/362–1616 | Reservations essential | Closed Mon.–Tues. in Nov. No lunch | $50 | AE, DC, MC, V.

Dorset Inn. Contemporary. The oldest continuously operating inn in Vermont (established in 1796) has a folk art–decorated dining room and a rustic tavern with fireplace. Delicious, straightforward updated American cuisine is on the menu. Try the yam fritters with maple syrup or the Apple Smoked Barbecue Chicken served with corn cakes and black beans. | 1 Church St. | 802/867–5500 | www.dorsetinn.com | Breakfast also available | $12–$20 | AE, MC, V.

Inn at Westview Farm. Contemporary. This mid-19th-century former farmhouse is a southern Vermont landmark. You can dine in the Auberge room or visit the casual Clancy's Tavern for lighter fare. Try the rack of lamb on herbed barley with a raisin chutney, or sautéed sesame shrimp with ginger and apricot beurre blanc. Tavern fare has smaller portions of fresh seafood, steaks, chops, stews, chicken, and salads. | 2928 Rte. 30 | 802/867–5715 or 800/769–4903 | www.innatwestviewfarm.com | No lunch | $16–$26 | MC, V.

Lodging

Barrows House. This antiques-filled inn sprawls over nine buildings and 11 acres. Some rooms have fireplaces. Restaurant, bar, picnic area. Some kitchenettes, some refrigerators, some in-room VCRs, no room phones, TV in some rooms. Pool. Sauna. Tennis. Bicycles. Cross-country skiing, downhill skiing. Library. Business services. Pets allowed. | Rte. 30, at corner of Dorset Hollow Rd. | 802/867–4455 or 800/639–1620 | fax 802/867–0132 | www.barrowshouse.com | 28 rooms in 9 houses | $90–$265, including dinner | MAP | AE, D, MC, V.

Cornucopia. Innkeepers welcome you at this 1880s colonial house with champagne. The gourmet breakfast is decorated with candles and flowers. All rooms include toiletries, terry robes, and either down comforters or quilts; three rooms have fireplaces. Complimentary breakfast. No smoking, room phones, TV in common area. No kids under 16. No pets. | 3228 Rte. 30 | 802/867–5751 or 800/566–5751 | fax 802/867–5753 | innkeepers@cornucopiaofdorset.com | www.cornucopiaofdorset.com | 5 rooms | $130–$270 | AE, MC, V.

Dorset Inn. Opened in 1796, this is Vermont's oldest continuously operated inn, right on the green in town. Rooms are carpeted, with a softer edge and a sprinkling of antiques. Restaurant, bar. No air-conditioning in some rooms, no room phones, no TV in rooms, TV in lounge. No kids. | Church and Main Sts. | 802/867–5500 | fax 802/867–5542 | www.dorsetinn.com | 31 rooms | $150–$200 | AE, MC, V.

Inn at Westview Farm. A big, rambling farmhouse that is ½ mi south of Dorset and has been made into an exquisite full-service inn. The public rooms and broad verandas are especially inviting. Restaurant, bar, complimentary breakfast. | 2928 Rte. 30 | 802/867–5715 | fax 802/867–0468 | westview@vermonttel.com | www.innatwestviewfarm | 10 rooms | $130–$170 | AE, MC, V.

Squire House. Abutting a wooded grove, this 1918 colonial house sits back from the road on 11 acres of land. The inn has spacious rooms and bathrooms, high ceilings, and wood paneling in its dining room. The three common rooms contain a piano and fireplaces. In summer, afternoon tea is served on one of two brick terraces. Complimentary breakfast. No air-conditioning, no smoking, no room phones, no TV in some rooms, TV in common area. No kids under 10. No pets. | 3395 Dorset West Rd. | 802/867–0281 | fax 802/867–2565 | rwsquire@ix.netcom.com | www.squirehouse.com | 4 rooms | $75–$135 | No credit cards.

FAIRLEE

MAP 11, F6

(Nearby town also listed: White River Junction)

Fairlee, tucked between the Connecticut River and brooding 600-ft cliffs, is a popular spot for golf and water sports—Lake Morey and much of Lake Fairlee lie within town limits. An early inhabitant, Samuel Morey, is credited with operating a rudimentary steamboat on the river and on Lake Morey in 1793, well before Robert Fulton steamed into history on the *Clermont*.

Information: Upper Valley Chamber of Commerce | Box 697, 61 Old River Rd., White River Junction, 05001 | 802/295–6200 | fax 802/295–3779 | www.uppervalleyvt.com.

Attractions

Chatman's Store. An eclectic range of products such as fishing tackle, fine wines, and old books are on sale at this Fairlee mainstay, which is also flanked by a greenhouse and an antiques shop. The store has been operated by the same family since 1922. | Main St. | 802/333–9709 | Mon.–Sat. 8–6, Sun. 8–5.

Fairlee Motel and Drive-in. Come and enjoy a movie at the country's oldest running motel and drive-in. The grassy field and surrounding green will remind you that you are still in Vermont. | 1809 Rte. 5 | 802/333–9192 | $5.50 | Mid-Apr.–mid-Sept., Fri.–Sun. nights.

ON THE CALENDAR

JUNE: *Vermont State Open Golf Tournament.* The pine tree–lined course with narrow fairways is noted for the constraints it places on players. | Lake Morey Inn Country Club, 179 Clubhouse Rd. | $250 for professionals, $125 for amateurs | 802/333–4800.

AUG.: *Lobster Festival.* Lobsters galore from Maine are devoured on Fairlee Common on the first weekend in August. $15 per person. | On Fairlee Common, Main St. | Mon.–Tues. 8:30–4:30, Wed.–Thurs. 10–6 | 802/333–4363.

Dining

Pot Latch Tavern. Austrian. The interior of this restaurant has wood paneling and wooden tables. The last Thursday of every month is German Night when all types of German specialties are served. The restaurant also serves many veal dishes, some vegetarian main courses, and fresh lobster from Maine in summer. | Rte. 5 | 802/333–4629 | Closed Tues. Memorial Day–Labor Day; Closed Mon.–Tues Sept.–Mar. | $8–$18 | MC, V.

Lodging

Fairlee Motel and Drive-In. The country's oldest operating motel and drive-in offers the best of both worlds. You can sit in a room and enjoy the feature film from your window (only on weekends in summer), or you can relax in the privacy of your room with the shades pulled. The lot is a grass field, thus reducing the sound pollution from the drive-in guests. There are picnic tables beside the lot. Microwaves, refrigerators, no smoking. No pets. | 1809 Rte. 5 | 802/333–9192 | 12 rooms | $40–$60 | Drive-in closed mid-Sept.–mid-Apr. | AE, MC, V.

Lake Morey Inn Country Club. A superb lakeside resort with four-season recreational opportunities. In the heart of the upper Connecticut River valley. Dining room, bar. In-room data ports, some refrigerators, room service, no TV in some rooms. Indoor-outdoor pool. Hot tub. Driving range, 18-hole golf, putting green, 2 tennis courts. Exercise equipment, hiking, beach, windsurfing, boating, waterskiing. Cross-country skiing, downhill skiing, ski shop, sleigh rides, snowmobiling, tobogganing. Video games. Children's programs (ages 3–12). Business services. | Clubhouse Rd. | 802/333–4311 or 800/423–1211 | fax 802/333–4553 | lakemoreyinn@msn.com | www.lakemoreyinn.com | 144 rooms, 22 cottages | $94–$127 weekdays, $108–$141 weekends; $80–102 cottages | MC, V.

Silver Maple. You can stay in a knotty pine–paneled cottage or in the main late-18th-century inn in this hotel 1 mi from Lake Morey. Complimentary Continental breakfast. No air-conditioning, no room phones, no TV in some rooms. Pets allowed. | 520 U.S. Rte. 5 S | 802/ 333–4326 or 800/666–1946 | www.silvermaplelodge.com | 8 rooms (2 with shared bath), 8 cottages | $56–$86 | AE, D, MC, V.

GRAFTON

MAP 11, E10

(Nearby towns also listed: Bellows Falls, Chester, Londonderry, Newfane, Rockingham)

The entire village of Grafton stands as testimony to the preservationist spirit in Vermont. Long neglected after its early-19th century heyday as a farming, manufacturing, and sheep-raising center, Grafton was resurrected by a private foundation that restored its centerpiece, the Old Tavern at Grafton, and other village structures. The celebrated Grafton cheese, one of Vermont's premier cheddars, is made here.

Information: **Grafton Information Center,** | Box 9, Daniels House, Grafton, 05146 | 802/ 843–2255 | fax 802/843–2245 | www.old-tavern.com.

Attractions

Grafton Historical Society Museum. Housing mostly 19th-century artifacts, this museum also has a special collection of soapstone artifacts and an assortment of different writing implements. | Main St. | 802/843–2584 or 802/843–2489 or 802/843–1010 | $3 | Memorial Day–Columbus Day, weekends and holidays 10–12 and 2–4; daily during foliage season 10–12, 2–4, and by appointment.

Grafton Ponds Cross-Country Skiing Center. With 20 mi of trails, the center even has its own snowmaking operation and mountain biking in summer. Lessons are available and there's a cozy lodge in which to relax. | Townshend Rd. | 802/843–2400 | fax 802/843–2245 | Daily 9–6 summer; 9–4 winter.

Historic Grafton Village. Restored 19th-century community. One of the finest examples of rural New England architecture and village life. | 92 Main St. | 802/843–2255 | fax 802– 843–2245 | www.old-tavern.com | Free | Daily.

The Old Tavern at Grafton. A splendid restoration of an 1801 inn, which is worth a look even if you aren't spending the night. | 92 Main St., at Townshend Rd. | 802/843–2231 | www.old-tavern.com | Jan.–Mar. and May–Dec., daily 8–11.

ON THE CALENDAR

AUG.: *House Tour.* For one weekend each August, 10 of this village's historic homes are open so you can view their carefully restored interiors. | 802/843–2255.

Dining

The Old Tavern. Contemporary. This inn is furnished with Early American antiques, old portraits, and Chippendale chairs. It has classic New England dishes and more contemporary Continental cuisine. Try the Soft Shell Crabs in a Champagne-Tarragon Butter with Wild Rice Cakes, the Pan-Roasted Chilean Sea Bass with Couscous and Swiss Chard, or the Lamb in a Sherry Demi-Glace. | 92 Main St. | 802/843–2231 or 800/843–1801 | Breakfast also available. Closed Apr. No lunch mid-Oct.–late May, weekdays | $19–$28 | AE, DC, MC, V.

Lodging

Butternut Acres Bed-and-Breakfast. This charming 1820s white clapboard house was originally a farmhouse. The house is surrounded by trees and flower-laden meadows and an outside staircase provides private access to the rooms. Complimentary breakfast. No air-conditioning, no smoking, no TV in some rooms. Pool. | 35 Theron Dr. | 802/843–2429 | 2 rooms | $85 | No credit cards.

The Old Tavern. Established in 1801, this historic country inn was once a stagecoach stop on the Boston-to-Montreal route, visited by literary luminaries such as Nathaniel Hawthorne, Thoreau, and Emerson. It is the centerpiece of Grafton village and is filled with gleaming

© Corbis

SAY CHEESE

Walk into any Vermont general store worthy of the name, and one of the first things you'll see is a big wheel of cheese resting under a glass dome on the counter. "Store cheese," the old-timers call it, but it's cheddar, pure and simple. Vermonters have made cheddar cheese for centuries. As recently as the early 1900s, most of the output of the state's dairy farms was transformed into butter and cheese, rather than sold as more perishable, hard-to-ship fluid milk. More than 40 varieties of cheese are made from cow's, goat's, and sheep's milk in Vermont, and, in fact, the state turns out more mozzarella than cheddar. But cheddar remains Vermont's signature cheese. Cheddar cheese originated in and around Cheddar, England, although far more cheddar is made in the United States than in England today. Some sources even use the term "cheddar" interchangeably with "American" cheese—although a good sharp cheddar, the kind Vermont is known for, has about as much in common with processed American cheese as fine Bordeaux does with jug wine. Vermont cheddar begins with cow's milk, treated with a special bacteria and heated so it ferments. Then the cheesemaker adds microbial rennet, grown from spores. The rennet causes the fermented milk to coagulate, separating into solid curds and liquid whey. The whey, which accounts for some 90 percent of the original milk volume, is drained from the curds and used as cattle feed. The next step is to mill the rubbery curds into slabs, which are then piled in vats and repeatedly turned and re-stacked. This process, called "cheddaring," extracts additional whey from the curds and gives it a firmer consistency. Then the slabs of curd are cut into pieces the size of French fries, and salt is added. The curds are compressed into wheels or blocks, which are wrapped and stored at 45°F for at least 60 days. That minimal aging would produce a very mild cheddar; for sharper varieties, six months to three years of aging is required, and one producer is introducing a four-year-old cheddar with an especially strong bite. Six Vermont producers turn out about 100 million pounds of cheddar a year. Cabot is by far the largest, and gives tours of its operation in the town of the same name. Other cheddar makers offering tours are Grafton, which takes its name from the restored southern Vermont village where it is located; Shelburne Farms, just south of Burlington; and Crowley, in tiny Healdville southeast of Rutland. (Crowley, which is made in the oldest cheese factory in the U.S., calls its product "Crowley cheese," not cheddar, but the process is the same.) Two smaller producers not offering tours—but selling cheese on their premises— are Butterworks Farm in Westfield, just south of Newport near the Canadian border and Orb Weaver Farm in New Haven, near Middlebury. Orb Weaver makes "Farmhouse cheese," but any connoisseur would recognize it as cheddar.

Chippendale chests and table and polished Windsor chairs. The pool is a converted pond. Dining room, bar, complimentary breakfast. TV in common area. Pond. Tennis. Cross-country skiing, downhill skiing. Kids over 7 only (except in 3 cottages). Laundry facilities. | 92 Main St. | 802/843–2231 or 800/843–1801 | fax 802/843–2245 | www.old-tavern.com | 66 rooms, 8 suites, 7 cottages | $205–225, $275 suites, $500–$830 cottages | Closed Apr. | MC, V.

Woodchuck Hill Farm. A fully restored colonial farmhouse, this is one of the oldest (1790) dwellings in the area, and is furnished with antiques. It is in the countryside, 2 mi from the village, with spectacular mountain views. Behind the barn is a large pond surrounded by rolling lawns that are ideal for sunning, with a platform dock in the swimming area, and a gazebo. Complimentary breakfast. No smoking, no room phones, no TV in some rooms, TV in common room. Sauna. Pond. Library. | Woodchuck Hill Rd. | 802/843–2398 | www.woodchuckhill.com | 10 rooms (2 with shared bath) | $89–$160 | AE, MC, V.

GREEN MOUNTAIN NATIONAL FOREST

MAP 11, C11

(Nearby towns also listed: Bennington, Manchester, Manchester Center, Rutland, Warren)

Green Mountain National Forest contains nearly 600,000 acres of woodland in its separate northern and southern units. Although short on federally designated wilderness acreage (wilderness areas include Lye Brook, in the south, and Bristol Cliffs farther north) and subject to periodic timber leasing, the National Forest is nevertheless a tremendous backcountry resource, containing many of the highest peaks of the state-long Green Mountain range. The Long Trail, a "footpath in the wilderness" managed by the Green Mountain Club in Waterbury, runs the length of Vermont, much of it on National Forest land.

Information: Headquarters, Green Mountain National Forest, | 231 N. Main St., Rutland, 05701 | 802/747–6700 | fax 802/747–5766 | www.fs.fed.us/r9/gmfl.

Attractions
Moosalamoo Recreation Area. A near-wilderness preserve 1 mi east of Ripton, laced with hiking, mountain biking, and cross-country ski trails. | Green Mountain National Forest | 802/747–6700 or 802/247–6401 | www.moosalamoo.com | $5 per night for a campsite | Daily.

Lodging
Old Hotel. Formerly the Long Run Inn, this hotel provides simple, affordable accommodations. Built in the 1840s as a hotel for lumberjacks, it evokes a bygone era with homemade quilts, braided rugs, hardwood floors, and antique glass. The Long Trail is nearby and the New Haven River rolls below. Complimentary breakfast. No air-conditioning, no smoking, TV in common area. | Lincoln Gap Rd., Lincoln | 802/453–2567 | 7 rooms (share 3 baths) | $55–$75 | MC, V.

HIGHGATE SPRINGS

MAP 11, C1

(Nearby town also listed: St. Albans)

Highgate Springs, the last Vermont town before the Canadian border along Interstate 89, was founded by Hessian veterans of the American Revolution who thought they were settling in Canada. After the boundary survey proved them wrong, they stayed anyway. At Highgate, you're equidistant from the equator and the North Pole.

Information: **Swanton Chamber of Commerce** | 20 S. River St., Swanton, 05488 | 802/868–7200 | fax 802/868–4744 | www.swantonchamber.com.

Attractions

Missisquoi National Wildlife Refuge. At the mouth of the Missisquoi River, 5 mi south of Highgate Springs, the refuge is one of Vermont's best birding and canoeing spots. | 371 N. River St., Swanton | 802/868–4781 | fax 802/868–2379 | Donations accepted | Office weekdays 8–4:30, refuge daily dawn–dusk.

ON THE CALENDAR

JULY: *Swanton Summer Festival.* Carnival rides, amusements, barbecues, fair activities, parades. | Village Green, downtown Swanton | Last week of July | 802/868–7200.

Lodging

Country Essence Bed-and-Breakfast. The 30 acres of landscaped grounds, 2 mi south of town, that encompass this 1850s white clapboard home and property are directly adjacent to the national wildlife refuge. The windows of one room overlook quiet meadows where geese and deer are sometimes seen. All rooms have antique furnishings. Complimentary Continental breakfast. No smoking, no TV, no room phones. Pool. Hiking. No pets. | 641 Rte. 7 N., Swanton | 802/868–4247 | amessier@together.net | www.countryessence.com | 2 rooms | $60 | No credit cards.

Highgate Manor Inn. This restored brick mansion, 10 mi south of Highgate Springs, is on the green of Highgate Falls. The rooms have period furniture that reflects the home's Victorian past. Complimentary breakfast. No smoking, no room phones, no TV. Library. No kids under 12. | Rte. 207, Highgate Falls | 802/868–5610 or 802/868–9007 | fax 802/868–5610 | 6 rooms | $75 | MC, V.

The Tyler Place on Lake Champlain. One of Vermont's top family resorts, with loyal returning clientele. Set on 165 acres, it has a private lakefront and nature trails. There are fireplaces in the cottages. Dining room, bar. Kitchenettes (in cottages), refrigerators, no TV in rooms, TV in common room. 2 pools (1 indoor), wading pool. Driving range, tennis. Gym, hiking, windsurfing, boating, waterskiing. Children's programs (ages 1–16). | Old Dock Rd., Highgate Springs | 802/868–3301 or 802/868–4000 | fax 802/868–7602 | www.tyler-place.com | 29 suites, 29 cottages | $300–$394 suite; $400–$484 cottage | Open Memorial Day–mid-Sept. | AP | D, MC, V.

ISLAND POND

MAP 11, G2

(Nearby town also listed: Newport)

Island Pond was a bustling railroad center back in the days when it marked the halfway point on the main line between Portland, Maine, and Montreal. It was also the site of a government armory, and the boyhood home of singer Rudy Vallee. As the only sizeable community in Vermont's empty northeastern corner (the municipality's technical name is Brighton), Island Pond is a service center for hunters, anglers, and snowmobilers. There is a pond—more like a small lake—and it does have an island in it.

Information: **Island Pond Chamber of Commerce** | Box 255, Island Pond, 05846 | 802/723–6300 | webmaster@islandpond.com | www.islandpond.com.

Attractions

Brighton State Park. This state park, located on the lake, has sandy beaches, picnic tables, grills, and boat rentals. | Lake Shore Dr. | 802/723–4360 | Mid-May–early Oct., daily 9–9.

KODAK'S TIPS FOR PHOTOGRAPHING LANDSCAPES AND SCENERY

Landscape
- Tell a story
- Isolate the essence of a place
- Exploit mood, weather, and lighting

Panoramas
- Use panoramic cameras for sweeping vistas
- Don't restrict yourself to horizontal shots
- Keep the horizon level

Panorama Assemblage
- Use a wide-angle or normal lens
- Let edges of pictures overlap
- Keep exposure even
- Use a tripod

Placing the Horizon
- Use low horizon placement to accent sky or clouds
- Use high placement to emphasize distance and accent foreground elements
- Try eliminating the horizon

Mountain Scenery: Scale
- Include objects of known size
- Frame distant peaks with nearby objects
- Compress space with long lenses

Mountain Scenery: Lighting
- Shoot early or late; avoid midday
- Watch for dramatic color changes
- Use exposure compensation

Tropical Beaches
- Capture expansive views
- Don't let bright sand fool your meter
- Include people

Rocky Shorelines
- Vary shutter speeds to freeze or blur wave action
- Don't overlook sea life in tidal pools
- Protect your gear from sand and sea

In the Desert
- Look for shapes and textures
- Try visiting during peak bloom periods
- Don't forget safety

Canyons
- Research the natural and social history of a locale
- Focus on a theme or geologic feature
- Budget your shooting time

Rain Forests and the Tropics
- Go for mystique with close-ups and detail shots
- Battle low light with fast films and camera supports
- Protect cameras and film from moisture and humidity

Rivers and Waterfalls
- Use slow film and long shutter speeds to blur water
- When needed, use a neutral-density filter over the lens
- Shoot from water level to heighten drama

Autumn Colors
- Plan trips for peak foliage periods
- Mix wide and close views for visual variety
- Use lighting that accents colors or creates moods

Moonlit Landscapes
- Include the moon or use only its illumination
- Exaggerate the moon's relative size with long telephoto lenses
- Expose landscapes several seconds or longer

Close-Ups
- Look for interesting details
- Use macro lenses or close-up filters
- Minimize camera shake with fast films and high shutter speeds

Caves and Caverns
- Shoot with ISO 1000+ films
- Use existing light in tourist caves
- Paint with flash in wilderness caves

From *Kodak Guide to Shooting Great Travel Pictures* © 2000 by Fodor's Travel Publications

Dining

Jennifer's Restaurant. American. Island Pond's only eatery, this restaurant sits in the middle of town, a stone's throw away from the water. It specializes in all kinds of seafood. | Cross St. | 802/723–6135 | $8–$13 | AE, D, MC, V.

Lodging

The Lake Front Inn and Motel. Sitting directly on the water, this inn is ideal for outdoor enthusiasts who wish to enjoy the lake. You can snowmobile in winter and swim, fish, and boat from the property in summer. Some kitchenettes, some microwaves, some refrigerators, no smoking, cable TV. Lake. Dock, water sports, boating. Fishing. Snowmobiling. | 127 Cross St. | 802/723–6507 | fax 802/723–6507 | lfinn@sover.net | www.thelakefrontinn.com | 20 rooms, 3 suites | $84–$295 | AE, MC, V.

Quimby Country. A Northeast Kingdom tradition since 1894, this inn feels like an old-time fishing lodge where hearty meals attract loyal family clientele. The hotel is on 650 acres tucked deep in the woods overlooking Forest Lake, 20 mi north of Island Pond, with larger Great Averill Pond nearby. No room phones. Lake. Tennis. Hiking, boating. Fishing. Children's program (ages 5 and up). Pets allowed. | Rte. 114, Forest Lake Rd., Averill | 802/822–5533 | fax 802/822–5537 | 20 cabins | $111–$126 (adults), $63–$74 (ages 9–16), $49–$52 (ages 3–8) | Closed Oct.–mid-May | AP | No credit cards.

JEFFERSONVILLE

MAP 11, D3

(Nearby town also listed: Stowe)

Jeffersonville, a settlement within the town of Cambridge, is the northern gateway to Smuggler's Notch. The "Mountain Road"—a climbing, twisting, often bloodcurdlingly narrow stretch of Vermont Route 108—heads south from the village to Stowe, passing beneath the brow of Mt. Mansfield. "Jeff" is the home of the popular Smuggler's Notch ski and summer resort, which dwarfs the village's small commercial center lying just off Route 15.

Information: **Smugglers' Notch Area Chamber of Commerce** | Box 364, Jeffersonville, 05464 | 802/644–2239 | www.smuggsinfo.com.

Attractions

Boyden Valley Winery. You can take a tour of this micro-winery on family farm in Lamoille River valley, 4 mi east of Jeffersonville. There are free wine tastings and a wine and cheese café where you can buy cheese, paté, coffee, and wine. There are wine and cheese canoe tours on request and local artisans' work on sale, including reproduction furniture. | At Rtes. 15 and 104, Cambridge | 802/644–8151 | fax 802/644–8212 | www.boydenvalley.com | Free, wine and cheese canoe tours $25 | June–Dec., Tues.–Sun. 10–5; Jan.–May, Fri.–Sun., 10–5.

★ **Smugglers' Notch.** Skiing and snowboarding on three mountains, 5 mi south of Jeffersonville, with a renowned instruction program, plenty of slope-side accommodations; great for families. | 4323 Rte. 108 S | 802/644–8851 or 800/451–8752 | www.smuggs.com | Dec.–Apr., daily.

Vermont Horse Park. This park across the street from the village of Smugglers' Notch has both mountain trails and canyon trails. You can give your kid a ride on a pony or take a romantic trip in an authentic horse-drawn sleigh. | Rte. 108 | 802/644–5347 | Daily.

ON THE CALENDAR

JULY: *Fourth of July Celebration.* Jeffersonville's Independence Day parade draws a large crowd from the surrounding area and includes a fair and fireworks on the mountain. | Main St. | 802/644–2239 | www.smugnotch.com/html/events/4th.htm.

Dining

Café Banditos Restaurant and Cantina. Mexican. This family restaurant across the road from Smuggler's Notch Resort has video games and movies for the kids. The traditional Mexican fare is complemented by vegetarian and seafood specials. | Rte. 108 | 802/644–5736 | banditos@sover.net | Closed Mon.–Wed. in Apr.–June. No lunch in winter | $8–$13 | AE, D, DC, MC, V.

Dinner's Dunn at the Windridge Bakery. American. This bakery is famous for its homemade breads and serves classic American fare daily. The Italian herb flatbread pizzas are a favorite among locals. | Main St. | 802/644–8219 or 802/644–5556 | Breakfast also available. No dinner Sun.–Tues. | $9–$15 | MC, V.

Plum and Main Restaurant. American. This eatery 10 mi east of Jeffersonville is housed in the Johnson's original post office, built in 1917. Prime-rib dinners, fresh seafood, and homemade soups complement the classic diner fare. | Main St., Johnson | 802/635–7596 | Breakfast also available. No dinner Sun. | $6–$14 | No credit cards.

Three Mountain Lodge. American/Casual. The dining room of this lodge has walls of exposed timber and a wood-burning fireplace. The restaurant offers steak and seafood dishes, homemade pastas, and vegetarian entrées as well as an extensive wine list and licensed bar. | Rte. 108 | 802/644–5736 | coco@threemountainlodge.com | virtualvermont.com/threemountainlodge | Closed Mon. | $13–$23 | D, DC, MC, V.

Lodging

Deer Run Motor Inn. In a rural wooded area, this property has clean, comfortable accommodations in a scenic landscape. The backyard area has room for picnicking and lounging as well as a swing set for the kids. Refrigerators, cable TV. Pool. Playground. Pets allowed. | Rte. 15 | 802/644–8866 or 800/354–2728 | 25 rooms | $70 | AE, D, MC, V.

Highlander. Just outside Jeffersonville village (1½ mi south) near the beginning of the winding road through Smugglers' Notch, this hotel is convenient to the resort and has views of the surrounding mountains. Restaurant, grill, picnic area. No air-conditioning, some refrigerators, cable TV. Pool. Sauna. Video games. Playground. | Rte. 108 S | 802/644–2725 or 800/367–6471 | fax 802/644–2725 | highlander@stowevt.net | 15 rooms | $45–$75 | MC, V.

Jefferson House Bed-and-Breakfast. A turn-of-the-20th-century house in downtown Jeffersonville that has a wraparound porch, two common areas, and an upstairs deck from which to view the dazzling night sky. The town's restaurants are within walking distance. Complimentary breakfast. TV in common area. No pets. | 71 Main St. | 802/644–2030 or 800/253–9630 | jeffhouse@pwshift.com | www.scenesofvermont.com/jeffhse/index.html | 3 rooms | $65–$75 | D, MC, V.

Mannsview Inn. This white clapboard former farmhouse built in 1865 is a 10-minute drive from Smugglers' Notch resort. In summer there are special canoeing tour packages. No air-conditioning, no smoking, no room phones, TV in common area. Cross-country skiing, downhill skiing. Kids over 7 only. | 916 Vermont Rte. 108 S | 802/644–8321, 888/937–6266 reservations | fax 802/644–2006 | www.mannsview.com | 6 rooms (4 with shared bath, 2 with shower only) | $65–$125 | AE, MC, V.

Sinclair Inn. A restored Queen Anne inn with a terrific multihued paint job amd a landscaped garden, this is convenient to Mt. Mansfield via Underhill State Park. Picnic area, complimentary breakfast. No smoking, no room phones. No kids under 12. | 389 Rte. 15, Jericho | 802/899–2234, 800/433–4658 reservations | fax 802/899–2234 | 6 rooms (4 with shower only) | $90–$145 | MC, V.

Smugglers' Notch Inn. Guest rooms are small but cheerful in this 18th-century inn. There are handmade quilts in some rooms. Downstairs, there's a cozy parlor. Dining room, picnic area, complimentary breakfast. No air-conditioning, no room phones, TV in common area. Cross-country skiing, downhill skiing. Library. | Church St. (Rte. 108) | 802/644–2412 or 800/845–3101 | smuginn@pwshift.com. | www.pbpub.com/smugglers/smuginn.htm | 11 rooms | $90–$125 | AE, MC, V.

Smugglers' Notch Ski and Tennis Resort. Consistently rated one of America's best family resorts, this hotel is 5 mi south of Jeffersonville. There are three ski mountains, a nearby state park, and access to many miles of hiking trails. Dining room, bar with entertainment. No air-conditioning in some rooms, some kitchenettes, some microwaves, cable TV, some in-room VCRs. Pool. Hot tub, massage. Miniature golf, 12 tennis courts (2 indoor). Exercise equipment, hiking. Bicycles, ice-skating. Cross-country skiing, downhill skiing, sleigh rides. Children's programs (ages 3–17), playground. Business services. Airport shuttle. | 4323 Vermont Rte. 108 S | 802/644–8851 or 800/451–8752 | fax 802/644–5913 | smuggs@smuggs.com | www.smuggs.com | 515 rooms, 25 suites | $95–$140, $130–$240 studios | AE, DC, MC, V.

Sterling Ridge Inn & Log Cabins. Built as an inn in 1988, this property also has eight cabins. It's surrounded by 80 acres and has mountain views. There are fireplaces in the cabins. Picnic area, complimentary breakfast. No air-conditioning, kitchenettes, some microwaves, no smoking, some in-room VCRs, no room phones. Pool. Cross-country skiing. | 1073 Junction Hill Rd. | 802/644–8265 or 800/347–8266 | www.vermont-cabins.com | 8 rooms, 8 cabins | $100–$150 cabins; $50–$89 rooms | MC, V.

Windridge Farms Inn. Slate floors, exposed timbers, and pine paneling are just some of the charms of this 18th-century inn. The period furniture complements this architectural theme, further evoking the colonial era. The inn is directly adjacent to the famous Windridge Bakery. No smoking, cable TV, no room phones, TV in common area. No pets. | Main St. | 802/644–8219 or 802/644–5556 | Ldunn@pshift.com. | www.virtualvermont.com/windridgeinn | 4 rooms, 1 suite | $75 | MC, V.

KILLINGTON

MAP 11, D8

(Nearby towns also listed: Bridgewater, Plymouth, Rutland, Woodstock)

Killington was the original name of the town of Sherburne, which is considering changing it back—so strong is the identification with the giant ski resort, the East's largest, which lies mostly within its borders. (The 4,241-ft summit of Killington Peak is in the adjacent town of Mendon.) Virtually all of Sherburne's businesses are skier-oriented;

KODAK'S TIPS FOR NIGHT PHOTOGRAPHY

Lights at Night
· Move in close on neon signs
· Capture lights from unusual vantage points

Fireworks
· Shoot individual bursts using a handheld camera
· Capture several explosions with a time exposure
· Include an interesting foreground

Fill-In Flash
· Set the fill-in light a stop darker than the ambient light

Around the Campfire
· Keep flames out of the frame when reading the meter
· For portraits, take spot readings of faces
· Use a tripod, or rest your camera on something solid

Using Flash
· Stay within the recommended distance range
· Buy a flash with the red-eye reduction mode

From *Kodak Guide to Shooting Great Travel Pictures* © 2000 by Fodor's Travel Publications

the two main drags are U.S. Route 4 and the Killington Access Road, although "transportation" hereabouts is just as likely to refer to gondolas and high-speed chairlifts.

Information: Killington and Pico Areas Association, | Box 114C, Rte. 4, Killington, 05751 | 802/773–4181 | fax 802/775–7070 | www.killingtonchamber.com.

Attractions

Gifford Woods State Park. You can camp at tent sites or lean-tos or hike along trails near the crest of the Green Mountains. | On Rte. 100 | 802/775–5354 | May–mid-Oct., daily 9–9.

Ground Zero. Snow tubing is the main attraction here. The center also has ice-skating, nighttime gondola rides, and other special events. | Snowshed Lodge Area, Killington Access Rd. | 802/422–6200 | Closed Dec.–Mar.

Pico Alpine Slide and Scenic Chairlift. Ride the chair to the top of the slide and guide your wheeled sled around breathtaking turns. | 802/422–6763 | $7; special rates for children | May–Oct., daily 10–6; call for winter information.

Ski Areas. Even when the snows have thawed, Vermont's mountain resorts offer outdoor activity in abundance.

Killington Ski and Summer Resort. This is the East's largest ski resort, with 205 trails on six mountains. In summer you can play golf, mountain bike, mountain board, or ride the water slide at the adventure park. | 4763 Killington Rd. | 802/422–3261 or 800/621–6867 | www.killington.com | Call for information on various packages and events | Nov.–Memorial Day, weekdays 9–4, weekends 8–4; Memorial Day–mid-June and Labor Day–Oct., weekends 10–6; mid-June–Labor Day, daily 10–6.

Pico. Killington's lower-key, slightly more laid-back next-door neighbor offers fine skiing and boarding. | On U.S. 4, 3 mi west of Rte. 100 | 802/422–6200 or 800/848–7325 | www.killington.com | Call for details of activity packages | Nov.–Apr., daily 8–4.

ON THE CALENDAR

AUG.: *Green Mountain 10-K Road Race.* A 6.2-mi endurance run which takes place on the first Sunday of August. You can register on the day of the race. | Summit Lodge | 802/422–3535 | www.summitlodgevermont.com | $18.

Dining

Cascades Lodge. Continental. Panoramic views set the scene for roast duck, Caribbean-style crab cakes, and paella. Kids' menu. No smoking. | 58 Old Mill Rd. | 802/422–3731 | www.cascadeslodge.com | Breakfast also available. Closed May. No lunch | $13–$25 | AE, D, MC, V.

Casey's Caboose. American/Casual. A replication of Casey Jones's caboose is joined to a 35-ton, turn-of-the-20th-century railroad snowplow car to make this cheerful and unique dining spot where a toy train runs continually across the top of the bar. If you're hungry enough, try the 16-ounce locomotive cut of prime rib; if not, the caboose cut is 4 ounces smaller. | Killington Rd. | 802/422–3795 | Closed May | $8–$23 | AE, D, MC, V.

Choices. Contemporary. Specializing in gourmet dinners served at the restaurant or for takeout, this eatery has such dishes as the rotisserie sampler: lamb, stuffed pork loin, and chicken. The intimate dining area is filled with high-back chairs, candles, and fresh-cut flowers. | Killington Rd. | 802/422–4030 | $13–$22 | AE, D, MC, V.

Grist Mill. American/Casual. This rendering of an early gristmill includes post-and-beam construction, a waterwheel, and a wraparound deck. Hearty New England fare is on the menu, including the berry-glazed chicken breast stuffed with artichoke hearts and cheese. | Killington Rd. | 802/422–3970 | $13–$20 | AE, D, MC, V.

★ **Hemingway's.** Contemporary. Guests can choose from three delightful rooms in this old Vermont farmhouse: the old-world wine cellar is the coziest, with its rustic stone wall and winepress. In the exposed-brick garden room, climbing ivy accents the windows overlooking an herb garden and patio. The peach-color vaulted room with its polished wood floor, dark upholstered chairs, and chandeliers is the most elegant. Try the homemade ravioli in pheasant stock with morels and the fillet of bass with vanilla butter sauce. | On U.S. 4 | 802/422–3886 | www.hemingwaysrestaurant.com | Closed mid-Apr.–mid-May, early Nov., and Mon.–Tues. No lunch | $50–$60, wine–tasting dinner $72 | AE, DC, MC, V.

Inn at Long Trail. Contemporary. A mammoth boulder sits on one side of the dining room as though it has just rolled thorugh the wall, while pictures illustrating the inn's history hang on the other walls. For dinner, try the mushroom and risotto strudel. Reservations are recommended. | Rte. 4 | 802/775–7181 or 800/325–2540 | Breakfast also available. Closed mid-Apr.–mid-June. No lunch | $11–$19 | AE, MC, V.

McGrath's Irish Pub. Irish. Part of the Inn at Long Trail, this pub serves traditional Irish fare and hosts live performances on Thursday and Saturday nights in winter and in the foliage season. The pub is known for its Guinness Beef Stew. | Rte. 4 | 802/775–7181 or 800/325–2540 | $4–$7 | AE, MC, V.

Mother Shapiro's Restaurant. American/Casual. Old church pews, beveled mirrors, and marble-top tables are some of the idiosyncratic charms of this casual eatery. The restaurant is known for its Jewish French toast. A game room offers distractions for the kids. | Killington Rd. | 802/422–9933 | Breakfast also available. Closed May–June weekdays | $7–$18 | AE, D, DC, MC, V.

Outback Pizza. Pizza. Alligators crawl on branches beneath the canvas-awning ceiling in this Australian-inspired pizzeria. The restaurant serves wood-fired pizzas like the Vermont BLT with cheddar, mozzarella, crumbled bacon, tomato slices, basil, and artichoke hearts. | Killington Rd. | 802/422–9885 | $10–$16 | AE, MC, V.

Peppers Bar and Grill. American/Casual. Reminiscent of a 1940s diner, this eatery has a stainless-steel facade and a steel-and-wood interior and serves some of Killington's most inexpensive fare. For dinner, try the broccoli over linguine with a mustard cream sauce. | Killington Rd. | 802/422–3177 | Breakfast also available | $11–$20 | AE, MC, V.

Red Clover Inn. Contemporary. The majestic views from this idyllic mountain setting on 13 acres, 5 mi west of Killington, might make you hesitate to forsake outdoor activities to go inside. Yet once settled in the candlelit colonial-style dining room with pine furniture, stenciled walls, and fireplace, you won't regret your decision. Try the Pheasant Ravioli, hand-rolled with wild mushroom pasta and served in a mushroom broth; Potato-Crusted Salmon; or Duck with a Ginger-Honey Glaze served with spaetzle. Homemade rolls and desserts. Wine cellar. No smoking. | 7 Woodward Rd., Mendon | 802/775–2290 or 800/752–0571 | Closed Easter–Memorial Day. No lunch | $18–$30 | D, MC, V.

Sugar House Café. American/Casual. Dine among electrically illuminated wall coverings, while gazing on the gorgeous Vermont peaks. Entrées include Angus steak and sun-dried tomato and basil ravioli. Reservations are recommended for dinner. | Killington Rd. | 802/422–4302 | Breakfast also available. Closed May–June and mid-Oct.–Nov. No lunch | $7–$19 | AE, D, DC, MC, V.

Vermont Inn. Continental. This cozy 1840s farmhouse, with warm wood tones, an original fieldstone fireplace, and linen-covered tables lit with oil lamps, has been a local favorite since the 1960s. You can enjoy spectacular mountain views from the greenhouse. Known for rack of lamb, salmon, and veal stuffed with spinach, shallots, Vermont bacon, and cheddar. Wine cellar. | Rte. 4 | 802/775–0708 or 800/541–7795 | www.vermontinn.com | Closed mid-Apr.–Memorial Day and Mon. No lunch | $25 | AE, MC, V.

Zola's Grille and Theodore's Tavern at the Cortina Inn. Contemporary. Overstuffed chairs, brass lamps, and flower-adorned tables offer optimum comfort after a day on the slopes. Excellent contemporary cuisine in Zola's Grille is punctuated with French and Mediterranean influences. Try the ever-popular fresh rainbow trout, pan-roasted and served with smoked shrimp and wild mushrooms, or the unique Antelope Chop with a Jack Daniels sauce served with maple corn bread. Theodore's Tavern, with its fireplace and adjoining billiard room, is an inviting stopover for burgers, sandwiches, soups, and salads. Sunday brunch. | 103 U.S. Rte. 4 E | 802/773–3333 or 800/451–6108 | No lunch | $11–$30 | D, MC, V.

Lodging

Cascades Lodge. This small hotel stands at 2,200 ft elevation. The views from here are terrific, and skiing is at the front door. Dining room, bar with entertainment, complimentary breakfast. No air-conditioning, in-room data ports, room service, cable TV, some in-room VCRs. Indoor pool. Hot tub. Exercise equipment. Video games. Business services. | 58 Old Mill Rd., Killington Village | 802/422–3731 or 800/345–0113 | fax 802/422–3351 | cascades@vermontel.com | www.cascadeslodge.com | 46 rooms | $139 weekdays, $199 weekends | AE, D, MC, V.

Comfort Inn Killington Centre. Gabled roofs give the six buildings of this inn the look of mountain chalets. Minikitchens, dining areas, and whirlpools are features of some rooms which can be joined into suites. Complimentary Continental breakfast. Some kitchenettes, some microwaves, some refrigerators, no smoking, cable TV. Pool. No pets. | Killington Rd. | 802/422–4222 or 800/257–8664 | fax 802/422–4226 | comfortk1@aol.com | www.comfortk1.com | 66 rooms | $125–$175 | AE, D, DC, MC, V.

Cortina Inn. A plush, full-service miniresort that is 10 minutes from Killington. Some rooms have fireplaces. Restaurant, bar with entertainment, picnic area, complimentary breakfast. In-room data ports, some refrigerators, room service, cable TV, some in-room VCRs. Indoor pool. Hot tub, massage. 8 tennis courts. Exercise equipment, hiking. Bicycles, ice-skating. Cross-country skiing, sleigh rides, snowmobiling. Playground. Business services. Airport shuttle. | 103 Rte. 4 | 802/773–3333 or 800/451–6108 | fax 802/775–6948 | cortina1@aol.com | www.cortinainn.com | 91 rooms, 6 suites | $109–$189, $209–$289 suites | AE, D, DC, MC, V.

Grey Bonnet Inn. A cozy little lodge on the quieter side of the Route 4–Route 100 intersection. Trails from the inn property connect to the Long Trail. Restaurant, bar. TV. 2 pools (1 indoor). Hot tub. Tennis. Exercise equipment. Cross-country skiing, downhill skiing. Playground. | 831 Rte. 100 | 802/775–2537 or 800/342–2086 | fax 802/775–3371 | www.greybonnetinn.com | 40 rooms | $59–$160 | Closed Apr.–mid-June, late Oct.–late Nov. | MAP | D, MC, V.

Inn at Long Trail. A 1938 rustic roadside lodge with massive boulders built into the walls. It has long been a favorite of the Killington–Pico ski crowd as well as Long Trail hikers. Restaurant, bar with entertainment, complimentary breakfast. Some room phones. Hiking. Cross-country skiing. | Rte. 4, at Sherburne Pass | 802/775–7181 or 800/325–2540 | fax 802/747–7034 | ilt@vermontel.net | www.innatlongtrail.com | 19 rooms | $89–$200 | Closed mid-Apr.–mid-June | MAP | AE, MC, V.

Inn of the Six Mountains. A big, deluxe inn convenient to Killington's wealth of recreational opportunities. It is popular with tours and there is complimentary ski area transportation. Dining room, bar, complimentary breakfast (winter only). In-room data ports, refrigerators, cable TV. Indoor/outdoor pool. Hot tub, massage. Tennis. Exercise equipment, hiking. Video games. Business services. | 2617 Killington Rd. | 802/422–4302, 800/228–4676 outside VT | fax 802/422–4321 | www.sixmountains.com | 103 rooms | $129–$189 | AE, D, DC, MC, V.

Killington Pico Motor Inn. A smaller, lower-key alternative to the larger Killington resorts, but still close to the slopes. Dining room, bar, complimentary breakfast. Refrigerators, cable TV. Pool. Hot tub. Video games. Business services. | 64 U.S. Rte. 4 | 802/773–4088 or 800/548–4713 | fax 802/775–9705 | www.killingtonpico.com or www.virtualvermont.com/hotel-motel/kpmotorinn | 29 rooms | $135 | AE, D, MC, V.

Killington Village Inn. A genuine New England inn with knotty pine paneling, a huge fieldstone fireplace, and a red clapboard exterior. The simple but comfortable rooms are complemented by the inn's cozy and inviting bar. Restaurant, bar, complimentary breakfast. No air-conditioning, no smoking, cable TV, no room phones. Hot tub. Video games. No pets. | Killington Rd. | 802/422–3301 or 800/451–4105 | fax 802/422–3971 | www.killingtonvillageinn.com | 20 rooms | $70–$120 | AE, D, DC, MC, V.

Mountain Sports Inn. This Austrian-style chalet provides clean, basic accommodations. Light-oak furniture with rose and lavender accents fill every room. Complementary Continental breakfast. No air-conditioning, no smoking, cable TV. Hot tub, sauna. Gym. No pets. | Killington Rd. | 802/422–3315 or 888/422–3315 | fax 802/422–8145 | info@mountainsportsinn.com | www.mountainsportsinn.com | 25 rooms | $58–$132 | AE, D, MC, V.

Peak Chalet. Close to Killington and Pico, but a world away from resort glitz—and, thankfully, a lot farther off the busy main roads than most of the larger establishments. Picnic area, complimentary Continental breakfast. No air-conditioning, no smoking, no room phones, TV in common area. Cross-country skiing. No kids under 12. | 184 S. View Path | 802/422–4278 | www.thepeakchalet.com | 4 rooms (shower only) | $85–$125 | AE, DC, MC, V.

Red Clover Inn. A mid-19th-century house-turned-inn on 13 acres. The restaurant has won a *Wine Spectator* award. The interior includes some antiques. Dining room. No smoking, some in-room hot tubs, some in-room VCRs, no TVs in some rooms, TV in common area. Pool. Library. No kids under 12. | 7 Woodward Rd., Mendon | 802/775–2290 or 800/752–0571 | fax 802/773–0594 | redclovr@vermontel.com | redcloverinn.com | 14 rooms | $215–$475 | D, MC, V.

Red Rob Inn. Relaxed, pleasant, and unpretentious are good descriptions of this classic hillside inn. Rooms are bright, done in a white and woodsy minimalist style, and most feature a balcony or deck. Restaurant, bar, complimentary breakfast. No air-conditioning, no smoking, cable TV. Indoor pool. Hot tub, sauna. Video games. Library. No pets. | 802/422–3303 or 800/451–4105 | info@redrob.com | www.redrob.com | 33 rooms | $75–$149 | AE, D, DC, MC, V.

Sherburne-Killington. A small inn with sublime mountain views, right at the crossroads of central Vermont ski country. Picnic area. Refrigerators, cable TV, in-room VCRs (and movies). Pool. Playground. | 1946 Rte. 4 | 802/773–9535 or 800/366–0493 | fax 802/773–0011 | 20 rooms | $120 | AE, D, MC, V.

Summit Lodge. Two friendly St. Bernards greet patrons of this cozy lodge where antiques mix with country-casual decor. There are formal and informal dining options. Some rooms have fireplaces. Dining room, bar. No air-conditioning, in-room VCRs (and movies). 2 pools. Hot tub, sauna, steam room. Tennis. Racquetball. Ice-skating. Video games. Library. Playground. Business services. Airport shuttle. | Killington Rd. | 802/422–3535 or 800/635–6343 | fax 802/422–3536 | summitlodge@killingtoninfo.com | www.summitlodgevermont.com | 45 rooms | $44–$179 | AE, DC, MC, V.

Tyrol Motor Inn. A small, independent motel, partway between Rutland and the Killington resort area, that is a reasonably priced family option. Picnic area, complimentary breakfast. No air-conditioning in some rooms, some refrigerators. Pool. Hot tub. Playground. | Rte. 4, Mendon | 802/773–7485 or 800/631–1019 | www.tyrolinn.com | 17 rooms | $48–$126 | AE, D, MC, V.

Val Roc. Another inexpensive option for overnight travelers who don't need one of the full-service resorts up on the mountain. Picnic area, complimentary Continental breakfast. No air-conditioning in some rooms, some kitchenettes, refrigerators, cable TV, some in-room VCRs. Pool. Hot tub. Tennis. Pets allowed. | 8006 Rte. 4 | 802/422–3881 or 800/238–8762 | www.valroc.com | 24 rooms | $59–$99 | AE, DC, MC, V.

Vermont Inn. This mid-19th-century inn has small but cheerful, charmingly refurbished rooms. It is on a 6-acre spread with fine mountain views and has a highly regarded restaurant. Bar, picnic area. No air-conditioning, no smoking, TV in common area. Pool. Hot tub, sauna. Tennis. Exercise equipment. Cross-country skiing, downhill skiing. No kids under 6. | 69 Rte. 4 | 802/775–0708 or 800/541–7795 | fax 802/773–2440 | www.vermontinn.com | 18 rooms | $140–$205 | AE, MC, V.

LONDONDERRY

(Nearby towns also listed: Grafton, Manchester, Manchester Center, Peru, Stratton Mountain, Weston)

Londonderry, a onetime mill town built along the banks of the West River, stands at the intersection of Vermont Routes 11 and 100. It is primarily a service center for nearby Stratton and Bromley ski areas.

Information: Londonderry Area Chamber of Commerce | Mountain Marketplace, Box 58, Londonderry, 05148 | 802/824–8178 | fax 802/824–5473 | www.londonderryvt.com.

ON THE CALENDAR

JULY: *Fourth of July Parade*. This Independence Day parade has live animals, cars, and street performers. From booths set up on either side of Main Street, vendors sell crafts, novelty items, and strawberry shortcake. | Main St. | 802/824–8178.

Dining

Frog's Leap Inn. Contemporary. This elegant colonial country inn 9 mi south of town is perched on a knoll of expansive lawn with beautiful views of Magic Mountain. French and Mediterranean influences enhance the dishes. For starters, try Stuffed Quail with Wild Elderberry Glaze, or the Crab and Goat Cheese Flan with Roasted Pepper Coulis. For entrées try the Home-Smoked Chamomile and Juniper Salmon or the veal medallions. Sunday brunch. No smoking. | Rte. 100 | 802/824–3019 or 877–FROGSLEAP | Reservations essential | Closed Mon.; closed Mon.–Wed. in Nov.–Mar. No lunch | $11–$29 | AE, MC, V.

Three Mountain Inn. Contemporary. Sit in one of two intimate dining rooms, warmed by fireplaces, and enjoy such entrées as the roasted Maine lobster, infused with a champagne-saffron butter sauce. The inn's cuisine, based in the classical French tradition, is complemented by many modern influences. | Rte. 30/Rte. 100, Jamaica | 802/874–4140 or 800/532–9399 | fax 802/874–4745 | threemtn@sover.net | www.threemountaininn.com | Closed Nov. and Tues. in Apr.–July | $20–$30 | AE, MC, V.

Three Clock Inn. Contemporary. This 200-year-old colonial exudes an unpretentious charm, decorated with antiques, art books, and potted plants. The menu reflects a French influence. For starters, try Frog Legs Provençal or Escargots Napolean. For main courses try Pistachio-Encrusted Seafood, rack of venison, or Squab Chicken with Portobello Mushrooms. No smoking. Guests may enjoy a cordial or coffee in the garden. Wine cellar. | Middletown Rd., South Londonderry | 802/824–6327 | www.threeclockinn.com | Closed 1st 3 wks Nov., late Apr.–mid-May, and Mon. No lunch | $18–$24 | AE, MC, V.

Lodging

Blue Gentian. A small alpine lodge in the heart of southern Vermont ski country. You can relax in the lounge with a fireplace. Complimentary breakfast. No air-conditioning, no smoking, cable TV, no room phones. Pool. Hot tub. Business services. | 29 Magic Mountain Rd. | 802/824–5908 or 800/456–2405 | fax 802/824–3531 | www.bluegentian.com | 13 rooms (2 with shower only) | $50–$85 | MC, V.

Dostal's. A family-friendly lodge with Austrian ambience, 3 mi east of Londonderry, that is convenient to skiing and Weston and Manchester attractions. Restaurant, bar. No air-conditioning in some rooms, cable TV. 2 pools (1 indoor). 2 hot tubs. Tennis. Video games. | Magic Mountain Rd. | 802/824–6700 or 800/255–5373 | fax 802/824–6701 | www.dostals.com | 50 rooms | $69–$139 | Closed mid-Mar.–mid June and mid-Oct.–mid-Dec. | AE, D, MC, V.

Frog's Leap Inn. A mid-19th-century colonial farmhouse on 32 acres between Londonderry and Weston. Dining room, complimentary Continental breakfast. No air-conditioning, cable TV in common area, no room phones. Pool. Tennis. Cross-country skiing, downhill skiing. | Rte. 100 | 802/824–3019 | fax 802/824–3657 | www.frogsleapinn.com | 17 rooms (2 with shared bath), 4 suites | $120–$215 | AE, MC, V.

Inn at Three Ponds. The rooms of this colonial-style inn have pine paneling and beautiful hardwood furniture. The large garden, three ponds, and three common areas are good for relaxing and lounging. A garden house at one end of the property offers a spectacular view of the ponds and the mountains. Complimentary breakfast. No smoking. Pond. Library. No pets. | Rte. 11 E | 802/824–9416 | inn3ponds@aol.com | www.innatthreeponds.com | 4 rooms | $100–$185 | AE, MC, V.

Londonderry Inn. A rambling 1826 farmhouse on a hillside above the West River in South Londonderry. You can relax over billiards in the tavern. Dining room, complimentary breakfast. No room phones, TV in common area. Pool. Cross-country skiing, downhill skiing. Business services. | Rte. 100, S. Londonderry | 802/824–5226 | fax 802/824–3146 | www.londonderryinn.com | 25 rooms (5 with shared bath) | $41–$116 | No credit cards.

Magic View Motel. This alpine-style motel has rooms with knotty pine paneling, wall-to-wall carpeting, and scenic views of Magic Mountain. A complimentary breakfast is offered during peak periods, including foliage season, ski season, hunting season, and summer weekends. No air-conditioning, refrigerators, no smoking, cable TV, no room phones. No pets. | Rte. 11 | 802/824–3793 | fax 802/824–3794 | magicview@tds.net | members.aol.com/magikview/index.htm | 18 rooms, 1 apartment | $79–$85 | MC, V.

Snowdon. A clean, inexpensive motel, 1½ mi east of Londonderry, where French, German, and Dutch are spoken (along with English). The motel is steps from golf, tennis, hiking, and skiing. Restaurant, picnic area. Cable TV. Business services. | Rte. 11 | 802/824–6047 or 800/419–7600 | fax 802/824–6047 | 12 rooms | $50–$85 | No credit cards.

Swiss Inn and Restaurant. Country-inn charm in a motel package 1½ mi west of Londonderry. The restaurant has Swiss specialties. Restaurant, bar, complimentary breakfast. Cable TV. Pool. Tennis. Cross-country skiing, downhill skiing. Playground. | Rte. 11 | 802/824–3442 or 800/847–9477 | fax 802/824–6313 | www.swissinn.com | 20 rooms | $54–$99 | AE, MC, V.

Three Mountain Inn. Built in the 1780s as part of a farm, this country inn 9 mi south of Londonderry boasts five fireplaces, two beehive ovens, period furniture, and wide-planked walls. There are captivating views of the Green Mountains and the surrounding woods and it is less than ½ mi to Jamaica State Park. Some rooms have fireplaces while others have their own private decks. Restaurant, complimentary breakfast. No smoking, in-room hot tubs, some in-room VCRs, no TV in some rooms. Pool. Library. No kids under 12. | Rte. 30, also Rte. 100, Jamaica | 802/874–4140 or 800/532–9399 | fax 802/874–4745 | threemtn@sover.net | www.threemountaininn.com | 14 rooms, 1 cottage | $125–$295 | AE, MC, V.

LUDLOW

MAP 11, D9

(Nearby towns also listed: Springfield, Weston)

Ludlow has transformed itself from a factory town with a ski area nearby into a ski town that used to have a factory—the rambling, onetime General Electric aircraft parts plant downtown is now honeycombed with restaurants and boutiques. The ski area is Okemo, just north of town.

Information: **Ludlow Area Chamber of Commerce** | Box 333, Okemo Marketplace Clocktower, Ludlow, 05149 | 802/228–5830 | fax 802/228–7642 | www.vacationinvermont.com.

Attractions

Crowley Cheese Factory. America's oldest operating cheese factory (1882) turns out its delicious sharp cheddar the old-fashioned way, in small batches. | Healdville Rd. | 802/259–

2340 | www.crowleycheesefactory.com | Free | Weekdays 8–4; call ahead for best time to view cheese making. Store open daily 10–5.

Okemo Mountain Ski Area. Okemo, 1 mi north of Ludlow, is a family-oriented resort with ample gentle terrain, but plenty of challenges for experienced skiers and boarders. | 77 Okemo Ridge Rd., Ludlow | 802/228–4041 or 800/78–OKEMO | fax 802/228–4558 | www.okemo.com | Call for rates and package information | Call for information for summer and winter schedules.

Okemo State Forest. Straddling the towns of Ludlow and Mount Holly, this 4,461-acre protected woodland is adjacent to Okemo Mountain ski area. A foot trail leads to the summit of 3,343-ft Okemo Mountain, with views reaching across Vermont, New York, Massachusetts, and New Hampshire. | Vermont Department of Forests, Parks, and Recreation, 103 S. Main St., Building 10S, Waterbury | 802/241–3650 | www.vtstatepars.com | Call for package and info | Mid-May–mid Oct.

ON THE CALENDAR
MAY: *Great River Century Ride.* A 25-, 50-, or 100-mi bicycle ride. | Starts at Cavendish Point Hotel, Proctorsville, 3 mi from Ludlow on Rte. 103 | 802/228–2722 | $20.

Dining
Brick House. Contemporary. This recent addition to Ludlow's culinary scene is in a historic 1835 brick Federal home 1 mi south of town. Good casual dining for hungry skiers, with a menu of Thai dishes and nightly specials along with the usual steaks, chops, and seafood. | Rte. 103 | 802/228–4249 | No lunch | $10–$22 | MC, V.

Cappuccino's. Italian. This charming and unpretentious trattoria, just off Ludlow's main drag, has inviting hoop-backed chairs, candlelit tables with flowers, and tasteful artwork. The moderately priced menu includes imported pastas and a nice selection of fresh seafood, beef, and chicken. Save room for one of their luscious desserts. | 41 Depot St. | 802/228–7566 | Closed Mon.–Tues. No lunch | $11–$21 | MC, V.

DJ's Restaurant. American. Main Street's best bargain. Families in ski clothes and with big appetites will feel welcome. It is known for prime rib and yummy chicken—fried or roasted, with french fries or mashed potatoes. | 146 Main St. | 802/228–5374 | No lunch | $10–$20 | MC, V.

Echo Lake Inn. Contemporary. A regal survivor of the Victorian-era lakeside resort, this four-story white clapboard inn 6 mi north of Ludlow has exposed beams that enhance the dining room's chic/rustic decor. An excellent selection of wines complements the varied cuisine of lamb, beef, veal, game, pastas, and fresh seafood—all with a graceful mingling of Yankee authenticity and European flair. | Rte. 100, Tyson | 802/228–8602 or 800/356–6844 | Closed mid-Oct.–late Nov., Apr.–mid-May. No lunch | $17–$23 | AE, MC, V.

Governor's Inn. Contemporary. In a late Victorian house with period ambience. Try the scallops in brandy sauce or veal in cabernet sauce. Only 1 dinner seating at 7. No smoking. | 86 Main St. | 802/228–8830 | Reservations essential | Closed Mon.–Tues. | $50 prix fixe | MC, V.

Harry's Café. Eclectic. With casual wooden booths and local artwork (most of which was donated by grateful customers), Harry's is the kind of eatery you just can't help falling in love with. The globe-trotting menu runs the gamut from Thai to Mexican, European to Middle Eastern. You can feast on duck that is crisp and juicy, or sample the fish-and-chips. Better, however, to venture forth into more interesting territory, such as grilled jerk scallops, Ravioli Diablo, lamb-watercress-scallion lo mein, Thai red curry, or their famous version of Pad Thai. It is 5 mi north of Ludlow. Kids' menu. No smoking. | On Rte. 103 | 802/259–2996 | Reservations essential on weekends in winter | Closed Mon.–Tues. No lunch | $6–$20 | AE, MC, V.

Nikki's. Contemporary. Each of the three dining rooms has its own distinctive feel, with stained glass, brick fireplaces, or a cozy table in the wood-paneled wine cellar. For starters try the salad of bib and red oak leaf lettuces topped with panfried leeks and Asiago cheese.

For entrées, don't miss the famous steak au poivre, which is drenched in black peppercorns and finished with a Grand Marnier reduction. Save enough room to at least look at the magnificent dessert tray. No smoking. | 44 Pond St. (Rte. 103) | 802/228–7797 | No lunch | $16–$40 | AE, DC, MC, V.

Sweet Brier Tavern. American/Casual. Farm implements and other country antiques ornament the dining room of the Cavendish Pointe Hotel. The smoked salmon and mixed seafood fra diavolo are both very popular. Kids' menu. | Rte. 103, Cavendish | 802/226–7688 or 800/438–7908 | Breakfast also available. Closed May. No lunch | $15 | AE, D, MC, V.

Wicked Good Pizza. Pizza. This New York–style pizza is, indeed, wicked good. And they serve slices! Delicious subs, salads, pastas, and calzones complete the menu. For pizzas try the Green Mountain Pesto or Wicked Good White. Roadkill is the meat-lover's pie and Loaded for Bear has everything. Or stay relatively fit with the Vermont Veggie. | 117 Main St. | 802/228–4131 | $6–$20 | No credit cards.

Lodging

Andrie Rose. Luxury suites with fireplaces are a welcome feature at this 1829 inn at the base of Okemo Mountain. Dining room, picnic area, complimentary breakfast. No air-conditioning in some rooms, some refrigerators, no smoking, cable TV, some in-room VCRs, some room phones. Business services. | 13 Pleasant St. | 802/228–4846 or 800/223–4846 | fax 802/228–7910 | andrierose@aol.com | www.andrieroseinn.com | 21 rooms, 9 suites | $120–$195, $280–$305 suites | AE, D, MC, V.

Cavendish Pointe Hotel. This hotel, 2½ mi east of Ludlow, has a living room with a two-story fireplace and numerous antiques. The indoor pool provides a source of relaxation year-round. Rooms have views of the lovely Okemo Mountain. Restaurant, bar. Refrigerators, no smoking, cable TV. Hiking. Cross-country skiing. Video games. Business services. Pets allowed. | Rte. 103, Cavendish | 802/226–7688 or 800/438–7908 | cavpnt@ludl.tds.net | www.okemo-cavendishpointe.com/contact.html | 70 rooms | $108–$199 | AE, D, MC, V.

Combes Family Inn. This 1850 farmhouse anchors 50 acres of woods and fields 4 mi north of Ludlow. As its name implies, the lodging has a homey feel, from the country antiques right down to the home-cooked meals. Three of the rooms are large enough to accommodate families. Dining room, picnic area, complimentary breakfast. No air-conditioning in some rooms, room service, no room phones, TV in common area. Cross-country skiing. Pets allowed. | 953 E. Lake Rd. | 802/228–8799 or 800/822–8799 | billcfi@ludl.tds.net | www.combesfamilyinn.com | 11 rooms | $60–$134 | AE, D, MC, V.

Echo Lake Inn. A Victorian inn, 5 mi north of Ludlow, that has the feel of an old-time resort hotel, because it was one, built in 1840 and now handsomely restored. There is a lake just across the road. Guests may make use of the canoes and rowboat available at the hotel. Dining room, bar, picnic area. Room service, some in-room hot tubs, cable TV in common area, no TV in some rooms. Pool, wading pool. Hot tub, steam room. Dock, boating. Business services. | Rte. 100, Tyson | 802/228–8602 or 800/356–6844 | fax 802/228–3075 | www.echolakeinn.com | 23 rooms, 2 suites, 7 apartments | $119–$199, $269–$329 suites, $270–$305 apartments | AE, D, MC, V.

Golden Stage Inn. Comfortable lodging in a onetime stagecoach stop 3 mi south of Ludlow. Dining room. No smoking. Pool. | 399 Depot St., Proctorsville | 802/226–7744 or 800/253–8226 | fax 802/226–7882 | goldenstageinn@tds.net | www.goldenstageinn.com | 10 rooms (2 with shared bath) | $89–$110 | D, MC, V.

Governor's. An elegant Victorian summer home of a former Vermont governor, with lovely period furnishings. Dining room. No smoking, no room phones. No kids. | 86 Main St. | 802/228–8830 | fax 802/228–2961 | www.thegovernorsinn.com | 8 rooms, 1 suite | $145–$195, $235–$265 suites | MC, V.

Okemo Inn. Sitting atop a hill 1 mi south of Ludlow, this country inn has scenic views of the valley below and its environs. The inn, built in 1810, has wood paneling, three common areas with fireplaces, and a wide front porch. Complimentary breakfast. No air-conditioning, no smoking, no room phones, TV in common area. Pool. Sauna. No kids under 6. No pets. | 61 Locust Hill Rd. | 802/228–8834 or 800/328–8834 | okemoinn@tds.net | www.oke-moinn.com | 10 rooms | $150 | AE, MC, V.

Okemo Mountain Lodge. Stay slopeside in this hotel and apartments. Downtown Ludlow is just a three-minute drive. Most apartments have fireplaces. Restaurant, bar. Kitchenettes, cable TV, some in-room VCRs. Cross-country skiing, downhill skiing. | 77 Okemo Ridge Rd. | 802/228–5571 or 800/786–5366 | fax 802/228–2079 | info@okemo.com | www.okemo.com | 184 condominiums | $370–$995 | AE, MC, V.

LYNDONVILLE

(Nearby town also listed: St. Johnsbury)

Lyndonville, a blue-collar town 8 mi north of St. Johnsbury, is the home of two distinctive institutions. One is the Dairy Association, manufacturers of the soothing salve called Bag Balm (meant for cows' udders, it's now a popular unguent for humans). The other is Lyndon State College, which has one of America's best meteorology programs—fitting, given the extremes of weather this part of the world receives.

Information: Lyndon Area Chamber of Commerce | Box 886, 51 Depot St., Lyndonville, 05851 | 802/626–9696 | fax 802/626–1167 | www.lyndonvermont.com.

Attractions

Burke Mountain Ski Area. Many U.S. Olympians have trained at this small but challenging area in Darling State Park. | In East Burke village | 802/626–3305 or 800/541–5480 | www.burkemountain.com.

Lake Willoughby. Five miles long by 1 mi wide and nestled between steep mountains, this deep northern lake (18 mi north of Lyndonville) looks like a landlocked fjord—and harbors monster lake trout. | Rte. 5A | 802/626–9696 | Daily.

Lyndonville Covered Bridges. Lyndonville is the proud home to five covered bridges, the highest concentration in Vermont. You can take a walking tour of all five bridges by first picking up a guidebook at the White Market, located on Depot Street. The guidebook gives the location of each bridge and a brief history. | Depot St. | 802/626–5339.

ON THE CALENDAR

JULY: *Stars and Stripes.* In the third week of July, Lyndonville hosts the Stars and Sripes celebration. The festival includes a parade, a craft show, a road race, a street dance, and a country breakfast. | On the Green | 802/626–9696.

Dining

Old Cutter Inn. Continental. The dining room of this inn, 7 mi northeast of Lyndonville, serves dishes such as roasted Long Island duck à l'orange and Swiss specialties like Rahm-schnitzel. The windows afford a spectacular view of the sunset across Willougby Gap. | 143 Pinkham Rd., East Burke | 802/626–5152 | www.pbpub.com/cutter.htm | Closed Apr., Nov., and Wed. No lunch | $16–$25 | D, MC, V.

River Garden Café. American/Casual. You can always eat outdoors on the café's enclosed porch, which overlooks a perennial garden. A wide range of entrées are available, from roasted rack of lamb to fresh fish. | Rte. 114, East Burke | 802/626–3514 | Closed Nov. and Mon. | $10–$20 | AE, D, MC, V.

The Tack Room. American/Casual. This restaurant in the Old Cutter Inn, 7 mi northeast of town, caters to the whole family, serving dishes like specialty burgers, cheese fondue, and mushroom toast. A kids' menu is also available. | 143 Pinkham Rd., East Burke | 802/626–5152 | www.pbpub.com/cutter.htm | Closed Apr., Nov., and Wed. No lunch | $5–$14 | D, MC, V.

Wildflower Inn. Contemporary. 1 mi north of Lydonville. A rambling complex of old farm buildings set on 500 acres. Homemade breads and vegetables from the inn's garden complement the country-style entrées. | Darling Hill Rd. | 802/626–8310 | Closed Apr., late Oct.–late Nov. | $14–$20 | MC, V.

Willough Vale Inn and Restaurant. American/Casual. In the main building of the inn and overlooking Lake Willoughby, 16 mi north of town, this relaxed dining spot has a wide range of different entrées, including vegetarian, and seafood dishes. Try the Willough Vale Chicken, stuffed with cabbage and aged cheddar, served with an apple cider sauce. Reservations are recommended. | Rte. 5A, Westmore | 802/525–4123 or 800/594–9102 | fax 802/525–4514 | info@willoughvale.com | www.willoughvale.com | Closed Sun.–Thurs. in May–June; Sun.–Mon. June–foliage season | $12–$20 | AE, MC, V.

Lodging

Branch Brook Bed-and-Breakfast. Built in the 1850s, this property is beautifully landscaped and overlooks a wandering brook. The B&B is near hiking and biking trails, as well as lakes and rivers. Complimentary breakfast. No air-conditioning, no smoking, no TV. No pets. | S. Wheelock Rd., Lyndon | 802/626–8316 or 800/572–7712 | fax 802/626–5722 | 5 rooms (2 with shared bath) | $65–$85 | MC, V.

Days Inn. A reasonably priced chain hotel just a short hop off Interstate 91 and near St. Johnsbury's attractions and Burke Mountain and Northeast Kingdom lakes. Complimentary Continental breakfast. Cable TV. | 28 Backcenter Rd. | 802/626–9316 | fax 802/626–1023 | 40 rooms | $50–$70 | AE, D, DC, MC, V.

Fox Hall. Sitting on 80 acres of land at the northwestern corner of Lake Willoughby, the second-story rooms in this bed-and-breakfast have views of the lake and mountains. Built in the 1890s as a summerhouse, the building has beautiful wood floors and paneling. Photographs, paintings, and sculptures of moose, the Northeast Kingdom's largest land animal, fill all the rooms. Complimentary breakfast. No air-conditioning, no smoking, no room phones, TV in common area. Lake. Dock, water sports, boating. Fishing. Cross-country skiing. No kids under 8. No pets. | 145 Fox Hall La. | 802/525–6930 | fax 802/525–1185 | spyden@sover.net | www.scenesofvermont.com/foxhall/ | 9 rooms | $79–$109 | MC, D, V.

Old Cutter Inn. A Swiss chef runs this inn 7 mi northeast of town with one of the Northeast Kingdom's most esteemed kitchens in an old farmhouse. Dining room, picnic area. No smoking, no TV in rooms, TV in common area. Pool. Cross-country skiing. Pets allowed. | 143 Pinkham Rd. | 802/626–5152 | fax 802/626–5152 | www.pub.com/cutter.htm | 9 rooms, 1 suite | $56–$70, $96–$150 suite | Closed Apr., Nov. | MAP | MC, V.

Wildflower. A 500-acre farm with sledding and great views, kids love the animals. The rooms are beautifully designed with hand-stenciled walls and country quilts with four-poster beds. Kids will love the teddy bear pancakes. Dining room, complimentary breakfast. No air-conditioning, kitchenettes in suites, no smoking, no room phones, no TV in rooms, TV in common room. Pool, wading pool. Hot tub, sauna. Tennis. Sleigh rides. Batting cages, basketball court. Children's programs (ages 3–12). Business services. | 2059 Darling Hill Rd. | 802/626–8310 or 800/627–8310 | fax 802/626–3039 | www.wildflowerinn.com | 22 rooms in 4 buildings, 11 suites | $125–$230 | Closed 2 wks in Apr. and Nov. | MC, V.

Willough Vale Inn. In an incomparable location at the northern end of Lake Willoughby (16 mi north of Lyndonville), this inn's big wraparound veranda invites lounging. The best inn rooms are in front and the rear suite lacks a view. All of the cottages are directly on the lake. Restaurant, bar. No air-conditioning in some rooms, some kitchenettes. | 793 Orleans Vermont, Rte. 5A, Westmore | 802/525–4123 or 800/594–9102 | fax 802/525–4514 | grnmtinn@aol.com | www.willoughvale.com | 8 rooms, 4 cottages | $69–$139, $189–$205 cottages; $1,295–$1,400 weekly rates for cottages | AE, MC, V | Closed Apr. and Nov.

MANCHESTER AND MANCHESTER CENTER

MAP 11, C10

(Nearby towns also listed: Arlington, Bennington, Dorset, Londonderry, Peru, Stratton Mountain)

Manchester, a favored summer retreat for well over a century, has reinvented itself over the past two decades. Manchester Center, which had been little more than a crossroads town with business catering to locals and visitors to Bromley and Stratton Mountain ski areas, courted a score or more of upscale designer discount outlets, making old-time residents grumble that the intersection of Routes 7 and 11 had become "Malfunction Junction." Just a couple of miles to the south, though, tranquil Manchester Village became even more so, when traffic was rerouted onto a new, limited-access Route 7. The tone here is set by the elegant, colonnaded Equinox hotel, and by Robert Todd Lincoln's gracious Hildene estate.

Information: Manchester and the Mountains Regional Chamber of Commerce | 5046 Main St., Manchester Center, 05255 | 802/362–2100 | fax 802/362–3451 | www.manchestervermont.net.

Attractions

American Museum of Fly-Fishing. Just up the road from the Battenkill River and the home of Orvis rods, the museum houses early tackle, some belonging to famous anglers. | 3657 Main St. | 802/362–3300 | www.amff.com | $3 | Daily 10–4.

Charles F. Orvis Co. A mecca for fly anglers and the manufacturer of exquisite rods made from graphite, fiberglass, and traditional bamboo. This store also has a complete line of sporting equipment and country clothing. You can also find stocked practice ponds and courses in fly-fishing and upland game shooting. | Historic Rte. 7A, Manchester | 802/362–3750 or 800/541–3541 | www.orvis.com | Free | Daily 8–6.

Emerald Lake State Park. Tucked right alongside Route 7 6 mi north of Manchester, with a nice swimming beach and wooded campsites. | U.S. 7, North Dorset | 802/362–1655 or 802/483–2001 | www.vtstateparks.com | $2 | Daily 10–9.

Equinox Sky Line Drive. One of New England's most exhilarating auto roads, 5 mi south of Manchester, leads to the summit of Mount Equinox with a small inn, foot trails, and views reaching way into Massachusetts and New York State. | Historic Rte. 7A | 802/362–1114 | $6 per car and driver | May 1–Oct. 31, daily.

Factory outlet stores. Manchester has become an outpost of designer apparel at bargain prices—look for Ralph Lauren, Armani, Cole-Han, Brooks Brothers, and many more. | Rtes. 11 and 30.

Historic Hildene. Robert Todd Lincoln, son of the president, built this stately summer mansion 2 mi south of downtown Manchester in 1902. There's a 1,000-pipe organ, a spectacular formal garden, and cross-country ski trails in winter. | Historic Rte. 7A | 802/362–1788 | www.hildene.org | $8 | May–Oct., daily 9:30–4.

Merck Forest and Farmland Center. This 2,800-acre, privately owned forest 10 mi northwest of Manchester has foot trails, organic farming and—in spring—a maple sugar-making operation. | Box 86, Rupert | 802/394–7836 | www.merckforest.org | Free | Daily dawn–dusk.

Southern Vermont Art Center. A rambling Georgian Revival former summer home 1 mi north of Manchester, offering a changing series of exhibitions of painting, graphics, and photography. Sculptures punctuate the rolling lawns. | West Rd. | 802/362–1405 | www.svac.org | $5 | Mid-May–Oct., Tues.–Sat. 10–5, Sun. noon–5; Dec.–Mar., Mon.–Sat. 10–5.

Tilting at Windmills Gallery. One of the area's largest collections, this gallery features a variety of works by established national and international artists, such as Andrew Wyeth and Marcel Favreau. | Rte. 11/30, Manchester Center | 802/362–3022 | fax 802/362–3550 | tilting@sover.net | www.tilting.com | Mon.–Sat. 10–5, Sun. 10–4.

ON THE CALENDAR

JULY–AUG.: *Manchester Music Festival.* The MMF sponsors a summer concert series in July and August at the Southern Vermont Arts Center as well as numerous other chamber music concerts throughout the year. | Manchester West Rd. | 802/362–1956 or 800/639–5868 | fax 802/362–0711 | mmf@vermontel.net | www.mmfvt.org | $15–$25.

Dining

Bistro Henry. Contemporary. The modest facade belies the quality of this restaurant's cuisine, one of the finest in southern Vermont. Try the daily risotto, rare grilled tuna, or merlot-braised lamb. No smoking. | Rte. 11/30, Manchester Center | 802/362–498 | Closed late Nov.–mid-Dec., mid-Apr.–mid-May, and Mon. No lunch | $16–$30 | AE, MC, V.

The Black Swan. Contemporary. This restaurant in a 19th-century brick colonial house serves fresh fish, game, beef, and pasta. The desserts are all homemade. | Rte. 7A, Manchester | 802/362–3807 | www.blackswanrestaurant.com | Closed Tues. and Wed. in Nov.–May, Wed. in June–Oct. | $15–$26 | AE, MC, V.

The Buttery. Contemporary. The restaurant is on the top floor of the Jelly Mill & Friends complex, so you need to be careful on the way up if you're an obsessive shopper. Fabulous sandwiches, homemade soups, and fresh salads make for an interesting mélange of inter-

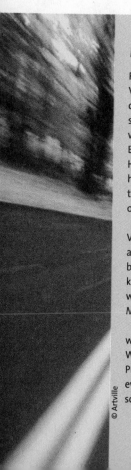

© Artville

MANCHESTER–WESTON AREA

Few regions offer as complete a sampling of the modern and traditional essence of Vermont as the area around Manchester, Londonderry, and Weston, in the south-central part of the state. Manchester has something of a dual personality. Its southerly portion, Manchester Village, maintains the resort feel of a century ago, with fly-fishing along the Battenkill, afternoons on the veranda of the stately old Equinox hotel, and strolls in the gardens surrounding Robert Todd Lincoln's estate, Hildene. But just up the road, Manchester Center is another world, a bargain-hunter's bonanza with a score of designer clothing outlets. After shopping, a visit to the Southern Vermont Art Center can provide a more contemplative moment—or perhaps an even heftier expenditure, if contemplation leads to purchase.

Just a few miles outside of town—via a long uphill drive—is Bromley, one of Vermont's oldest ski resorts. Still favored for its gentle, southward slopes, Bromley also offers summer fun on its exhilarating alpine slide. The nearby village of Peru boasts another popular summer spot, Hapgood Pond, with campsites and a sandy, kid-friendly beach. Peru is also a gateway to the Long Trail, Vermont's premier wilderness footpath, and to the 14-mi Mt. Tabor auto road through the Green Mountain National Forest.

Weston was one of the first Vermont hamlets to promote itself just for what it was—a picture-book village set serenely around a classic Yankee common. Weston's allure has been enhanced by its respected summer theater, the Weston Playhouse, and by the Vermont Country Store, an old-time emporium that sells everything your New Englander great-grandparents could have wanted, and then some.

national delights. Try the gourmet chili with sour cream, avocado, and red onion. | Rte. 7A | 802/362–3544 | Breakfast also available. No lunch | $4–$9 | AE, D, DC, MC, V.

Candeleros. Mexican. The attractive rough-wood and tile decor makes you feel as though you're in an upscale Mexican cantina. There are excellent salads, grilled chicken, and fish choices as well as great margaritas—the restaurant has over two dozen tequilas on hand. Open-air dining at tables overlooking town. Kids' menu. No smoking. | Rte. 7A, Manchester Center | 802/362–0836 | Closed Nov.–mid-May. No lunch Mon.–Thurs. | $10–$18 | DC, MC, V.

Garlic John's. Italian. This dependable Italian cuisine features enough pasta entrées and generous portions to suit any hungry après-ski family. Good seafood, chicken, veal, and beef. Kids' menu. No smoking. | Rte. 11/30, Manchester Center | 802/362–9843 | No lunch | $8–$20 | AE, MC, V.

Equinox. Continental. The recently restored 200-year-old Equinox Hotel presides over Manchester Village like a benevolent Queen Mum, with its white colonnaded facade and marble sidewalks. The traditional New England fare is dependably good, but not superb. You can dine on sirloin, lobster, turkey, and salmon in the casual Tavern or the more formal Colonnade. No smoking. | 3567 Main St. | 802/362–4700 or 800/362–4747 | Breakfast also available | $28–$35 | AE, MC, V.

Laney's. American/Casual. A great family environment where the kids won't be bored and the parents won't leave broke. Memorabilia abounds here and each dish has been given a handle from a famous movie *Cactus Flower*—garden salad; *Gone with the Wind*—rib sampler with chicken; *Oliver Twist*—pasta primavera; and the ever-popular *Adam's Ribs*—yes, you guessed it, a rack of baby backs. No smoking. | Rte. 11/30, Manchester Center | 802/362–4456 | Closed Mon.–Tues. No lunch | $10–$16 | AE, D, MC, V.

Little Rooster. Contemporary. A quaint European-style eatery with blue-checkered tablecloths that has creative luncheon specials and baguette sandwiches. Try the baked Portobello mushroom with goat cheese Brie and artichoke-tomato sauce, the delicious waffles, or a designer omelet. No smoking. | Rte. 7A, Manchester | 802/362–3496 | Breakfast also available. Closed late Nov. and late Apr. No dinner | $7–$9 | No credit cards.

Mark Anthony's Ye Olde Tavern. American. The wide floorboards creak in this vintage spot ½ mi north of Manchester and you can't help but feeling as though you have to duck as you walk beneath the exposed beams. Traditional Yankee food is on the menu for dinner, with more casual fare at lunch. Try blackened cider-glazed ham, the filet mignon with béarnaise sauce, or the pork with Cajun cream sauce. No smoking. | U.S. 7 N/Main St. | 802/362–0611 or 800/450–1790 | $13–$27 | AE, DC, MC, V.

Mt. Tabor Inn and Tavern. American. This tavern, 10 mi north of Manchester, was originally a barn. It has a fireplace, wood floors, and a post-and-beam construction. The menu has traditional fare such as steaks, burgers, and seasonal seafood specials. During summer and peak seasons, the tavern serves breakfast and lunch daily. | Rte. 7, Mt. Tabor | 802/293–5907 or 877/658–2267 | mttaborinn@aol.com | www.mttaborinn.com | $8–$20 | AE, D, DC, MC, V.

Mulligan's. American/Casual. Here's a place where you'll feel right at home with a brew and the sports section. The tavern has a big-screen TV as well as a couple of additional TV sets over the substantial wood and brass-railed bar. The main dining rooms are comfortable and less sports-minded than the tavern. Standard American fare of steaks, chops, seafood, and pasta is surprisingly good for a restaurant that serves so many different choices. | Rte. 7A | 802/362–3663 | $10–$21 | AE, MC, V.

The Perfect Wife. Contemporary. This restaurant and tavern in an old colonial home are surrounded by gardens and lawns. The creative cuisine has Cajun and Pacific Rim influences. In the tavern, try jerk chicken sandwich and deep-fried Cajun crawfish. In the dining room, the sesame-crusted yellowfin tuna, sautéed crab cakes, and pepper-seared filet mignon are popular favorites. | 2594 Depot St. | 802/362–2817 | www.perfectwife.com | Closed Mon. | Tavern $6–$12, dining room $12–$20 | MC, V.

MANCHESTER AND
MANCHESTER
CENTER

INTRO
ATTRACTIONS
DINING
LODGING

Reluctant Panther. Continental. Don't be put off by the purple facade and yellow shutters: this is one of the best country inns in Vermont and the cuisine is superb, an elegant fusion of Swiss and European fare with modern American variations. Try the chilled mussels with a jalapeño-lime salsa, raclette, Port-Wine-Braised Lamb Shank over Creamy Garlic-Parmesan Polenta, or Arctic Char in Potato Crust over Watercress Vichyssoise. Wine cellar. No smoking. | 39 West Rd. | 802/362–2568 or 800/822–2331 | No lunch | $22–$26 | AE, D, DC, MC, V.

Sirloin Saloon. Steak. This full-service steak house in a former mill serves consistently good, traditional American cuisine. Salad bar. Kids' menu. No smoking. | At Rte. 11/Rte. 30 | 802/362–2600 | No lunch | $15–$25 | AE, D, DC, MC, V.

Village Country Inn. French. Candlelight and white trellises make the Rose Room a perfect place for a romantic dinner. Try the sautéed New England venison scaloppine with a bourbon shallot glaze. | 3835 Main St., Manchester | 802/362–1792 or 800/370–0300 | fax 802/362–7238 | www.villagecountryinn.com | $12–$26 | AE, D, MC, V.

Wilburton Inn. Continental. Formerly a billiard room, the inn's dining room has wood paneling, a fireplace, and elegant table settings. All the breads are baked on the premises and nicely complement the food, including the mahi tuna with sesame seeds, served with wasabi and an Asian barbecue sauce. | River Rd., Manchester Village | 802/362–2500 or 800/648–4944 | fax 802/362–1107 | www.wilburton.com | $23–$27 | AE, D, MC, V.

Lodging

Aspen. Inexpensive little motel and cottage that has been run by the same family for 24 years, just north of Manchester Center. Picnic area. Refrigerators available, cable TV. Pool. | Rte. 7A N | 802/362–2450 | fax 802/362–1348 | www.thisisvermont.com/aspen | 24 rooms, 1 cottage with fireplace | $75–$105 | AE, D, MC, V.

Barnstead Innstead. Stay in this early-19th-century reddish hay barn, just two blocks from the Manchester shopping whirl. No smoking, cable TV. Pool. Skiing. | Rte. 30 | 802/362–1619 | www.barnsteadinn.com | 14 rooms | $95–$150 | MC, V.

Battenkill Inn. A high-ceilinged, tall-windowed yellow-clapboard Victorian 3 mi south of Manchester on the banks of the eponymous trout stream. Complimentary breakfast. No room phones. Cross-country skiing. | 6342 Rte. 7A, Sunderland | 802/362–4213 or 800/441–1628 | fax 802/362–0975 | www.battenkillinn.com | 11 rooms | $100–$165 | AE, DC, MC, V.

Brittany Motel. A tidy, little, independently owned motel at the base of Mt. Equinox. Picnic area. Refrigerators, cable TV. | 1056 Main St. (Rte. 7A), Manchester Center | 802/362–1033 | fax 802/362–0551 | www.thisisvermont.com/brittany | 12 rooms | $68–$83 | AE, D, MC, V.

The Chalet Motel. The rooms in this motel 1 mi from downtown Manchester are clean and comfortable with many modern amenities. Restaurant. Refrigerators, no smoking, cable TV. No pets. | 1875 Depot St., Manchester Center | 802/362–1622 or 800/343–9900 | fax 802/362–1753 | chalet@sover.net | www.thechaletmotel.com | 43 rooms | $100–$120 | AE, D, DC, V, MC.

1811 House. Light a fire in the fireplace or sink into a high four-poster bed with a canopy overhead in this vintage charmer next to a golf course. Bar, complimentary breakfast. Cross-country skiing, downhill skiing. Library. No kids under 16. | Rte. 7A, Manchester | 802/362–1811 or 800/432–1811 | fax 802/362–2443 | www.1811house.com | 14 rooms | $180–$230 | AE, D, MC, V.

Equinox. One of Vermont's premier resorts. The oldest part of the inn, where Vermonters fomented anti-British sentiment before the Revolution, dates from the 1700s. Mrs. Abraham Lincoln vacationed in the stately, colonnaded main building, which was rescued from destruction when it was listed on the National Register of Historic Places. A famous golf course occupies only part of the property's 2,000 acres. Restaurant, bar with entertainment. Some kitchenettes, cable TV, some in-room VCRs. 2 pools (1 indoor). 18-hole golf course, putting green, tennis. Gym. Cross-country skiing, downhill skiing. Library. Business services. | 3567 Main St. | 802/362–4700 or 800/362–4747 | fax 802/362–4861 | postmaster@equinoxresort.com | www.equinoxresort.com | 183 rooms, 27 suites | $179–$589, $589–$899 suites | MAP | AE, D, DC, MC, V.

Eyrie Motel. An East Dorset motel set on 22 hillside acres with a panorama of the Valley of Vermont between the Green Mountain and Taconic ranges. Picnic area, complimentary Continental breakfast. Refrigerators. Pool. Hiking. | 158 Bowen Hill Rd. | 802/362–1208 | fax 802/362–2948 | www.thisisvermont.com/eyriemotel | 12 rooms | $75–$100 | AE, D, MC, V.

The Four Winds Country Motel. This motel 2½ mi north of Manchester Center and near Manchester outlet shopping has spacious rooms, tastefully appointed with antiques. After shopping, you can relax by the fire in the parlor. Complimentary Continental breakfast. Refrigerators, cable TV. Pool. Cross-country skiing, downhill skiing. | 7379 Historic Rte. 7A | 802/362–1105 | fax 802/362–0905 | www.fourwindscountrymotel.com | 18 rooms | $66–$115 | AE, MC, V.

Inn at Manchester. Period furnishings, a grand porch, and a marble terrace distinguish this many-gabled Victorian inn just south of town. Dining room, picnic area, complimentary breakfast. TV in common area. Pool. No kids under 12. | Rte. 7A | 802/362–1793 | fax 802/362–3218 | www.innatmanchester.com | 18 rooms | $120–$176 | AE, D, MC, V.

The Inn at Willow Pond. Built in the 1770s as a dairy farm, this inn has 20 acres and is surrounded by the scenic Green Mountains. Rooms have wood furniture, handmade quilts, marble baths, and fireplaces. Restaurant, complimentary Continental breakfast (only weekdays). In-room data ports, refrigerators, cable TV, some in-room VCRs. Pool. Sauna. Gym. Cross-country skiing. Business services. No pets. No smoking. | Rte. 7A, Manchester | 802/362–4753 or 800/533–3533 | fax 802/362–4737 | info@innatwillowpond.com | www.innatwillowpond.com | 40 rooms | $138–$208 | AE, D, DC, MC, V.

Inn atop Mount Equinox. An unusual, secluded property atop Mt. Equinox that can be accessed by a toll road and is surrounded by 8,000 pristine acres laced with hiking trails. Restaurant, picnic area, complimentary breakfast. No air-conditioning, no room phones, TV in common area. No kids under 12. Business services. | Skyline Dr., Arlington | 802/362–1113 | fax 802/362–3057 | inn@mountequinox.org | www.mountequinox.org | 19 rooms | $120–$140 | Closed late Oct.–early May | MC, V.

Manchester Highlands. A century-old home with a secluded feel despite a short walk to shopping. There are views of Mt. Equinox from the rear veranda. Picnic area, complimentary breakfast. No smoking, no room phones, TV in common room. Pool. | 216 Highland Ave., Manchester | 802/362–4565 or 800/743–4565 | fax 802/362–4028 | www.highlandsinn.com | 15 rooms (10 with shower only) | $104–$149 | AE, MC, V.

Manchester View. A motel on 14 acres 2 mi north of Manchester, with a setting that lives up to the name. There are 18 fireplaces throughout the building. In-room data ports, refrigerators, some in-room hot tubs, cable TV, some in-room VCRs. Pool. Business services. | Rte. 7A, at High Meadows Way | 802/362–2739 | fax 802/362–2199 | www.manchesterview.com | 26 rooms, 10 suites | $90–$220; $170 and above for suites with fireplaces, $180 and above with hot tubs | AE, D, DC, MC, V.

Mt. Tabor Inn and Restaurant. This inn 10 mi north of Manchester is directly across from the Green Mountains National Forest and has spectacular views of the nearby mountains. The spacious, individually decorated rooms are bright and sunny, each with a mountain view. Restaurant. Cable TV, no room phones. | Rte. 7, Mt. Tabor | 802/293–5907 or 877/658–2267 | mttaborinn@aol.com | www.mttaborinn.com | 12 rooms | $85 | AE, D, DC, MC, V.

North Shire Motel. The motel's spacious, chalet-style rooms have cathedral ceilings, spectacular views of the mountains, and private patios. You can see gorgeous sunsets from your room or from the large front lawn. Complimentary Continental breakfast. Refrigerators, no smoking, cable TV. Pool. No pets. | Rte. 7A, Manchester | 802/362–2336 | info@northshiremotel.com | www.northshiremotel.com | 14 rooms | $95–$110 | AE, D, MC, V.

MANCHESTER AND
MANCHESTER
CENTER

INTRO
ATTRACTIONS
DINING
LODGING

Olympia Motor Lodge. Deer and wild turkeys wander onto the back lawns of this small motel with an inn ambience, 2½ mi north of Manchester. Bar. In-room data ports, cable TV. Pool. Tennis. Business services. | 7259 Main St., Manchester Center | 802/362–1700 | fax 802/362–1705 | www.olympia-vt.com | 24 rooms | $85–$115 | AE, D, MC, V.

Ormsby Hill. This pre-Revolutionary house once sheltered Ethan Allen from the British before becoming an Underground Railroad stop. The rooms have antiques and fireplaces and some offer mountain views. Complimentary breakfast. In-room hot tubs. Cross-country skiing, downhill skiing. | Historic Rte. 7A, Manchester Center | 802/362–1163 or 800/670–2841 | fax 802/362–5176 | ormsby@vermontel.com | www.ormsbyhill.com | 10 rooms | $165–$305 | D, DC, MC, V.

Palmer House. A resort motel on 22 well-tended acres. It makes for a comfortable weekend getaway with its sparkling pool and plexicushion tennis courts. Complimentary Continental breakfast. Refrigerators, cable TV. 2 heated pools (1 indoor). Hot tub. 9-hole par-3 golf course, tennis. Fishing. Business services. | Main St. (Rte. 7A), Manchester Center | 802/362–3600 | www.palmerhouse.com | 40 rooms, 10 suites | $120–$165, $180–$220 suites | AE, D, MC, V.

The Quail's Nest Bed-and-Breakfast Inn. This inn in the center of Danby, 10 mi north of Manchester, exudes a warm country charm. The hostess serves the four-course, complimentary breakfast in full period costume. Rooms have antique furniture, handmade quilts, and wood floors. The inn has received awards from the governor for its attention to environmental concerns. Complimentary breakfast. No smoking, no room phones, TV in common area. No kids under 4. No pets. | 81 S. Main St., Danby | 802/293–5099 or 800/599–6444 | fax 802/293–6300 | quailsnest@quailsnestbandb.com | www.quailsnestbandb.com | 6 rooms | $70–$115 | AE, D, MC, V.

Reluctant Panther. Strikingly painted on the outside and exquisitely furnished within, the Panther has sustained a reputation for fine dining for a quarter-century. Some rooms have fireplaces. Dining room, complimentary breakfast. Some in-room hot tubs, cable TV. No kids. | 39 West Rd., Manchester Village | 802/362–2568 or 800/822–2331 | fax 802/362–2586 | panther@silver.net | www.reluctantpanther.com | 10 rooms, 11 suites | $159–$229, $259–$399 suites | AE, MC, V.

River Meadow Farm. This 90-acre farm adjacent to the Battenkill River is home to two horses, two cows, and a sugarhouse. You can relax beside a fire or play the piano in winter and lounge in the glassed-in porch in summer. Complimentary breakfast. No smoking, no room phones, TV in common area. Hiking. Cross-country skiing. No pets. | Sugar House La., Manchester Center | 802/362–1602 | 5 rooms (share 2 baths) | $60 | No credit cards.

Seth Warner Inn. Built as an inn, this structure has been lodging travelers for over 200 years. Rooms have exposed beams and contain period antiques and quilts. The duck pond and gardens in the backyard make this an ideal romantic getaway. Complimentary breakfast. No smoking, no room phones, TV in common area. No pets. | 2353 Main St., Manchester | 802/362–3830 | fax 802/362–1268 | leettetreault@compuserve.com | www.sethwarnerinn.bizonthe.net | 5 rooms | $105 | AE, MC, V.

Silas Griffith Inn. Built in 1891 for Vermont's first millionaire, with the detailing he demanded, this inn is 12 mi north of Manchester. Each room is distinctive and several can combine as suites. There are fireplaces in every room. Dining room, bar, complimentary breakfast. No smoking, cable TV in common area, no room phones, no TV in some rooms Heated pool. Massage, outdoor spa. Library. | 178 S. Main St., Danby | 802/293–5567 or 800/545–1509 | fax 802/293–5559 | www.silasgriffith.com | 16 rooms | $149–$249 | MC, V.

Stamford Motel. A small, inexpensive motel in Manchester Center. Picnic area. Some refrigerators, cable TV. Pool. | 6458 Main St. (Rte. 7A N), Manchester Center | 802/362–2342 | fax 802/362–1935 | www.stamfordmotel.com | 14 rooms | $60–$70 | AE, D, DC, MC, V.

Toll Road Motor Inn. A small motel tucked off the highway 2¼ mi east of Manchester, along the route from Manchester Center to Bromley ski area. Refrigerators, no room phones. Pool.

| 2220 Depot St., Manchester Center | 802/362–1711 | fax 802/362–1715 | 16 rooms | $79–$109 | AE, D, DC, MC, V.

Village Country Inn. A small, restored 19th-century hotel 1 mi south of Manchester near Orvis and designer outlets. Rocking chairs line the piazza and the bedrooms are a Victorian confection. There are also formal gardens with fountains. Dining room, bar, complimentary breakfast. No air-conditioning in some rooms, no TV in some rooms. Pool. Tennis. | 3835 Main St. (Rte. 7A), Manchester | 802/362–1792 or 800/370–0300 | fax 802/362–7238 | www.villagecountryinn.com | 33 rooms | $150–$375 | AE, D, MC, V.

Weathervane Motel. A standard circa-1960 motel 2½ mi south of Manchester that's been kept up nicely. Complimentary Continental breakfast. In-room data ports, some refrigerators, cable TV, VCR available. Pool. Putting green. Business services. | Historic Rte. 7A, Manchester Village | 802/362–2444 or 800/262–1317 | fax 802/362–4616 | www.weathervanemotel.com | 22 rooms | $76–$145 | AE, MC, V.

Wedgewood Motel. A clean, serviceable Manchester Center overnighter that's fine for a few days when you're hitting the slopes or outlet-shopping. Picnic area, complimentary Continental breakfast. Refrigerators, cable TV. Pool. No pets. | 5927 Main St. | 802/362–2145 or 800/254–2145 | fax 802/362–0190 | www.thisisvermont.com/wedgewood | 12 units | $68–$118; kids 12 and under stay for free | AE, D, DC, MC, V.

Wilburton Inn. This shingle-style Manchester Village inn on 20 acres was built in 1906 as the area's largest estate. Now it's owned by a Greek-born psychiatrist and his wife, Georgette, who's sister to playwright Wendy Wasserstein. Dining room, bar, complimentary breakfast, room service (in season). Some refrigerators, no TV in some rooms. Pool. Tennis. | River Rd., Manchester Village | 802/362–2500 or 800/648–4944 | fax 802/362–1107 | www.wilburton.com | 35 rooms | $170–$225 | AE, MC, V.

MARLBORO

MAP 11, D11

(Nearby towns also listed: Brattleboro, Wilmington)

Marlboro, a tidy village just off southern Vermont's scenic Molly Stark Trail (Route 9), is the home of Marlboro College, an excellent small liberal arts institution, and its summertime Marlboro Music Festival, founded by pianist Rudolf Serkin.

Information: Brattleboro Area Chamber of Commerce | 180 Main St., Brattleboro, 05301 | 802/254–4565 | fax 802/254–5675 | www.brattleboro.com.

Attractions

Marlboro College. Home of the celebrated summer music festival, founded by Rudolf Serkin in 1950 and long graced by the late Pablo Casals. | South Rd. | 802/257–4333 | www.marlboro.edu | Free, some events will have a charge.

Southern Vermont Natural History Museum. More than 500 specimens in 80 dioramas constitute one of New England's largest mounted bird collections, along with a complete mounted collection of northeastern mammals. One exhibit allows you to view a variety of live hawks and owls up close. A newly discovered gem in southern Vermont, this museum began as the private collection of taxidermist Luman Nelson. | Rte. 9, Marlboro | 802/464–0048 | $3 | Memorial Day–Oct., daily 10–5; Nov.–May, weekends 10–4.

ON THE CALENDAR

JULY–AUG.: *Marlboro Music Festival.* Seven weeks of chamber works rehearsed and performed by distinguished artists and gifted young musicians 10 mi west of Brattleboro. Programs are selected only a few days in advance of each performance and there are up to 80 performances per week. | Persons Auditorium, Marlboro College | 802/254–2394 in season; 215/569–4690 in winter | Tickets $5–$25 | Concerts at 2:30 and 8:30 weekends. **JULY:** *Civil War Days.* Vermont's largest civil war event, this celebration features reenactments of skirmishes and camp life, artillery demonstrations, and an array of artifacts. | Rte. 9 | 802/254–4565.

Dining

Colonel Williams Inn. Contemporary. The dining room of this 18th-century farmhouse contains a wood-burning fireplace and overlooks the Green Mountains. House specialties include the grilled, marinated Vermont lamb chops with a rosemary jus. | Rte. 9 | 802/257–1093 | fax 802/257–4460 | colwminn@sover.net | www.colonelwilliamsinn.com | $12–$22 | AE, D, MC, V.

Lodging

Colonel Williams Inn. The rooms in this 1796 white clapboard inn, originally built as part of a sheep farm, have wide-plank wood floors and antique furniture. Four of them also have wood-burning fireplaces. The innkeepers are NECI graduates and prepare delicious breakfasts and dinners. Restaurant, bar, complimentary breakfast. No air-conditioning in some rooms, some kitchenettes, some refrigerators, no smoking, no room phones, TV in common area. Pond. Fishing. Ice-skating. Cross-country skiing. Pets allowed (in efficiencies). | Rte. 9 | 802/257–1093 | fax 802/257–4460 | colwminn@sover.net | www.colonelwilliamsinn.com | 9 rooms, 4 efficiencies | $100–$140 | AE, D, MC, V.

Whetstone Inn. Stagecoaches once halted at this 1700s inn in the heart of Marlboro village. There are fireplaces in the public rooms. Restaurant, picnic area. No air-conditioning, some kitchenettes, some refrigerators. Pond. Pets allowed. | South Rd. | 802/254–2500 | www.whetstone | 11 rooms (3 with shared bath) | $60–$80 | No credit cards.

MIDDLEBURY

(Nearby towns also listed: Brandon, Bristol, Vergennes)

Middlebury is the consummate college town. Middlebury College, one of the nation's most prestigious liberal arts schools, grew up with the community; it was founded in 1800, just 13 years after Middlebury was settled. The campus itself lies on the outskirts of town, while the downtown clusters around the falls of Otter Creek and is distinguished by an 1809 Congregational church crowned by Vermont's most beautiful spire. You'll also find the fine 1830 Middlebury Inn, resplendent in mellowed brick, a lively, compact business center with the excellent Vermont Bookshop (38 Main St.; 802/388–2061), and the eminently browsable Vermont State Craft Center at Frog Hollow.

Information: Addison County Chamber of Commerce | 2 Court St., Middlebury, 05753 | 802/388–7951 or 800/SEE–VERMONT | fax 802/388–8066 | www.midvermont.com.

Attractions

Congregational Church. Completed in 1809, the church has a 136-ft spire considered by many to be the most graceful and elegant in Vermont. | Main St., at Rte. 7 | 802/388–7634 | Daily; summer services, Sun. 10.

Historic Middlebury Village Walking Tour. A self-guided walk around the center of this lively, compact college town, taking in local architectural and historical highlights. You can pick up a map from the Addison Chamber of Commerce. | 2 Court St. | 802/388–7951 | www.midvermont.com | Free | Daily.

Middlebury College. The college was founded in 1800 and is especially renowned for its language program. | Old Chapel Rd. | 802/443–5000 | www.middlebury.edu.

Bread Loaf School of English. The site of Middlebury College's celebrated summer creative writing program (10 mi east of Middlebury), which attracts some of America's finest novelists and poets as instructors. The site is not open to the public, but there are occasional summer readings to which visitors are welcome. Call for details. | Bread Loaf Campus, Rte. 125, Ripton | 802/388–7945 | www.blse.middlebury.edu | Free | Call for details.

Emma Willard House. Home of the pioneer women's educator, who operated a school here early in her career. The house was built in 1809 and in 1959 became the property of Middlebury College, now serving as its admissions office. There are no exhibits, but visitors are welcome to stop by and look inside. | 131 S. Main St. | 802/443–3000 | www.middleburry.edu | No charge | Weekdays 7:45–4:30.

Henry Sheldon Museum of Vermont History. A window on small-town life a century and a half ago, with furnishings, tools, and portraits. | 1 Park St. | 802/388–2117 | www.middlebury.edu/~shel-mus | $4 | Mon.–Sat. 10–5.

Middlebury College Museum of Art. The museum has Rodin sculptures, along with the work of the respected 19th-century Vermont sculptor Hiram Powers. | Rte. 30 | 802/443–3168 | www.middleburry.edu/~museum | Tues.–Sun. weekdays 10–5, weekends 12–5.

Old Stone Row. The campus's oldest, most architecturally distinguished corner, centered on 1816 Painter Hall, given by college founder Gamaliel Painter. | Old Chapel Rd. | 802/443–5000 | www.middlebury.edu.

Middlebury College Snow Bowl. Open to the public, the college's slopes 13 mi east of Middlebury are a pleasant, low-priced alternative to the larger ski areas. | Rte. 125, Hancock | 802/388–4356 | $25–$30 day passes | Dec.–Mar., daily 9–4.

Starr Library. The century-old library, built of six kinds of Vermont marble, houses an impressive collection of American first editions. | Old Chapel Rd. | 802/443–5494 | www.middlebury.edu/lib | Free | Weekdays 8 AM–1 AM, weekends 9 AM–11 PM during school year; weekdays 8AM–12PM, weekends 9AM–11PM during interim periods.

Robert Frost Interpretive Trail. A pathway through woods and meadows 10 mi east of Middlebury, marked with quotations from Frost poems influenced by his residence in nearby Ripton and other northern New England locations. Picnic area across the street and ¼ mi east. | Rte. 125, Ripton | 802/388–4362 | Free | Daily.

Shoreham Co-op Apple Picking. Choose from among several varieties at this orchard 13 mi southwest of Middlebury in the heart of Vermont apple country. | 3442 Rte. 22A, Shoreham | 802/897–7400 or 802/388–4921 | Free | Mid-Aug.–mid-May., daily.

UVM Morgan Horse Farm. The university's farm, just outside town, raises Morgans and gives visitors a close-up look at specimens of Vermont's state animal—all of whom are descended from a single stallion, Figure, who lived 200 years ago. There is a complimentary tour and video on request. | 74 Battell Dr., Weybridge | 802/388–2011 | ctr.uvm.edu/cals/farms/mhfarm.htm | $4 | May–Oct., daily 9–4.

Vermont Folklife Center. The center has photographs, audiotapes, manuscripts, folk art, and other artifacts of Vermont life past and present. In 1801 this was the home of Gamaliel Painter, founder of Middlebury College. | 3 Court St. | 802/388–4964 | www.vermontfolklifecenter.org | Free | Nov.–Apr., weekdays 9–5; May–Oct., weekdays 9–5, Sat. 11–4.

Vermont State Craft Center at Frog Hollow. Shop here for the best work of Vermont woodworkers, jewelers, printmakers, potters, glassmakers, and more. | 1 Mill St. | 802/388–3177 | www.froghollow.org | Free | Jan.–Apr., Mon.–Sat. 10–5; May–Dec., Mon.–Thurs. 9:30–5:30., Fri.–Sat. 9:30–6, Sun. 11–5.

ON THE CALENDAR

JULY: Festival on the Green. A weeklong celebration in the center of Middlebury that has an antiques sale, nightly entertainment, and a street dance. | On the Green | 802/388–7951 or 800/SEE–VERMONT.

Dining

Dog Team Tavern. American. This eatery 4 mi north of Middlebury is famous for its hand-hooked rugs and local crafts, its sticky buns, and its generous portions of hearty fare you order from the blackboard before sitting. You won't go wrong with a steak or a regional New England dish. Kids' menu. No smoking. | Dog Team Rd. | 802/388–7651 | www.dogteam-tavern.com | No lunch | $11–$17 | AE, D, DC, MC, V.

Fire and Ice. American. With 10 different dining areas, this lively establishment is dominated by a 22-ft mahogany motorboat perched near the 55-item "salad ballroom," the separate salad bar. Options include steaks, chops, seafood, and some teriyaki and stir-frys. Salad bar. Kids' menu. No smoking. | 26 Seymour St. | 802/388–7166 or 800/367–7166 | No lunch Mon. | $15–$25 | AE, D, DC, MC, V.

Mister Up's. Contemporary. Exposed brick and dark wood surround the large bar area. The dining level encircles an excellent salad bar. Riverfront greenhouse dining along Otter Creek is a treat. The consistently dependable fare is simple yet satisfying. Try the baked onion soup. Sunday brunch. | 25 Bakery La. | 802/388–6724 | $9–$14 | AE, D, MC, V.

Roland's Place. Continental. Originally a stagecoach tavern, the dining room is part of the 1796 house and has dramatic pastoral views from its windows. Fresh Vermont produce and meats are used in entrées like pan-seared tenderloin with a juniper-berry sauce and a hearty venison pie. In summer and fall, lunch and dinner are served in an outdoor dining area beneath an old maple tree. Four miles north of Middlebury. | 3629 Ethan Allen Hwy./Rte. 7, New Haven | 802/453–6309 | rolands@together.net | www.virtualcities.com/vt/rolands.htm | Closed Mon.–Wed. in Nov.–Apr. | $12–$18 | AE, DC, MC, V.

Waybury Inn. Contemporary. The TV series *Newhart* once made this landmark inn famous. Dependable hospitality, good food, and a convenient location keep visitors returning. The cuisine is a combination of traditional New England favorites and modern variations, all complemented by herbs from the garden out back. There is traditional fare in the pub while the more formal dining room is known for rack of lamb, excellent trout, and a surf-and-turf of steak and shrimp. Be sure to try the pecan-fried calamari as an appetizer. No smoking. Sunday brunch. | Rte. 125, East Middlebury | 802/388–4015 or 800/348–1810 | No lunch | $18–$28 | AE, D, MC, V.

Woody's. Contemporary. This restaurant has some of the nicest porch dining in Vermont. With Otter Creek running toward the falls, you may feel as though you're on a riverboat traveling upstream. The excellent contemporary cuisine can suffer from minor lapses of inconsistency if chef/owner Woody Danforth is not on the premises. However, this is a small quibble given the overall pleasant dining experience. Try the burgers or house steak and the steamed Prince Edward Island mussels are a great starter. Sunday brunch. No smoking. | 5 Bakery La.; just off Main St. | 802/388–4182 | $9–$20 | AE, MC, V.

Lodging

Blue Spruce Motel. A reasonably priced motel 3 mi south of town with mountain views. Some kitchenettes, cable TV. | 2428 Rte. 7 S | 802/388–4091 | fax 802/388–3003 | 21 rooms, 6 cottages | $58–$125 | AE, D, DC, MC, V.

Greystone Motel. A clean, pleasant motel 2 mi south of Middlebury village. Picnic area. Cable TV. | Rte. 7 S | 802/388–4935 | 10 rooms | $55–$75 | AE, D, MC, V.

Inn on the Green. Built in 1803, this comfy inn sits conveniently on the green, in the center of Middlebury, offering easy access to the many shops and restaurants. All the rooms have period furnishings and some are handicap accessible. Complimentary Continental breakfast. No smoking, cable TV, room phones. No pets. | 71 S. Pleasant St. | 802/388–7512 or 888/244–7512 | fax 802/388–4075 | innkeeper@innonthegreen.com | 11 rooms | $155 | AE, D, DC, MC, V.

Lemon Fair Bed & Breakfast. This pleasant little B&B housed in a former meetinghouse (1796) moved to its present site on the village green in 1819. Four miles from Lake Champlain, it is 8 mi west of Middlebury. Complimentary breakfast. No room phones. | Crown Point Rd., Bridport | 802/758–9238 | fax 802/758–2135 | limewalk@together.net | www.lime-walk.com/lemonfair | 4 rooms, 1 suite | $75–$95 | No credit cards.

Linens and Lace Bed-and-Breakfast. Sterling silver heirlooms, antiques, and fresh flowers decorate this Victorian property. You can enjoy afternoon tea or lemonade in summer on the wraparound porch overlooking the perennial garden or stroll to the green, only three blocks away. Complimentary breakfast. No smoking, no room phones, TV in common area. No kids under 8. No pets. | 29 Seminary St. | 802/388–0832 or 800/808–3897 | www.mid-vermont.com/html/Lodgin/_lodg_fs.htm | 3 rooms | $99–$119 | No credit cards.

Middlebury Inn. One of Vermont's most distinguished small hotels, the inn has been a fixture of this town since the early 19th century. The best rooms are on upper floors of the main building, facing west. Lunch is served on the porch in summer. Restaurants, bar, complimentary Continental breakfast. Cable TV. Business services. Pets allowed (fee). | 14 Court House Sq | 802/388–4961 or 800/842–4666 | fax 802/388–4563 | midinnut@sover.net | www.middlebury-inn.com | 66 rooms, 9 suites | $86–$195, $195–$355 suites | AE, D, DC, MC, V.

The 1796 House. This house 9 mi north of Middlebury was built in 1796 by one of Ethan Allen's Green Mountain Boys and offers lodging upstairs from one of Vermont's finest restaurants, which is owned by the chef. Restaurant, complimentary breakfast. No room phones. | 3629 Ethan Allen Hwy., New Haven | 802/453–6309 | rolands@together.net | www.virtualcities.com/vt/rolands.htm | 3 rooms | $75–$105 | AE, DC, MC, V.

Sugarhouse Motel. When it's warm enough, this motel allows you to build a campfire on the front lawn and cook your dinner on it. Standing on the crest of a hill, it affords beautiful views of the sunrise and sunset across the mountains. Prices are very reasonable during nonpeak times. Microwaves, refrigerators, no smoking, cable TV. Pets allowed (fee). | Rte. 7 | 802/388–2770 or 800/SUGARHOUSE | fax 802/388–8616 | ars@together.net | 14 rooms | $99 | MC, V.

Swift House Inn. This stately Federal-style home was built some 200 years ago for a prominent local family, and rooms—there and in two annexes—are full of period-style pieces, with fireplaces in some. Complimentary Continental breakfast, room service. Some in-room hot tubs. Sauna. Business services. | 25 Stewart La. | 802/388–9925 | fax 802/388–9927 | www.swifthouseinn.com | 21 rooms in 3 buildings | $90–$205 | AE, D, DC, MC, V.

Waybury Inn. An inn since 1810, this East Middlebury landmark became well known when its facade was featured in the TV series *Newhart*. Restaurant, bar, complimentary breakfast. No air-conditioning in some rooms, no TV in rooms, no room phones, TV in common area. | Rte. 125, East Middlebury | 802/388–4015 or 800/348–1810 | fax 802/388–1248 | wayburyinn@together.net | www.wayburyinn.com | 14 rooms | $95–$150 | D, DC, MC, V.

MONTGOMERY CENTER

MAP 11, E2

(Nearby town also listed: Newport)

Montgomery Center lies at the gateway to Jay Peak, Vermont's northernmost ski resort. Devastated by the 1997 flash flooding of the Trout River, the town and its cozy inns are back to normal, complete with a new downtown bridge. Although the old steel-and-concrete span was carried away by the flood, Montgomery's claims to fame—seven wooden covered bridges, the most of any town in Vermont, all more than 100 years old—were undamaged.

Information: Jay Peak Area Association | R.R. 2, Box 137, Jay, 05859 | 802/988–2259 or 800/882–7460 | fax 802/326–3194 | www.jaypeakvermont.org.

Attractions

Jay Peak Ski Resort. Sticking up out of the flat farmland, Jay averages 332 in of snowfall a year—more than any other Vermont ski area. Jay Peak is in fact two mountains with 66 trails, the highest reaching nearly 4,000 ft with a vertical drop of 2,153 ft. The smaller mountain has more straight-fall-line, expert terrain, and the tram-side peak has many curving and meandering trails perfectly suited for intermediate and beginning skiers. Every morning at 9 the ski school offers a free tour, from the tram down one trail. Jay has 75% snowmaking coverage. The area has a halfpipe and snowboard terrain for snowboarders. A touring center at the base of the mountain has 32 km (20 mi) of groomed cross-country trails. There is a $5 trail fee. | Rte. 242, Jay, | 802/988–2611; 800/451–4449 outside VT | fax 802/988–4049 | www.jaypeak.com | $49 Adults, $39 Students, $34 Child | early to mid-Nov–late April.

Jay Peak Tram Rides. Climbing 2,100 ft to the summit, the tram affords views of the mountains and surrounding country. From the top of the mountain you can see New York, New Hampshire, Maine, and Canada. | Jay Peak Resort, Rte. 242, Jay | 802/988–2611 or 800/451–4449 | $8 | July–Columbus Day, daily 10–4.

ON THE CALENDAR

JULY–AUG.: *Concert on the Commons.* Held in the Historical Society building, a reconverted 19th-century church, this series of concerts features an array of classical music. | Rte. 118 | 802/326–4720 or 802/326–4404 | $10.

Dining

Black Lantern Inn. Contemporary. Wide-plank floorings and wood paneling add to the charm of the inn's historic dining room, 2 mi northwest of Montgomery Center. Windows look toward the early 19th-century Episcopal church across the main street. The menu includes such delectables as potato-crusted horseradish salmon. | Rte. 118, Montgomery Village | 802/326–4507 or 800/255–8661 | fax 802/326–4077 | blantern@together.net | www.black-lantern.com | $12–$20 | AE, D, MC, V.

Lemoine's Restaurant and Pub. American/Casual. The dining room of this 100-year-old establishment, part of the Inn on Trout River, is decorated in a Victorian motif. You can choose from a full range of American and Continental dishes, or opt for one of the heart-healthy entrées. You will particularly enjoy the sautéed medallions of pork, served with a mustard and wine sauce, seasoned with shallots and peppers. | 241 Main St. (Rte. 118) | 802/326–4391 or 800/338–7049 | fax 802/326–4077 | info@troutinn.com | www.troutinn.com | Reservations essential | No lunch | $13–$19 | AE, D, MC, V.

Lodging

Black Lantern Inn. This inn 2 mi northwest of Montgomery Center was built as a hotel for mill workers in 1803. It has a village location and the country decor has sophisticated touches in main building and annex. Some in-room hot tubs, no room phones. | Rte. 118, Montgomery Village | 802/326–44507 or 800/255–8661 | fax 802/326–4077 | blantern@together.net | www.blacklantern.com | 10 rooms, 6 suites | $85–$145 | MAP | AE, D, MC, V.

Hazen's Notch Bed-and-Breakfast. This renovated red clapboard farmhouse in the middle of the Green Mountains has scenic views of the surrounding mountain meadows and forests. The property is only steps away from hiking, biking, and cross-country skiing trails. Complimentary breakfast. No air-conditioning, no smoking, no room phones, TV in common area. Pond. Library. Pets allowed. | Rte. 58/Hazen's Notch Rd. | 802/326–4708 | hazens@together.net | www.pbpub.com/hazensnotch.htm | 3 rooms | $60–$70 | No credit cards.

Hotel Jay and Jay Peak Condominiums. The hotel is decorated with ski-lodge simplicity. Rooms have views of both Jay Peak and the valley and upper floors have balconies. If you come in winter, you must purchase a package which includes a lift ticket, breakfast, dinner, lodging, and ski school. Restaurant, bar, complimentary Continental breakfast (summer only). No air-conditioning, no smoking, cable TV. Pool. Hot tub, sauna. 2 tennis courts. Cross-country skiing, downhill skiing. No pets (in winter). | Rte. 242, Jay | 802/988–2611 or 800/451–4449 | fax 802/988–4049 | jaypeak@together.net | www.jaypeakresort.com | 48 rooms, 120 condos | $60–$163 Apr.–Nov.; $599 and up (min. 2 night) Dec.–late Mar. | MAP | AE, D, MC, V.

Inn on Trout River. A century-old inn with back lawns rambling down to the Trout River. The restaurant (Lemoine's Restaurant and Pub) is known for heart-healthy/diabetic options as well as a full menu. One room has a potbellied stove; all have down quilts and flannel sheets. Llama treks are arranged for groups. There are also kayaking and mountain biking packages, as well as teddy bear creation packages (a class and practicum on how to make a teddy bear and outfit it as well). Restaurant, bar, complimentary breakfast. No room phones. Fishing. Library. | 241 Main St. (Rte. 118) | 802/326–4391 or 800/338–7049 | fax 802/326–3194 | info@troutinn.com | www.troutinn.com | 10 rooms | $103–$125 | MAP available | AE, D, MC, V.

MONTPELIER

(Nearby towns also listed: Barre, Waterbury)

Montpelier is the nation's least-populous state capital, with fewer than 9,000 residents. Aside from the Vermont National Life Insurance Company, on a hillside overlooking the town, Montpelier's business is government, ensconced in a building that writer (and part-time Vermonter) John Gunther called "the most beautiful statehouse in America." Built in 1836 of Barre granite and topped with a statue of the Roman goddess of agriculture, the gold-domed capitol is the home of a citizens' legislature whose rank-and-file members don't even have private offices—head inside during a session and you'll see senators and representatives meeting with their constituents in the hallways.

Montpelier is so confined by the steep walls of the Winooski River valley that just about everything in town is concentrated along State and Main streets, within scant blocks of the capitol and the river. It's a lively little place, with interesting shops, museums of art and history, and a clutch of good restaurants operated by the New England Culinary Institute.

Information: Central Vermont Chamber of Commerce | Box 336, Beaulieu Pl., Stewart Rd., Barre, 05641 | 802/229–4619 | fax 802/229–5713 | www.central-vt.com.

Driving Around Town: Due to the small size of the city, traffic congestion is seldom an issue. While there are a number of narrow side streets, major thoroughfares crisscross the city and make sightseeing by car easy and comfortable. If you want to park your car, you can do so on the street or in one of the many parking lots or garages in the downtown area. The only detail you should keep in mind is that since Montpelier is the state capital, many of the parking slots are taken during the weekdays. On weekends and nights, parking is easily found. Feed the parking meters. The speed limit is 25 mph throughout the city. Although you are permitted to turn right on red as a general rule, there are a number of intersections, particularly downtown, where this is forbidden.

Attractions

ART AND ARCHITECTURE

State House. Vermont's gold-domed capitol, topped by a statue of the goddess of agriculture, was built in 1836. Its later Victorian interior has since been restored. Free guided tours are offered Mon.–Fri. from 8 to 3:30, every ½ hour. | 115 State St. | 802/828–2228 | www.leg.state.vt.us | Free | Weekdays 8–4, Sat. 11–3.

BEACHES, PARKS, AND NATURAL SIGHTS

Hubbard Park. A quiet little retreat 1 mi northwest of America's smallest state capital. No camping. | Winter St. | 802/223–5141 or 802/223–7335 | Free | Daily 7–dusk, closed to cars late Mar.–Apr.

MUSEUMS

Camp Meade Victory Museum. Once a Civilian Conservation Corps camp in the early 1930s, this is now the site of a museum focusing on the Great Depression and World War II. There are over 25 exhibits, including films, audio recordings, and memorabilia. The museum is next to the Camp Meade Motor Court, 4 mi northwest of Montpelier. | Rte. 2, Middlesex | 802/223–5537 | www.campmeade.com | $5 | May–mid-Oct., Mon.–Sat. 9–5, Sun. 9–3.

Thomas Waterman Wood Art Gallery. Nineteenth-century portraits and landscapes are on display here and there is also a contemporary gallery. On the Vermont College Campus | College Hall, 36 College St. | 802/828–8743 | $2, free on Sun. | Tues.–Sun. 12–4.

Vermont Museum. Vermont's primary historical repository has a changing series of exhibits alongside its main collection. | 109 State St. | 802/828–2291 | www.state.vt.us/vhs | $3 | Tues.–Fri. 9–4:30, Sat. 9–4, Sun. 12–4.

OTHER POINTS OF INTEREST

Morse Farm. The seventh generation of a Vermont farm family carries on the maple-sugaring tradition on this farm 3 mi north of Montpelier. There are plenty of informative displays, a guided tour, and a video. | 1168 County Rd. | 802/223–2740 or 800/242–2740 | www.morsefarm.com | Free/Daily 8–6:30 in season; 9–5 in winter.

Vermont College of Norwich. An array of brick buildings and turn-of-the-20th-century mansions encircle the sprawling lawn of this small campus. Based on the ideas of John Dewey, the school offers numerous opportunities for those seeking education in the progressive tradition. | 36 College St. | 802/828–8500.

ON THE CALENDAR

JULY: *Independence Day Celebration.* The Fourth of July is celebrated in the state capital with full flare. A parade, foot race, street dance, and a host of street vendors fill State Street in front of the capitol building. A spectacular fireworks display finishes the day-long festivities. | State St. | 802/229–4619.

Dining

INEXPENSIVE

Horn of the Moon. Vegetarian. Plants and local art fill the bright airy interior of this restaurant, rendering it a pleasant and relaxed spot for dining. The cuisine is flavored with Mexican and Italian flourishes, and does not include too much tofu. | 8 Langdon St. | 802/223–2895 | Breakfast also available. Closed Mon. | $5–$9 | No credit cards.

Sarducci's. Italian. Bright, cheerful rooms overlooking the Winooski River are a perfect place to enjoy pizza fresh from wood-fired ovens, wonderfully textured homemade breads, and creative pasta dishes such as pasta pugliese, which marries penne with basil, black olives, roasted eggplant, Portobello mushrooms, and sun-dried tomatoes. | 3 Main St. | 802/223–0229 | No lunch Sun. | $8–$15 | AE, MC, V.

MODERATE

Chef's Table. Continental. Students and instructors at the New England Culinary Institute are responsible for the exquisite game, pastas, and salmon here. No smoking. | 118 Main St. | 802/229–9202 | Closed Sun. No lunch weekends | $25–$35 | AE, D, DC, MC, V.

Lobster Pot. Seafood. The nautical theme rules here—the salad bar is in a converted rowboat. Kids' menu. | 1028 Rte. 302 | 802/476–9900 | $20–$30 | AE, D, DC, MC, V.

Lodging

INEXPENSIVE

Camp Meade Motor Court. A Civilian Conservation Corps camp in the early 1930s, this unique lodging 4 mi northwest of Montpelier is adjacent to the Camp Meade Victory Museum. It has a canteen and nightly campfires. There is no charge at the museum for those staying at the motor court. Restaurant. No air-conditioning in some rooms, cable TV. Pool. No pets. | Rte. 2, Middlesex | 802/223–5537 | cmpmeade@together.net | www.campmeade.com | 19 cabins | $48 | Closed mid-Oct.–Apr. | MC, V.

La Gue Inns. A modern hotel 3 mi north of downtown Montpelier. It has access to VAST snow-mobile trails. Restaurant, bar, picnic area. Some refrigerators, cable TV, and in-room movies. Pool. Business services. | 394 Fisher Rd. | 802/229–5766 | fax 802/229–5766 | www.lagueinc.com | 80 rooms | $45–$80 | AE, D, MC, V.

Montpelier Guest Home. A Victorian home with simple, affordable accommodations in a residential neighborhood. The rooms are decorated with antiques and handmade quilts. A large garden with decks, benchs, hammocks, and a waterfall affords a secluded space for lounging. No air-conditioning, no smoking, no room phones, no TV. No pets. | 138 North St. | 802/229–0878 | fax 802/229–0878 | kitzmill@together.net | www.guesthome.com | 3 rooms | $45 | D, MC, V.

MODERATE

Betsy's Bed and Breakfast. An antiques-filled Victorian lodging convenient to the state capitol and the New England Culinary Institute restaurants. Complimentary breakfast. No air-conditioning, some kitchenettes, no smoking, cable TV. Exercise equipment. | 74 E. State St. | 802/229–0466 | fax 802/229–5412 | www.central-vt.com/web/betsybb | 12 rooms | $80–$100 | AE, MC, V.

Capitol Plaza. Montpelier's only full-service downtown hotel is across the street from the state capitol and office buildings. Restaurant, bar. In-room data ports, cable TV. Beauty salon. Business services. | 100 State St. | 802/223–5252 or 800/274–5252 | fax 802/229–5427 | www.capitolplaza.com | 47 rooms (3 with shower only) | $79–$149 | AE, D, MC, V.

Econo Lodge Montpelier. This motel just off Interstate 89 has clean rooms with a full range of modern amenities. Some microwaves, some refrigerators, no smoking, cable TV. Pets allowed. | 101 Northfield St. | 802/223–5258 or 800/553–2666 | fax 802/223–0716 | 54 rooms | $98 | AE, D, DC, MC, V.

The Inn at Montpelier. A sparkling inn with a wraparound front porch, sitting rooms, paintings, some fireplaces. Complimentary Continental breakfast. In-room data ports, cable TV. Business services. | 147 Main St. | 802/223–2727 | fax 802/223–0722 | www.innat-montpelier.com | 19 rooms | $124–$177 | AE, DC, MC, V.

Northfield Inn. An antiques-filled Victorian inn on a hillside, with plush European feather beds, porches, and a patio, overlooking Northfield village and the mountains, an apple orchard, and a woodland pond, 10 mi south of Montpelier. Complimentary breakfast. No air-conditioning, no smoking, some in-room VCRs. Business services. | 228 Highland Ave., Northfield | 802/485–8558 | www.pbpub.com/northfield or www.bbdirectory.com/inn/northfieldinn | 14 rooms, 2 suites | $103–$119 | MC, V.

MORRISVILLE

MAP 11, E3

(Nearby town also listed: Stowe)

Morrisville is the main market town for Lamoille County, and as such has experienced a small community's version of suburban sprawl. While the town was once concentrated within a few blocks of the Lamoille River, where a cinema and several small businesses and restaurants still thrive, most of its commercial life has gravitated to a pair of malls on the outskirts. Just 10 mi north of Stowe, it's the best bet for nonboutique shopping and serious grocery stock-ups for residents and kitchenette-equipped visitors to the resort town.

Information: **Lamoille Valley Chamber of Commerce** | 43 Portland St., Tegu Building, Morrisville, 05661 | 802/888–7607 or 800/849–9985 | fax 802/888–5006 | www.stowes-mugglers.org.

Attractions

Johnson Woolen Mills. This mill, 7 mi west of Morrisville, has been making rugged woolenware for 150 years. They specialize in the pants, jackets, and vests favored by Vermont hunters and loggers, along with blankets, kids' clothes, and country casual wear. | 51 Lower Main St., Johnson | 802/635–7185 | www.johnsonwoolenmills.com | Free | Mon.–Sat. 9–5.

Stowe Soaring. Glider rides and lessons, as well as scenic airplane rides 4 mi south of Morrisville. You get gorgeous hawk's-eye views of Mt. Mansfield and surrounding area while on one of the rides that last anywhere from 10 minutes to 1 hour. | 2305 Whitcomb Aviation, Laporte Rd., Morrisville-Stowe Airport | 802/888–7845 | www.together.net/~whitav/homepage.htm | Airplane rides $89 for up to 3 passengers; glider rides from $54 for a 10-minute ride, to $169 for a 1-hr ride | Mid-Apr.–Oct., daily. Call for details.

ON THE CALENDAR

JUNE–AUG.: *Morrisville Military Band Concert.* Each Thursday at 7 PM in summer, the Morrisville Military Band holds a free concert in the amphitheater of the local high school, the People's Academy. | Copley St. | 802/888–3919.

Dining

Hilary's Restaurant. American/Casual. The interior of this eatery is ornamented with wood trim and potted plants. The dining room's many nooks provide opportunities for intimate dining. There is a huge selection of dishes, including soups, salads, and vegetarian items. Particularly popular are the creative burgers. | 65 Northgate Plaza | 802/888–5352 | Breakfast also available | $12–$16 | AE, D, MC, V.

Lodging

Sunset Park Motor Inn. From the windows of this lodge you can gaze out on the scenic landscape of the Green Mountains. The rooms are clean and comfortable and the property also has lawns and playgrounds. The inn rents out a house, equipped with a full kitchen. Restaurant, bar, picnic area. Some refrigerators, some in-room hot tubs, cable TV. Pool. Playground. No pets. | Rte. 15 W, off Rte. 100 | 802/888–4956 or 800/544–2347 | fax 802/888–3698 | sunset@together.net | www.homepages.together.net/~sunset/index.htm | 55 rooms, 1 house | $125, $175 for the house | AE, D, DC, MC, V.

NEWFANE

MAP 11, D11

(Nearby towns also listed: Brattleboro, Grafton, Putney)

Newfane is one of Vermont's white villages—its Greek Revival homes and public buildings seem to get a fresh coat of snowy paint every night. The most beautiful of the structures that line Route 30 is the 1825 County Courthouse, chastely pillared and porticoed. Near the manicured village green also stand a town hall, a Congregational church of the 1830s, and two fine inns—the 1793 Old Newfane Inn and the aptly named Four Columns. Newfane is prime antiques country, with no fewer than four dealers in the village.

Information: Brattleboro Area Chamber of Commerce | 180 Main St., Brattleboro, 05301 | 802/254–4565 | fax 802/254–5679 | www.brattleboro.com.

Attractions

Jamaica State Park. A pleasant stop 26 mi north of Brattleboro along scenic Route 30, with campsites, swimming, and foot trails. | 285 Salmon Hole Rd. | 802/874–4600 or 802/885–8891 | $2 | Apr.–Columbus Day, daily 8:30 AM–9 PM.

The Old Village on Newfane Hill. Stone obelisks commemorate the original town of Newfane, which was moved to the valley in the early 1800s. To get to this remote place, drive south on Route 30 to Grimes Hill Road. Go west on Grimes Hill Road to Newfane Hill Road and go up the hill. The obelisks are on the east side of the road. | Newfane Hill Rd.

Scott Covered Bridge. Closed to traffic and maintained as a state historic site, the Scott Bridge 5 mi north of Newfane was built in 1870 and extends 276 ft. There's good swimming below: leap off the bridge for a splash. | On Rte. 30 north of Townshend | Free.

Townshend State Park. A trail to the top of 1,680-ft Bald Mountain affords fine views of the West River valley in this park 6 mi north of Newfane. There are tent sites available. | 2755 State Forest Rd. | 802/365–7500 or 800/2996–3071 | www.vtstateparks.com | Free | Memorial Day–Columbus Day, daily until dusk.

COVERED BRIDGES

Despite all the publicity surrounding a certain book and movie about covered bridges in Iowa, most people still associate the quaint old structures with New England—particularly Vermont. And the one question nearly everyone asks is, how come covered bridges are covered?

Sooner or later, everyone gets the same answer: "To keep the horses from getting frightened as they crossed the river." But that answer is wrong. Vermont's 100-plus surviving covered bridges were given walls and roofs for the same reason bridges were covered in medieval Europe—to keep their framework and roadbeds from suffering the effects of weather. Given Vermont's climate, covering bridges was an especially sensible approach.

For many years, covered bridge building was a matter of art and engineering tackled by skilled craftsmen who often traveled from town to town and who tended to become associated with one style of bridge building or another. The Franklin County town of Montgomery, which is often considered to be Vermont's covered bridge capital (it has six of the structures, with a seventh just over the line in Enosburg), was the home of the renowned Jewett brothers. Between 1863 and 1890 the brothers fashioned nine wooden spans in their hometown alone, using a system called the "Town Lattice Truss," named after its inventor, Ithiel Town. This approach called for erecting two crosshatched frames, spanning each side of the bridge. Other builders favored steam-bent arches, or variations on the post-and-beam construction once used in houses and barns—and again gaining favor today.

The Jewetts and their like built to last. When covered bridges succumb, it's usually because of arson, neglect, or the need for a wider span. Keep the roof in repair, and the frame may well outlast steel and concrete.

© Corbis

Windham County Courthouse. Vermont's most handsome county courthouse was built in 1825 and exemplifies the chaste Greek Revival style. | 7 Court St. | 802/365–7979 | Free | Weekdays 8:30–4:30.

Windham County Historical Society Museum. The museum displays all kinds of artifacts from towns in Windham County, dating from the late 1700s through the early 1900s, in a two-story brick building. Activities include four to six programs May to Oct. Not accessible to the disabled. | Main St. (Rte. 30) | 802/365–4148 | Memorial Day–late Oct., Wed.–Sun. 12–5.

ON THE CALENDAR
OCT.: *Heritage Festival.* Held each Columbus Day weekend, this festival includes a parade, vendors, and craft exhibits. The Morris dancers are also annual guests, celebrating the fall with European ritual dances. | On the Green.

Dining
Four Columns Inn. Contemporary. This graceful Greek Revival mansion has hand-hewn beams, a massive brick fireplace, and comfortable antique furniture. For starters try the Spicy Vermont Quail with Greens, Goat Cheese, and Smoked Bacon and move onto the Local Free-Range Chicken with Porcini Sauce or Seared Venison Loin with a Spiced Zinfandel Glaze and Sun-Dried Cherries. No smoking. | 21 West St. | 802/365–7713 or 800/787–6633 | Closed late Apr. and Tues. No lunch | $18–$29 | AE, D, MC, V.

The Inn at South Newfane. Contemporary. A fireplace occupies a corner of the dining room, on the other side of which six double windows look onto the sleepy village. The menu includes both light and hearty fare. Try the tournedos wrapped in bacon and served with asparagus and a lobster tail with béarnaise sauce. | 369 Dover Rd., South Newfane | 802/348–7191 | fax 802/348–9325 | thecullens@innatsouthnewfane.com | www.innatsouthnewfane.com | Closed Wed.; closed Mon.–Tue. Dec.–Mar. | $12–$24 | AE, D, MC, V.

Old Newfane Inn. Continental. Set on the Newfane green, this historic colonial inn was established in 1787. From king crab flambé to frogs legs Provençal, curry and goulash to beef, veal, and game birds, the dependably good fare has established a well-deserved reputation. | 4 Court St. on Rte. 30 | 802/365–4427 or 800/789–4427 | Closed Apr.–late May, Nov.–mid-Dec., and Mon. No lunch | $17–$27 | No credit cards.

Lodging
Four Columns Inn. This Greek Revival mansion dating from 1830 faces Newfane's much-photographed green. It is filled with antique furniture. Dining room, bar, complimentary breakfast. No smoking, cable TV in lounge, no TV in rooms. Pool. Business services. Pets allowed. | 21 West St. | 802/365–7713 | fax 802/365–0022 | www.fourcolumnsinn.com | 15 rooms, 4 suites | $140–$175, $195–$270 suites | AE, D, MC, V.

The Inn at South Newfane. In the middle of the sleepy community of South Newfane, 3 mi south of Newfane, this inn offers quiet, secluded accommodations. Built in the 1840s as a summer home, the inn sports a large backyard porch overlooking a pond and 100 acres of scenic property. Rooms are furnished with antiques, quilts, and comforters. Dining room, bar, complimentary breakfast. No air-conditioning, no smoking, no room phones, TV in common area. Pond. | 369 Dover Rd., South Newfane | 802/348–7191 | fax 802/348–9325 | thecullens@innatsouthnewfane.com | www.innatsouthnewfane.com | 6 rooms | $115–$130 | AE, D, MC, V.

Old Newfane Inn. A quietly formal inn dating from the late 18th century in lovely Newfane village, full of period antiques. Several rooms have fireplaces. Restaurant, bar, complimentary Continental breakfast. No air-conditioning, no room phones. Kids over 10 only. | 4 Court St., Village Common | 802/365–4427 | www.oldnewfaneinn.com | 10 rooms (2 with shared bath) | $125–$155 | Closed Apr.–late May, Nov.–mid-Dec., and Mon. | No credit cards.

Sugarhouse Suite. Stay in an actual sugarhouse. Located just off Route 30, this suite features a cathedral ceiling, fireplace, its own kitchenette, and a private patio. The secluded rural surroundings make this a perfect romantic getaway. Kitchenettes, refrigerators, no smoking, no room phones, no TV. Hiking. No pets. | Redway Hill Rd. | 802/365–7762 or 888/741–2022 | fax 802/365–7762 | shs@sover.net | www.sover.net./~shs | 1 suite | $150 | No credit cards.

Windham Hill Inn. This brick 1825 house 12 mi north of Newfane overlooks the West River valley. The rooms are distinctively furnished with antiques and original art. The music room has a grand piano. A hiking trail threads through the surrounding 160-acre property. Dining room. No smoking, TV in common area. Pool. Tennis court. Cross-country skiing. No kids under 12. Business services. | 311 Lawrence Dr., West Townshend | 802/874–4080 or 800/944–4080 | fax 802/874–4702 | www.windhamhill.com | 21 rooms | $245–$370 | MAP | AE, D, DC, MC, V.

NEWPORT

(Nearby town also listed: Island Pond)

Long dormant as its economic fortunes declined, Newport has revived and begun to pay attention to its greatest asset—its splendidly scenic Lake Memphremagog waterfront. With a new marina, community boathouse, and an excursion vessel, the old lumber town now looks to tourism as its economic engine. Many of the visitors sail in from Quebec; along the dock on a summer day you'll hear as much French as English. To the north, the lake shimmers beneath steep wooded hills; just 3 mi of its length is in the United States, with the remaining 30 mi extending across the border into Canada.

Information: Vermont's North Country Chamber of Commerce | The Causeway, Newport, 05855 | 802/334–7782 | www.vtnorthcountry.com.

Attractions

Goodrich Memorial Library. This turreted brick 1899 structure houses Newport's main library collections, along with a stuffed animal exhibit. | 202 Main St. | 802/334–7902 | Free | Mon.–Wed. and Fri. 9:30–5, Thurs. 9:30–8, Sat. 9:30–3.

Haskell Opera House and Library. The international border actually runs right through this recently restored venue for cultural events, 8 mi north of Newport. | 96 Caswell Ave., Derby Line | 802/873–3022 | www.haskellopera.org | $2 (suggested donation) | Library Tues., Wed., Fri., Sat. 10–5; Thurs. 10–8.

Newport Boardwalk. This brick and wooden boardwalk has benches and gazebos for sitting or fishing. Biking is also a popular pastime along the lake. | Lake Memphremagog.

Old Stone House. An 1830s granite school dormitory built by headmaster Alexander Twilight, the first African-American college graduate (Middlebury College) in this country. The house is in the heart of the Brownington County historic district, 15 mi south of Newport. There is an exhibit celebrating Twilight's life and guided tours on request. | 28 Old Stone House Rd., Brownington | 802/754–2022 | homepages.together.net/~osh/ | $5 | Mid-May–June and Sept.–mid-Oct., Fri.–Tues. 11–5; July–Aug., daily 11–5.

Stardust Princess. The *Princess* offers excursions on Lake Memphremagog, a 33-mi-long jewel that extends north into Canada. | City Dock | 802/334–6617 | Cruises started at $9.95/ Memorial Day weekend through Labor Day weekend, daily 10–7:30; Sept.–Oct., weekends 10–6.

ON THE CALENDAR

JULY: *International Swim.* Each July, swimmers from around the world gather in New-port to swim the entire distance of the lake, from Newport to Magog in Canada. | Proudy Beach | 802/334–6345.

Dining

The East Side. American/Casual. This popular lakeside eatery is buoyant and bustling. The large main dining room and deck, along with a spacious tavern, make for a lively mood on a summer weekend. Fresh seafood, steaks, chops, and prime rib dominate the menu. Kids' menu. No smoking. | 47 Landing St. | 802/334–2340 | Breakfast also available on week-ends. Closed Mon. | $10–$27 | AE, D, MC, V.

Lodging

Bay View Lodge and Motel. Reasonably priced lodgings near downtown Newport and its revitalized lakefront. The lodge's verandas have views of Lake Memphremagog and North-east Kingdom mountains. Golf, marina, shops, and beaches nearby. Restaurant, bar. Cable TV. Hot tub. Video games. Library. | 501 Pleasant St. (Rte. 5), Newport | 802/334–6543 | fax 802/334–6781 | 18 rooms | $39–$49 | AE, MC, V.

Inn at the Hill/Top of the Hills Motel and Inn. The individually appointed rooms of this late Victorian house share a country motif. A full range of modern amenities complements these rustic charms and makes the inn a comfortable and relaxing retreat. Complimen-tary Continental breakfast. Cable TV, in-room VCRs. Laundry facilities. Business services.

© Corbis

MAPLE SYRUP

Before you pour that stuff on your pancakes, check the label. Is it pure Vermont maple syrup?

Vermont is the United States' largest producer of the liquid gold offered up by *acer saccharum*, the sugar maple tree. But the trees don't give maple syrup; they give maple sap. Converting this watery, only vaguely sweet substance into syrup—an art learned from Native Americans—is a time-consuming, labor-intensive industry that remains remarkably decentralized and low-tech, even at the dawn of the 21st century.

You'll often hear maple producers talk about how many "taps" they have. They're referring to the number of holes drilled and taps inserted into mature sugar maples (a tree should be 10 inches in diameter before it receives even a single tap), so that sap can be harvested when it rises in the trees at winter's end. A few very small pro-ducers still hang metal buckets on their taps and collect the sap each day by towing a vat behind a tractor, or even on a sled drawn by horses. But most sap nowadays is collected through a system of plastic tubing that links all of the taps in the "sugar-bush" and routes the liquid to a storage tank right at the sugarhouse.

Once collected, the sap is boiled in a big steel pan called an evaporator. As it seeps through a series of baffles, it thickens, darkens, and grows sweeter. When the sap is flowing—a phenomenon associated with warm days and subfreezing nights, usually in March and April—producers will work around the clock in the steamy sugarhouses, stoking their fires and keeping a close eye on the syrup. A practiced eye will know when it's ready—and, along with equally practiced taste buds, will know how it ranks according to Vermont's strict, state-enforced grading system. Grade A Fancy has a fine but almost elusive flavor; most Vermonters prefer darker, more robust grades.

Pets allowed ($10 fee). | 1724 E. Main St. | 802/334–6748 or 800/258–2748 | fax 802/334–1463 | iath@together.net | www.innatthehill.com | 15 rooms | $65–$75 | AE, D, MC, V.

Super 8 Motel. A clean, cheerful, and economical motel 4 mi north of downtown Newport. Complimentary Continental breakfast. Cable TV. Business services. | 4412 Rte. 5, Derby | 802/334–1775 | fax 802/334–1994 | www.super8.com | 52 rooms | $61–$66 | AE, D, DC, MC, V.

NORTH HERO

(Nearby town also listed: Burlington)

North Hero, along with its sister town, South Hero, on the Champlain islands, is alleged to have been named for the Allen brothers, Ethan and Ira. North Hero and Knight Point state parks have incomparable Lake Champlain locations; throughout the island town, there are spectacular views of the Green Mountains and New York's Adirondacks. Stop for a picnic at City Bay near the old stone court house and look west across the lake toward Mt. Mansfield.

Information: Lake Champlain Islands Chamber of Commerce | Box 213, North Hero, 05474 | 802/372–5683 | fax 802/372–3205 | www.champlainislands.com.

Attractions

Ed Weed State Fish Hatchery. At this state-of-the-art hatchery 10 mi south of North Hero trout are raised to stock size and exhibits tell about fish species native to Vermont. | 14 Bell Hill Rd. | 802/372–3171 | Free | Daily 7:30–4.

Grand Isle–Plattsburgh Ferry. At 12 minutes, the ride seems too short for all this scenery. The ferry, 10 mi south of North Hero, is a good route to the northern Adirondacks via Plattsburgh, New York. | Ferry Dock, Rte. 314 | 802/864–9804 | www.ferries.com | 1-way fare: $7 car and driver, $2.25 each additional passenger | Daily 24 hrs.

North Hero State Park. This gorgeous lakeside location, 6 mi north of North Hero, has campsites, swimming, and Green Mountain views. | 802/372–8727 or 802/879–5674 | $2 | Memorial Day–Labor Day, daily 9–9.

Royal Lipizzan Stallions. Expertly trained white stallions perform precise maneuvers of Austrian dressage traditions, ridden by three generations of the Herrmann family. | Lipizzan Park, Rte. 2, 1½ mi past the drawbridge that crosses Lake Champlain | 802/372–5683 | www.champlainislands.com | $15 | Performances July–Aug., Thurs. and Fri. at 6, Sat. and Sun. at 2:30.

St. Anne's Shrine. A Roman Catholic shrine on site of Vermont's oldest settlement. There's a striking statue of Samuel de Champlain as well as a chapel, picnic area, and beach. | 92 St. Anne's Rd., Isle La Motte | 802/928–3362 | Free | Mid-May–mid-Oct., daily.

ON THE CALENDAR

JULY–AUG.: *Royal Lipizzan Stallions of Austria.* Expertly trained white stallions perform precise maneuvers of Austrian dressage traditions, ridden by three generations of the Herrmann family. | Rte. 2, North Hero | Performances July–Aug., Thurs. and Fri. at 6, Sat. and Sun. at 2:30 | 802/372–5683 | www.champlainislands.com.

AUG.: *North Hero Pipers' Gathering.* This bagpipe festival includes concerts, workshops, and dances. Vendors also come to sell different types of bagpipes. The events take place in buildings throughout North Hero; the concerts are held in the Town Hall. | Town Hall | 207/363–7924 | www.celticfire.com.

Dining

Margo's Pastry and Café. Café. Ten miles south of North Hero, Margo's serves coffees and juices as well as an assortment of pastries and light fare including soups, salads, quiches, pastas, focaccias, and wraps. You can dine in the café, take it home, or eat outside watching the lake and a nearby farm. | 200 Rte. 2, Grand Isle | 802/372–6112 | Breakfast also available. Closed Nov.–Apr. No dinner | $4–$8 | No credit cards.

North Hero House. Contemporary. On a scenic island in Lake Champlain, the inn (1891) was originally a stopover for steamship travelers. Today the spacious colonial dining room is tastefully decorated with antiques and collectibles. Nouvelle American cuisine is distinguished by many fresh, creatively presented ingredients. Delicious salads and daily seafood specials. Lunch is served on the pier. Sunday brunch. No smoking. | Rte. 2 | 802/372–4732 or 888/525–3644 | www.northherohouse.com | Breakfast also available | $13–$26 | AE, D, MC, V.

Shore Acres Restaurant. Contemporary. Wherever you sit in the dining room, you will gaze on lovely Lake Champlain and the Green Mountains. The regionally inspired cuisine includes dishes like slow-roasted rack of lamb served with garlic port rosemary sauce. | 237 Shore Acres Dr. | 802/372–8722 | www.shoreacres.com | Closed mid-Oct.–Apr. | $15–$24 | MC, V.

Lodging

Aqua Vista. The cabins of this lodge have a rustic antique interior and are suited to couples. Windows look east toward the lake, its islands, and Mt. Mansfield. The property is directly on the water, but also offers 64 acres of untamed land for bird-watching or hiking. No air-conditioning, refrigerators, no smoking, no room phones. Hiking, beach. No pets. | Rte. 2 | 802/372–6628 | 6 cabins | $75 | No credit cards.

Charlie's Northland Lodge. Sitting directly on the lake, this lodge is designed for outdoor enthusiasts who wish to pursue fishing, swimming canoeing, kayaking, and boating. The house was built in the 1800s and has a screened-in porch and a living room with a fireplace. Complimentary Continental breakfast. No air-conditioning, refrigerators, no smoking, no room phones. Beach, dock, boating. Fishing. No kids under 10. No pets. | Rte. 2 | 802/372–8822 | dorcrik@aol.com | 3 rooms (share a bath) | $65–$70 | MC, V.

North Hero House. A hotel with a superb lakeside location that offers Green Mountain views. There's a private beach with dockage, Sunfish and canoe rentals. The main house was built at the begining of the 19th century. Restaurant, bar, complimentary Continental breakfast. Tennis. | Rte. 2 | 802/372–4732 or 888/525–3664 | fax 802/372–4735 | nhh-lake@aol.com | www.northherohouse.com | 26 rooms, 2 suites | $89–$179, $199–$249 suites | AE, D, MC, V.

Ruthcliffe Lodge. In a remote location on the smallest of the Lake Champlain Islands, this lodge's rooms are all on the lakeside. You can dine in the lodge or on a lakeside patio. Restaurant, picnic area, complimentary breakfast. No air-conditioning, no smoking, no room phones, TV available. Boating. Bicycles. | 1002 Old Quarry Rd., Isle La Motte | 802/928–3200 or 800/769–8162 | fax 802/928–3200 | www.virtualcities.com/~virtual | 7 rooms | $81–$96 | Closed mid-Oct.–mid-May | AE, D, MC, V.

Shore Acres Inn and Restaurant. At this inn property, lawns sweep down to Lake Champlain, and you can contemplate the sweeping views from sparkling white Adirondack chairs. The restaurant known for steak, chops, seafood. Restaurant, bar. No air-conditioning in some rooms, some refrigerators, cable TV. Golf course, 2 tennis courts, croquet. Pets allowed. | 237 Shore Acres Dr. | 802/372–8722 | www.shoreacres.com | 23 rooms | $87–$129 | Closed mid-Oct.–mid-Apr. | D, MC, V.

Thomas Mott Homestead Bed & Breakfast. Small and inviting, this vintage farmhouse-turned-inn draws guests from as far as Europe. There are lake views on three sides of the house, regular quilting on weekends, and complimentary Ben and Jerry's ice cream—all you can eat—every Friday. Complimentary breakfast. No air-conditioning, no smoking, TV in common area. Cross-country skiing. | 63 Blue Rock Rd., Alburg | 802/796–3736 or 800/

348–0843 | fax 802/796–3736 | tmott@together.net | www.thomas-mott-bb.com | 5 rooms | $79–$105 | D, MC, V.

NORWICH

(Nearby towns also listed: White River Junction; Hanover, NH)

Norwich is a quiet Connecticut River valley town, today serving in large part as a bedroom community for Dartmouth College, across the river in Hanover, New Hampshire. It is the home of Sands, Taylor, and Wood, the two-century-old firm that manufactures King Arthur's flour, and maintains an amply stocked gourmet baking supply shop on Route 5.

Information: **Upper Valley Chamber of Commerce** | Box 697, 61 Old River Rd., White River Junction, 05001 | 802/295–6200 | fax 802/295–3779 | www.uppervalleyvt.com.

Attractions

King Arthur Flour Baking Center. The center includes an outlet store, a bakery, and a bakery school. The store, which has been in business since 1790, sells tools, specialty grains, and flours. At the bakery you can watch bakers at work. | Rte. 5 S | 802/649–3361 | Mon.–Sat. 9–6, Sun. 11–4.

Montshire Museum of Science. One of the finest museums in New England, the Montshire Museum houses exhibits on space, technology, and nature. A 100-acre woodland, laced with trails, allows you to observe a living eco-system up close. | Montshire Rd. | 802/649–2200 | $5.50 | Daily 10–5.

Dining

Jasper Murdoch Alehouse. American/Casual. Antique bottles and beer posters cover the walls of this pleasant Victorian pub within the Norwich Inn. The pub, known for its own fresh, house-brewed beer, serves dishes like a smoked chicken sandwich on house-made pepperjack brioche. | Main St. | 802/649–1143 | Closed Mon. | $6–$9 | AE, D, DC, MC, V.

Norwich Inn. Contemporary. The elegant, candlit dining room of this Victorian inn serves such entrées as roast Long Island duckling with wild rice flan and ginger rhubarb sauce. Breakfast and lunch are served on an enclosed porch. | Main St. | 802/649–1143 | Breakfast also available. Closed Mon. | $16–$22 | AE, D, DC, MC, V.

Lodging

Norwich Inn. This Victorian inn in the center of sleepy Norwich has 23 rooms, 16 of which are in the original house, and seven of which are in an adjacent motel. An additional four suites, all with kitchens, are perfect for families. The rooms are individually appointed but all have basic modern amenities. Restaurant, bar, complimentary Continental breakfast. Some kitchenettes, no smoking, cable TV. | Main St. | 802/649–1143 | 23 rooms, 4 suites | $69–$149 | AE, D, DC, MC, V.

PERU

(Nearby towns also listed: Londonderry, Manchester, Manchester Center, Stratton Mountain)

Peru is a sedate village in the heart of the Green Mountain National Forest's southern section. Within the town's borders are Bromley ski area, known for its southward

PERU

INTRO
ATTRACTIONS
DINING
LODGING

slopes and family amenities, and Hapgood Pond State Recreation Area, a secluded spot offering fishing, swimming, camping, and nature trails.

Information: **Manchester and the Mountains Chamber of Commerce** | 2 Main St., Peru, 05255 | 802/362–2100 | fax 802/362–3451 | www.manchestervermont.net.

Attractions
Bromley Alpine Slide. Unlike some alpine slides, this one offers different tracks for novices and speed demons. It is the country's longest alpine slide at ²/₃ mi. Slow, medium, or fast-track runs are yours for the taking and the simple-to-use brake means that you're always in control. | Rte. 11 | 802/824–5522 | www.bromley.com | $6.50 | Late May–mid-June and mid-Sept.–mid-Oct., weekends 10–6; mid-June–mid-Sept., Sun.–Fri. 10–5, Sat. 10–6.
Bromley Mt Ski Area. One of Vermont's oldest ski areas is 2 mi southwest of Peru and favored for its southward slopes and diverse terrain. Also a variety of summer activities: scenic chair-lift rides, miniature golf, hiking, children's theater. | Rte. 11, Peru | 802/824–5522 | www.brom-ley.com | $47 for weekend lift ticket | Summer activities mid-June–mid-Oct., winter activities mid-Nov.–mid-Apr.

J.J. Hapgood Village Market. Come in and get a slab of sharp Vermont cheddar from the enormous wheel on the counter. Maple syrup, jams, jellies, and Vermont produce are also for sale. | Main St., Peru | 802/824–5911 | Mon.–Sat. 7–6, Sun. 8:30–1.

Wild Wings Ski Touring Center. Within the Green Mountain National Forest this center, 2¹/₂ mi north of Peru, has 13 mi of groomed trails. | North Rd., Peru | 802/824–6793 | $12 full day, $9 half day | Mid-Dec.–Mar., daily 9–4.

ON THE CALENDAR
SEPT.: *Peru Fair.* Held on the fourth Saturday of September, this fair includes a parade, a pig roast, crafts demonstrations, flea market, pony rides, musical entertainment, and street performers. | Main St. | 802/824–6336.

Dining
Ginger Tree. Chinese. Traditional Cantonese and Hunan specialties are served up in the Wiley Inn, a charming colonial inn near Bromley Mountain. To start, try the shrimp and vegetable soup made with succulent Ecuadorian shrimp. Spicy Shanghai noodles and aromatic chicken are both winning entrées. No smoking. | Rte. 11, Bromley Mountain | 802/824–5500 | Closed Mon.–Tues. No lunch | $35 for 5–course dinner; prix fixe | AE, D, MC, V.

Johnny Seesaw's. Continental. The rustic, hand-hewn main lodge was originally built by Russian logger Ivan Sesow, who dubbed it the Wonderview Log Pavillion. Raucous Saturday-night dances, homemade moonshine, and sin cabins helped fuel a reputation for debauchery in its early days. Today Johnny Seesaw's maintains the Prohibition-era charm of this mountain getaway while serving terrific Yankee cuisine. Live acoustic guitar on Saturday evenings. Known for prime rib and Cornish game hen. Kids' menu. No smoking. | Rte. 11 | 802/824–5533 or 800/424–CSAW | Closed Apr.–late May. No lunch | $14–$25 | D, MC, V.

Lodging
The Bromley View Inn. Eight miles east of Manchester, and encircled by forests, this inn provides comfortable accommodations in the heart of the Green Mountains. Rooms overlook the breathtaking landscape. Amenities in the common area include a jukebox and a pool table. Bar, complimentary breakfast. No air-conditioning, no room phones, TV in common area. Pond. Video games. Library. | Rte. 30, Bondville | 800/297–1459 | fax 802/297–3676 | bvi@sover.net | www.bromleyviewinn.com | 13 rooms | $90–$130 | AE, D, MC, V.

Johnny Seesaw's. This snug, log lodge was a dance hall in the 1920s. It has long been a favorite with skiers who gather around the big circular fireplace. The cottages also have fireplaces. Restaurant, complimentary breakfast. Some refrigerators, some room phones. Pets allowed. | Rte. 11, Peru | 802/824–5533 | fax 802/824–5533 | gary@jseesaws.com | www.jseesaw.com

| 8 rooms, 8 suites, 4 cottages | $160, $170 suites, $190 cottages | Closed mid-Apr.–late May | D, MC, V.

The Wiley Inn. Built in 1835, the house has served as a residence, stagecoach stop, and teahouse. Some rooms have fireplaces, others contain large windows and canopy beds. Rooms overlook the mountains and wooded forests. The property also includes two ponds filled with trout, and 10 acres of wooded land. Restaurant, complimentary breakfast. No smoking, some in-room hot tubs, no room phones, TV in common area. Pool, 2 ponds. Hot tub. No pets. | Rte. 11 | 888/843–6600 | fax 802/824–4195 | wileyinn@sover.net | www.wileyinn.com | 16 rooms | $95–$185 | AE, D, MC, V.

PLYMOUTH

MAP 11, D8

(Nearby towns also listed: Bridgewater, Killington, Ludlow, Woodstock)

Of all America's presidential shrines, Plymouth presents perhaps the clearest and most poignant portrayals of a chief executive's boyhood. Calvin Coolidge was born here on July 4, 1872, and the village of Plymouth Notch—a state historic site—has been kept as it was when he was growing up. Along with the family store, residence, and barns, visitors can see the room where Coolidge's father, a justice of the peace, swore in his son as president by kerosene light, upon learning of the death of President Warren Harding. Coolidge's burial plot is nearby.

Information: **President Calvin Coolidge Historic Site** | Coolidge Memorial Dr., Plymouth Notch, 05056 | 802/672–3773 | www.historicvermont.org.

Attractions

Calvin Coolidge State Forest. Several 3,000-ft-plus peaks dot this preserve, 1 mi north of Plymouth, near the president's birthplace. | Rte. 100A (Calvin Coolidge Memorial Hwy.) | 802/672–3612 or 802/886–2434 | www.vtstatepark.com | $2 | Memorial Day–Columbus Day, daily 9–9.

Plymouth Cheese Factory. This small cheddar-making operation right at the Coolidge homestead was owned by the former president's family. You can buy all types of Vermont cheeses here. | 802/672–3773 | Late May–mid.-Oct., daily 9:30–5.

President Calvin Coolidge Homestead. An entire 19th-century preserved village 1 mi northeast of Plymouth that includes Coolidge's birthplace, the house where he was inaugurated, and a visitor center with historical exhibits. | 1 Coolidge Memorial Dr. | 802/672–3773 | $5 | Memorial Day–Columbus Day, daily 9:30–5.

The Wilder Barn. Antique farm tools, old carriages, and the cheese factory's original equipment are exhibited here. The barn itself is a relic; built in 1875, it has hand-hewn beams held together with pegs. | Plymouth Notch | 802/672–4313 | $6 | Late May–mid-Oct.

ON THE CALENDAR

JULY: *President Calvin Coolidge's Birthday Parade.* President Coolidge is the only president to have been born on July 4th. This parade, which begins on the Village Green and ends at his grave, is a celebration of both the president and the nation. A chicken barbecue is held afterwards at the Wilder House. | Plymouth Notch | 802/672–3773.

Dining

Hawk Inn and Mountain Resort. Contemporary. A relaxing inn restaurant within the large resort. Dishes include Full Roast Pork Loin with Hot Pear Chutney, Pan-Seared Salmon with Roast Beet Vinaigrette, and Dijon Rosemary Rack of Lamb. | 75 Billings Rd. | 802/672–3811 | Reservations essential | $14–$29 | AE, MC, V.

The Wilder House. Delicatessen. The restaurant was originally a tavern, built in the 1830s, and also the home of the president's mother who in 1868 became engaged to the president's father in the sitting room. A fireplace is the central focus of the dining room and park benches and lawns around the house provide places for eating in the open air. The restaurant serves an assortment of sandwiches, soups, baked goods, and salads. | Plymouth Notch | 802/672–4313 | Breakfast also available. Closed Columbus Day–Memorial Day. No dinner | $5–$6 | No credit cards.

Lodging

Farmbrook. This the motel 3 mi north of Plymouth is most convenient to the Coolidge Birthplace. It's inexpensive and has a quiet, stream-side setting. Grill, picnic area. Some kitchenettes, no room phones. | Rte. 100A | 802/672–3621 | www.farmbrook.com | 12 rooms | $45–$65 | No credit cards.

Hawk Inn and Mountain Resort. Inn, apartments, and freestanding cottages, luxuriously appointed and hidden amid wooded hillsides. Maid service in the cottages and apartments. Fieldstone fireplaces. Dining room, bar, picnic area, complimentary breakfast, room service (inn rooms). In-room data ports, minibars, refrigerators, cable TV, in-room VCRs (and movies). 2 pools (1 indoor), swimming pond. Hot tub, massage. Tennis. Exercise equipment, hiking, boating. Fishing. Bicycles, ice-skating. Cross-country skiing, sleigh rides, tobogganing. Children's programs (ages 5–12), playground. Business services. Airport shuttle, free parking. | 75 Billings Rd. | 802/672–3811 or 800/685–4295 | fax 802/672–5582 | www.hawkresort.com | 50 rooms, 20 mountain villas, 18 town houses | $290–$350, $350–$650 apartments, $369–$470 cottages | MAP | AE, D, DC, MC, V.

Plymouth Towne Inn Bed-and-Breakfast. Breakfasts are served in a greenhouse dining room at this 1850s farmhouse. You can spend evenings in front of the fireplace. Rooms are individually appointed with oak and wicker furniture. Complimentary breakfast. No air-conditioning, no smoking, no room phones, TV in common area. Hot tub. No pets. | Rte. 100, Plymouth | 802/672–3059 | 4 rooms | $80 | No credit cards.

Salt Ash Inn. The colorful history of this inn dating from 1830 includes service as a stagecoach stop, post office, and dance hall. Dining room, bar, picnic area, complimentary breakfast. No air-conditioning, no smoking, cable TV. Pool. No kids under 5. | 1800 Salt Ash, at Rte. 100 and 100A | 802/672–3748, 800/725–8274 reservations | innkepr@aol.com | www.vermontvacation.com | 18 rooms (9 with shower only) | $69–$145, $275–$395 weekend package | MC, V.

PUTNEY

MAP 11, E11

(Nearby towns also listed: Bellows Falls, Newfane)

Putney, home of Landmark College, lies just north of Brattleboro along the Connecticut River. It was a destination of choice for 1960s counterculturists, many of whom have grown gray here; it's as easy a place as any in the state to find organic produce. Vermont's great governor and senator George Aiken hailed from Putney, where he operated a nursery.

Information: **Brattleboro Area Chamber of Commerce** | 180 Main St., Brattleboro, 05301 | 802/254–4565 | fax 802/254–5675 | www.brattleboro.com.

Attractions

Green Mountain Spinnery. At Exit 4 off Interstate 91 this factory is opposite the Putney Inn. Tours are given of the spinnery at 1:30 on the first and third Tuesday of every month. A factory-shop sells yarn, knitting accessories, and patterns. | 7 Brickyard La. | 802/387–4528 or 800/321–9665 | $2.

Harlow's Sugar House. This sugarhouse 2 mi north of Putney manufactures cider and maple syrup. A gift shop sells the products as well as seasonal fruit. | Rte. 5 | 802/387–5852/Daily 9–5.

JUNE–AUG.: *Yellow Barn Music School and Festival.* From late June to early August, the Yellow Barn Music School hosts between three and seven chamber concerts a week in Putney and the surrounding communities. The musicians include outstanding graduate-level students, internationally known faculty, and guest artists. | Concert Barn, Main St. | 800/639–3819 | ybarn@sover.net | www.yellowbarn.org.

Dining

Putney Inn Restaurant. American/Casual. The inn's relaxed and comfortable dining room is part of the original 1752 farmhouse and contains such details as hand-hewn beams and a brick hearth. The cuisine is inspired by regional produce and meats. Try the locally raised fresh turkey with apple maple pecan stuffing. | 57 Putney Landing Rd. | 802/387–5517 or 800/653–5517 | www.putneyinn.com | $13–$22 | AE, D, MC, V.

Putney Summit Restaurant. American/Casual. Within the Putney Summit Inn, this restaurant serves an array of homemade New England dishes including soups, salads, sandwiches, fish, beef, and pastas. Especially popular is the veal Wiener schnitzel. | Rte. 5 | 802/387–5806 | Breakfast available Sun. Closed Mon.—Tues. and 1st 2 wks Nov. | $9–$19 | AE, DC, MC, V.

Lodging

Beckwood Pond Bed-and-Breakfast. This property on 10 acres of wooded land offers opportunities for hiking, snowshoeing, and cross-country skiing. An additional 4 acres are landscaped, providing picnic areas and places to lounge in summer. Rooms are appointed with period furnishings, antiques, and heirlooms. Complimentary breakfast. No air-conditioning, no smoking, no room phones, TV in common area. No kids under 13. No pets. | 1107 Rte. 5 | 802/254–5900 | fax 802/254–8456 | beckwood@sover.net | www.beckwood-pond.com | 5 rooms | $130–$160 | AE, D, MC, V.

Hickory Ridge House Bed & Breakfast. A National Register Federal-style mansion (1808) with Palladian window and country antiques. The rooms in front are the most spacious and it has a rural, 12-acre setting near Connecticut River. German, Russian, and French are spoken. Complimentary breakfast. Hiking. Cross-country skiing. | 53 Hickory Ridge Rd. S | 802/387–5709 or 800/380–9218 | fax 802/387–4051 | www.hickoryridgehouse.com | 6 rooms, 1 cottage | $145–$175, $350 cottage | MC, V.

Putney Inn. This post-and-beam farmhouse, built in the 1750s by one of the first settlers of the area, houses a restaurant and public rooms. The guest rooms in annex are furnished with Queen Anne reproductions. The 13-acre site has Connecticut River valley views. The restaurant is highly regarded. Restaurant, bar. Cable TV. Pets allowed. | 57 Putney Landing Rd. | 802/387–5517 or 800/653–5517 | fax 802/387–5211 | putneyinn@sover.net | www.putneyinn.com | 25 rooms | $88–$158 | MAP available off-season | AE, D, MC, V.

Putney Summit Inn. This inn sits 1 mi north of Putney Village within a lovely rural landscape. Perennial gardens surround the inn and provide a lush space for relaxing in summer. The rooms are each appointed with a unique selection of antiques. The four rooms in the inn are available throughout the year, but the cottages are open only from Memorial Day to the third week in October. Restaurant, complimentary breakfast. No air-conditioning, no smoking, cable TV, no room phones. | Rte. 5 | 802/387–5806 | 4 rooms, 6 cottages | $60 | Closed Mon. and 1st 2 wks Nov. | AE, DC, MC, V.

Ranney-Crawford House. This bed-and-breakfast is housed in an early-19th-century brick house, 4½ mi north of Putney. The rooms, some of which have their own fireplaces, are done in period furniture and antiques. Windows overlook the surrounding meadows and mountains. Complimentary breakfast. No air-conditioning, no smoking, no room phones,

TV in common area. No kids under 10. No pets. | 1097 Westminster West Rd. | 802/387–4150 or 800/731–5502 | www.ranney-crawford.com | 4 rooms | $120 | AE, MC, V.

Room with a View. The rural location of this fully furnished apartment (4 mi north of Putney) makes it a perfect place for those seeking seclusion or outdoor recreation. The room has an outdoor deck and the windows overlook the spectacular New Hampshire mountains. No air-conditioning, microwaves, refrigerators, no smoking, cable TV, room phones. No kids under 10. | 119 Warden Rd. | 802/387–5291 | lmccorm@sover.net | welcome.to/roomwithaview | 1 room | $145 | No credit cards. .

RANDOLPH

MAP 11, E6

(Nearby towns also listed: Montpelier)

Randolph, near Vermont's geographical center, was a prime candidate to become state capital prior to Montpelier's selection in 1805. Later Randolph became a railroad town. Randolph Center, an older settlement east of today's main population center, is the home of Vermont Technical College.

Information: Randolph Area Chamber of Commerce | Box 9, 66 Central St., Randolph, 05060 | 802/728–9027 | fax 802/728–4705 | www.randolph-chamber.com.

Attractions

Porter Music Box Museum and Greystone Gift Shop. The world's only manufacturer of large-disk music boxes, this site has a museum that exhibits music boxes from the 1700s to the present. Some are played for you on the tour. The museum is housed in a mansion built by Albert Chandler. | Rte. 66 | 800/811–7087 | info@portermusicbox.com | www.portermusicbox.com | $5 | May–Dec., Mon.–Sat. 9:30–5 (mid-Aug.–mid-Oct., also Sun. noon–4).

ON THE CALENDAR
SEPT.: *New World Festival.* Held on the Sunday before Labor Day each September, the New World Festival is a celebration of Celtic and Franco music and dance. The festival begins at noon and continues until midnight with dancing, concerts, crafts, and vendors. | Chandler Music Hall, Main St. | 802/728–9694 | $17.50 for the whole day, $6 after 10 PM.

Dining
Lippitt's Restaurant and Morgan's Pub. American/Casual. Part of the Three Stallion Inn, this restaurant and pub offer the same menu. The dining room overlooks the back lawn behind which mountains loom. Included on the menu are such succulent dishes as bourbon molasses pork chops. | Green Mountain Stock Farm | 802/728–5575 or 800/424–5575 | fax 802/728–4036 | tsi@quest-net.com | www.3stallioninn.com | Closed 1 wk in Apr. and 1 wk in Nov. No lunch | $16–$26 | AE, D, MC, V.

Lodging
Three Stallion Inn. This inn on 1,300 acres is perfect for outdoor enthusiasts; the property's 50 km (30 mi) of trails pass through woods, streams, and meadows. The rooms are adorned with floral pattern wallpaper and bedcovers which complement the rural landscape seen from the windows. The inn is just off Interstate 89 at Exit 4. Complimentary Continental breakfast. No air-conditioning, no smoking, no room phones, TV in common area. Pool. Hot tub, sauna. Tennis courts. Gym, hiking. Fishing. Cross-country skiing. Pets allowed (fee). | Green Mountain Stock Farm | 802/728–5575 or 800/424–5575 | fax 802/728–4036 | tsi@quest-net.com | www.3stallionsinn.com | 15 rooms | $147 | Closed 1 wk in Apr. and 1 wk in Nov. | AE, D, MC, V.

ROCKINGHAM

(Nearby towns also listed: Bellows Falls, Chester, Grafton, Springfield)

Rockingham, the Connecticut River valley town of which Bellows Falls is the main settlement, is best known for its 1787 Rockingham Meetinghouse, one of the purest expressions of early New England architecture. With its box pews, steeple-less exterior, and absence of all decoration, the meetinghouse is a hymn to simplicity.

Information: **Great Falls Region Chamber of Commerce** | Box 554, Village Sq, Rockingham, 05101 | 802/463–4280 | www.gfrcc.org.

Attractions

Rockingham Meetinghouse. The meetinghouse, part of the old village of Rockingham that no longer stands, is the country's oldest community meetinghouse still in use. Many of its features, like the glass and the box pews, are original to the 1787 structure. The building is 4 mi north of Bellows Falls, just off Route 103. | Meeting House Rd. | 802/463–4280.

ON THE CALENDAR

AUG.: *Rockingham Old Home Days.* Held on the weekend of August's first Sunday, this festival celebrates the history of the town and its surrounding villages. The festivities include bands, one of the Northeast's largest fireworks displays, and a pilgrimage to the meetinghouse. | Bellows Falls, Rockingham | 802/463–4280.

RUTLAND

(Nearby towns also listed: Brandon, Killington)

Rutland is Vermont's "second city" and perennial runner-up to Burlington. Nevertheless it is the commercial anchor and main population center of the central part of the state. Owing its early prosperity to its location in the middle of Vermont's marble belt and to the Rutland Railroad (later the Vermont Railway), Rutland welcomed a number of heavy industries during the late 19th and early 20th centuries. Enough of this industrial base survives to give the town a grittier, less "typical Vermont" cast. Rutland has in fact been feuding with Woodstock, that classic emblem of the tourists' Vermont, over the issue of longer trucks being allowed on Route 4, which serves both communities. Rutland argues that the bigger rigs are vital to the city's industries, while Woodstock detests having them rumble through its manicured streets.

Even Rutland, though, sees a future in which tourism and service industries are as important as manufacturing. After years of decline, the Edward Hopperesque downtown is being revitalized; Rutland scored a point against suburban mall developers when it lured a Wal-Mart into existing space in the city center. There are even plans to rehabilitate downtown's surviving movie palace as an arts center.

Perhaps most important for Rutland's future, it stands at the western gateway to the enormous Killington-Pico ski resort complex. Stand at the intersection of Routes 7 and 4, and it's almost possible to feel the gravitational pull of the "megamountain" on Rutland's eastward expansion.

Information: **Rutland Region Chamber of Commerce** | 256 N. Main St., Rutland, 05701 | 802/773–2747 | fax 802/773–2772 | www.rutlandvermont.com.

Attractions

Chaffee Center for the Visual Arts. Artist members of the Center offer their works for sale in the galleries of a Victorian mansion. | 16 S. Main St. | 802/775–0356 | www.chaffeecenter.org | $2 suggested donation | Mon. and Wed.–Sat. 10–5, Sun. 12–4; closed Tues.

Farrow Gallery and Studios. Ten miles west of Rutland in Castledon, a late-19th-century church is home to this gallery which exhibits the sculpture and jewelry of Patrick Farrow and other Vermont artists. | 835 Main St., Castleton | 802/468–5683 | www.vermontel.net/~farogal/index.html | May–Dec., Wed.–Mon. 10–5; Jan.–Apr., call ahead.

Half Moon State Park. This park on Town Road offers opportunities for boating and canoeing on its lake, as well as trails and campsites. A quiet woodsy park. It is 3½ mi off Route 30, 10 mi west of Rutland. | Black Pond Rd., Hubbardton | 802/273–2848 | Mid-May–Columbus Day Daily 8–10.

Hubbardton Battlefield and Museum. British forces sustained heavy losses while winning a July 1777 battle fought at this site 7 mi west of Rutland. The battlefield area is encircled by a walking trail that is about ½ mi in length. Along the trail are several markers that describe the battle and mark positions of the American and British forces. Today it's a remote and beautiful site. | E. Hubbardton Rd. | 802/273–2282 | $1 | Wed.–Sun. 9:30–5:30.

Mountain Top Cross Country Ski Resort. A 1,300-acre, self-contained resort high in the Green Mountains above Rutland. | 195 Mountain Top Rd., off Rte. 7 | 802/483–2311 or 800/445–2100 | www.mountaintopinn.com | Dec.–Mar. and May–Oct., daily.

New England Maple Museum. Displays tell the story of maple sugaring in Vermont, from the days of wooden sap buckets to the present. | Rte. 7, Pittsford | 802/483–9414 | $2.50 | Mid-Mar.–May and Oct.–Dec. daily 10–4; closed Jan.–mid-Mar.

Norman Rockwell Museum. An exhibit of Rockwell's published work 2 mi east of Rutland, that places a special emphasis on the illustrator's Vermont years. (*See* also the Norman Rockwell Exhibition in Arlington.) | 654 Rte. 4 E, Rutland | 802/773–6095 | www.norman-rockwellvt.com | $4 | Daily 9–5.

Vermont Marble Exhibit. Much of central Vermont sits above a vein of marble. This exhibit, 2 mi west of Rutland, tells how it's quarried and polished, and provides examples of fine carving. | 61 Main St., Proctor | 802/459–2300 or 800/427–1390 | $5 | Memorial Day–late Oct., daily 9–5:30.

Wilson Castle. A local nabob built this 32-room extravaganza in 1888. The furnishings, wood paneling, and stained glass are superb. | W. Procter Rd. | 802/773–3284 | www.wilsoncastle.com | $7 | Memorial Day–Oct., daily 9–6.

ON THE CALENDAR

MAY–OCT.: *Craft Fair and Flea Market.* Craft vendors sell everything from pottery to homemade jams at this market, while others hawk their antiques on the Rutland Fairgrounds. The market takes place every weekend throughout the summer. | Rutland Fairgrounds, Rte. 7 | Weekends 9–4 | 802/492–2013.

JULY: *Green Mountain Festival.* Rodeo and Independence Day Celebrations, magicians, balloons, fly-overs, clowns, fireworks are all part of this event. | Rutland Fairgrounds, Rte. 7 | 802/773–2747 | $10.

SEPT.: *Vermont State Fair.* A mainly agricultural fair with rodeos, demolition derby. It begins on Labor Day weekend and runs through the following weekend. | Rutland Fairgrounds, Rte. 7 | 802/775–5200 | $10.

Dining

Countryman's Pleasure. German. This early-19th-century farmhouse charmer 3 mi east of town serves roast duckling, pecan-crusted tuna, and scallops St. Christopher. There's open-air dining on the sunporch. Kids' menu, early-bird suppers. | Townline Rd., Mendon | 802/773–7141 | No lunch | $15–$25 | AE, DC, MC, V.

Little Harry's. Eclectic. This agreeable café in the heart of the business district serves a unique variety of dishes, most with Thai accents. Try the Duck Choo Chee—duck served in a curry sauce. Kids' menu. | 121 West St. | 802/747–4848 | $11–$17 | AE, MC, V.

Mountain Top Inn. American. The dining room of this mountain inn has dramatic views of the Chittenden Reservoir and the mountains. The menu includes roast pork tenderloin, rack of lamb, and seafood. | 195 Mountain Top Rd., Chittenden | 802/483–2311 or 800/445–2100 | fax 802/483–6373 | info@mountaintopinn.com | www.mountaintopinn.com | Breakfast also available. Closed mid-Mar.–mid-May and mid-Oct.–mid-Dec. No lunch | $18–$24 | AE, MC, V.

The Palms. Italian. Since it opened on Palm Sunday, 1933, this restaurant has been run by the Sabataso family. Specialties include the chef's own creation: veal à la Palms—veal scallops topped with mushrooms, two kinds of cheese, and a special tomato sauce. | 36 Strongs Ave. | 802/773–2367 | Closed Sun. | $10–$16 | AE, DC, MC, V.

Royal's 121 Hearthside. Contemporary. Some cooking in this rustic 1800s colonial inn is on the open hearth. Try the chicken stuffed with goat cheese or the pecan-crusted swordfish and don't miss the popovers—they're famous. Early-bird suppers. | 37 N. Main St. (U.S. 7) | 802/775–0856 | $16–$23 | AE, D, DC, MC, V.

Sirloin Saloon. Steak. This full-service steak house has consistently good, traditional American cuisine. All the steaks are excellent as is the wood-grilled fresh seafood. Salad bar. Kids' menu. No smoking. | 200 S. Main St. (U.S. 7) | 802/773–7900 | www.sirloinsaloon.com | No lunch | $10–$25 | AE, D, DC, MC, V.

Lodging

Best Western Inn and Suites. A reasonably priced motel with both rooms and suites 3 mi east of Rutland. It's near Killington and Pico. Complimentary Continental breakfast. In-room data ports, some kitchenettes, cable TV, some in-room VCRs. Pool. Tennis. Laundry facilities. Business services. | Rte. 4 E | 802/773–3200 | fax 802/773–3200 | www.bestwestern-rutland.com | 56 rooms, 56 suites | $79–$149, $99–$169 suites | AE, D, DC, MC, V.

Comfort Inn. Just off Rte. 7 near downtown; popular with tours. Complimentary Continental breakfast. In-room data ports, cable TV. Indoor pool. Hot tub, sauna. Business services. | 19 Allen St. | 802/775–2200 | fax 802/775–2694 | 104 rooms | $40–$151 | AE, D, DC, MC, V.

Finch & Chubb. Built in preparation for the War of 1812, this place is 24 mi east of Rutland in sleepy Whitehall. Restaurant, complimentary Continental breakfast. Cable TV. Pool. | 82 N. Williams St., Whitehall | 518/499–2049 | fax 518/499–2049 | fin._chubb@msn.com | www.visitwhitehall.com | 6 rooms | $59–$79 | AE, D, DC, MC, V.

Harvest Moon Bed-and-Breakfast. This property 3 mi north of town is surrounded by pastures and hay fields. Once a farmhouse, the B&B has a wraparound porch, a parlor with piano, and hiking trails on Pine Hill. Drive north on Merchant's Row in Rutland, which becomes Grove Street. Complimentary Continental breakfast. No air-conditioning, no smoking, no room phones, TV in common area. Hiking. Library. No pets. | 1659 N. Grove St. | 802/773–0889 | info@harvestmoonvt.com | www.harvestmoonvt.com | 2 rooms | $125 | D, MC, V.

Holiday Inn Center of Vermont. This is Rutland's largest hotel, just south of downtown, off the busy Route 7 strip. Restaurant, bar with entertainment. In-room data ports, room service, cable TV. Indoor pool. Hot tub. Gym. Laundry facilities Business center. Airport shuttle. | 476 U.S. Rte. 7 S | 802/775–1911 | fax 802/775–0113 | www.holidayinn-vermont.com | 150 rooms | $119–$299 | AE, D, DC, MC, V.

Howard Johnson Inn. A standard chain entry on busy Route 7 just south of downtown. Complimentary Continental breakfast. Cable TV, some in-room VCRs. Indoor pool. Sauna. Video games. Laundry facilities. | 378 S. Main St. | 802/775–4303 | fax 802/775–6840 | 98 rooms | $64–$149 | AE, D, DC, MC, V.

The Inn at Rutland. A gracious B&B in one of the imposing Victorian homes that line Rutland's Main Street (Route 7). Each room is distinctively furnished with antiques and designer linens. Complimentary breakfast. No smoking, cable TV. | 70 N. Main St. | 802/773–0575 or 800/808–0575 | fax 802/775–3506 | www.innatrutland.com | 12 rooms (4 with shower only) | $110–$185 | AE, D, DC, MC, V.

Maplewood Inn. A rambling 1843 Greek Revival farmhouse 18 mi west of Rutland that is handsomely furnished. Some rooms can be combined as suites and four of them have fireplaces. Complimentary Continental breakfast. Cable TV. Business services. | Rte. 22A S, Fair Haven | 802/265–8039 or 800/253–7729 | fax 802/265–8210 | www.sover.net/~maplewd | 5 rooms | $80–$145 | AE, MC, V.

Mountain Top Inn and Resort. This secluded, 1,300-acre resort 10 mi from Rutland has one of Vermont's most dramatic settings, overlooking Chittenden Reservoir and the Green Mountains. There's a lively equestrian center and, in winter, some 100 km (60 mi) of trails for cross-country skiing. Dining room, bar. Room service, TV in common area. Pool. Sauna. Golf course, putting green, tennis. Hiking. Boating. Fishing, ice-skating. Cross-country skiing, sleigh rides. | 195 Mountain Top Rd., Chittenden | 802/483–2311 or 800/445–2100 | fax 802/483–6373 | info@mountaintopinn.com | www.mountaintopinn.com | 34 rooms, 6 cottages, 6 chalets | $196–$268 | Closed Apr. and Nov. | AE, MC, V.

Nordic Hotel Suites. Suites at this hotel have fireplaces, spiral staircases, modern amenities, and private decks. It is surrounded by the Green Mountains and is 1 mi east of Rutland and only 6 mi east of Killington. Kitchenettes, microwaves, refrigerators, no smoking, cable TV, room phones. No pets. | Rte. 4 E | 802/773–7964 | fax 802/775–6624 | wswt.com/nordic | 24 suites | $95–$185 | AE, D, MC, V.

The Phelps House. The first Frank Lloyd Wright house built in Vermont, this B&B has five common rooms with fireplaces and stoves. The large guest rooms are elegantly appointed with canopy beds, oriental rugs, and antiques. Complimentary breakfast. No air-conditioning, no smoking, no room phones, TV in common area. Tennis court. Library. No pets. | 19 North St. | 802/775–4480 | dphelps@together.net | 8 rooms | $75–$100 | No credit cards.

Pine Tree Lodge. A comfortable motel that provides clean and affordable accommodations throughout the year. During the peak season, the price of a room includes a complimentary Continental breakfast. In summer guests can enjoy the beautiful garden flowers. Picnic area. Refrigerators, no smoking, cable TV. Pool. No pets. | 154 Woodstock Ave./Rte. 4 E | 802/773–2442 or 800/773–2441 | fax 802/773–0220 | www.pinetreelodge.com | 14 rooms | $54–$109 | AE, D, MC, V.

Ramada Limited. Conveniently located outlet of this popular chain. Complimentary Continental breakfast. Some kitchenettes, cable TV. Indoor pool. Sauna. | 253 S. Main St. (U.S. 7) | 802/773–3361 | fax 802/773–4892 | 75 rooms | $74–$139 | AE, D, DC, MC, V.

Tulip Tree Inn. This 1842 antique inn 10 mi north of Rutland was the home of a millionaire inventor who got out of the market just before the crash in 1929. The inn is filled with antiques and Chittenden Reservoir is nearby if you want water sports. Dining room, bar. No room phones. Library. No kids. | 49 Dam Rd., Chittenden | 802/483–6213 or 800/707–0017 | fax 802/483–2623 | ttinn@sover.net | www.tuliptreeinn.com | 9 rooms | $189–$399 | Closed Apr.–mid-May and 1st 2 wks Nov. | MAP | MC, V.

ST. ALBANS

MAP 11, C2

(Nearby town also listed: Highgate Springs)

St. Albans was once known as the Rail City, so important were its railroad offices, yards, and roundhouses. Today St. Albans is still the northern terminus for Amtrak's daily *Vermonter*, but the old "Rail City" sobriquet survives only as the name of a local microbrew. Like many a small Vermont city, St. Albans has had to fight to keep its downtown vibrant;

it survives with a mix of small businesses and restaurants, and a sturdy stock of Victorian commercial and public buildings at its core. Taylor Park, with its ornate fountain, forms a fine central focus for downtown's grander structures. St. Albans Bay State Park, on Lake Champlain, is just 3 mi east.

St. Albans has the odd distinction of being the northernmost site of hostilities in the Civil War. On October 19, 1864, Confederate raiders in civilian clothes staged the "St. Albans Raid"—a simultaneous robbery of all the city's banks. The rebels escaped over the Canadian border with $200,000. They were acquitted in Canada on grounds that they were belligerents in wartime, but the Canadians reimbursed the banks ¼ of the stolen sum after an American outcry.

Information: **St. Albans Area Chamber of Commerce** | 2 N. Main St., St. Albans, 05478 | 802/524–2444 | fax 802/527–2256 | www.stalbanschamber.com.

Attractions

Burton Island State Park. One of Vermont's most unusual state parks, it is only accessible by boat. Here you can enjoy swimming and camping in a car-free setting. Visitors may use their own boats to reach the island, or they may take a passenger ferry, which leaves Kamp Kill Kare State Park 3 mi southwest of St. Albans. | On island in Lake Champlain | 802/524–6353 or 802/879–6565 | $2 | Memorial Day–Labor Day, daily 8–8.

Chester A. Arthur Historic Site. The 21st president spent his earliest days on this site 10 mi west of St. Albans. The present building is a re-creation of the parsonage where Arthur's minister father lived with his family. | Chester Arthur Hwy., off Rte. 36 | 802/828–3211 | $2 | Memorial Day–Columbus Day, Wed.–Sun. 10–4.

Lake Carmi State Park. Swimming, camping, and a boat launch are available at this lakeside park 15 mi northeast of St. Albans. | 460 Marsh Farm Rd., Enosburg Falls | 802/933–8383 or 802/879–5674 | www.state.vt.us/anr/ftr/park/ | $2 | Mid-May–Labor Day 10–dusk; check in after 2, depart by 11.

Missisquoi Valley Rail Trail. The 26 mi of trail follows an old railroad bed to the Canadian border. The trail is perfect for hikers, bikers, and cross-country skiiers. | Rte. 7 N | 802/524–2444.

St. Albans Historical Museum. Exhibits chronicle local history, including the colorful railroad days. One room recreates an old-time country doctor's office. | 7 Church St. | 802/527–7933 | $3 | May–Oct., weekdays 1–4 or by appointment.

ON THE CALENDAR

APR.: *Maple Festival.* The last weekend in April brings carnival time in St. Albans: maple syrup and pancakes help fuel the activities, which include a banquet, an antiques show, a talent show, arts and crafts, and a parade. | Downtown St. Albans | 802/524–5800 | www.vtwebs.com/maplefest.

JUNE–SEPT.: *Summer Sounds Concert Series.* From the last Sunday in June to the first Sunday in September, this county-wide festival appears in five different towns, including Highgate and St. Albans. All kinds of music are represented, including folk, pop, blues, country, and opera. The concerts that take place at 7 on Sunday are always free. | The Village Green | 802/868–3351.

JULY: *Bay Day.* Triathlon race with kids' events and activities. | St. Albans Bay | 802/524–2444.

Dining

Old Foundry Restaurant. American/Casual. This restaurant in a foundry that used to produce railcar wheels is decorated with old photographs and memorabilia. The eatery's fare has a steak and seafood emphasis. Breads and desserts are homemade. | Corner of Lake and Federal Sts. | 802/524–9665 | $10–$16 | MC, V.

Lodging

Cadillac. A traditional, independent motel just south of downtown St. Albans. It is surrounded by 3½ acres of landscaped grounds and has a rock garden and a waterfall. Restaurant, picnic area. Refrigerators, cable TV. Pool. Pets allowed. | 213 S. Main St. | 802/524–2191 | fax 802/527–1483 | www.motel-cadillac.com | 54 rooms, 5 suites, 1 honeymoon suite | $55–$70, $75–$85 suites | AE, D, DC, MC, V.

Comfort Inn and Suites. One of St. Albans' newest lodgings, this chain hotel has direct access to Interstate 89 and is a short drive from downtown. It is a Choice Hotels Gold award winner. Picnic area, complimentary Continental breakfast. In-room data ports, some microwaves, refrigerators, cable TV, some in-room VCRs. Indoor pool. Exercise equipment. Video games. Laundry facilities. Business services. | 813 Fairfax Rd. | 802/524–3300 | fax 802/524–3300 | comfort2@together.net | www.selectvermont.com/comfortinn | 63 rooms, 17 suites | $90–$131 | AE, D, DC, MC, V.

Econo Lodge in St. Albans. This chain motel provides warm, inviting accommodations at affordable prices. Some rooms are handicap accessible and pets are allowed in other rooms. Complimentary Continental breakfast. Refrigerators, cable TV. Pets allowed (fee). | 287 S. Main St. | 802/524–5956 or 800/55–ECONO | fax 802/524–5956 | econolake@aol.com | www.econolodge.com/hotel/vt022 | 29 rooms | $99 | AE, D, DC, MC, V.

ST. JOHNSBURY

MAP 11, F4

(Nearby town also listed: Lyndonville)

St. Johnsbury, the only town in the world so named, is the informal capital of the sparsely populated three-county region known as the Northeast Kingdom, and the birthplace of an industry that weighed the world's goods: it was here in 1830 that Thaddeus Fairbanks invented the platform scale. Both the scale business and the Fairbanks family prospered over the following decades, and their beneficence created the two landmarks—the Fairbanks Museum and Planetarium, and the St. Johnsbury Athenaeum (a library) and Art Gallery—for which the city is best known today.

St. Johnsbury is a neatly bifurcated city, with its struggling commercial district at the bottom of a steep hill near the Passumpsic River and the old railroad yards; and its Victorian public buildings—the Athenaeum, Museum, and Court House—arranged along Main Street atop the hill. Also enjoying a hilltop location is St. Johnsbury Academy (founded, of course, by the Fairbanks family), which serves the unusual dual role of public high school and highly regarded private academy.

Information: **Northeast Kingdom Chamber of Commerce** | 357 Western Ave., Suite 2, St. Johnsbury, 05819 | 802/748–3678 | fax 800/639–6379 | www.vermontnekchamber.org.

Attractions

Cabot Creamery Cooperative. Watch Vermont cheddar being made at the state's biggest cheese producer, 20 mi west of St. Johnsbury. There's a film, free tastings, and a cheese shop. | Main St. (Rte. 215), Cabot | 800/837–4261 | www.cabotcheese.com | $1 | June–Oct., daily 9–5; Nov.–Dec. and Feb.–May, Mon.–Sat. 9–4.

Fairbanks Museum and Planetarium. An imposing Romanesque Revival structure that houses a fascinating collection of Vermontiana, mounted animal and bird specimens, and international ethnography. There is also a children's room and a small planetarium. | 1302 Main St., at Prospect St. | 802/748–2372 | www.fairbankmuseum.org | Museum $5, planetarium $2 | Sept.–May, Mon.–Sat. 10–4, Sun. 1–5; July–Aug., Mon.–Sat. 10–6, Sun. 1–5; planetarium shows Mon.–Fri. 11 and 1:30, Sat.–Sun 1:30.

Maple Grove Farm of Vermont. One of Vermont's biggest maple producers shows how it's done. Guided tours are available on request. | 1052 Portland St. | 802/748–5141 | www.maplegrove.com | $1 | Weekdays 8–4.

St. Johnsbury Athenaeum and Art Gallery. Adjoining the city library is a gallery of art unchanged in 125 years. The 19th-century portrait and landscape collection's highlight is Bierstadt's enormous *Domes of the Yosemite*. | 1171 Main St., at Eastern Ave. | 802/748–8291 | $2 (suggested donation) | Mon. and Wed. 10–8; Tues., Thurs., Fri. 10–5:30; Sat. 9:30–4.

ON THE CALENDAR

JUNE–AUG.: *St. Johnsbury Town Band.* The town band gives Monday evening concerts from 8 to 9 | St. Johnsbury Academy Amphitheater, off Main St. | Mon. 8–9 | Free | 603/638–4961.

OCT.: *Fall Foliage Festival.* Part of a weeklong, traveling celebration, this festival appears for one day in St. Johnsbury and includes street performers, live music, craft vendors, and a farmers' market. | Main St. | 802/748–3678.

Dining

Creamery. American. This eatery in the center of Danville village (7 mi west of St. Johnsbury) is in a late 1800s creamery. It is adorned with old milk cans, memorabilia, and photographs and divided into an upstairs dining room and downstairs pub. The chalkboard menu changes everyday but consistently lists fresh fish, chicken, and beef dishes. Kids' menu. | Hill St., Danville | 802/684–3616 | Closed Sun.– Mon. | $12–$16 for dining room, $6–$12 for pub | AE, MC, V.

Rabbit Hill Inn. Contemporary. An elegant, candlelit restaurant in a famous old inn. Live entertainment, a flutist or harpist, on Saturday during dinner. Wine cellar. No smoking. | 48 Lower Waterford Rd. | 802/748–5168 | Reservations essential | Breakfast also available. No lunch | $37 prix fixe | AE, MC, V.

Surf and Sirloin Restaurant. American/Casual. The stained wood interior of this mid-1800s dining room produces a cozy environment within which to enjoy a variety of steak and seafood dishes. A kids' menu is also available. | 264 Portland St. | 802/748–5412 | Breakfast also available | $10–$14 | MC, V.

Lodging

Aime's Motel. A 1950s theme dominates this independent motel, just outside the city center. Each room has a screened-in porch. You can also relax on lawn furniture in the backyard next to the Moose River. Cable TV. | 46 Rte. 18 | 802/748–3194 or 800/504–6663 | aimmotel@hcr.net | 18 rooms, 1 apartment | $55–$70, $100 apartment | AE, D, MC, V.

Albro Nichols House Bed-and-Breakfast. Built in 1848 on a farm, this building has since been moved to the center of town. It offers easy access to St. Johnsbury's restaurants and attractions. The porch, backyard patio, and formal gardens are all comfortable spaces for relaxing. Complimentary breakfast. No air-conditioning, no smoking, cable TV, some in-room VCRs, some room phones. No pets. | 53 Boynton Ave. | 802/751–8434 | 3 rooms (2 with shared bath) | $55–$65 | No credit cards.

Echo Ledge Farm Bed-and-Breakfast. This property 5 mi east of town used to be a dairy farm. The farmhouse dates from the late 18th century and is decorated country home comfortable and cozy. Woods and fields surround the house, and from the windows you can gaze on the neighboring farmlands. Complimentary breakfast. No air-conditioning in some rooms, no smoking, no room phones, TV in common area. No pets. | Rte. 2 E, East St. Johnsbury | 802/748–4750 | 6 rooms (2 with shared bath) | $47–$87 | MC, V.

Holiday Motel. Recently renovated independent motel just north of city center. Picnic area. Cable TV. Pool. | 222 Hastings St. | 802/748–8192 | fax 802/748–1244 | 34 rooms | $89–$95 | AE, D, MC, V.

Injun Joe Court. Tidy cabins in a scenic location on Joe's Pond, 10 mi west of St. Johnsbury. Kitchenettes. Beach, boating. Fishing. Pets allowed. | 3251 Rte. 2, West Denvill | 802/684–3430 | 15 cabins | $40–$48 cabins | Closed mid-Oct.–mid-May | MC, V.

Rabbit Hill Inn. This rambling 200-year-old inn is an elegant upcountry oasis, 10 mi south of St. Johnsbury. It has a serene village location and its dining is renowned. Some rooms have fireplaces. Restaurant, bar. No air-conditioning in some rooms, no smoking, some in-room hot tubs, no room phones. Pond. Cross-country skiing. No kids under 12. | On Rte. 18, Lower Waterford Rd., Lower Waterford | 802/748–5168 or 800/762–8669 | fax 802/748–8342 | rabbit.hill.inn@connriver.net | www.rabbithillinn.com | 21 rooms, 19 suites | $240–$270, $330–$375 suites | MAP | AE, MC, V.

SHELBURNE

MAP 11, C4

(Nearby towns also listed: Burlington, Charlotte, Vergennes)

Shelburne, a prosperous Burlington suburb just south of the city along Lake Champlain, is the home of two institutions associated with the Webb family and its railroad fortune. The Shelburne Museum, a trove of Americana, was the gift of Electra Havemeyer Webb; while Shelburne Farms, containing the mansions and show barns of her father William Seward Webb, is now a family-owned agricultural education center on the point that separates Shelburne Bay from the main body of the lake.

Information: Lake Champlain Regional Chamber of Commerce | 60 Main St., Suite 100, Burlington, 05401 | 802/863–3489 | fax 802/863–1538 | www.vermont.org.

Attractions

Charlotte–Essex Ferry. This car ferry 8 mi south of Burlington makes the 20-minute crossing of Lake Chaplain to the picturesque village of Essex, New York, at the gateway to the Adirondack Mountains. | Ferry Dock at end of Rte. F5 | 802/864–9804 | www.ferries.com | 1-way fare: $7 car and driver, $2.25 per passenger | Apr.–Jan., or when lake is ice-free.

Shelburne Farms. A Victorian millionaire's estate dating from 1887, with cavernous restored barns, a sumptuous inn and restaurant, a working farm, and its own celebrated brand of cheddar. | 1611 Harbor Rd., at Bay Rd. | 802/985–8686 or 802/985–8442 | $5 | Mid-May–mid-Oct., daily 9–5.

Shelburne Museum. Hailed as New England's Smithsonian, this is Vermont's premier collection of Americana, folk art, and period buildings. Seven historic houses (1773–1840) have been moved here from northern New England and New York—and filled with artifacts of everyday life. Also on the property is the lake steamer *Ticonderoga*. | 6000 Shelburne Rd. | 802/985–3346 | www.shelburnemuseum.org | $17.50 | Late May–mid-Oct., daily 10–5; late Oct.–Dec., daily 1–4; closed Jan.–Mar.

Vermont Teddy Bear Company. At North America's largest teddy bear manufacturer, you can watch the little characters being made and then take one home or ship one to anywhere in the world. The classic 15-inch bruin costs $49. | 6655 Shelburne Rd. | 802/985–3001 | www.vermontteddybear.com | $1 | Mon.–Sat. 9–6, Sun. 10–5.

ON THE CALENDAR

MAY: *Shelburne Museum Lilac and Gardening Weekend.* The 400 lilac bushes clustered on the museum grounds are the center of attention at this celebration which includes garden tours, demonstrations, lectures, carousel rides, music, dancing, and children's activities. | Shelburne Museum, 6000 Shelburne Rd. | 802/985–3346 | www.shelburnemuseum.org.

Dining

Café Shelburne. French. A satisfying, if pricey bistro. Try the asparagus and endive salad or rabbit salad on haricots verts, or the roast lamb. | Rte. 7 | 802/985–3939 | Closed Sun.–Mon. No lunch | $18–$22 | AE, MC, V.

Chef Leu's House. Chinese. This restaurant is consistently praised as the area's best for Chinese. Among the specialties are the orange-accented dishes. | 2545 Shelburne Rd./Rte. 7 | 802/985–5258 | $7–$13 | AE, D, DC, MC, V.

Inn at Shelburne Farms. French. A country inn with relaxed surroundings and decor. The traditional cuisine including filet mignon, steamed Atlantic salmon with shrimp, poached duck, vegetarian options. No smoking. | 1611 Harbor Rd. | 802/985–8498 | No lunch | $17–$25 | AE, MC, V.

Lodging

Days Inn. A chain option near the Shelburne Museum. Complimentary Continental breakfast. Cable TV. Pool. | 3229 Shelburne Rd. | 802/985–3334 | fax 802/985–3419 | 58 rooms | $50–$140 | AE, D, DC, MC, V.

★ **Inn at Shelburne Farms.** Amid the pastures and woodlands of this 1,400-acre working farm, a turn-of-the-20th-century inn perches on Saxton's Point, overlooking Lake Champlain and the Adirondacks. A unique selection of period antiques and wallpaper give each room its own distinct character. Some rooms face the lake and provide views of breathtaking sunsets. Restaurant, bar, picnic area. No air-conditioning, no smoking, no TV. Tennis court. Hiking, beach. Library. No pets. | 16 Harbor Rd. | 802/985–8498 | fax 802/985–8123 | www.shelburnefarms.org | 24 rooms (7 with shared bath), 2 cottages | $105–$350 | Closed mid-Oct.–mid-May | AE, D, MC, V.

T-Bird Motor Inn. A clean and modern motor inn ¾ mi north of Shelburne that provides discount tickets for nearby Shelburne Museum. Picnic area, complimentary Continental breakfast. Some refrigerators, cable TV. Pool. | 4405 Shelburne Rd. | 802/985–3663 or 800/335–5029 | 24 rooms | $58–$120 | Closed Nov.–mid-May | AE, MC, V.

SPRINGFIELD

MAP 11, E9

(Nearby towns also listed: Chester, Grafton, Ludlow, Rockingham)

Springfield was, until quite recently, the capital of the upper Connecticut River valley's machine-tool industry. Given its start with the help of the Black River's water power around the time of the American Revolution, Springfield—named after Springfield, Massachusetts—eventually achieved an industrial importance out of all proportion to its size. At one time the machines that cut most of the gears for America's cars were made here. As was true elsewhere, industry and immigration went hand in hand in Springfield: a century ago, one-third of the town's population had been born in eastern Europe, and a strong Polish strain survives in this part of Vermont. The machine-tool industry, however, does not.

Information: Springfield Chamber of Commerce | 14 Clinton St., Springfield, 05156 | 802/885–2779 | fax 802/885–6826 | www.springfieldvt.com.

Attractions

Eureka Schoolhouse. A restored 1790s school that is now Vermont's oldest one-room schoolhouse. | Rte. 11 (Charleston Rd.) | 802/885–2779 | www.cit.state.vt.us/dca/historic/hp_ites | Free | May–mid-Oct., Wed.–Mon. 11–5.

Reverend Dan Foster House and Old Forge. This house 6 mi north of Springfield is run by the Weathersfield Historical Society and exbihits the artifacts of Weathersfield's citizens. There is an old kitchen and individual rooms focusing on different regional families. The exibits change each summer. | 2656 Weathersfield Center Rd. | 802/263–5230 | Donations accepted | Late June–Sept., Thurs.–Mon. 2–5.

Springfield Art and Historical Society. This museum has early-American tableware and everyday objects as well as primitive paintings and contemporary art exhibits. | 9 Elm Hill | 802/885–2415 | Donations accepted | Mid-Apr.–Nov., Tues.–Fri. 10–4, Sat. 2–5.

ON THE CALENDAR

JUNE: *Weathersfield Antiques Show and Sale.* One of Vermont's longest-running roundups of antiques dealers comes together on the last Saturday of the month at the Old Meetinghouse. There is a snack bar on site. | Weathersfield Center Rd., Weathersfield | 802/263–9462.

OCT.: *Apple Festival.* Apples are at the core of this autumnal celebration which includes a craft show, apple games, a petting zoo, food vendors, and a climbing wall. The festival takes place each year on the Columbus Day weekend. | Riverside Middle School, Rte. 11 | 802/885–2779 | $2.

Dining

B.J. Brickers. American. This comfortable, family-oriented restaurant specializes in seafood and prime rib. Kids' menu and kids under 12 eat for half price. | 282 River St. | 802/885–9186 | $8–$15 | AE, D, MC, V.

Hartness House Inn. Continental. In a turn-of-the-20th-century inn, this marble dining room is spacious yet cozy. It's known for its fresh seafood. In summer there's open-air dining on a deck. Early-bird suppers. No smoking. | 30 Orchard St. | 802/885–2115 | www.hart-nesshouse.com | Breakfast also available | $13–$20 | AE, DC, MC, V.

Inn at Weathersfield. Contemporary. The flickering light of candles illuminates this inn's dining room which was originally a carriage house. The menu changes daily but might include such dishes as oven-baked pork tenderloin with apple-apricot brandy. | Rte. 106, Perkinsville, Weathersfield | 802/263–9217 | Closed May, Nov., and Mon.–Tues. No lunch | $11–$24 | AE, D, DC, MC, V.

Johnathon's. American. The city's friendliest staff waits on you at this riverside family restaurant. Although it serves a variety of dishes like hamburgers and steaks, the eatery specializes in seafood. | 244 River St. | 802/885–9231 | Breakfast also available | $9–$13 | MC, V.

Lodging

Baker Road Inn. Privacy, comfort, and quiet are the prime draws of this simple inn. A large deck surrounds an outdoor pool and is perfect for relaxing in summer. Two bunk rooms are available for parents traveling with children. Complimentary breakfast. No air-conditioning, no smoking, no room phones, no TV. Pool. No pets. | 29 Baker Rd. | 802/886–2304 | 4 rooms | $55 | No credit cards.

Bull Run Farm Bed-and-Breakfast. This early 1800s farmhouse 5 mi north of Springfield is part of a small farm which raises cows, geese, and chicken. The gardens and pool provide a convenient place for escape and contemplation. Complimentary breakfast. No air-conditioning, no room phones, no TV. Pool. No pets. | 903 French Meadow Rd., North Springfield | 802/886–8470 | 2 rooms | $55 | No credit cards.

Hartness House Inn. A sprawling former country estate that was built around the turn of the 20th century. The industrialist, inventor, and Vermont governor, James Hartness, who called it home, included an observatory for star-watching, which you can still do today. Restaurant, complimentary Continental breakfast, room service. Pool. Business services. |

30 Orchard St. | 802/885–2115 | fax 802/885–2207 | www.hartnesshouse.com | 40 rooms in 2 buildings | $89–$150 | AE, DC, MC, V.

Holiday Inn Express. A smaller, no-frills representative of chain that's just off Interstate 91 at Exit 7. Restaurant, bar, picnic area, complimentary Continental breakfast. In-room data ports, microwaves, some refrigerators, cable TV. Indoor pool. Exercise equipment. Business services. Pets allowed. | 818 Charlestown Rd. | 802/885–4516 | fax 802/885–4595 | hix-press@aol.com | 88 rooms | $125 | AE, D, DC, MC, V.

Hugging Bear. Teddy bears and other vintage pieces fill this antebellum Victorian house, which is next door to a shop that has over 9,000 teddy bears. Complimentary breakfast. No air-conditioning in some rooms, no smoking, no room phones, TV in common area. Cross-country skiing, downhill skiing. | 244 Main St., Chester | 802/875–2412 or 800/325–0519 | www.vbv-online.com/huggingbear | 6 rooms | $85–$125 | AE, D, MC, V.

Inn at Weathersfield. This late-18th-century inn has been a stagecoach stop and station on the Underground Railroad during its long life. There are antiques in the guest rooms and most rooms have fireplaces. Dining room, complimentary breakfast. No TV in some rooms, TV in common area. Pond. No kids under 8. | Rte. 106, Perkinsville in Weathersfield | 802/263–9217 or 800/477–4828 | fax 802/263–9219 | www.weathersfieldinn.com | 11 rooms, 1 suite | $95–$185 | AE, D, DC, MC, V.

Stone Hearth Inn. Curl up in front of the eponymous fireplace in this farmhouse-turned-inn built in the early 19th century. Exposed beams, wide-board pine floors, and a casual common space in the attached barn give this B&B an informal appeal. Dining room, bar, picnic area, complimentary breakfast. No air-conditioning. No room phones, TV in common area. Hot tub. Cross-country skiing, downhill skiing, snowmobiling. | 698 Rte. 11 W Chester | 802/875–2525 or 888/617–3656 | fax 802/875–4688 | www.virtualvermont.com/shinn | 10 rooms | $60–$100 | MAP available | AE, D, MC, V.

STOWE

MAP 11, D4

(Nearby towns also listed: Jeffersonville, Morrisville, Waterbury)

When a college librarian made the first ski descent of Mt. Mansfield in 1914, the village of Stowe meant no more to the world outside Vermont than any other farm town up in the hills. By the 1930s crews were cutting the mountain's first downhill trails, and Stowe's resort mystique was born.

There is Stowe the village—a collection of shops and restaurants occupying no more than a few blocks at the intersection of Routes 100 and 108—and Stowe Mountain resort, the official name of the ski area that sprawls across Spruce Peak and the east face of Mt. Mansfield. Here are the runs that have challenged generations of skiers: the National, the Goat, the Liftline, the Nosedive, and dozens of others.

Connecting the village and the resort is Route 108, the Mountain Road, a string of eateries, taverns, nightspots, and stylish shops that may not be Aspen or Chamonix—but that define après-ski, Vermont style.

Information: Stowe Area Association | Box 1320, Main St., Stowe, 05672 | 802/253–7321 or 800/24–STOWE | fax 802/253–2159 | www.gostowe.com.

Attractions

Elmore State Park. This park has campsites and a nice swimming beach on Lake Elmore. The trails lead to summit of 2,608-ft Elmore Mountain. | 856 Rte. 12, at Lake Elmore | 802/888–2982 or 802/479–4280 | $2 | Mid-May–Columbus Day, daily 10–sunset.

Mt. Mansfield State Forest. A rugged backcountry preserve containing the summits of Mt. Mansfield, and extending south to Waterbury Reservoir with its Little River State Park. At

4,393 ft, Mt. Mansfield is Vermont's highest peak, visible throughout the northern part of the state. It is said to resemble the profile of a reclining man and has summits named Chin and Nose. | 802/244–7103 or 802/479–4280.

Mt. Mansfield Gondola. A breathtaking ascent to just below the "Nose" of Mt. Mansfield, site of the Cliff House restaurant. | 5781 Mountain Rd., Rte. 108, north of Stowe Village | 802/253–3500 or 800/253–4SKI | www.stowe.com | Summer gondola rides $11 | June–Sept., daily 10–5; winter, daily 9–4.

Sterling Falls Gorge. To reach one of Vermont's most spectacular natural landmarks, drive 1 mi north on Route 100, then turn onto Stagecoach Road and continue another 1½ mi until Sterling Gorge Road. Drive another 1½ mi to the gorge. | Sterling Gorge Rd. | 802/253–7321 or 800/24–STOWE.

Stowe Mountain Auto Road. This toll road, 6 mi northwest of Stowe, leads from Route 108 to just below the Nose on Mt. Mansfield. From there you can hike along trails that range all over the mountain. | 5781 Mountain Rd., Rte. 108 | 802/253–3500 | www.stowe.com | $14/ vehicle | Mid-May–mid-Oct., daily 10–5.

Stowe Mountain Resort. Known to skiers everywhere simply as Stowe, this legendary resort is 6 mi north of Stowe village and offers the challenging "Front Four" trails on Mt. Mansfield as well as many others. | 5781 Mountain Rd., Rte. 108 | 802/253–3500 or 800/253–4SKI | www.stowe.com | Mid-Nov.–Apr., weekdays 8–4, weekends 7:30–4; mid-May–mid-Oct., daily 10–5.

Alpine Slide. Ride down Spruce Peak on a wheeled sled 2,300 ft along a slick, winding track. The ski area chairlift makes the run to the top. | 5781 Mountain Rd., Rte. 108 | 802/253–3500 | www.stowe.com | $8 | June–Sept., daily 10–5.

Stowe Recreation Path. A 5½-mi paved path for walking, running, cycling, and rollerblading, beginning in town and ranging through the countryside. | Starts at Stowe Community Church on Main Street | 802/253–7321 | www.gostowe.com | Free | Daily.

Trapp Family Lodge. The ski center at this lodge offers over 100 km (60 mi) of groomed and backcountry trails, lessons, and ski rentals. You can ski to a cabin in the woods which serves snacks and lunch. | 700 Trapp Hill Rd. | 802/253–8511 or 800/826–7000 | fax 802/253–5740 | www.trappfamily.com.

ON THE CALENDAR

JAN.: *Winter Carnival* in Stowe. Vermont's oldest winter fest, with a hockey tournament, snowshoe race, cross-country race, snow golf and volleyball, and more. | 802/253–7321.

JULY: *Stoweflake Balloon Festival.* Over 20 balloons are launched continuously at this event. | Stoweflake Resort Field, Rte. 108 | 2nd weekend in July | 802/253–7321.

JUNE–AUG.: *Trapp Family Meadow Concerts.* Summer concerts in the Trapp Family meadow at the Trapp Family Lodge. | 700 Trapp Hill Rd. | Sun. evenings | 802/253–8511 | $20 adults, $12 kids.

AUG.: *Stowe Antique Classic Car Meet.* Cars in categories ranging from horseless carriages to the age of fins compete for best in show at this two-day July meet. There are plenty of parts and paraphernalia for sale. | Nichols Field | 8 AM to dark | 802/426–3265.

Dining

Blue Moon Café. Contemporary. Light jazz and original paintings by local artists set the stage for the café's gustatory masterpieces like the marinated leg of lamb with pine-nut crust and braised sweet onions. The restaurant is open daily during most of the year, and only on weekends in late fall and early spring. | 35 School St. | 802/253–7006 | $16–$22 | AE, D, DC, MC, V.

Buttertub Bistro. American/Casual. This comfortable eatery, overlooking the resort's gardens, serves hearty salads, grilled sandwiches, and special pastas. It is across the hall from the Buttertub Bar, a cigar-friendly tavern. | 4000 Mountain Rd. | 802/253–8585 or 800/451–8686 | fax 802/253–9263 | www.topnotch-resort.com | $9–$19 | AE, D, DC, MC, V.

Cactus Café. Mexican. A local favorite, this restaurant has Mexican, Southwestern, and American dishes. Specials often include fresh seafood. It is in a 19th-century redbrick building, the interior of which is decorated like a Southwestern pueblo. | 2160 Mountain Rd. | 802/253–7770 | No lunch | $8–$15 | MC, V.

Cliff House Restaurant. Contemporary. This restaurant sits atop Mt. Mansfield and is accessible only through the gondola. When calling for a reservation, leave your phone number in case weather prevents the gondola from running. The fixed price includes the gondola ticket, appetizer, salad, entrée, and dessert. A popular entrée is the marinated Vermont venison with cherry port-wine sauce. | Mt. Mansfield | 802/253–3000 | www.stowe.com | Reservations essential | Closed from the end of ski season to Memorial Day | $40 prix fixe | AE, D, DC, MC, V.

Depot Street Malt Shoppe. American/Casual. This 1950s-style diner serves a variety of American inspired dishes, including burgers, sandwiches, cherry cokes, and egg creams. Try the La Bamba burger with chili and cheese. | 57 Depot St., next to post office, Stowe Village | 802/253–4269 | $7–$8 | No credit cards.

Edson Hill Manor. Contemporary. Walls of windows afford views of the property's rolling hills, behind which lay the spectacular Green Mountains. Wildflower paintings and climbing vines complement the bucolic landscape. The highly designed food includes such dishes as pan-seared salmon and rack of lamb. There is also an extensive wine list. | 1500 Edson Hill Rd. | 802/253–7371 or 800/621–0284 | fax 802/253–4036 | www.stowevt.com | Closed Sun.–Thurs. in Apr. and May. No lunch | $18–$24 | AE, D, MC, V.

Foxfire Inn. Italian. The intimate, candlelit dining rooms of this inn are perfect for romantic evenings. Try the chicken ripieno—stuffed chicken breast with figs, pancetta, and Gorgonzola cheese, served with a creamy marsala sauce. | Rte. 100 | 802/253–4887 | No lunch | $12–$20 | AE, D, MC, V.

Gazebo. American/Casual. This poolside eatery, from which you can see both gardens and mountains, serves light, sun-inspired food like cold soups and salads, as well as grilled items such as hamburgers and pizzas. | 4000 Mountain Rd. | 802/253–8585 or 800/451–8686 | fax 802/253–9263 | www.topnotch-resort.com | Closed Labor Day–Memorial Day | $7–$15 | AE, D, DC, MC, V.

Gracie's Restaurant. American/Casual. A dog theme gives this eatery its fun and funky tenor. The restaurant is best known for its lineup of "Just Doggone Good Burgers," including the Chihuahua, with tomato and guacamole, and the Blazing Beagle, with spicy Cajun seasoning. Homemade breads and an array of fresh fish complete the menu. | Rte. 100, in the Carlson Building, Stowe Village Center | 802/253–8741 | Reservations essential for 6 or more | $7–$19 | AE, D, MC, V.

Isle de France. French. The dining room here is modeled after the Ritz-Carlton in Paris and there is also a more relaxed bistro. Try the rack of New Zealand lamb. | 1899 Mountain Rd. | 802/253–7751 | www.stoweinfo.com | Closed Mon. No lunch | Dining room $17–$26, bistro, $14–$17 | AE, D, DC, MC, V.

Maxwell's. Contemporary. While you dine on the regionally inspired cuisine, floor to ceiling windows afford views of Mt. Mansfield and the surrounding mountains. The restaurant boasts of its fresh produce and meats and its heart-healthy fare, such as seared tuna with roasted roma tomatoes, olives, capers, and artichoke hearts. The wine list is extensive. | 4000 Mountain Rd. | 802/253–8585 or 800/451–8686 | fax 802/253–9263 | www.topnotch-resort.com | Breakfast also available. No lunch | $18–$38 | AE, D, DC, MC, V.

Miguel's Stowe Away. Mexican. The more traditional Mexican fare of this restaurant is complemented by tasty surprises like coconut-fried shrimp. A front room has a pool table which requires no quarters. The establishment is kid-friendly and offers a separate kids' menu. | 3148 Mountain Rd. | 802/253–7574 or 800/245–1240 | fax 802/253–5192 | www.miguels.com | No lunch in spring and fall | $8–$18 | AE, D, DC, MC, V.

Mr. Pickwick's Restaurant. English. Located in Ye Olde England Inn, this pub is decorated with authentic brass-, copper-, and stonework. Among the authentic British dishes served here are fish-and-chips, beef Wellington, and Cornish pasty. For entertainment, there is a table-side magician. | 433 Mountain Rd. | 802/253–7558 or 800/477–3771 | fax 802/253–8944 | englandinn@aol.com | www.englandinne.com | $15–$30 | MC, V.

Olives Bistro. Mediterranean. Candlelight and linen spreads set the tone at this intimate restaurant. Try the Greek lasagna, with layers of spinach, onion, feta cheese, olives, pine nuts, tomatoes, ricotta, and mozzarella. The seafood specials are also popular. | Mountain Rd., Stowe Center Complex | 802/253–2033 | Closed Sun. No lunch | $10–$18 | AE, MC, V.

Partridge Inn. Seafood. This inn has white tablecloths and fireplaces and is known for its Maine lobster, baked and stuffed or broiled. Kids' menu. No smoking. | 504 Mountain Rd. | 802/253–8000 | Closed 1st 3 wks Nov. No lunch | $20–$30 | AE, D, DC, MC, V.

The Shed. American. A rustic barn with a relaxed brewpub, airy Garden Room, and open-air dining on the deck in summer. The menu has a range of entrées and includes the World Famous Shed Burger, marinated in the house beer and served on an English muffin. Kids' menu. Sunday brunch. No smoking. | 1859 Mountain Rd. | 802/253–4364 | $10–$20 | AE, D, DC, MC, V.

Swisspot of Stowe. Swiss, American. Fondue is the thing at this restaurant, although you will also find other carnal fare such as steak and Wiener schnitzel on the menu. A deck allows you to sit and dine amid flower baskets. Kids' menu. No smoking. | 128 Main St. | 802/253–4622 | Closed mid-Apr.–mid-June and mid-Oct.–mid-Dec. | $9–$16 | AE, D, DC, MC, V.

Ten Acres Lodge. Continental. The intimate and candlelit dining rooms of this inn serve delectable dishes such as roast free-range duckling with apricot sauce, served with applewood smoked bacon and Israeli couscous. | 14 Barrows Rd. | 802/253–7638 or 800/327–7357 | fax 802/253–6589 | $15–$23 | AE, D, DC, MC, V.

Whip Bar and Grill. American/Casual. Part of the Green Mountain Inn, this restaurant has a tack-room theme and hanging buggy whips form a partition between the dining room and the bar. Dark green Scottish plaid, carriage lamps, and 19th-century horse prints adorn the walls. The menu concentrates on upscale pub food, including shepherd's pie, ribs, burgers, sandwiches, soups, and salads. Tofu-vegetable stir-fry is also an option. | 18 Main St. | 802/253–7301 or 800/786–9346 | fax 802/253–5096 | grnmtinn@aol.com | www.greenmountaininn.com | Breakfast also available | $8–$20 | AE, D, MC, V.

Whiskers. Continental. The dining rooms of this eatery are ornamented with country antiques and fresh wild flowers, supplied from the restaurant's garden. In warm weather, you can dine on a deck which overlooks this wild flower garden. Prime rib, lobster, and barbecued ribs are the specialties here, though filet mignon, pasta, and chicken dishes are also served. Salad bar. Kids' menu. Sunday brunch. | 1652 Mountain Rd. | 802/253–8996 | No lunch | $17–$25 | AE, D, DC, MC, V.

Lodging

Buccaneer Country Lodge. This was the home of Olympic ski star Billy Kidd. Today it has antiques-filled lounges and flower gardens. Some rooms have fireplaces and the suites have decks. It's on Mountain Road, near the ski area. Picnic area, complimentary breakfast. Some kitchenettes, refrigerators, cable TV. Pool. Hot tub. Library. | 3214 Mountain Rd. | 802/253–4772 or 800/543–1293 | fax 802/253–4752 | www.buccaneerlodge.com or www.stowe-info.com/buccaneer | 12 rooms, 4 suites | $79–$139 | MC, V.

Butternut Inn. A charming inn, full of period pieces, that is a quiet retreat. Its 8 acres of gardens are crisscrossed by nature trails, a pond, fountain, and arbors. There's also a sun-room and a billiard room overlooking the West Branch River. Adults preferred. Dining room, picnic area, complimentary breakfast. No smoking, cable TV. Pool. Hot tub. Library. | 2309 Mountain Rd. | 802/253–4277 or 800/328–8837 | fax 802/253–5263 | www.butternutinnvt.com | 18 rooms | $85–$170 | MC, V.

Commodores Inn. A big, modern motel just south of Stowe village. Restaurant, complimentary Continental breakfast (off season). In-room data ports, some refrigerators, cable TV, some in-room VCRs. 2 pools (1 indoor), wading pool. Hot tubs. Exercise equipment. Video games. Business services. Pets allowed (fee). | 823 S. Main St. | 802/253–7131 or 800/44–STOWE | fax 802/253–2360 | www.commodoresinn.com | 50 rooms | $112–$138 | AE, D, DC, MC, V.

Edson Hill Manor. This brick house, 6 mi north of Stowe, was built on 225 rolling acres in the 1940s, with beams hewn for Ethan Allen. It's filled with oriental rugs, and there is a secluded carriage house in back. The rooms are pine paneled, and many have fireplaces. Dining room, bar. No air-conditioning in some rooms. Pool. Fishing. Cross-country skiing. | 1500 Edson Hill Rd. | 802/253–7371 or 800/621–0284 | fax 802/253–4036 | www.stowevt.com | 25 rooms | $110–$170 | AE, D, MC, V.

Foster's Place. An affordable lodge on 18 acres with spectacular views of Mt. Mansfield. It has numerous amentities—not only is there a swimming pool, there is also a swimming hole and trout stream. In winter, the property's proximity to the ski resort is an added bonus. No smoking, no room phones, TV in common area. Pool. Spa. Hiking, volleyball. Fishing. Video games. Laundry facilities. Pets allowed (fee). | Rte. 108/4986 Mountain Rd. | 802/253–9404 or 800/330–4880 | fax 802/253–4470 | info@fosters-place.com | www.fosters-place.com | 32 rooms (6 with private bath), 3 houses | $39–$55 | AE, MC, V.

Foxfire Inn. Once a farmhouse, the inn now plays off its country charms. The rooms offer basic, comfortable lodging above a spectacular Italian eatery. The living room has a fireplace for cold evenings. Dining room, complimentary breakfast. No smoking, no room phones, no TV. No pets. | Rte. 100 | 802/244–5288 | fax 802/253–7016 | foxfireinn@aol.com | 5 rooms | $90 | AE, D, MC, V.

The Gables. Barn board, exposed beams, and antiques are some of the rustic charms of this 19th-century farmhouse. A fireplace warms the common area where you can laze and chat. The rooms, individually appointed, are all comfortable and inviting. Complimentary breakfast. No smoking, some room phones, no TV in some rooms. Pool. Hot tub. Volleyball. No pets. | 1457 Mountain Rd. | 802/253–7730 or 800/422–5371 | fax 802/253–8989 | 12 rooms, 2 suites, 4 carriage-house rooms | $110–$235 | AE, D, DC, MC, V.

Golden Eagle. This sprawling, family-owned resort is a good place to bring your kids. Guests may rent fishing poles or bring their own to fish in the trout pond and there are nature trails you can take advantage of. Restaurant, bar, picnic area. Some kitchenettes, microwaves available, refrigerators, some in-room hot tubs, cable TV, some in-room VCRs. 3 pools (1 indoor). Hot tub, massage. Tennis. Gym, hiking. Fishing. Library. Children's programs (ages 4 and up), playground. Business services. | 511 Mountain Rd. | 802/253–4811 or 800/626–1010 | fax 802/253–2561 | stoweagle@aol.com | www.stoweagle.com | 71 rooms, 11 suites, 2 cottages, 5 apartments | $99–$109; $149–$159 suites, cottages, apartments | AE, D, DC, MC, V.

Green Mountain Inn. This 1833 inn, filled with antiques, is right in the center of Stowe and has a year-round heated outdoor pool. Rooms are in the main inn and an annex. Dining room, bar. Cable TV, in-room VCRs (and movies). Pool. Hot tub, massage. Exercise equipment. Business services. Pets allowed. | 18 Main St. | 802/253–7301 or 800/786–9346 | fax 802/253–5096 | grnmtinn@aol.com | www.greenmountaininn.com | 54 rooms, 24 suites, 1 house | $115–$209, $179 suites, $200 carriage house | AE, D, MC, V.

Grey Fox Inn & Resort. There are a variety of room types at this resort. Some have mountain views and others are apartments. It is home to the famous Dutch Pancake Cafe and near Stowe Mountain Resort skiing. Dining room, picnic area. In-room data ports, some kitchenettes, some microwaves, cable TV, some in-room VCRs. 2 pools (1 indoor). Hot tub. Exercise equipment. Bicycles. Cross-country skiing. Video games. Laundry facilities. Business services. | 990 Mountain Rd. | 802/253–8921 or 800/544–8454 | fax 802/253–8344 | www.stowegreyfoxinn.com | 41 rooms | $85–$152 | AE, D, MC, V.

Hob Knob Inn. Motel accommodations on a hillside 2½ mi north of Stowe. The restaurant known for steak and fresh fish. Some rooms have fireplaces. Restaurant, bar, complimentary breakfast (winter), complimentary Continental breakfast (summer). Some kitchenettes, refrigerators. Pool. | 2364 Mountain Rd. | 802/253–8549 or 800/245–8540 | fax 802/253–7621 | www.hobknob.com | 20 rooms, 1 suite, 1 cottage | $58–$98, $110–$150 suites, $90–$130 cottage | Closed Nov. and Apr.–May | AE, D, MC, V.

Honey Wood Lodge. A small B&B inn on 9 acres. Complimentary breakfast. No smoking, some in-room hot tubs, no room phones, TV in common area. 2 pools. Cross-country skiing. Kids over 10 only. | 4583 Mountain Rd. | 802/253–4846 or 800/659–6289 | fax 802/253–7050 | honeywd@aol.com | www.honeywoodinn.com | 8 rooms, 2 suites | $85–$169, $145–$229 suites | AE, MC, V.

Inn at the Brass Lantern. An exquisitely restored early-19th-century farmhouse with quilts, Mt. Mansfield views and fireplaces in some rooms. Complimentary breakfast. No smoking, no TV, no room phones, some in-room hot tubs. Library. | 717 Maple St. | 802/253–2229 or 800/729–2980 | fax 800/253–7425 | brasslntrn@aol.com | www.brasslanterninn.com | 9 rooms | $165–$210 | AE, MC, V.

Inn at the Mountain. A medium-size lodge that is superbly situated with a ski lift just outside the inn. You can see the slopes from many of the rooms. Restaurant, bar. Refrigerators, room service, cable TV. 3 pools. Hot tub. Tennis. Exercise equipment. Bicycles. Cross-country skiing, downhill skiing, ski shop, snow boarding. Business services. | 5781 Mountain Rd. | 802/253–7311 or 800/253–4754 | fax 802/253–3659 | www.stowe.com | 34 rooms | $173 | AE, D, DC, MC, V.

Innsbruck Inn. This mountainside inn with European flair, 4 mi west of Stowe has private accommodations in the chalet in addition to rooms in main lodge. Restaurant, bar, picnic area. Some kitchenettes, refrigerators, cable TV, some in-room VCRs. Pool. Hot tub. Exercise equipment. Cross-country skiing. Video games. Business services. Pets allowed (fee). | 4361 Mountain Rd. | 802/253–8582 or 800/225–8582 | fax 802/253–2260 | www.innsbruckinn.com | 28 rooms | $74–$169 | AE, D, MC, V.

Miguel's Stowe Away. Wide-planked floors and barn-board walls original to the 18th-century structure mix with a subtle Southwestern influence to give this lodging its unique charm. Restaurant, bar, complimentary breakfast. No smoking, cable TV, no room phones. Pool. Hot tub. Pets allowed. | 3148 Mountain Rd. | 802/253–7574 or 800/245–1240 | fax 802/253–5192 | www.miguels.com | 6 rooms | $80 | AE, D, DC, MC, V.

Mount Mansfield Hostel. Built by Civilian Conservation Corps in the 1930s, this hostel provides the bare essentials, with the area's lowest rates. Cozy dorm-style accommodations are run by Vermont Department of Forests and Parks, way up on the Mountain Road. It is away from resort bustle but the closest lodging to Stowe's slopes. Bring sleeping bag or rent sheets. Cross-country skiing, downhill skiing. | 6992 Mountain Rd. | 802/253–4010 | skidorm@together.net | www.hostel.com or www.hostel.together.net | 2 dorm rooms (male and female) sleep 22 each | $15–$24 | Closed Apr.–May | AE, D, MC, V.

Mountain Road Resort. Small, well-appointed resort tucked away on flower-filled property, 1 mi north of Stowe. The French pétanque court is an unusual offering. It is the French equivalent to bocce ball, played on a flat, hard, gravel surface with metal and wood balls. Picnic area. Some kitchenettes, some microwaves, refrigerators, some in-room hot tubs, cable TV, VCR available. 2 pools (1 indoor). Hot tub. Tennis. Exercise equipment. Bicycles. Playground. Laundry facilities. Business services. Pets allowed (fee). | 1007 Mountain Rd. | 802/253–4566 or 800/367–6873 | fax 802/253–7397 | stowevt@aol.com | www.stowevtusa.com | 30 rooms, 7 suites, 7 apartments | $95–$189, $189–$380 suites, $179–$235 apartments | AE, D, DC, MC, V.

Mountainside Resort at Stowe. Condo accommodations with up to four bedrooms in each unit that are off the main road and 2½ mi from skiing. Some units have fireplaces. There's a minimum two-night stay in winter. Picnic area. No air-conditioning. Indoor pool. Hot tub, saunas. Tennis. Playground. Laundry facilities. Business services. | 171 Cottage Club Rd. | 802/253–8610 or 800/458–4893 | fax 802/253–7838 | mtside@together.net | www.mountainsideresort.cc | 88 apartments | $190–$229 | AE, MC, V.

Notch Brook Condominium. This 16-acre compound with spectacular Mt. Mansfield views has a range of accommodations including three-bedroom apartments. There are fireplaces in some units. Complimentary Continental breakfast (in season). No air-conditioning, some kitchenettes, cable TV. Pool. Saunas. Tennis. Laundry facilities. Business services. Pets allowed (fee). | 1229 Notch Brook Rd. | 802/253–4882 or 800/253–4882 | fax 802/253–4882 | nbrook@sover.net | www.stoweinfo.com/saa/notchbrook | 49 rooms | $76–$195 | AE, DC, MC, V.

Riverside Inn. This inn, originally an 18th-century farmhouse, provides clean, tidy, and affordable accommodations next to a golf course and the Trapp Family Lodge. Ten rooms are in the main house and another six are part of a more recently built motel-style lodging. The common room has books and a fireplace. No air-conditioning in some rooms, no smoking, cable TV, some room phones, TV in common area. Hiking. Fishing. Cross-country skiing. Pets allowed. | 1965 Mountain Rd. | 802/253–4217, 800/966–4217, or 800/548–7568 | fax 802/253–4117 | rivinn@aol.com | www.gostowe.com/saa/riverside | 16 rooms (6 with shared bath) | $59–$89 | AE, MC, V.

Scandinavia Inn and Chalets. A Mountain Road lodge and chalets with as many as six bedrooms that is 3³/₄ mi north of Stowe. The Scandinavian motif extends to an extensive collection of trolls. Dining room, picnic area. No air-conditioning in some rooms, no smoking, cable TV. Pool. Hot tub. Exercise equipment. Laundry facilities. | 3576 Mountain Rd. | 802/253–8555 or 800/544–4229 | fax 802/253–8555 | scandi@plainfiell.bypass.com | www.scandinaviainn.com | 18 rooms, 4 chalets | $99–$140, $235–$296 chalets | Closed mid-Oct.–late Nov. | AE, D, MC, V.

Siebeness. Tasteful pine and maple antique furnishings, small artifacts, and pieces of art give these rooms a quiet, homey charm. The studios have fireplaces and decks, making them ideal for romantic getaways. Complimentary breakfast. Some refrigerators, no smoking, some in-room hot tubs, no TV in some rooms. Pool. Hot tub. Hiking. Cross-country skiing. No pets. | 3681 Mountain Rd. | 802/253–8942 or 800/426–9001 | fax 802/253–9232 | siebeness@aol.com | www.siebeness.com | 10 rooms, 2 studios | $125–$250 | AE, MC, V.

Stowe Inn and Tavern at Little River. This inn is just a short walk from downtown, Mountain Road shops, and recreation path. Restaurant, bar, complimentary Continental breakfast. Some kitchenettes, some refrigerators, cable TV. Pool. Hot tub. Business services. Pets allowed. | 123 Mountain Rd. | 802/253–4836, 800/227–1108 eastern U.S | fax 802/253–7308 | www.stoweinn.com | 43 rooms | $99–$130 | AE, MC, V.

Stowe Motel and Snowdrift. A moderately priced option halfway between the village and the ski area, this hostelry looks out on the mountains from its expansive grounds—16 landscaped acres. You can opt for quarters with a fireplace. Picnic area. In-room data ports, some kitchenettes, refrigerators, cable TV. 2 pools. Hot tub. Tennis. Bicycles. Cross-country skiing. Business services. | 2043 Mountain Rd. | 802/253–7629 or 800/829–7629 | stowemotel@aol.com | www.stowemotel.com | 54 rooms; 6 apartments | $92–$178, $100–$325 apartments | D, DC, MC, V.

Stoweflake Mountain Resort & Spa. Lodge, motel, and town-house accommodations next to a golf course on Mountain Road, 1¹/₂ mi north of Stowe. The apartments have fireplaces. Restaurant, bar, room service. Cable TV. In-room data ports, some microwaves, some refrigerators. 2 pools (1 indoor). Hot tub. Driving range, putting green, tennis. Exercise equipment. Library. Business services. | 1746 Mountain Rd. | 802/253–7355 or 800/253–2232 | fax 802/253–4419 | stoweflk@sover.net | www.stoweflake.com | 70 rooms, 24 apartments | $153–$340, $225–$675 apartments | AE, D, DC, MC, V.

Stowehof Inn. In this alpine farmhouse on a back road above Stowe village, no two rooms are alike and some have fireplaces. The restaurant serves fine French cuisine. There is a trout pond; bring your own equipment. Dining room, bar, complimentary breakfast. Cable TV, some in-room VCRs. Pool. Hot tub, sauna. Tennis. Fishing. Cross-country skiing, sleigh rides. Library. Business services. | 434 Edson Hill Rd. | 802/253–9722 or 800/932–7136 | fax 802/253–7513 | www.stowehofinn.com | 50 rooms | $138–$250 | MAP | AE, D, DC, MC, V.

Sun and Ski Motor Inn. A motel on 9 acres with mountain views that is 1½ mi north of Stowe and next to the recreation path. Picnic area, complimentary Continental breakfast. Refrigerators, cable TV. Pool. Sauna. Fishing. Bicycles. | 1613 Mountain Rd. | 802/253–7159 or 800/448–5223 | fax 802/253–7150 | www.stowesunandski.com | 28 rooms | $88–$120 | AE, MC, V.

Sunset Motor Inn. A clean, independently owned motel at the busy Morrisville intersection halfway between Stowe (10 mi north) and Smugglers Notch skiing. There is a restaurant next door. Picnic area. Refrigerators, some in-room hot tubs, cable TV, some in-room VCRs. Pool. Playground. | 160 Rte. 15 W | 802/888–4956 or 800/544–2347 | fax 802/888–3698 | sunset@together.net | www.gostowe.com/saa/sunset | 55 rooms | $92–$130 | MAP | AE, D, DC, MC, V.

Ten Acres Lodge. This warm and inviting New England–style clapboard lodge is in a pastoral landscape. The rooms are elegant and stylish; some contain a fireplace. The cottages have more room and come with a kitchenette and fireplace. Restaurant, bar, complimentary breakfast. Some kitchenettes, no room phones, no TV. Pool. Cross-country skiing, downhill skiing. Playground. Airport shuttle. | 14 Barrows Rd. | 802/253–7638 or 800/327–7357 | fax 802/253–6589 | 17 rooms, 2 cottages | $230–$260 | MAP | AE, D, DC, MC, V.

Topnotch at Stowe Resort & Spa. One of Vermont's best resorts. The lobby is imposing with its floor-to-ceiling windows, freestanding circular fieldstone fireplace, and cathedral ceiling, and the rooms live up to the first impression. The spa is tops in the area. Dining rooms, bar with entertainment, room service. No air-conditioning in some rooms, some kitchenettes, microwaves available, some refrigerators, cable TV, some in-room VCRs. 2 pools (1 indoor). Beauty salon, hot tub, spa. 14 tennis courts (4 indoor). Gym, horseback riding. Bicycles. Cross-country skiing. Libraries. Children's programs (ages 5–12). | 4000 Mountain Rd. | 802/253–8585 or 800/451–8686 | fax 802/253–9263 | www.topnotch-resort.com | 60 rooms, 12 suites, 18 townhouses | $220–$300, $270–$750 town houses | MAP | AE, D, DC, MC, V.

Town and Country Resort. A resort motel 1 mi north of Stowe that is between the village and skiing. It has Stowe's largest outdoor pool. Restaurant, bar. Some refrigerators, cable TV. 2 pools (1 indoor), wading pool. Sauna. Tennis. Business services. | 876 Mountain Rd. | 802/253–7595 or 800/323–0311 | fax 802/253–4764 | tnc@together.net | www.tcstowe.com | 45 rooms | $58–$135 | MAP | AE, D, DC, MC, V.

Trapp Family Lodge. Once owned by the Trapp family of *The Sound of Music* fame, this lodge is renowned for its cross-country skiing. Dining room, bar with entertainment, tea shop. No air-conditioning. 3 pools (1 indoor). Tennis. Exercise equipment, hiking. Cross-country skiing, ski shop, sleigh rides. Library. Business services. | 700 Trapp Hill Rd. | 802/253–8511 or 800/826–7000 | fax 802/253–5740 | www.trappfamily.com | 93 rooms, 100 cottages | $210–$329, $1,500/wk cottages | AE, D, DC, MC, V.

Winding Brook Lodge. A snug lodge that was constructed from logs and fieldstone, circa 1940. The property also has a three-bedroom town house. It's a rustic, charming location with warm and gracious hospitality. Taproom, picnic area, complimentary breakfast. No smoking, TV in common areas. Outdoor pool and hot tub. Business services. | 199 Edson Hill Rd. | 802/253–7354 or 800/426–6697 | fax 802/253–8429 | www.stoweinfo.com/saa/walkabout | 15 rooms | $65–$135, $350 town house | AE, MC, V.

Ye Olde England Inne. The British owners go all out to create a "jolly old" English mood in this Tudor-style inn, ¼ mi from the village, right down to the Laura Ashley decor. The pub stocks many British ales. Dining room, bar with entertainment, grill, picnic area. Some in-room hot tubs, cable TV, some in-room VCRs. Pool. Hot tub. Business services. | 433 Mountain Rd. | 802/253–7558 or 800/477–3771 | fax 802/253–8944 | englandinn@aol.com | www.old-englandinne.com | 30 rooms, 10 suites, 3 cottages | $179–$239, $349 cottages | AE, MC, V.

STRATTON MOUNTAIN

(Nearby towns also listed: Londonderry, Manchester, Manchester Center, Peru)

Stratton Mountain was just another remote peak in the southern Green Mountains until 1959, when all that verticality was put to use in the name of alpine skiing. Today the 3,936-ft peak is served by a high-speed gondola and an assortment of other lifts, and the resort that has grown up around its base operates year-round; among summer offerings are a golf school and events on the pro tennis tour.

Information: **Manchester and the Mountains Regional Chamber of Commerce** | 5046 Main St., Suite 1, Manchester Center, 05255 | 802/362–2100 | fax 802/362–3451 | www.manchestervermont.net.

Attractions

Horses for Hire. This stable, 1 mi from Stratton, offers private, personal horseback rides, riding lessons, and sleigh rides. Open daily, weather permitting, you should call first for an appointment. | Diers Rd., off Rte. 30, Rawlsonville | 802/297–1468.

Skiing. Stratton Mountain. With 90 trails and a dozen lifts for downhillers, Stratton also has fine cross-country skiing as well as summer golf, tennis, and an arts festival. | On Stratton Mountain access road, off Rte. 30 | 802/297–4000, 802/297–2200, or 800/STRATTON | Dec.–Mar., daily.

ON THE CALENDAR

SEPT.: *Labor Day Street Festival.* Specialty foods, imported beers, and children's activities. | Labor Day weekend | 802/STRATTON.

Dining

Haig's Black Angus Steakhouse. American/Casual. Hanging plants and a wall of glass brighten this airy dining room. Among the many items on the menu are pastas, veal, lobster, fish, and, of course, Black Angus steak. The restaurant also has a kids' menu. | River Rd./Rte. 30, Bondville | 802/297–1300 or 800/897–5894 | fax 802/297–3000 | haigs@vermontel.net | www.haigs.com | Closed mid-Apr.–mid-May. No lunch | $9–$27 | AE, D, MC, V.

Partridge in a Pantry. Delicatessen. You can enjoy your sandwich, soup, or salad among this deli's charming cow paraphernalia and antiques or, alternatively, you can call ahead to order something and pick it up. | Village Sq. | 802/297–9850 | Breakfast also available. No dinner | $5–$9 | AE, MC, V.

Red Fox Inn. Contemporary. The inn's dining room is actually a restored barn, the windows of which afford views of Stratton and Magic mountains. The upstairs dining room has a refined menu, including dishes like penne à la vodka with shrimp and lobster, while the downstairs tavern serves burgers, pizzas, and pastas. On the weekends the tavern hosts musicians. | Winhall Hollow Rd., Bondville | 802/297–2488 | fax 802/297–2156 | foxlog@sover.net | Closed May. No lunch | $6–$26 | AE, D, DC, MC, V.

Sage Hill Restaurant. American/Casual. A floor-to-ceiling stone fireplace towers above you in this restaurant within the Stratton Mountain Inn. The traditional American menu of steaks, chops, and seafood is given an extra spark with specials such as lobster and alligator. | Middle Ridge Rd. | 802/297–2500 or 877/887–3767 | fax 802/297–1778 | sales@strattonmountain.com | www.strattonmountain.com | Breakfast also available. No lunch | $15–$30 | AE, D, DC, MC, V.

The Tavern. American. This casual spot within the Stratton Mountain Inn serves light fare such as salads, sandwiches, chicken wings, and hamburgers. Video games, a pool table, and five TVs are available for your or your kids' amusement. | Middle Ridge Rd. | 802/297–

2500 or 877/887–3767 | fax 802/297–1778 | sales@strattonmountain.com | www.stratton-mountain.com | No lunch | $7–$20 | AE, D, DC, MC, V.

Lodging

Haig's. Opened in 1973, the early American-style lodge has large, well-furnished rooms, many of which contain stone fireplaces. The lodge is connected to three bars, a restaurant, and an indoor golfing range. In addition, on weekends and holidays, a separate facility houses a dance club. Restaurant, bar. No air-conditioning, cable TV. No pets. | River Rd./Rte. 30, Bondville | 802/297–1300 or 800/897–5894 | fax 802/297–3000 | haigs@ver-montel.net | www.haigs.com | 30 rooms | $105–$107 | AE, D, MC, V.

Liftline Lodge. Right at the Stratton slopes, this European-style chalet is a perfect place for skiiers. Rooms are appointed with fine furnishings, richly colored carpets, fireplaces, stoves, and refrigerators. Restaurant. No air-conditioning in some rooms, in-room data ports, cable TV, some in-room VCRs. 2 outdoor pools. Hot tubs, saunas. Driving range, putting green. Exercise equipment. Business services. Pets allowed. | Stratton Mountain Rd., Stratton | 802/297–6100 or 800/STRATTON | fax 802/297–2949 | www.stratton.com | 77 rooms | $75–$150, $150–$300 apartments | AE, MC, V.

Ober Tal Condominiums. Each bedroom unit of this lodging has a wood-burning field-stone fireplace, complete kitchen, washer-dryer, and private deck. Large, comfortable furniture fills the rooms. Kitchenettes, microwaves, refrigerators, cable TV. Laundry facilities. | Stratton Mountain Rd. | 802/297–2200 or 800/787–2886 | fax 802/297–4300 | www.stratton.com | 27 rooms | $90–$320 | AE, D, DC, MC, V.

Red Fox Inn. Built as a farmhouse in the early 1800s, this inn is surrounded on all sides by woods and mountains. Neither telephones nor TV spoil the remote, rustic charms evoked by the antiques and central fireplace. Restaurant, bar. No air-conditioning, no smoking, no room phones, no TV. No pets. | Winhall Hollow Rd., Bondville | 802/297–2488 | fax 802/297–2156 | foxlog@sover.net | 10 rooms | $100–$175 | AE, D, DC, MC, V.

Stratton Mountain Inn. This complex in the heart of the Stratton Mountain Resort is the largest lodging on the mountain. The exposed brick-and-beam construction gives the hotel a traditional New England feel. Rooms are modern and well maintained, with solid wood furnishings complementing the New England theme. Restaurant, bar. In-room data ports, no smoking, cable TV. Pool. Hot tub, sauna. Golf course, tennis courts. Gym. Video games. No pets. | Middle Ridge Rd. | 802/297–2500 or 877/887–3767 | fax 802/297–1778 | sales@strattonmountain.com | www.strattonmountain.com | 120 rooms | $89–$450 | AE, D, DC, MC, V.

Stratton Village Lodge. The only slopeside ski-in, ski-out lodge on the mountain, the Stratton Village is just up the hill from the Stratton Mountain Inn. It has a modern New England style; each of the rooms is equipped with a range of modern amenities. Restaurant, bar. In-room data ports, minibars, microwaves, refrigerators, no smoking, cable TV. Pool. Hot tub, sauna. Golf course, tennis courts. Gym. Video games. No pets. | Middle Ridge Rd. | 802/297–2500 or 877/887–3767 | fax 802/297–1778 | sales@strattonmountain.com | www.strattonmountain.com | 91 rooms | $89–$450 | AE, D, DC, MC, V.

Village Watch. The valley and mountain are both visible from this contemporary wooden condo complex. Two-, three-, and four-bedroom condos are available, each with a complete kitchen, fieldstone fireplace, and sundeck. Kitchenettes, microwaves, refrigerators. Cable TV, in-room VCRs. No pets. | Stratton Mountain Village | 802/297–2200 or 800/727–2886 | fax 802/297–4300 | www.stratton.com | 35 units | $140–$480 | AE, D, DC, MC, V.

VERGENNES

(Nearby towns also listed: Bristol, Charlotte, Middlebury, Shelburne)

Vergennes is the smallest chartered city in Vermont (1 square mi) and the third-oldest in New England. Nestled on the banks of Otter Creek some 6 mi from its mouth at Lake Champlain, the vest-pocket downtown boasts several fine examples of Victorian architecture. Vergennes is a handy jumping-off place for several nearby attractions, including the Lake Champlain Maritime Museum, Button Bay State Park (so named because of the perforated stone "buttons" found along the lakeshore), and the plush, expansive Basin Harbor Resort.

Information: **Vergennes Chamber of Commerce** | Box 335, Vergennes, 05491 | 802/877–0080 | www.virtualvermont.com/chamber/vergennes.

Attractions

Button Bay State Park. Camp and swim on Lake Champlain, 6 mi south of Vergennes, and look for the little stone "buttons" that give the bay its name. There's also a swimming pool if you'd rather swim there. | Button Bay Rd., just south of Basin Harbor | 802/475–2377 | $2 | Memorial Day–Columbus Day, daily 10–dusk.

Chimney Point State Historic Site. The days of French exploration of the Champlain Valley, along with Native American artifacts, are the focus of exhibits in a restored 1700s tavern, 6 mi south of Vergennes. | 7305 Rte. 125, at Rte. 17, Addison | 802/759–2412 | www.historicvermont.org | $2 | Memorial Day–Columbus Day., Wed.–Sun. 9:30–5:30.

John Strong Mansion. The Georgian mansion of an early settler, built in 1798 on bricks fired on the site, 6 mi southwest of Vergennes. There's a secret room behind the chimney. | 6656 Rte. 17 W, Addison | 802/759–2309 | $3 | May–Labor Day, Fri.–Sun. 9–5.

Kennedy Bros. Factory Marketplace. The focus is on woodenware and furnishings at this outlet, but there's lots more for sale: antiques and crafts in 43,000 square ft of space. | 11 Main St. | 802/877–2975 | www.kennedy-brothers.com | Free | Daily 9:30–5:30.

Lake Champlain Maritime Museum. Come discover why Lake Champlain is considered the most historic body of water in North America. Climb aboard a 54-ft replica of Benedict Arnold's gunboat, *Philadelphia II*, rigged, armed, and afloat in the museum's North Harbor. Visit the fully interactive Revolutionary War exhibit, and watch craftsmen continue traditional maritime skills of boatbuilding and blacksmithing. | 4472 Basin Harbor Rd. | 802/475–2022 | www.lcmm.org | $8 | May–mid-Oct., daily 10–5.

Rokeby Museum. Nineteenth-century Vermont author Rowland Robinson wrote his dialect-humor stories in this house 3 mi north of Vergennes, and also sheltered runaway slaves headed for Canada. | Rte. 7, Ferrisburgh | 802/877–3406 | $4 | Mid-May–mid.-Oct., Thurs.–Sun. 11–3:30.

ON THE CALENDAR
AUG.–SEPT.: *Reflections on Basin Harbor Weekend.* A one-week exhibit that includes works by Vermont artisans who draw inspiration from the lake and its environs. | Basin Harbor Club, Basin Harbor Rd. | 802/475–2311 or 800/622–4000 | www.basinharbor.com | Free.

Dining
Christophe's. French. In this unpretentious antique French country place chef Christophe Lissarrague serves traditional fare on beautiful china set on crisp white linen. Try the grilled halibut served with braised scallions, parsnip/potato puree, and maché or the sauteed lamb morsels with potato gratiné, haricots vert, and paloise sauce. | On the Green in Vergennes | 802/877–3413 | Closed mid-Oct.–mid-May. No lunch | $38, (prix fixe) | MC, V.

Main Dining Room at the Basin Harbor Club. Contemporary. Windows take up the entire west wall of the dining room and provide breathtaking views of the sunsets across Lake Champlain and the Adirondacks. The prix fixe dinner comes in five courses and might include as its entrée roast Misty Knoll poussin with sun-dried cherry vinaigrette. The menu emphasizes fresh Vermont products. Pastries, desserts, and breads are all baked on the premises. A kids' menu is also available. | Basin Harbor Rd. | 802/475–2311 or 800/622–4000 | fax 802/475–6545 | info@basinharbor.com | www.basinharbor.com | Jacket and tie | Closed mid-Oct.–mid-May. No lunch | $33 | MC, V.

Red Mill Restaurant at the Basin Harbor Club. American/Casual. This restaurant in what was originally a tractor barn and sawmill, next to a grass airstrip, has a more casual environment than the Main Dining Room. It serves a variety of dishes, including roasted vegetable grinder, Pad Thai, Vermont farm salad, and Philly cheese steak. | Basin Harbor Rd. | 802/475–2311 or 800/622–4000 | fax 802/475–6545 | info@basinharbor.com | www.basinharbor.com | Closed mid-Oct.–mid-May | $6–$19 | MC, V.

Lodging

Basin Harbor Club. A tidy and genteel traditional summer resort that sprawls away from its waterfront on Lake Champlain. There are fine views along the footpaths that meander among the cottages and to the main lodge and various sports facilities. A lovely place. Dining room, bar. Some refrigerators, TV in common area. Outdoor heated pool. Massage. 18-hole golf course, putting green, tennis. Gym, hiking, beach, dock, boating. Bicycles. Children's programs (ages 3–13). Laundry facilities. Business services. Airport shuttle. Pets allowed. | Basin Harbor Rd. | 802/475–2311 or 800/622–4000 | fax 802/475–6545 | res@basinharbor.com | www.basinharbor.com | 40 rooms, 77 cottages | $210–$270, $305–$425 cottages | Closed mid-Oct.–mid-May | MAP | MC, V.

Emerson's Guest House. This 1850 Victorian residence is in the heart of Vergennes, near shopping and restaurants. The property is also adjacent to hiking trails. On the inn's 4 acres you can laze among lilac or rosebushes and gaze out at the Adirondacks. All the rooms have hardwood floors, Persian rugs, and antique furnishings. Complimentary breakfast. No air-conditioning in some rooms, no smoking, no room phones, TV in common area. No kids under 3. | 82 Main St. | 802/877–3293 or 800/653–3034 | emersons@sover.net | www.emersonhouse.com | 6 rooms (2 with shower only, 4 with shared bath) | $65–$105 | MC, V.

Skyview Motel. There are fine Adirondack views at this small independent motel that is 2 mi north of Vergennes and convenient to the Maritime Museum. Picnic area. Some kitchenettes, refrigerators, cable TV. Playground. | 2956 Rte. 7 | 802/877–3410 | 15 rooms | $60–$85 | AE, MC, V.

Strong House Inn. You can see the Green Mountains and the Adirondacks from this early-19th-century inn. Some rooms have fireplaces. Dining room, complimentary breakfast, room service. No smoking, some room phones, no TV in some rooms. No kids under 8. | 94 W. Main St. | 802/877–3337 | fax 802/877–2599 | innkeeper@stronghouseinn.com | www.stronghouseinn.com | 14 rooms | $95–$305 | AE, MC, V.

Whitford House. This property, 12 mi south of Vergennes, occupies 37 scenic acres. The rooms of this restored 1790s farmhouse all have windows that survey the surrounding meadows, gardens, and mountains. Fresh flowers decorate the rooms each day throughout the year. The B&B is home to six sheep, so if you would like to bring your pet, be sure to call in advance. Complimentary breakfast. No air-conditioning, no smoking, no room phones, no TV. Hiking, boating. Bicycles. Cross-country skiing. Library. | 912 Grandey Rd., Addison | 802/758–2704 or 800/746–2704 | fax 802/758–2089 | whitford@together.net | www.whitfordhouseinn.com | 3 rooms, 1 guest house | $110–$200 | MC, V.

Way Ahead

- ❏ Devise a trip budget.
- ❏ Write down the five things you want most from this trip. Keep this list handy before and during your trip.
- ❏ Book lodging and transportation.
- ❏ Arrange for pet care.
- ❏ Photocopy any important documentation (passport, driver's license, vehicle registration, and so on) you'll carry with you on your trip. Store the copies in a safe place at home.
- ❏ Review health and home-owners insurance policies to find out what they cover when you're away from home.

A Month Before

- ❏ Make restaurant reservations and buy theater and concert tickets. Visit fodors.com for links to local events and news.
- ❏ Familiarize yourself with the local language or lingo.
- ❏ Schedule a tune-up for your car.

Two Weeks Before

- ❏ Create your itinerary.
- ❏ Enjoy a book or movie set in your destination to get you in the mood.
- ❏ Prepare a packing list.
- ❏ Shop for missing essentials.
- ❏ Repair, launder, or dry-clean the clothes you will take with you.
- ❏ Replenish your supply of prescription drugs and contact lenses if necessary.

A Week Before

- ❏ Stop newspaper and mail deliveries.
- ❏ Pay bills.
- ❏ Stock up on film and batteries.
- ❏ Label your luggage.
- ❏ Finalize your packing list—always take less than you think you need.
- ❏ Pack a toiletries kit filled with travel-size essentials.
- ❏ Check tire treads.
- ❏ Write down your insurance agent's number and any other emergency numbers and take them with you.
- ❏ Get lots of sleep. You want to be well-rested and healthy for your impending trip.

A Day Before

- ❏ Collect passport, driver's license, insurance card, vehicle registration, and other documents.
- ❏ Check travel documents.
- ❏ Give a copy of your itinerary to a family member or friend.
- ❏ Check your car's fluids, lights, tire inflation, and wiper blades.
- ❏ Get packing!

During Your Trip

- ❏ Keep a journal/scrapbook as a personal souvenir.
- ❏ Spend time with locals.
- ❏ Take time to explore. Don't plan too much. Let yourself get lost and use your Fodor's guide to get back on track.

WAITSFIELD

(Nearby towns also listed: Warren, Waterbury)

Waitsfield is one of two principal commercial, lodging, and dining centers of the Mad River valley (the other is Warren). The town is also the gateway to Mad River Glen, which is a skiing world apart: owned by a limited shareholders' cooperative, it boasts the last single chairlift in America, depends primarily on natural snow, and is alone among Vermont resorts in banning snowboards.

Information: **Sugarbush Chamber of Commerce** | Box 173, Waitsfield, 05673 | 802/496–3409 or 800/828–4748 | fax 802/496–5420 | www.madrivervalley.com.

Attractions

Lareau Swimhole Park. Across the road from the Lareau Farm Country Inn and Featherbed Inn, this park is a delightful spot for frolicking in the river, picnicking, or canoeing. | Rte. 100 | 802/496–3409 or 800/828–4748.

★ **Mad River Glen Ski Area.** No snowboards, almost no snowmaking, the rough-and-ready base lodge, and narrow, often challenging trails make this place feel a little like a New England ski resort of bygone days—not to mention the last of the single chairlifts. There's plenty of gentle, lovely terrain for beginners, and the ski school is as small and manageable as the parking lot. | Rte. 17 | 802/496–3551 or 802/496–2001 | www.madriverglen.com | Mid-Dec.–mid-Apr., weekdays 9:30–4, weekends 8:30–4.

Valley Players Theatre. This community theater in an 1800s brick building is host to musical performances, children's workshops, and plays put on by the Valley Players themselves. | Rte. 100 | 802/583–1674 or 802/496–9612 | $6–$12.

ON THE CALENDAR

AUG.: *Festival of the Arts.* The towns of Waitsfield and Warren are host to a month-long celebration of the arts. The wide range of activities includes visits to artists' studios, dances, exhibits, theatrical performances, and chamber music concerts. | Waitsfield–Warren | 800/517–4247.

Dining

American Flatbread. Pizza. Cooked in a wood-fired, primitive earthen oven, this pizza is unequivocally the best in Vermont, and arguably some of the best in the world. The chewy, sometimes oddly shaped flatbread crusts are reminiscent of the famous pizzas of Wooster Square in New Haven, but these contain locally grown organic vegetables and nitrate-free meats. Go early to avoid crowds. In the Lareau Farm Country Inn. | 46 Lareau Rd., off Rte. 100 south of Rte. 17 | 802/496–8856 | Closed Sun.–Thurs. No lunch | $10–$17 | MC, V.

Chez Henri. French. This romantic, Parisienne-style bistro has won a loyal following through the years with traditional dishes like onion soup, cheese fondue, and rack of lamb with rosemary-garlic sauce. The accommodating chef also prepares other entrées to please his clientele, including vegetarian courses and hamburgers. During good weather, you can sit outside by a purling brook. Kids are welcome. | Sugarbush Village | 802/583–2600 | $13–$24 | AE, MC, V.

The Den. American. A giant bank safe is on the right as you enter this ultrapopular spot full of knotty pine, with seating at booths and tables. Burgers, pork chops, and sandwiches star at lunch, Texas ribs and steaks are the best choices for dinner. | Rte. 100 | 802/496–8880 | $10–$14 | AE, MC, V.

Jay's Restaurant and Pizzeria. Italian. This local hangout has a variety of dishes, from pizza, calzones, and pasta to more eclectic fare like Jamaican jerk chicken or shrimp

Provençal. During the warm weather you can dine outside under an apple tree. | Mad River Green Shopping Center, Rte. 100 | 802/496–8282 | Reservations not accepted | Breakfast also available | $7–$14 | D, MC, V.

Millbrook Inn. American/Casual. The restaurant of this inn serves not only traditional Vermont meals, like rack of lamb, but also traditional Indian dishes like "Vegetable Thali," vegetables cooked in curry and spices. | Rte. 17/533 McCullough Hwy. | 802/496–2405 or 800/477–2809 | fax 802/496–9735 | millbrkinn@aol.com | www.millbrookinn.com | $12–$18 | AE, MC, V.

The Steak Place. American/Casual. This restaurant is part of the Tucker Hill Lodge and offers a variety of dishes in addition to their steak entrées. They are locally known for their wood-smoked baby back spare ribs. The work of local artists and artisans decorates the dining room walls. | 65 Marble Hill Rd. | 802/496–3025 | tuckhill@tuckerhill.com | www.tuckerhill.com | $7–$28 | AE, MC, V.

Lodging

1824 House. A 10-gabled white house that's on the National Register of Historic Places, with 22 acres of woodland and a hillside pasture along which the Mad River runs. Complimentary breakfast. No smoking, no room phones. Hot tub. | 2150 Main St. | 802/496–7555 or 800/426–3986 | fax 802/496–7559 | 1824@madriver.com | www.1824house.com | 8 rooms | $100–$150 | AE, D, MC, V.

Featherbed Inn. Built in the early 1800s, this old farmhouse has such charms as wide-planked wood floors, exposed beams, and a fieldstone fireplace. The rooms are all tastefully outfitted with antiques, memorabilia, and of course featherbed mattresses. The surrounding 27 acres provide room for lounging and strolling. Complimentary breakfast. No air-conditioning in some rooms, no smoking, no room phones, TV in common area. No kids under 10. No pets. | 5864 Main St. (Rte. 100) | 802/496–7151 | fax 802/496–7933 | featherbedinn@madriver.com | www.featherbedinn.com | 10 rooms | $100–$150 | AE, MC, V.

Inn at the Round Barn Farm. A 12-sided barn is the focal point of this serenely luxurious hostelry with a down comforter on every bed, many amenities, and beautiful grounds. Surprisingly, most guests are not skiers. Complimentary breakfast. No air-conditioning in some rooms, no smoking, some room phones, TV in common area. Indoor pool, ponds. Cross-country skiing. Business services. | 1661 E. Warren Rd. | 802/496–2276 | fax 802/496–8832 | roundbarn@madriver.com | www.innattheroundbarn.com | 12 rooms | $135–$220 | AE, MC, V.

Lareau Farm Country Inn. A vintage, New England farm-turned-inn, with 60 acres of meadows and an enduringly popular, and unique, pizza kitchen, the American Flatbread. The inn was first built in 1794 and then rebuilt in 1830 in a Greek Revival style. You can swim in one of the four swimming holes or in the river. Picnic area, complimentary breakfast. No air-conditioning, no room phones, TV in common area. | 46 Lareau Rd., off Rte. 100 | 802/496–4949 or 800/833–0766 | fax 802/296–7979 | lareau@lareaufarminn.com | www.lareaufarminn.com | 13 rooms (2 with shared bath) | $80–$135 | MC, V.

Mad River Inn. Built as a farmhouse in the 1860s, this inn is 1 mi north of Waitsfield, just off Route 100. The rooms are comfortably furnished in a Victorian theme with period antiques and featherbeds. Complimentary breakfast. No air-conditioning, no smoking, no room phones, no TV in some rooms. No pets. | Tremblay Rd. | 802/496–7900 or 800/832–8278 | fax 802/496–5390 | madriverinn@madriver.com | www.madriverinn.com | 10 rooms | $95–$135 | AE, MC, V.

Millbrook Inn. Wide, worn pink plank floors greet you as you enter this Cape-style farmhouse. Rooms are individually appointed with period furniture, antique objets d'art, and handmade quilts. The price of the rooms includes breakfast and dinner during the peak seasons. Restaurant, complimentary breakfast. No air-conditioning, no smoking, no room phones, no TV. No kids under 6. Pets allowed. | Rte. 17/533 McCullough Hwy. | 802/496–2405 or 800/477–2809 | fax 802/496–9735 | millbrkinn@aol.com | www.millbrookinn.com | 7 rooms | $120–$140 | AE, MC, V.

Tucker Hill Inn. This hillside inn on 14 acres has the appeal of a country home. Rooms are have antique furnishings, quilted beds, and floral-pattern wallpaper. Gardens and trails await you outside. Restaurant, bar, complimentary Continental breakfast. No air-conditioning, cable TV, in-room VCRs. Pool. Tennis courts. Hiking. Cross-country skiing. | 65 Marble Hill Rd. | 802/496–3983 or 800/543–7841 | tuckerhill@tuckerhill.com | www.tuckerhill.com | 16 rooms | $129–$199 | AE, MC, V.

Waitsfield Inn. This former parsonage built in 1825 in the village has ornate woodwork and many country antiques. Complimentary breakfast. No air-conditioning, no smoking, no room phones, no TV. Cross-country skiing. No kids under 5. | Rte. 100 | 802/496–3979 or 800/758–3801 | fax 802/496–3970 | waitsfieldinn@madriver.com | www.waitsfieldinn.com | 14 rooms | $120–$140 | Closed 1 wk in Apr. | AE, D, MC, V.

WARREN

(Nearby towns also listed: Waitsfield, Waterbury)

Warren is one of two principal commercial, lodging, and dining centers of the Mad River valley. (The other is Waitsfield.) The town serves as a gateway to the Sugarbush ski area. Much larger and more modern than neighboring Mad River Glen, Sugarbush occupies parts of two separate mountains and offers a full range of summer activities.

Information: Sugarbush Chamber of Commerce | Box 173, Waitsfield, 05673 | 802/496–3409 or 800/828–4748 | fax 802/496–5420 | www.madrivervalley.com.

Attractions

Parade Gallery. This gallery exhibits oil, watercolor, and acrylic paintings, photographs, ceramics, and sculpture by Vermont and New England artists. | Main St. | 802/496–5445 | www.paradegallery.com | Free | Thurs.–Tues. 10–5:30.

Sugarbush Golf Course. An 18-hole course set amid some of Vermont's most distractingly beautiful scenery that is 3 mi northwest of the town center. | Golf Course Rd. | 802/583–6725 | Greens fee $52 | May–Oct., daily.

★ **Sugarbush Resort.** A two-mountain, year-round resort with 18 lifts and 112 trails that is 3 mi northwest of the town center. An express quad connects the twin peaks. | Sugarbush Access Rd. | 800/53–SUGAR, 800/583–SNOW, or 802/583–2381 | www.sugarbush.com | Daily 9–4:30.

Sugarbush Soaring Association. You can take glider rides and have lessons in the heart of the Green Mountains at this site 2 mi northeast of Warren. | Sugarbush Airport | 802/496–2290 | www.soaratsugarbush.org | May–Oct., daily.

Sugarbush Sports Center. This complex three mi northwest of Rte. 100 in Sugarbush Village has a pool, fitness center, squash and racquetball courts, saunas, and a 30-ft climbing wall. | Sugarbush Village Rd. | 802/583–2391 | $13 | Weekdays 6:30–9, weekends 8–8.

ON THE CALENDAR

JULY: *Fourth of July Celebration.* The Independence Day festival in Warren begins with a parade, winding down Main Street. A street party is held at the country store and a fair takes place simultaneously next to the local elementary school. The fair, which includes pony rides, a climbing wall, and vendors, is the site of the world championship cherry-pit spitting contest. | Main St. | 800/517–4247 | $1.

Dining

Bass Restaurant. American/Casual. This restaurant in a building originally designed for theatrical presentations has three different levels for dining. Hints of the Mediterranean flavor the American cuisine in dishes like the New England fisherman's stew—lobster, shrimp, scallops, and black mussels in an herb-infused tomato broth. | Sugarbush Access Rd. | 802/583–3100 | Closed Wed. June–Oct. No lunch | $11–$24 | AE, D, MC, V.

The Common Man. Continental. This elegantly rustic 19th-century barn, with a massive stone fireplace and crystal chandeliers hung from soaring hand-hewn rafters, offers regional European dishes. Don't miss the Escargot Maison appetizer and try one of the famous rabbit dishes. Kids' menu. Wine cellar. No smoking. | 3209 German Flats Rd. | 802/583–2800 | Closed Mon. Apr.–Dec. No lunch | $13–$23 | AE, D, MC, V.

Grill Down Under. American/Casual. The central focus of this warm and welcoming bistro, part of the Sugarbush Inn, is its grill. Subdued lighting and small tables contribute to a feeling of intimacy. Subtle flourishes like lime-cilantro butter and mustard-maple syrup give color to the assortment of grilled dishes like hamburgers, chops, and fish. | Sugarbush Inn, Sugarbush Access Rd. | 802/583–2301 or 800/53–SUGAR | fax 802/583–3209 | www.sugarbush.com | Closed mid-Apr.–Memorial Day. No lunch | $12–$22 | AE, D, MC, V.

Michael's. Contemporary. Pleasant and sunny with Mediterranean hues, original paintings of island scenes, and salsa-flavored music, this eatery 1 mi from Warren specializes in global fare. While flavors from the Caribbean and southeast Asia predominate, you can also get a great Delmonico steak or Maine salmon. Try the breast of duckling or the tinga— slow-cooked and shredded pork with black beans and rice. Kids' menu. | Rte. 100, Warren | 802/496–3832 | Closed Mon.–Wed. Closed mid-Oct.–mid-Dec. and Apr.–May. No lunch | $20 | MC, V.

The Pitcher Inn. Contemporary. The numerous windows of the inn's two dining rooms offer spectacular views of the stream purling below. The cuisine is inspired by locally grown produce and wild game, and the breads are all baked on the premises. For fun, you can arrange to have dinner in the inn's wine cellar, one of the largest in the state. | 275 Main St. | 802/496–6350 or 888/867–4824 | fax 802/496–6354 | pitcher@madriver.com | www.pitcherinn.com | Closed mid-Apr.–mid-May and Tues. | $20–$32 | AE, MC, V.

The Warren House Restaurant. American/Casual. The restaurant's rustic interior—barn board, stone fireplace, and antiques—has a true Vermont flavor. The menu has a variety of entrées, including steaks, unique pastas, and seafood. Families are welcome. | Sugarbush Access Rd. | 802/583–2421 | Closed Tues. | $14–$19 | AE, MC, V.

Lodging

Beaver Pond Farm Inn. This tidy little 1840 farmhouse nestles in the meadows of the Mad River valley. A huge deck offers fine views. The innkeeper is a fly-fishing guide. Complimentary breakfast. | 1225 Golf Course Rd. | 802/583–2861 | fax 802/583–2860 | beaverpond@madriver.com | www.beaverpondfarminn.com | 5 rooms | $85–$125 | MAP available | MC, V.

Bridges Resort and Racquet Club. One of the state's most popular tennis resorts, this property has 45 acres of grounds and one- to three-bedroom apartments and is 2¼ mi west of Warren. The rooms have fireplaces. Picnic area. No air-conditioning, kitchenettes, cable TV, some in-room VCRs. 3 pools (1 indoor). 12 tennis courts (indoor and outdoor). Exercise equipment, hiking. Children's program (ages 3 and up), playground. Business services. | 202 Bridges Circle (Rte. 100) | 802/583–2922 or 800/453–2922 | fax 802/583–1018 | bridgesresort@madriver.com | www.bridgesresort.com | 100 apartments | $110–$390 | AE, MC, V.

Deer Meadow Inn. The inn is 1 mi north of Warren on a 35-acre property that contains woods, two stocked ponds, and landscaped lawns. The spacious rooms have fine, wooden antiques and afford views of the mountains and property. A wraparound porch provides a relaxed spot to soak in the scenery. Complimentary breakfast. No air-conditioning, no smoking, cable TV. 2 ponds. Hiking. Fishing. Ice-skating. Cross-country skiing. No pets. | Airport Rd./E. Warren Rd. | 802/496–2850 or 888/459–9183 | fax 802/496–2850 | majorell@accessvt.com | www.deermeadowinn.com | 3 rooms | $125–$130 | MC, V.

Golden Lion Riverside Inn. A motel on the ski area access road with a private river beach. Picnic area, complimentary breakfast. No air-conditioning, some kitchenettes, cable TV. Pets allowed. | 731 Rte. 100 | 802/496–3084 | fax 802/496–7438 | gldnlion@madriver.com | www.madriver.com/lodging/goldlion | 15 rooms | $49–$98 | AE, D, MC, V.

The Pitcher Inn. An exquisite Relais & Chateaux property. Each room was designed by a different architect and has a different motif. There are fireplaces in most rooms. Formal dining room focuses on local produce and game and has one of Vermont's best wine cellars. Restaurant. In-room data ports, in-room hot tubs, cable TV, in-room VCRs. | 275 Main St. | 802/496–6350 or 888/867–4824 | fax 802/496–6354 | pitcher@madriver.com | www.pitcherinn.com | 9 rooms, 2 suites | $300–$500, $600 suites | AE, MC, V.

Powderhound Inn. A 19th-century farmhouse at the intersection of Route 100 and the Sugarbush Access Road, two of the main drags through the area. All guest quarters are apartments. Restaurant (in season only), picnic area. No air-conditioning, kitchenettes, cable TV. Pool. Hot tub. Tennis. Pets allowed (fee). | Rte. 100 | 802/496–5100 or 800/548–4022 | fax 802/496–5163 | www.powderhoundinn.com | 44 apartments | $70–$145 | AE, D, MC, V.

Sugarbush Inn. Pillars adorn the front of this charming yellow inn—the area's only full-service hotel. Floral prints, matching quilts, and first-rate antique reproductions make the rooms warm and inviting. Most rooms have decks with spectacular mountain views. A cozy sitting room contains a library and a fireplace. 2 restaurants, bar, complimentary Continental breakfast. No air-conditioning in some rooms, no smoking, cable TV. Pool. Gym. Shop. Library. No pets. | Sugarbush Access Rd. | 802/583–2301 or 800/53–SUGAR | fax 802/583–3209 | www.sugarbush.com | 46 rooms | $115–$208 | AE, D, MC, V.

Sugarbush Village Condominiums. These one- to five-bedroom apartments and houses, many with fireplaces or woodstoves, are right at the ski slopes—you can ski in and ski out. All are privately owned so the decor varies. No air-conditioning, kitchenettes, some microwaves, refrigerators, cable TV, some in-room VCRs. Pool. Laundry facilities. | 76 Mountainside Dr. | 802/583–3000 or 800/451–4326 | fax 802/583–2373 | segares@madriver.com | www.sugarbushvillage.com | 150 apartments | $90–$440 | AE, D, MC, V.

Sugartree Inn. A small, cozy lodge that is 3 mi north of Warren. The rooms have canopied and brass beds. The breakfasts are made from prize-winning original recipes, such as thick french toast with homemade orange honey sauce. Complimentary breakfast. No air-conditioning in some rooms. No smoking. No kids under 7. Business services. | 2440 Sugarbush Access Rd. | 802/583–3211 or 800/666–8907 | fax 802/583–3203 | sugartree@madriver.com | www.sugartree.com | 9 rooms | $95–$150 | Closed 3 wks in Apr. | AE, D, DC, MC, V.

West Hill House Bed-and-Breakfast Inn. This 1850s farmhouse, just 1¼ mi west of Warren, is on 9 acres and is surrounded by woods, meadows, and mountains. You can relax in the library, the sunroom, or the living room inside; or if you prefer, the inn also has a front porch and back deck for lounging. Six of the rooms have gas fireplaces. Complimentary breakfast. No smoking, some in-room hot tubs, cable TV, in-room VCRs, no room phones. Pond. Hiking. Library. No kids under 12. No pets. | 1496 W. Hill Rd. | 802/496–7162 or 800/898–1427 | fax 802/496–6443 | westhill@madriver.com | www.westhillhouse.com | 7 rooms | $115–$160 | AE, D, MC, V.

WATERBURY

MAP 11, D4

(Nearby towns also listed: Barre, Montpelier, Stowe, Waitsfield, Warren)

Waterbury, a crossroads town at the juncture of Interstate 89 and Route 100 (which leads, depending on whether you head north or south, either to Stowe or the Sugarbush–Mad River Glen region), was long associated with the Vermont State Hospital complex, now all but closed and replaced by state offices. Much of the town is taken up by Mt. Mansfield State Forest, which includes Little River State Park (camping, swimming) and the adjacent Waterbury Reservoir, popular with canoeists.

Information: **Waterbury Tourism Council,** | Box 468, Waterbury, 05676 | 800/684–8210 | fax 802/244–7822.

Attractions

Ben and Jerry's Ice Cream Factory. You can watch the super-premium stuff being made during a ½-hour tour and then stop for a sundae or cone at the boys' ice-cream shop. There are activities for children in summer, including a table for making bubbles, spin art, and a playground. Fully accessible to the mobility-impaired | Rte. 100, Waterbury | 802/244–TOUR | www.benjerry.com | $2 | Daily 9–8, tours every 10 mins until 6, then every ½ hr until 8.

Cabot Annex Store. Sample one of the many cheeses for which Cabot is famous or watch a video that demonstrates how the cheese is made. Cheese and other Vermont specialties are sold here. | 2653 Waterbury-Stowe Rd., Waterbury Center | 802/244–6334.

Camel's Hump Mt. Vermont's third-highest peak is 8½ mi northwest of Waterbury. The 4,083-ft summit of Camel's Hump is accessible via a 3½-mi trek up Monroe Trail. | Camel's Hump Rd. | 802/244–7037 | www.greenmountainclub.org | Free.

Cold Hollow Cider Mill. Watch cider being made in enormous batches at this mill 3½ mi north of Waterbury. The adjacent store sells dozens of products made from apples and more. | Rte. 100 | 802/244–8771 or 800/327–7537 | www.coldhollow.com | Free | June–Oct., daily 8–7; Nov.–May, daily 8–6.

Little River State Park. One of north-central Vermont's most popular spots for camping, swimming (registered campers only), and canoeing is 2 mi west of Waterbury. | 3444 Little River Rd. | 802/244–7103 or 802/479–5280 | www.vtstateparks.com | $2; special rates for children | May–Columbus Day, daily 9–9.

ON THE CALENDAR

JULY: *Fourth of July Celebration.* One of the biggest Independence Day festivals in the state, this celebration includes a parade, pony rides, Ferris wheels, dancing, musical performances, and a large fireworks display. Floats, marching bands, and fire trucks all participate in the parade which begins on Main Street and finishes at a recreation center. | Main St. | 800/244–8533 | $1.

Dining

Arvad's. American/Casual. Using primarily Vermont products, this restaurant serves an assortment of entrées, including chicken wings, stir-fry, fish scampi, and burritos. It boasts of the largest beer selections in Vermont, over 110 different varieties from which to choose. In summer, you can dine beneath an awning on an outdoor deck. | 3 S. Main St. | 802/244–8973 or 800/599–8973 | $6–$16 | AE, D, DC, MC, V.

Black Bear Inn. Contemporary. The inn's dining room is lit from above by skylights and overlooks a lush garden. The prix fixe dinners might include delectables such as grilled Atlantic salmon with a maple-Dijon mustard glaze. | Bolton Access Rd., Bolton | 802/434–2126 or 800/395–6335 | fax 802/434–5161 | blkbear@wcvt.com | www.blkbearinn.com | $25 | MC, V.

Old Stagecoach Inn. American. The dining room of this 19th-century inn is filled with English and European antiques that recall the days before trains and cars. The regional cuisine is made with Vermont products. A particular favorite is the slow roast sampler—barbecued beef, pork, and chicken. A patio on the side of the inn, away from the street, permits outdoor dining in summer. | 18 N. Main St. | 802/244–5056 or 800/262–2206 | fax 802/244–6956 | lodging@oldstagecoach.com | www.oldstagecoachinn.com | Closed Sun.–Tues. No lunch | $11–$12 | AE, D, MC, V.

Thatcher Brook. French. A charming rustic setting in a Victorian inn. Try the Parmesan-crusted salmon, the shrimp and scallop Provençal, or the filet mingon bordelaise. In summer there is open-air dining on the 400-ft covered porch. Kids' menu. No smoking. | 1017 Waterbury-Stowe Rd. | 802/244–5911 | No lunch | $14–$25 | AE, D, DC, MC, V.

★ **Villa Tragara.** Italian. You can order tapas or pastas made at this vintage farmhouse. No smoking. | Rte. 100 | 802/244–5288 | No lunch | $15–$25 | AE, MC, V.

Lodging

Black Bear Inn. This mountaintop inn is in Bolton, 7 mi west of Waterbury. It is decorated with teddy bears of all shapes and sizes. Many of the rooms have gas fireplaces and balconies. Some have hot tubs. Restaurant, complimentary breakfast. No smoking, some in-room hot tubs, cable TV, no room phones. Pool. Hot tub. Tennis courts. Hiking. Pets allowed. | Bolton Access Rd., Bolton | 802/434–2126 or 800/395–6335 | fax 802/434–5161 | blkbear@wcvt.com | www.blkbearinn.com | 24 rooms | $135 | MC, V.

Black Locust. Built as a farmhouse in 1832, this inn affords views of Sugarbush, Mt. Mansfield, and the Green Mountains between the surrounding black locust trees. Rooms are given individual character with different themes, such as the Ashley-Rose Room. The inn is on 3 acres and is 5 mi north of Waterbury. Complimentary breakfast. No smoking, no room phones, TV in common area. Cross-country skiing, downhill skiing. Kids over 12 only. | 5088 Waterbury-Stowe Rd., Waterbury Center | 802/244–7490 or 800/366–5592 | fax 802/244–8473 | blklocst@sover.net | www.blacklocustinn.com | 6 rooms | $100–$150 | Closed Apr. and Nov. | AE, D, MC, V.

Grunberg Haus Bed and Breakfast. This hand-built Austrian chalet and immense fireplace anchors 14 acres of gardens and woods. No air-conditioning, no room phones. Hot tub. Cross-country skiing. | 94 Pine St., Rte. 100 | 802/244–7726 or 800/800–7760 | grunhaus@aol.com | www.grunberghaus.com | 13 rooms (6 with shared bath), 2 cabins | $59–$115, $89–$135 cabins | D, MC, V.

Holiday Inn. A full-service chain that is right off Interstate 89 and near Ben and Jerry's and Cold Hollow Cider Mill. Restaurant, bar with entertainment, picnic area, room service. In-room data ports, cable TV, some in-room VCRs. Pool. Sauna. Tennis. Video games. Laundry facilities. Business services. Pets allowed. | 45 Blush Hill Rd. | 802/244–7822 | fax 802/244–7822 | 79 rooms | $79–$109 | AE, D, DC, MC, V.

Inn at Blush Hill. Waterbury's oldest hostelry was built in 1790 and was once a stagecoach stop. It is furnished in period style and some rooms have fireplaces. Picnic area, complimentary breakfast. No air-conditioning, cable TV in common area, no room phones. Cross-country skiing, downhill skiing. Library. | Blush Hill Rd. | 802/244–7529 or 800/736–7522 | fax 802/244–7314 | www.blushhill.com | 5 rooms | $89–$130 | AE, D, MC, V.

Old Stagecoach Inn. This 1820s inn is in the center of town. Antiques from America and abroad fill the rooms and common areas, giving the inn an authentic country flavor. The more inexpensive rooms share a bath. Dining room, bar, complimentary breakfast. No air-conditioning in some rooms, some kitchenettes, some refrigerators, no smoking, some room phones, TV in common area. Library. Pets allowed (fee). | 18 N. Main St. | 802/244–5056 or 800/262–2206 | fax 802/244–6956 | lodging@oldstagecoach.com | www.oldstagecoachinn.com | 8 rooms (3 share bath), 3 efficiencies | $55–$200 | AE, D, MC, V.

Thatcher Brook Inn. A rambling country inn built in 1899. It has twin gazebos and a front porch and is on a busy road. 2 restaurants, complimentary breakfast. No air-conditioning, no smoking. Cross-country skiing, downhill skiing. Business services. | Rte. 100 N | 802/244–5911 or 800/292–5911 | fax 802/244–1294 | info@thatcherbrook.com | www.thatcherbrook.com | 22 rooms (3 with shower only) | $80–$180 | AE, D, DC, MC, V.

BEN & JERRY'S FROZEN ASSETS

It was a match made in heaven . . . or rather in Vermont, which natives and visitors alike often think of as the same thing. There were all those cows, grazing in lush pastures and turning out millions of gallons of high-quality milk. There was the army of young, countercultural emigrés pouring into the state (although "army," back in the '6os and '70s, wasn't a word they particularly cared for). And there was America's sweet tooth.

The year was 1978. Ben Cohen and Jerry Greenfield, two natives of New York's Long Island, had been rattling around trying to find work that would be fun, and maybe vaguely lucrative. They took a correspondence course in ice cream making and looked around for a college town where they might open up shop. The idea was that if we all scream for ice cream, college students screamed the loudest.

Ben and Jerry rented a former gas station on the corner of St. Paul and College streets in Burlington. Using fresh Vermont cream and local ingredients (well, maybe crushed candy bars weren't local), they hand-cranked their product in small batches for a clientele that quickly became passionate about the new ice cream parlor in town. Before long, the boys were packing pints for distribution to outlets throughout northern Vermont. Eventually, production had to be mechanized, and Ben & Jerry's trucks began shipping all over New England and beyond. The old gas station was history, but a whole new chain of "scoop shops" appeared. There's one on Church Street, in Burlington, today. During all their years of phenomenal growth, Ben and Jerry stayed true to the idea of creating flavors so offbeat they bordered on the bizarre. If there's a unifying principle behind such concoctions as Cherry Garcia, Dastardly Mash, Chubby Hubby, Rainforest Crunch, Phish Food (named for the band with Burlington roots), and Cool Brittania, it's that texture matters as much as flavor. Company lore has it that behind this devotion to things that go crunch in your mouth lies Ben Cohen's poor sense of taste and smell; in inventing new flavors, Ben has said, he's always relied heavily on texture. Not, of course, that the world has found anything wrong with his ice cream's taste. Ben & Jerry's other guiding principle has been its devotion to what it calls its "social mission," which has always centered on donation of a percentage of pretax profits to charity. The company has also always prided itself on being one of the largest purchasers of Vermont milk, thus helping family farms stay in business. These ideals survived the company's transition from gas station to publicly-traded corporation, and are touted as vigorously as the ice cream itself at the firm's flagship plant in Waterbury—one of Vermont's leading tourist destinations. Now, Vermonters (and ice cream fans everywhere) watch to see what happens as Ben & Jerry's joins the wider corporate world. Early in 2000, multinational consumer products giant Unilever bought the company. They've promised to run things as they've always been run, to keep production in Vermont, and to honor the social mission. Ben and Jerry, meanwhile, are still directly involved. But they don't turn the crank anymore.

© Corbis

WEST DOVER

MAP 11, D11

(Nearby town also listed: Wilmington)

West Dover, on the southern fringes of the Green Mountain National Forest, is—at 1,720 ft—one of Vermont's loftiest villages. Like a number of other Vermont towns, it has been transformed in a few short decades from hamlet to condo haven—in this case, the catalyst was the nearby Mt. Snow ski resort. Mt. Snow, with some 80 trails and connections to smaller Haystack farther south, has spread its appeal year-round with a golf course and affiliated school. As you'd expect, West Dover is home to a number of inns, some sumptuous and some merely cozy.

Information: **Mount Snow Valley Chamber of Commerce** | W. Main St., Wilmington, 05363 | 802/464–8092 | fax 802/464–0287 | www.visitvermont.com.

Attractions

Mount Snow Ski Area. Southernmost of Vermont's major downhill resorts, Mt. Snow is 9 mi north of West Dover and offers 134 trails and plenty of intermediate and expert terrain. | Rte. 100, in Green Mountain National Forest | 802/464–2151, 802/464–8501, or 800/245–SNOW | fax 802/464–4136 | www.mountsnow.com | Nov.–early May, daily.

ON THE CALENDAR

JUNE: *Wicked Wild Mountain Bike Festival and World Cup.* Riders compete in Downhill, Dual Slalom, and Cross Country. Outdoor festival and activities for the whole family. | Mount Snow Resort, Rte. 100 N | 802/464–3333 or 800/245–7669 | www.mountsnow.com.
SEPT.: *Brewer's Fest.* Enjoy live music and great food while sampling some of the over 60 microbrews showcased at this festival. | Mount Snow Resort, Rte. 100 N | 802/464–8092.

Dining

Deerhill Inn and Restaurant. Contemporary. Of all the eating establishments in the Mt. Snow Valley, this one between Haystack and Mt. Snow is among the best. The views are breathtaking, the decor is tasteful, and there's traditional jazz worthy of any four-star restaurant. Try the Portobello mushroom stuffed with crab and lobster or the chicken stuffed with pesto and sun-dried tomatoes. | Valley View Rd. | 802/464–3100 or 800/99–DEER9 | Closed Wed. No lunch | $22–$34 | AE, MC, V.

The Doveberry Inn and Restaurant. Italian. The handmade quilted cloths on the tables change with the seasons in the unpretentious Doveberry just down the road from Mt. Snow. Try the wood-grilled veal chop with wild mushrooms, the rare grilled tuna with mascarpone tomato drizzle, or the roast pork loin in a balsamic glaze. No smoking. | Rte. 100 | 802/464–5652 or 800/722–3204 | Reservations essential on winter weekends | Closed Mon.–Tues. in Apr.–May. No lunch | $19–$29 | AE, MC, V.

Gregory's at the West Dover Inn. Contemporary. Hand-hewn wooden beams support the roof of this dining room—originally a stable—decorated with dark paneling. Focusing primarily on local produce and meat, the menu showcases indigenous Vermont flavors. The grilled roast duck with port-wine demi-glace is outstanding. The restaurant also has an extensive wine list. | 108 Rte. 100 | 802/464–5207 | fax 802/464–2173 | wdvrinn@sover.net | www.westdoverinn.com | Closed mid-Apr.–Memorial Day and Tues.–Wed. No lunch | $17–$24 | AE, D, MC, V.

Harriman's Restaurant. Contemporary. Part of the Grand Summit Hotel, the restaurant serves a number of dishes, catering to the diverse interests of the hotel's clientele. Not only does the restaurant have upscale entrées like stuffed chicken, venison, and roast duck, but it also offers lighter fare like burgers, salads, and sandwiches. | Grand Summit Hotel and

Conference Center, Mt. Snow | 802/464–6600 ext. 6032 | Breakfast also available. No lunch | $8–$25 | AE, D, DC, MC, V.

Inn at Sawmill Farm. Continental. Traditional fare mixes with contemporary American selections on the menu in these lovely warm dining rooms. The inn's 36,000-bottle cellar has a thoughtful selection of options to complement your meal. The Indonesian curried chicken and seared salmon in saffron or tenderloin in a black truffle Madeira sauce are standouts. No smoking. | Rte. 100 at Crosstown Rd. | 802/464–8131 or 800/493–1133 | Closed Apr.–May. No lunch | $27–$35 | AE, DC, MC, V.

The Silo. American/Casual. This unique restaurant occupies what was once a silo, hay barn, and windmill. From its walls and ceiling hang dried flowers, quilts, and Vermont antiques, complementing the intrinsic rustic beauty of the building. The restaurant serves steaks, burgers, barbecued chicken and ribs, salads, homemade soups, sandwiches, and pastas. | 324 Rte. 100 | 802/464–2553 | Closed mid-Apr.–mid-May and Tues.–Wed. June–Oct. No dinner weekends | $9–$28 | AE, D, DC, MC, V.

Tony's Pizza. Pizza. This pizzeria offers a variety of dishes—cold subs, pasta, homemade soups, salads, and pizza—all to take out. | Rte. 100 | 802/464–8669 | $5–$15 | No credit cards.

Lodging

Deerhill Inn. An English-style inn with views of Mt. Snow slopes that is 6 mi north from Wilmington. Some rooms have hand-painted murals. There's a fireplace in the living room. Ski, golf, and fishing packages are available. Restaurant, bar, complimentary breakfast. Pool. | Valley View Rd. | 802/464–3100 or 800/99–DEER9 | fax 802/464–5474 | deerhill@sover.net | www.deerhill.com | 13 rooms, 2 suites | $120–$195, $220–$290 suites | AE, MC, V.

Doveberry Inn. A cheerful, spacious, welcoming inn, 7 mi north of Wilmington near the Mt. Snow access road. Après ski, everyone gathers around the fireplace in the living room. Restaurant, complimentary breakfast. Cable TV, in-room VCRs. | Rte. 100 | 802/464–5652 or 800/722–3204 | fax 802/464–6229 | duveberry@aol.com | www.doveberryinn.com | 8 rooms | $85–$175 | MAP | AE, MC, V.

Grand Summit Hotel and Conference Center. This hotel at the base of Mt. Snow has a diverse range of rooms and condo units. The units are especially convenient for those desiring the permanence of a second home since they all contain kitchens. The furnishings are cheerful complements to the comfortable and spacious rooms. The hotel runs many different family activities throughout the year. Restaurant, bar, room service. Some kitchenettes, some refrigerators, no smoking, cable TV, in-room VCRs. Pool. Hot tub, spa, sauna. Gym, hiking. Downhill skiing, sleigh rides. Video games. Baby-sitting. Laundry facilities. Business services. No pets. | Rte. 100, Mt. Snow | 800/451–4211 | fax 802/464–4192 | www.mountsnow.com | 200 rooms | $205–$281 | AE, D, DC, MC, V.

Gray Ghost Inn. This inn, 1 mi from Mount Snow, has a true family feel. Local pottery and art ornament some rooms, while others are paneled with tongue-and-groove cypress. Handmade quilts and maple nightstands complement this homeyness. Dining room, complimentary breakfast. No air-conditioning, no smoking, no room phones, TV in common area. Sauna. Library. | Rte. 100 | 802/464–2474 or 800/745–3615 | fax 802/464–5236 | innkeeper@grayghostinn.com | www.grayghostinn.com | 26 rooms | $62–$102 | AE, D, MC, V.

Inn at Mount Snow. This small country inn is directly adjacent to the resort. The rooms, half of which provide spectacular mountain views, are individually appointed and decorated, many with floral motifs, some with fireplaces. The living room has a large fireplace and big windows. An antique pool table with leather pockets is the pride of the billiards room. Picnic area, complimentary breakfast. No air-conditioning, no smoking, some in-room hot tubs, cable TV, no room phones. Pool. No pets. | Rte. 100 | 802/464–3300 or 800/577–7669 | fax 802/464–3396 | www.innatmountsnow.com | 14 rooms | $125–$300 | AE, D, MC, V.

Inn at Quail Run. An inn on 12 acres in the Green Mountains, with fine valley views. Convenient to Mt. Snow. Picnic area, complimentary breakfast. No air-conditioning, no smok-

WEST DOVER

INTRO
ATTRACTIONS
DINING
LODGING

ing, cable TV, no room phones. Pool. Sauna. Cross-country skiing. Playground. Business services. | 106 Smith Rd. | 802/464–3362 or 800/34–ESCAPE | fax 802/464–7784 | quailrunvt@aol.com | www.bbonline.com/vt/quailrun | 13 rooms | $190–$220 | AE, D, MC, V.

Inn at Sawmill Farm. This rustic farmhouse and its outbuildings have been transformed into a luxurious country inn with soaring rough-hewn post and beams, early-American portraits, and plentiful floral arrangements. No two rooms are alike, and there are many antiques throughout. Half of the rooms have wood-burning fireplaces. The dining room is lovely—and justly famous. Restaurant, bar. No room phones, TV in common area. Pool. Tennis. Cross-country skiing, downhill skiing. Business services. | Crosstown Rd. at Rte. 100 | 802/464–8131 or 800/493–1133 | fax 802/464–1130 | www.vermontdirect.com/sawmill | sawmill£sover.net | 20 rooms | $350–$520 | Closed Apr.–May | MAP | AE, DC, MC, V.

Red Cricket Inn. A small, inexpensive inn on Route 100. Picnic area. Video games. Business services. | 45 Rte. 100 N | 802/464–8817 or 800/733–2742 | fax 802/464–0508 | redcrick@sover.net | www.redcricketinn.com | 24 rooms (20 with shower only) | $50–$130 | AE, D, MC, V.

West Dover Inn. Originally a stagecoach stop and a tavern, this Greek Revival inn in the center of the village has been a lodging for travelers since the mid-1800s. The interior of the structure—the wainscoting, the wide-planked wood floors, and the moldings—are all original. Antiques and hand-sewn quilts in the rooms complement these details. The inn also has two porches and a patio. Dining room, complimentary breakfast. No air-conditioning, cable TV, no room phones. No kids under 8. | 108 Rte. 100 | 802/464–5207 | fax 802/464–2173 | wdvrinn@sover.net | www.westdoverinn.com | 12 rooms, 4 suites | $100–$135, $150–$200 suites | Closed mid-Apr.–Memorial Day | MAP | AE, MC, V.

WESTON

(Nearby towns also listed: Londonderry, Ludlow)

Weston, standing snug around its tidy, iron-fenced commons and near the headwaters of the West River, was one of the first towns in the state to present itself to the outside world as the beau ideal of a Vermont village. The original attraction was the Weston Playhouse, which began presenting summer theater in 1937. In the years just after World War II, Vrest Orton chose Weston as the site for his Vermont Country Store. Playhouse and store still prosper—the latter now anchors a huge mail-order business, but retains its penny candies and bolts of calico—and have been joined by a host of craft and specialty shops. Remarkably, the comfortable village character survives.

Information: **Londonderry Area Chamber of Commerce** | Mountain Marketplace Box 58, Londonderry, 05148 | 802/824–8178 | fax 802/824–5473 | www.londonderryvt.com.

Attractions

Farrar–Mansur House Museum. This 1797 tavern was one of Weston's earliest gathering places. The exhibits tell the story of the village in pre-tourism days. | Rte. 100 | 802/824–6375 | $2 | July 4th–Labor Day, Wed.–Sun. 1–4, then weekends until Columbus Day.

Greendale Camping Area. A small and secluded campground deep in the Green Mountain National Forest. | 2 mi north of Weston on Rte. 100, then 2 mi west on Greendale Rd. in Green Mountain National Forest | 802/362–2307 | fax 802/362–1251 | $5 per night | Memorial Day–Labor Day, daily.

Todd Gallery. The gallery exhibits the arts and crafts of Vermont artists, including photographs, paintings, prints, baskets, pottery, and wooden work. | 614 Main St. (Rte. 100) | 802/824–5606 | www.toddgallery.com | Thurs.–Mon. 10–5; closed Apr.

Vermont Country Store. For more than 50 years, the Orton family has celebrated the old-time general store tradition; the cracker barrel, potbellied stove, and penny-candy counter here are the heart of a big mail-order operation based on time-honored goods. | Rte. 100 | 802/824–3184 | www.vermontcountrystore.com | Free | Mon.–Sat. 9–5.

Weston Playhouse. This venerable summer stock institution started out in a converted church 60 years ago. Several plays are performed each summer in playhouse on the Common. | On the Green, Rte. 100 | 802/824–8167 or 802/824–5288 | www.westplay.com | $24–$30 | Late June–Sept., performances held Tues.–Sat. at 8, Sun. at 7, Wed. and Sat. at 3.

ON THE CALENDAR
OCT.: *Weston Craft Show.* Each Columbus Day weekend nearly 50 vendors come to Weston to sell and exhibit their crafts, including baskets, ironwork, and pottery. | Weston Playhouse, Rte. 100 | 802/824–5606 | $5.

Dining
The Bryant House. American. New England dishes like chicken pie, smoked ham, and homemade soups are the specialty of this lunchtime eatery. The turn-of-the-20th-century soda fountain also serves locally made ice cream and desserts. | Main St. (Rte. 100) | 802/824–6287 | Closed Sun. No dinner | $6–$9 | D, MC, V.

Inn at Weston. Continental. A converted, 1848 farmhouse houses this inn where you can find intimate ambience beneath a warming red ceiling. Try the Veal Weston, steak au poivre, and fresh seafood. Filet mignon with a chipotle hollandaise is a specialty, as is the salmon served on angel hair pasta with a pink sherry cream sauce. No smoking. | Rte. 100 | 802/824–5804 | Breakfast also available. Closed 2 wks in Apr. No lunch | $18–$30 | AE, MC, V.

Lodging
Colonial House. A pleasant inn–motel hybrid just south of Weston village. Restaurant, complimentary breakfast. No air-conditioning, cable TV in common area, no room phones, no TV in some rooms. | 287 Rte. 100 | 802/824–6286 or 800/639–5033 | fax 802/824–3934 | choinn@sover.net | www.cohoinn.com | 6 rooms in inn (all with shared bath), 9 rooms in motel | $70 inn rooms, $70–$100 motel rooms | D, MC, V.

The Darling Family Inn. This early-19th-century inn, ½ mi north of the village green, is surrounded by pastoral land, woods, and mountains. The rooms of the inn each contain a tasteful selection of American and English country antiques. Two cottages, in which are permitted pets and kids of any age, sit atop a knoll and overlook the inn. Picnic area, complimentary breakfast. No air-conditioning, no smoking, no room phones, no TV. Pool. Library. No kids under 10. No pets. | 815 Rte. 100 | 802/824–3223 | dfi@vermontel.net | home.att.net/~darlingfamilyinn/ | 5 rooms, 2 cottages | $85–$145 | No credit cards.

Friendly Acres Motel and Inn. A motel on 7 acres of wooded land that looks onto both Stratton and Magic mountains. You can lounge outside on picnic tables and chairs which surround the motel. The inn is kid friendly and can accommodate families of up to six persons. Rooms are embellished with hand-painted stenciling and quilts. Picnic area, complimentary breakfast. No air-conditioning, no smoking, no room phones, TV in common area. No pets. | 913 Rte. 100 | 802/824–5851 | fax 802/824–6114 | shultz@friendlyacres.com | www.friendlyacres.com | 10 rooms | $100 | MC, V.

Inn at Weston. A 1848 inn that is just a short walk from the shops and playhouse. The larger rooms in the older front section have the most character. Restaurant, bar, picnic area. Hiking. | Rte. 100 | 802/824–5804 | www.innweston.com | 13 rooms | $185–$295 | Closed late Nov.–early Dec. and 2 wks in Apr. | AE, D, MC, V.

Wilder Homestead Inn. This inn in a vintage house near the village green and on the West River has an English-style pub and restaurant. Complimentary breakfast. No air-conditioning, no smoking, cable TV in common area, no room phones. No kids under 12. | 25 Lawrence

Hill Rd. | 802/824–8172 | fax 802/824–5054 | wilder@sover.net | www.wilderhomestead.com | 7 rooms (2 with shared bath) | $85–$150 | MAP | MC, V.

WHITE RIVER JUNCTION

MAP 11, F7

(Nearby towns also listed: Norwich, Windsor, Woodstock)

White River Junction is just what it sounds like—an old railroad town, proud enough of its heritage to have an antique steam locomotive standing in front of the Amtrak station. Often bypassed by interstate highway travelers (Interstate 91 and Interstate 89 have a junction here, too), the old downtown is worth a look for its period-piece Coolidge Hotel, for the old Boston and Maine steam locomotive that stands in front of the Amtrak station, and for a vintage Italian delicatessen that serves as a reminder of the immigrants who made all those trains run.

Information: **Upper Valley Chamber of Commerce** | 61 Old River Rd., White River Junction, 05001 | 802/295–6200 | fax 802/295–3779 | www.uppervalleyvt.com.

Attractions

Montshire Museum of Science. A bright, lively museum with hands-on exhibits exploring technology, natural history, ecology. There are also living habitats with creatures such as snakes and honeybees. Outdoors, the trails wind through 100 acres of meadow and forest. | Montshire Rd. | 802/649–2200 | www.montshire.net | $5.50 | Daily 10–5.

Quechee Gorge. It's 165 ft straight down from the highway bridge to the rushing Ottauquechee River at this gorge 8 mi west of White River Junction. Foot trails follow a winding route to the floor of the gorge. | U.S. 4.

25,000 Gifts and Woolens. One of Vermont's oldest and largest gift and woolen apparel shops. | At the junction of U.S. 4 and 5 | 802/295–3575 | Mid-May–mid-Jan., Mon.–Sat. 9–5, Sun. 10–5.

ON THE CALENDAR

AUG.: *Quechee Scottish Festival*. Scottish music, food, and traditional games honor the upper Connecticut River valley's Caledonian settlers. | Polo Field, Quechee | 802/295–7900 | $8 | 4th Sat. in Aug.

Dining

A.J.'s. American. Tables are made from recycled ship's hatches in this casual restaurant warmed with woodstoves and a fireplace. Especially popular is the steamed seafood fantasy platter for two. It's four blocks east of Interstate 89 and Interstate 91. Salad bar. Kids' menu. No smoking. | 40 Bowling La., off Sykes Ave. | 802/295–3071 | No lunch | $12–$26 | AE, DC, MC, V.

Gillam's Restaurant. American. The soups, breads, and salad dressings are homemade at this popular local eatery. The menu offers a range of dishes including steak, hamburger, and seafood. The chef and owner attended the Culinary Institute of America in New York City. | Sykes Ave. | 802/296–3071 | Breakfast also available | $4–$16 | AE, D, MC, V.

Tastes of Africa. African. Carvings, masks, and jewelry adorn the walls of this unusual Vermont eatery. The menu offers dishes from across Africa, including curried goat and peanut chicken stew. Wednesday is Ethiopian night and Sunday is soul food night. | 1 S. Main St. | 802/296–3756 | www.tastingafrica.com | Closed Mon.–Tues. No lunch | $10–$17 | D, MC, V.

Lodging

Best Western at the Junction. A representative of chain that is convenient to Interstates 89 and 91. Some microwaves, cable TV. Indoor pool, wading pool. Hot tub. Exercise equipment. Playground. Laundry facilities. Pets allowed (fee). | 306 N. Hartland Rd. | 802/295–3015 | fax 802/296–2581 | bestwesternjunct@cgnetworks.net | www.bestwestern.com | 112 rooms | $69–$139 | AE, D, DC, MC, V.

Comfort Inn. Near Interstates 89 and 91. Complimentary Continental breakfast. In-room data ports, some microwaves, cable TV. Pool. Laundry facilities. Business services. | 8 Sykes Ave. | 802/295–3051 | fax 802/295–5990 | 94 rooms | $69–$125 | AE, D, DC, MC, V.

Hotel Coolidge. They haven't torn down all the small-town hotels across from the train station yet. This one thrives and is just a hop and skip from the Amtrak stop. There's a genteel, immaculate lobby and a serviceable coffee-and-sandwich shop (other restaurants nearby). Guest rooms are modest but clean and comfortable. No smoking, cable TV. Shop. | 39 S. Main St. | 802/295–3118 or 800/622–1124 | fax 802/291–5100 | hotel.coolidge@valley.net | www.coolidge.com | 30 rooms | $59–$79, $18–$21 hostel | AE, D, DC, MC, V.

House of Seven Gables. Just 2 mi north of White River Junction in Hartford, this 1890 Victorian inn overlooks the White River. Intricate wood paneling, original to the structure, adorns the walls and ceilings, surrounding the Italian-tile fireplace. You can lounge by the fire, read a book, or watch TV in one of the five common areas, or enjoy the fresh air from the back deck or porch. The comfortable rooms have antique furnishings. Complimentary breakfast. No air-conditioning in some rooms, no smoking, no room phones, TV in common area. Library. | 25 Maple St., Hartford | 802/295–1200 | fax 802/295–8949 | house7gables@email.com | 6 rooms (4 with shared bath) | $125–$135 | AE, MC, V.

Pleasant View Motel. From the rooms of this family-owned motel you can spy the mountainside village of Hartford and the White River below. Three giant cedar trees provide a shady spot to picnic or have a drink. Picnic area. Some refrigerators, cable TV. No pets. | 583 Woodstock Rd. | 802/295–3485 | 15 rooms | $52–$72 | AE, D, MC, V.

Ramada Inn. A full-service chain operation near Interstate 89 and Interstate 91. Restaurants, bar with entertainment. Room service, cable TV. Indoor pool. Hot tub. Putting green. Exercise equipment. Downhill skiing. Video games. Business services. Pets allowed. | 259 Holiday Dr. | 802/295–3000 | fax 802/295–3774 | 136 rooms | $135 | AE, D, MC, V.

Stonecrest Farm. Originally part of a dairy farm, this country inn, 1 mi north of White River Junction, is surrounded by red clapboard barns and towering evergreens. The charms of the house's interior include exposed beams, a spiral staircase, a fireplace, and a baby grand piano. Antiques, quilts, and down comforters fill each bedroom. Complimentary breakfast. No air-conditioning, no smoking, some room phones. Kids over 8 only. Business services. | 1187 Christian St., Wilder | 802/296–2425 or 800/730–2425 | fax 802/295–1135 | gail.sanderson@valley.net | www.stonecrestfarm.com | 6 rooms (4 with shower only) | $129–$144 | Closed wk of Dec. 25 | AE, MC, V.

WILMINGTON

MAP 11, D11

(Nearby towns also listed: Bennington, Brattleboro, Marlboro, West Dover)

Standing roughly at the halfway point of the east–west Molly Stark Trail (Route 9) between Bennington and Brattleboro, Wilmington is just a few miles south of Haystack ski area and the public, Desmond Muirhead–designed Haystack Golf Club. The White House of Wilmington, which has its own system of cross-country ski trails, sets the standard among local inns.

Information: **Mount Snow Valley Chamber of Commerce** | Box 3, W. Main St., Wilmington, 05363 | 802/464–8092 | fax 802/464–0287 | www.visitvermont.com.

Attractions

Haystack Ski Area. A smaller, family-oriented ski resort, 3 mi northwest of Wilmington, that is now affiliated with Mount Snow. Haystack can be skied by ticketholders at the larger area. | Off Coldbrook Rd. | 802/464–8501, 802/464–2151, or 800/245–7669 | Dec.–Mar., daily.

Memorial Hall Center for the Arts. The Center for the Arts sponsors numerous visual arts exhibits, theatrical performances, film festivals, workshops, and concerts throughout the year, all of which are held in Memorial Hall in the heart of Willmington. | Main St. | 802/464–8411 | www.visitvermont.com/memorialhall.

Molly Stark State Park. A small park, with camping facilities, alongside the Molly Stark Trail (Route 9), 4 mi east of Wilmington. | Rte. 9 | 802/464–5460 or 802/886–2434 | www.vtstateparks.com | $2 | May–Oct., daily 9–9.

North River Winery. Fruit wines such as Green Mountain Apple and Vermont Pear are produced on the premises in a converted farmhouse and barn, 6 mi south of Wilmington. A tour explains the process. | Rte. 112, Jacksonville | 802/368–7557 | Free | Late May–Dec., tours daily 10–5.

ON THE CALENDAR

JULY–AUG.: *Art on the Mountain.* Over 200 exhibitors come each year to Haystack mountain in order to showcase and sell their fine art and crafts. | New Haystack Base Lodge | 802/464–5475.

AUG.: *Deerfield Valley Farmers Day Exhibition.* An old-fashioned country fair complete with a midway, horse shows, competitions, agricultural events, rides, and food. | Wilmington Middle/High School's Baker Field, School St. | 3rd weekend in Aug. | 802/464–5277.

DEC.: *Christmas Eve Sleigh Ride at Adams Farm.* Experience the nostalgia of yesteryear with your family and friends; take a sleigh-ride journey into the woods, to an old log cabin. Enjoy a warm-up by the wood fire, a steaming cup of hot chocolate, and Christmas carols at the piano. Reservations required. | Adams Farm, 15 Higley Hill Rd. | Rides at 7, 7:45, 8:30, and 9:15; call for reservations | 802/464–3762.

Dining

Dot's Restaurant. American/Casual. Locally renowned for her great home cooking and baking, Dot serves up a range of daily specials, including baked stuffed sole, chicken stuffed with jack cheese and broccoli, pastas, homemade soups, and sandwiches. Hollywood memorabilia and movie stills ornament the knotty pine walls. | Main St. | 802/464–7284 | $4–$13 | MC, V.

Hermitage Inn. Continental. The colonial-style Hermitage has a 200-seat dining room adorned with the world's largest collection of Michel Delacroix lithographs and original paintings, as well as hundreds of antique and decorative decoys. The menu is known for game birds, venison, and fresh fish, all of which are superb. Try the homemade game pâté made from pheasant, duck, and venison liver, or the homemade venison sausage in a bordelaise sauce. Sunday brunch. Wine cellar. | Coldbrook Rd. | 802/464–3511 | www.hermitage.com | No lunch | $16–$25 | AE, DC, MC, V.

Le Petit Chef. French. This charming restaurant in an 18th-century farmhouse has three intimate dining rooms. Though the menu changes from season to season, there is always a variety of choices—veal, poussin, duck, rack of lamb, and a vegetarian entrée. A particular favorite is the sautéed loin of venison, served with currant sauce, rhubarb-and-cherry chutney, and caramelized endive. | Rte. 100 | 802/464–8437 | Closed mid-Apr.–Memorial Day, end of Oct.–Thanksgiving, and Tues. No lunch | $18–$30 | AE, MC, V.

Poncho's Wreck. American/Casual. In the heart of quaint Wilmington, this unique structure mixes the aesthetics of a Victorian residence, a beachcomber's Hall of Fame, and the New York Yacht Club's medal room. The food, which is as quirky and inventive as the interior, includes south-of-the-border specialties as well as steak, chicken, and seafood dishes. | S. Main St. | 802/464–9320 | $12–$20 | AE, D, MC, V.

White House Inn. Continental. This neoclassical mansion (1915), 1 mi east of the village of Wilmington, has numerous fireplaces, original French wallpaper, Victorian fixtures, and antiques. Have a drink in the patio lounge overlooking the sweeping lawn and the Green Mountains. The excellent cuisine in the wood-paneled dining room is distinguished by consistently good steaks, veal, seafood, lamb, and superb duck. Try the steak Medici, a pan-seared fillet with port wine, shallots, garlic, and mushrooms. Sunday brunch. | 178 Rte. 9 E | 802/464–2135 or 800/541–2135 | www.whitehouseinn.com | Breakfast also available. Closed Apr.–mid June. No lunch | $19–$23 | AE, D, DC, MC, V.

Lodging

Hermitage Inn. A fine country inn set regally amid formal gardens at the base of Haystack Mountain, about 5 mi from Wilmington. Many rooms have fireplaces, and there's an art gallery. Restaurant, bar. Tennis. Cross-country skiing. Business services. | Coldbrook Rd. | 802/464–3511 | fax 802/464–2688 | hermitage@sover.net | www.hermitage.com | 15 rooms | $225–$250 | MAP | AE, DC, MC, V.

Horizon Inn. A homey, moderately priced inn-motel on the Molly Stark Trail. Picnic area. Cable TV. Indoor pool. Hot tub. Exercise equipment. Snowmobiling. Video games. Business services. | Rte. 9 | 802/464–2131 or 800/336–5513 | fax 802/464–8302 | horizon@sover.net | www.horizoninn.com | 27 rooms | $75–$150 | AE, D, MC, V.

Misty Mountain Lodge. Built in 1803 as a farmhouse, this lodge has 150 acres of meadows and woodland. All guest rooms have a spectacular view of the valley and the Green Mountains. A fieldstone fireplace, wide pine flooring, and a tasteful assortment of antiques enhance the lodge's inherent rustic charm. But the truly unique feature of this lodge is the proprietor who has a beautiful voice and enjoys singing and playing guitar in front of the fire. Dining room, complimentary breakfast. No air-conditioning, no smoking, no room phones, no TV in some rooms. Hot tub. Hiking. Cross-country skiing, snowmobiling. No pets. | 326 Stowe Hill Rd. | 802/464–3961 | mistymtn@together.net | homepages.together.net/~mistymtn | 8 rooms (4 with shared bath) | $70–$116 | AE, D, MC, V.

Nordic Hills Lodge. Off the main road, this 1967 lodge is popular with tours in summer and fall. Complimentary breakfast. No air-conditioning, no room phones. Pool. Hot tub, sauna. Cross-country skiing, downhill skiing. | 34 Look Rd. | 802/464–5130 or 800/326–5130 | fax 802/464–8248 | 27 rooms | $60–$105 | Closed Apr.–mid-May, late Oct.–late Nov. | MAP | AE, D, DC, MC, V.

Nutmeg Inn. Built as a farmhouse in the 1770s, this inn sits on the western edge of town, 3/4 mi from the center of Wilmington. Rooms are appointed with four-poster beds, antique furniture, handmade quilts, and colorful throw rugs. Many also have wood-burning fireplaces. During the warmer months, you can sit beneath apple trees or go for a hike on the expansive grounds. Complimentary breakfast. In-room data ports, no smoking, some in-room hot tubs, cable TV. Hiking. Library. No kids under 13. No pets. | Rte. 9 | 802/464–7400 or 800/277–5402 | fax 802/464–7331 | nutmeg@sover.net | www.nutmeginn.com | 10 rooms, 4 suites | $119–$189 | AE, D, MC, V.

Trail's End, A Country Inn. On a remote road, 4 mi north of Wilmington, this bed-and-breakfast has all the charms of a 1950s ski lodge—wood trim, knotty pine paneling, a stone fireplace, and stone floors. Laura Ashley prints and curtains fill the rooms, some of which have wood-burning fireplaces. A trout-stocked pond in the back awaits your fishing rod. Complimentary breakfast. No air-conditioning, no room phones, no TV in some rooms. Outdoor pool, pond. Tennis. Cross-country skiing. | 5 Trail's End La. | 802/464–2727 or 800/859–2585 | fax 802/464–5532 | trailsnd@together.net | www.trailsendvt.com | 15 rooms | $110–$200 | AE, MC, V.

White House of Wilmington Inn. This Colonial Revival house built in 1915 is 9 1/2 mi east of Wilmington center and has handsome, spacious public rooms and luxurious guest quarters with valley views. Restaurant, bar, complimentary Continental breakfast. No air-conditioning, some in-room hot tubs, no room phones, TV in common area. 2 pools (1 indoor).

Sauna. Cross-country skiing. | 178 Rte. 9 E | 802/464–2135 | fax 802/464–5222 | whitehse@sover.net | www.whitehouseinn.com | 23 rooms (16 in inn, 7 in guest house cottage), 1 suite | $162–$250, $218 suite, $98–$118 cottage | Closed Apr. | MAP | AE, DC, MC, V.

WINDSOR

(Nearby towns also listed: White River Junction; Cornish, NH)

Windsor bills itself as the "birthplace of Vermont," and it was in fact here, at the building now known as the Old Constitution House, that delegates met in July 1777 to adopt a constitution for the Republic of Vermont. That republic lasted as a sovereign state for 14 years, until in 1791 Vermont joined the United States as the 14th state. Windsor also boasts the Vermont entrance to the state's longest covered bridge, an 1866 span shared with New Hampshire, on the Connecticut River's opposite shore.

Information: **Upper Valley Chamber of Commerce** | Box 697, 61 Old River Rd., White River Junction, 05001 | 802/295–6200 | fax 802/295–3779 | www.uppervalleyvt.com.

Attractions

American Precision Museum. Housed in a former factory, the museum tells the story of the American machine-tool industry and the rise of "Yankee Ingenuity." | 196 Main St. | 802/674–5781 | www.americanprecision.org | $5 | Memorial Day–early Nov., daily 10–5.

Ascutney Mountain Resort. Skiing is the attraction in winter at this four-season resort, 5 mi west of Windsor. The rest of the year the resort provides hiking and mountain biking trails, tennis courts, and swimming pools. | Rte. 44, Brownsville | 802/484–7711 or 800/243–0011.

Covered bridge. The longest of the surviving covered bridges over the Connecticut River, this 1866 span carries auto traffic to Cornish, New Hampshire. | off U.S. 5.

Lake Runnemede and Paradise Park. Behind the Old Constitution House, this nature park has an antique gazebo in which you can enjoy your lunch or simply sit and take in the view. | Main St.

Mt. Ascutney State Park. This park, 3 mi south of Windsor, has campsites and a trail to the summit of 3,150-ft Mt. Ascutney for Connecticut River valley views. | Rte. 44A | 802/674–2060 or 802/886–2434 | $2 | Mid-May–Columbus Day, daily 8–dusk.

Old Constitution House. The constitution for the Republic of Vermont was drawn up in this house in 1777. Exhibits tell how that independent nation evolved into the Green Mountain State. | N. Main St. | 802/672–3773 | www.historicvermont.org | $2 | May–Columbus Day, Wed.–Sun. 11–5.

Vermont State Craft Center at Windsor House. One of several galleries showcasing the work of Vermont's finest artisans; everything on exhibit is for sale. | 54 Main St. | 802/674–6729 | Free | Tues.–Sat. 10–5, Sun. 12–5; closed Mon.

Wilgus State Park. A small park nestled against the Connecticut River that is 6 mi south of Windsor. There are tent sites and foot trails. | 3985 Rte. 5 | 802/674–5422 or 802/886–2434 | $2 | Memorial Day–Columbus Day, daily 9–dusk.

ON THE CALENDAR

JULY: *Windsor Heritage Days/Republic of Vermont.* This festival, which occurs on the weekend closest to July 8th, celebrates the constitution of Vermont with historic reenactments, an equestrian parade, folk music performances, horse and carriage rides, and free ice cream. | Main St. | 802/674–5910 or 802/674–5041 | www.windsorvt.com.

Dining

Biscotti's. Italian. Open only in winter, this restaurant is in the Ascutney Mountain Resort, 5 mi west of Windsor, and caters primarily to skiers who want a lunch or early evening bite. Pizza is served by the slice or pie; calzones, sandwiches, and wraps are also available. | Ski Tow Rd., Brownsville | 802/484–7711 or 800/243–0011 | fax 802/484–3117 | info@ascutney.net | www.ascutney.com | Closed Apr.–mid-Dec. | $2–$10 | AE, MC, V.

Brown's Tavern/Harvest Inn. American/Casual. Part of the Ascutney Mountain Resort that is 5 mi west of Windsor, this pair of restaurants, which serve the same menu, are adjacent to one another and overlook the slopes. The fare includes burgers, salmon fillets, steaks, and light salads. | Ski Tow Rd., Brownsville | 802/484–7711 or 800/243–0011 | fax 802/484–3117 | info@ascutney.net | www.ascutney.com | Breakfast also available. Closed mid-Apr.–mid-May | $10–$18 | AE, MC, V.

Depot Square. American/Casual. A small deli, across the street from the Windsor Station, that serves hearty breakfasts and sandwiches. An outdoor picnic bench provides outdoor seating. | Depot Ave. | 802/674–2675 | No dinner | $3–$8 | AE, MC, V.

Juniper Hill Inn. American. The Juniper Hill Inn dining room has one dinner sitting each evening at 7. Specialty dishes include herb-crusted rack of lamb and pork tenderloin with caramelized apples and garlic. The decor is Colonial Revival, and the property dates from 1902. | 153 Pembroke Rd. | 802/674–5273 | Reservations essential | No lunch | $33 prix fixe | D, MC, V.

Windsor Station. American/Casual. Sitting in this restaurant's booths, created from the high-back benches of the depot, you can imagine what the rail station might have been like when it was built in the 19th century. Among the entrées are such main-line favorites as chicken Kiev, filet mignon, and prime rib. | Depot Ave. | 802/674–2052 | Closed Mon. in autumn, winter, and spring. No lunch | $12–$19 | AE, MC, V.

Lodging

Ascutney Mountain Resort Hotel. The mountainside hotel, 5 mi west of Windsor, has suites and condos in a range of configurations and sizes—some with kitchens, fireplaces, and decks. The condos on the slope side have three bedrooms, three baths, and private entrances. The three restaurants within the complex provide a variety of convenient dining options. 3 restaurants, 2 bars. No air-conditioning, some kitchenettes, some microwaves, some refrigerators, no smoking, cable TV, in-room VCRs. Pool. Tennis. Gym, health club, racquetball. Ice-skating. Cross-country skiing, downhill skiing. Video games. Baby-sitting, children's programs (3–10). Laundry facilities. No pets. | Ski Tow Rd., Brownsville | 802/484–7711 or 800/243–0011 | fax 802/484–3117 | info@ascutney.net | www.ascutney.com | 115 rooms, 100 suites | $75–$129 rooms, $165–$640 suites | AE, MC, V.

WHAT TO PACK IN THE TOY TOTE FOR KIDS

- ❏ Audiotapes
- ❏ Books
- ❏ Clipboard
- ❏ Coloring/activity books
- ❏ Doll with outfits
- ❏ Hand-held games
- ❏ Magnet games

- ❏ Notepad
- ❏ One-piece toys
- ❏ Pencils, colored pencils
- ❏ Portable stereo with earphones
- ❏ Sliding puzzles
- ❏ Travel toys

*Excerpted from *Fodor's: How to Pack: Experts Share Their Secrets*
© 1997, by Fodor's Travel Publications

Juniper Hill Inn. A National Register turn-of-the-20th-century mansion on a secluded site, this inn has gardens and Mt. Ascutney views. Some of the rooms have fireplaces. Dining room, bar. No smoking, no room phones, TV in common area. Pool. | 153 Pembroke Rd. | 802/674–5273 or 800/359–2541 | fax 802/674–2041 | innkepper@juniperhillinn.com | www.juniperhillinn.com | 16 rooms | $95–$175 | D, MC, V.

Mill Brook Bed-and-Breakfast. This 1878 farmhouse is directly across from the Mt. Ascutney ski slopes. The four sitting rooms and bedrooms have antiques and contemporary furnishings and are ornamented with such architectural details as scrolling on the baseboards. There's a gazebo next to the brook that provides a quiet, secluded place for lounging. Picnic area, complimentary breakfast. No air-conditioning, no smoking, no room phones, no TV. Hot tub. Volleyball. Fishing. Pets allowed (fee). | Rte. 44, Brownsville | 802/484–7283 | millbrook@outboundconnection.com | 2 rooms, 3 suites | $79–$129 | AE, MC, V.

Windsor Motel. This motel among the pine trees is 1 mi south of Windsor and provides simple, affordable accommodations with views of Mt. Ascutney. Picnic tables and lawn chairs are put outside during the warmer seasons. Picnic area. Some refrigerators, cable TV, no room phones. Pool. | Rte. 5, Ascutney | 802/674–5584 | 11 rooms | $45 | MC, V.

WOODSTOCK

MAP 11, E8

(Nearby towns also listed: Barnard, Bridgewater, Killington, Plymouth, White River Junction)

Woodstock enjoys a distinctive place in Vermont skiing history. Although no local ski area has ever grown larger than the tiny Suicide Six just outside of town, it was here that America's first mechanical lift—a rudimentary rope tow—was installed in 1934. Woodstock also has a reputation as perhaps the poshest Vermont village. Its social tone is set by the magnificent Woodstock Inn, developed by Laurance Rockefeller, just west of the town center. Rockefeller has also left his mark on his adopted home through the donation of 500-plus acres for what has become Vermont's first national park, Marsh-Billings, just a short walk from the tidy streets, chic shops, and beautifully kept homes of the village.

Information: Woodstock Area Chamber of Commerce | Box 486, Woodstock, 05091 | 888/496–6378 | 802/457–3555 | www.woodstockvt.com.

Attractions

Billings Farm and Museum. A model 1890s farm, ½ mi north of Woodstock, with a barn full of period machinery and informative displays, the farm manager's house, and year-round demonstrations of farm work and animal husbandry. | Rte. 12 | 802/457–2355 | $8 | May–late Oct., daily 10–5.

Covered bridge. The 139-ft "Middle Bridge" in the center of Woodstock crosses Kedron Brook, and was built in 1969 according to time-honored methods. It replaced an iron bridge that had been condemned. | Center of village | 802/457–3555.

Huneck Gallery. Vermont artist Stephen Huneck specializes in whimsical animal wood carvings—dogs, fish, penguins, rabbits, and other creatures—freestanding, in relief, or in furniture. Huneck's prints wonderfully capture canine expressions and foibles. The artist is present on Saturdays to sign prints and talk about his work. | 49 Central St. | 802/457–3206 | www.huneck.com | Free | Mon.–Sat. 10–5, Sun. 11–4.

Kedron Valley Stables. You can get lessons, go on trail rides, including inn-to-inn, take sleigh and wagon excursions at this stable. | Rte. 106 S | 802/457–1480 | www.kedron.com | Daily 10–4.

IN LAND WE TRUST

Vermont's greatest asset is its unspoiled rural landscape. In large part, it has been the centuries-long stewardship of small, family-owned farms that has enabled the Green Mountain State to sustain the character of a peaceable agrarian kingdom. In recent years, though, it has become increasingly difficult to maintain small farms. Rising costs of nearly everything a farmer needs to do business, combined with lagging dairy prices and relentless development pressure, have convinced many farmers that selling their land is far more lucrative than trying to coax a profit from it.

Over the past 50 years, the number of Vermont dairy farms has shrunk from 11,000 to roughly 1,600. Admittedly, a lot of those vanished farms were marginal ten-cow operations, and new types of agriculture have taken root in the state. But the threat to farmland—and the green vistas it creates and preserves—is very real. Helping to save those open spaces, along with the family farm lifestyle, is the job of the Vermont Land Trust.

Although it seldom buys land outright, the Trust has managed to protect from development more than 350,000 acres since its founding in 1977—an amount equal to nearly six percent of the land area of Vermont. The Trust accomplishes its mission by buying—or accepting as donations—conservation easements, also known as development rights, on land that remains in the hands of private owners. A conservation easement is a legal document perpetually restricting the uses to which a piece of property may be put—in other words, it may require that a piece of prime agricultural acreage continues to be used as farmland, or at the very least is kept open and undeveloped. The Trust also obtains easements on forest lands and other ecologically valuable tracts.

The formula is a simple one. If a landowner wishes to sell a conservation easement, he or she negotiates with the Trust to arrive at a sum representing the difference between the property's value if it were to be sold for development, and its value as farmland or other open space. This is the amount the owner receives in return for surrendering the development rights. Or, a landowner may donate the easement outright, or leave it to the Trust in his or her will.In several states, the business of purchasing development rights as a means of protecting open land has been entirely financed by the government. The Vermont Land Trust, however, represents a creative partnership involving both the public and private sectors. Roughly a quarter of operating funds comes from the dues and contributions of Trust members. A similar amount is derived from foundation and government grants. The remainder of the costs is split between capital bequests and endowment income, and contributions to cover specific projects."

Imagine Vermont 100 years from now," suggests a Land Trust brochure. Thanks to that spark of imagination, that 22nd-century landscape should still retain a healthy component of forests and fields.

Marsh-Billings-Rockefeller National Historical Park. America's newest—and Vermont's only—national park is the first to focus on conservation and stewardship of natural resources. There are 20 mi of carriage ways and hiking trails. | 54 Elm St. | 802/457–3368 | www.nps.gov/mabi | Park free, mansion $6 | Memorial Day–late Oct., daily 10–5.

Simon Pearce. Constructed in 1981 in an old wool mill, the furnaces of this glassblowing workshop are fueled by the Ottauquechee River. Visitors can watch artisans handcrafting clear glass vessels in the workshop and, afterwards, can retire to the store where the wares are sold. A restaurant is also housed in the mill. | The Mill, Main St., Quechee | 802/295–2711 or 800/774–5277 | www.simonpearce.com | Store daily 9–9; workshop weekdays 9–9, weekends 9–5.

Silver Lake State Park. You can swim in lovely Silver Lake or pitch you tent in one of the sites at this park 10 mi northwest of Woodstock. | Silver Lake | 802/234–9451 or 802/886–2434 | $2 | Memorial Day–Labor Day, daily 10–9.

Joseph Smith Birthplace. First prophet and founder of the Church of Jesus Christ of Latter Day Saints, Joseph Smith (1805–44), was born on this site. The granite memorial exhibit and historic trail commemorate his endeavors. A picturesque 350-acre site. | 357 LDS La., off Dairy Hill Rd. | 802/763–7742 | fax 802/763–7612 | Free | May–Oct., daily 9–7; Nov.–Apr., Mon.–Sat. 9–5, Sun. 1:30–5.

Suicide Six Ski Area. While there's not much vertical rise (650 ft) here, there are 23 challenging trails. The area, 3 mi north of Woodstock, is affiliated with the Woodstock Inn. | Stage Rd., S. Pomfret | 802/457–6666 and 802/457–6661 | www.woodstockinn.com | Call for details | Dec.–Mar., daily 9–4.

Vermont Institute of Natural Science. You can see exhibits on the plants, birds, and animals of the region at this museum. There's also a fascinating Raptor Center, with live specimens of birds of prey. Outside there are nature trails. | 2723 Church Hill Rd. | 802/457–2779 | www.vinsweb.org | $6 | May–Oct., daily 10–5; Nov.–Apr., Mon.–Sat. 9–4.

Walking Tours around Woodstock. A pleasant way to get acquainted with one of Vermont's most architecturally distinguished towns. Each guided walking tour lasts about an hour and a half. | Information booth on the Green in the center of Woodstock | 802/457–1042 or 888/496–6378 | $6 | June–Oct., daily 10:30 and 1:30.

Woodstock Country Club. Part of the Woodstock Inn and ¾ mi south of Woodstock, this club has an 18-hole, Robert Trent Jones course and tennis courts. | 14 The Green | 802/457–6672 or 802/457–6674 | www.woodstockinn.com | $60 weekdays, $79 weekends | May–Oct., daily 7–7; closed Apr. and Nov.

Woodstock Historical Society. A historic 19th-century dwelling that is the site of a local history exhibit. Guided tours of the house are available. | 26 Elm St. | 802/457–1822 | $2 for tour of the whole building | May–Oct., Mon.–Sat. 10–4, Sun. 12–4.

ON THE CALENDAR

SEPT.: *All About Apples.* Cider pressing, apple butter making, apples on a string, horse-drawn wagon rides. | Billings Farm and Museum | 802/457–2355.

Dining

Barnard Inn. French. An elegant establishment with four cozy dining rooms in a handsome 1792 brick house featuring exposed beams, fireplaces, and exquisite table settings that is 8 mi north of Woodstock. It's known for roast duckling, but also try bold dishes such as venison tenderloin served with a raspberry vinegar and bitter chocolate sauce. No smoking. | Rte. 12, Barnard | 802/234–9961 | Closed Sun.–Mon. No lunch | $21–$27 | AE, MC, V.

Bentley's. Contemporary. This popular eatery in downtown Woodstock is filled with plush Victorian sofas, oriental rugs, and antique lamps. For lunch, try the Cajun burger or the Portobello mushroom sandwich. For dinner try the Jack Daniels steak, a New York Strip au poivre flamed table-side with whiskey; or the Maple Leaf Farms duckling with the raspberry Chambord sauce. Kids' menu. Live entertainment on some weekends, as well as dancing every Saturday. Sunday brunch. | 3 Elm St. | 802/457–3232, 877/457–3232 in VT | $9–$20 | AE, D, DC, MC, V.

The Jackson House Inn. Contemporary. The late-Victorian-style Jackson House (1890) is 1½ mi west of Woodstock. It has hardwood floors, fine European antiques, and oriental rugs, and has been an elegant stopover for guests since the 1940s. The new American cuisine fuses local ingredients and classic French techniques. For starters, try the Yellowfin Tuna Tartar Served with Pickled Ginger and Wasabi Tobikko, or the Pan-Seared Foie Gras with Polenta Rostini, Black Grapes and Pomegranate Syrup. For an entrée try free range chicken with mushroom risotto or saffron bouillabaisse. | 114 Senior La. | 802/457–2065 | Closed early Dec., last 2 wks Apr., and Mon.–Tues. No lunch | $49 prix fixe | AE, MC, V.

Kedron Valley Inn. Continental. A romantic spot with candlelit dinners, private tables, and antiques that is 5 mi south of Woodstock. The walls are covered in antique quilts. Two fireplaces and linen table cloths complete the setting. Try the Norwegian Salmon Stuffed with Herb Seafood Mousse in Puff Pastry. Homemade sorbet. Kids' menu. | Rte. 106 | 802/457–1473 | Breakfast also available. Closed Apr. and for 10 days before Thanksgiving. No dinner Tues. and Wed. from Nov.–Aug. | $18–$24 | AE, D, MC, V.

Lincoln Inn. Contemporary. The inn's dining room is painted a soft gold which gives the room a bright, almost springlike air. Famous for its fillets of beef tenderloin, the restaurant serves a range of entrées including fresh fish, chicken, and veal dishes. | 530 Woodstock Rd. (U.S. 4) | 802/457–3312 | fax 802/457–5808 | lincon2@aol.com | www.lincolninn.com | Closed Mon. No lunch | $13–$23 | D, MC, V.

Pane and Salute. Italian. Regional Italian breads are this eatery's specialty, but pizzas, soups, sandwich specials, and dishes such as penne with spinach, pine nuts, raisins, and Parmesan are also served. | 61 Central St. | 802/457–4882 | Reservations not accepted | Breakfast also available. No dinner Sept.–June or Mon.–Thurs. and Sun. July–Sept. | $4–$9 | MC, V.

The Parker House. Contemporary. This imposing brick Victorian house has notable American comfort food and alfresco dining in warm months. Try the spinach salad with grilled Portobello mushroom and warmed Vermont goat cheese, and the rack of lamb in Cabernet-rosemary sauce. No smoking. | 1792 Main St., Quechee | 802/295–6077 | Closed Tues. June–Oct. and Sun.–Thurs. Nov.–May. No lunch | $18–$22 | AE, MC, V.

Prince and the Pauper. Continental. The romantic, candlelit dining room is accented with dark wood and original oils. Dishes range from traditional French to Italian, American, and Pacific rim. Try the roast duck in blueberry sauce, or the rack of lamb served in a puff pastry with spinach and mushroom duxelles, finished with bordelaise sauce. Sunday brunch. | 24 Elm St. | 802/457–1818 | No lunch | $38 prix fixe | AE, D, MC, V.

Quechee Inn at Marshland Farm. Continental. A charming 18th-century farmhouse overlooking the Ottauquechee River. The menu of accessible American food is enhanced by local game, vegetables, baked goods, and cheeses. An appetizer is a must with choices such as Venison Pastrami, Maine crab salad with avocado and tomato on watercress, or duck confit tart. For an entrée try the locally raised, free-range chicken on a salad of haricots verts, or caramelized sea scallops. No smoking. | Quechee Main St. | 802/295–3133 or 800/235–3133 | No lunch | $15–$25 | AE, D, DC, MC, V.

Simon Pearce. Continental. This restaurant, in a 150-year-old restored mill perched over the Ottauquechee River, has views of the falls that flow through Quechee's covered bridge and is 10 mi east of Woodstock. The menu blends Continental, contemporary, and American comfort food. Try the Maine salmon in phyllo with shiitake mushrooms and spinach or roast duck with mango chutney. The award-winning wine list has over 1,000 selections. No smoking. Open-air dining on an enclosed terrace. Wine cellar. | Main St., Quechee | 802/295–2711 | $19–$29 | AE, D, DC, MC, V.

WOODSTOCK

INTRO
ATTRACTIONS
DINING
LODGING

Village Inn of Woodstock. Contemporary. Traditional and innovative New England fare is served beneath tin ceilings and stained-glass windows in the inn's dining room. A fireplace and oak mantel add rustic charm to the interior. A particularly popular dish is the roast Vermont turkey, served with maple-bourbon candy yams and apple-leek stuffing. | 41 Pleasant St. | 802/457–1255 or 800/722–4571 | fax 802/457–3109 | villageinn@aol.com | www.villageinnofwoodstock.com | Closed mid-Oct.–mid-May | $16–$22 | AE, D, MC, V.

Woodstock Inn. Continental. In one of the more genteel inns in Vermont, this restaurant serves nouveau New England cuisine. The rack of lamb with sun-dried tomato and whole grain mustard crust is a signature dish. Or try the unique veal tenderloin Wellington with mushroom duxelles and foie gras, finished with Madeira wine. Live piano music most evenings. Sunday brunch. No smoking. | 14 the Green | 802/457–1100 | Jacket required | $19–$26 | AE, MC, V.

Lodging

Applebutter Inn. This small inn occupies a nicely restored 1830 house on 12 acres, 3 mi east of Woodstock. The hearty natural-foods breakfasts are a major hit with all who visit. Complimentary breakfast. No smoking, no room phones, TV in common room. | Happy Valley Rd., Taftsville | 802/457–4158 or 800/480–1734 | aplbtrn@aol.com | www.bbonline.com/vt/applebutter | 6 rooms | $90–$150 | MC, V.

Ardmore Inn. The 1850s Victorian Greek Revival inn takes its name from the Irish phrase for "great house," and in keeping with this theme, the interior is ornamented with numerous Irish antiques, giving each room its own special flair. You can relax in the sun on the veranda or in the gardens. Complimentary breakfast. No smoking, no TV. No pets. | 23 Pleasant St. | 802/457–3887 or 800/497–9652 | ardmoreinn@aol.com | www.ardmoreinn.com | 5 rooms | $110–$175 | AE, D, MC, V.

Braeside Inn. A comfortable motel 1 mi east of downtown Woodstock. Picnic area. Cable TV, some in-room VCRs. Pool. | Rte. 4 E | 802/457–1366 | fax 802/457–1366 | 12 rooms | $58–$98 | AE, D, MC, V.

Canterbury House Bed & Breakfast. This inviting 1880 Victorian house is close to antiques shops and restaurants. Country floral patterns dominate in most rooms, which are furnished with period antiques. There is a patio overlooking a garden where you can sit on lounge chairs beneath the pine tree in summer. Complimentary breakfast, picnic area. No smoking, no room phones, TV in common area. No kids under 17. | 43 Pleasant St. | 802/457–3077 | innkeeper@thecanterburyhouse.com | www.thecanterburyhouse.com | 8 rooms (4 with shower only) | $135 | AE, MC, V.

The Carriage House of Woodstock. Built as a carriage workhouse, barn, and residence, this relaxed inn dates from the early 18th century. Rooms, each named after a different covered bridge, have their own character, which is accented through period antiques. Scenic landscapes surround the property and fill each window. Complimentary breakfast. No smoking, no TV. No pets. | Woodstock Rd., Rte. 4 W | 802/457–4322 or 800/791–8045 | fax 802/457–4322 | stanglin@sover.net | www.carriagehousewoodstock.com | 9 rooms | $120–$170 | AE, D, MC, V.

Charleston House. In a Greek Revival house in the Woodstock Historic District. Complimentary breakfast. No smoking, no room phones. | 21 Pleasant St. | 802/457–3843 or 888/475–3800 | fax 802/457–2512 | nohl@together.net | www.charlestonhouse.com | 9 rooms | $110–$205 | AE, MC, V.

Deer Brook Inn. This inn on 5 acres of land, which were once part of a dairy farm, is 5 mi west of Woodstock's village green. A hill in the back of the property affords splendid views of the Ottauquechee valley. Rooms have pine floors, handmade quilts, antiques, and hand-stenciled patterns. Complimentary breakfast. No smoking, no room phones, no TV in some rooms. No pets. | 535 Rte. 4 | 802/672–3713 | www.bbhost.com/deerbrookinn | 9 rooms | $110–$130 | AE, MC, V.

The Jackson House Inn. An elegant Victorian (1890) inn 1½ mi. west of Woodstock, with European antiques, Oriental rugs, and French crystal. Two new wings house suites and a cathedral-ceiling restaurant with a big granite fireplace. There's also a formal parlor and cozy library. Restaurant, complimentary breakfast. No smoking, some room phones, TV in common area. Pond. Spa. Library. | 114 Senior La. | 802/457–2065 or 800/448–1890 | fax 802/457–9290 | innkeeper@jacksonhouse.com | www.jacksonhouse.com | 9 rooms, 6 suites | $180–$220, $260–$340 suites | Closed early Dec. and 2 wks in Apr. | AE, MC, V.

Kedron Valley Inn. There are fireplaces and woodstoves in some of the rooms at this riding-happy inn 5 mi south of Woodstock. The rooms also have queen-size canopy beds and gorgeous quilts. Restaurant, bar. No air-conditioning in some rooms, no room phones. Pond. Business services. Pets allowed. | Rte. 106, South Woodstock | 802/457–1473 or 800/836–1193 | fax 802/457–4469 | kedroninn@aol.com | www.innformation.com/vt/kedron | 28 rooms | $120–$230 | Closed Apr. | MAP | D, MC, V.

Lincoln Inn. This inn, built in the 1860s, is 2½ mi west of the village on 6 acres of land and is bordered by the Ottauquechee River. The proprietors will welcome you with a bottle of wine, which you can drink in the gazebo next to the river. The rooms have period antiques. Restaurant, complimentary breakfast. No air-conditioning in some rooms, no smoking, no room phones, TV in common area. Cross-country skiing. Library. Business services. | 530 Woodstock Rd. (U.S. 4) | 802/457–3312 | fax 802/457–5808 | lincon2@aol.com | www.lincolninn.com | 6 rooms | $125–$175 | AE, D, MC, V.

Ottauquechee Motor Lodge. This small, inexpensive motel overlooks the river and is 4½ mi west of Woodstock. Refrigerators, cable TV. | Rte. 4 | 802/672–3404 | www.ottauquechee.com | 15 rooms | $49–$160 | D, DC, MC, V.

Parker House. This inn, 5 mi east of Woodstock, is in an old house dating from 1857 and has period furnishings. Restaurant, complimentary breakfast. No air-conditioning in some rooms, no room phones, TV in common area. Library. | 1792 Main St., Quechee | 802/295–6077 | fax 802/296–6696 | parkerhouseinn@valley.net | www.theparkerhouseinn.com | 7 rooms | $115–$145 | MC, V.

Pond Ridge. A small, moderately priced motel on 6 acres by the Ottauquechee River. Picnic area. Some kitchenettes, cable TV. Swimming. | 60 U.S. 4 W | 802/457–1667 | fax 802/457–1667 | prm4vt@aol.com | www.vtliving.com/pondridgemotel | 15 rooms, 5 apartments | $39–$99, $79–$250 apartments | AE, DC, MC, V.

Quechee Inn at Marshland Farm. This late-18th-century farmhouse just above Quechee Gorge was the home of Vermont's first lieutenant governor, Joseph Marsh. Restaurant, bar, complimentary breakfast. Cable TV, no room phones. Boating. Fishing. Bicycles. Cross-country skiing. Business services. | Quechee Main St. | 802/295–3133 or 800/235–3133 | fax 802/295–6587 | quecheeinn@pinnacle-inns.com | www.quecheeinn.com | www.pinnacle-inns.com/quecheeinn/ | 24 rooms, 2 suites | $80–$170, $120–$240 suites | AE, D, DC, MC, V.

Quechee Lakes. Fully furnished apartments and freestanding homes 5 mi west of Woodstock. The apartments have one to four bedrooms, some with a fireplace. Dining room, bar. Kitchenettes, microwaves, cable TV, some in-room VCRs. 2 pools (1 indoor). Hot tub, massage. Driving range, 2 18-hole golf courses, putting green. Gym, hiking, private beach, boating. Bicycles. Cross-country skiing, downhill skiing, sleigh rides, tobogganing. Video games. Children's programs (3–12), playground. Laundry facilities. | The farmhouse, Rte. 4 | 802/295–1970 or 800/745–0042 | fax 802/296–6852 | qlrc@valley.net | www.pbpub.com/quecheelakes/ | 87 2- to 8-person apartments | $300–$800 per 2 nights (2–night minimum) | MC, V.

Shire Motel. A Woodstock village location with motel convenience. Refrigerators, cable TV. Business services. | 46 Pleasant St. | 802/457–2211 | fax 802/457–5836 | dotcall@aol.com | www.shiremotel.com | 33 rooms | $95–$175 | AE, D, MC, V.

Three Church Street. The unique charms of this Georgian mansion include a 19th-century music room, adorned with chandeliers, couches, and a Steinway. Although the inn is in the middle of the village, the porch overlooks the Ottauquechee River and Mount Tom. Rooms have such details as four-poster beds and antiques. Complimentary breakfast. No smoking, no room phones, no TV in some rooms, TV in common area. Pets allowed. | 3 Church St. | 802/457–1925 | fax 802/457–9181 | 3chrch@aol.com | www.scenesofvermont.com/3church | 11 rooms | $80–$115 | MC, V.

Village Inn of Woodstock. Brass beds, wicker furniture, and Laura Ashley prints fill the rooms of this Victorian country inn. Two common areas provide room for watching TV or relaxing next to a fire. A shaded perennial garden occupies the backyard where you can relax and enjoy the afternoon. Complimentary breakfast. No smoking, some in-room hot tubs, no room phones, no TV in some rooms, TV in common area. Pets allowed. | 41 Pleasant St. | 802/457–1255 or 800/722–4571 | fax 802/457–3109 | villageinn@aol.com | www.villagein-nofwoodstock.com | 8 rooms | $130–$240 | AE, D, MC, V.

Winslow House. This secluded farmhouse built in 1872 once presided over a dairy farm that reached down to the banks of the Ottauquechee River. Guest quarters are uncommonly spacious, with separate sitting rooms and attractive antiques. Complimentary breakfast. Refrigerators, no smoking, cable TV. Cross-country skiing, downhill skiing. Pets allowed. | 492 Woodstock Rd. | 802/457–1820 | fax 802/457–1820 | www.pbpub.com/winslow-house | 5 rooms | $115–$150 | D, DC, MC, V.

The Woodbridge Inn. A little over 6 mi west of Woodstock's village green, this Victorian inn offers numerous special amenities. Perhaps its most unique element is the option of having a ride on a horse-drawn carriage or sleigh, driven by the proprietor in traditional dress. The inn does its own baking, and uses organic ingredients in its breakfasts, picnic lunches, and custom dinners. The rooms have views of Mt. Killington, wood floors, hand-hooked rugs, and antiques. Complimentary breakfast. No air-conditioning, no smoking, no room phones, no TV. Sleigh rides. | Rte. 4, West Woodstock | 802/672–5070 or 800/611–5070 | olexandr@sover.net | www.thewoodbridgeinn.com | 6 rooms | $140 | MC, V.

Woodstock Inn. With its fieldstone fireplace and massive wood-beam mantels, the lobby here embodies the spirit of New England, as do the patchwork quilts on the beds in every room. The furnishings are institutional but of high-quality, belying the large contingent of corporate conference attendees among the clientele. Dining room, bar with entertainment, room service. Some refrigerators, cable TV, some in-room VCRs. 2 pools (1 indoor). Hot tub, massage. Driving range, 18-hole golf course, putting green, tennis. Gym. Business services. | 14 The Green | 802/457–1100 or 800/448–7900 | fax 802/457–6699 | www.wood-stockinn.com | woodstock.resort@connriver.net | 143 rooms, 8 suites | $165–$204, $325–$535 suites | AE, MC, V.

Woodstocker Bed & Breakfast. Just a stroll from the covered bridge and village green, this 1830s B&B offers welcome and comfort you'd expect in a friend's living room, with big leather couches that invite lounging. Rooms are scattered with antiques, including brass and iron four-poster beds. Complimentary breakfast. No air-conditioning in some rooms, kitchenettes, cable TV in common area, no room phones. Hot tub. | 61 River St. | 802/457–3896 or 800/457–3896 | fax 802/457–4432 | woodstocker@valley.net | www.scenesofvermont.com/wood-stocker | 9 rooms | $85–$155 | MC, V.

Index

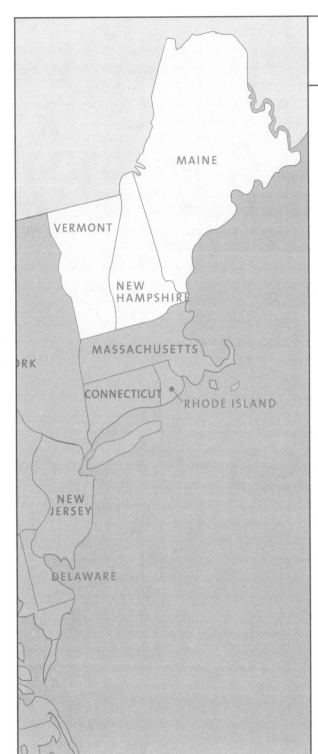

Atlas

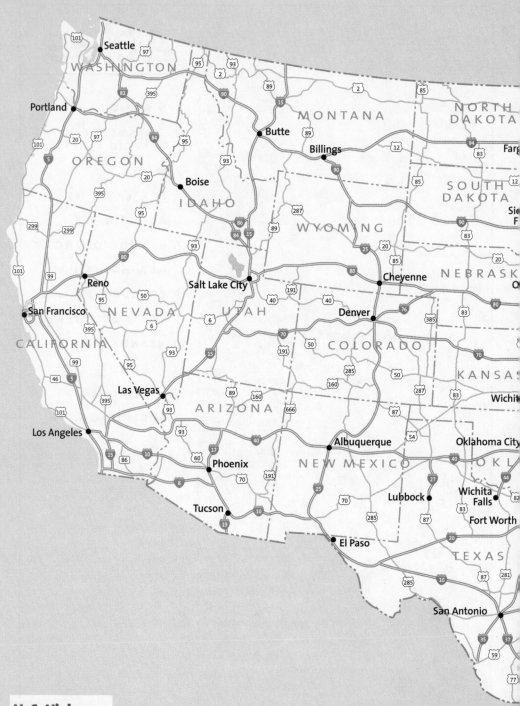

U. S. Highways

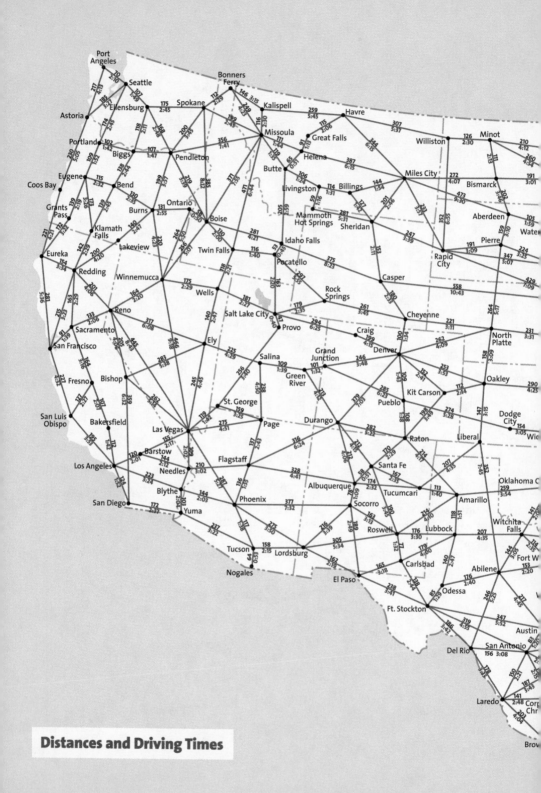

Distances and Driving Times

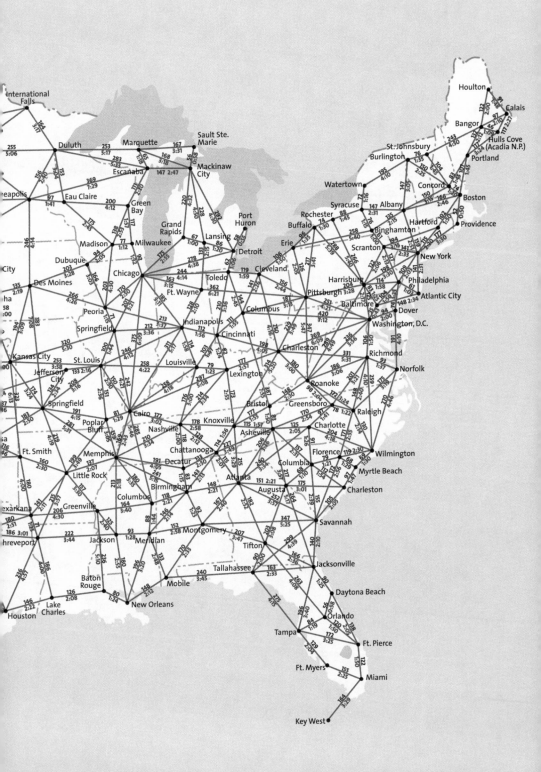

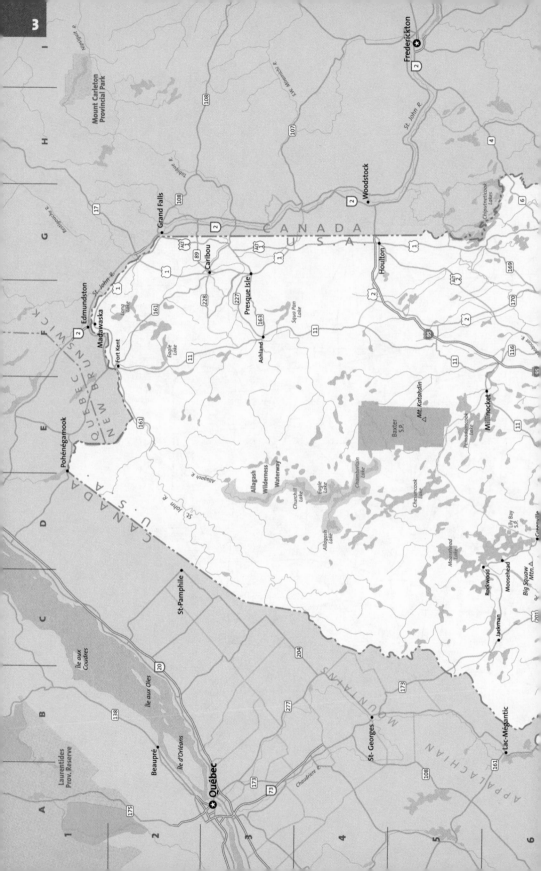

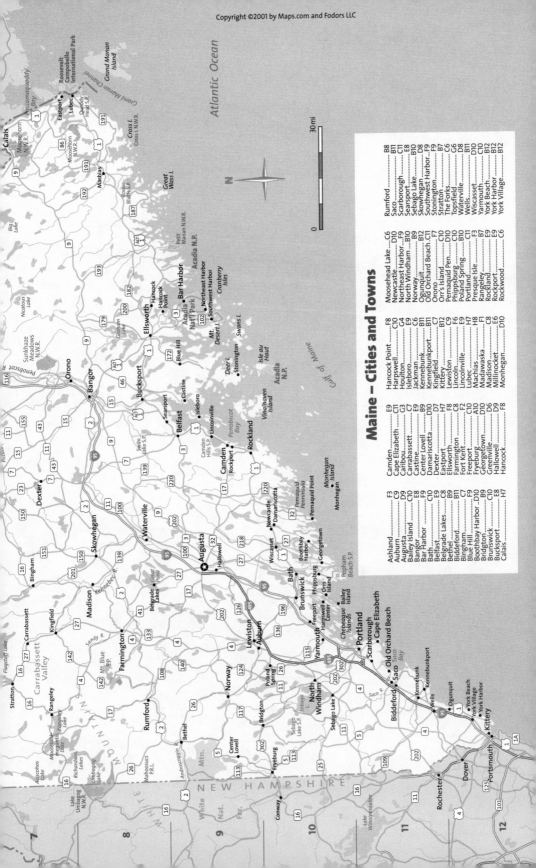

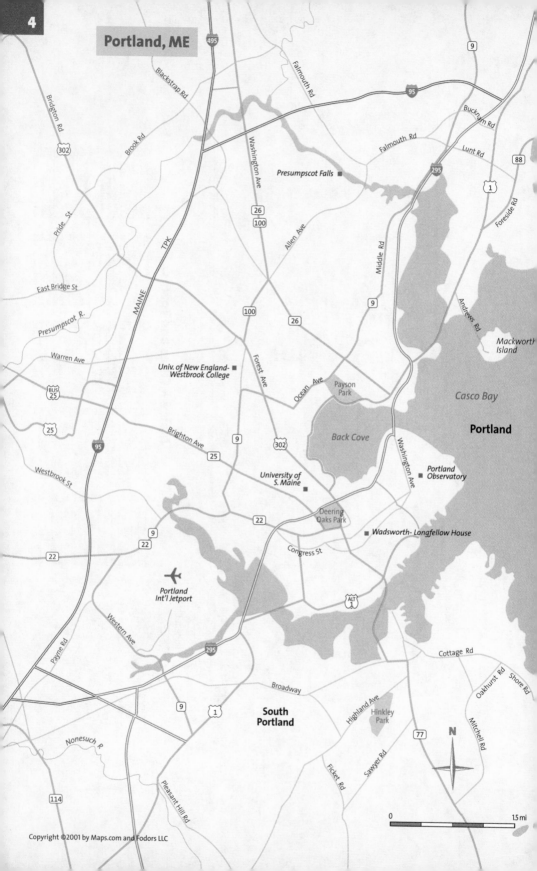

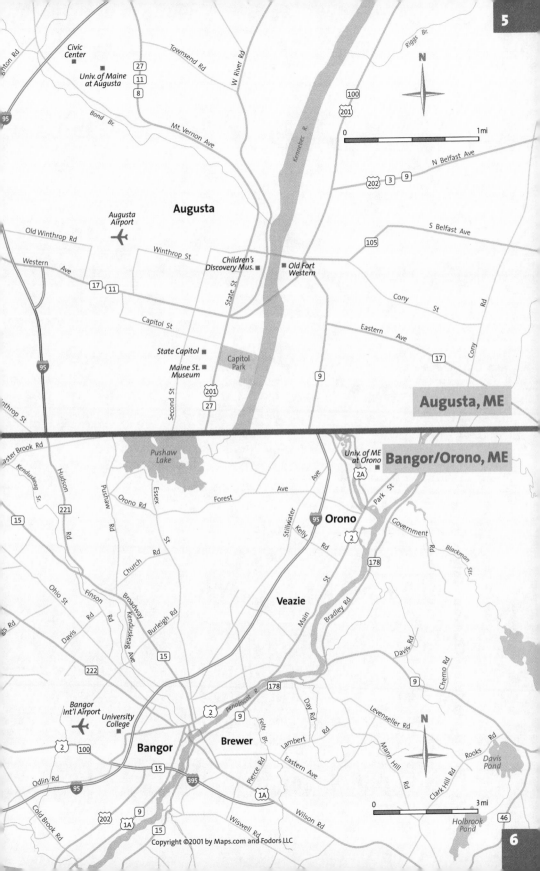

Riggs Br.

N

95

Civic
Center

Townsend Rd

W River Rd

100

201

27

Univ. of Maine
at Augusta

11

8

Bond Br.

Mt. Vernon Ave

0   1mi

N Belfast Ave

Augusta

202 3 9

Old Winthrop Rd

Augusta
Airport
✈

S Belfast Ave

Western   Ave

Winthrop St

Children's
Discovery Mus.

Old Fort
Western

105

17 11

Kennebec R.

Cony   St   Rd

Capitol St

State Capitol

Maine St.
Museum

Capitol
Park

Eastern   Ave

17 Cony

95

Second St

201

27

9

Augusta, ME

inthrop St

aster Brook Rd

Bangor/Orono, ME

Pushaw
Lake

Univ. of ME
at Orono

2A

Park St

Kenduskeag St.

Hudson

221

Pushaw Rd

Orono Rd

Essex

Forest

Ave

Ave

Stillwater

Kelly

95 **Orono**

2

Government Rd

Blackman Str.

15

178

Church Rd

Veazie

Main St.

Bradley Rd

Davis Rd

Chemo Rd

Ohio St

Finson Rd

Broadway

Burleigh Rd

Day Rd

Rd

9

Davis

15

Kenduskeag Ave

178

Levenseller Rd

N

222

Penobscot R.

Bangor
Int'l Airport
✈

University
College

2

9

Felts Br.

Lambert

Eastern Ave

Mann Hill Rd

Clark Hill Rd

Rooks Rd

Davis
Pond

2 100

Bangor

Brewer

Pierce Rd

15

395

Odlin Rd

95

1A

Wilson Rd

0   3mi

Cold Brook Rd

202 1A

9

15

Wiswell Rd

Holbrook
Pond

46

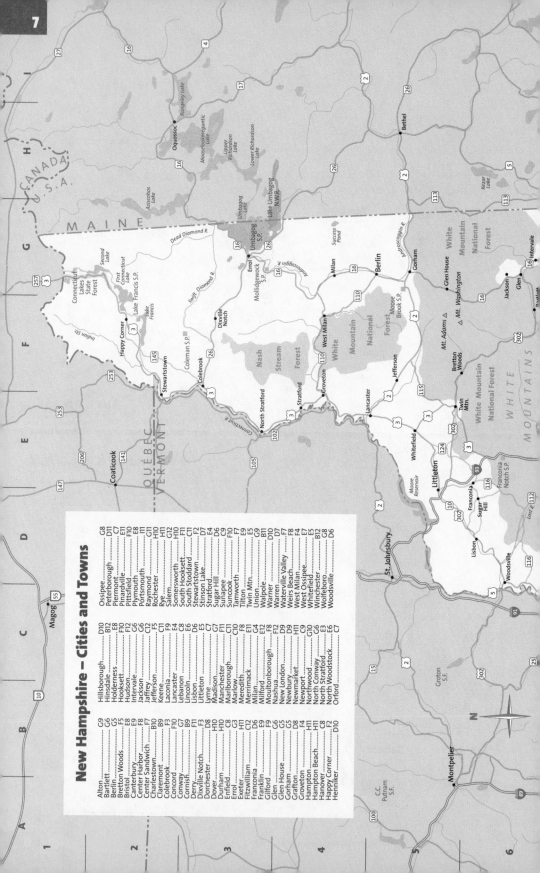

New Hampshire – Cities and Towns

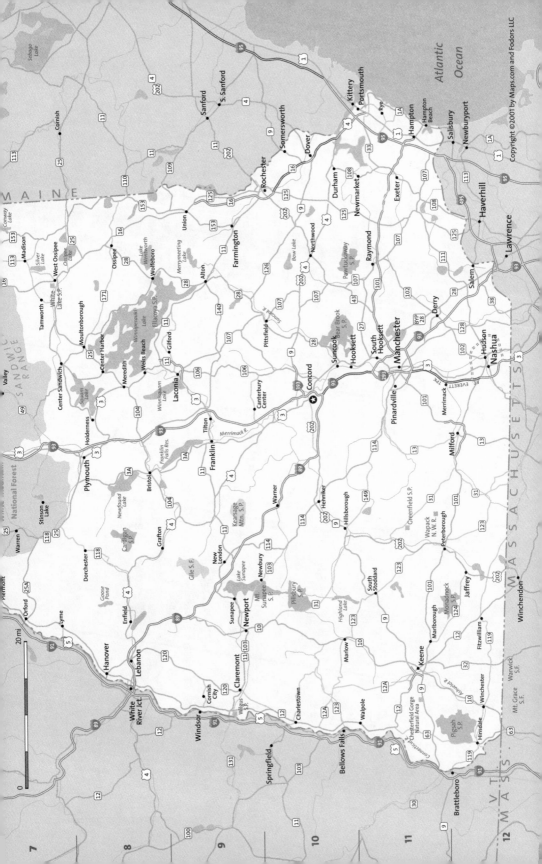

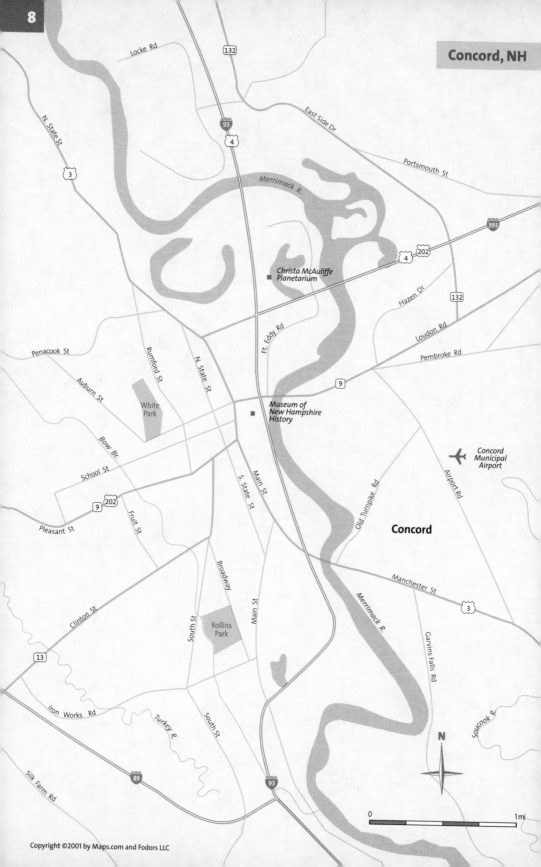

Concord, NH

Locke Rd

132

93

4

N. State St

3

East Side Dr

Portsmouth St

Merrimack R.

393

4 202

Christa McAuliffe
Planetarium

Hazen Dr

132

Ft. Eddy Rd

Loudon Rd

Penacook St

Pembroke Rd

Rumford St

N. State St

9

Auburn St

White
Park

Museum of
New Hampshire
History

Concord
Municipal
Airport

Bow Br.

School St

Airport Rd

9 202

S. State St

Main St

Old Turnpike Rd

Pleasant St

Fruit St

Concord

Broadway

Manchester St

3

Clinton St

South St

Rollins
Park

Main St

Merrimack R.

Garvins Falls Rd

13

Iron Works Rd

Turkey R.

South St

N

89

93

Silk Farm Rd

Soucook R.

0   1mi

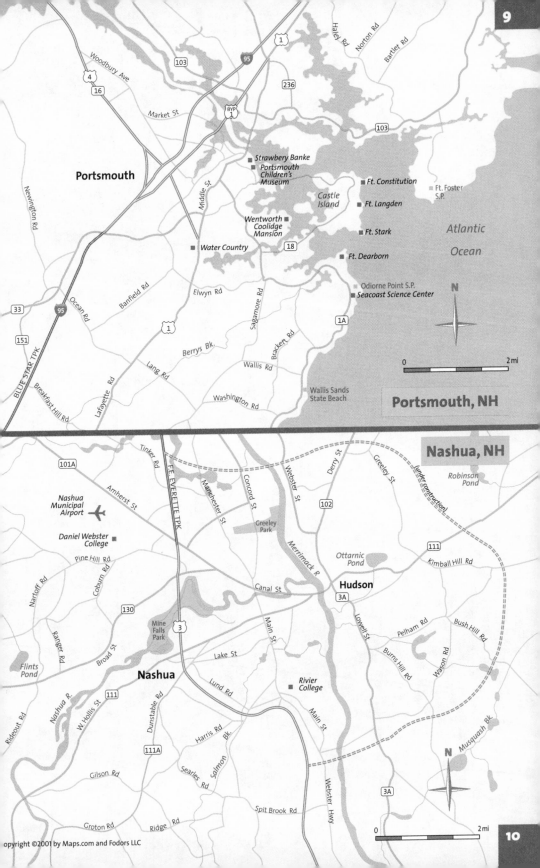

Portsmouth

Woodbury Ave
4
16
103
1
95
Market St
236
BYP 1
103
Haley Rd
Norton Rd
Bartlet Rd
Newington Rd

Strawbery Banke
Portsmouth Children's Museum

Castle Island

Ft. Constitution
Ft. Foster S.P.
Ft. Langden

Middle St

Wentworth Coolidge Mansion

Ft. Stark

Water Country

18

Ft. Dearborn

Atlantic Ocean

33
95
151
BLUE STAR TPK
Ocean Rd
Banfield Rd
Elwyn Rd
Sagamore Rd
1
Berrys Bk.
Brackett Rd
Lang Rd
Lafayette Rd
Breakfast Hill Rd
Wallis Rd
Washington Rd

Odiorne Point S.P.
Seacoast Science Center

N

1A

Wallis Sands State Beach

0   2 mi

Portsmouth, NH

Nashua, NH

101A
Tinker Rd
F.E. EVERETTE TPK
Amherst St
Concord St
Webster St
Derry St
Greeley St
(under construction)
Robinson Pond

Nashua Municipal Airport

Manchester St

102

Greeley Park

Daniel Webster College

Pine Hill Rd
Coburn Rd

Merrimack R.

Ottarnic Pond

111
Kimball Hill Rd

Nartoff Rd

130

Canal St

Hudson

3A

Lowell St
Pelham Rd
Bush Hill Rd

Ranger Rd
Broad St

Mine Falls Park

3

Main St
Lake St

Burns Hill Rd
Wason Rd

Flints Pond

111
W. Hollis St

Nashua R.

Nashua

Dunstable Rd
Lund Rd

Rivier College

Rideout Rd

Harris Rd
Salmon Bk.

Musquash Bk.

111A
Gilson Rd
Searles Rd
Ridge Rd
Spit Brook Rd
Groton Rd

Main St
Webster Hwy

N

3A

0   2 mi

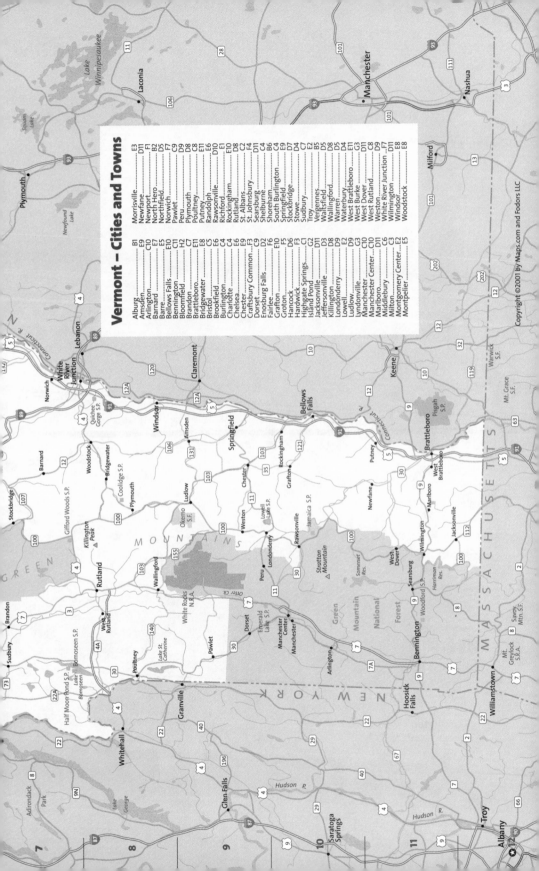

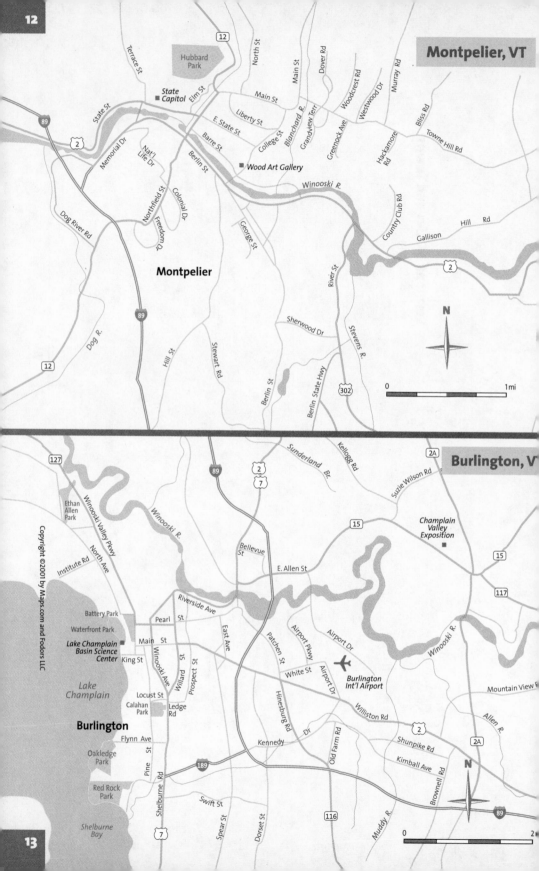

12

Hubbard Park

Terrace St

North St

Main St

Dover Rd

Woodcrest Rd

Westwood Dr

Murray Rd

Montpelier, VT

State Capitol

State St

Elm St

Main St

Liberty St

Blanchard R.

Grandview Terr

Greenock Ave

Hackamore Rd

Bliss Rd

Towne Hill Rd

89

2

Memorial Dr

Nat'l Life Dr

E. State St

Barre St

College St

Berlin St

Wood Art Gallery

Northfield St

Colonial Dr

Freedom Ct

Winooski R.

Country Club Rd

Gallison

Hill

Rd

Dog River Rd

Montpelier

George St

River St

2

89

12

Dog R.

Hill St

Stewart Rd

Sherwood Dr

Stevens R.

Berlin St

Berlin State Hwy

302

N

0   1mi

127

89

2

7

Sunderland Br.

Kellogg Rd

2A

Burlington, VT

Ethan Allen Park

Winooski R.

Winooski Valley Pkwy

North Ave

Institute Rd

Bellevue St

E. Allen St

Suzie Wilson Rd

15

Champlain Valley Exposition

15

117

Riverside Ave

Winooski R.

Battery Park

Pearl

St

East Ave

Patchen St

Airport Pkwy

Airport Dr

Mountain View

Waterfront Park

Lake Champlain Basin Science Center

Main

St

King St

Winooski Ave

Willard St

Prospect St

White St

Airport Dr

Burlington Int'l Airport

Lake Champlain

Locust St

Calahan Park

Ledge Rd

Hinesburg Rd

Williston Rd

2

Allen R.

2A

Burlington

Flynn Ave

Pine St

Kennedy

Dr

Old Farm Rd

Shunpike Rd

Kimball Ave

Brownell Rd

N

Oakledge Park

Shelburne Rd

189

Red Rock Park

Swift St

Spear St

Dorset St

116

Muddy R.

89

Shelburne Bay

7

0   2